HANDBOOK OF INDUSTRIAL ORGANIZATION
VOLUME II

HANDBOOKS IN ECONOMICS

10

Series Editors

KENNETH J. ARROW
MICHAEL D. INTRILIGATOR

NORTH-HOLLAND
AMSTERDAM · NEW YORK · OXFORD · TOKYO

HANDBOOK OF INDUSTRIAL ORGANIZATION

VOLUME II

Edited by

RICHARD SCHMALENSEE
Massachusetts Institute of Technology

and

ROBERT D. WILLIG
Princeton University

1989

NORTH-HOLLAND
AMSTERDAM • NEW YORK • OXFORD • TOKYO

ISBN North-Holland for this set 0 444 70436 1
ISBN North-Holland for this volume 0 444 70435 3

Publishers
ELSEVIER SCIENCE PUBLISHERS B.V.
P.O. Box 1991
1000 BZ Amsterdam
The Netherlands

Sole distributors for the U.S.A. and Canada
ELSEVIER SCIENCE PUBLISHING COMPANY, INC.
655 Avenue of the Americas
New York, N.Y. 10010
U.S.A.

Library of Congress Cataloging-in-Publication Data

Handbook of industrial organization/edited by Richard Schmalensee and Robert Willig.
p. cm. — (Handbooks in economics; 10)
Includes bibliographies.
ISBN 0-444-70434-5 (v. 1). ISBN 0-444-70435-3 (v. 2). ISBN 0-444-70436-1 (set)
1. Industrial organization (Economic theory)—Handbooks, manuals, etc. I. Schmalensee, Richard. II. Willig, Robert D., 1947– III. Series: Handbooks in economics; bk. 10.
HD2326.H28 1988
338.6—dc 19 88-25138
CIP

PRINTED IN THE NETHERLANDS

INTRODUCTION TO THE SERIES

The aim of the *Handbooks in Economics* series is to produce Handbooks for various branches of economics, each of which is a definitive source, reference, and teaching supplement for use by professional researchers and advanced graduate students. Each Handbook provides self-contained surveys of the current state of a branch of economics in the form of chapters prepared by leading specialists on various aspects of this branch of economics. These surveys summarize not only received results but also newer developments, from recent journal articles and discussion papers. Some original material is also included, but the main goal is to provide comprehensive and accessible surveys. The Handbooks are intended to provide not only useful reference volumes for professional collections but also possible supplementary readings for advanced courses for graduate students in economics.

CONTENTS OF THE HANDBOOK

VOLUME I

PREFACE TO THE HANDBOOK

Purpose and motivation

The *Handbook of Industrial Organization* aims to serve as a source, reference, and teaching supplement for industrial organization (or industrial economics), the broad field within microeconomics that focuses on business behavior and its implications both for market structures and processes, and for public policies towards them.[1] Our purpose has been to provide reasonably comprehensive and up-to-date surveys of recent developments and the state of knowledge in the major areas of research in this field as of the latter part of the 1980s, written at a level suitable for use by non-specialist economists and students in advanced graduate courses.

We feel that the preparation and publication of the *Handbook of Industrial Organization* is particularly timely due to the confluence of several exciting trends in this field of economics. First, industrial organization is a primary locus of the recent and ongoing revolution that is re-examining all microeconomic phenomena as strategic interactions with explicitly-specified (and often asymmetric) information structures. This trend alone has generated an unprecedented burst of theoretical research on industrial organization, with new answers to old questions rivalled in quantity only by the volume of new answers to new questions.

Second, new waves of empirical and experimental work in industrial organization are gathering momentum, driven by clarified views of the limitations of the previous focus on cross-sectional interindustry studies, and by the profusion of new hypotheses and possibly testable conclusions produced by the explosion of theoretical work.

Third, the boundaries between historically distinct fields of economics, such as international trade and macroeconomics, and industrial organization, have recently become blurred. The perfectly competitive model traditionally central to other fields is being replaced by explicit models of imperfect competition derived from industrial organization. As a consequence, important new results are being generated in these fields, and significant new issues for the field of industrial organization are emerging.

[1] This Handbook attempts to cover only those themes and issues that have been prominent in what de Jong (1986) has called "Anglo-Saxon thinking" in industrial organization. He presents an interesting overview of the rather different continental European tradition.

Finally, a bevy of significant policy issues squarely in the domain of industrial organization has been at the forefront of public and political attention in recent years. Takeover and merger activity, the movement towards deregulation, increasing globalization of competition, and concerns about national competitiveness have all been powerful stimuli to theoretical, empirical, and policy research, and have increased awareness of the magnitude of the work still to be done in industrial organization.

These trends both make the field of industrial organization exciting and enhance the value that this Handbook can provide by communicating the state-of-the-art in that field to those who seek to contribute to it or to apply it to their own concerns. This potential value has motivated us as editors and has induced the authors of the chapters that follow to contribute so generously of their enormously productive efforts.

Organization

The organization of the *Handbook of Industrial Organization* reflects our perspectives on the principal topics in the field that have recently received intensive research attention or that otherwise are most needful of a new integrative survey. Each of the chapters in the Handbook can be read independently, though they are organized into Parts with some logic, and many pairs are close complements.

Part 1 begins the Handbook with four chapters on the firm. In much of economics, the firm has been viewed as just a black box that maximizes profits subject to an exogenous production or cost function. Because firm behavior is so important in industrial organization, scholars in this field have been productively working to open that box. John Panzar (Chapter 1) focuses on the impact of costs and technology on the organization of production among firms in an industry. He surveys the body of theoretical results on the connections between detailed properties of multiproduct cost functions and details of firm and market structure, and discusses methods of applying these results in empirical analyses of such industries as electric power and telecommunications.

Bengt Holmstrom and Jean Tirole (Chapter 2) consider the implications of imperfect information for the behavior of firms viewed as organizations of self-interested owners, managers, and employees. They summarize the burgeoning body of research that formally analyzes from this perspective the existence, scope, financing, internal structure, control, and objectives of firms. In a complementary chapter, Oliver Williamson (Chapter 3) analyzes the consequences of the minimization of transactions costs for the structures of firms and for the locations of boundaries between firms and markets. Martin Perry (Chapter 4) focuses on vertical integration as an important dimension of firm structure. His presentation surveys the long line of research on the incentives for and effects of vertical integration, and connects this body of work to the perspectives of transactions costs and information asymmetries.

A solid understanding of the firm is a logical prerequisite to answering what has long been the central research question in industrial organization: "How can behavior and performance in a market be understood and predicted on the basis of observable data?" Scholars who attempt to answer this question generally deal also with its sequel: "Can government policy somehow improve market performance?" Parts 2–5 of this Handbook concentrate on these questions. Antitrust policy issues are discussed as they arise in the chapters in Parts 2–4 (and in several of the chapters in Part 1); Part 5 focuses on economic and social regulation.

Part 2 is devoted to the theoretical literature on market behavior and performance, which has grown explosively in the last decade and a half, and to the implications of this research for antitrust policy.[2] Much of this work draws on recent developments in noncooperative game theory, especially the theory of dynamic games of incomplete or imperfect information. Drew Fudenberg and Jean Tirole (Chapter 5) present an overview of the game-theoretic tools that have been most widely applied in this spate of new research, and employ representative models as examples of the analytic techniques.

The next two chapters provide complementary analyses of the determinants of the intensity of rivalry among sellers in a market. Carl Shapiro (Chapter 6) integratively summarizes the state of oligopoly theory, running the gamut from the classical models of Cournot and Bertrand to the latest models set in the context of repeated games with imperfect information. Alexis Jacquemin and Margaret Slade (Chapter 7) consider related theoretical work focusing on cartels, explicit and implicit collusion, and mergers, and the implications of this work for antitrust policy.

The following two complementary chapters are concerned with the process of market entry. Richard Gilbert (Chapter 8) focuses on structural barriers to entry and mobility, bridging the gaps between the classical treatments of Bain and Stigler and the recent treatments that formally model the strategic incentives of both incumbents and potential entrants. Janusz Ordover and Garth Saloner (Chapter 9) emphasize rational strategic behavior designed to prevent or remove competition and use this theory to analyze antitrust policy towards "predatory" business behavior.

The next four chapters in Part 2 cover economic models of the "Four P's" of traditional marketing textbooks: Product, Price, Promotion (mainly advertising), and Place (distribution). Hal Varian (Chapter 10) summarizes and integrates the

[2]The reader interested in theoretical work in industrial organization should also consult Tirole (1988). One could argue that this Part might have contained a chapter on the theory of auctions and bargaining, which has advanced rapidly in recent years.

large literature on price discrimination, describes how a wide variety of selling practices are analytically equivalent when viewed through the lens of price discrimination, and contrasts the results of welfare analyses of such pricing with its treatment by antitrust policy. Michael Katz (Chapter 11), in a chapter that complements several of the chapters in Part 1, analyzes contracts between manufacturing firms and the wholesalers and retailers who distribute their wares. The formal treatment covers a host of vertical restraints and practices and their welfare effects. Curtis Eaton and Richard Lipsey (Chapter 12) survey models of product choice and product differentiation, focusing on the positive and normative implications unavailable from less structured models of oligopoly. Joseph Stiglitz (Chapter 13) focuses on the consequences of imperfectly informed buyers for the way that markets work, with specific attention to the implications for pricing, advertising, and other modes by which information is conveyed in market equilibria.

The last two chapters in Part 2 are concerned with issues of great empirical and policy importance that have recently begun to receive serious theoretical attention. Jennifer Reinganum (Chapter 14) provides a survey of game-theoretical work on competition in the processes of R&D and the dissemination of its technological fruits, focusing on both analytical technique and on the economic meaning of assumptions and results. Dennis Carlton (Chapter 15) considers evidence on price rigidity, industrial organization theories that are consistent with that evidence, and the associated implications for macroeconomics.

Part 3 contains four surveys of market-oriented empirical studies that bear on the issues raised in Part 2.[3] Until the start of this decade, industry-level cross-section studies of profitability differences dominated empirical work in industrial organization. Richard Schmalensee (Chapter 16) provides an overview of these and related studies, assessing the underlying methodologies and highlighting the robust regularities found in the data. Timothy Bresnahan (Chapter 17) contributes an integrative treatment of the tools and results that are emerging from the rapidly expanding stream of research devoted to building and testing structural models of firm behavior in individual markets. Wesley Cohen and Richard Levin (Chapter 18) survey the broad, interdisciplinary empirical literature on the determinants of technical progress. Their chapter is a natural complement to Chapter 14. Charles Plott (Chapter 19) concludes this Part of the Handbook with an overview of the methods, results, and analyses of the new wave of laboratory experiments designed to test industrial organization hypotheses.

[3] We had hoped that Part 3 would contain a chapter on the theoretical and empirical tools from modern finance theory that have proven valuable in industrial organization. For a useful discussion of one important aspect of the relation between these fields, see Schwert (1981). Some other aspects of this relation are discussed by Bengt Holmstrom and Jean Tirole in Chapter 2.

Part 4 consists of two chapters that take an explicitly global view of industrial organization. Paul Krugman (Chapter 20) describes recent theoretical work on imperfect competition in open economies. His analysis, relating closely to several chapters in Part 2, shows how the theory of international trade can be enriched with foundations drawn from the field of industrial organization, and how the international context raises new issues of theory and application for the field. Richard Caves (Chapter 21) explores the use of international comparisons in empirical research. This chapter, closely related to Chapter 16, shows the value of a broader perspective on industrial organization issues than is provided by the experience of any single nation.

Part 5 provides overviews of theoretical and empirical studies of regulatory policy.[4] Roger Noll (Chapter 22) contributes a chapter on the economic analysis of the political–economic determination of regulatory policies and other government interventions in the marketplace. The next three chapters consider economic regulation of price, entry, and conditions of sale, regulation which is nominally intended to limit the exercise of monopoly power. Ronald Braeutigam (Chapter 23) reviews and interprets the literature on optimal pricing for natural monopolies (whether regulated or publicly owned). David Baron (Chapter 24) provides an overview of recent formal research on the design of optimal regulatory mechanisms and institutions when information is asymmetric, connecting this literature to the classical treatment of rate-of-return regulation. Paul Joskow and Nancy Rose (Chapter 25) survey and critique the voluminous empirical literature on the effects of economic regulation. Howard Gruenspecht and Lester Lave (Chapter 26) conclude the *Handbook of Industrial Organization* with an overview of the economic rationales and effects of social regulatory policies directed at health, safety, environmental, and related problems.

Historical overviews

Because most of the individual chapters in the *Handbook of Industrial Organization* provide historical overviews of the topics they cover, it seems redundant to provide a general overview here. For additional discussions of the historical development of the field of industrial organization, see Scherer (1980), Bresnahan and Schmalensee (1987), Hay and Morris (1979), Schmalensee (1982, 1988), and Roberts (1987).

[4] We must again note a gap in coverage; we had hoped that this Part would contain an overview and analysis of competition (antitrust) policies and their enforcement.

Acknowledgements

Our primary debt is, of course, to the authors of the chapters in the *Handbook of Industrial Organization*. We appreciate the care, skill, and imagination with which they carried out their assignments, their willingness to take our comments seriously, and their efforts to meet our deadlines. Many also provided us with useful advice and comments. We are also indebted to Louis Phlips for his many hours of work on this project; it is our fault and the reader's loss that he is not among the Handbook authors.

RICHARD SCHMALENSEE
Massachusetts Institute of Technology

ROBERT D. WILLIG
Princeton University

References

Bresnahan, T.F. and R. Schmalensee (1987) 'The empirical renaissance in industrial economics: An overview', *Journal of Industrial Economics*, 35:371–378.

Hay, D.A. and D.J. Morris (1979) *Industrial economics: Theory and evidence*. Oxford: Oxford University Press.

de Jong, H.W. (1986) 'European industrial organization: Entrepreneurial economics in an organizational setting', in: H.W. de Jong and W.G. Shepherd, eds., *Mainstreams in industrial organization, Book I*. Boston: Kluwer.

Roberts, D.J. (1987) 'Battles for market share: Incomplete information aggressive strategic pricing, and competitive dynamics', in: T. Bewley, ed., *Advances in economic theory, Fifth World Congress*. Cambridge: Cambridge University Press.

Scherer, F.M. (1980) *Industrial market structure and economic performance*, 2nd edn. Chicago: Rand McNally.

Schmalensee, R. (1982) 'The new industrial organization and the economic analysis of modern markets', in: W. Hildenbrand, ed., *Advances in Economic Theory*. Cambridge: Cambridge University Press.

Schmalensee, R. (1988) 'Industrial economics: An overview', *Economic Journal*, 98:643–681.

Schwert, G. W. (1981) 'Using financial data to measure the effects of regulation', *Journal of Law and Economics*, 24:121–158.

Tirole, J. (1988) *The theory of industrial organization*. Cambridge: MIT Press.

CONTENTS OF VOLUME II

Chapter 19

An Updated Review of Industrial Organization: Applications of Experimental Methods

PART 4 – INTERNATIONAL ISSUES AND COMPARISONS

Chapter 20

Industrial Organization and International Trade

PART 3

EMPIRICAL METHODS AND RESULTS

Chapter 16

INTER-INDUSTRY STUDIES OF STRUCTURE AND PERFORMANCE

RICHARD SCHMALENSEE*

Massachusetts Institute of Technology

Contents

*The first version of this chapter was written while I was visiting the Harvard Business School, and it benefitted from my access to Baker Library there. In preparing the current version, I have been helped enormously by exceptionally useful comments from Dennis Carlton, Richard Caves, William Dickens, Henry Farber, Franklin Fisher, Paul Geroski, Jerry Hausman, Alexis Jacquemin, Paul Joskow, Robert Masson, Dennis Mueller, David Ravenscraft, Jean Tirole, Leonard Weiss, Robert Willig, and audiences at Princeton, the 1986 EARIE Conference, and Penn State.

Handbook of Industrial Organization, Volume II, Edited by R. Schmalensee and R.D. Willig

1. Introduction

This chapter is concerned with inter-industry studies of the relations among various measures of market structure, conduct, and performance.[1] Prior to the seminal work of Bain (1951, 1956), most empirical research in industrial organization involved detailed case studies of particular industries. These were time-consuming, involved a great deal of subjective judgement, and covered only a small sample of industries, in many of which antitrust litigation had made data available. Bain's inter-industry, cross-section approach seemed to make possible rapid and objective analysis of large samples of markets. Research interest accordingly shifted from industry studies to inter-industry work during the 1960s.

In a comprehensive survey written at the start of the 1970s, Weiss (1974) discussed 46 cross-section studies of the correlates of seller concentration. Ten years later, Gilbert (1984) found 45 such studies of the U.S. banking industry alone. But during this same decade a number of critics effectively challenged the data and methods used in inter-industry research, as well as the conventional interpretation of its findings. Interest shifted to work on the theory of imperfectly competitive markets and, more recently, to econometric industry studies employing formal models of conduct. Inter-industry studies are now out of fashion.

While some feel that fashion is unjust because cross-section research can reveal the structural parameters that determine market conduct and performance, others contend that the cross-section approach is inherently incapable of producing anything useful. In the next section I argue for an intermediate position: cross-section studies rarely if ever yield consistent estimates of structural parameters, but they can produce useful stylized facts to guide theory construction and analysis of particular industries. They typically fail to be persuasive when they attempt to do much more than this. Inter-industry research can complement industry studies by describing robust relations that hold across large samples of markets.

Cross-section studies also fail to be persuasive when they ignore serious measurement problems. Section 3 considers some of these, focusing on the problem of measuring profitability. Again I take an intermediate view: these problems deserve to be taken seriously but, if handled sensibly, they are not so severe as to render cross-section work valueless.

[1]Other chapters in this Handbook discuss related work on the dynamics of pricing behavior (Chapter 15 by Dennis Carlton), technical change (Chapter 18 by Wesley Cohen and Richard Levin), and international comparisons (Chapter 21 by Richard Caves). Chapter 17 by Timothy Bresnahan considers single-industry studies concerned with many of the issues treated here.

Sections 4–6 discuss the main empirical regularities that have been uncovered in inter-industry research. The discussion is organized by dependent variable: Section 4 describes studies that attempt to explain differences in profitability, Section 5 considers studies of prices and costs, and Section 6 discusses studies of concentration, advertising intensity, and conduct-related variables. Section 7 contains a few concluding remarks.

The literature discussed here is enormous, and this chapter is inevitably incomplete despite its length. The reference list at the end is biased toward recent works (and full, book-length presentations) in which earlier contributions are discussed. A number of previous surveys treat some topics in more depth than is possible here.[2]

2. Method and interpretation

2.1. Long-run equilibria and the endogeneity problem

The usual presumption in cross-section work in all fields of economics is that observed differences across observations reflect differences in long-run equilibrium positions.[3] Thus, for instance, cross-section studies of demand are usually interpreted as producing estimates of long-run elasticities.

In general, in order to use cross-section data to estimate long-run relations, deviations from long-run equilibrium must be uncorrelated with the independent variables employed. If this strong requirement (discussed further below) is satisfied, and if theoretically sound structural equations can be formulated and identified, simultaneous equations techniques can be employed to yield consistent estimates of long-run structural parameters. In order to estimate any structural equation consistently, one must generally have at least as many available instrumental variables as there are variables on the right-hand side of the equation. Instrumental variables must be exogenous – that is, uncorrelated with the structural residual. If an equation has K endogenous variables and L exogenous variables on the right-hand side, consistent estimation requires at least K additional instrumental variables that (a) can be excluded from the equation on theoretical grounds and (b) are correlated with one or more of the included

[2]Useful surveys of portions of the cross-section literature include Weiss (1971, 1974), Ferguson (1974), Jacquemin and deJong (1977), Comanor and Wilson (1979), Hay and Morris (1979, chs. 7 and 12), Scherer (1980, chs. 4 and 9), Brozen (1982), Geroski (1983), Curry and George (1983), Gilbert (1984), Waterson (1984, ch. 10), and Caves (1985).

[3]For general discussions of the cross-section approach, see Phillips (1976), Cowling (1976), Caves, Porter, and Spence (1980, ch. 1), Sawyer (1982), and Donsimoni, Geroski and Jacquemin (1984), in addition to the surveys cited in footnote 2, above. Caves and Pugel (1980) provide a nice discussion of the long-run equilibrium presumption and use it explicitly to structure their analysis.

endogenous variables. I now argue that the instruments necessary for consistent estimation are rarely available in inter-industry empirical work in industrial organization.

Inter-industry studies in industrial organization are part of an enterprise that seeks tools, based on either deductive or inductive analysis, that permit one to make useful predictions about real markets based on relatively stable, observable variables. These quantities, which together comprise *market structure*, are loosely divided into two sets. *Intrinsic* structural variables [called *basic conditions* by Scherer (1980)] are more or less completely determined by the nature of the product and the available technologies for production and marketing. Other elements of market structure are *derived* in that they may reflect government policy, business strategies, or accidents of history, as well as the relevant intrinsic variables. List of derived structural variables usually include seller concentration, conditions of entry, buyer concentration, and product differentiation.

In any complete market model, such as the textbook models of monopoly and competition, market structure determines *market conduct* – the behavioral rules followed by buyers, sellers, and potential entrants to choose the variables under their control. *Market performance* is assessed by comparing the results of market conduct to first-best ideals, such as perfect competition, or feasible alternatives.

Most of the cross-section literature has been concerned with the effects of intrinsic structural variables on derived structure and with the effects of structure as a whole on conduct and performance. But, except in textbook competitive markets, derived market structure is clearly affected by market conduct in the long run. Mergers and investments alter seller concentration; marketing strategies may affect product differentiation; the attractiveness of entry depends on the actual and expected conduct of established sellers. And, though the linkages may be looser, intrinsic structure is also affected by conduct in the long run. Invention and innovation can change the nature of the product and the available technologies. Industry-specific aspects of government policy are generally affected by industries' lobbying and other political activity and may also be affected by observed performance.

Thus, in the long-run equilibria with which cross-section studies must be primarily concerned, essentially all variables that have been employed in such studies are logically endogenous. This means that there are in general no theoretically exogenous variables that can be used as instruments to identify and estimate any structural equation. (Even if one is willing to argue that intrinsic structure is approximately exogenous, one has only a small number of potential instrumental variables. And these are difficult to observe because actual characteristics of existing firms or plants are not determined only by intrinsic structure.) Moreover, recent theoretical work emphasizes the complexity of market conduct and its determinants and thus makes it difficult to argue strongly for the exclusion of any variable from any structural equation.

Several authors, beginning with Strickland and Weiss (1976), have estimated three-equation models, with profitability, advertising and concentration all treated as endogenous.[4] An examination of some of the specification and exogeneity assumptions made in a leading example of this approach makes the basic endogeneity problem clear. Martin (1979a) needs two instruments to identify and estimate his profitability equation. He employs a durable good dummy variable and lagged values of concentration and profitability. Given the long-run equilibrium presumption and the likelihood that departures from long-run equilibrium are serially correlated, it seems unlikely that lagged endogenous variables are generally valid instruments in cross-section studies. He treats the ratio of imports to sales as exogenous, even though high domestic prices should attract imports [Geroski (1982), Caves (1985)]. And he also treats as exogenous three variables that depend on the technologies actually employed by the industry's firms. Since these depend on seller conduct as well as the menu of available technologies, they are unlikely to be valid instruments.

Martin excludes the three technology-based variables mentioned above from his structural equation for advertising intensity, even though it is unclear in theory why marketing decisions should not depend on production technology. He uses these three variables, along with a regional markets dummy and lagged profitability and concentration, as instruments. The validity of all these seems suspect, with the possible exception of the regional dummy. Similar problems affect Martin's concentration equation.

Some authors have treated additional variables as endogenous.[5] The longer the list of endogenous variables in any model, the more difficult it is to obtain valid instruments from available data. It seems very unlikely that the endogeneity problem posed here can be solved by more elaborate model specifications. Nor can this problem be simply dismissed by the observation that least-squares and simultaneous equations methods generally yield very similar estimates. The relation between these estimates is entirely determined by the set of variables used as instruments.[6] And specification tests of the sort employed by Geroski

[4]Martin (1979a, 1979b) has pointed out that the original Strickland–Weiss (1976) model is not identified, even if one assumes all their judgements about exogeneity are correct.

[5]Studies using simultaneous equations methods include Comanor and Wilson (1974), Geroski (1982), Marvel (1980), Caves, Porter and Spence (1980), Martin (1983), and Connolly and Hirschey (1984).

[6]But the general similarity between the coefficient estimates produced by least squares and simultaneous equations techniques in cross-section studies does present something of a puzzle. (I am indebted to Jerry Hausman for posing this problem and for suggesting the development that follows.) Consider the simplest possible structural equation: $y = \beta x + \varepsilon$, where y, x, and ε have mean zero, and β is a constant. Suppose that x is correlated with ε, as is a proposed instrumental variable, z. Let β_o and β_i be the ordinary least squares and instrumental variables estimates of β, respectively. Then a

(1982), Connolly and Hirschey (1984), and others to test for endogeneity are valid only if one has available a sufficient number of instruments known a priori to be valid.

Consistent structural estimation is possible without instrumental variables in recursive systems,[7] but arguments for recursivity are rarely made in this literature. Similarly, panel data, in which a set of firms or industries is observed over time, can yield consistent structural estimates if an explicit model of disequilibrium behavior is employed. But this has rarely been done; almost all inter-industry studies have had only a cross-section dimension, and studies using panel data have generally had a non-structural, descriptive focus.

2.2. Design and interpretation

Even if cross-section studies in industrial organization generally can only describe relations among long-run equilibrium values of endogenous variables, such studies can make a contribution. But they should be designed, executed, and interpreted with due regard for their limitations.

A simple example will help to structure the discussion. Consider a competitive market in which data are available only on price, P, and quantity, Q, both endogenous v⁻·iables. Suppose, further, that it is considered reasonable to work with linear approximations to the supply and demand curves:

$$Q^s = a + bP + e, \tag{2.1a}$$

$$Q^d = \alpha - \beta P + \varepsilon \tag{2.1b}$$

---

bit of algebra shows that the probability limit of $(\beta_i - \beta_o)/\beta_o$ is given by

$$\left[(1 - R_o^2)/R_o^2\right]^{1/2}\left[(\rho_{z\varepsilon}/\rho_{zx}) - \rho_{x\varepsilon}\right]/\left[1 - (\rho_{x\varepsilon})^2\right]^{1/2},$$

where R_o^2 is the least-squares R^2, and the ρ's are correlations. In time-series studies with trendy variables, ρ_{xz} and R_o^2 will be close to one, so that even if z is a terrible instrument (so that $\rho_{z\varepsilon}$ and $\rho_{x\varepsilon}$ are approximately equal), the difference between least squares and instrument variables estimates will generally be small. In cross-section data, however, ρ_{xz} and R_o^2 are generally well below one, so that large changes in coefficients would be expected to be the rule even with poor instruments.

[7]Suppose the structural equation for some variable, y, involves a set of independent variables, X, some of which are endogenous, and a disturbance term, ε. This equation can be consistently estimated by least squares as long as y does not enter the structural equations for the endogenous elements of X *and* ε is uncorrelated with the disturbances of those equations. That is, y must not affect X directly, and the unobservable variables determining X and y must be uncorrelated.

where e and ε summarize the effects of the exogenous variables affecting supply and demand, respectively. Working with the reduced form of (2.1), it is easy to see that the variances of price and quantity and the covariance between them implied by this model are as follows:

$$(b+\beta)^2\sigma_{PP} = \sigma_{\varepsilon\varepsilon} + \sigma_{ee} - 2\sigma_{e\varepsilon}, \tag{2.2a}$$

$$(b+\beta)^2\sigma_{QQ} = b^2\sigma_{\varepsilon\varepsilon} + \beta^2\sigma_{ee} + 2b\beta\sigma_{e\varepsilon}, \tag{2.2b}$$

$$(b+\beta)^2\sigma_{PQ} = b\sigma_{\varepsilon\varepsilon} - \beta\sigma_{ee} + (\beta - b)\sigma_{e\varepsilon}. \tag{2.2c}$$

These three equations in five unknowns (b, β, σ_{ee}, $\sigma_{\varepsilon\varepsilon}$, and $\sigma_{e\varepsilon}$) cannot generally be solved for unique estimates of b or β. But this does not mean that data on price and quantity provide no useful information.

In early studies of the demand for agricultural products, for instance, it was argued that σ_{ee} was much larger than $\sigma_{\varepsilon\varepsilon}$. In this case least squares estimation of (2.1b) yields an approximately consistent estimate of β. Alternatively, suppose that one feels that $\beta = 0$ but observes $\sigma_{PQ} < 0$. Equation (2.2c) shows immediately that $\rho_{e\varepsilon} = \sigma_{e\varepsilon}/[\sigma_{ee}\sigma_{\varepsilon\varepsilon}]^{1/2}$ must be positive. The plausibility of this implication can perhaps be evaluated on the basis of theory and evidence from other contexts. More formally, with $\beta = 0$, equations (2.2) can be solved for $\rho_{e\varepsilon}$ as a function of σ_{PP}, σ_{QQ}, σ_{PQ}, and b. Using this relation, and allowing for sampling variability, one can ask whether plausible values of the elasticity of supply are consistent with plausible values of $\rho_{e\varepsilon}$.

The first point of this example is that data on endogenous variables do provide information, though not the sort that can be handled by commonly employed estimation techniques. For models noticeably more complex than (2.1), such information can be quite difficult to interpret. [Explicit latent variable models may be useful here; see Aigner, Hsiao, Kapteyn and Wansberg (1984).] The second point is that even in simple models, the interpretation of relations among endogenous variables requires a good deal of prior information. Since the prior information one brings to any empirical study is derived both from theory and from previous empirical work, this suggests (correctly, I think) that progress is often made by assembling pieces of theory and evidence from a variety of sources, rather than through definitive tests of critical hypotheses.

All this implies that the primary objective in cross-section studies must be to describe the main patterns in the data set employed as clearly and completely as possible. The appropriate mind-set, which some recent work seems clearly to reflect, is accordingly that of descriptive statistics, not structural hypothesis testing. Of course, all correlations are not created equal. Theory and previous empirical work must determine what is worth studying and how it should be measured. Structural hypotheses must inevitably play a key role at the design stage, even when the endogeneity problem prevents structural estimation and testing. On the other hand, strong and robust relations among variables with economic content should always be reported, even if they do not make sense in light of existing theory; they may be central to the development of better theory.

Regression analysis may be an appropriate technique for data description in many cases. But in a world of what Krasker, Kuh and Welsch (1983) describe as "dirty data and flawed models", ordinary least squares (and other methods based on second moments) should be supplemented by the techniques they and others have developed for detecting and dealing with extreme observations. [For a striking example of the effects of outliers in cross-section data, see Cohen, Levin and Mowery (1987).] And if statistical analysis is to be used as a tool to summarize data, rather than to estimate structural models, it is important to let the data speak. This points toward the use of relatively simple specifications and careful treatment of specification uncertainty [Leamer (1983), Bothwell, Cooley and Hall (1984), Connolly and Hirschey (1984)].

The almost exclusive attention paid to *t*- and *F*-statistics in much cross-section work is inconsistent with the methodological viewpoint taken here. Such statistics do help the reader sort out the impact of sampling variation, of course. But the relation between structural hypotheses and estimated coefficients is often unclear or controversial. (Indeed, the existence of competing structural explanations for the findings of many cross-section studies is both a reason why this line of research has fallen from favor and a symptom of the general impossibility of structural estimation in this context.) From the descriptive point of view, equal interest usually attaches to the magnitude of estimated coefficients and to the contribution of particular independent variables to explaining the variance of the dependent variable. In the supply–demand example, the *t*-statistic on the slope coefficient in a least squares estimate of (2.1a) would be of interest, but it would provide only a small fraction of the information in the data. In the present context, one would like to know not just whether concentrated industries are on average more profitable than unconcentrated industries, but also whether the difference (if any) is large or trivial.

In general, descriptive work should be concerned with measurement and data summarization in the broadest sense. Convincing evidence on the validity of structural hypotheses rarely emerges from a single empirical study – here or in other branches of economics. Progress is facilitated if the main features of individual data sets are fully described, so that diverse studies can be compared and contrasted. Improvements in data collection and measurement methods are likely to add more value than refinements in the specification of underidentified structural equations.

Because it is often not clear how best to measure many variables suggested by theory, the most interesting empirical relations are those that are robust to plausible variations in measurement methods as well as to variations in specification. And because different countries often have different accounting conventions and construct official data in different ways, and we seek economic laws that hold across national boundaries, international replications are especially valuable. [The use of matched Canadian and U.S. industries by Caves, Porter and Spence (1980), Baldwin and Gorecki (1985), and a few others is noteworthy in this context.]

Finally, it is important to recall that if departures from long-run equilibrium are correlated with the independent variables, cross-section studies will produce a biased picture of relations among long-run equilibria. And such correlations are often plausible. Capital-intensive industries tend to be concentrated and to have cyclically sensitive profitability, for instance. New industries or those that have been disturbed by major innovations are likely to be farther from equilibrium than others, with the direction of departure from equilibrium dependent on the source and nature of the innovation. All of this points to the desirability of attempting to control for departures from equilibrium in cross section, of using replication to check for robustness with respect to sample selection and period of study, and of employing panel data creatively. Panel data sets make it possible in principle to control for or to study cyclical and secular disequilibria and to analyze directly the long-run differences among industries.[8] Panel data share another very desirable feature with data on geographically-separated markets in a single industry: they make it possible to control for unobservable industry-specific variables by focusing on differences over time or across space.

The descriptive orientation presented here implies that cross-section studies in industrial organization should be modest, both in their goals and in their conclusions, since it is generally impossible to estimate structural models complex enough to be theoretically defensible. Modesty would go a long way toward making cross-section studies persuasive, thus putting them on the same plane as good cross-section work in other fields. Consistent with this orientation, I concentrate in Sections 4–6 on empirical regularities that seem to be robust to variations in specification, time period, country, and plausible changes in variable definition.[9] Theory enters in discussions of measurement and specification choice, but I do not attempt to provide definitive structural interpretations of results.

[8] At the simplest level, industry averages over relatively long time periods shed more light on long-run differences than observations for any single year. More generally, modern econometric techniques make it possible to combine intertemporal (within-unit) and inter-industry (between-unit) information efficiently and to perform revealing specification tests; see Hausman and Taylor (1981).

[9] Assmus, Farley and Lehmann (1984) and the references they cite discuss formal approaches to the analysis of multiple studies, the use of which is effectively precluded here by the breadth of the literature covered.

3. Measuring key variables

Most of the cross-section literature focuses on relations involving one or more of the following variables: profitability, concentration, and barriers to entry. Subsections 3.1 and 3.2 consider measures of profitability that have been employed (and attacked) in this literature. Subsections 3.3 and 3.4 discuss measurement of concentration and barriers to entry, respectively.

3.1. Measures of profitability

The many measures of profitability that have been employed in the cross-section literature fall into four basic classes. First, Bain (1951, 1956) argued that the relevant theory deals with the ability of firms to hold price above long-run average cost, where "cost" is defined as usual to include competitive returns on capital employed. Since most firms (and plants) produce multiple products, this suggests using the ratio of excess profit to sales revenue. Only Qualls (1972) and a few others have used accounting-based estimates of this measure of profitability, perhaps because it requires an estimate of the competitive rate of return on capital employed.

Second, many studies have employed accounting rates of return on assets or equity. Bain (1951, 1956) used the after-tax rate of return on equity because of data limitations, and other authors have employed the before-tax rate of return on equity and the before- and after-tax rates of return on assets. [Returns on assets are most naturally defined to include both interest payments and profits; see Schmalensee (1976).] Before-tax measures are undistorted by peculiarities of tax systems, though long-run (risk-adjusted) after-tax (economic) rates of return should be equalized under the null hypothesis of perfect competition. Increases in leverage make the residual return to equity more variable, and in competitive capital markets investors must generally be paid higher average returns to compensate. Rates of return on assets, on the other hand, will mainly reflect operating results, not capital structure decisions.

Third, Collins and Preston (1968, 1969) introduced and employed the so-called price–cost margin (PCM), which can generally be computed for more narrowly-defined industries than accounting rates of return. Consider a firm with long-run constant returns to scale, and let v = variable cost per unit, δ = depreciation rate of capital, ρ = competitive rate of return, P = price, Q = output, and K = dollar value of capital employed. Then the markup of price over long-run average (and marginal) cost is given by

$$\frac{P - v - (\rho + \delta)(K/Q)}{P} = \frac{PQ - vQ}{PQ} - (\rho + \delta)\frac{K}{PQ}. \tag{3.1}$$

The first quantity on the right, (revenue − variable cost)/revenue, is the PCM.

Under competitive conditions, the PCM should on average equal the second quantity on the right of equation (3.1), the required rental on assets employed per dollar of sales. Many authors have used the PCM as the dependent variable in linear regressions and included the ratio of assets (sometimes depreciable assets) to revenue among the independent variables. In light of (3.1), this procedure amounts to assuming that both the competitive rate of return, ρ, and the rate of depreciation, δ, are the same for all industries in the sample.

Fourth, measures that employ the market value of a firm's securities (often, because of data limitations, only its common stock) are attractive because, under the widely-accepted hypothesis of capital market efficiency, the market value of a firm's securities reflects all available information about its future profitability [Schwert (1981)]. In an early study, Stigler (1963) employed the ratio of the market value of a firm's equity to its inflation-adjusted book value. Two other measures have been widely used. Tobin's q, defined as the ratio of the market value of a firm to the replacement cost of its tangible assets, should on average equal one under the competitive null hypothesis if (and only if) intangible assets are not present [Lindenberg and Ross (1981), Salinger (1984)]. The excess value ratio (EVR), defined as (market value − book value)/revenue, was introduced by Thomadakis (1977) as a measure of the ratio of (capitalized) excess profits to sales. [Smirlock, Gilligan, and Marshall (1984) compare these two measures.]

Are all these measures so highly correlated with one another that debates about their relative merits are pointless? At least for the last three classes of measures, the answer seems to be as follows:[10]

Stylized Fact 3.1

Correlations among accounting rates of return are high, and regression results are usually not sensitive to which measure of this type is employed. Correlations of accounting rates of return with the PCM and with measures based on market values are lower, and regression results often depend on which type of measure is used.

The weak correlation between the PCM and the ratio of accounting profits to sales reported by Liebowitz (1982a) and others suggests important inter-industry differences in rates of depreciation and competitive rates of return.

3.2. *Accounting problems*

All of the profitability measures mentioned above rely on accounting data, even those also using data on securities prices [Schwert (1981)]. As Benston (1985)

[10]See, for instance, Ornstein (1972), Caves, Porter and Spence (1980), Lindenberg and Ross (1981), Liebowitz (1982a), Martin (1979b), Salinger (1984), and Hirschey (1985).

demonstrates, it is easy to list many reasons why accounting data yield noisy measures of economic variables. (The PCM is particularly easy to criticize because it omits capital costs.) Important problems arise because large firms are generally active in many markets. Firm-level data are thus multi-market aggregates, while data constructed at the plant level do not reflect costs incurred at the firm level, and the allocation of those costs to individual lines of business is inevitably somewhat arbitrary.[11]

On the other hand, it is unlikely that accounting numbers are pure noise: firms use accounting data (though perhaps not the aggregates in published reports) in decision-making, and many studies in the finance and accounting literatures find that the stock market reacts to the publication of accounting reports. While the signal to noise ratio in accounting data is of interest, the more important question is the extent to which errors in accounting data are correlated (positively or negatively) with independent variables used in regression analysis. If such correlations are important, coefficient estimates will be biased, and statistical studies, even with large samples, may miss real relations involving true, economic profitability and report spurious relations that are mere artifacts of accounting practices.

Stigler (1963) noted that owners of small U.S. corporations have an incentive to pay themselves high salaries, and thus to understate their accounting profits, in order to avoid the double taxation of dividend income. His results indicate that small corporations tend to account for a larger share of industry assets the lower is concentration. [See also Kilpatrick (1968) on adjusting for the effects of this incentive.] One can argue on theoretical grounds that managers have strategic and public relations incentives to understate high profits and overstate low profits, though the extent of such behavior has apparently not been systematically studied.

More recently, considerable attention has been focused on capitalization and depreciation practices and inflation as sources of bias. Much of the relevant theoretical literature [see especially Stauffer (1971) and Fisher and McGowan (1983)] has considered a firm composed of a large number of identical investment projects. Each project requires an initial outlay of one dollar and produces a net cash flow of $\pi(\tau)$ dollars when it is τ periods old, with all dollar figures deflated to some base period. Suppose there are no taxes and the following relation holds:

$$1 = \int_0^\infty \pi(\tau)e^{-r\tau}\,d\tau, \tag{3.2}$$

so that r is the real, economic rate of return on the firm's operations.

[11]These problems apply in the United States to data published by the Internal Revenue Service, the Census of Manufactures, and the Federal Trade Commission's Line-of-Business program, respectively.

To see how r relates to accounting rates of return, let $I(t)$ be the number of projects the firm starts in period t, and let $P(t)$ be the ratio of prices in period t to those in the base period. Thus, $P(t)I(t)$ is the current dollar value of the firm's investment in period t. Let $b(\tau, t)$ be the book value in period t of a dollar invested in period $t-\tau$, and let $d(\tau, t)$ be the accounting depreciation charged against this investment. Then the firm's accounting rate of return on assets in year t is given by cash flow minus depreciation, all over the book value of assets:

$$r_a(t) = \frac{\int_0^\infty I(t-\tau)P(t)\pi(\tau)\,d\tau - \int_0^\infty I(t-\tau)P(t-\tau)d(\tau,t)\,d\tau}{\int_0^\infty I(t-\tau)P(t-\tau)b(\tau,t)\,d\tau}. \tag{3.3}$$

In the simplest case prices are constant, so that $P(t) = 1$ for all t, and that accounting depreciation is not time-dependent, so that $b(\tau, t) = b(\tau)$ and $d(\tau, t) = d(\tau)$ for all τ and t. Then in order for r_a to equal r for all possible investment paths, $I(t)$, it follows from (3.3) that the following equation be satisfied for all τ:

$$-d(\tau) = rb(\tau) - \pi(\tau). \tag{3.4}$$

As Hotelling (1925) first demonstrated and many others have independently discovered since, (3.4) will be satisfied with $b(0) = 1$ and $-d(\tau) = b'(\tau)$ for all τ if and only if the asset's net book value is given by

$$b_e(\tau) = \int_\tau^\infty \pi(x)e^{-r(x-\tau)}\,dx. \tag{3.5}$$

That is, depreciation is *exact* if the asset's book value is equal to the net present value, computed at the economic rate of return, of its future net cash flows. Then exact or economic depreciation is just the decline in book value: $d_e(\tau) = -d[b_e(\tau)]/d\tau$.

If prices are changing, equation (3.4) is replaced by

$$-P(t-\tau)d(\tau,t) = rP(t-\tau)b(\tau,t) - P(t)\pi(\tau). \tag{3.6}$$

It is easy to see that (3.6) is satisfied for all t and τ and for any price trajectory, $P(t)$, if both Hotelling book values and Hotelling depreciation deductions are adjusted to take into account inflation since the asset was purchased:

$$b(\tau,t) = [P(t)/P(t-\tau)]b_e(\tau), \tag{3.7a}$$

$$d(\tau,t) = [P(t)/P(t-\tau)]d_e(\tau). \tag{3.7b}$$

[See Shalchi and Smith (1985) for an overview of the accounting literature on methods for handling price changes in practice.]

To see what happens when exact depreciation and inflation adjustments are not employed, it is convenient and traditional (but somewhat unrealistic) to consider steady-state growth paths. Suppose prices rise at rate i and investment grows at rate g, and define the Laplace transform, $f^*(s)$, of any function of time, $f(t)$, by

$$f^*(s) = \int_0^{\infty} f(t)e^{-st}dt, \tag{3.8}$$

where s is a constant [Stauffer (1971)]. Then, if depreciation is not time-dependent, substitution in (3.3) and integration by parts allow the steady-state accounting rate of return to be rewritten as

$$r_a = g + i + \frac{\pi^*(g) - 1}{b^*(g+i)} = (g+i)\frac{\pi^*(g) - d^*(g+i)}{1 - d^*(g+i)}. \tag{3.9}$$

Since $\pi^*(r) = 1$ by definition, equation (3.9) shows that when $g = r$ the accounting rate of return overstates the economic rate of return by exactly the rate of inflation. It thus provides an unbiased estimate of the firm's *nominal* rate of return, which can be related to observed nominal interest rates, for instance. In the *usual case* in which $r > g$ and $\pi^*(g)$ thus exceeds one, r_a exceeds $g + i$ but may be greater or less than $r + i$ in general [Fisher and McGowan (1983)]. More rapid depreciation, perhaps taking the form of expending some of the initial investment, will reduce $b^*(g+i)$ and $d^*(g+i)$. As long as $\pi^*(g) > 1$, it follows that the steady-state accounting rate of return will be *increased*, even though both profits and assets will be reduced.

In the very special case of exponential decay, $\pi(\tau) = (r+\delta)e^{-\delta\tau}$. Then if $b(\tau) = e^{-d\tau}$, where d and δ may differ, equation (3.9) becomes:

$$r_a = r + i + [i + (d - \delta)]\left[\frac{r-g}{g+\delta}\right]. \tag{3.10}$$

Depreciation is exact if and only if $d = \delta$.[12] If $d = \delta$, r_a is equal to the nominal rate of return, $r + i$, for very short-lived assets ($\delta \to \infty$) and approaches $r + i(r/g)$ as asset longevity increases ($\delta \to 0$). In the usual case in this example, at least, the steady-state bias is thus worse for longer-lived assets. Similarly, as long as $r > g$, the bias is a decreasing function of the firm's growth rate for fixed r.

[12] One should not be misled by this example: in general the time-path of Hotelling depreciation does *not* have the form of the cash-flow profile – nor, necessarily, of standard accounting depreciation schemes.

It is clear that if accounting data are to be used to measure economic profits, an inflation adjustment of the sort described by equations (3.8) is appropriate. Bain (1951) recognized this point, and Stigler (1963) adjusted his data for the effects of inflation. Few later authors have followed suit. The analysis above indicates that failure to adjust for inflation will induce bias if asset lifetimes or firm growth rates are correlated with independent variables employed in profitability regressions.

Outlays for advertising, research, and development are treated as current expenses in conventional accounting, as are costs of producing firm-specific human capital, even though all these outlays are expected to produce future cash flows. The analysis above indicates that in the usual case, these procedures tend to understate firms' capital stocks (by depreciating more rapidly than is economic) and overstate rates of return (see Subsection 4.4 below).

Firms have some discretion over the accounting procedures they employ. Studies of choices of accounting methods [Zmijewski and Hagerman (1981), Holthausen and Leftwich (1983)] consistently support

Stylized Fact 3.2

Large U.S. firms are more likely than small ones to adopt accounting practices (like accelerated depreciation) that lower current profits and increase steady-state accounting rates of return.

Salamon (1985) argues that this phenomenon is the source of the correlation between firm size and accounting profitably detected by Hall and Weiss (1967) and some other authors. On the other hand, there is little support for the existence of a correlation between accounting method choices and industry concentration [Hagerman and Senbet (1976), Zmijewski and Hagerman (1981), Holthausen and Leftwich (1983)].

All this suggests that empirical work on profitability should take accounting biases seriously. In some cases it may be sufficient to use alternative profitability measures that are likely to be biased in different directions. Sometimes controls for accounting distortions can be included among the regressors [Telser (1972, ch. 8), Salinger (1984)]. Alternatively, it may be possible to construct subsamples that differ in the likely direction or importance of accounting biases and to check for stability among the subsamples [Demsetz (1979)]. Inflation-related distortions can be corrected, at least approximately, on a fairly routine basis.[13] One can either exclude small corporations [Kilpatrick (1968)] or attempt to adjust their

[13] For instance, under the assumptions made to derive equation (3.10), if $d = \delta$, then δ equals the observed accounting depreciation/assets ratio, and the inflation-induced bias in the rate of return on assets can be corrected by multiplying both assets and depreciation by $(g + \delta + i)/(g + \delta)$.

accounting profits for excessive salaries [Stigler (1963)]. A number of authors have attempted to adjust accounting data for depreciation-related biases using the steady-state framework presented above [e.g. Weiss (1969), Stauffer (1980), and Salamon (1985)]. Such adjustments require considerable prior information, since the basic cash flow profile, $\pi(\tau)$, cannot be directly estimated from aggregate accounting data.

3.3. Measures of concentration

Two questions are of central importance here: Which measure of concentration should be employed? And how should geographic and product market boundaries be drawn?

A number of authors have presented axiomatic arguments for particular concentration measures; see Hannah and Kay (1977), Curry and George (1983), and Waterson (1984). Ideally, of course, the appropriate measure of concentration should be derived from oligopoly theory. As Cowling and Waterson (1976), among others, have observed, the H-index of concentration, equal to the sum of squared market shares, emerges as an endogenous correlate of industry profitability in a Cournot oligopoly with (exogenous) cost differences. Saving (1970) shows that concentration ratios (the aggregate shares of domestic output or employment of, for instance, the four or eight largest sellers) emerge similarly under alternative behavioral assumptions. But the usual hypotheses of interest involve the effect of concentration on behavior, and this argues against assuming the mode of behavior in advance. Stigler (1964) suggests that the H-index provides a reasonable measure of the ease of detecting cheating on collusive agreements, but his arguments are not fully rigorous. In short, received theory does not dictate the choice of concentration measure.

Most authors use concentration ratios because they are available in government-supplied data and because many studies have found alternative concentration measures to be highly correlated. But the choice among even highly correlated concentration measures can affect the results obtained [Kwoka (1981), Sleuwaegen and Dehandschutter (1986)]. And concentration ratios can be used to develop good estimates of the H-index [Schmalensee (1977), Michelini and Pickford (1985)], so that good estimates of other measures may also be obtainable from published data.

Many authors have also simply used the market boundaries provided by the compilers of official data. As antitrust cases make clear, it is often difficult to choose among market definitions, and the official definitions are often inappropriate. (Geographic market boundaries in official data usually coincide with national boundaries, and product markets boundaries are often based mainly on similarity of production technologies.) Bain (1951) chose to drop from his sample those officially-defined "markets" for which geographic or product boundaries did not seem sensible. This reduced his sample size from 149 to 83. Most subsequent authors have been unwilling to sacrifice so many degrees of freedom to obtain well-defined markets. [But see Mann, Henning, and Meehan (1967).]

Most investigators (but not all) do drop catch-all industries with such terms as "not elsewhere classified" or "miscellaneous" in their descriptions. Some also adjust published concentration ratios for the existence of regional markets [see Shepherd (1974) and, especially, Weiss and Pascoe (1986)]; others include dummy variables for products that are rarely shipped long distances. Going in the other direction, it is common to allow for foreign competition by using the ratio of imports to domestic production [Caves (1985)]. But Leitzinger and Tamor (1983) and others note that if a product is already imported in non-trivial quantities, and if there are no non-tariff barriers preventing an increase in imports, imports can respond to domestic price changes, so that it may be better to work with world markets (and world concentration) rather than domestic markets.

A few studies have considered the relation between *buyer* concentration and seller profitability. The basic Bainian argument here is that buyers who are large relative to the market should be able to destabilize collusion in concentrated industries and push sellers' prices and profits down toward competitive levels. On the other hand, if a seller faces few buyers because he sells to a single concentrated industry and if the concentration–collusion hypothesis is valid, downstream input demand may be less elastic that it would be under competitive conditions, tending to offset increased downstream bargaining power [Waterson (1980)]. Measurement of buyer concentration has proven to be difficult in practice [compare Lustgarten (1975), Guth, Schwartz and Whitcomb (1976), and Waterson (1980)] and tightly constrained by data availability.

3.4. *Measures of entry barriers*

The cross-section literature has taken three different approaches to measuring the elements of market structure that Bain (1956) argued affected the ability of established firms to prevent supra-normal profits being eroded by entry. First, Bain (1956) performed a detailed structural analysis of each of the industries in his sample and classified them according to the height of the barriers to entry in each. This approach is labor-intensive, and subjective judgement must be used to integrate the information on each industry into an overall estimate of the height of entry barriers. For these reasons, only a few subsequent authors [notably Mann (1966) and Qualls (1972); see also Palmer (1973)] have used this approach.

Second, Orr (1974a), using 1964–67 Canadian data, estimated a model of the following sort:

$$\Delta N = \gamma(r - r^*), \tag{3.11}$$

where ΔN is the gross increase in the number of sellers over the period, γ is a positive constant measuring the speed of adjustment, r is the average observed profit rate, and r^* is the profit rate at which entry would cease. Orr (1974a) substituted for r^* a linear function of variables designed to measure the conditions of entry. In a later study, Orr (1974b) used the estimated coefficients of this function to construct a measure of entry barriers for each industry in his sample. Only Masson and Shaanan (1982) and a few others have adopted this two-step approach.

Third, the most common approach to the treatment of entry barriers in studies of profitability appears to be due to Comanor and Wilson (1967). They investigated regression equations of the following form:

$$r = \beta_0 + \beta_1(CON) + \beta_2(BE_1) + \cdots + \beta_{N+1}(BE_N), \tag{3.12}$$

where r is a measure of profitability, the β's are unknown coefficients, CON is a measure of seller concentration, and the BE's are variables designed to measure the structural determinants of entry barriers. BE variables that appear in the literature generally correspond to three of the four possible sources of entry barriers discussed by Bain (1956): scale economies, capital requirements, and product differentiation advantages of established sellers. [Bain (1956) found the fourth possible source, absolute cost advantages of established sellers, to be the least important in his sample.]

Comanor and Wilson (1967, 1974) and many others have measured the importance of *scale economies* by the ratio of the output of a *plant* of minimum efficient scale (MES) to the output of the market as a whole. [Only Neumann, Bobel and Haid (1979) and a few others have attempted to measure minimum efficient *firm* scale.] MES is most commonly measured as either the average size of the largest plants accounting for half the industry's output or the size of the smallest of these plants. Both measures rest on the assumption that the distribution of observed plant sizes relative to MES does not vary systematically across industries, though Weiss (1976) and Baldwin and Gorecki (1985) find evidence that this assumption is false. And Davies (1980) shows that the differences between MES measures based on the size distribution of existing plants and MES measures computed using either survivorship methods or the interesting approach of Lyons (1980) tend to be positive and to be positively correlated with concentration. [See also Ornstein, Weston, Intriligator and Shrieves (1973) on MES measures.]

Caves, Khalizadeh-Shirazi and Porter (1975) argued that even if MES is large relative to the market, small-scale entry may be attractive unless the cost penalty for operation at suboptimal scale is substantial. They compute a cost disadvantage ratio (CDR) by taking the ratio of value-added per worker in plants below MES to that in larger plants, and they propose multiplying the

MES/market ratio by a zero/one dummy variable that equals one only when CDR is small. [Chappel and Cottle (1985) use firm-level data in this fashion.] This procedure tends to overstate the cost disadvantages of small plants, since capital/labor ratios typically rise with scale [Caves and Pugel (1980)] – but CDRs above unity are not uncommon in U.S. data. It is unclear why a zero/one specification is preferable to some sort of continuous interactive form. Some studies employ a CDR-based dummy variable by itself in linear equations; the theoretical rationale is not apparent.

Bain (1956) argued that a potential entrant might be deterred if the *capital requirements* of entry were large in absolute terms. The hypothesis that capital markets are seriously imperfect, on which Bain rested his argument, does not now command much respect. But recent theory implies that entry will be deterred if a large fraction of entry costs are sunk (i.e. cannot be recovered upon exit), and the relative importance of sunk cost may be correlated with the absolute level of capital requirements [see Kessides (1986)]. Capital requirements are often handled in the Comanor–Wilson (1967) framework by including among the regressors a variable measuring the capital cost of a plant of minimum efficient scale. Some authors multiply this quantity by a CDR-based dummy variable.

Finally, Bain (1956) attributed the greatest importance to *product differentiation advantages of established sellers*. Comanor and Wilson (1967) introduced the idea of using an industry's advertising/sales ratio to measure this structural feature; they and others have also employed advertising spending per firm for this purpose. [Cowling (1976) and Porter (1976a) compare these measures.] Some studies have also used research and development spending as a percentage of sales or patents/sales, and Neumann, Bobel and Haid (1985) used the ratio of registered trademarks to owners' equity. All of these variables are basically measures of conduct and thus clearly endogenous in the long run.

4. Profitability

Bain (1951) began the literature considered in this section by arguing that if high seller concentration facilitates collusion, firms in highly concentrated industries should on average earn supra-competitive profits. He found support for this hypothesis using data on leading U.S. firms in the 1936–40 period.[14] In a second seminal study, Bain (1956, esp. pp. 190–191) argued that both high concentration and high barriers to entry were necessary to produce excess profits in long-run equilibrium. He found support for this interactive hypothesis using data on leading U.S. firms in 1936–40 and 1947–51. Bain (1951, 1956) is still worth

[14]For detailed discussions if Bain's (1951) study, see Brozen's (1970, 1971) critique and the responses by Qualls (1974) and Weiss (1974).

reading today for his careful handling of data and his thoughtful discussion of many of the hypotheses, problems, and results that have dominated the subsequent literature.

Subsection 4.1 discusses some descriptive statistics on differences in measured profitability, and Subsection 4.2 considers control variables that have been employed in cross-section studies of profitability levels. Subsections 4.3–4.5 present the main results that have been obtained in these studies, and Subsection 4.6 discusses studies concerned with the variability of profits.

4.1. *Descriptive statistics on profitability*

Are many firms sufficiently profitable as to suggest large percentage differences between price and average cost? Analysis of U.S. data on accounting rates of return [Alberts (1984)] and Tobin's q's [Salinger (1984)], along with the generally small estimates of monopoly welfare losses based on cross-section differences in profit rates, imply

Stylized Fact 4.1

Differences among observed accounting rates of return and market/book ratios in the U.S. are generally too low to be easily reconciled with the existence of textbook monopolies.

The 1936–40 profitability data reported in Bain (1951) support this observation. The average after-tax rate of return on equity in Bain's 20 unconcentrated industries is 6.9 percent. If this is the competitive rate of return, r_c, any other firm's excess after-tax return on equity is given by

$$r - r_c = \frac{(1-\tau)(R-C)}{E} = \left[\frac{(1-\tau)R}{E}\right]\left[\frac{R-C}{R}\right], \tag{4.1}$$

where r is the actual after-tax rate of return on equity, τ is the corporate tax rate, R is revenue, C is total cost (including normal profit), and E is owners' equity. Data from the U.S. Internal Revenue Service *Statistics of Income, 1938* indicate that $[(1-\tau)R/E]$ averages about 1.12 for manufacturing firms in Bain's sample. Thus an observed r of 16 percent corresponds to a markup over total cost $[(R-C)/R]$ of about 8.1 percent $[= (16.0 - 6.9)/1.12]$, which would be chosen by a monopoly facing a demand elasticity of about 12. A firm with such an elastic demand curve has little monopoly power, and yet only 3 of Bain's 22 concentrated industries had r's above 16 percent. The highest r in Bain's sample was for "aircraft and parts", an industry far out of equilibrium in the 1930s; it corresponds to a demand elasticity of about 8.

On the other hand, Mueller (1977, 1986) and Connolly and Schwartz (1985), using both accounting rates of return and the EVR, find that profit rates of large U.S. firms to not converge over time to a common mean [see also Stigler (1963)], and Odagiri and Yamawaki (1986) and Geroski and Jacquemin (1988) report similar results for large Japanese and U.K. firms, respectively. Some studies of other countries (discussed below) cannot reject convergence in the limit, but none finds rapid convergence.

Stylized Fact 4.2

Accounting profitability differences among large firms tend to persist for long periods.

Connolly and Schwartz (1985) find that highly profitable U.S. firms regress toward the mean noticeably more slowly than others.

There appear to be important international differences in profit dynamics. Geroski and Jacquemin (1988) cannot reject the null hypothesis that profitabilities of large French and German firms converge to a common value in the limit, and Odagiri and Yamawaki (1986) find more dispersion in asymptotic profit rates in the United States than in Japan. These studies also argue that rates of convergence are more rapid in Japan than in the United States and more rapid in France and Germany than in the United Kingdom. Odagiri and Yamawaki (1987) find the United States to have the largest asymptotic differences and the slowest convergence in a larger set of countries.

The importance of industry differences in the determination of profitability has been studied by Gort and Singamsetti (1976), using firm-level data for the United States in 1970, and by Schmalensee (1985), Scott and Pascoe (1986), Ross (1986), and Kessides (1987) using U.S. Federal Trade Commission Line of Business data for the mid-1970s. All employed dummy variables for each industry in the sample, and all support

Stylized Fact 4.3

At the firm or business unit level in the United States, industry characteristics account for only about 10–25 percent of the cross-section variation in accounting rates of return.[15]

[15]Gort and Singamsetti (1976) and Kessides (1987) come up with 10 percent, Schmalensee (1985) with 20 percent, and Ross (1986) with 30 percent. [The Scott–Pascoe (1986) estimates are not strictly comparable.] Mueller (1986, pp. 218–219) argues plausibly that the Schmalensee and Ross estimates may be unusually high because of the extraordinary impact of the first oil shock in 1975, the year covered by their data.

This suggests that Stylized Fact 4.2 reflects more than industry-specific accounting biases and stable mixes of firms' activities, though it does not rule out persistent differences in growth rates or accounting practices as sources of long-lived differences.[16] Recent work by Cubbin and Geroski (1987) with a panel of 217 large U.K. firms over the 1951–77 period finds that changes in firms' profit rates are not well explained by industry averages; their estimates reveal important firm-specific dynamic effects. On the other hand, Schmalensee (1985) found that industry characteristics accounted for about 75 percent of the variation in industry average accounting rates of return, suggesting that the industry is at least a valid unit of analysis.

Gort and Singamsetti (1976) attributed the variation in rates of return not explained by industry dummy variables to firm characteristics. But Schmalensee (1985) found that knowing a firm's profitability in one industry provided no information on the likely profitability of its other businesses. This is consistent with Mueller's (1986) finding that the only detectable impact of merger activity in a sample of large U.S. firms during the 1950–72 period was to hasten the regression of acquiring firms' profitability toward the mean. Recently, however, Scott and Pascoe (1986) and Kessides (1987) have detected significant firm effects in the FTC Line of Business data.

4.2. *Control variables*

Many control variables have been employed in cross-section studies of profitability. [Ravenscraft (1983) and Bothwell, Cooley and Hall (1984) provide long lists.] Following Comanor and Wilson (1967), many authors have used some measure of recent sales growth in order to control for the effects of disequilibrium.[17] This variable almost always "works" statistically [see, especially, Bothwell, Cooley and Hall (1984)]:

Stylized Fact 4.4

Recent growth in revenue is positively correlated with measured profitability.

Bradburd and Caves (1982) argue that only unanticipated growth should affect profitability, but they find support for this hypothesis only among uncon-

[16] Imel, Behr and Helmberger (1972) demonstrate that heteroskedasticity is almost certainly present in regression analysis of the profitability of diversified firms. Unfortunately, the data needed to estimate the disturbance covariance matrix consistently are rarely available. But even if fully efficient estimation is not possible, White's (1980) techniques can be used to avoid biased inferences.

[17] Mueller (1986) controls for disequilibrium by using time series data to estimate the steady-state profitability of each firm in his sample.

centrated U.S. industries in 1972. Liebowitz (1982b) examines the dynamic effects of several alternative measures of disequilibrium on the rate of return on assets in U.S. data for the 1960s. He concludes that revenue growth over a one- or two-year period if the best available measure. (Growth rates over longer periods may serve as crude controls for growth-related accounting biases.) Liebowitz (1982b) also finds that his measures of disequilibrium are generally uncorrelated with concentration, so that estimates of the concentration–profitability relation may not be biased by failure to control for disequilibrium.

Studies using the PCM to measure profitability generally employ the capital/revenue ratio as a control. The coefficient of this variable is usually plausible and statistically significant. But significant negative estimates have been reported by a number of authors [e.g. Ornstein (1975), Liebowitz (1982a), Domowitz, Hubbard and Petersen (1986a, 1986b)] especially when U.S. data for the 1970s are employed.

Pagoulatos and Sorenson (1981) and Harris (1986) present evidence that PCMs are lower in industries with more elastic demand, and Bradburd (1982) finds that PCMs are lower in producer goods industries selling inputs that are important to downstream buyers (and for which demand elasticities should accordingly be high). But Bradburd finds no support for the plausible hypothesis that demand elasticity is negatively related to PCM only in concentrated industries.

Finally, a number of authors have attempted to control for differences in risk, using a variety of measures and obtaining a variety of significant [Bothwell and Keeler (1976), Neumann, Bobel and Haid (1979, 1985), Harris (1984, 1986)], insignificant [Grabowski and Mueller (1978), Bothwell, Cooley and Hall (1984), Hirschey (1985)], and perverse [Thomadakis (1977), Mueller (1986)] results. This state of affairs is somewhat surprising a priori, since investors must generally be compensated for bearing risk. Part of the problem may be that firms with inherently risky demand find it optimal to charge a lower price, all else equal, in order to maximize their market value [Harris (1986)].

4.3. Concentration and profitability

Weiss (1974) examined 46 studies that had been published by the early 1970s and noted that 42 of them had found a positive relation between concentration and profitability. [See also the reviews by Collins and Preston (1968) and Phillips (1971).] He took this as providing strong support for the concentration–collusion hypothesis, though he did note that the concentration–profitability relation was generally statistically weak. [See, for instance, Stigler (1963) and Collins and Preston (1968).]

The economic effects of concentration implied by the early literature were also generally small. Employing equation (4.1) as above, for instance, Bain's (1951) results imply an average markup over long-run cost of only 4.6 percent in the concentrated industries in his preferred sample. For other samples (see his table 3), implied markups varied from 0.9 to 3.2 percent, and the corresponding profitability differences were generally statistically insignificant.

Weiss (1971) noted that Bain's (1956) hypothesis called for interactive (concentration × barriers) specifications, but surprisingly few authors have employed models of this sort. Mann (1966) and Qualls (1972) found support for Bain's hypothesis in U.S. data, as did Jenny and Weber (1976) in French data. Orr (1974b) and Caves, Porter and Spence (1980), however, found that interactive specifications did not perform noticeably better than simple linear models with Canadian data. Salinger (1984) argued that Bain's hypothesis implied that (3.12) should be replaced by interactive regression models of the form:

$$r = \beta_0 + CR\left[\beta_1(BE_1) + \cdots + \beta_N(BE_N)\right] + \beta_{N+1}(G) + \cdots, \tag{4.2}$$

where G is a measure of past sales growth, and the ellipses indicate additional variables discussed below. Salinger found that such models had essentially no ability to explain variations in the market/book ratios of large U.S. firms in 1976. Thus, the relevant literature does not provide strong support for Bain's interactive hypothesis.

Using linear models, like equation (3.12), a number of studies published after Weiss (1971, 1974) wrote found positive relations between domestic concentration and profitability; these include studies of Japan [Caves and Uekusa (1976)], Pakistan [White (1974)], France [Jenny and Weber (1976)], West Germany [Neumann, Bobel and Haid (1979, 1985)] and several studies of U.S. manufacturing industries.[18] Gilbert (1984) concluded that analyses of U.S. banking markets support the existence of a positive – though economically trivial – relation.

But many later studies of U.S. data, particularly those using multivariate specifications, found no statistically significant linear relation between domestic concentration and profitability, even when market share (see Subsection 4.5) was not included among the regressors.[19] Several studies [Porter (1976a), Grabowski and Mueller (1978), Connolly and Hirschey (1984), Hirschey (1985)] reported

[18]See Imel, Behr and Helmberger (1972), Telser (1972, ch. 8), Lustgarten (1975), Peltzman (1977), Thomadakis (1977), LaFrance (1979), Marvel (1980) and Masson and Shaanan (1982). de Melo and Urata (1986) find a positive relation in Chilean data in 1979 but not in 1967.

[19]Examples include Comanor and Wilson (1967, 1974), Ornstein (1972, 1975), Vernon and Nourse (1973), Boyer (1974), Gort and Singamsetti (1976), Cattin and Wittink (1976), Porter (1976a, ch. 6), Strickland and Weiss (1976), Martin (1979a, 1979b), Lindenberg and Ross (1981), and Bradburd (1982).

statistically significant *negative* concentration coefficients with U.S. data. And, while Weiss (1971, 1974) noted the tendency of the concentration–profitability relation to weaken during inflationary periods [see, for instance, Stigler (1963)], Domowitz, Hubbard and Petersen (1986a, 1986b) found that this relation essentially vanished in the United States during the 1970s. [See also Scott and Pascoe (1986) and Schmalensee (1987).]

Non-U.S. data have also produced negative results. Phillips (1971) failed to detect a concentration–profitability relation in French, Belgian, or Italian data, and Jacquemin, de Ghellinck and Huveneers (1980) confirmed his results for Belgium. With the exception of the theoretically interesting study of the relation between changes in the *H*-index of concentration and changes in profitability by Cowling and Waterson (1976), most studies of the United Kingdom have failed to find a positive linear relation between concentration and profitability [Hart and Morgan (1977), Hart and Clarke (1980), Clarke (1984)]. And the Cowling–Waterson (1976) results are apparently not robust to changes in the sample of industries studied [Hart and Morgan (1977)].

Most of these studies adopt specifications in which one or another concentration ratio is linearly related to profitability. Alternative concentration measures and functional forms sometimes yield stronger results.[20] Stigler (1964), for instance, found the *H*-index outperformed the four-firm concentration ratio. Most other studies have not detected sharp differences among these and other frequently discussed (and highly correlated) measures. Kwoka (1979, 1981), however, found that the shares of the two leading firms are noticeably more closely related to industry PCMs than broader concentration ratios. [See also Kwoka and Ravenscraft (1986).]

Bain (1951) argued that his data seemed to show the existence of a critical concentration ratio, above which profitability increased discontinuously. Changes in concentration above or below this level had no discernible effect. A number of studies using U.S. data have found some support for a relation of this form [Dalton and Penn (1976), White (1976), Kwoka (1979); but see Sleuwaegen and Dehandschutter (1986)]. In the most sophisticated study of this sort, Bradburd and Over (1982) find evidence for two critical levels. If concentration was previously low, they find that profits do not increase with increases in concentration until the leading four firms account for 68 percent of industry sales. But if

[20]Theory suggests that the conduct, and thus the profitability, of multi-product firms that encounter each other in multiple markets ought to be affected by these contracts, as well as by concentration in the relevant markets. Scott (1982) finds strong support for an interactive version of this hypothesis in data on U.S. manufacturing markets in 1974, but Gilbert (1984) notes that (generally less sophisticated) investigations of this hypothesis using data on banking markets have produced relatively weak results.

concentration was previously high, profits do not drop until the four-firm ratio falls below 46 percent. Finally, however, Geroski's (1981) work indicates that the critical concentration ratio hypothesis fares no better in U.K. data than the hypothesis of a linear relation.

At the very least, these mixed results make it clear that a researcher cannot expect a strong, positive concentration–profitability relation to leap out from cross-section data:[21]

Stylized Fact 4.5

The relation, if any, between seller concentration and profitability is weak statistically, and the estimated concentration effect is usually small. The estimated relation is unstable over time and space and vanishes in many multivariate studies.

Several studies have found a negative linear relation between the imports/consumption ratio and profitability.[22] But, even if foreign competition can erode domestic market power, the long-run profitability of a competitive industry should be unaffected by imports. This argues for an interactive specification [Pugel (1980a), Caves (1985)]. And several authors have indeed found that the negative impact of imports on domestic profitability is stronger when domestic concentration is high.[23]

Stylized Fact 4.6

The ratio of imports to domestic consumption tends to be negatively correlated with the profitability of domestic sellers, especially when domestic concentration is high.

[21] Hay and Kelley (1974) find that explicit collusion in the United States tends to occur most frequently in concentrated industries (especially where products are homogeneous) and to involve only a few firms. This generally supports the notion that concentration facilitates collusion. But explicit collusion is illegal and apparently relatively rare in the United States, and if concentration made *tacit* collusion easy, sellers in concentrated industries would not need to break the law.

[22] Examples include Geroski's (1982) study of the United Kingdom, Chou's (1986) study of Taiwan, work on West German data by Neumann, Bobel and Haid (1979, 1985), and studies of the United States by Martin (1979a) and Marvel (1980). de Melo and Urata (1986) find a positive relation for Chile, which they attribute to quantitative import restrictions.

[23] Examples include studies of U.S. data by White (1976), Pugel (1980a), and Domowitz, Hubbard and Petersen (1986a), a study of Belgian data by Jacquemin, de Ghellinck and Huveneers (1980), a study of Chile by de Melo and Urata (1986) and work by Caves, Porter and Spence (1980) with Canadian data.

Pugel (1980a) also finds that import penetration has a stronger negative relation with domestic profitability when conventional measures of entry barriers are high. The success of interactive specifications involving import penetration contrasts sharply with the (concentration × barriers) work discussed above.[24]

The arguments in the preceding paragraph suggest that increases in tariff protection should have a positive structural impact on long-run profits only in concentrated industries. But, while Round (1983) finds an empirical relation of this sort for Australia, Bloch (1974b) finds none for Canada. A number of authors have employed the ratio of exports to domestic production in profitability regressions. It is hard to provide a convincing theoretical rationale for this specification [Caves (1985)], and significant coefficients of both signs have been reported [compare Neumann, Bobel and Haid (1979, 1985) with Geroski (1982) and Martin (1983)], along with many insignificant results. Finally, Leitzinger and Tamor (1983) find that a (weak) proxy for world market concentration strongly outperforms U.S. domestic concentration for a sample of widely-shipped goods in 1972, and Yamawaki (1986) finds that the profit margin on Japanese exports is positively related to concentration in the corresponding U.S. industry.

Lustgarten (1975) found that *buyer* concentration was negatively related to PCMs in the 1963 U.S. data. LaFrance (1979) noted that buyer concentration is theoretically irrelevant under perfect competition and found evidence that the negative effect of buyer concentration increases with seller concentration in Lustgarten's data. But Guth, Schwartz and Whitcomb (1976) argued that Lustgarten's measure of buyer concentration was flawed and that correcting the flaws eliminated his results. And Ravenscraft (1983) and Martin (1983) report significant *positive* coefficients of buyer concentration in U.S. data for the mid-1970s. In the most theoretically sophisticated study of buyer concentration, Waterson (1980), using data on changes between 1963 and 1968 in the United Kingdom and measures of buyer concentration based on the *H*-index, finds evidence supporting both a negative effect of buyer concentration on profits and a positive effect of downstream margins. But Bradburd (1982) finds that downstream margins have a negative effect on PCMs in 1972 U.S. data. It seems fair to conclude that no robust relation has yet emerged from studies of buyer concentration.

[24]It is worth noting that most studies in which import penetration is the dependent variable find it positively related to both domestic concentration and profitability; see Marvel (1980), Caves, Porter and Spence (1980), and Caves (1985). [Chou (1986) does not detect these relations in data for Taiwan, however.] It is also interesting to note that specification tests tend to signal the endogeneity of imports, while not flagging other logically endogenous variables [Geroski (1982)]. Finally, in related work, Feinberg (1986) reports that when the German mark fell sharply in 1977–83, so that import competition generally declined, domestic prices rose *less* in more concentrated industries.

4.4. *Entry barriers and profitability*

Since the MES/market measure of scale economies and the MES-based measure of capital requirements are highly correlated with each other [and with seller concentration; see, for instance, Comanor and Wilson (1967)], both rarely if ever have statistically significant coefficients in profitability regressions. It is common, however, for either scale economies [e.g. Ornstein (1972)] or capital requirements [e.g. Comanor and Wilson (1967, 1974)] to have a significant negative coefficient. Most of the studies cited in Subsection 4.3 support

Stylized Fact 4.7

Measures of scale economies or capital requirements tend to be positively correlated with industry-level accounting profitability.

Studies using CDR-based dummy variables [e.g. Kwoka (1979)] generally obtain stronger results. The robustness of the relation described by Stylized Fact 4.7 is somewhat surprising; simple models of entry deterrence suggest that the structural MES/market coefficient should be at most equal to the competitive rate of return [Schmalensee (1981)], implying an effect small enough to be difficult to detect in the data.

Comanor and Wilson (1967, 1974) first reported a strong, positive relation between the advertising/sales ratio and industry-level profitability (measured as the after-tax of return on equity) for U.S. consumer goods industries. This finding has proven to be unusually robust.[25]

Stylized Fact 4.8

In broad samples of manufacturing industries producing consumer goods, advertising intensity is positively related to industry-average accounting profitability.[26]

A comparison of the least-squares and fixed effects estimates reported for consumer goods industries by Domowitz, Hubbard and Petersen (1986a, 1986b),

[25]Replications include the work of Caves and Uekusa (1976) with Japanese data, Round's (1983) study of Australian data, studies of U.K. data by Cowling, Cable, Kelly and McGuinness (1975) and Geroski (1982), and analyses of U.S. data by Imel, Behr and Helmberger (1972), Vernon and Nourse (1973), Strickland and Weiss (1976), Carter (1978), Martin (1979a, 1979b), Marvel (1980), Pagoulatos and Sorenson (1981), Masson and Shaanan (1982), Harris (1984), Bothwell, Cooley and Hall (1984), and Domowitz, Hubbard and Petersen (1986a, 1986b).

[26]Since advertising is usually omitted from variable costs in calculating the PCM, the relevant null hypothesis in studies using his measure of profitability is that the coefficient of the advertising/sales ratio is equal to unity. Coefficients above unity imply a positive relation between advertising intensity and profits net of advertising outlays; coefficients below unity imply a negative relation.

based on U.S. panel data covering the 1958–81 period, indicates that long-run average advertising intensity is positively related to average profitability, as the cross-section studies indicate, but year-to-year changes in these quantities are negatively related across industries.

The results of Bradburd and Caves (1982) and Domowitz, Hubbard and Petersen (1986a) [see also Cattin and Wittink (1976)] imply that in producer goods industries, advertising intensity is negatively related to profitability in both the long and short runs. Advertising is not the dominant component of selling costs in these industries [Weiss, Pascoe and Martin (1983)], so that the measurement error involved in using advertising as a proxy for selling costs may bias the advertising coefficient substantially toward zero.

Salinger (1984) and Hirschey (1985) obtain significant positive coefficients for both advertising intensity and research and development intensity with data on U.S. firms, and Stonebraker (1976) reports similar results at the industry level. Grabowski and Mueller (1978) and Connolly and Hirschey (1984) provide further support at the industry level and also report a significant and robust negative relation between profitability and the product of concentration and R&D intensity. Despite the contrary results obtained by Martin (1983), there seems enough evidence to assert

Stylized Fact 4.9

In broad samples of U.S. manufacturing industries, research and development intensity is positively related to profitability. The relation may weaken or change sign when concentration is high.

Two alternatives to the Bainian interpretation of Stylized Fact 4.8 have been widely discussed [Comanor and Wilson (1979)]; both also apply in principle to the first part of Sylized Fact 4.9. The *endogeneity* interpretation is based on standard models of optimal advertising spending [Schmalensee (1972, 1976)]. These imply that the farther is price above marginal cost, the more profitable is an additional sale, and the higher is the optimal advertising/sales ratio. Thus, the advertising–profitability correlation may reflect differences in the intensity of price competition not explained by other variables included in profitability regressions.

Vernon and Nourse (1973), using a sample of large U.S. firms in the 1960s, bound that industry-average advertising/sales ratios were more strongly correlated with firm profitability than were the firms' own ratios [see also Mueller (1986)], but Schmalensee (1976) showed that this was consistent in principle with the endogeneity interpretation. The arguments of Section 2 imply that the robustness of the advertising–profitability relation to the use of simultaneous equations methods [Comanor and Wilson (1974), Strickland and Weiss (1976),

Martin (1979a, 1979b), Pagoulatos and Sorenson (1981)] does not effectively rebut this interpretation either.

The second alternative interpretation is that the advertising–profitability correlation is simply an *accounting artifact*. The argument can be developed using the steady-state framework developed in Subsection 3.2, neglecting inflation for simplicity. [See also Weiss (1969) and Demsetz (1979).] Suppose that an investment of \$1 in physical capital produces a cash flow of $ce^{-\delta\tau}$ when it is τ periods old, where c is a constant, as long as the ratio of the firm's "goodwill stock", which is increased by advertising and depreciates exponentially at a rate $\lambda > \delta$, to its physical capital is (at least) α. Thus, the firm must invest $\$\alpha$ in advertising when it invests \$1 in physical capital and must support that investment with advertising spending equal to $\$\alpha(\lambda - \delta)e^{-\delta\tau}$ when it is τ periods old. Then if r is the firm's economic rate of return, c must equal $[(r + \delta) + \alpha(r + \lambda)]$.

If the firm is growing steadily at rate g, its advertising spending at time t must equal $I(t)\alpha(g + \lambda)/(g + \delta)$, where $I(t)$ is investment in physical capital at time t. Then if advertising is expensed and physical capital is depreciated at a rate d, the firm's steady-state accounting rate of return on assets, r_a, will be given by

$$r_a - r = (d - \delta)\left[\frac{r - g}{g + \delta}\right] + A\left[\frac{r - g}{g + \lambda}\right], \tag{4.3}$$

where $A = \alpha(g + \lambda)(g + d)/(g + \delta)$ is the ratio of advertising to the *accounting* value of the firm's physical capital.

The first term on the right of (4.3) [which also appears in (3.10)] is the bias due to inappropriate depreciation of physical capital. The second term, which is positive when $r > g$ (the *usual case*), measures the bias due to expensing advertising. This term is large, indicating substantially overstated profitability, if advertising is important (A is large), if it depreciates slowly (λ is small), or if r is much larger than g.

Weiss (1969) dealt with this second bias by adjusting accounting rates of return using (essentially) equation (4.3) and assuming an advertising depreciation rate of 30 percent per year. This adjustment did not remove the advertising–profitability relation. [Grabowski and Mueller (1978) depreciated both advertising and R&D and obtained similar results.] When Bloch (1974a) used a 5 percent depreciation rate, however, the relation vanished. Equation (4.3) explains the difference: the lower is the depreciation rate, λ, the larger is the implied adjustment to the profitability of advertising-intensive firms. Time-series studies of advertising and demand generally suggest that Weiss' assumption is more plausible [Lambin (1976), Comanor and Wilson (1979), Assmus, Farley and Lehmann (1984)], but the issue is not settled.

Demsetz (1979) observed that (4.3) implies that for any λ, the importance of the accounting bias is directly related to $(r - g)$ and thus approximately related to $(r_a - g)$. Dividing his sample according to the latter variable, Demsetz found a positive relation between the rate of return on equity and advertising intensity only when ($r_a - g$) was large. In another indirect test of the accounting artifact interpretation, Salinger (1984) included measures of the ratio of advertising and R&D capital [computed as in Grabowski and Mueller (1978)] to the book value of assets in equation (4.2). He argued that linear relations between these variables and the market/book ratio are implied by the accounting artifact interpretation, while Bain's (1956) hypothesis predicts a positive coefficient for interaction terms involving the products of these variables and seller concentration. He found strong linear relations and insignificant coefficients of the interaction terms. On the other hand, the finding that firm profitability is more closely related to industry advertising intensity than to the firm's own advertising/sales ratio [Vernon and Nourse (1973), Mueller (1986)] appears inconsistent with the accounting artifact interpretation. [See also the discussion of advertising and entry in Subsection 6.3.]

Moreover, neither the endogeneity interpretation nor the accounting artifact interpretation imply that the advertising–profitability relation should vary with market structure or type of advertising, and numerous variations of this sort have been reported. As noted above, the relation is apparently different in consumer- and producer-good industries. Boyer (1974) found a *negative* advertising–profitability relation among U.S. local service industries, and White (1976) found a positive relation only in unconcentrated U.S. manufacturing industries. Porter (1976a, 1976b, 1979) analyzed consumer good industries in the United States and reported a positive advertising–profitability relation for convenience goods (for which buyers do not rely heavily on retailers for information) but not for non-convenience goods, for network television but not for other media [consistent with Boyer (1974), newspaper advertising was negatively related to profitability], and for leading firms but not for followers. All of this suggests that the endogeneity and accounting artifact interpretations are incomplete, but the reported results also seem inconsistent with the view that advertising is always associated with entry barriers.

4.5. *Intra-industry differences*

In a widely-cited early study of firm-level data, Hall and Weiss (1967) found that absolute firm size was positively related to profitability in U.S. manufacturing, even after controlling for industry characteristics, and Caves and Uekusa (1976) reported a similar relation for all but the largest Japanese firms. But a number of studies have failed to replicate this finding in U.S. data [e.g. Ornstein (1972), Imel, Behr and Helmberger (1972), and Vernon and Nourse (1973)],[27] and

[27]Indeed, Leonard Weiss reports (personal communication to the author, July 1986) that he has been unable to replicate the Hall and Weiss (1967) findings with more recent and more complete data.

negative firm size effects have been reported in studies of France [Jenny and Weber (1976)], West Germany [Neumann, Bobel and Haid (1979)], and large European and Japanese firms [Jacquemin and Saez (1976)]. [See also Salamon (1985).] There seems to be no support for a general relation between absolute firm size and profitability.

Gale (1972) found a strong positive relation between the weighted average market share and profitability of large U.S. firms in the 1963–67 period. This seems inconsistent with the general view that economies of scale in most industries are exhausted at output levels corresponding to low market shares [Scherer (1980, ch. 4)]. But Gale's results are consistent with the existence of long-lived efficiency differences among firms in the same industry, with more efficient firms attaining larger equilibrium market shares.[28] And Demsetz (1973, 1974) argued that efficiency differences provide an alternative explanation for the positive relation between concentration and profitability that many investigators had detected. [See Mancke (1974) for a related formal analysis stressing differences in luck.]

To illustrate this argument, consider a market in which firms produce a homogeneous product under constant returns to scale but have different unit costs. [This development follows Schmalensee (1987); see also Cowling and Waterson (1976) and Clarke, Davies and Waterson (1984).] Let us use the conjectural variation formalism to summarize conduct and asume that each firm acts as if it expects its rivals to increase their aggregate output by λ in response to a unit increase in its own output. Higher values of λ correspond to less intense rivalry. It can be shown that in long-run equilibrium, the accounting rate of return on assets (neglecting accounting biases) of a typical firm i is given by

$$r_i = \rho + [(1+\lambda)/Ek_i]\,MS_i, \tag{4.4}$$

where ρ is the competitive rate of return, E is the market elasticity of demand, k_i is firm i's capital/revenue ratio, and MS_i is firm i's market share. If $k_i = k$ for all i, the industry-average rate of return is given by

$$r_I = \sum MS_i r_i = \rho + [(1+\lambda)/Ek]\,H, \tag{4.5}$$

where H is the H-index of concentration. Concentration is endogenous here; it is determined by exogenous cost differences and industry conduct (λ). [Donsimoni, Geroski and Jacquemin (1984) discuss implications of this point.]

One way of interpreting Bain's (1951) concentration–collusion hypothesis is that λ in this model should be positively related to H across industries. And one

[28] Of course these results are also consistent with the hypotheses that collusion is common and that large firms tend to benefit disproportionately from it.

way of interpreting Demsetz' (1973, 1974) argument is that even if λ is the same for all firms in all industries, (4.5) predicts a positive correlation between concentration and profitability across industries. In fact, since E and k vary across industries, it predicts a weak correlation and is thus broadly consistent with the mixed results reported in Subsection 4.3. The rest of this subsection focuses on work aimed at distinguishing between these two view of the world. [See also Brozen (1982).]

Demsetz' view implies that only leading firms, with efficiency advantages, should earn supra-normal profits in concentrated industries. And Bain (1951, p. 320) noted that in his data, "Smaller firms tended to fare about the same regardless of industry concentration; the dominant firms in general had earnings rates that were positively influenced by concentration." Subsequent work by Collins and Preston (1969), Carter (1978), Porter (1979), Chappel and Cottle (1985), and others [see also Weiss (1974)] also supports

Stylized Fact 4.10

The profitability of industry leaders in U.S. manufacturing may be positively related to concentration; the profitability of firms with small market shares is not.[29]

The weak results obtained by many industry-level studies (Stylized Fact 4.5) may thus reflect in part averaging over small and large firms, with the presence of the former tending to mask a positive concentration–profitability relation involving the latter.

This pattern may not generally hold outside the United States. While Round (1975) finds a positive relation between concentration and differences between the profitability of large and small firms in Australia, Clarke, Davies and Waterson (1984) find no support for Stylized Fact 4.10 in the United Kingdom, and Neumann, Bobel and Haid (1979) report exactly contrary results for West Germany.

Two non-Demsetzian interpretations of Stylized Fact 4.10 have been offered. Bain (1956, p. 191) argued that the observed profitability of small firms is generally contaminated by failure to take full advantage of scale economies. Porter (1979), who found a number of differences between profitability equation estimates for industry leaders and for smaller firms, interpreted his findings in terms of the theory of strategic groups. This theory, which stresses barriers to

[29]Demsetz (1973, 1974) obtained similar results using absolute firm size instead of market share [see also Kilpatrick (1968)], but, as Daskin (1983) showed, these findings do not bear directly on the differential efficiency hypothesis that he presents. Note also Porter's (1979) finding that the inter-industry standard deviation in profit rates of leading firms was about 80 percent larger than the standard deviation of smaller firms' profit rates.

mobility that prevent other sellers from imitating the industry leaders, is supported by Newman's (1978) findings that the concentration–profitability relation holds only when leading firms are in the same businesses and that heterogeneity along this dimension lowers profits only in concentrated industries. [See also Oster (1982).]

Weiss (1974) argued that the most natural way to discriminate between the Bain and Demsetz views was to include both concentration and market share in the same equation. Results with specifications of this sort strongly support the following:[30]

Stylized Fact 4.11

In samples of U.S. firms or business units that include many industries, market share is strongly correlated with profitability; the coefficient of concentration is generally negative or insignificant in regressions including market share.

On the other hand, Demsetz' argument implies [see equation (4.4)] that a positive intra-industry relation between profitability and market share should generally hold in U.S. manufacturing. But, though positive relations are somewhat more common than negative ones in most periods [but see Schmalensee's (1987) results for 1972], intra-industry studies of the United Kingdom by Clarke, Davies and Waterson (1984) and of the United States by several authors unanimously support the following:[31]

Stylized Fact 4.12

Within particular manufacturing industries, profitability is not generally strongly related to market share.

These latter results suggest that estimates supporting Stylized Fact 4.11 may be dominated by a small number of industries with unusually strong positive

[30]Examples include Bothwell and Keeler (1976), Gale and Branch (1982), Martin (1983), Ravenscraft (1983), Bothwell, Cooley and Hall (1984), Harris (1984), Smirlock, Gilligan and Marshall (1984), Schmalensee (1985), Smirlock (1985), Mueller (1986), Ross (1986), and Kessides (1987). Shepherd (1974, ch. 4) and Thomadakis (1977) found positive coefficients of both share and concentration, but their sample selection procedures have been questioned [Hirschey (1985)]. On the other hand, Neumann, Bobel and Haid (1979) report a positive and significant concentration coefficient along with a significant *negative* market share effect in West German data. [See also Scott and Pascoe (1986).]

[31]See, for instance, Collins and Preston (1969), Comanor and Wilson (1974), Cattin and Wittink (1976), Porter (1979), Caves and Pugel (1980), Daskin (1983), and Schmalensee (1987). Using FTC lines of business data, Ross (1986) finds that market share is more strongly related to profitability in consumer goods industries than in producer goods, and Kessides (1987) strongly rejects the hypothesis that the market share–profitability relation is stable across industries.

relations between share and profitability. The results of Ross (1986) and, especially, Kessides (1987) tend to support this suggestion.

Collins and Preston (1969) find that differences between the profitability of large and small firms are not related to subsequent changes in concentration, as the Demsetz view would suggest. Salinger (1984) argues that, while Bain predicts that only (concentration × barriers) interaction terms should be positively related to market/book ratios, Demsetz predicts a positive relation involving concentration by itself. Salinger's data are inconsistent with both predictions.

Gale (1972) found that the impact of profitability on market share was positively related to concentration, suggesting that λ in (4.4) is an increasing function of concentration. But this finding has not proven robust.[32] Comanor and Wilson (1974, ch. 10) argued that the gap between the profits of large and small firms in consumer goods industries tended to be positively related to the industry advertising–sales ratio. The results of Caves and Pugel (1980), Ravenscraft (1983), Mueller (1986), and Schmalensee (1987) also support:[33]

Stylized Fact 4.13

The estimated effect of market share on profitability in U.S. manufacturing industries is positively related to the industry advertising/sales ratio.

Finally, recent work by Martin (1983), Kwoka and Ravenscraft (1986), Mueller (1986), Cotterill (1986), and Scott and Pascoe (1986) suggests a variety of complex firm-specific intra-industry effects not easily explicable by either Bain's or Demsetz' hypotheses. (See also the discussion of Stylized Fact 4.2, above.) While the industry may be a valid unit of analysis, systematic differences among firms deserve more attention than they have generally received.

4.6. Variability of profit rates

Stigler (1963) hypothesized that, since one would expect effective collusion to occur only in some concentrated industries, the cross-section variance of profit rates should be higher in concentrated than unconcentrated industries. He found

[32] Ravenscraft (1983) and Smirlock (1985) report negative coefficients of concentration–share interaction terms, for instance; see also Caves and Pugel (1980), Daskin (1983), Rhoades (1985), and Schmalensee (1987). But Mueler (1986) reports a robust negative coefficient of [(1-share) × concentration].

[33] Stonebraker (1976) finds that measures of small firm distress are positively related to large firm profitability when industry growth is controlled for. These same measures are positively correlated with industry advertising and R & D intensity. This suggests that Stylized Fact 4.13 can be extended to include R & D, as do the results of Mueller (1986).

only weak support for this hypothesis. But his data did suggest that the intertemporal variance in profit rates was lower in more concentrated industries. This finding is apparently at odds with the view that collusion/warfare cycles are not uncommon when concentration is high. Subsequent work has focused on the intertemporal variance, but no clear picture of the industry-level correlates of earnings variability have emerged. Perhaps this is because most studies have not attempted to control for differences in the variability of exogenous disturbances.

Confirming Stigler (1963), Gort and Singamsetti (1976) and Rhoades and Rutz (1982) find negative relations between concentration and the intertemporal variance in studies of U.S. manufacturing and banking, respectively, and Sullivan (1978) finds a negative relation for U.S. manufacturing firms between concentration and the beta-coefficient measure of systematic risk. But Round (1983) and Clarke (1984) report (weak) positive relations between concentration and intertemporal variability in data on Australia and the United Kingdom, respectively, and Shepherd (1974) reports a positive relation for a sample of large U.S. firms.

Winn (1977) finds that the simple correlation between concentration and profit variability is negative in U.S. data, but concentration has a positive, significant coefficient in a regression that includes a control for firm size [see also Daskin (1983)]. This implies a strong negative relation between firm size and the intertemporal variance. Such a relation has been reported by Jacquemin and Saez (1986) and other authors and is consistent with the strong negative relation generally observed between firm size and the cross-section variance [e.g. Hall and Weiss (1967)]:

Stylized Fact 4.14

Firm size tends to be negatively related to the intertemporal and cross-section variability of profit rates.

Of course, the intertemporal variance is not necessarily a good measure of riskiness. Geroski and Jacquemin (1986) find that large U.K. firms tend to have larger intertemporal variances than large French and German firms, but a smaller residual variances in regressions involving lagged profitability, and the residual variance is the better measure of the extent to which profits are unpredictable. Lev (1983) considered autoregressive models of both sales and accounting profits and found a strong negative relation between firm size and the residual variance, along with a positive relation between barriers to entry [as assessed by Palmer (1973)] and the serial correlation of sales and earnings. This last result is broadly consistent with the finding of Lustgarten and Thomadakis (1980) that the stock market responds more strongly to changes in accounting earnings announced by firms in concentrated industries, presumably because earnings changes are expected to be more persistent in those industries.

On the other hand, the profits of concentrated industries are not particularly stable over the business cycle, at least in the United States [Domowitz, Hubbard and Petersen (1986a, 1986b, 1987)], Germany [Neumann, Bobel and Haid (1985)], Japan [Odagiri and Yamashita (1987)]. The U.S. results in particular strongly support.

Stylized Fact 4.15

Price–cost margins tend to be more strongly pro-cyclical in more concentrated industries.

5. Prices and costs

Instead of studying profitability, some authors have chosen to analyze its basic components: price and cost. Subsection 5.1 surveys cross-section studies of prices, and Subsection 5.2 examines related work on cost and its determinants.

5.1. Price levels

Studies that compare price levels among geographically separated markets in the same industry are immune to the serious accounting problems that affect profitability studies, and one can expect that omitted market-specific variables are less important (and thus less likely to cause large biases) when attention is focused on a single industry. On the other hand, biased results may be obtained if adequate controls for exogenous determinants of cost are not included. The relation between concentration and price has been studied in numerous markets.[34] This work generally provides strong support for:[35]

[34]These include life insurance [Cummins, Denenberg and Scheel (1972)], banking services [Gilbert (1984) provides a survey], cement [Koller and Weiss (1986)], off-shore oil and timber auctions [Brannman, Klein and Weiss (1987)] air transportation [Bailey, Graham and Kaplan (1985)], newspaper advertising [Stigler (1964), Thompson (1984)], radio advertising [Stigler (1964)], groceries [Lamm (1981), Geithman, Marvel and Weiss (1981), Cotterill (1986)], gasoline [Marvel (1978), Geithman, Marvel and Weiss (1981)], and bond underwriting [Geithman, Marvel and Weiss (1981), Brannman, Klein and Weiss (1987)].

[35]It is worth noting, however, that Cummins, Denenberg and Scheel (1972) find that premiums for group life insurance do not rise with concentration. And, while Marvel (1978) finds that the lowest price charged for gasoline in any area rises with concentration, the relation involving the highest price is statistically insignificant.

Stylized Fact 5.1

In cross-section comparisons involving markets in the same industry, seller concentration is positively related to the level of price.

Price studies that search for critical concentration ratios [Geithman, Marvel and Weiss (1981), Thompson (1984)] obtain mixed results. And while some authors find a small concentration effect [e.g. Stigler (1964), Gilbert (1984), Bailey, Graham and Kaplan (1985)], others find quite large effects [e.g. Marvel (1978), Thompson (1984)].

The relation between concentration and price seems much more robust statistically than that between concentration and profitability. Since studies of price have fewer obvious weaknesses than studies of profitability, Stylized Fact 5.1 seems to provide the best evidence in support of the concentration–collusion hypothesis.[36]

Bloch (1947b) and Hazledine (1980) found that higher Canadian tariffs raised the ratio of Canadian to U.S. prices only when Canadian concentration was high. Nickell and Metcalf (1978) found that the ratio of the prices of proprietary to store-brand grocery products rose with seller concentration and the advertising/sales ratio in U.K. data. They interpreted store-brand prices as a control for costs, but their results also seem consistent with inter-brand differences in quality and consumer information.

Lamm (1981) reports that the three-firm concentration ratio is the best predictor of grocery prices in U.S. cities. Using market shares instead, he finds that the leader's share is insignificant, the shares of the second- and third-ranked firms are positive and highly significant, and the share of the fourth-largest firm is significantly negatively related to price. [Compare Kwoka's (1979) results for manufacturing PCMs.] On the other hand, Cotterill (1986) finds that the H-index is the best predictor of individual grocery stores' prices in Vermont.

Studies of the relation between prices and legal restrictions on local advertising by eyeglass vendors [Benham (1972)] and retail pharmacies [Cady (1976)] have produced strong results supporting:

Stylized Fact 5.2

Legal restrictions on local advertising in the United States are associated with higher retail prices.

[36]Domowitz, Hubbard and Petersen (1987) find that even though margins are more pro-cyclical in more concentrated industries, prices move counter-cyclically in concentrated producer-goods industries with high average margins. These findings are reconciled by observing that cost movements are especially strongly counter-cyclical for the latter industries.

Kwoka (1984) finds that legal restrictions are unrelated to the average quality of optometric services but negatively related to the dispersion in quality levels available. Albion (1983) finds no relation between advertising intensity at the manufacturing level and average retail markup across product categories in data supplied by a U.S. supermarket chain, but within categories he detects a negative relation, especially for highly-advertised, widely-used products.

5.2. Costs and productivity

The shortcomings of accounting data might account for the apparently stronger association between concentration and price than between concentration and profitability. Another explanation might be that costs in concentrated industries tend to be above minimum levels. This would occur if rent-seeking efforts to attain or protect monopoly power elevated costs in these industries substantially, if non-price competition were generally sufficiently intense to erode profits, or if high prices in concentrated industries tended to attract inefficiently small producers.

The first two hypotheses have apparently not been systematically tested. On the third hypothesis, Weiss (1976) found that the fraction of industry output produced in plants below (engineering/interview estimates of) minimum efficient scale in U.S. manufacturing industries was *negatively* related to concentration. Baldwin and Gorecki (1985) obtained similar results for Canada, as did Scherer, Beckstein, Kaufer and Murphy (1975) in a detailed analysis of 6 nations and 12 industries.

On the other hand, Baldwin and Gorecki (1985) also found that concentrated industries with strong tariff protection tended to have more inefficient capacity, all else equal, and Bloch's (1974b) analysis of Canadian/U.S. cost differences points in the same direction. This suggests that cost elevation may occur only in concentrated industries protected from entry by tariffs or other barriers.

A number of authors have employed data on U.S. local banking markets to study the hypothesis that concentration is positively related to cost. [See Gilbert (1984) for an overview.] Edwards (1977) found that banks in concentrated markets demanded 76 percent more labor than other comparable banks; he argued that this reflected the ability of managers in concentrated markets to exercise their preference for larger staffs. Hannan and Mavinga (1980), who also looked at spending on furniture and equipment and on office space, found a positive interaction between concentration and a dummy variable indicating dispersed ownership and thus (presumably) management control. But Smirlock and Marshall (1983) found that concentration was unrelated to labor demand when bank size was controlled for.

Time-series studies over long periods do not find a positive relation between changes in concentration and changes in costs. Instead, what emerges from the work of Peltzman (1977), Lustgarten (1984), and Gisser (1984) is

Stylized Fact 5.3

Over time, U.S. manufacturing industries that experience large increases *or* decreases in concentration tend to show above-average increases in productivity and below-average increases in price.

Gisser (1984) finds that increases in concentration have stronger estimated effects than decreases in initially unconcentrated industries, while the reverse is true in concentrated industries. These results suggest that major product, process, or marketing innovations are associated with large absolute changes in concentration, with the sign of the change depending on the source of the innovation.

Finally, one might hypothesize that costs in concentrated industries are too high because firms in such industries have weak incentives to resist union demands for supra-competitive wages. And Rose (1987) finds that trucking deregulation in the United States, which increased competition in that industry, lowered truck drivers' wages substantially. The large inter-industry literature has produced less clear-cut results, however.

Weiss (1966) observed that wage rates were positively related to both concentration and unionization in the United States in 1959; Phlips (1971) also found positive relations between wages and concentration for Belgium, France, and Italy. But Weiss found that when worker characteristics were added to his regression, the concentration effect vanished, and the estimated impact of unionization was weakened. The subsequent literature [surveyed by Dickens and Katz (1986)] reveals a more complex pattern. Dickens and Katz (1986) show that in U.S. data unionization and concentration are strongly correlated with a number of other factors that might plausibly affect wages (such as plant size, for instance), so that estimates of the effects of concentration are very sensitive to the data set and specification employed. Thus even though there do appear to be industry-level differences in wages that cannot be explained by differences in employee characteristics, the exact source of these differences is difficult to identify with available cross-section data.[37]

Pugel (1980b) found that a measure of excess profit per labor hour was more strongly positively related to U.S. industry-average wage rates than was con-

[37]Landon (1970) finds that printers' wages are *lower* in cities with more concentrated newspaper markets. But since newspaper unions are very strong and almost all U.S. newspaper markets very highly concentrated (many are monopolies), it is not clear how general this result is.

centration; Caves, Porter and Spence (1980) obtained similar results with Canadian data. Pugel argued that his estimates implied that labor on average captured 7–14 percent of excess profits. Karier (1985) added unionization to a standard PCM equation for 1972 and argued that his estimates implied that unions captured about 60 percent of excess profits. Voos and Mishel (1986) obtained a significant negative coefficient of a (concentration × unionization) interaction term in a study of supermarket profits. Their estimates implied that unions captured about 30 percent of profit increases due to concentration. And when Salinger (1984) allowed unionization to interact with (concentration × entry barriers) terms, he found that complete unionization served to eliminate essentially all excess returns. On the other hand, Clark (1984) and Domowitz, Hubbard and Petersen (1986b) find no support for the argument that increases in unionization have a stronger negative effect on profitability in high-concentration industries.

Several studies report important differences in the cyclical behavior of wages in concentrated and unconcentrated industries. Haworth and Reuther (1978) found that in U.S. industry-level wage equations with controls for worker characteristics, concentration was positively related to wages in 1958, when unemployment was high, but not in prosperous 1967. They obtained similar results for unionization and for a (concentration × unionization) interaction variable. Analyses of a 1958–81 panel data set for U.S. manufacturing by Domowitz, Hubbard and Petersen (1986a, 1986b) strongly confirm these findings. They first (1986a) observe that movements in aggregate demand affect PCMs more strongly than movements in industry sales, suggesting cyclical effects operating through economy-wide input markets. They then (1986b) find that, especially in producer goods industries, the coefficient of a (unionization × concentration × unemployment rate) interaction is negative, implying that PCMs of highly unionized, highly-concentrated industries are compressed relative to those of all industries on average during periods of low aggregate demand. These findings together indicate that labor costs in concentrated, unionized industries are less cyclically sensitive than average.

6. Structure and conduct

As Section 2 noted, seller concentration and advertising intensity are determined at least in part by market processes. Subsections 6.1 and 6.2, respectively, consider studies in which these quantities appear as dependent variables. Subsections 6.3 and 6.4 deal with two additional conduct-related phenomena: entry into and exit from industries, and the stability of market shares and market positions within industries.

6.1. *Seller concentration*

International comparisons of concentration levels for the 1950s [Bain (1966)] and 1960s [Pryor (1972)] point to

Stylized Fact 6.1

Rank correlations of manufacturing industries' concentration levels between industrialized nations are very high. Among large industrialized nations, concentration levels do not decline much with increases in the size of the economy.

The first sentence suggests that similar processes operate to determine concentration levels everywhere, while the second indicates that firm size and market size tend to be positively related internationally. On this latter relation and its structural basis, see Scherer, Beckstein, Kaufer and Murphy (1975).

Most studies of seller concentration begin with some measure of minimum efficient plant scale, often derived from the size distribution of existing plants. [See Subsection 3.5 and, for a valuable survey, Curry and George (1983).] Studies of Canada [Caves, Porter and Spence (1980)], the United Kingdom [Hart and Clarke (1980)], Belgium [Jacquemin, de Ghellinck and Huveneers (1980)], Japan [Caves and Uekusa (1976)], Germany [Neumann, Bobel and Haid (1979)], and the United States [e.g. Comanor and Wilson (1967), Strickland and Weiss (1976), Martin (1979a), Geroski, Masson and Shaanan (1987)] support

Stylized Fact 6.2

Levels of seller concentration are positively related to estimates of the market share of a plant of minimum efficient scale (MES).

Some studies report a positive relation between concentration and MES-based estimates of the capital required to build an efficient plant,[38] but generally this variable performs less well than MES/market estimates [Curry and George (1983)]. One might take Stylized Fact 6.2 as suggesting that concentration is determined largely by production technology, but there are several reasons why this inference is not completely justified.

First, the relation between MES/market ratios and concentration is much weaker in first-differences than in levels in U.K. [Hart and Clarke (1980)] and U.S. [Levy (1985), Martin (1979b)] data. This is consistent with the second part

[38]See, for instance, Comanor and Wilson (1967), Caves, Porter and Spence (1980), and Pagoulatos and Sorenson (1981).

of Stylized Fact 5.1 and with the generally weak relation between market growth and changes in concentration over time.[39]

Second, frequently-used measures of minimum efficient plant scale derived from the size distribution of existing plants are suspect for a variety of reasons, as Subsection 3.5 noted. Ornstein, Weston, Intriligator and Shrieves (1973) argue that the capital–labor ratio is a better indicator of the underlying technology; they and others [e.g. Collins and Preston (1969), Caves and Uekusa (1976)] provide strong support for

Stylized Fact 6.3

Capital-intensity is positively correlated with concentration among U.S. manufacturing industries.

Third, what ought to matter for seller concentration is scale economies at the firm level, not at the plant level. But Neumann, Bobel and Haid (1979) are almost the only ones to employ a measure of minimum efficient firm scale in this context. In U.K. data, concentration is positively related to the extent of multi-plant operations [Hart and Clarke (1980), Curry and George (1983)], but there is an element of tautology in this relation. [See also Scherer, Beckstein, Kaufer and Murphy (1975) on the determinants of plant scale and multi-plant operation.]

A number of authors have argued that there are scale economies in advertising, so that minimum efficient firm size and thus concentration in advertising-intensive industries should be higher than production scale economies suggest. Several studies have found positive relations between concentration and advertising intensity in U.S. data.[40] And Cowling, Cable, Kelly and McGuinness (1975) find a positive relation between advertising per firm and (survivorship estimates of) minimum efficient firm size, controlling for (survivorship estimates of) minimum efficient plant size. But other studies report no relation between advertising and concentration changes in multivariate studies [Hart and Clarke (1980), Curry and George (1983), Levy (1985)].

Mueller and Rogers (1980) find that when they divide advertising spending among media, only the ratio of television advertising to sales is positively related to changes in U.S. concentration over the 1958–72 period. This suggests that only television advertising involves important scale economies – presumably deriving

[39]See Martin (1979b), Mueller and Rogers (1980), Pagoulatos and Sorenson (1981), Levy (1985), Curry and George (1983); but see also Ornstein, Weston, Intriligator and Shrieves (1973).

[40]Examples include Ornstein, Weston, Intriligator and Shrieves (1973), Strickland and Weiss (1976), Caves, Porter and Spence (1980), Mueller and Rogers (1980), Pagoulatos and Sorenson (1981), and Connolly and Hirschey (1984); see also the studies discussed in Subsection 6.2, in which advertising intensity is the dependent variable.

from the large minimum outlays necessary to use this medium efficiently. But Lynk (1981) finds that concentration tended to fall in those U.S. industries that most rapidly increased the fraction of their advertising spending going to television when the cost of TV fell in the 1950s and early 1960s.

Fourth, most engineering/interview estimates of the importance of firm-level scale economies suggest that existing levels of concentration, particularly in the United States, are higher than they would be if the leading sellers were of minimum efficient scale [Scherer (1980, ch. 4)]. This, again in combination with the second part of Stylized Fact 6.1, suggests that other forces have operated to increase concentration.

If a number of firms have attained efficient scale thus have constant unit cost, it may be reasonable to model their growth rates and sizes as determined by stochastic processes. In the most famous model of this sort, called Gibrat's Law, period-to-period changes in the logarithm of firm size are independent, normal random variables. It follows that the distribution of firm sizes will tend toward lognormality, with increasing variance (and thus rising concentration) over time. Depending on assumptions about growth, birth, and death, stochastic models can also generate the Pareto and other skewed size distributions; see Ijiri and Simon (1977) for an overview.

Studies of actual size distributions in the United States [Quandt (1966), Silberman (1967), Kwoka (1982)] and the United Kingdom [Clarke (1979), Davies and Lyons (1982)] concentrate on the lognormal and Pareto distributions and generally support:

Stylized Fact 6.4

Size distributions of firms and plants are highly skewed; all families of distributions so far tried fail to describe at least some industries well.

Neither the lognormal nor the Pareto consistently outperforms the other [Curry and George (1983)].

Early studies of firms' growth rates in the United States [Hymer and Pashigian (1962), Mansfield (1962)] generally supported Gibrat's Law. But several recent studies, using new, large data sets, have found that mean growth rates decline with firm size and age [Evans (1987a, 1987b), Hall (1987), Dunne, Roberts and Samuelson (1988a, 1988b)], as does the probability of failure.

Stylized Fact 6.5

In U.S. data, mean firm growth rates and failure probabilities decline with firm size and age. The standard deviation of growth rates declines with size, but less rapidly than the reciprocal of the square root of size.

Results on mean growth abroad are mixed. Singh and Whittington (1975) found a weak positive relation between size and mean growth in the United Kingdom, while Jacquemin and Saez (1976) found a negative relation for large European firms, but no relation for large Japanese firms.

To understand the significance of the second part of Stylized Fact 6.5, note that if Gibrat's Law held exactly and large firms were simply collections of small firms with uncorrelated growth, the standard deviation of growth rates would decline as $[\text{firm size}]^{-1/2}$. The slower decline observed in many studies suggests that large firms specialize in correlated activities. But Daskin (1983) finds that larger U.S. firms have more stable growth even after controlling for diversification patterns.

It is important to recognize that variations in growth rates alone do not determine firm size distributions: entry, exit, and mergers may also be important. Until recently, antitrust restrictions on horizontal mergers in the United States were quite strict, and such mergers were a relatively unimportant source of increases in concentration. For the United Kingdom, however, Hannah and Kay (1977) conclude that, while stochastic rate growth differences were an important source of increases in concentration, mergers were much more important. Muller (1976) also argues that mergers were important in maintaining high concentration in West Germany despite rapid market growth. While controversy remains, it seems safe [Curry and George (1983)] to assert

Stylized Fact 6.6

Outside the United States, mergers have been an important source of increases in seller concentration.

6.2. *Advertising intensity*

Numerous regression analyses in which advertising intensity is the dependent variable have confirmed the positive advertising–profitability relation discussed in Subsection 4.4.[41] Telser (1964) found that advertising/sales ratios were unrelated to concentration in the United States, but Mann, Henning and Meehan (1967) found a positive relation. [Comanor and Wilson (1979) discuss the interpretation of this relation.] Subsequent studies generally support the existence

[41]See, for instance, Comanor and Wilson (1974), Strickland and Weiss (1976), Martin (1979a, 1979b), Farris and Buzzell (1979), Caves, Porter and Spence (1980), and Pagoulatos and Sorenson (1981); but see Martin (1983), who reports a negative relation.

of a positive concave or inverted-U relation:[42]

Stylized Fact 6.7

Among consumer goods industries, advertising intensity increases with concentration at low levels of concentration; the relation may vanish or change sign at high levels of concentration.

The observation that advertising intensity may decrease with increases in concentration in concentrated industries suggests, somewhat implausibly, that sellers in such industries not infrequently collude to reduce advertising outlays.

Ornstein (1977) argued that the positive relation between advertising intensity and concentration in the United States was roughly as strong in producer goods industries as in consumer goods industries. But Bradburd (1980) showed that when these two groups were defined more strictly (using the fraction of sales made to retailers), a positive, concave relation emerged for consumer goods, but no relation was apparent for producer goods. [See also Weiss, Pascoe and Martin (1983).] Buxton, Davies and Lyons (1984) posited different relations for pure producer and consumer goods industries and used data on the fraction of sales made to retailers to estimate an interactive model for industries selling both. They reported no relation for producer goods in U.K. data and an inverted-U relation for consumer goods.[43]

Within consumer good industries, Comanor and Wilson (1974) found that leading firms had higher advertising/sales ratios than followers when the industry advertising/sales ratio was low, but that leaders spent a smaller percentage of revenue on advertising when the industry ratio was high. The latter pattern has been found by Lambin (1976) in European data and by Farris and Buzzell (1979) in a study of advertising and promotion outlays.

6.3. *Entry and exit*

Basic price theory implies that entry will occur if and only if potential entrants expect post-entry prices to be at least equal to their costs. Bain (1956) argued that entrants' expectations are determined by the height of pre-entry profits relative to

[42]Examples include studies of Canadian [Caves, Porter and Spence (1980)], U.K. [Cowling, Cable, Kelly and McGuinness (1975)], and U.S. data [Strickland and Weiss (1976), Martin (1979a, 1979b), Pagoulatos and Sorenson (1981), and Connolly and Hirschey (1984)]; see also Lambin (1976).

[43]Arterburn and Woodbury (1981) studied the frequency with which price was mentioned in national magazine ads for 37 consumer goods in the United States in the early 1970s. They found that price was more likely to be mentioned the higher was the industry PCM and the lower was concentration. The coefficient of the industry advertising/sales ratio was negative for convenience goods but positive for non-convenience goods.

structural entry barriers; recent theoretical work has shown that strategic behavior of incumbent firms can also affect entrants's expectations.

Official data usually considerable entry (and exit) in almost all industries by firms that attain (or relinquish) small market shares [Baldwin and Gorecki (1987), Dunne, Roberts and Samuelson (1988a, 1988b)], so empirical work seeks to explain differences in the importance of entry across industries. This has been measured by the absolute or relative, gross or net change in the number of firms [Mansfield (1962), Orr (1974a), Deutsch (1975), Gorecki (1975, 1976)], by the occurrence of substantial entry [Harris (1976a)], and by the market share achieved by entrants [Harris (1976b), Masson and Shaanan (1982), MacDonald (1986)]. [See Geroski (1983) for useful survey and Dunne, Roberts and Samuelson (1988a, 1988b) on relations among alternative measures of entry and exit.] While the last of these seems the most satisfactory, Hause and Du Rietz (1984) use both the number of entrants and their share of industry employment and report broadly similar results for both measures in Swedish data.

Mansfield (1962) studied four industries (steel, petroleum, tires, and autos) over time and found that the ratio of new firms at the end of a decade to firms at the start was positively related to profitability during the period and negatively related to the capital cost of a firm of minimum efficient scale. While some subsequent studies also report a positive effect of profits [Harris (1976a, 1976b), Masson and Shaanan (1982)], insignificant coefficients seem at least as common [Orr (1974a), Deutsch (1975), Gorecki (1976)]. Since behavior designed to deter entry can be expected to lower pre-entry profits, the lack of a robust relation between pre-entry profits and the level of entry may not be terribly surprising.

Similarly, while some studies [Deutsch (1975), Hause and Du Rietz (1984), MacDonald (1986)] report a positive relation between growth and entry, others find no relation [Orr (1974a), Harris (1976b), Masson and Shaanan (1982)]. Gorecki (1976) finds that growth is positively related to foreign entry into Canadian manufacturing industries but unrelated to domestic entry. [Gorecki (1975) reports significant differences between the correlates of entry into U.K. industries by new firms and by those established elsewhere.] On theoretical grounds one would expect anticipated and unanticipated growth to have different effects on entry, but Bradburd and Caves (1982) did not find this distinction helpful in explaining profitability differences.

Harris (1976b) examined entry during the 1950–66 period into U.S. industries for which structural entry barriers had been assessed by Bain (1956) and Mann (1966). Nine of the 18 industries with above-average pre-entry profitability experienced substantial entry; of the nine industries classed has having "very high" entry barriers, four experienced substantial entry.[44] The Bain/Mann

[44] Harris (1976b) found that substantial entry tended to lower profitability, though industries with very high barriers (which tended to have high advertising/sales ratios) were still more profitable than average even after substantial entry.

judgements about overall entry barriers did not seem to predict the actual occurrence of entry terribly well.

Following Mansfield (1962), a number of authors have employed measures of the market share or capital cost of a plant of minimum efficient scale to capture the impact of scale-related entry barriers. And, as in the profitability literature, both are rarely significant, but at least one usually is:[45]

Stylized Fact 6.8

Measures of scale economies or capital requirements tend to be negatively related to entry.

Harris (1976b) found substantial entry into only two of the 12 industries in which product differentiation was held to be an important source of barriers by Bain (1956) and Mann (1966), and into only one of the seven of these industries with above-average profits. Since advertising intensity is highly correlated in this sample with high estimated product differentiation barriers, this is consistent with other work that supports:[46]

Stylized Fact 6.9

Advertising intensity is negatively related to entry in manufacturing industries.

Some studies have included concentration in equations designed to explain entry; see Kessides (1986) for a discussion. Positive [Deutsch (1975)], negative [Orr (1974a), Kessides (1986)], and insignificant [Harris (1976a)] coefficients have been reported. Hause and Du Rietz (1984) find the existence of a cartel agreement to be negatively related to entry in Swedish manufacturing industries.

Mansfield (1962) also studied the incidence of exit. He found that the fraction of firms leaving an industry was negatively related to the ratio of average size to minimum efficient scale and to industry profitability. Marcus (1967) found that

[45]Studies finding a negative effect of capital requirements include Orr (1974a), Gorecki (1976), Hause and Du Rietz (1984), and MacDonald (1986). [Gorecki (1976) finds a significant effect only for domestic entrants. Hause and Du Rietz (1984) use the mean employment in plants built by entrants.] Studies by Gorecki (1975), Harris (1976a), and Masson and Shaanan (1982) find a negative effect of MES/market.

[46]Support is provided by studies of Canadian [Orr (1974a), Gorecki (1976)] and U.S. data [Deutsch (1975), Harris (1976a), Masson and Shaanan (1982)]. [See also Kessides (1986).] But MacDonald (1986) fails to detect an advertising effect in his study of U.S. food processing industries during the 1970s. And Gorecki (1975) finds that specialist entry into U.K. manufacturing industries is negatively related to advertising per firm but positively related to the industry advertising/sales ratio.

the incidence of accounting losses was a better predictor of exit than the average level of profits, and he found that small, young firms were the most likely to incur losses. Dunne, Roberts and Samuelson (1988a, 1988b) report exit rates that decline sharply with age. Studies of exit from unprofitable, declining industries by Caves and Porter (1976) and Harrigan (1986) suggest that exit is delayed by the existence of tangible and intangible industry-specific assets, as well as by managerial and strategic factors.

Finally, Dunne, Roberts and Samuelson (1988b), using plant-level U.S. Census panel data, find systematic differences between entry by new and by diversifying firms. Using similar Canadian data, Baldwin and Gorecki (1987) support this finding and also report differences related to the nationality of diversifying entrant firms.

6.4. Share and rank stability

Mueller (1986) observes that in 41 percent of 350 U.S. manufacturing industries with essentially the same official definition in 1950 and 1972, the leading firm was the same in both years. (Note that industries in which technical change has been important are underrepresented in samples of this sort.) He finds that leaders' market shares tend to persist over long periods as well [see also Shepherd (1974)]. While stable market shares and firm ranks are consistent in principle with either collusion or competition, most would argue that unstable shares and ranks are inconsistent with effective collusion. Unfortunately, data limitations have kept the empirical literature on rank and share stability thin.

In an early study of rank changes, Mansfield (1962) found that small firms were less likely to grow to exceed the size of previously larger rivals in older, more concentrated industries. A number of studies of rank changes among leading banks (mobility) and changes in the identity of the leaders (turnover) have reported negative relations between concentration and both mobility and turnover [Gilbert (1984)]. But, as Marlow, Link and Trost (1984) point out, the measures used in these studies are counts of changes, and least squares is inappropriate for such discrete, bounded dependent variables. Using non-linear methods with data on U.S. savings and loan associations, they find no relation between concentration and turnover. While they do detect a weak negative relation between concentration and mobility, it has very little explanatory power.

Studies of market share stability generally employ sums across firms of the absolute values of either absolute or relative changes in shares to measure instability. Gort (1963) found a positive relation between concentration and share stability but no relation involving (judgemental estimates of) product differentiation or profitability. His work, along with the studies discussed in the previous paragraph and the results of Caves and Porter (1978) and Heggestad and Rhoades (1978), points toward

Stylized Fact 6.10

In manufacturing industries and local banking markets in the United States, market shares tend to be more stable the higher is concentration.

Telser (1964) found a negative relation between advertising intensity and stability in a small sample of industries. While Reekie (1974) found a negative relation for markets within two product classes, he detected a positive relation within two others. And, consistent with Gort's (1963) results, Lambin (1976) and Caves and Porter (1976) found no relation between advertising/sales ratios and share stability.

7. Conclusions and implications

I have argued that inter-industry research in industrial organization should generally be viewed as a search for empirical regularities, not as a set of exercises in structural estimation. And I have attempted to show that research in this tradition has indeed uncovered many stable, robust, empirical regularities. Inter-industry research has taught us much about how markets *look*, especially within the manufacturing sector in developed economies, even if it has not shown us exactly how markets *work*.

This literature has also produced an impressive, if implicit, agenda for future research. It seems difficult to reconcile the set of Stylized Facts discussed above with any familiar simple view of the world; some Stylized Facts seem difficult to reconcile with each other. Work in some areas has produced no clear picture of the important patterns in the data, and non-manufacturing industries have not received attention commensurate with their importance. The literature is full of interesting results that beg for attempts at replication.

But cross-section studies are limited by serious problems of interpretation and measurement. Future inter-industry research should adopt a modest, descriptive orientation and aim to complement case studies by uncovering robust empirical regularities that can be used to evaluate and develop theoretical tools. Finally, it is important to note that much of the most persuasive recent work relies on non-standard data sources, particularly panel data (which can be used to deal with disequilibrium problems) and industry-specific data (which mitigate the problem of unobservable industry-specific variables).

References

Aigner, D.J., Hsiao, C., Kapteyn, A. and Wansberg, T. (1984) 'Latent variable models in econometrics', in: Z. Griliches and M. Intriligator, eds., *Handbook of econometrics*, vol. 2, Amsterdam: North-Holland.

Alberts, W.W. (1984) 'Do oligopolists earn 'noncompetitive' rates of return?', *American Economic Review*, 74:624–632.

Albion, M.S. (1983) *Advertising's hidden effects*. Cambridge: Auburn House.

Arterburn, A. and Woodbury, J. (1981) 'Advertising, price competition, and market structure', *Southern Economic Journal*, 47:763–775.

Assmus, G., Farley, J.U. and Lehmann, D.R. (1984) 'How advertising affects sales: A meta-analysis of econometric results', *Journal of Marketing Research*, 21:65–74.

Bailey, E.E., Graham, D.R. and Kaplan, D.P. (1985) *Deregulating the airlines*. Cambridge: MIT Press.

Bain, J.S. (1951) 'Relation of profit rate to industry concentration: American manufacturing, 1936–1940', *Quarterly Journal of Economics*, 65:293–324.

Bain, J.S. (1956) *Barriers to new competition*. Cambridge: Harvard University Press.

Bain, J.S. (1966) *International differences in industrial structure*. New Haven: Yale University Press.

Baldwin, J.R. and Gorecki, P.K. (1985) 'The determinants of small plant market share in Canadian manufacturing industries in the 1970s', *Review of Economics and Statistics*, 67:156–161.

Baldwin, J.R. and Gorecki, P.K. (1987) 'Plant creation versus plant acquisition: The entry process in Canadian manufacturing', *International Journal of Industrial Organization*, 5:27–42.

Benham, L. (1972) 'The effect of advertising on the price of eyeglasses', *Journal of Law and Economics*, 15:337–352.

Benston, G.J. (1985) 'The validity of profits-structure with particular reference to the FTC's line of business data', *American Economic Review*, 75:37–67.

Bloch, H. (1974a) 'Advertising and profitability: A reappraisal', *Journal of Political Economy*, 82:267–287.

Bloch, H. (1974b) 'Prices, costs and profits in Canadian manufacturing: The influence of tariffs and concentration', *Canadian Journal of Economics*, 7:594–610.

Bothwell, J.L. and Keeler, T.E. (1976) 'Profits, market structure and portfolio risk', in: R.T. Masson and P.D. Qualls, eds., *Essays in industrial organization in honor of Joe S. Bain*. Cambridge: Ballinger.

Bothwell, J.L., Cooley, T.F. and Hall, T.E. (1984) 'A new view of the market structure – market performance debate', *Journal of Industrial Economics*, 32:397–417.

Boyer, K. (1974) 'Informative and goodwill advertising', *Review of Economics and Statistics*, 56:541–548.

Bradburd, R. (1980) 'Advertising and market concentration: A re-examination of Ornstein's spurious correlation hypothesis', *Southern Economic Journal*, 46:531–539.

Bradburd, R. (1982) 'Price–cost margins in producer goods industries and 'the importance of being unimportant' ', *Review of Economics and Statistics*, 64:405–412.

Bradburd, R.M. and Caves, R.E. (1982) 'A closer look at the effect of market growth on industries' profits', *Review of Economics and Statistics*, 64:635–645.

Bradburd, R.M. and Over, A.M. (1982) 'Organizational costs, 'sticky' equilibria and critical levels of concentration', *Review of Economics and Statistics*, 64:50–58.

Brannman, L., Klein, J.D. and Weiss, L.W. (1987) 'The price effects of increased competition in auction markets', *Review of Economics and Statistics*, 69:24–32.

Brozen, Y. (1970) 'The antitrust task force deconcentration recommendations', *Journal of Law and Economics*, 13:279–292.

Brozen, Y. (1971) 'Bain's concentration and rates of return revisited', *Journal of Law and Economics*, 14:351–369.

Brozen, Y. (1982) *Concentration, mergers, and public policy*. New York: Macmillan.

Buxton, A.J., Davies, S.W. and Lyons, B.R. (1984) 'Concentration and advertising in consumer and producer markets', *Journal of Industrial Economics*, 32:451–464.

Cady, J.F. (1976) 'An estimate of the price effects of restrictions on drug price advertising', *Economic Inquiry*, 14:493–510.

Carter, J.R. (1978) 'Collusion, efficiency, and antitrust', *Journal of Law and Economics*, 21:435–444.

Cattin, P. and Wittink, D.R. (1976) 'Industry differences in the relation between advertising and profitability', *Industrial Organization Review*, 4:156–164.

Caves, R.E. (1985) 'International trade and industrial organization: Problems, solved and unsolved', *European Economic Review*, 28:377–395.

Caves, R.E. and Porter, M.E. (1976) 'Barriers to exit', in: D.P. Qualls and R.T. Masson, eds., *Essays in industrial organization in honor of Joe Bain*. Cambridge: Ballinger.

Caves, R.E. and Porter, M.E. (1978) 'Market structure, oligopoly and stability of market shares', *Journal of Industrial Economics*, 27:289–312.

Caves, R.E. and Pugel, T.A. (1980) *Intraindustry differences in conduct and performance: Viable strategies in U.S. manufacturing industries*. New York: New York University, Salomon Brothers Center.

Caves, R.E. and Uekusa, M. (1976) *Industrial organization in Japan*. Washington: Brookings Institution.

Caves, R.E., Khalizadeh-Shirazi, J. and Porter, M.E. (1975) 'Scale economies in statistical analyses of market power', *Review of Economics and Statistics*, 57:133–140.

Caves, R.E., Porter, M.E. and Spence, A.M. (1980) *Competition in the open economy: A model applied to Canada*. Cambridge: Harvard University Press.

Chappel, W.F. and Cottle, R.L. (1985) 'Sources of concentration-related profits', *Southern Economic Journal*, 51:1031–1037.

Chou, T.-C. (1986) 'Concentration, profitability and trade in a simultaneous equation analysis: The case of Taiwan', *Journal of Industrial Economics*, 34:429–443.

Clark, K.B. (1984) 'Unionization and firm performance: The impact on profits, growth, and productivity', *American Economic Review*, 74:893–919.

Clarke, R. (1979) 'On the lognormality of firm and plant size distributions', *Applied Economics*, 11:415–433.

Clarke, R. (1984) 'Profit margins and market concentration in U.K. manufacturing industry', *Applied Economics*, 16:57–71.

Clarke, R., Davies, S.W. and Waterson, M. (1984) 'The profitability–concentration relation: Market power or efficiency?' *Journal of Industrial Economics*, 32:435–450.

Cohen, W.M., Levin, R.C. and Mowery, D.G. (1987) 'Firm size and R & D intensity: A re-examination', *Journal of Industrial Economics*, 35:543–566.

Collins, N.R. and Preston, L.E. (1968) *Concentration and price–cost margins in manufacturing industries*. Berkeley: University of California Press.

Collins, N.R. and Preston, L.E. (1969) 'Price-cost margins and industry structure', *Review of Economics and Statistics*, 51:271–286.

Comanor, W.S. and Wilson, T.A. (1967) 'Advertising, market structure and performance', *Review of Economics and Statistics*, 49:423–440.

Comanor, W.S. and Wilson, T.A. (1974) *Advertising and market power*. Cambridge: Harvard University Press.

Comanor, W.S. and Wilson, T.A. (1979) 'The effect of advertising on competition: A survey', *Journal of Economic Literature*, 17:435–476.

Connolly, R.A. and Hirschey, M. (1984) 'R&D, market structure and profits: A value-based approach', *Review of Economics and Statistics*, 66:678–681.

Connolly, R.A. and Schwartz, S. (1985) 'The intertemporal behavior of economic profits', *International Journal of Industrial Organization*, 4:365–472.

Cotterill, R.S. (1986) 'Market power in the retail food industry: Evidence from Vermont', *Review of Economics and Statistics*, 68:379–386.

Cowling, K. (1976) 'On the theoretical specification of industrial structure–performance relationships', *European Economic Review*, 8:1–14.

Cowling, K. and Waterson, M. (1976) 'Price–cost margins and market structure', *Economica*, 43:267–274.

Cowling, K., Cable, J., Kelly, M. and McGuinness, T. (1975) *Advertising and economic behavior*. London: MacMillan.

Cubbin, J. and Geroski, P.A. (1987) 'The convergence of profits in the long run: Inter-firm and inter-industry comparisons', *Journal of Industrial Economics*, 35:427–442.

Cummins, J.D., Denenberg, H.S. and Scheel, W.C. (1972) 'Concentration in the U.S. life insurance industry', *Journal of Risk and Insurance*, 39:177–199.

Curry, B. and George, K.D. (1983) 'Industrial concentration: A survey', *Journal of Industrial Economics*, 31:203–255.

Dalton, J.A. and Penn, J.W. (1976) 'The concentration–profitability relationship: Is there a critical concentration ratio?', *Journal of Industrial Economics*, 25:133–142.

Daskin, A.J. (1983) 'Essays on firm diversification and market concentration', unpublished dissertation, MIT.

Davies, S. (1980) 'Minimum efficient size and seller concentration: An empirical problem', *Journal of Industrial Economics*, 28:287–302.

Davies, S. and Lyons, B.R. (1982) 'Seller concentration: The technological explanation and demand uncertainty', *Economic Journal*, 92:903–919.

de Melo, J. and Urata, S. (1986) 'The influence of increased foreign competition on industrial concentration and profitability', *International Journal of Industrial Organization*, 4:287–304.

Demsetz, H. (1973) 'Industry structure, market rivalry, and public policy', *Journal of Law and Economics*, 16:1–10.

Demsetz, H. (1974) 'Two systems of belief about monopoly', in: H.J. Goldschmid, H.M. Mann and J.F. Weston, eds., *Industrial concentration: The new learning*. Boston: Little, Brown.

Demsetz, H. (1979) 'Accounting for advertising as a barrier to entry', *Journal of Business*, 52:345–360.

Deutsch, L.L. (1975) 'Structure, performance, and the net rate of entry into manufacturing industries', *Southern Economic Journal*, 41:450–456.

Dickens, W.T. and Katz, L.F. (1986) 'Interindustry wage differences and industry characteristics', in: K. Lang and J. Leonard, eds., *Unemployment and the structure of labor markets*. Oxford: Basil Blackwell.

Domowitz, I., Hubbard, R.G. and Petersen, B.C. (1986a) 'Business cycles and the relationship between concentration and price–cost margins', *Rand Journal of Economics*, 17:1–17.

Domowitz, I., Hubbard, R.G. and Petersen, B.C. (1986b) 'The intertemporal stability of the concentration–margins relationship', *Journal of Industrial Economics*, 35:13–34.

Domowitz, I., Hubbard, R.G. and Petersen, B.C. (1987) 'Oligopoly supergames: Some empirical evidence on prices and margins', *Journal of Industrial Economics*, 35:379–398.

Donsimoni, M.-P., Geroski, P.A. and Jacquemin, A. (1984) 'Concentration indices and market power: Two views', *Journal of Industrial Economics*, 32:419–434.

Dunne, T., Roberts, M.J. and Samuelson, L. (1988a) 'The growth and failure of U.S. manufacturing plants', Pennsylvania State University, mimeo.

Dunne, T., Roberts, M.J. and Samuelson, L. (1988b) 'Patterns of firm entry and exit in U.S. manufacturing industries', *Rand Journal of Economics*, 19: forthcoming.

Edwards, F.R. (1977) 'Managerial objectives in regulated industries: Expense-preference behavior in banking', *Journal of Political Economy*, 85:147–162.

Evans, D. (1987a) 'Tests of alternative theories of firm growth', *Journal of Political Economy*, 95:657–674.

Evans, D. (1987b) 'The relationship between firm growth, size, and age: Estimates for 100 manufacturing industries', *Journal of Industrial Economics*, 35:567–581.

Farris, P.W. and Buzzell, R.D. (1979) 'Why advertising and promotional costs vary: Some cross-sectional analyses', *Journal of Marketing*, 43:112–122.

Feinberg, R.M. (1986) 'The interaction of foreign exchange and market power effects on German domestic prices', *Journal of Industrial Economics*, 35:61–70.

Ferguson, J.M. (1974) *Advertising and competition*. Cambridge: Ballinger.

Fisher, F.M. and McGowan, J.J. (1983) 'On the misuse of accounting rate of return to infer monopoly profits', *American Economic Review*, 73:82–97.

Gale, B.T. (1972) 'Market share and rate of return', *Review of Economics and Statistics*, 54:412–423.

Gale, B.T. and Branch, B.S. (1982) 'Concentration versus market share: Which determines performance and why does it matter?', *Antitrust Bulletin*, 27:83–106.

Geithman, F.E., Marvel, H.P. and Weiss, L.W. (1981) 'Concentration, price, and critical concentration ratios', *Review of Economics and Statistics*, 63:346–353.

Geroski, P.A. (1981) 'Specification and testing the profits-concentration relationship: Some experiments for the U.K.', *Economica*, 48:279–288.

Geroski, P.A. (1982) 'Simultaneous equations models of the structure–performance paradigm', *European Economic Review*, 19:145–158.

Geroski, P.A. (1983) 'The empirical analysis of entry: A survey', University of Southampton, mimeo.

Geroski, P.A. and Jacquemin, A. (1988) 'The persistence of profits: A European comparison', *Economic Journal*, 98:375–389.

Geroski, P.A., Masson, R.T. and Shaanan, J. (1987) 'The dynamics of market structure', *International Journal of Industrial Organization*, 5:93–100.

Gilbert, R.A. (1984) 'Bank market structure and competition: A survey', *Journal of Money, Credit and Banking*, 16:617–645.

Gisser, M. (1984) 'Price leadership and dynamic aspects of oligopoly in U.S. manufacturing', *Journal of Political Economy*, 92:1035–1048.

Gorecki, P.K. (1975) 'The determinants of entry by new and diversifying enterprises in the U.K. manufacturing sector, 1958–1963', *Applied Economics*, 7:139–147.

Gorecki, P.K. (1976) 'The determinants of entry by domestic and foreign enterprises in Canadian manufacturing', *Review of Economics and Statistics*, 58:485–488.

Gort, M. (1963) 'Analysis of stability and change in market shares', *Journal of Political Economy*, 71: 51–63.

Gort, M. and Singamsetti, R. (1976) 'Concentration and profit rates: New evidence on an old issue', *Explorations in Economic Research*, 3:1–20.

Grabowski, H.G. and Mueller, D.C. (1978) 'Industrial research and development, intangible capital stocks, and firm profit rates', *Bell Journal of Economics*, 9:328–343.

Guth, L.A., Schwartz, R.A. and Whitcomb, D.K. (1976) 'The use of buyer concentration ratios in tests of oligopoly models: Comment', with 'Reply' by S. Lustgarten, *Review of Economics and Statistics*, 58:488–494.

Hagerman, R.L. and Senbet, L.W. (1976) 'A test of accounting bias and market structure', *Journal of Business*, 49:509–514.

Hall, B.H. (1987) 'The relationship between firm size and firm growth in the U.S. manufacturing sector', *Journal of Industrial Economics*, 35:583–606.

Hall, M. and Weiss, L.W. (1967) 'Firm size and profitability', *Review of Economics and Statistics*, 49:319–331.

Hannah, L. and Kay, J. (1977) *Concentration in modern industry*. London: MacMillan.

Hannan, T.H. and Mavinga, F. (1980) 'Expense preference and managerial control: The case of the banking firm', *Bell Journal of Economics*, 11:671–682.

Harrigan, K.R. (1986) 'Strategic flexibility', in L.G. Thomas, ed., *The economics of strategic planning*. Cambridge: Ballinger.

Harris, M.N. (1976a) 'Entry and barriers to entry', *Industrial Organization Review*, 4:165–174.

Harris, M.N. (1976b) 'Entry and long-term trends in industry performance', *Antitrust Bulletin*, 21:295–314.

Harris, F.H.deB. (1984) 'Growth expectations, excess value, and the risk adjusted return to market power', *Southern Economic Journal*. 51:166–179.

Harris, F.H.deB. (1986) 'Market structure and price–cost performance under endogenous profit risk', *Journal of Industrial Economics*, 35:35–60.

Hart, P.E. and Clarke, R. (1980) *Concentration in British industry: 1935–1975*. Cambridge: Cambridge University Press.

Hart, P.E. and Morgan, E. (1977) 'Market structure and economic performance in the United Kingdom', *Journal of Industrial Economics*, 25:177–193.

Hause, J.C. and Du Rietz, G. (1984) 'Entry, industry growth, and the microdynamics of industry supply', *Journal of Political Economy*, 92:733–757.

Hausman, J.A. and Taylor, W.E. (1981) 'Panel data and unobservable individual effects', *Econometrica*, 49:1337–1398.

Haworth, C.T. and Reuther, C. (1978) 'Industry concentration and interindustry wage determination', *Review of Economics and Statistics*, 60:85–95.

Hay, D.A. and Morris, D.J. (1979) *Industrial economics: Theory and evidence*. Oxford: Oxford University Press.

Hay, G.A. and Kelley, D. (1974) 'An empirical survey of price fixing conspiracies', *Journal of Law and Economics*, 17:13–38.

Hazledine, T. (1980) 'Testing two models of pricing and protection with Canada/U.S. data', *Journal of Industrial Economics*, 29:145–154.

Heggestad, A.A. and Rhoades, S.A. (1978) 'Multi-market interdependence and local market competition in banking', *Review of Economics and Statistics*, 60:523–532.

Hirschey, M. (1985) 'Market structure and market value', *Journal of Business*, 58:89–98.

Holthausen, R. and Leftwich, R. (1983) 'The economic consequences of accounting choice', *Journal of Accounting and Economics*, 5:77–117.

Hotelling, H. (1925) 'A general mathematical theory of depreciation', *Journal of the American Statistical Association*, 20:340–353.

Hymer, S. and Pashigian (1962) 'Firm size and rate of growth', *Journal of Political Economy*, 60:556–569.

Ijiri, Y. and Simon, H.A. (1977) *Skew distribution functions*. Amsterdam: North-Holland.

Imel, B., Behr, M.R. and Helmberger, P.G. (1972) *Market structure and performance*. Lexington, Mass.: Lexington.

Jacquemin, A. and deJong, H.W. (1977) *European industrial organization*. New York: Wiley.

Jacquemin, A. and Saez, W. (1976) 'A comparison of the performance of the largest European and Japanese industrial firms', *Oxford Economic Papers*, 28:271–283.

Jacquemin, A., de Ghellinck, E. and Huveneers, C. (1980) 'Concentration and profitability in a small, open economy', *Journal of Industrial Economics*, 29:131–144.

Jenny, R. and Weber, A.P. (1976) 'Profit rates and structural variables in French manufacturing industries', *European Economic Review*, 7:187–206.

Karier, T. (1985) 'Unions and monopoly profits', *Review of Economics and Statistics*, 67:34–42.

Kessides, I.N. (1986) 'Advertising, sunk costs, and barriers to entry', *Review of Economics and Statistics*, 68:84–95.

Kessides, I.N. (1987) 'Do firms differ much? Some additional evidence', University of Maryland, mimeo.

Kilpatrick, R.W. (1968) 'Stigler on the relationship between industry profit rates and market concentration', *Journal of Political Economy*, 76:479–488.

Koller, III, R.H. and Weiss, L.W. (1986) 'Price levels and seller concentration: The case of Portland Cement', University of Wisconsin, Madison, mimeo.

Krasker, W.S., Kuh, E. and Welsch, R.E. (1983) 'Estimation for dirty data and flawed models', in: Z. Griliches and M.D. Intriligator, eds., *Handbook of econometrics*, vol. 1. Amsterdam: North-Holland.

Kwoka, Jr., J.E. (1979) 'The effect of market share distribution on industry performance', *Review of Economics and Statistics*, 59:101–109.

Kwoka, Jr., J.E. (1981) 'Does the choice of concentration measure really matter?', *Journal of Industrial Economics*, 29:445–453.

Kwoka, Jr., J.E. (1982) 'Regularity and diversity in firm size distributions in U.S. industries', *Journal of Economics and Business*, 34:391–395.

Kwoka, Jr., J.E. (1984) 'Advertising and the price and quality of optometric services', *American Economic Review*, 74:211–216.

Kwoka, Jr., J.E. and Ravenscraft, D. (1986) 'Cooperation v. rivalry: Price–cost margins by line of business', *Economica*, 53:351–363.

LaFrance, V.A. (1979) 'The impact of buyer concentration – an extension', *Review of Economics and Statistics*, 59:475–476.

Lambin, J.J. (1976) *Advertising, competition and market conduct in oligopoly over time*. Amsterdam: North-Holland.

Lamm, R.M. (1981) 'Prices and concentration in the food retailing industry', *Journal of Industrial Economics*, 29:67–78.

Landon, J.H. (1970) 'The effect of product-market concentration on wage levels: An intra-industry approach', *Industrial and Labor Relations Review*, 23:237–247.

Leamer, E.E. (1983) 'Model choice and specification analysis', in: Z. Griliches and M.D. Intriligator, eds., *Handbook of econometrics*, vol. 2. Amsterdam: North-Holland.

Leitzinger, J.J. and Tamor, K.L. (1983) 'Foreign competition in antitrust law', *Journal of Law and Economics*, 26:392–415.

Lev, B. (1983) 'Some economic determinants of time-series properties of earnings', *Journal of Accounting and Economics*, 5:31–48.

Levy, D. (1985) 'Specifying the dynamics of industry concentration', *Journal of Industrial Economics*, 34:55–68.

Liebowitz, S.J. (1982a) 'What do census price–cost margins measure?', *Journal of Law and Economics*, 25:231–246.

Liebowitz, S.J. (1982b) 'Measuring industrial disequilibria', *Southern Economic Journal*, 49:119–136.

Lindenberg, E.B. and Ross, S.A. (1981) 'Tobin's q ratio and industrial organization', *Journal of Business*, 54:1–32.

Lustgarten, S. (1975) 'The impact of buyer concentration in manufacturing industries', *Review of Economics and Statistics*, 57:125–132.

Lustgarten, S. (1984) *Productivity and prices: The consequences of industrial concentration.* Washington: American Enterprise Institute.

Lustgarten, S. and Thomadakis, S.B. (1980) 'Valuation response to new information: A test of resource mobility and market structure', *Journal of Political Economy*, 88:977–993.

Lynk, W.J. (1981) 'Information, advertising, and the structure of the market', *Journal of Business*, 54:271–303.

Lyons, B.R. (1980) 'A new measure of minimum efficient plant size in U.K. manufacturing industry', *Economica*, 47:19–34.

MacDonald, J.M. (1986) 'Entry and exist on the competitive fringe', *Southern Economic Journal*, 52:640–658.

Mancke, R.B. (1974) 'Causes of interfirm profitability differences: A new interpretation of the evidence', *Quarterly Journal of Economics*, 88:181–193.

Mann, H.M. (1966) 'Seller concentration, barriers to entry, and rates of return in 30 industries', *Review of Economics and Statistics*, 48:296–307.

Mann, H.M., Henning, J.A. and Meehan, Jr., J.W. (1967) 'Advertising and concentration: An empirical investigation', *Journal of Industrial Economics*, 16:34–45.

Mansfield, E. (1962) 'Entry, Gibrat's law, innovation and the growth of firms', *American Economic Review*, 52:1023–1051.

Marcus, M. (1967) 'Firms' exit rates and their determinants', *Journal of Industrial Economics*, 16:10–22.

Marlow, M.L., Link, J.P. and Trost, R.P. (1984) 'Market structure and rivalry: New evidence with a non-linear model', *Review of Economics and Statistics*, 66:678–682.

Martin, S. (1979a) 'Advertising, concentration and profitability: The simultaneity problem', *Bell Journal of Economics*, 10:639–647.

Martin, S. (1979b) 'Entry barriers, concentration and profit', *Southern Economic Journal*, 46:471–488.

Martin, S. (1983) *Market, firm, and economic performance: An empirical analysis.* New York: New York University, Salomon Brothers Center.

Marvel, H.P. (1978) 'Competition and price levels in the retail gasoline market', *Review of Economics and Statistics*, 60:252–258.

Marvel, H.P. (1980) 'Foreign trade and domestic competition', *Economic Inquiry*, 18:103–122.

Masson, R.T. and Shaanan, J. (1982) 'Stochastic–dynamic limit pricing: An empirical test', *Review of Economics and Statistics*, 64:413–422.

Michelini, C. and Pickford, M. (1985) 'Estimating the Herfindahl index from concentration ratio data', *Journal of the American Statistical Association*, 80:301–305.

Mueller, D. (1977) 'The persistence of profits above the norm', *Economica*, 44:369–380.

Mueller, D. (1986) *Profits in the long run*. Cambridge: Cambridge University Press.

Mueller, W.F. and Rogers, R.T. (1980) 'The role of advertising in changing concentration in manufacturing industries', *Review of Economics and Statistics*, 62:89–96.

Muller, J. (1976) 'The impact of mergers on concentration: A study of eleven West German industries', *Journal of Industrial Economics*, 25:113–132.

Neumann, M., Bobel, I. and Haid, A. (1979) 'Profitability, risk and market structure in West German industries', *Journal of Industrial Economics*, 27:227–242.

Neumann, M., Bobel, I. and Haid, A. (1985) 'Domestic concentration, foreign trade and economic performance', *International Journal of Industrial Organization*, 3:1–19.

Newman, H.H. (1978) 'Strategic groups and the structure–performance relationship', *Review of Economics and Statistics*, 60:417–427.

Nickell, S. and Metcalf, D. (1978) 'Monopolistic industries and monopoly profits or, are Kellogg's cornflakes overpriced?', *Economic Journal*, 88:254–268.

Odagiri, H. and Yamawaki, H. (1986) 'A study of company profit-rate time series: Japan and the United States', *International Journal of Industrial Organization*, 4:1–23.

Odagiri, H. and Yamawaki, H. (1987) 'The persistence of profits: International comparison', International Institute of Management, Berlin, mimeo.

Odagiri, H. and Yamashita, T. (1987) 'Price mark-ups, market structure, and business fluctuation in Japanese manufacturing industries', *Journal of Industrial Economics*, 35:317–342.

Ornstein, S.I. (1972) 'Concentration and profits', *Journal of Business*, 45:519–541.

Ornstein, S.I. (1975) 'Empirical uses of the price–cost margin', *Journal of Industrial Economics*, 24:105–117.

Ornstein, S.I. (1977) *Industrial concentration and advertising intensity*. Washington: American Enterprise Institute.

Ornstein, S.I., Weston, J.F., Intriligator, M.D. and Shrieves, R.E. (1973) 'Determinants of market structure', *Southern Economic Journal*, 39:612–625.

Orr, D. (1974a) 'The determinants of entry: A study of the Canadian manufacturing industries', *Review of Economics and Statistics*, 56:58–66.

Orr, D. (1974b) 'An index of entry barriers and its application to the market structure–performance relationship', *Journal of Industrial Economics*, 23:39–50.

Oster, S. (1982) 'Intraindustry structure and the ease of strategic change', *Review of Economics and Statistics*, 64:376–383.

Pagoulatos, E. and Sorenson, R. (1981) 'A simultaneous equations analysis of advertising, concentration and profitability', *Southern Economic Journal*, 47:728–741.

Palmer, J. (1973) 'The profit–performance effects of the separation of ownership from control in large U.S. industrial corporations', *Bell Journal of Economics*, 4:293–303.

Peltzman, S. (1977) 'The gains and losses from industrial concentration', *Journal of Law and Economics*, 20:229–263.

Phillips, A. (1976) 'A critique of empirical studies of relations between market structure and profitability', *Journal of Industrial Economics*, 24:241–249.

Phlips, L. (1971) *Effects of industrial concentration*. Amsterdam: North-Holland.

Porter, M.E. (1976a) *Interbrand choice, strategy and bilateral market power*. Cambridge: Harvard University Press.

Porter, M.E. (1976b) 'Interbrand choice, media mix and market performance', *American Economic Review*, 66:398–406.

Porter, M.E. (1979) 'The structure within industries and companies' performance', *Review of Economics and Statistics*, 61:214–227.

Pryor, F.L. (1972) 'An international comparison of concentration ratios', *Review of Economics and Statistics*, 54:130–140.

Pugel, T.A. (1980a) 'Foreign trade and U.S. market performance', *Journal of Industrial Economics*, 29:119–129.

Pugel, T.A. (1980b) 'Profitability, concentration and the interindustry variation in wages', *Review of Economics and Statistics*, 62:248–253.

Qualls, D. (1972) 'Concentration, barriers to entry and long-run economic profit margins', *Journal of Industrial Economics*, 20:146–158.

Qualls, D. (1974) 'Stability and persistence of economic profit margins in highly concentrated industries', *Southern Economic Journal*, 40:604–612.

Quandt, R.E. (1966) 'On the size distribution of firms', *American Economic Review*, 56:416–432.

Ravenscraft, D.J. (1983) 'Structure–profit relationships at the line of business and industry level', *Review of Economics and Statistics*, 65:22–31.

Reekie, W.D. (1974) 'Advertising and market share mobility', *Scottish Journal of Political Economy*, 21:143–158.

Rhoades, S.A. (1985) 'Market share as a source of market power: Implications and some evidence', *Journal of Economics and Business*, 37:343–363.

Rhoades, S.A. and Rutz, R.D. (1982) 'Market power and firm risk', *Journal of Monetary Economics*, 9:73–85.

Rose, N.L. (1987) 'Labor rent-sharing and regulation: Evidence from the trucking industry', *Journal of Political Economy*, 95:1146–1178.

Ross, D.R. (1986) 'Do markets differ much: Comment – markets differ by stage of processing', Williams College, mimeo.

Round, D.K. (1975) 'Industry structure, market rivalry and public policy: Some Australian evidence', *Journal of Law and Economics*, 18:273–281.

Round, D.K. (1983) 'Intertemporal profit margin variability and market structure in Australian manufacturing', *International Journal of Industrial Organization*, 1:189–209.

Salamon, G.L. (1985) 'Accounting rates of return', *American Economic Review*, 75:495–504.

Salinger, M.A. (1984) 'Tobin's q, unionization and the concentration–profits relationship', *Rand Journal of Economics*, 15:159–170.

Saving, T.R. (1970) 'Concentration ratios and the degree of monopoly', *International Economic Review*, 11:139–146.

Sawyer, M.C. (1982) 'On the specification of structure–performance relationships', *European Economic Review*, 17:295–306.

Scherer, F.M. (1980) *Industrial market structure and economic performance*, 2nd edn. Chicago: Rand-McNally.

Scherer, F.M., Beckstein, A., Kaufer, E. and Murphy, R.D. (1975) *The economics of multi-plant operation*. Cambridge: Harvard University Press.

Schmalensee, R. (1972) *The economics of advertising*. Amsterdam: North-Holland.

Schmalensee, R. (1976) 'Advertising and profitability: Further implications of the null hypothesis', *Journal of Industrial Economics*, 25:45–54.

Schmalensee, R. (1977) 'Using the H index of concentration with published data', *Review of Economics and Statistics*, 59:186–193.

Schmalensee, R. (1981) 'Economies of scale and barriers to entry', *Journal of Political Economy*, 89:1228–1238.

Schmalensee, R. (1985) 'Do markets differ much?', *American Economic Review*, 75:341–351.

Schmalensee, R. (1987) 'Collusion versus differential efficiency: Testing alternative hypotheses', *Journal of Industrial Economics*, 35:399–425.

Schwert, G.W. (1981) 'Using financial data to measure effects of regulation', *Journal of Law and Economics*, 24:121–158.

Scott, J.T. (1982) 'Multimarket contact and economic performance', *Review of Economics and Statistics*, 64:368–375.

Scott, J.T. and Pascoe, G. (1986) 'Beyond firm and industry effects on profitability in imperfect markets', *Review of Economics and Statistics*, 68:284–292.

Shalchi, H. and Smith, C.H. (1985) 'Research on accounting for changing prices: Theory, evidence, and implications', *Quarterly Review of Economics and Business*, 25:5–37.

Shepherd, W.G. (1974) *The treatment of market power*. New York: Columbia University Press.

Silberman, I.H. (1967) 'On lognormality as a summary measure of concentration', *American Economic Review*, 57:807–831.

Singh, A. and Whittington, G. (1975) 'The size and growth of firms', *Review of Economic Studies*, 42:15–26.

Sleuwaegen, L. and Dehandschutter, W. (1986) 'The critical choice between the concentration ratio and the H-index in assessing industry performance', *Journal of Industrial Economics*, 35:193–198.

Smirlock, M. (1985) 'Evidence on the (non) relationship between concentration and profitability in banking', *Journal of Money Credit and Banking*, 17:69–83.

Smirlock, M. and Marshall, W. (1983) 'Monopoly power and expense-preference behavior: Theory and evidence to the contrary', *Bell Journal of Economics*, 14:166–178.

Smirlock, M., Gilligan, T. and Marshall, W. (1984) 'Tobin's q and the structure–performance relationship', *American Economic Review*, 74:1051–1060.

Stauffer, T.R. (1971) 'The measurement of corporate rates of return: A generalized formulation', *Bell Journal of Economics and Management Science*, 2:434–469.

Stauffer, T.R. (1980) *The measurement of corporate rates of return*. New York: Garland.

Stigler, G.J. (1963) *Capital and rates of return in manufacturing industries*. Princeton: Princeton University Press.

Stigler, G.J. (1964) 'A theory of oligopoly', *Journal of Political Economy*, 72:44–61.

Stonebraker, R.J. (1976) 'Corporate profits and the risk of entry', *Review of Economics and Statistics*, 58:33–39.

Strickland, A.D. and Weiss, L.W. (1976) 'Advertising, concentration and price–cost margins', *Journal of Political Economy*, 84:1109–1121.

Sullivan, T.G. (1978) 'The cost of capital and the market power of firms', *Review of Economics and Statistics*, 60:209–217.

Telser, L.G. (1964) 'Advertising and competition', *Journal of Political Economy*, 72:537–562.

Telser, L.G. (1972) *Competition, collusion, and game theory*. Chicago: Aldine.

Thomadakis, S.B. (1977) 'A value based test of profitability and market structure', *Review of Economics and Statistics*, 59:179–185.

Thompson, R.S. (1984) 'Structure and conduct in local advertising markets', *Journal of Industrial Economics*, 33:241–249.

Vernon, J.M. and Nourse, R.E.M. (1973) 'Profit rates and market structure of advertising intensive firms', *Journal of Industrial Economics*, 22:1–20.

Voos, P.B. and Mishel, L.R. (1986) 'The union impact on profits in the supermarket industry', *Review of Economics and Statistics*, 68:513–517.

Waterson, M. (1980) 'Price–cost margins and successive market power', *Quarterly Journal of Economics*, 94:135–150.

Waterson, M. (1984) *Economic theory of industry*. Cambridge: Cambridge University Press.

Weiss, L.W. (1966) 'Concentration and labor earnings', *American Economic Review*, 56:96–117.

Weiss, L.W. (1969) 'Advertising, profits, and corporate taxes', *Review of Economics and Statistics*, 51:421–430.

Weiss, L.W. (1971) 'Quantitative studies of industrial organization', in: M.D. Intriligator, ed., *Frontiers of quantitative economics*. Amsterdam: North-Holland.

Weiss, L.W. (1974) 'The concentration–profits relationship and antitrust', in: H.J. Goldschmid, H.M. Mann and J.F. Weston, eds., *Industrial concentration: The new learning*. Boston: Little, Brown.

Weiss, L.W. (1976) 'Optimal plant size and the extent of suboptimal capacity', in: R.T. Masson and P.D. Qualls, eds., *Essays in honor of Joe S. Bain*. Cambridge: Ballinger.

Weiss, L.W. and Pascoe, Jr., G.A. (1986) *Adjusted concentration ratios in manufacturing, 1972 and 1977*. Washington: Federal Trade Commission.

Weiss, L.W., Pascoe, Jr., G.A. and Martin, S. (1983) 'The size of selling costs', *Review of Economics and Statistics*, 65:668–672.

White, H. (1980) 'A heteroskedasticity-consistent covariance matrix estimator and a direct test for heteroskedasticity', *Econometrica*, 48:817–838.

White, L.J. (1974) *Industrial concentration and economic power in Pakistan*. Princeton: Princeton University Press.

White, L.J. (1976) 'Searching for the critical industrial concentration ratio: An application of the 'switching of regimes' technique', in: S.M. Goldfeld and R.E. Quandt, eds., *Studies in nonlinear estimation*. Cambridge: Ballinger.

Winn, D.N. (1977) 'On the relations between rates of return, risk, and market structure', *Quarterly Journal of Economics*, 91:157–163.

Yamawaki, H. (1986) 'Exports, foreign market structure, and profitability in Japanese and U.S. manufacturing', *Review of Economics and Statistics*, 63:618–627.

Zmijewski, M.E. and Hagerman, R.L. (1981) 'An income strategy approach to the positive theory of accounting standard setting/choice', *Journal of Accounting and Economics*, 3:129–149.

Chapter 17

EMPIRICAL STUDIES OF INDUSTRIES WITH MARKET POWER

TIMOTHY F. BRESNAHAN*

Stanford University

Contents

*I owe a tremendous debt to the editors of this handbook for their encouragement and comments. Their contribution is so large that it would be diminished if I named any of the other very helpful friends and colleagues who contributed ideas and discussion. Though Richard E. Quandt's name does not appear in the reference list, his influence on the field shows in dozens of papers. The remaining errors are mine.

Handbook of Industrial Organization, Volume II, Edited by R. Schmalensee and R.D. Willig

1. Introduction

This chapter treats econometric studies of market power in single markets and in groups of related markets. The recent increase in the number of such studies and substantial advances in the methods for carrying them out constitute a dramatic shift in the focus of empirical work in the industrial organization (IO) field. The new literature treated here is based largely on time series data from single industries, or on data from closely related markets. It has taken a markedly different view of what can be observed, and how economic quantities are to be measured, than earlier work did. At some risk of oversimplifying a growing and varied literature, I summarize the new approach as having these central ideas:

- Firms' price–cost margins are not taken to be observables; economic marginal cost (MC) cannot be directly or straightforwardly observed. The analyst infers MC from firm behavior, uses differences between closely related markets to trace the effects of changes in MC, or comes to a quantification of market power without measuring cost at all.
- Individual industries are taken to have important idiosyncracies. It is likely that institutional detail at the industry level will affect firms' conduct, and even more likely that it will affect the analyst's measurement strategy. Thus, practitioners in this literature are skeptical of using the comparative statics of variations across industries or markets as revealing anything, except when the markets are closely related.
- Firm and industry conduct are viewed as unknown parameters to be estimated. The behavioral equations by which firms set price and quantity will be estimated, and parameters of those equations can be directly linked to analytical notions of firm and industry conduct.
- As a result, the nature of the inference of market power is made clear, since the set of alternative hypotheses which are considered is explicit. The alternative hypothesis of no strategic interaction, typically a perfectly competitive hypothesis, is clearly articulated and is one of the alternatives among which the data can choose.

This "new empirical industrial organization" (NEIO) is clearly somewhat different than the previously dominant empirical method in the field, the structure–conduct–performance paradigm (SCPP).

For the quarter century following the pioneering work of Bain (1951), the focus of the SCPP was the cross-section study of many industries. Industry and firm profits were predicted from various structural measures. The NEIO is partly motivated by dissatisfactions over three maintained hypotheses in the SCPP: (i) economic price–cost margins (performance) could be directly observed in accounting data, (ii) cross-section variation in industry structure could be captured by a small number of observable measures, and (iii) empirical work should be aimed at estimating the reduced-form relationship between structure and performance.[1] Furthermore, the SCPP has been caught in a kind of gridlock over the question of whether high accounting profits are to be interpreted as a sign of good or of bad performance.[2] The SCPP did, however, introduce something into the field of tremendous value: systematic statistical evidence. The NEIO is an attempt to continue the use of such evidence while returning to the study of single (or related) industries. On its more optimistic days, the NEIO therefore sees itself as taking the best from the two great empirical IO traditions: SCPP and industry case studies.

A typical NEIO paper is first and foremost an econometric model of an industry. Thus the new literature has been able to draw closely on economic theory to guide specification and inference in the empirical models. Quite a bit of this chapter will treat method: it will attempt to provide a review of the manner in which theory has been applied, and the way in which economic inferences have been drawn from the empirical work. Much of the work in the literature has been focused on one set of issues, those surrounding price and quantity determination in oligopoly. The major subtopics covered include the formation and enforcement of tacitly collusive arrangements, the nature of noncooperative oligopoly interaction in the world, the degree of single-firm market power under product differentiation, and the size and determinants of the industry price–cost margin. The next two sections take up the question of measuring market power in concentrated single product industries; Section 2 reviews the various empirical models of monopoly power and of oligopoly interaction, and Section 3 covers the theoretical and empirical arguments for why it is monopoly power that is being measured. Section 4 takes up the question of measuring market power in the presence of product differentiation. These three sections form the bulk of the chapter, as the material they cover forms the bulk of the literature. The chapter has two conclusions. The first is a review of what the NEIO has learned about the extent of market power, the second a biased view of where the literature should go to learn more about the sources of market power.

[1] This is the extreme "structuralist" view associated primarily with Bain. [See Scherer (1980, ch. 1) for the label.] Other positions which take more of a view that conduct is sometimes observable are not importantly different for my purposes. The SCPP and NEIO remain very distinct on how performance and conduct are to be measured in any view.

[2] See Demsetz (1974) and Schmalensee, Chapter 16 in this Handbook. The conventional story is that high profit measures poor performance, i.e. measures the Lerner index ($\mathscr{L}$). Demsetz' alternative interpretation was that high profits measure good performance, i.e. low costs, an argument he buttressed by the observation that much of the profit in concentrated industries goes to large firms. These firms might therefore be large because of cost advantages. Bain (1951) had already provided a "poor performance" interpretation of this observation, however.

2. Oligopoly theory and the measurement of market power

Many of the advances in methodology for measuring market power can be seen most clearly in a stylized econometric model of oligopoly interaction in a single-product industry. The central inference in the stylized model is about firm and industry conduct: the goal is the estimation of parameters measuring the degree of competition. In parallel to laying out the stylized model, I will follow a single specific treatment, namely Porter's (1984) study of strategic interaction among nineteenth-century railroads. This organization is slightly repetitive, but permits the simultaneous treatment of two topics: the relationship of the empirical inferences to oligopoly theory, and their relationship to the data.

The stylized model has three sets of unknown parameters: costs, demand, and firm conduct. The observable variables that are endogenous to the industry equilibrium include industry price and each firm's quantity (sometimes only industry quantity) in time series; price–cost margins are not taken to be directly observable. This focus was reflected early in the rhetoric of the literature: in his title, Rosse (1970) cast the econometrician's problem as "Estimating Cost Function Parameters Without Using Cost Data". The observables are also taken to include variables that shift cost and demand functions.[3] Oligopoly theory is used to specify the equations of the model to be estimated. In this section, the use of theory to specify the model will be emphasized over inference. Inferences about market power will be identified only through refutable implications of the theory contained in the comparative statics or comparative dynamics of oligopoly equilibrium. Another paper title is symptomatic of the form of departure from tradition: Panzar and Rosse (1977a) "Structure, Conduct and Comparative Statics". The question of exactly how the comparative statics identify the conduct parameters is sufficiently important to deserve discussion in a separate section.

The stylized model's specification of demand functions and of cost functions tends to follow fairly standard applied econometrics treatments, so I will be terse in describing them. Specification of conduct parameters is more novel, less standardized, and less well understood, so I will treat it at somewhat greater length.

2.1. *Notation, cost, and demand*

The dependent variables of the stylized model are market price P_t, and each firm's quantity Q_{it}. Throughout, i will index firms and t will index observations,

[3]A few studies have also included variables which can be interpreted as directly shifting firm conduct: changes in regulation, entry (or the number of firms), mergers, and so on. These kinds of variation is much more prevalent in the studies of closely related markets than in single-industry time series.

normally taken to be in time series. Since we are treating the single-product case, $Q_t = \Sigma_i Q_{it}$ is well defined. For clarity, it is also useful to assume that the demand function for the product contains no intertemporal linkages from durability, habits, learning or other sources. It is convenient to write the demand function in inverse form:

$$P_t = D(Q_t, Y_t, \delta, \varepsilon_{dt}), \tag{1}$$

where Y_t are all variables shifting demand, δ are unknown parameters of the demand function. The demand equation econometric error terms ε_{dt} are written as entering in a potentially nonlinear way and not necessarily treated as a scalar.

In Porter's (1984) study of an 1880s railroad cartel, Q_t is grain shipped by rail from Chicago to the East Coast, measured in tons.[4] The time index t refers to a week between the first week of 1880 and the sixteenth week of 1886. The price data, P_t, are based on a weekly poll taken by the cartel of its members; given the possibility of secret price cutting, P_t is probably to be interpreted as if it were a weighted average of list prices. The demand function takes the constant elasticity form:[5]

$$\log P_t = \delta_0 + \delta_1 \log Q_t + \delta_2 L_t + \varepsilon_{dt}, \tag{1'}$$

where L_t, the only demand-side exogenous variable, is a dummy variable equal to 1 if the Great Lakes were open to navigation. (Shipment by water is a seasonal competitor to the railroads.)

Returning to the stylized model, the treatment of costs similarly takes a familiar form. For reasons of later convenience, we start from the total cost function:

$$C_{it} = C(Q_{it}, W_{it}, Z_{it}, \Gamma, \varepsilon_{cit}), \tag{2}$$

where W_{it} is the vector of factor prices paid by firm i at observation t, Z_{it} are other variables that shift cost, Γ are unknown parameters, and ε_{cit} are econometric error terms, treated as in (1). The distinction between factor prices and other cost shifters is maintained because many important developments in the literature concern the comparative statics of market equilibrium in W. I have put an i subscript on Z and W, since in some applications the comparative statics of equilibrium in the costs of a single firm or subgroup of firms are emphasized.

[4]Porter provides an argument for why this industry should be treated as a single-product one on pp. 302–303. He considers the aggregation of all grain, the dropping of all nongrain shipments, and the dropping of all westbound shipments.

[5]I shall mention a consistent notation throughout, rather than adopting the notation of individual papers. (1′) is Porter's (1) in inverse form.

More commonly, however, Z and W will not have an i subscript, since they will be measured at the industry level. In applications where the cost function being treated is a short-run cost function, Z will include the (SR) fixed factors. The definition of marginal cost follows from (2):

$$MC = C_1(Q_{it}, W_{it}, Z_{it}, \Gamma, \varepsilon_{cit}), \tag{3}$$

where the nonlinearity of cost in the econometric error has been exploited for the first time. $C_1(\cdot)$ is written as random, just as $C(\cdot)$. The error term in (3) is (harmlessly) written the same as (2), though obviously an additive error in the cost function will not appear in MC.

Outside the perfectly competitive model, firms do not have supply curves.[6] Instead, price- or quantity-setting conduct follows more general supply relations:

$$P_t = C_1(Q_{it}, W_{it}, Z_{it}, \Gamma, \varepsilon_{cit}) - D_1(Q_t, Y_t, \delta, \varepsilon_{dt})Q_{it}\theta_{it}. \tag{4}$$

Since $P - D_1Q$ is monopoly MR, (4) has the interpretation of MC = "perceived" MR for oligopoly models. The parameters θ index the competitiveness of oligopoly conduct. As θ_{it}, a positive unknown parameter, moves farther from 0, the conduct of firm i moves farther from that of a perfect competitor. At first glance, (4) appears to contain MC, even though I have said the approach assumes that MC is unobservable. The contradiction is not real, however, only apparent. Marginal cost, $C_1(\cdot)$, in (4) appears as a function of unknown parameters, Γ, not as an accounting datum. Only after Γ has been somehow estimated can MC be calculated; most of the methods described below draw inferences about Γ and θ in the same econometric step.

The next section will take up the conduct interpretation of θ at some length. Obviously letting θ vary both by firm and observation results in an overparameterized model. It is written here in such generality to permit nesting all of the known theories of oligopoly. Any empirical study will put some structure on the way θ varies across time and firms.

In Porter's railroad study, the constant-elasticity demand assumption implies that (4) can be written with the explicit Q_{it} terms substituted out. Furthermore, (4′) is not estimated for the individual firms, but rather aggregated to industry-wide data:

$$\log(P_t(1 + \delta_1\theta_t)) = MC = \Gamma_0 + \Gamma_1 \log Q_t. \tag{4′}$$

It is assumed that firms have heterogeneous marginal costs arising from a log-linear cost function, but that there are no exogenous shifts in the level of

[6] By a supply curve, I mean a solution for Q as a function of P of the equation $P = MC(Q)$.

costs over time. Thus, MC in (4′) is interpreted as the marginal cost of the average firm in the industry at time t. The overparameterization of θ_{it} is solved by aggregation: the interpretation of θ_t is as the average of the conduct parameters of the firms in the industry. Since there is some entry and some acquisition activity during the sample period, the average firm's marginal cost can be expected to shift over time: this is captured by a series of structural dummies S_t, which enter as $\langle \Gamma_2, S_t \rangle$.[7] Similarly, these changes in industry structure may have changed conduct: this is captured in the same dummies. The lack of other cost shifters (factor prices) or demand shifters (the price of lake shipping) is dealt with not by new data but by a close reading of the estimation results in light of the likely omitted variable biases.

To Porter, a crucial question is whether θ_t varies over time because of changes in industry conduct. High θ_t periods are to be interpreted as successful cartel cooperation, low θ_t times as price wars or similar breakdowns in cooperation. Furthermore, it is assumed that the probability of successful collusion is $1 - \pi$. After a transformation, the supply relation ultimately estimated takes the form:

Supply relation	*Probability*	
$\log P_t = \Gamma_0 + \alpha^{\mathrm{a}} + \Gamma_1 \log Q_t + \langle \Gamma_2, S_t \rangle + \varepsilon_{cit}$	π	(4″)
$\log P_t = \Gamma_0 + \alpha^{\mathrm{a}} + \alpha^{\mathrm{b}} + \Gamma_1 \log Q_t + \langle \Gamma_2, S_t \rangle + \varepsilon_{cit}$	$1 - \pi$	

where α^{a} is a transformation of the conduct parameter in periods of successful collusion, and α^{b} measures the change in conduct when collusion breaks down.[8] Of course, it is clear that α^{a} cannot be separately estimated from Γ_0 on the basis of estimating these equations, but there is considerable interest in estimating α^{b}, the percentage amount by which a breakdown in the cartel changes prices. As the form of (4″) suggests, Porter estimates the system (1′, 4″) by "switching equations" methods, in which the probability π as well as the regular parameters are estimated from the data.

In general, the endogenous variables of the stylized model are P_t and Q_{it}. Many empirical studies, like Porter's, use only industry-wide data and thus have endogenous variables P_t and Q_t. In either event, the core econometric methods are those for simultaneous equations. Some empirical studies proceed by estimating (1) and (4) directly as structural equations: this is attractive, as the supply parameters θ are of primary interest. Other studies, however, may lack data on price or quantity or on firm-specific quantity. In the first case, some reduced form

[7] The four structural dummies capture the entry by the Grand Trunk railway and the entry by the Chicago and Atlantic, an addition to the New York Central and the departure of the Chicago and Atlantic from the Cartel. The $\langle\ ,\ \rangle$ notation is the inner product.

[8] Let θ_t be able to take on one of two values, θ^{a} and θ^{b}. Then $\alpha^{\mathrm{a}} = -\log(1 + \theta^{\mathrm{a}} \delta_1)$ and $\alpha^{\mathrm{a}} + \alpha^{\mathrm{b}} = -\log(1 + \theta^{\mathrm{b}} \delta_1)$.

will be estimated. In the second, aggregate data will be used. For both purposes, it is useful to briefly define a few related functions. If (1) and (4) are solved simultaneously for all firms, they yield the reduced forms for price and each firm's quantity:

$$P_t = P^*(W_t, Z_t, Y_t, \Omega, \varepsilon_t), \tag{5}$$

$$Q_{it} = Q_i^*(W_t, Z_t, Y_t, \Omega, \varepsilon_t), \tag{5'}$$

where $\Omega = (\delta, \Gamma, \theta)$ is the vector of all parameters, ε_t is the vector of all structural error terms, W_t is the superset of all the W_{it},[9] and Z_t and Y_t are similarly defined. Similarly, we have the reduced form equation for industry quantity, $Q^*(\cdot)$, and so on.

Discussion of the results of these analyses in general must be delayed until after the discussion of the interpretation of the parameters θ. Porter's results, however, will be discussed briefly here. The value of α^{b} estimated in (4″) implies that price was raised about 40 percent by successful collusion in the industry. The implicit estimates of θ are consistent with collusive behavior approximately as anticompetitive as that implied by the Cournot model.[10] The implicit fraction of the time that the cartel broke down was 28 percent; both the amount and timing of cartel breakdown activity differed somewhat from the patterns detected by earlier scholars and by contemporaneous sources.

The advantages of the modelling technique embodied in (1) and (4) seem to me to be threefold. The first is that the econometric approach is structural. Each parameter has an economic interpretation, and substantial departures of the estimated parameters from expected values can serve as clues to difficulties with or shortcomings of the analysis. For example, Porter estimates a negative Γ_1; he provides an argument for why MC might be downward-sloping, an argument that is more convincing in the context of railroads than it might be in many others. The second advantage of the approach I take up in the next section: if the interpretation of θ is correct, the relationship of the estimates of conduct to theory will be clear. A third advantage is in the section after that: given the structural nature of the econometrics, the reason why the data identify the conduct parameters can be made clear.

[9] If there are only market factor prices, $W_t = W_{1t}$ without any loss of information. If all firms buy factors at different prices, then $W_t = (W_{1t}, W_{2t}, \dots)$.

[10] The assertion about Cournot depends on the (unidentified) inference that noncooperative behavior is approximately price-taking.

2.2. *Alternative treatments of firm conduct and of θ*

Supply relations are more general than supply equations because they permit the possibility of nonprice taking conduct, captured in the strategic interaction parameters (θ). Clearly the form in which this nonprice taking conduct is modelled will be central to the inferences about market power drawn in any particular study. The approach covered in Subsection 2.2.1 takes the specification of θ directly from a theory or group of theories. The logical extension of that approach, testing a small number of distinct theories of oligopoly interaction, is covered in Subsection 2.2.2. Another group of papers, covered in Subsection 2.2.3, has had a looser connection to oligopoly theory. A typical paper in it reports its inferences as "estimating oligopoly conjectural variations". There has been enormous confusion about the interpretation of this work, however, primarily because of a language gap. To resolve the confusion, the phrase "conjectural variations" has to be understood in two ways: it means something different in the theoretical literature than the object which has been estimated in the empirical papers. A brief subsection, 2.2.4, discusses the interpretation of estimates when only industry-wide data are used, another area of some confusion. Throughout, individual papers will be used to illustrate how the analytical ideas are actually carried out in the data.

2.2.1. *Supply relations from single, specific theories*

The first approach to writing (4) and specifying θ uses explicitly theoretical language. Important examples include Rosse (1970), in which the supply relation is derived from the theory of monopoly. Bresnahan (1981) has product differentiation with Bertrand pricing. Porter (1984) uses the Green and Porter (1984) version of Stigler's (1964) theory of collusive oligopoly over time to specify (4); since that theory implies that both collusive and price-war periods will be seen in the data, θ varies over time in the empirical model. After the specification of models based on a single oligopoly theory, I discuss the specification of alternative models based upon a small number of different solution concepts (Bertrand, collusion, etc.) each of which leads to a different version of (4), as in Bresnahan (1980). Geroski (1983) applies this approach to the coffee industry data of Gollop and Roberts (1979), specifying theories in which conduct (and therefore θ) varies across firms (such as Stackelberg leader/follower models). All of the studies which take this approach to specifying the supply relation impose dramatically more structure on the way θ enters (4) than the way I have written it, the structure implied by the theory or theories used. More generally this approach focuses on the estimation of specific models of strategic conduct. The flavor of this analysis can be gotten by considering a few examples. The first of these is monopoly and the Cournot model, or (in a higher or at least higherfaulting theoretical language) one-shot Nash equilibrium with quantities as the strategic choice variables. This takes the form $\theta_{it} = 1$ for all i, t:

$$P_t = C_1(Q_{it}, W_{it}, Z_{it}, \Gamma, \varepsilon_{cit}) - D_1(Q_t, Y_t, \delta, \varepsilon_{dt})Q_{it}. \tag{6}$$

When there are several firms in the industry, (6) provides an estimating equation for each firm. When there is only one firm in the industry, Cournot behavior (among others) is the same as monopoly behavior. Thus, $\theta = 1$ for monopoly, and (6) holds.

Rosse's (1970) study of American newspapers estimated an equation like (6) simultaneously with one like (1). In his work, Q_{it} is taken to be a three-vector: column inches of advertising, Q_t^{a}; circulation, Q_t^{c}; and column inches of "editorial" (nonadvertising) material, Q_t^{a}. There are two prices associated with these variables: the price of circulation is measured as the average price per subscription copy, and the price of advertising is the average price charged per inch.[11] It is reasonable to expect that the amount of circulation affects advertisers' demand; and that the amount of editorial material and the amount of advertising affect subscribers' demand for the newspaper itself. Using superscripts on prices for advertising and for circulation, the demand equation (1) takes the form:

$$\begin{aligned} P_t^{\mathrm{a}} &= D^{\mathrm{a}}(Q_t^{\mathrm{a}}, Q_t^{\mathrm{c}}, Y_t, \delta, \varepsilon_{\mathrm{a}t}) \qquad \text{(advertising demand)}, \\ P_t^{\mathrm{c}} &= D^{\mathrm{c}}(Q_t^{\mathrm{a}}, Q_t^{\mathrm{c}}, Q_t^{\mathrm{e}}, Y_t, \delta, \varepsilon_{\mathrm{c}t}) \quad \text{(circulation demand)}. \end{aligned} \tag{1'}$$

The treatment of MR needs also to reflect this interdependence. The appropriate definition of MR is the derivative of the firms' entire revenue with respect to a single product's quantity. For example, the form of (6) for circulation is:

$$P_t = MC^{\mathrm{c}} - Q_t^{\mathrm{c}} D_2^{\mathrm{c}}(Q_t^{\mathrm{a}}, Q_t^{\mathrm{c}}, Q_t^{\mathrm{e}}, \dots) - Q_t^{\mathrm{a}} D_2^{\mathrm{a}}(Q_t^{\mathrm{a}}, Q_t^{\mathrm{c}}, \dots), \tag{6^{c}}$$

where the last term on the right is the unusual MR term: the advertising-price effect of higher circulation. Simultaneous estimation of cost function and supply relation exploits the cross-equation restrictions between demand and MR. If demand can be estimated, and MR thereby inferred, an estimate of monopoly MC can be obtained from $MC = MR$. This permits Rosse to take a very sophisticated view of the MC function. For example, his treatment permits transitory shocks to the sizes of firms in his sample to drive a wedge between

[11] Clearly, this three-product approach to the newspaper involves some aggregation of products, such as the different sizes of advertisement that can be purchased. Also, in the interest of uniform notation, I have suppressed some of the details of Rosse's treatment, and have written the demand equations in inverse form.

$LRMC$ and $SRMC$. Obviously, the degree to which such an analysis is convincing depends on the quality of the demand estimates and on the reliability of the MR inference; a linear demand specification (like Rosse's) may fit well, yet provide poor estimates of MR. As (6^c) suggests, the ability to support this inference against criticism turns on a sophisticated use of the institutional detail of the industry, in this case newspapers.

The other static, noncooperative, symmetric oligopoly model to receive attention is that of Bertrand (one-shot Nash equilibrium with prices as the strategic variables). Since this model is not interestingly distinct from perfect competition in the case of single product industries with flat marginal costs, the greatest attention has been focused on the product-differentiated case. Bresnahan (1981) estimates such a model on 1977 and 1978 cross-sections of automobiles by type. The demand system comes from a spatial treatment of the demand for automobiles by type. Automobiles of different types are assumed to lie in a one-dimensional space, and consumers are assumed to be distributed according to a one-dimensional parameter describing differences in their demands.[12] The own-price and cross-price elasticities are determined by how close products are in this space. Letting X_i be the quality of good i, the demand for a typical good is given by

$$Q_i = \delta_0\big((P_j - P_i)/(X_j - X_i) - (P_i - P_h)/(X_i - X_h)\big) + \varepsilon_{di}, \tag{7}$$

where products h, i, j are adjacent in quality space. Here the price of automobile i is the manufacturer to dealer list price, which is identical to the transactions price for the vast majority of sales. Quantity is model–year production, and the unit of observation (i) is now not the firm but the product. Quality is taken to be ex ante unknown, but to be a hedonic function of observable characteristics:

$$X_i = f(Z, \delta_1) + \varepsilon_{xi}, \tag{8}$$

where Z is a vector of the typical hedonic characteristics: length, weight, horsepower, etc. Under Bertrand competition, the equivalent of (6) is given by

$$\begin{aligned} Q_i = {} & (P_i - MC_i)\,\delta_0\big(1/(X_j - X_i) - 1/(X_i - X_h)\big) \\ & + d_{ij}P_j\,\delta_0/(X_j - X_i) + d_{ih}P_h\,\delta_0/(X_i - X_h) + \varepsilon_{si}, \end{aligned} \tag{6''}$$

where d_{ij} is a dummy for whether the firm that produces product i also produces product j. As in the Rosse treatment, the definition of MR is taken on a

[12] The demand system is that of "vertical product differentiation"; see Prescott and Visscher (1977).

whole-firm basis. In this cross-section work, marginal cost is a function only of product type Z, not of factor prices. It is clear from (6″) that the closeness of competitive products is the key determinant of market power in such a model. Bresnahan (1981) reports two related findings: the large price–cost margins appear to be on the larger vehicles, and the larger vehicles appear to be much farther apart in product–quality space.[13] The obvious problem with this kind of modelling is the highly restrictive assumptions made about the form of the demand system. Bresnahan (1980, 1981), like Rosse (1970), attempts to deal with these primarily by analysis of the residuals; the devices include introducing firm dummies, adding ε_{xi} to (7), and so on.

A second class of models of some importance have separate leaders and followers. Of these, the first is the Stackelberg leader model. I adopt the notational convention that there are I firms in the industry, so $i = 1, \ldots, I$. The Stackelberg model writes (6) for firms $2, \ldots I$, but for the "leader," firm 1 writes:

$$P_t = C_1(Q_{1t}, W_{1t}, Z_{1t}, \Gamma, \varepsilon_{c1t}) - D_1(Q_t, Y_t, \delta, \varepsilon_{dt}) Q_{1t}(1 + \theta_S), \qquad (7)$$

where θ_S is obtained by first solving (6) simultaneously for all firms except firm 1; this yields functions $Q_i(Q_1, \ldots)$. Then θ_S is the derivative of the sum of these with respect to Q_{1t}.

A closely related model, the dominant firm model, has been estimated by Suslow (1986). In her treatment, there is a fringe of firms that are price-takers, the producers of "scrap" or recycled aluminum. The dominant firm is Alcoa, and the sample refers to the interwar period in which Alcoa had a monopoly on the production of new aluminum. In a general dominant firm model, the fringe firms have supply relations which are supply curves. Without loss of generality, the supply curve of the entire fringe is determined by its collective MC:

$$P_t = C_1(Q_{ft}, W_{ft}, Z_{ft}, \Gamma, \varepsilon_{cft}), \qquad (10)$$

$$Q_{ft} = S(P_t, W_{ft}, Z_{ft}, \Gamma, \varepsilon_{cft}), \qquad (10')$$

where $Q_{ft} = \sum_{i=2, I} Q_{it}$, and W and Z are taken to be common to all firms in the fringe: the function in (10′) is the inverse of that in (10). Suslow (1986) permits the dominant firm and the fringe to sell somewhat differentiated products. For clarity I will assume they sell the same product. In her paper, Q_{ft} is the physical quantity of "secondary" aluminum recycled, and P_{ft} the recycled price. The demand shifters Z_{ft} include an estimate of the stock of aluminum available for recycling. The leader in a dominant firm model is taken to be sophisticated, and

[13]This confirms the view of many industry observers, based on accounting profits data. It received further confirmation from a study of auto dealers' (as well as manufacturers') prices in Bresnahan and Reiss (1985).

to set:

$$P_t = C_1(\cdot) + D_1(\cdot)Q_{1t}(1 + S_D), \tag{11}$$

$$S_D = D_1(\cdot)S_1(\cdot)/(1 - D_1(\cdot)S_1(\cdot)). \tag{11'}$$

In Suslow's paper, Alcoa's *MC* is shifted by cost variables, such as the firm's accounting average variable cost, which clearly do not enter the supply function of the fringe. Price is measured by realized average revenue, quantity by sales in physical units.[14] She finds that Alcoa enjoyed considerable monopoly power, despite the competition of the fringe, since the quantity S_D is estimated to be small. This approach has some of the same interpretational difficulties as the earlier one: *MR* still needs to be carefully selected. There is also the need to establish or test that the selected firm is in fact the leader; Suslow accomplishes this by arguing from the industry structure of new aluminum (monopoly) and of recycling (many firms).

Leaving static noncooperative theories, leads us to dynamic theories. The problem of repeated oligopoly interaction has received a great deal of theoretical attention, since it is reasonable to presume that long-run considerations might reduce the competitiveness of oligopoly conduct. Oligopolists might go along with a collusive arrangement, even though deviations are profitable, if they recognize that deviations will lead to a general breakout of competition. A pathbreaking model is that of Stigler (1964): if it is purely this self-interest which holds collusive arrangements together, they should be expected to sometimes break down as the parties grow suspicious of each others' motives and behavior. In an uncertain environment, firms will not always know whether secret price-cutting has occurred, and this will lead to some price wars even if there is no actual secret price-cutting. Thus, one should expect cartels to break up and to reform: data on a cartelized or tacitly collusive industry should show both periods of successful cooperation and periods of outright competition. Empirically, of course, this will show up as time-varying θ.

Several recent formalizations have put considerably more structure on the theory, and on the pattern of industry equilibrium over time. The first of these is Green and Porter (1984) (GP). In their theory, price wars actually break out because of shocks that firms cannot observe. When profit drops in the *SR*, firms cannot tell with certainty whether this is because of chiselling on the cartel agreement or because the aggregate situation has worsened. Bad enough shocks will trigger price wars. GP, and a later paper by Porter (1983) treat the problem of "design" of a cartel arrangement. In their theory, firms decide (collectively)

[14] Suslow's treatment of the marginal cost of a monopolistic that can produce to store as inventory is somewhat shortchanged by this discussion.

how high to raise prices in collusive periods, how trigger happy to be, and how long price wars should be. The degree of competition in a price war is taken as exogenous (it is assumed to take the Cournot form). The theory predicts that there will be alternating periods of price war and of successful collusion. The length of the price wars and the size of a shock needed to trigger a price war are picked to maximize industry profit. The intuition of these and of other Stigler-esque theories comes from incentive economics. Why should collusive firms not raise price all the way to the monopoly level? If they did, it would give too much of an incentive to deviate from the cartel arrangement. Why should price wars last a while before the cartel is reformed? Otherwise, the possibility of a price war could not deter any opportunistic behavior.

Abreu et al. (1986) find cartel designs that are even more profitable for firms than the GP ones, by permitting more complex arrangements among firms. These designs still have alternating periods of successful collusion and of price wars, but now there are "triggers" both for beginning a price war and for ending one. Thus, the length of price wars is random. Furthermore, the amount of competition in a price war is endogenous to the model: it, too, is optimized to maximize the returns to the colluders. Rotemberg and Saloner (1986) take a somewhat different tack. In their model, the environment in which firms operate shifts over time. As a result, the optimal cartel price shifts as well. Suppose (as in the analysis they provide) that current demand is not a predictor of future demand. Then in boom periods, the gain from defecting from a cartel is unusually large at any given price. Therefore the cartel must set an unusually low price to reduce the incentive to defect. The reverse line of argument holds in demand busts.

These various theories have in common the idea that in an imperfectly informed world, "successfully" collusive industries will have periods of cartel pricing and periods of competition.[15] In general, they imply models with θ_{it} not necessarily equal to $\theta_{i\tau}$. The theories differ somewhat in the expected time-series behavior of these two regimes, as the exact equations determining passage from one regime to the other vary between theories. Green and Porter theories, for example, seem to suggest that θ changes from the collusive to the competitive value when there is an unanticipated shock to demand, and that returns to collusion will follow with a fixed lag. Abreu et al. have θ following a time-series process driven by demand shocks as well, but the process is Markov. The Rotemberg and Saloner theory suggests endogenous strategic variation in conduct within the collusive regime. It is easy to imagine other theories of success or failure in tacit collusion which predict different patterns; taking all of these theories at once would lead to even more complex potential time-series behavior for θ.

[15]Rotemberg and Saloner do not write their theory in this way, because they assume that there is no imperfect information. This is clearly an assumption of convenience (irrelevant to the point they are making) rather than a central feature of the model.

I have already discussed the details of Porter's (1983) approach to time-varying θ, and the discussion of the previous paragraph begins the discussion of the relationship of that approach to theory. For clarity, let me reprint (4″) here. The supply relation estimated in Porter (1983) [see also Lee and Porter (1984)] is

Supply relation	*Probability*	
$\log P_t = \Gamma_0 + \alpha^{a} + \Gamma_1 \log Q_t + \langle \Gamma_2, S_t \rangle + \varepsilon_{cit}$	π	(4″)
$\log P_t = \Gamma_0 + \alpha^{a} + \alpha^{b} + \Gamma_1 \log Q_t + \langle \Gamma_2, S_t \rangle + \varepsilon_{cit}$	$1 - \pi$	

By estimating only a single probability of colluding or competing, π, Porter puts less structure on the problem than the theories suggest. Estimation of π in (4″) can tell us how frequently cartels break down, but cannot tell us what predicts breakdowns and reformations – the area in which the theories disagree. At a minimum, one would like π to be state dependent. Alternatively, whether changes in markup from regime b to regime a appear statistically to be the same event as shocks to demand could be investigated. An initial attempt to investigate the time-series behavior of the regimes is contained in Porter (1985). Rotemberg and Saloner (1986) provide a somewhat less structural analysis of the same question, using Porter's reported regime shifts as well as the time-varying pattern of automobile industry competition and collusion reported in Bresnahan (1987). I see little in these investigations that differentiates among the various theories; the time-series behavior of conduct is harder to estimate than the average level of conduct.

It will be surprising (to me, anyway) if further similar investigations succeed in strongly differentiating among the theories. Investigations of the question, Do there seem to be price wars?, can essentially take advantage of the data in all periods. The investigator is trying to find out that there are two distinct regimes. On the other hand, an investigation of the question, What sets price wars off and what stops them?, necessarily will have a much smaller sample size. Instead of having the number of observations equal to the number of sample periods, it has the number of observations equal to the number of price wars. This low assessment of the success probability of further testing is not particularly troubling (to me, anyway) since the various theories are identical for practical purposes.

A final remark on this subsection goes better here than anywhere else. Industrial organization economists have frequently felt that their field was data-starved, or at least starved of appropriate data. The studies reviewed here show this to be false. The dissertation of work of Rosse, Bresnahan and Suslow each involved collection of data from industry sources in the public domain, with no reliance on government sources for endogenous variables. Porter's work, too, is based on industry sources.

2.2.2. *Supply relations from a small set of theories*

The papers treated in the previous subsection took a single (in the last case, complex!) theory as a starting point for the specification of the supply relation. A closely related development has been attempts to estimate the supply relations of a small number of different theories and to test among them. This is the approach of Bresnahan (1980, 1987). The data used are again cross-sections of automobiles, this time from the mid-1950s. The demand equations are exactly as in (7). But the supply relations for joint monopoly pricing as well as those for Bertrand pricing are estimated. These differ from (6″) only in that $d_{ij} = 1$ whether the neighboring products are produced by the same firm or not. (MR for a joint monopoly of all firms is the derivative of industry revenue with respect to quantity.) The estimates, otherwise much like those described above, show collusive behavior in some years, but competitive (Bertrand) behavior in 1955. This provides a strategic explanation of part of the large expansion of auto production in that model year. In related work, Geroski (1983) and Roberts (1983) put the structure implied by a small number of leader–follower type theories on the data for coffee roasting firms in the United States, finding that the smaller firms in the industry are price-taking followers. The leading firms do not appear to joint profit maximize (even given the constraint implied by the fringe's supply curve) but do behave less competitively than Cournot firms.

Since each of the theories reviewed up to now in this section is associated with different values of the parameters in θ, one might decide to treat θ as a continuous-valued parameter and estimate it. This approach is the one discussed in the next section. It risks the possibility that values of θ which are "in between" existing theories will be estimated, but that is hardly a disaster. The distinction between the continuous-valued θ and the distinct θ's from several theories is purely econometric. The researcher who has estimated θ from a continuum will test theories by nested methods. The other researcher will use non-nested tests to distinguish among the few theories entertained, as I did in the work described in the previous paragraph.[16]

2.2.3. *Supply equations in "conjectural variations" language*

The second approach to specification of (4) uses "conjectural variations" (CV) language and treats conduct as a continuous-valued parameter to be estimated. In this language, the parameters describing firms' conduct are not written in the form of θ in (4). Instead, the parameters are described in terms of firms' conjectural variations, that is, their "expectations" about the reaction of other firms to an increase in quantity. These parameters are typically allowed to take

[16] See Geroski, Phlips and Ulph (1985) for a different position on this issue.

on any values in a broad range. An important early paper is Iwata (1974), whose title "Measurement of Conjectural Variations in Oligopoly" is illustrative of the thrust of the literature.[17] He saw the question as inferring where, in the continuum between perfect competition and monopoly, the Japanese plate glass industry lay. Another important early paper was Gollop and Roberts (1979), which permitted conjectures to vary across firms. Later work by Spiller and Favaro (1984) and Gelfand and Spiller (1987) on banking continued this emphasis on heterogeneity of firm conduct.

In the CV language, the empirical supply relationship is written in the form:

$$P_t = C_1(\cdot) - D_1(\cdot)Q_{it}\big(1 + r_i(Q_{it}, Q_{jt}, Z_{it}, \Phi)\big). \tag{12}$$

Here Q_{jt} is the vector of all other firms' quantities, and the dependence of cost and demand on exogenous variables and parameters can be temporarily suppressed. Note first that the only difference between (4) and (12) is that the term θ_{it} in (4) has been replaced by the term $1 + r(\cdot)$. This does suggest some practical differences between the papers discussed in the previous subsection and the CV papers. The CV papers tend to permit all values of r_i, not just those associated with particular theories. There is clearly nothing fundamental about this: as discussed above, one could easily treat θ in (4) as lying in a continuum. Second, the CV papers have tended to emphasize the relationship between firm size and conduct: hence the explicit dependence of $r_i(\cdot)$ on quantities in (12). There is also an implicit dependence: different values of Φ are often permitted firms in different size classes.

As a matter of logic, there is absolutely no difference between (4) and (12) in general, since the identity $\theta_{it} - 1 = r_i(Q_{it}, Q_{jt}, Z_{it}, \Phi)$ implies that the two specifications can nest the same models. (Nothing in the previous subsection implied that θ_{it} needed to be a constant, though many theoretical models have constant θ_{it}.) Therefore I will use θ to mean $1 + r$, and vice versa according to convenience, in the rest of this chapter. I cannot overemphasize this point: there is *no difference* between saying what the "conjectural variation" is and saying what theory of oligopoly holds in the data. Misunderstandings of the phrase "conjectural variations" to mean something other than it does mean in the empirical papers has been rife, however.

There are some cases where no misunderstandings arise: for example, the Cournot model is labelled "zero conjectural variations". It is usually innocent to think of Cournot firms as ones that "expect" other firms' quantities to be

[17] Iwata (1974) differs from many of the papers surveyed here in that it assumes that accounting data reveal PCMs. Its role in using the data to try to draw inferences about conduct was very influential, however.

constants. Similarly, $r(\cdot)$ of -1 is perfect competition, and it is completely correct to say of a competitive firm that it "expects" price to be a constant.

The linguistic difficulties arise in other cases because allusion to underlying theoretical models is typically made in the same "expectations" or "conjectures" language. Suppose we think of (12) as the derivative of a single-firm profit function:

$$\max_{Qi} D\left(\sum_j Q_{jt}(Q_i), \ldots\right) Qi - C(Q_i, \ldots) \tag{13}$$

Equation (13) has every other firm's quantity as a function of Q_i. Then we read $1 + r_i$ in (12) by

$$1 + r_i(\cdot) = \mathrm{d}Q_i/\mathrm{d}Q_i + \sum_j \mathrm{d}Q_j/\mathrm{d}Q_i, \tag{14}$$

where the sum over firms j is $j \neq i$. Some minor variations in language occur, but the typical understanding is that the $\mathrm{d}Q_j/\mathrm{d}Q_i$ terms measure the way firm i "expects" firm j to "react" to an increase in quantity.[18]

It is when the estimated "conjectures" are ones which lead to prices close to the collusive level that the simple "expectations" interpretation is suspect. The point can be seen under the assumption that all firms have the same cost curves and "conjectures". Let there be I firms in the industry. Suppose we get the conjectures associated with the collusive level of output, $(1 + r_i) = I$:

$$P + C_1(\cdot) - D_1(\cdot) I Q_i \tag{15}$$

for each firm, since that particular value is the solution to the problem "maximize the profits of all I firms". How, then, are we to interpret $1 + r_i = I$? Taken literally, the coefficient says that the firm picks its output to maximize industry profits because it "expects" the other firms in the industry to match its output: $r_i > 0$ is an expectation of matching behavior, and the r_i of (15) imply an expectation of proportional matching: $\mathrm{d}Q_j/\mathrm{d}Q_i = 1$.

In a great many treatments of oligopoly as a repeated game, firms produce output in most periods according to (15), but the reason they do is that they *expect* deviations from that level of quantity to lead to a general breakdown in restraint. (The exact form this would take varies among the theories: see Subsec-

[18]Some papers describe estimates of (11) as "estimating conjectural variations", other as "estimating firms' first-order conditions". If (11) is solved for Q_i it is "estimating firms' reaction functions". Adding up the first-order conditions and interpreting the result in light of Cournot theory even leads to the language "estimating the equivalent number of firms". Obviously, there are no important distinctions between these languages.

tion 2.2.1 above, and see Shapiro, Chapter 6 in this Handbook, for a much fuller treatment.) Thus, the matching behavior is unobserved; firms expect that if they deviate from the collusive arrangement, others will too. This expectation deters them from departing from their share of the collusive output.

The crucial distinction here is between (i) what firms believe will happen if they deviate from the tacitly collusive arrangements and (ii) what firms do as a result of those expectations. In the "conjectural variations" language for how supply relations are specified, it is clearly (ii) that is estimated. Thus, the estimated parameters tell us about price- and quantity-setting behavior; if the estimated "conjectures" are constant over time, and if breakdowns in the collusive arrangements are infrequent, we can safely interpret the parameters as measuring the average collusiveness of conduct.[19] The "conjectures" do *not* tell us what will happen if a firm autonomously increases output (and thereby departs from the cartel agreement), the normal sense in which theoretical papers would use "conjectural variations".

A second set of interpretive questions arises when the variation across firms in r_i is modelled by estimating Φ in $r_i(Q_{it}, Q_{jt}, Z_{it}, \Phi)$, as in Gollop and Roberts (1979), Spiller and Favaro (1984), and Gelfand and Spiller (1987). A speculative interpretation is that the dependence of the $r_i(\cdot)$ on own quantity tells us something about "mutual forbearance". The notion here is that one can read the derivative of $r_i(\cdot)$ with respect to own quantity as revealing something about how competition would change if firms were to deviate from agreed production. This seems to trip over the distinction just raised between what the conjectures enforce and what they are. I would therefore not use the "mutual forbearance" language.

The use of different strategic parameters for firms of different sizes suggests that the CV models may provide a strategic explanation of the size distribution of firms, since their endogenous variables include the quantity produced or market share of each firm. By permitting the firms to have different conduct, such models permit ex ante identical firms to be of different sizes in equilibrium. For example, the three papers just listed all permit different conjectural variations for different size classes of firms. When economies of scale are permitted (as in these papers) this can provide information about the details of large-firm–small-firm interaction. It was this which motivated Geroski (1983) and Roberts (1983) to test specific theories in this context: they were particularly interested in questions

[19]All of these theories of going along with a collusive arrangement suggest that it is not necessarily the fully collusive outcome that will arise. Somewhat smaller r_i's than in (13), and therefore somewhat larger equilibrium output, can also arise (when worse information makes collusive arrangements harder to enforce, for example.) In these circumstances, firms' "expectations" about what would happen if they deviated from planned output might be exactly the same, but their production levels would be different. That is to say, there is *no information* about firms' expectations contained in the estimates of the $r_i(\cdot)$. The $r_i(\cdot)$ tell us how close to a completely collusive outcome the expectations induce. The only thing they tell us about expectations is that the expectations are sufficient to deter departure from the normal arrangement.

like: "Are large firms, taken as a group, leaders and small firms followers?" I think this very interesting line of research is still incomplete, since alternative explanations of the size distribution of firms have yet to be introduced. In particular, it would seem important to let different firms have different cost functions. Then it would be possible to test the alternative hypothesis that the size distribution is driven by relative costs despite identical conduct parameters.[20]

2.2.4. *Work with aggregate industry data and aggregate conduct*

In many circumstances, the lack of single-firm data will prohibit estimation of supply relations for individual firms. Instead aggregate industry data must be used. One approach is to simply rewrite (4) in aggregate form:

$$P_t = C_1(Q_{it}, W_{it}, Z_{it}, \Gamma, \varepsilon_{cit}) - D_1(Q_t, Y_t, \delta, \varepsilon_{dt})Q_{it}\theta_{it} \tag{4}$$

becomes

$$P_t = C_1(Q_t, W_t, Z_t, \Gamma, \varepsilon_{ct}) - D_1(Q_t, Y_t, \delta, \varepsilon_{dt})Q_t\theta_t. \tag{16}$$

This approach is familiar from as different works as Appelbaum (1979) and Porter (1984). Under the null hypothesis of no market power, $\theta = 0$, the interpretation of C_1 as industry marginal cost is clear. When there is market power, however, different firms will almost certainly have different marginal costs in equilibrium. Analysis like that of Cowling and Waterson (1976) shows that noncooperative oligopoly will tend to have variation in price–cost margins across firms unless they have identical, constant *MC*. In these circumstances, a stable industry marginal cost curve need not exist, and interpretation of (16) may be clouded.

There are clearly some circumstances in which industry-wide marginal costs are equal to each firm's *MC*; consider the example of a cartel that succeeds in rationalizing production. Generally, however, (16) will need to be interpreted as some sort of average. In this context, an error in the interpretation of (16) has crept into the literature: the assertion that $\theta_{it} = \theta_{jt}$ is an implication of theory.[21] This is clearly incorrect, as there is nothing in the logic of oligopoly theory to force all firms to have the same conduct. It is better to follow Cowling and Waterson (1976) and interpret the aggregate θ_t in (16) as industry average conduct, and $(P - C_1)/P$ as the industry average markup.

[20] This is not a trivial task. The existing specifications of a common cost function with scale economies do permit heterogeneity in the level of *MC* across firms. The interesting hypothesis turns on whether firms of different sizes would have similar *MC* at the same output, a tricky measurement problem.

[21] Appelbaum (1982) made this argument; it has been picked up by Lopez (1984).

2.2.5. *Final thoughts on θ and r_i*

Both the work closely based on economic theory and the conjectural variations work has overwhelmingly cast its (logical) tests of theories of strategic interaction as (statistical) hypothesis tests about θ. These studies tend to state their problem as one of measuring conduct or strategic interaction rather than as of measuring market power. Thus, they focus on hypothesis tests about θ or r_i. In this connection, an important observation was made by Appelbaum (1979): setting the entire vector θ to zero in (4) or (equivalently) setting all of the r_i to -1 imposes the restriction of price-taking conduct. Thus all approaches to specifying (4), even those which do not use explicitly theoretical language, can be thought of as "Testing Price-Taking Behavior", Appelbaum's title. This would not be particularly interesting, except that the particular alternative hypothesis against which price-taking has been rejected is one with market power.

The next section treats the question of what constitutes an adequately rich specification of cost and demand so as to permit a reasonably convincing case that a strategic interaction hypothesis is in fact being tested. The section will show that the hypothesis of market power is in fact identified on reasonable data. This is an important step: if it were merely true that perfect competition were rejected, and that no positive indicia of power over price were found, the observation that the results might be a statistical artifact would be compelling. For now, however, let me point out an extremely important advance implicit in this approach. The alternative hypothesis includes price-taking behavior: when it is rejected, it is rejected against specifications based on theories in which firms succeed in raising prices above *MC*. Only econometric problems, not fundamental problems of interpretation, cloud this inference about what has been determined empirically.

3. How the data identify market power

An advantage of the use of structural econometric models and explicit theories of industry equilibrium is that the class of models the data are allowed to treat is made explicit. Thus, the class of alternatives within which the inference of monopoly power has been drawn can be clearly stated. This in turn limits the number of alternative explanations which can be reasonably advanced. More importantly, however, this procedure permits an explicit answer to a central question: Why is the economic inference of monopoly power identified by the data? What implication of the theory of perfect competition has been found to be false when market power is measured by these methods? These questions do not arise for SCPP methods, of course, since SCPP takes price–cost margins to be observable. In the NEIO, PCMs are to be estimated, and it is therefore of immediate interest what observable feature of the data, and what natural experiments, reveal them to the analyst. To date, there are four new classes of identification arguments: (i) comparative statics in demand, (ii) comparative statics in cost, (iii) supply shocks, and (iv) econometric estimation of MC. This section takes up these arguments in turn. There is a fifth area, the comparative statics in industry structure, which is familiar in its logic; price is predicted as a function of the number of firms or of other concentration measures. This area is, I believe, awaiting its identification arguments, for reasons I lay out in Subsection 3.5.

3.1. Comparative statics in demand

A natural empirical procedure is to write out a system consisting of (1) and of one (4) for each firm, under one of the parameterizations of θ from the previous section. Some appropriate econometric method yields estimates of δ, Γ and especially θ, under the assumption that they are all separately identified. Thus, the same data, and inferences based on the comparative statics of equilibrium, provide estimates of cost, demand and conduct parameters. This natural procedure, however, should make clear why it is that it works. What idiosyncratic implication of perfect competition has been rejected, what idiosyncratic implication of market power or oligopoly interaction has been observed in the data? The first approach to this question was to ask whether the comparative statics of monopoly, oligopoly, and perfect competition models are logically distinct, and if so how.

The encouraging answer to this question can be seen in a very simple model, in which only an aggregate supply relation is estimated and in which θ is taken to be a constant over time.[22] To further simplify, assume that the econometric errors enter both demand and supply in an additive way, and that the slope of the demand curve does not depend on Q_t. Then we write (1) and (4) as:

$$P_t = D(Q_t, Y_t, \delta) + \varepsilon_{dt}, \tag{17}$$

$$P_t = C_1(Q_t, W_t, Z_t, \Gamma) + \varepsilon_{ct} - D_1(Y_t, \delta)Q_t\theta. \tag{18}$$

Obviously, δ can be estimated: (17) has only quantity as an included endogenous variable, and instruments are available from the cost function. Call any estimate which has been obtained δ^*. Then one could calculate the "datum" $D_{it}^* =$

[22] The analysis of this section is based on Bresnahan (1982) and Lau (1982), which make the argument presented here in a more precise way.

$D_1(Y_t, \delta^*)$, and consider estimation of the equation:[23]

$$P_t = C_1(Q_t, W_t, Z_t, \Gamma) + \varepsilon_{ct} - D_{it}^* Q_t \theta. \tag{19}$$

This has two endogenous variables: Q_t, which occurs in cost, and $D_{it}^* Q_t$, the variable whose coefficient is θ. When can θ be estimated? Econometrically, two conditions must hold. First, the two endogenous variables must not be perfectly correlated. The definition of D_{it}^* makes clear that they will in fact be perfectly correlated unless D_1, the slope of the demand curve, depends on Y_t. Second, instruments must be available for both endogenous variables. This will obviously be the case if Y_t is a two-vector, with one element of Y_t entering D_1, the other not. More generally, Lau (1982) has shown that a sufficient condition for identification is that the inverse demand function $D(\cdot)$ cannot be written in a way such that Y_t is separable from Q_t; since Q_t is a scalar, this clearly requires that Y_t be a two- (or more) vector.

The economics of this argument can be stated very simply. The comparative statics of models with market power have a particular role for changes in the slope of the demand curve. Suppose that the exogenous variables entering demand can (in principle) perform a particular natural experiment: they can rotate the demand curve around a given point, say the industry equilibrium point. Under perfect competition, this will have no effect: supply and demand intersect at the same point before and after the rotation. Under any oligopoly or monopoly theory, however, changes in the elasticity of demand will shift the perceived marginal revenue of firms. Equilibrium price and quantity will respond. Thus, the comparative statics of models with monopoly power do have idiosyncratic predictions, and the market comparative statics of perfect competition are distinct from those of monopoly.

The papers that have relied on this identification principle are those that have had a good natural experiment shifting the demand equations in an appropriate way. In Just and Chern (1980), it is the buying side which has the market power: a concentrated manufacturing industry buys tomatoes from atomistic farmers. The crucial exogenous variable was a change in harvesting technology, one which they argued changed the elasticity of supply.[24] In Bresnahan (1981, 1987) the firms possibly having market power are sellers of automobiles: demand elasticities depend on how close to one another firms' products are in a product space. More generally, we might think about the most attractive applications of this identification argument. The two elements of Y_t might be something measuring the size of the economy, such as national income, and a second variable

[23] This is describing an econometric procedure so ugly that no one would ever undertake it: it does however, show that and why more powerful techniques can identify.

[24] Just and Chern treat the case of oligopsony, so it is the supply elasticity which is shifted by the technical change. This has no effect on the logic of the argument.

measuring the price of a substitute or substitutes.[25] Use of this method of identification obviously turns on the ability to estimate the demand elasticities in a reliable way. The analyst will need to answer such criticisms in any particular case with standard econometric techniques for investigation of the robustness of results. Many observers have noted that alternative interpretations of the Just and Chern technology shift are available. The dependence of the Bresnahan automobile results on the exact ordering of the products in quality space is frequently pointed out. Equation (8), above, introduces an unobserved error into product quality, thereby relaxing the assumption that the ordering of products can be determined solely on the basis of observable proxies for quality.

A further refinement of this line of reasoning is available if one is prepared to assume that marginal cost is homogeneous of degree one in observed factor prices.[26] Then the θ in (17) or the more general (4) is clearly identified. The analyst interprets the coefficients of Q_t that are interacted with cost shifters to be part of MC, and those that are not to be part of the perceived marginal revenue term with coefficient θ. (Since MC is homogeneous of degree one in factor prices, Q_t cannot enter MC in a way such that it is not interacted with one or more elements of W.) Implicitly, this is how early papers like Appelbaum (1979, 1982) obtained identification. The homogeneity property is guaranteed if MC is obtained by differentiation of a total cost function, possibly one of the forms (translog, generalized Leontief, etc.) commonly used in factor demand system estimation. Then all coefficients in the supply relation which are *not* functions of factor prices are interpreted as indicators of market power. This line of argument obviously leans very hard on the assumption that the functional form of MC is correct and that all of the true marginal prices of the inputs can be observed. The true marginal price of capital is a potential problem for such studies. The way for such a study to rebut alternative interpretations of the results is to explore the robustness of the results to alternative treatments of MC: alternative functional forms, alternative treatments of the quasi-fixity of capital and labor, nonaccounting definitions of the cost of capital, etc.

3.2. *Comparative statics in cost*

An alternative comparative statics analysis is that of Panzar and Rosse (1977a, 1977b, 1987) (PR). PR propose two separate ideas: first, that an appropriate method for analysis is estimation of the reduced form, with particular attention given to the coefficients of factor prices W_t. The second idea is that reduced-form

[25] Clearly, this idea leans on an older line of thought, especially in connection with cartelization in the markets for primary commodities. See Scherer (1980, pp. 229ff).

[26] See the discussion of duality and cost below, and in Panzar and Rosse (1987).

revenue equations are likely to be estimable in many circumstances, since revenue is likely observable even where price and quantity are not. In light of this, let us begin with the reduced-form revenue equation, called $R^*(\cdot)$. This is the total revenue for a single firm. R^* is equal to equilibrium quantity (which depends on cost, demand and conduct) times equilibrium price (which has the same determinants). The observable shifters of cost and demand – Z, W, and Y – all enter this function. In the case of monopoly, solve the single firm's (1) and (4) for the price and quantity as a function of exogenous variables, parameters, and error terms, and then continue by calculating revenue. This yields a reduced-form revenue function of the form:

$$R_{it} = R^*(W_{it}, Z_{it}, Y_t, \text{params}, \varepsilon_t). \tag{20}$$

Equation (20) will be written in the same form when there is more than one firm in the market, and (1) and (4) have been simultaneously been solved for several firms. It will depend on the exogenous variables for all firms, of course. Let $R_W(W_{it}, Z_{it}, Y_t, \text{params}, \varepsilon_t)$ be the vector of derivatives with respect to all inputs, and let $\langle , \rangle$ be the inner product. The PR statistic is

$$H_R = \langle W_{it}, R_W(\cdot)\rangle / R^*(\cdot), \tag{21}$$

the sum of the elasticities of the reduced-form revenues with respect to all factor prices.[27] The PR statistic requires little data on endogenous variables in the system, although it does need *all* of the variables which shift demand or cost. The analyst proceeds by estimating the reduced-form revenue equation, R^* including all available information on W, Z and Y. Then H_R is calculated.[28] A particular advantage of estimating only a revenue equation is that no quality correction need be made to define a true price for the industry. The product may be better in some markets, so that its price per pound overstates its true price there. Yet this tricky data problem does not affect the reduced-form revenue equation. More generally, H_R can obviously be calculated whenever the structural system (1), (4) has been estimated. But $R^*(\cdot)$ can also be estimated in many circumstances when the structural equations, especially the supply relations, cannot.

The PR statistic has a clear economic interpretation in several cases. First, suppose that the market studied is a monopoly. Then $H_R < 0$. A very general proof is available in PR: the intuition, however, can be seen here, for the case of

[27] Existing applications have either parameterized the reduced form so that this statistic is a constant or have reported estimates near the center of the sample in some sense.

[28] The idea that W are the only exogenous variables needed to estimate H_R has been somewhat oversold. In some circumstances, the estimating equation for revenue is misspecified when only cost variables are included as exogenous variables. As the results discussed below imply, it is appropriate to omit demand shifters only when the hypothesis being tested is perfect competition. The test for monopoly requires a revenue function with all exogenous variables.

"elementary" monopoly. By elementary monopoly I mean simply the case in which a single firm picks only a single quantity. I will suppress the econometric errors and the parameters. Let $R(Q, Y)$ be monopolist's revenue function in the usual sense, so that R_Q is MR.[29] Then the monopolist solves:

$$R^*(W, Z, Y) = \max_Q R(Q, Y) - C(Q, W, Z)$$

$$= QD(Q, Y) - C(Q, W, Z). \tag{22}$$

Let R_k^* be the derivative of equilibrium revenue with respect to the kth factor price, and W^k be the kth factor price. A comparative statics analysis of (22) implies:

$$H_R = \sum_k R_k^* W^k / R = (R_Q)^2 (R_{QQ} - C_{11})^{-1} / R \leq 0. \tag{23}$$

Thus, the statistic H_R is signed for the elementary monopolist. The intuition of the simple result is straightforward. The H_R statistic gives the percentage change in equilibrium revenues that would follow from a 1 percent increase in all of the firm's factor prices. A 1 percent increase in all factor prices must lead to a 1 percent upward shift in MC. Thus H_R reveals the percentage change in equilibrium revenue that would follow from a 1 percent change in cost. Elementary monopoly theory tells us that a monopolist's optimal revenue will always fall when costs rise: otherwise, the monopolist's quantity was too large before the cost rise.

PR show, in a powerful result, that this finding generalizes to the case of a monopolist that has many choice variables, including both the case where the variables are the outputs of many products and the case where the variables include variables such as quality, advertising, etc.

Even this straightforward implication of monopoly theory has important uses. Suppose we have a sample of "monopolists" that face competition from sellers of other related products. A natural question is whether they are in fact monopolists, or whether the competition from other firms means that they should be treated as in a larger, more competitive market. The PR statistic speaks directly to this question; if they are monopolists, H_R should be negative. Unfortunately, it is not necessarily true that H_R has to be positive if the firms are not monopolists. PR show that in some specific models of oligopoly and of monopolistic competition, H_R must be positive. Thus, it is appropriate to see H_R as a statistic which has some ability to discriminate among alternative competitive hypotheses. There can, however, easily be a false finding of monopoly, since $H_R < 0$ can occur for reasons other than monopoly.

[29] $R(Q, Y)$ is distinct from $R^*(\cdot)$, the reduced-form equation for revenue.

A second economic hypothesis that can be cast as a test on H_R comes when the markets studied are in LR perfectly competitive equilibrium in the strong sense: free entry has driven out inefficient firms, and remaining firms produce at the bottom of their *LRAC* curves. Then $H_R = 1$. Let *MAC* be minimum average cost, and *QMAC* be the quantity which minimizes *AC*. A proportional shift in all factor prices will raise *MAC* by the same proportion without changing *QMAC*. The estimation of H_R proceeds using data on the revenue for single firms. At the firm level, revenue will shift proportionately to cost in LR equilibrium. At the industry level, revenue will expand less than proportionately to cost, as the increase in price will lead to lower quantity demanded: in this LR theory, the supply adjustment comes through entry and exit. Furthermore, the use of single-firm data is warranted, since the only determinants of price and of firm revenue in LR equilibrium are *MAC* and *QMAC*.[30] On the same argument, $R^*(\cdot)$ should not be a function of demand variables in a test of this hypothesis. Thus, the reduced-form revenue equation, estimated on firm data, has two distinct testable restrictions under the hypothesis of LR perfect competition.

The LR flavor of the comparative statics analysis in the PR analysis, both of monopoly and of competition, is reflected in the existing applications of the PR statistic, which are on cross-section data in similar local markets. Panzar and Rosse (1977b) treat the case of newspaper firms in local media markets. An observation is a newspaper, with its revenue as the dependent variable (of course, the majority of revenue is from advertising). If newspapers are monopolies, it is because they do not face intense competition from other media. They are able to reject the hypothesis that newspapers are monopolies even when they are the only newspaper in the market: the interpretation goes to the importance of competition from other media. Shaffer (1982) applies the PR analysis to a cross-section of banking firms in New York State in 1979, finding that the hypothesis of monopoly as well as the hypothesis of LR perfect competition could be rejected. How convincing these studies are depends on two areas: whether estimates on the cross-section of local areas reveals differences in LR equilibrium, and whether all of the variables which shift cost have been identified and correctly entered. The first of these points has been thought through: see Rosse (1970) on the "permanent plant hypothesis". At a minimum, it is clearly important to treat the cases of markets with rising demand separately from those with falling demand. The second point is very similar to one discussed in the previous section.

Recent work by Sullivan (1985) and Ashenfelter and Sullivan (1987) has extended the PR comparative statics in W idea to circumstances where variables other than revenue are observable: the results are based in the comparative

[30] Thus, it is appropriate to use only cost shifter exogenous variables in a test of LR perfect competition, and the reduced-form equations are not misspecified under the null if all demand variables are omitted.

statics of market price and quantity in factor prices. As a result of the additional observables, they can treat the oligopoly estimation problem of attempting to draw inferences about conduct. It will be most convenient to write the supply relation for a typical oligopolist in the conjectural variations form:

$$P_t = C_1(Q_t, W_t, Z_t, \Gamma, \varepsilon_{ct}) + D_1(\cdot)Q_i(1 + r_i(\cdot)). \tag{24}$$

In Sullivan's treatment, only market-wide data on price and quantity, and exogenous variables are available. Solving (24) for all firms simultaneously with the demand curve will yield reduced-form equations for P and Q, call these P^* and Q^*. Following PR, estimation of these reduced-form equations could yield H_Q and H_p, the elasticities of Q and of P with respect to marginal cost, possibly measured by a comparative statics exercise involving a proportional increase in all factor prices. Assume that all firms have common marginal cost, and let $\mathscr{L} = (P - C_1)/P$ be the Lerner index. In our notation, Sullivan shows:

$$\sum_i (1 + r_i)^{-1} \geq -H_P/(H_Q \mathscr{L}) \geq -H_P/H_Q, \tag{25}$$

where the last inequality follows because $\mathscr{L}$ must be less than or equal to unity with non-negative MC.

The left-hand inequality in (25) relates one unobservable quantity to another, because only H_P and H_Q are estimated by the technique: no estimates of marginal costs or of the price–cost margin are formed. However, under assumptions that MC is no less than zero, the right-hand inequality of (25) does imply a bound on the competitiveness of conduct. The statistic on the far right can be estimated. The larger is the statistic on the far left, the closer is conduct to competition. Thus, (25) can permit rejection of the hypothesis of successful collusion, though not of competition.

In his empirical work, Sullivan (1985) uses a cross-section (states of the United States) time series (years) on the cigarette industry. The crucial exogenous variable is state taxes, which clearly proxy for MC; all other exogenous variables are captured in an ANOVA procedure. The analysis obtains a slightly tighter bound than (25) by assuming costs are at least as large as taxes (paid by the seller), and is able to reject the hypothesis that cigarette prices are set as if by a cartel. Ashenfelter and Sullivan (1987) take a nonparametric approach to the same data, using year-to-year changes in tax rates and in the endogenous variables in the same state to estimate H_P and H_Q. In thinking about this approach, it is clear that its main potential problems in application are similar to those of PR: Has it been established that the variables which shift MC are not acting as proxies for any other variables? Is the quantitative relationship between these variables and MC certain? The use of tax data is obviously particularly strong on the second point. I suspect that the first point will usually turn on a detailed argument from the institutional detail of the particular industry at hand, from econometric investigations of robustness, and from ancillary data.

Why is it that the comparative statics in cost can only lead to inequality restrictions on oligopoly conduct, while comparative statics in demand variables provide an estimate of the degree of oligopoly power? [Compare (25) and (18).] The answer follows directly from the nature of the econometric exercise in each case. Consider the two-equation system determining industry price and quantity: there is a demand equation, and a supply relation. The conduct parameters we are particularly interested in are in the supply relation. When demand is shifted by some exogenous variable, it tends to trace out the supply relation, which is after all what we are trying to estimate. The statistic based on the comparative statics in cost could very easily identify the demand equation. They can only cast indirect light on parameters in the supply relation.

3.3. Estimation of marginal cost more directly

The two methods discussed in the previous subsections have in common that they treat the comparative statics of the industry or market equilibrium in isolation. Price and quantity are the only endogenous observables. To the extent that price–cost margins are estimated, the inference is based on the supply behavior of firms. I now turn to an alternative approach, which attempts to econometrically estimate MC from cost data or from factor demand data. This approach uses the methods of cost and factor demand function estimation using flexible functional forms. It relies heavily on the economic theory of cost as dual to production.[31]

The pioneering work in this area was done by Gollop and Roberts (1979) and Appelbaum (1979, 1982). Their approaches start from the total cost function, $C(\cdot)$ [see (2)]. To the observables of the stylized model they add quantity demanded of factors of production: typically broken down only into labor, capital and materials (sometimes energy is separate from other materials inputs). I label the demand for a particular factor of production x_k, that for all factors taken together as X. The key to the approach is to note that MC is the derivative of $C(\cdot)$ with respect to quantity, $C_1(\cdot)$ and that (using standard duality results) the factor demand equations are the derivatives of $C(\cdot)$ with respect to factor prices.[32] Then the approach estimates the demand equation, the supply relation,

[31] Obviously, this approach and the ones described in Subsection 3.1 are complements rather than substitutes.

[32] This follows from Shephard's lemma: see Diewert (1971).

and appends to that system the factor demand equations:

$$P_t = D(Q_t, Y_t, \delta, \varepsilon_{dt}), \tag{26}$$

$$P_t = C_1(Q_{it}, W_{it}, Z_{it}, \Gamma, \varepsilon_{cit}) - D_1(Q_t, Y_t, \delta, \varepsilon_{dt})Q_{it}\theta_{it}, \tag{27}$$

$$X_t = C_W(Q_{it}, W_{it}, Z_{it}, \Gamma, \varepsilon_{cit}). \tag{28}$$

Clearly, appending equations (28) to the system offers at least the possibility of substantial increases in the precision with which *MC* can be estimated, since there will be cross-equation restrictions between the factor demand equations and the supply relations; the cost parameters Γ appear in both. It is reasonable to expect these restrictions to be quite powerful. Since $C(\cdot)$ is necessarily homogeneous of degree 1 in W, its derivatives $C_W(\cdot)$ will (taken together) depend on all of the parameters of $C(\cdot)$. Thus, all of the parameters in *MC* also appear in the factor demand equations.

Clearly, the important questions about the utility of this technique in practice turn on the success in estimating *MC*. Questions of the appropriate functional form for $C(\cdot)$ can probably be addressed by trying several alternatives, or by using prior information about the industry at hand to specify the technology. To the extent that (28) includes a demand equation for capital, users of this approach must face the problem of valuing the capital assets of the firm: capital needs to be decomposed into the price of capital services and their quantity. Thus, the body of criticisms of the SCPP which centered on the accounting treatment of capital will likely reappear as criticisms of the cost function approach. Furthermore, if all factors are treated as *SR* variable in (28), the price–cost margins will need to be interpreted as price relative to *LRMC*.

Another approach to using factor demand information has recently been introduced by Hall (1986). He starts from the attractive notion that *MC* could be directly observable by the conceptual experiment of changing quantity produced, holding everything else constant, and measuring by how much expenditures on inputs changed. As the empirical analog of this, Hall works with data on the rates of change of output and of the labor input. One way to think of this is that average incremental cost is revealed by the data: the discrete changes in outputs that occur between sample periods lead to discrete changes in inputs, and the resulting empirical *AIC* is taken to be the estimate of *MC*. The second notion in Hall is that changes in the labor input alone can reveal *MC*. Under the assumption of (LR) constant returns, the wage rate times the change in labor demand divided by labor's share in cost should be *AIC*. To date, this approach has been largely implemented on aggregate data.[33]

[33] Hall only attempts to estimate $\mathscr{L}$; Shapiro (1987) extends the same logic to estimate θ as well.

This approach has clearly closely related to the previous one, in much the same way that index number approaches to cost and productivity are related to econometric cost and production functions, and therefore shares many of the same advantages and disadvantages. Some of the problems of interpretation have been overcome: the use of the labor demand only helps somewhat with the problem of capital valuation, though labor's share in cost still needs to be calculated. The index-number flavor adds another potential difficulty: if MC is not flat, AIC can be a poor proxy for it. Since the MC curve of interest is $SRMC$, it is unlikely to be flat in applications.

Although I said earlier that the methods described in this section were a complement to, rather than a substitute for, other methods, empirical practice done not yet reflect this. There are two regularities in scholarly practice to note. First, none of the papers cited in this subsection uses industry detail to provide a defense of its maintained hypothesis. Second, all of the papers in the literature can be divided into two classes: those cited in this subsection, which argue identification argument only from the restrictions between MC and factor demands, and all other papers described in this chapter, none of which tried to use factor demands to get better estimates of MC.

3.4. Supply shocks

I argued above that a core implication of modern theories of cartels, as well as an ancient empirical assertion about them, is that their conduct is not constant over time. I would now like to return to Porter's (1983) [Lee and Porter (1984)] switching regressions method for determining this. The question will be: What is it in the data that identifies the inference that cartels break up and reform? I will write (4″) slightly differently. Under the assumption that there are two kinds of conduct, which I think of as "price wars" and "collusion", there are two supply relations that hold in the data:

$$P = C_1(\,) - D_1(Y_t, \delta) Q \theta_r, \quad \text{during price wars,} \tag{29}$$

$$P = C_1(\,) - D_1(Y_t, \delta) Q \theta_c, \quad \text{during periods of collusion.} \tag{30}$$

Porter completes the model by specifying the (constant) probability π that (29) holds vs. (30). In price-war periods, prices and quantities are determined by the intersection of (29) and of the demand curve (1), while in periods of successful collusion, these are determined by (30) and (1). The analyst does not know whether there are in fact these two different regimes in the data: that inference is to be drawn from the pattern of prices, quantities and exogenous variables.

A natural question to ask is why this inference can in fact be drawn. I believe that the inference comes from a particular shape of the joint distribution of P

and Q conditional on Z, W and Y. Let us hold all of those exogenous variables fixed at some arbitrary levels. Let the P and Q which solve (29) and (1) be called P_r and Q_r, and those which solve (30) and (1) be called P_c and Q_c. These are random variables, since all of (29), (30), and (1) have econometric error terms. But the two different random variables have two different centers of distribution. In the r-regime, the mean of price will be lower and the mean of quantity will be higher: the regimes differ only in that the r-regime has a lower supply relation than the c-regime. If θ_c is much larger than θ_r, i.e. of collusion is successful at all, we should expect these two means to be far apart.

Now consider the entire distribution of P and Q conditional on the exogenous variables. It has two local modes: one each at (P_r, Q_r) and (P_c, Q_c). Empirical techniques for dealing with bimodal distributions, of which the switching regressions method is a leading example, will be able to detect the presence of the two modes. Thus, the Stigler-esque theories do have an idiosyncratic implication about the shape of the distribution of prices and of quantities. This line of inference departs somewhat from those described above, where the emphasis was on the comparative statics in observable exogenous variables. Here, the variable describing which regime the industry is in was taken to be unobservable. The implications of the theory for the data were drawn by making a simple assumption about that unobservable: that it took on two distinct values. Thus, the nature of the inference here comes from identifying a specific component in the error term: a component that enters the system as a supply shock.

The main potential difficulty with this inference is this: some unobserved shock other than changes in conduct may be moving in the supply equation. Since the inference is based on an error component, there is nothing in the procedure itself to guarantee that the conduct interpretation is the right one. If there are uncaptured changes in factor prices (recall Porter has no factor-price data) or shocks to technology, these could shift the supply relation as well. The size of the effect in the railroad data – the shocks lead to changes in both price and quantity on the order or 50 percent – makes it appear likely that the conduct interpretation is the right one, particularly in light of the extensive contemporaneous discussion of cartel adherence.[34]

3.5. Comparative statics in industry structure

The methods for identification of market power described in the previous four subsections yield estimates of the degree of power over price of a particular

[34] The alternative approach is to decide a priori on the sample split, and then attempt to separately estimate θ_c and θ_r, as in Bresnahan (1987). This has the substantial disadvantage of requiring prior information, but the advantage of being able to more directly assess whether the apparent shocks to supply are due to changes in conduct.

industry in its particular setting. The industry's structure, in the SCPP sense, is a given of the analysis. Substantial time-series changes in industry structure are rare events; thus, the single-industry case study method only rarely, and only on some bodies of data, permits the question of how changes in market structure affect conduct and performance. Methods based on cross-sections of similar markets have also cast some new light on the relationship between industry structure and market power. Unlike earlier mainstream work, which used accounting profit as the dependent variable, many recent studies use price or a price index as the dependent variable. The goal of the investigation is to see how concentration affects prices. Let me briefly outline the work in this area before discussing its interpretation.

The cross-section study of similar markets has been focused on businesses that are geographically local. The dependent variable is price, either a price index or one of the prices of a multi-product firm. The estimating equation is typically a reduced form for price. The industries studied include banking, for which Rhoades (1982) lists dozens of studies, retail food [Cotterill (1986), Lamm (1981)], gasoline suppliers [Marvel (1978)], airline city-pair markets [Graham, Kaplan and Sibley (1983)], cement [Koller and Weiss (1986)] and no doubt others. These studies typically take concentration to be exogenous.[35] The equation they estimate is therefore close to the reduced-form equation for price, departing from it only in that quantity (as transformed into a concentration measure) is included as exogenous. These studies confirm the existence of a relationship between price and concentration, which is at least suggestive of market power increasing with concentration. An interesting variant uses time-series changes in industry structure: see Barton and Sherman (1984) on the effects of a merger in the microfiche film industry on prices and profits.

Most of these studies offer the interpretation that the empirically estimated relationship can be interpreted to cast light on the prediction of almost all theories of oligopoly that higher concentration causes higher price–cost margins by changing conduct. I have seen no careful defense of this interpretation, and I am troubled by it; I offer a series of interpretational difficulties here not because I believe they are true but because they have not yet been rebutted.

If markets are less concentrated when they are larger, and more firms will "fit", then what relationship are we seeing in the data? Take the stark case of free entry as soon as entrants' profits are positive. We interpret the relationship in the data as being about concentration and $P - MC$, yet there is another equation in the model: $P = AC$ for entrants. In the larger markets, firms are also larger, have

[35]An important exception is Graham et al. (1983) which tests for the exogeneity of its concentration measures. Exogeneity is not rejected, even though the coefficients of the concentration measures change substantially when they are treated as endogenous. This suggests that exogeneity cannot be rejected because the test has little power, rather than because the assumption is substantively innocuous.

lower (average) costs, but everywhere firms break even. This reinterpretation is not necessarily a hostile one, but the welfare economics are somewhat different: price and concentration are related in a way that has no obvious bad effects, and does not imply entry barriers.

A somewhat different endogeneity problem arises within industries with the same number of firms. If the firms are selling the same products, then the more concentrated industry likely has more heterogeneity in costs. Greater heterogeneity in costs might interact with conduct in a way that increases prices or it might not.[36]

Even given the exogeneity of concentration, if firms are heterogeneous in their cost functions, markets with more firms allow more statistical "draws" on the lowest-cost firm. One should expect, on average, that the lowest-cost firm out of five has lower costs than the lowest out of three. If the lowest-cost firm is particularly important in the determination of price, as in some competitive models as well as in some oligopoly models, then this purely statistical effect will result in lower P in less concentrated markets. Since estimates that link price to concentration are necessarily on market-wide data, we are in the world of Subsection 2.2.4. The crucial equation is:

$$P = \text{Average}[MC] + D_1(\cdot)Q\,\text{Average}[\theta], \tag{17'}$$

where the notation Average[$\cdot$] means share-weighted average taken over firms in the market. In general, we do not know whether it is Average[MC] or Average[θ] or both that is lower in the less concentrated markets. It is the latter interpretation most authors have in mind. Furthermore, there can be links between these two: a firm with a substantial cost advantage may have less competitive conduct than it would facing more equal competition.

That last point can be fleshed out with some observations of the way actual heterogeneity has been sometimes explicitly measured. Consider the Graham et al. (1983) finding that not only concentration affects price in airline city-pair markets, but also that who the competitors are matters. Markets in which one or some competitors are new entrants into the airline business overall have lower prices than other markets, all else equal. It is extremely likely (see Graham et al., section 5) that these entrants have lower MC. It is also possible that their presence changes the conditions of competition. Which is it? The analysis of the paper cannot say. Exactly the same question applies to the interpretation of the industry structure dummies used in Porter (1983) [see (4″) above].

These questions of interpretation are not unanswerable; the previous four subsections discussed explicitly methods of telling MC from θ. The questions are, however, unanswered.

[36]Spiller and Favaro (1984) escape the problem of endogeneity in their time-series study of Uruguayan banking. Their sample period includes a change in the regulation of entry into their industry. They find that freer entry shifts the supply relation downward.

3.6. *On the identification of market power*

This section has reviewed a large body of method, all developed in the recent past, for empirical investigation of the hypothesis of market power. Several distinct lines of argument have been advanced, each of which relies on a distinct implication of market power for identification.[37] This variety reflects the variety in the data available in different industry studies. In any particular industry, the available information and institutional detail allows different kinds of analysis and different defenses of different analyses. We can therefore expect some continuing variation in desired method. It also reflects the great many implications of the comparative statics of equilibrium in markets with market power which are not found in competitive markets.

4. Market power in product-differentiated industries

Product differentiation raises two kinds of empirical questions, loosely divisible into the SR and LR. In the SR, the stock of products offered by firms and the attributes of these products is fixed. In the SR the measurement question of interest is how much monopoly power firms have because of existing product differentiation. This is (at least) a two-part question. First, as firms' products grow more distinct, each firm's profits will depend less on the policies of other firms. This first part of the question can be adequately answered by investigation of the elasticities of demand, including the cross-elasticities. Second, as products grow more distinct, each firm will respond less to competitive moves by rivals. Understanding this part of the question requires an empirical model of competitive interaction. The measurement of this SR market power has seen tremendous progress in recent times, and that forms the subject of this section.

The market power conceptual issues associated with the SR product differentiation questions are not all that distinct from those in the single-product case. The measurement problems are more severe, however. There are more demand parameters to be estimated: even under the assumption of constant elasticity (or slope) and symmetry, an N-product industry has N own-price elasticities, N income elasticities, and $(N-1)N/2$ cross-price elasticities. There is almost no industry for which the position that there are more than 100 products is untenable: without putting more structure on the problem, the analyst could need to estimate literally thousands of elasticities. On the cost side, the fact that firms produce multiple products suggests the existence of economies of scope: the cost

[37]At least one false identification argument has been proposed, as well. Koutsoyiannis (1982) argues that sales maximization by oligopolists can be empirically distinguished from entry-deterring behavior and from static profit-maximizing behavior. His model assumes monopoly rather than oligopoly: see his equation (26).

function may have some new complexities as well. The use of prior information to guide the specification of the model becomes crucial in such circumstances. Fortunately, in many contexts, prior information will be available from sources like industry trade journals, marketing studies, and so on. As a result of the industry specificity of this prior information, there is considerable variation across industries in the way one would like to proceed with the analysis.[38]

Far and away the most common technique for apparently product-differentiated industries is to assume that the products in the industry are basically fairly close substitutes, use an index of several products' prices as the observable price, and proceed.[39] This procedure is not inherently wrong. It may, however, result in the attribution of market power to noncompetitive conduct when in fact the source of the market power is differentiated products.

When the analyst wishes to study the product-differentiation issues directly, some procedure to reduce the complexity of the analysis from its full size must be employed. There is some experience with three general forms: modelling the product choice part of the demand system, aggregating similar products until there are only a few left in the system, and estimating only a few functions of the parameters of interest.

Tools for the product choice elements of demand have been a major topic of econometric theory and practice in recent times. The work of McFadden (1982) and others on discrete choice has provided a framework for modelling *individuals'* choices of products. These techniques, such as nested logit models, are clearly appropriate in circumstances where there is prior information about groupings of products, such as when industry sources emphasize the existence of distinct product segments within which competition is much more direct than without. A parallel literature, in the theory of "spatial" product differentiation, has concentrated on the relationship between heterogeneity in consumers' tastes and the demand curves facing differentiated oligopolists. It is more appropriate to industries in which there are no clear segment boundaries, i.e. where the fact that products A and B are both important parts of the competitive environment of C need not imply that A is an important part of B's environment. The spatial models thus emphasize the localization of competition as a way to reduce the number of demand parameters, while the discrete choice models emphasize grouping.[40] Both modelling approaches treat product quality similarly. Not

[38]Some other approaches have been attempted as well. Haining (1984) uses the spatial autocorrelation of prices of retail gasoline stations to attempt to infer something about the pattern of interaction among them. I could see not relationship between his statistical hypotheses – "pure competition" is the name of one and "supply and demand" is another – and any economic hypothesis.

[39]See, for example, Gollop and Roberts (1979), Roberts (1983), and Geroski (1983) on roast coffee; Appelbaum (1982) on tobacco and textiles; Sullivan (1985) and Ashenfelter and Sullivan (1987) on cigarettes.

[40]In the limit, models like multinomial logit (without any nests) have the entire industry forming the market segment. Then competition is completely symmetric.

surprisingly, there has been considerable interest in these models in the marketing field; Schmalensee and Thisse (1986) provide an overview of both the relevant economics and marketing literatures.

Empirical examples of this approach can be found in Bresnahan (1981, 1987), which use a spatial model of the demand for automobiles by type as the demand system. The flavor of this approach is that explicit functional form assumptions are made about the distribution of demands across individuals. These distributions, in turn, determine the form of the aggregate demand system. As in econometric work in discrete choice, typical distributional assumptions lead to empirical models with many fewer parameters than the unstructured approach described above. The degree to which such an analysis is convincing turns critically on the quality of the information used to specify the demand system. The best procedure for this is undoubtedly a close reading of the industry trade journals and of typical marketing practice.

Nonetheless, any approach which begins with a highly structured demand system naturally raises questions about the appropriateness of the particular structure. The distinction between localized competition and more systematic or segmented models is particularly important in this regard. Schmalensee (1985) devises test statistics for competitive localization that uses only the measurable movements of endogenous variables, the prices and quantities of particular brands. If exogenous shocks to the system are either market wide (i.e. shift the demand or supply of all products together) or are product-specific, then the extent to which particular products' prices and quantities tend to move together are an indicator of competitive localization. In an application to the ready-to-eat breakfast cereal industry, Schmalensee is able to decisively reject the symmetric model in which all products compete equally. The particular pattern of localization implied by his estimates leads him to doubt the (covariance) restrictions that identify the degree of localization, however.

The approach of aggregating products until there are only a few elasticities to be estimated was taken up by Gelfand and Spiller (1987), Suslow (1986), and Slade (1987). Gelfand and Spiller use data on banking firms competing to make loans of a great many different types. They aggregate the loans until only two types are left, and investigate the demand elasticities in the resulting two-by-two system. An important advance in their work is a model of interrelated oligopoly in the multiple markets, as firms' profits in each market are affected by strategies of other firms in both markets, or even possibly strategies that link the two markets.[41] Presumably such effects can only be studied when the number of markets has been reduced to a reasonably small level. Slade's (1987) treatment of gasoline station "majors" and "independents" is quite similar. The work of

[41] Gelfand and Spiller cast this intermarket interdependence in CV form: each firm has "conjectures" about how other firms will "react" in each of the two markets.

Suslow (1986) aggregates outputs into two: all of those produced by the dominant firm (Alcoa in the aluminum industry before the Second World War) and those produced by the fringe. The dominant firm's *MR* is a function of the degree of substitutability between its product and the product sold by the fringe, as well as by the usual determinants, the market demand elasticity and the fringe supply elasticity.

A third approach to the problem of multiple products has been taken by Baker and Bresnahan (1983, 1985). In their approach, the problem of estimating all of the cross-elasticities of demand is avoided by estimating only the interesting summary statistics of the demand for that product. To estimate the market power associated with a particular product, it is unnecessary to estimate all of the effects of all of the other products' prices in the market. Instead, only the total effect of competition from other products as a brake on the pricing power of the firm owning a particular product is of interest. Consider the seller of product 1, facing the demand system:[42]

$$P_1 = D(Q_1, P_2, \ldots, P_N, Y, \delta), \tag{31}$$

where $P_2, \ldots, P_N$ are the prices of products of competitors and econometric errors are suppressed for convenience.

The measurement problem is that the demand parameter vector δ can be very long, containing the cross-elasticity of demand with each of the $2, \ldots, N$ products. Baker–Bresnahan substitute out $P_2, \ldots, P_N$ in (31) by solving the supply and demand equations for each of them. Suppose that there are $(N-1)$ more equations like (31), one for each of the other products. Also, there is a supply relation for each of products $2, \ldots, N$:

$$P_i = C_1(Q_i, W_i, Z_i, \Gamma_i) - D_1(Q, Y, \delta)Q_i\theta_i, \quad i = 2, \ldots, N, \tag{4^{d}}$$

where Q is the vector of all firms' (and equivalently, all products') quantities. The $2*(N-1)$ equations (31), (4^{d}) can be solved for the prices and quantities of products $2, \ldots, N$. Call the solution for P:

$$P_i = P_i^*(Q_1, W_N, Z_N, \Gamma_N, \theta_N, Y, \delta),$$

where the dependence on Q_1 arises because *only* products $2, \ldots, N$ have been solved out, and the subscript I refers to the superset of all the subscripts i. The equation to be estimated is:

$$\begin{aligned} P_1 &= D(Q_1, P_2^*(\cdot), \ldots, P_N^*(\cdot), Y, \delta) \\ &= D^{\mathrm{R}}(Q_1, W_n, Z_N, \Gamma_N, \theta_N, Y, \delta), \end{aligned} \tag{32}$$

[42]This is slightly unfamiliar notation. It would be more familiar to write quantity for this product as a function of the prices of all products: the function presented is simply the inverse of that.

the residual demand curve for product 1. There are two immediate observations here. First, an enormous amount of information has been lost here by substituting out the prices of all the other products; it will be impossible to estimate all of the separate elements of δ from (32), much less all of the other parameters in it. But this is of little importance. The elasticity of D^{R} with respect to Q_1 tells us how much power the firm has over product 1's price, taking into account the adjustment of all other firms' prices and quantities.

A somewhat similar example may clarify the technique. Suppose that (4^{d}) takes the form $P_i = MC_i(W_i)$ for all the other firms: they are price-takers. Equation (32) then predicts the price of product 1 as a function of its quantity, and variables shifting the costs of all other products. If firm 1 has no market power in this product, the prices (and in this example, the costs) of other products will determine its price. In the no-market-power case, the elasticity of D^{R} with respect to Q_1 will be zero.

Thus, the Baker–Bresnahan approach estimates the demand elasticity facing the single firm or product, taking into account the competitive reaction of all other firms in the market. This demand elasticity summarizes the market power of the firm: knowing it is insufficient to determine the sources of that market power.[43]

The relationship between the Gelfand–Spiller or Suslow approach and the Baker–Bresnahan approach is this: in the first approach, all of the elasticities of demand, supply, and competitive interaction are estimated. From them the market power of any particular firm could be calculated. Of course, for practical implementation this approach requires specifying a relatively small number of different products. The second approach works when there are a large number of products, but does not yield estimates of all of the elasticities, only of the summary statistics relating to each firm's market power.

4.1. "Market definition", policy analysis, and product differentiation

Some of the techniques for assessing market power have been applied to the problem of "market definition" in antitrust analysis. In antitrust applications, it is frequently of some importance to determine whether a group of firms *would* have any market power if they chose to act in concert, or in other contexts whether a single firm in fact has any market power.[44] The latter question can be

[44]These questions are well-posed, even where the usual method of answering them, defining a "relevant market" and calculating market shares in it, is senseless.

[43]All of this presumes that the residual demand curve can be estimated. The condition for that is that firm 1's costs have moved independently of all other firms' costs. An obvious application of the technique, therefore, is in the international context. One would ask how steep the demand curve facing producers in a single country was; the natural experiment for estimating that quantity would be good if, for example, exchange rate movements had moved real relative costs in different countries.

directly answered by the Baker–Bresnahan technique. Scheffman and Spiller (1987) extend the Baker–Bresnahan technique to estimate the elasticity of demand facing a group of firms, thereby providing an answer to the former question. Baker and Bresnahan (1985) ask how much steeper the demand curve facing two firms would be post-merger than the pre-merger level. If two firms sell products that are very close substitutes, then each likely provides an important part of the competitive brake on the other, unless there are several other firms providing similar products as well. The increase in the steepness of the residual demand curve measures this effect.

Methods based on the Panzar–Rosse statistic have also been used in this connection.[45] Panzar and Rosse (1987) give a new interpretation to their monopoly test which is directly relevant here. Suppose a particular firm (firms) has been studied by PR methods. A rejection of "monopoly" for this firm (group of firms) implies that it (they) cannot be treated as acting in isolation. Other firms must be interacting with the firm (firms) at hand.

In a slightly different context, Schmalensee and Golub (1983) examine the spatial product differentiation of firms in the electricity market. They use models of the demand for electricity, the costs of transmission, and of competition to assess the likely impact of deregulation.

4.2. Product differentiation in the LR

In the LR, firms can add products, change their attributes (either physically or in consumers' perceptions) or new firms can enter with new products or imitations. This is a very complex area, full of hypotheses. Strategic interaction effects of many kinds are possible: preemption by establishment of a reputation for product superiority, preemption by filling out the product space, coordination of investment in distinct product types so as to reduce competition, and so on. Essentially nothing empirical is known about any of these hypotheses. Furthermore, the welfare implications of SR market power in a product differentiated industry are not transparent. In the Chamberlinian tangency of monopolistic competition, every firm has market power in the sense of this section. Yet that does not establish that there is any inefficiency, once the need to cover the fixed costs of product design are taken into account. The crucial issue here is an adequate empirical treatment of the supply curve of new firms and of new, different products. Empirical work on this area is likely to be forthcoming soon, but little exists now.[46]

[45] See Shaffer (1983) and Slade (1983).

[46] Many of the relevant analytical issues to support empirical work can be found in Panzar and Rosse (1981). Bresnahan and Reiss (1986) estimate an equation for the entry of a second product differentiated firm into a monopoly.

5. What has been learned about market power?

However useful its methodological contributions, the industry case-study nature of much work in the NEIO has raised questions of interpretation. How general are the results? What do these studies, taken together, reveal about market power in the economy as a whole? What have we learned about the conditions under which market power tends to arise? What is known about the easily measured correlates of market power, such as concentration? In short, a single industry case study cannot paint a broad picture; it can only reveal the nature of industry conduct and performance in the industry studied. The original idea of the SCPP was that empirical research would estimate a function mapping structural characteristics into measures of conduct (where that is possible) and of performance (more commonly). Empirical knowledge of this map is obviously valuable. It contains information about the sources as well as the location of market power. It could be used to guide policy in those areas, such as merger policy, where it could influence structure rather than conduct directly. An industry case study, whether done by the methods of the 1930s or the 1980s, can hope to reveal at most one point on the function. The integration of different case studies to give a unified picture of the whole map is an obviously attractive prospect. It can only be partially carried out now, even though the empirical papers described in this chapter have treated well over a dozen industries. In Table 17.1 I reproduce the estimated price cost margins ($\mathscr{L}$) from several different NEIO studies reviewed

Table 17.1
Summary of existing empirical work

Author	Industry	$\mathscr{L}$
Lopez (1984)	Food processing	0.504
Roberts (1984)	Coffee roasting	0.055/0.025[a]
Appelbaum (1982)	Rubber	0.049[c]
Appelbaum (1982)	Textile	0.072[c]
Appelbaum (1982)	Electrical machinery	0.198[c]
Appelbaum (1982)	Tobacco	0.648[c]
Porter (1983)	Railroads	0.40[b]
Slade (1987)	Retail gasoline	0.10
Bresnahan (1981)	Automobiles (1970s)	0.1/0.34[d]
Suslow (1986)	Aluminum (interwar)	0.59
Spiller–Favaro (1984)	Banks "before"[e]	0.88/0.21[f]
Spiller–Favaro (1984)	Banks "after"[e]	0.40/0.16[f]

[a] Largest and second largest firm, respectively.
[b] When cartel was succeeding: 0 in reversionary periods.
[c] At sample midpoint.
[d] Varies by type of car; larger in standard, luxury segment.
[e] Uruguayan banks before and after entry deregulation.
[f] Large firms/small firms (see their table 2).

here.[47] Different scholars will undoubtedly differ on the extent to which it offers answers to the questions of the last paragraph. A few preliminary conclusions, however, are available. These are cast in somewhat guarded language primarily because of the limited coverage of the available studies.

Conclusion A

There is a great deal of market power, in the sense of price-cost margins, in some concentrated industries.

The conclusion seems almost forced by the last column of Table 17.1. Several studies have found substantial power over price. Available data do not permit a systematic assignment of concentration indexes to the industries listed in Table 17.1, since they are not drawn from the economic censuses; several are based on the primary data gathering of different scholars. A glance down the list of industries, however, is sufficient to demonstrate that they are overwhelmingly drawn from the highly concentrated end of the industrial spectrum.

Finding A, I think, cannot be controversial, particularly with its qualification that it refers to "some" concentrated industries. The finding would be less controversial without the "some", and I think this is right. There are at least two reasons to suspect the generality of the findings in the papers reviewed in this chapter. First, authors who invent methods for the detection of market power are likely to first apply them in industries where they expect to find it. Thus, the existing studies have largely treated quite concentrated industries, industries where there were known or suspected cartels, industries where a solid old-style case study suggested anticompetitive conduct, and so on. The field is now ripe for revisionism! Or at least for continued expansion of the set of industries in which conduct and performance are well measured.

Second, the list of industries studied to date is special in another sense. Since the data are often drawn from trade journals, regulatory bodies, court proceedings or similar sources, the industries covered may be unrepresentative. Consider the industries with excellent trade journals; they are ones in which information about what competitors are doing is quite good. Thus the repeated finding of successful collusive arrangements might reflect the particular information structure of these industries. Similarly, Suslow's ability to mine the trial transcript in

[47]A few papers were left out of the table because their estimates were not given in such a form as to permit calculation of the Lerner index. (These papers heavily emphasize conduct over performance, of course.) Panzar–Rosse methods and Sullivan methods are excluded because they do not provide an estimate of the Lerner index. Instead, they provide an estimate of conduct parameters or a test of certain hypotheses about conduct. (Comments on a draft of this chapter suggest that this is not well understood: see Subsection 3.2, above.) Baker–Bresnahan methods are excluded because the demand elasticity estimates they provide correspond exactly to the Lerner index only in certain circumstances. (See Section 4.)

Alcoa for data arose *because* there was reason to suspect that firm had substantial market power. More new data sources are needed!

Conclusion B

One significant cause of high price-cost margins is anticompetitive conduct.

The studies under review distinguish between conduct, in the sense of firms' behavioral rules for price-fixing, and performance, in the price–cost margin sense. It is not the case that, systematically, we see tiny departures of conduct from price-taking plus very steep demand curves leading to large departures of performance from the competitive standard. Instead, some of the studies appear to be finding conduct well toward the collusive end of the spectrum. For example, Porter (1983) and Bresnahan (1987) both find explicitly collusive behavior. I should emphasize that conduct is not uniform. Roberts (1984), for example, finds that most of the firms in his industry should be classified in an (essentially) price-taking fringe. The largest firms have much less competitive conduct, but have not succeeded in raising prices to the profit maximizing level given the fringe's behavior. The variety of conduct across industries, as well as the variety of performance, suggest the importance of the continued study of market power as a phenomenon.

Conclusion C

Only a very little has been learned from the new methods about the relationship between market power and industrial structure.

There are two points here, one implicit in the discussion below Conclusion A. Table 17.1 is drawn mostly from the highly concentrated end of the industry spectrum. We therefore have new information about the map from structure to conduct and performance over only a very limited range. The second point is that the causes of market power have not been addressed by very many of these studies. One presumes, for example, that long-surviving market power is an indicator of some failure of the entry process to discipline conduct. Yet entry has hardly been discussed in the papers. That leads, naturally enough, to my final section.

6. The future: The sources of market power

This should properly be a short section: although the NEIO has had a great deal to say about measuring market power, it has had very little, as yet, to say about the causes of market power. In particular, the topics of entry, predation, entry deterrence, and strategic competition in the LR generally have not yet been extensively taken up in empirical work with explicit theoretical foundations. These topics, then, remain primarily for the future. There are a few scattered contributions.

6.1. Predation

Burns (1986) casts considerable light on the possibility and profitability of predatory pricing in a study of the tobacco trust. He finds that acquisitions of competitors made by the trust became cheaper after predatory incidents. Since predation has long been believed not to be an equilibrium phenomenon, this is a useful and important contribution. It relies on nineteenth-century data, perhaps the unique data available for its method. The tobacco trust often thought it was predating; in that era before antitrust law prevented such self-revelation, the trust left a solid documentary record of when the predatory incidents took place. Investigations of the trust's behavior by the Federal government and the courts yielded a rich data source for Burns' study. More circumspect modern firms will be less well documented. We have not yet taken the methodological step of discovering the empirical implications of predatory conduct when acts of predation must be inferred, not observed.

6.2. Entry

The problem of entry has received some useful methodological contributions have been made in working papers. Panzar and Rosse (1977b) work out an empirical model of LR entry, treating the number of firms in the industry as a continuous variable. They argue that the comparative statics of monopolistically competitive industry equilibrium have distinctive, testable implications. The key to their argument is the addition of a third set of equations to (1), demand, and (4), pricing. The new equations take the form:

$$P = LRAC(W, Y) \tag{33}$$

for the marginal firm. The application of this model, or similar ones, in monopolistic competition contexts is obviously an attractive prospect.

Bresnahan and Reiss (1986b) take up the problem of econometric models of entry with an integer number of firms. They provide an empirical application to monopolies and duopolies on a sample of automobile dealers in small, isolated towns. They model the entry decision of each of the first two firms into a market, and exploit the comparative statics of the level of firm profits in the size of the market to draw inferences about monopoly and duopoly conduct and entry behavior. Like Panzar and Rosse, they argue strongly that the right kind of sample for the study of entry is a cross-section of closely related markets. The particular characteristics of those markets in which more firms have entered will reveal the determinants of firm profitability.

Clearly much more work is needed on the determinants of, and the effects of, entry. In Subsection 3.4, above, I discussed the existing literature on the effects of entry and concentration on price in cross-sections of related markets. A careful working out of the analytics of the number of firms in an industry, their sizes, and so on, is a crucial step in the successful analysis of the effects of entry. This is one area in which we do not lack for data; many studies treating entry as exogenous have already been carried out.

6.3. Final remark

In stating the need for further study so strongly, I do not mean to suggest that the accomplishments to date are small. By departing from the tradition of treating performance as observable in accounting cost data, the *NEIO* has provided a new form of evidence that there is substantial market power in the economy, a form of evidence that is not susceptible to the standard criticisms of earlier approaches. Furthermore, the individual studies of particular industries are specific and detailed enough that alternative explanations of the findings can be rebutted. The current state of affairs is quite encouraging: we know that there is market power out there, and need to know a lot more about exactly where. We know essentially nothing about the causes, or even the systematic predictors, of market power, but have come a long way in working out how to measure them.

References

Abreu, D., Pearce, D. and Stacchetti, E. (1986) 'Optimal cartel equilibria with imperfect monitoring', *Journal of Economic Theory*, 39:251–269.

Anderson, J. (1984) 'Identification of interactive behavior in air service markets: 1973–76', *Journal of Industrial Economics*, 32:489–507.

Anderson, J. and Kraus, M. (1984) 'An econometric model of regulated airline flight rivalry', *Research in the Economics of Transportation*, 2.

Appelbaum, E. (1979) 'Testing price taking behavior', *Journal of Econometrics*, 9:283–294.

Appelbaum, E. (1982) 'The estimation of the degree of oligopoly power', *Journal of Econometrics*, 19:287–299.

Ashenfelter, O. and Sullivan, D. (1987) 'Nonparametric tests of market structure: An application to the cigarette industry', *Journal of Industrial Economics*, forthcoming.

Bain, J.S. (1951) 'Relation of profit rate to industry concentration: American manufacturing, 1936–40', *Quarterly Journal of Economics*, 65:293–324.

Baker, J. and Bresnahan, T. (1983) 'Estimating the elasticity of demand facing a single firm: Evidence for three brewing firms', mimeo.

Baker, J. and Bresnahan, T. (1985) 'The gains from merger and collusion in product differentiated industries', *Journal of Industrial Economics*, 33:427–444.

Barton, D. and Sherman, R. (1984) 'The price and profit effects of horizontal merger: A case study', *Journal of Industrial Economics*, 33:165–177.

Bresnahan, T.F. (1980) 'Three essays in the American automobile oligopoly', dissertation, Princeton University.

Bresnahan, T.F. (1981) 'Departures from marginal-cost pricing in the American automobile industry: Estimates for 1977–1978', *Journal of Econometrics*, 11:201–227.

Bresnahan, T.F. (1982) 'The oligopoly solution concept is identified', *Economics Letters*, 10:87–92.

Bresnahan, T.F. (1987) 'Competition and collusion in the American automobile oligopoly: The 1955 price war', *Journal of Industrial Economics*, forthcoming.

Bresnahan, T.F. and Reiss, P. (1985) 'Dealer and manufacturer margins', *Rand Journal of Economics*, 16:253–268.

Bresnahan, T.F. and Reiss, P. (1986) 'Entry in monopoly markets', mimeo.

Bulow, J. and Pfleiderer, P. (1983) 'A note on the effect of cost changes on prices', *Journal of Political Economy*, 91:182–185.

Burns, M. (1986) 'Predatory pricing and acquisition cost of competitors', *Journal of Political Economy*, 94:286–296.

Chamberlin, E.H. (1933) *The theory of monopolistic competition*. Mass.: Harvard University Press.

Cotterill (1986) 'Market power in the retail food industry: Evidence from Vermont', *Review of Economics and Statistics*, 68:379–386.

Cowling, K. and Waterson, M. (1976) 'Price cost margins and market structure', *Economica*, 43:267–274.

Demsetz, H. (1974) 'Two systems of belief about monopoly', in: H.J. Goldschmid, H.M. Mann and J.F. Weston, eds., *Industrial concentration: The new learning.* Mass.: Little, Brown.

Diewert, E. (1971) 'Application of Shephard's duality theorem', *Journal of Political Economy*, 79:481–507.

Gelfand, M.J. and Spiller, P. (1987) 'Entry barriers and multi-product oligopoly', *International Journal of Industrial Organization*, forthcoming.

Geroski, P. (1983) 'The empirical analysis of conjectural variations in oligopoly', mimeo.

Geroski, P., Phlips, L. and Ulph, A. (1985) 'Oligopoly, competition and welfare: Some recent developments', *Journal of Industrial Economics*, 33:369–386.

Gilbert, R. (1984) 'Bank market structure and competition – a survey', *Journal of Money, Credit and Banking*, 16:617–645.

Gollop, F. and Roberts, M. (1979) 'Firm interdependence in oligopolistic markets', *Journal of Econometrics*, 10:313–331.

Graham, D.R., Kaplan, D.P. and Sibley, D.S. (1983) 'Efficiency and competition in the airline industry', *Bell Journal of Economics*, 14:118–138.

Green, E.J. and Porter, R.H. (1984) 'Noncooperative collusion under imperfect price information', *Econometrica*, 52:87–100.

Haining, R. (1984) 'Testing a spatial interacting-markets hypothesis', *Review of Economics and Statistics*, 66:576–583.

Hall, R. (1986) 'The relationship between price and cost in U.S. industry', mimeo.

Iwata, G. (1974) 'Measurement of conjectural variations in oligopoly', *Econometrica*, 42:947–966.

Just, R. and Chern, W. (1980) 'Tomatoes, technology and oligopsony', *Bell Journal of Economics*, 11:584–602.

Koller, R. and Weiss, L. (1986) 'Price levels and seller concentration: The case of Portland Cement', mimeo.

Koutsoyiannis, A. (1982) 'Goals of oligopolistic firms: An empirical test of competing hypotheses', *Southern Economic Journal*, 51:540–567.

Lamm, R. (1981) 'Prices and concentration in the food retailing industry', *Journal of Industrial Economics*, 30:67–78.

Lau, L. (1982) 'On identifying the degree of competitiveness from industry price and output data', *Economics Letters*, 10:93–99.

Lee, L.F. and Porter, R.H. (1984) 'Switching regression models with imperfect sample separation information – with an application on cartel stability', *Econometrica*, 52:391–418.
Lerner, A. (1934) 'The concept of monopoly and the measurement of monopoly power', *Review of Economic Studies*, 11:157–175.
Lopez, R.E. (1984) 'Measuring oligopoly power and production responses of the Canadian food processing industry', *Journal of Agricultural Economics*, 35:219–230.
Marvel, H. (1978) 'Competition and price levels in the retail gasoline market', *Review of Economics and Statistics*, 60:252–258.
McFadden, D. (1982) 'Econometric models of probabilistic choice', in: C. Manski and D. McFadden, eds., *Structural analysis of discrete data with econometric application*. Cambridge, Mass.: MIT.
Panzar, J. and Rosse, J. (1977a) 'Structure, conduct and comparative statics', mimeo.
Panzar, J. and Rosse, J. (1977b) 'Chamberlin vs. Robinson: An empirical test for monopoly rents', mimeo.
Panzar, J. and Rosse, J. (1987) 'Testing for 'monopoly' equilibrium', *Journal of Industrial Economics*, forthcoming.
Porter, R.H. (1983) 'A study of cartel stability: The joint executive committee, 1880–1886', *Bell Journal of Economics*, 14:301–314.
Porter, R.H. (1984) 'Optimal cartel trigger price strategies', 29:313–338.
Porter, R.H. (1985) 'On the incidence and duration of price wars', *Journal of Industrial Economics*, 33:415–426.
Prescott, E.C. and Visscher, M. (1977) 'Sequential location among firms with foresight', *Bell Journal of Economics*, 8:378–393.
Roberts, J. (1984) 'Testing oligopolistic behavior', *International Journal of Industrial Organization*, 2:367–383.
Roberts, M. (1983) 'Testing oligopolistic behavior: An application of the variable profit function', *International Journal of Industrial Organization*, 2:367–383.
Rhoades, S. (1982) 'Structure–performance studies in banking: An updated summary and evaluation', FRB staff studies no. 119, see also Federal Reserve Bulletin.
Rosse, J.N. (1970) 'Estimating cost function parameters without using cost data illustrated methodology', *Econometrica*, 38:256–275.
Rotemberg, J. and Saloner, G. (1986) 'A supergame-theoretic model of business cycles and price wars during booms', *American Economic Review*, 76:390–407.
Scheffman, D. and Spiller, P. (1987) 'Geographic market definition under the DOJ guidelines', *Journal of Law and Economics*, forthcoming.
Scherer, F.M. (1980) *Industrial market structure and economic performance*, 2nd edn. Chicago: Rand McNally.
Schmalensee, R. (1985) 'Econometric diagnosis of competitive localization', *International Journal of Industrial Organization*, 3:57–70.
Schmalensee, R. and Golub, B. (1983) 'Estimating effective concentration in deregulated wholesale electricity markets', *Rand Journal of Economics*, 5:12–26.
Schmalensee, R. and Thisse, J.F. (1986) 'Perceptual maps and the optimal location of new products', Center of Operations Research and Econometrics, core reprint no. 8620.
Shaffer, S. (1982) 'A nonstructural test for competition in financial markets', in: *Proceedings of a conference in bank structure and competition*. Chicago: Federal Reserve Bank of Chicago.
Shapiro, M. (1987) 'How (monopolistically) competitive is U.S. industry', mimeo.
Slade, M. (1987) 'Conjectures, firm characteristics and market structure: An analysis of Vancouver's gasoline-price wars', mimeo.
Spiller, P. and Favaro, E. (1984) 'The effects of entry regulation on oligopolistic interaction: The Uruguayan banking sector', *Rand Journal of Economics*, 15:244–254.
Stigler, G.J. (1964) 'A theory of oligopoly', *Journal of Political Economy*, 72:44–61.
Sullivan, D. (1985) 'Testing hypotheses about firm behavior in the cigarette industry', *Journal of Political Economy*, 93:586–598.
Sumner, D. (1981) 'Measurement of monopoly behavior: An application to the cigarette industry', *Journal of Political Economy*, 89:1010–1019.
Suslow, V. (1986) 'Estimating monopoly behavior with competitive recycling: An application to Alcoa', *Rand Journal of Economics*, 17:389–403.

Chapter 18

EMPIRICAL STUDIES OF INNOVATION AND MARKET STRUCTURE

WESLEY M. COHEN

Carnegie Mellon University

RICHARD C. LEVIN*

Yale University

Contents

*We are grateful for the support of the Division of Policy Research and Analysis of the National Science Foundation, for the research assistance of Diane Owen, David Roth, and Somi Seong, for the helpful comments of Steven Klepper, Alvin Klevorick, Richard Nelson, and F. M. Scherer, and, above all, for the patience of the editors of this Handbook.

Handbook of Industrial Organization, Volume II, Edited by R. Schmalensee and R.D. Willig

1. Introduction

A central question in the field of industrial organization is how firms and markets should be organized to produce optimal economic performance. Empirical estimates of the costs of static resource misallocation attributable to suboptimal market organization range from miniscule [0.07 percent of GNP, as estimated by Harberger (1954)] to substantial [4-13 percent of GNP, as estimated by Cowling and Mueller (1978)]. Even the largest of these estimated costs, however, might be worth incurring in return for modest improvements in the rate of technological progress. The potential tradeoff between static and dynamic efficiency is therefore central to evaluating the performance of alternative modes of firm and market organization.

The idea that technological progress facilitated economic growth and improved welfare was appreciated long before economists became concerned with quantifying its impact. In the classical political economy of Ricardo, Mill, and Marx, technological progress was the principal force offsetting the tendency of capital accumulation to depress the rate of profit. For Ricardo and Mill, if not for Marx, technological progress was the principal impediment to the onset of a "stationary state" in which economic growth ceased.

It remained, however, for Schumpeter (1942) to argue for a sharp distinction between the organization of firms and markets most conducive to solving the static problem of resource allocation and those organizational forms most conducive to rapid technological progress. In Schumpeter's view, the atomistic firm operating in a competitive market may be a perfectly suitable vehicle for static resource allocation, but the large firm operating in a concentrated market was the "most powerful engine of progress and ... long-run expansion of total output". In this respect, he continued, "perfect competition is inferior, and has no title to being set up as a model of ideal efficiency" [Schumpeter (1942, p. 106)].

Schumpeter's assertions inspired what has become the second largest body of empirical literature in the field of industrial organization, exceeded in volume only by the literature investigating the relationship between concentration and profitability (surveyed in this Handbook by Schmalensee in Chapter 16). Most of this literature focuses on testing two hypotheses associated with Schumpeter: (1) innovation increases more than proportionately with firm size and (2) innovation increases with market concentration.

In focusing on these hypotheses, the profession, abetted partly by Schumpeter himself, has done some disservice to one of Schumpeter's central research missions, the development of a broader understanding of the nature and economic consequences of technological progress. With some notable exceptions, the profession, particularly industrial organization economists of the Harvard school [e.g. Mason (1951)], became preoccupied with investigating the effects of firm size and market concentration on innovation, most probably because Schumpeter's propositions appeared to offer a direct challenge to antitrust orthodoxy. Specifically, the proposition that an industrial organization of large monopolistic firms might have decisive welfare advantages cut sharply against the grain of antitrust thinking. As a result, the more general task of identifying and evaluating other, perhaps more fundamental, determinants of technological progress in industry has received little attention relative to the effort devoted to exploring the effects of size and market structure.

Indeed, we find that the empirical results bearing on the Schumpeterian hypotheses are inconclusive, in large part because investigators have failed to take systematic account of more fundamental sources of variation in the innovative behavior and performance of firms and industries. In this survey, we review the traditional empirical literature, but we also discuss the growing literature on the fundamental determinants of interindustry differences in innovation. We classify these determinants under three headings; the structure of demand, the nature and abundance of technological opportunity, and the conditions governing appropriability of the returns from innovation.

Our review finds the empirical literature on Schumpeter's hypotheses pervaded by methodological difficulties. Equations have been loosely specified; the data have often been inadequate to analyze the questions at hand; and, until recently, the econometric techniques employed were rather primitive. To the extent that preoccupation with the effects of firm size and concentration on innovation encourages omission of important and potentially correlated explanatory variables, estimates of these very effects have tended to be biased. Despite some recent advances in model specification, data collection, and statistical techniques, the results of this literature must be interpreted with caution.

Given the literature's methodological pitfalls, we can at best hope to identify robust findings. Relationships among important economic variables that prove robust to variations in sampling, specification, statistical techniques, and measurement are the "stylized facts" from which theory, and ultimately the formulation of precise and falsifiable hypotheses, develop. A lack of robustness can also advance understanding; although it is too rarely undertaken, thorough diagnosis of the reasons for inconsistent results across samples, specifications, techniques, or measures can produce valuable insights for theory construction. Also, as Schmalensee argues in his related chapter, the search for robust findings should focus not simply on the issue of statistical significance, but on the magnitude of estimated parameters and the contribution of particular variables to explaining variance in the dependent variable. Relationships that are persistently *significant* but miniscule in magnitude and unimportant in the explanation of variance are probably not worth much attention in the formulation of either theory or policy.

This survey critically reviews the empirical literature on the characteristics of markets and firms that influence industrial innovation. In addition to the econometric literature, we will also selectively review the case study and institutional literature that provides a richer, more subtle interpretation of the relationships among innovation, market structure, and industry and firm characteristics. Although the literature considered here is extensive, the survey is primarily confined to industrial organization in a narrow sense. We will not consider the effects on technical advance of national or economy-wide characteristics such as tax policy or the supply of trained engineers. We will not examine the substantial and important economic literatures on productivity measurement and growth, induced innovation, the adoption and diffusion of innovation, and the nature and organization of the R&D process. Nor will we discuss the vast sociological and social-psychological literatures on the innovation process and the effects of internal organization on the generation, adoption, and diffusion of innovations.[1]

In Section 2 we discuss the problems associated with measuring innovative effort and output. We then proceed, in Section 3, to review, thematically and critically, the literature that examines the effects of firm size and concentration upon innovation, as well as the related literature that considers the influence of selected firm characteristics. In Section 4 we discuss the literature on three sources of interindustry variation in innovative behavior and performance: demand, technological opportunity, and appropriability conditions. We pause here more frequently than in the previous section to provide specific details because the literature is less familiar to most industrial organization economists and has been less thoroughly reviewed elsewhere. In the concluding section, we consider the relationship of the econometric literature on innovation and market structure to the theoretical literature, and we suggest directions for future research.

2. Measurement

A fundamental problem in the study of innovation and technical change in industry is the absence of satisfactory measures of new knowledge and its contribution to technological progress. There exists no measure of innovation that permits readily interpretable cross-industry comparisons. Moreover, the value of an innovation is difficult to assess, particularly when the innovation is embodied in consumer products [see Griliches (1979)]. Despite these difficulties, a variety of measures of innovation have been employed by empiricists. They may be broadly classified as measures of either innovative inputs or outputs.

[1]For a recent review of the literature on productivity measurement and growth, see Link (1987). The literature on induced innovation, adoption and diffusion is surveyed by Thirtle and Ruttan (1987). Dosi (1988) covers aspects of the innovation process from the perspective of institutional economics. For an overview of the innovation process that covers the literature of other social sciences, see the survey prepared by the National Science Foundation (1983).

Direct measures of innovative output are the most scarce. Innovation counts have been assembled on a cross-industry basis for the United States by Gellman Research Associates (1976), and for the United Kingdom by a group of researchers at the Science Policy Research Unit (SPRU) at the University of Sussex [see Townsend et al. (1981) and Robson and Townsend (1984) for a description of the U.K. data]. Both of these efforts involved an elaborate process of using technical experts to identify significant innovations. Unavoidably, the innovations thus identified are heterogeneous in economic value, and despite the care taken in assembling the data, they are likely to reflect numerous unexamined biases. Little work has been done with the Gellman data, but the SPRU data have been quite fruitfully exploited [e.g. Pavitt (1983, 1984), Pavitt et al. (1987), Robson et al. (1988)].

Data on significant innovations have been assembled for particular industries. Mansfield (1963), for example, developed innovation counts for the steel, petroleum refining, and bituminous coal industries. In the pharmaceutical industry, data on the number of new chemical entities developed by firm and by year are readily available and have been widely used [e.g. Baily (1972), Peltzman (1973), Schwartzman (1976)]. Data on significant innovations in the semiconductor industry have been assembled by Tilton (1971) and Wilson et al. (1980).

Patent counts have been used most frequently to approximate the innovative output of firms or industries. A few early studies required considerable effort to assemble the data [e.g. Scherer (1965a), Grabowski (1968)]. More recently, automation of the U.S. Bureau of the Census' Patent File has facilitated the use of patent data, especially at the level of the firm [see Bound et al. (1984) and Griliches et al. (1987)].

There are significant problems with patent counts as a measure of innovation, some of which affect both within-industry and between-industry comparisons. Most notably, the economic value of patents is highly heterogeneous. A great majority of patents are never exploited commercially, and only a very few are associated with major technological improvements. Moreover, a patent may consist of several related claims, each of which might be filed as a separate patent. Indeed, although the quantity of patents is often used to measure national technological advantage [see National Science Board (1987)], comparisons are distorted by the tendency of U.S. inventors to bundle claims in one patent, while Japanese inventors typically file separate patents for each claim.[2]

Other difficulties specifically reduce the value of patent data in cross-industry applications. The propensity to patent varies considerably across industries. In

[2]Even if patents were homogeneous in economic value, their use as a measure of innovation in econometric studies would require special care. Because patents are integer-valued and because their distribution across firms or business units is highly skewed, standard assumptions about the distribution of the error term in a regression explaining patenting activity cannot be maintained. Solutions to this problem are suggested by Hausman, Hall and Griliches (1984).

the electronics industries, entire categories of economically significant innovations are typically not patentable. Computer software, for example, is normally eligible for copyright but not patent protection, and integrated circuit designs are neither patentable nor copyrightable.[3] Even where patents are available, the nature of an industry's technology and its competitive conditions tend to govern the tradeoff between patenting innovations and keeping them secret. In some industries, but not in others, patents reveal to competitors technological information that cannot be readily ascertained by other means (such as reverse engineering the product). In such cases, patenting may be inhibited and secrecy favored. By contrast, patents may be preferred where they serve as "signals" of technological competence to suppliers of capital, a phenomenon of particular importance to small firms.[4]

There have been several attempts to measure the value of innovations by examining the stock market's response to patent grants [Griliches (1981), Pakes (1985), and Cockburn and Griliches (1988)]. Cockburn and Griliches found that the stock market responds more strongly to changes in a firm's R&D spending than to changes in the stock of patents, although the valuation of both R&D and patents is significantly influenced by the "effectiveness" of patents in the firm's principal industry.[5] A promising alternative approach to measurement of the value of patents was taken by Schankerman and Pakes (1986) and Pakes (1986), who estimated the distribution of patent values from European data on annual patent renewals. The renewal data, however, have not yet been studied at the industry level because most national patent offices do not classify patents by industry. There is also evidence, recently developed by Trajtenberg (1987) for the computed tomography scanner industry, that a measure weighting patents by their citations in other patent applications may provide a relatively accurate index of the value of innovations within an industry.

In the majority of studies concerned with the effects of firm size or market structure on innovation, the dependent variable is a measure of input to the innovation process, rather than a measure of innovative output. Most commonly, innovative effort is measured by expenditures on R&D or by personnel engaged in R&D. Although both measures are intended to represent the current flow of resources devoted to the generation of innovation, both are flawed. R&D employment excludes flows of services from research equipment and laboratory materials, which may be combined with labor in variable proportions, while

[3]In the United States, passage of the Semiconductor Chip Protection Act in 1984 made integrated circuit designs (as represented on photolithographic "masks") eligible for a special form of intellectual property right that is neither a patent nor a copyright.

[4]For additional discussion of the strengths and weaknesses of patents as a measure of innovation, see Kuznets (1962), Pavitt (1985), Basberg (1987), and Griliches, Hall and Pakes (1987).

[5]Cockburn and Griliches used data on the effectiveness of patents developed by Levin et al. (1987) from a survey of R&D managers in 130 industries. The survey results are discussed in greater detail in Section 4.

R&D expenditures include the purchase of long-lived equipment that is expensed rather than capitalized under current accounting rules. R&D employment and expenditure data are also subject to considerable error in reporting, because the definitions used for financial reporting give firms considerable latitude in the classification of activities. Even the more rigorous definitions used in the annual National Science Foundation survey are subject to misinterpretation. Moreover, the discrepancy between the NSF definitions and the rules governing financial reporting leads to systematic differences across widely used data sets.[6]

Some investigators, notably Griliches (1979), have argued that the proper measure of innovative input is not the knowledge generated in any one period, but the services of an accumulated stock of knowledge upon which the firm draws. The construction of an operational measure of a knowledge stock, sometimes referred to as R&D capital, is problematic. Griliches identified three issues: (1) the determination of an appropriate depreciation rate, (2) the specification of the lags with which current R&D effort is added to the stock, and (3) the extent to which spillovers of knowledge generated by other firms, other industries, government agencies, or universities supplement the knowledge created by a firm's own R&D.

Despite some impressive efforts to grapple with these measurement problems, it remains unclear whether a meaningful index of a firm's or an industry's knowledge stock can be constructed. If, as Griliches suggested, the private rate of depreciation depends on obsolescence and the extent of spillovers to competitors, then the depreciation rate is not a given technological parameter; it is endogenous to the process of innovation and dynamic competition. In any event, it is clear that – to the extent that depreciation rates, lag structures, and spillovers differ systematically across industries – even a correctly measured flow of current R&D effort will not serve as an adequate proxy for the services of R&D capital in cross-industry comparisons.

Moreover, it is heroic to assume that even a properly measured representation of R&D stock or flow can fully summarize a firm's effort devoted to technological innovation. Hollander's (1965) account of incremental innovation on the shop floor, as well as numerous studies of learning by doing [e.g. Hirsch (1952) and Lieberman (1984)], indicate that considerable effort is devoted to technological innovation outside a firm's formal R&D operation. Moreover, many small firms simply have no formal R&D operation; effort devoted to technological innovation is typically an unmeasured fraction of the time worked by the firm's engineers and managers [see, for example, Kleinknecht (1987)].

[6]Cohen and Mowery (1984) found that Standard and Poor's Compustat data indicate that firms conduct 12 percent more R&D, on average, than indicated by the Federal Trade Commission's Line of Business Program data covering the same firms and years. The FTC applies the more restrictive NSF definition of R&D, while the Compustat data is derived from firms' annual 10-K reports to the Securities and Exchange Commission, which permits a more liberal definition.

A final problem common to the use of input as well as output measures of innovation is that when such measures are used, inventive effort and innovations are usually assumed to be qualitatively homogeneous. In most studies, process innovation is not distinguished from product innovation; basic and applied research are not distinguished from development. Such homogeneity assumptions, Lunn (1986) has emphasized, make it difficult to specify correctly an empirical model; some variables expected to influence process innovation, for example, may be thought to have no influence on product innovation. The importance of particular explanatory variables may also differ across types of activities. For example, the availability of patent protection would be expected to have a stronger effect on product R&D than on process R&D [Levin et al. (1987)], and a firm's degree of diversification would be expected to have a stronger effect on basic research than on applied research and development [Nelson (1959)].

For many purposes, data that distinguish types of inventive activity are unavailable. The National Science Foundation publishes a breakdown of expenditures for basic research, applied research, and development at a relatively high level of aggregation (corresponding mainly to two-digit industries, with some subdivision into groups of three-digit industries). Mansfield (1981) and Link (1982, 1985) have collected and analyzed a limited amount of data distinguishing basic research from applied research and development at the firm level. Although there are no official sources of data on the relative effort devoted to process and product innovation, Scherer (1982a, 1984a) classified all U.S. patents granted within a 15-month period in the mid-1970's by industry of origin and industry of use. In this framework, process innovations are those represented by patents used in their industry of origin. Scherer's data provide an interesting picture of interindustry flows of technology, and they have been used by Scherer (1982b, 1982c, 1983a, 1983b) and others for numerous purposes.[7]

3. Empirical studies in the Schumpeterian tradition

In this section we examine empirical research on the central Schumpeterian relationships between innovation, on the one hand, and firm size and market structure, on the other. We also discuss methodologically similar work that considers the influence on innovative activity of corporate characteristics that are correlated with size, such as diversification and financial capability. Three recent

[7]In some applications, Scherer's data have been used to divide an industry's R&D expenditures between process and product R&D [Lunn (1986), Levin and Reiss (1988)] by assuming that each industry devotes to processes a percentage of R&D equal to the percentage of its patents assigned to processes. This assumption is suspect to the extent that process innovations are less likely to be patented (and more likely to be protected by trade secrecy) than are product innovations.

literature surveys [Scherer (1980), Kamien and Schwartz (1982), and Baldwin and Scott (1987)] have ably summarized findings concerning the two "Schumpeterian" hypotheses and related propositions. For this reason, our summary of results will be brief. We focus instead on the methodological issues raised by this substantial body of work.

3.1. *Firm size and innovation*

A literal reading of Schumpeter's (1942) classic discussion suggests that he was primarily impressed by the qualitative differences between the innovative activities of small, entrepreneurial enterprises and those of large, modern corporations with formal R&D laboratories. Nonetheless, the empirical literature has interpreted Schumpeter's argument as a proposition that there exists a continuous, positive relationship between firm size and innovation. With a few exceptions [e.g. Nelson et al. (1967), Gellman Research Associates (1976), Pavitt et al. (1987)], the Schumpeterian hypothesis about firm size has been tested by some type of linear regression of a measure of innovative activity (input or output) on a measure of size.

Several arguments (only some of which were suggested by Schumpeter) have been offered to justify a positive effect of firm size on inventive activity. One claim is that capital market imperfections confer an advantage on large firms in securing finance for risky R&D projects, because size is correlated with the availability and stability of internally-generated funds. A second claim is that there are scale economies in the technology of R&D. Another is that the returns from R&D are higher where the innovator has a large volume of sales over which to spread the fixed costs of innovation. Finally, R&D is alleged to be more productive in large firms as a result of complementarities between R&D and other nonmanufacturing activities (e.g. marketing and financial planning) that may be better developed within large firms.

Counterarguments to the proposition have also been suggested. Perhaps the most prominent is that, as firms grow large, efficiency in R&D is undermined through loss of managerial control. Also, as firms grow large, the incentives of individual scientists and entrepreneurs become attenuated as their ability to capture the benefits from their efforts diminishes. Indeed, Schumpeter (1942) himself suggested that this feature of the bureaucratization of inventive activity could undermine capitalist development.

The balance of evidence on the relationship between firm size and innovation has shifted over the past twenty-five years. In the mid-1960s, the studies of Horowitz (1962), Hamberg (1964), and Comanor (1967) found that R&D intensity, the ratio of R&D to firm size (usually measured by sales), increased weakly with size. Mansfield (1964), however, found little evidence of such a relationship.

Scherer (1965a, 1965b) suggested a more subtle relationship – that inventive activity, whether measured by input (personnel) or output (patents), increased more than proportionally with size up to a threshold, whereupon the relationship was either weakly negative or did not exist.

Several subsequent cross-sectional studies found evidence of a positive, monotonic relationship between size and R&D [Soete (1979), Link (1980), Loeb (1983), and Meisel and Lin (1983)]. Also a number of studies found a positive relationship in selected industries, particularly chemicals [Mansfield (1964), Grabowski (1968)]. Despite the lack of unanimity, Scherer's findings, confirmed to varying degrees by a number of other investigators [Phlips (1971), Malecki (1980), and Link (1981)], were widely regarded as the profession's tentative consensus by the early 1980's.[8]

Recent work has cast doubt on the basis for this consensus. Employing data from the FTC's Line of Business Program for 1974, Scherer (1984b) himself found that business unit R&D intensity increased with business unit size in about 20 percent of the sample lines of business; no size effect was detected in most of the remaining industries. A different dissenting note was sounded by Bound et al. (1984). Using a larger and more comprehensive sample of American firms than any previously employed to study the size-innovation relationship at the firm level, they found that R&D intensity first falls and then rises with firm size. Both very small and very large firms were found to be more R&D intensive than those intermediate in size. Cremer and Sirbu (1978), using data on French firms, obtained similar results.

Using data from the FTC's Line of Business Program combined with the Levin et al. (1987) survey of appropriability and technological opportunity conditions in industry, Cohen et al. (1987) resurrected the earlier consensus, although in a slightly different form. They showed that once care was taken to control for industry effects and distinguish between the size of the firm and that of the business unit, neither size variable significantly affected R&D intensity in the (selected) sample of R&D performers.[9] A threshold effect was found, however, though different from that found earlier by Scherer. Using Tobit and probit estimation techniques, Cohen et al. concluded that the size of the business unit – but not that of the firm as a whole – affected the decision of the business unit to engage in R&D. They also highlighted a point neglected by other studies in this tradition. The importance of the size variables was found to be minute,

[8]See, for example, the review of the literature by Kamien and Schwartz (1982), as well as Scherer's (1980) own account in his widely used textbook.

[9]Cohen et al. found, however, that their results were surprisingly sensitive to the presence of a mere seven outliers in a sample of over 2000 business units. Each of these observations appeared to be subject to some form of measurement error. When these observations are included in the sample, firm size had a very small, but marginally significant effect on R&D intensity. When the outliers were excluded, the effect vanished.

both in terms of variance explained (less than 1 percent) and magnitude of the coefficients (a doubling of mean firm size increased R&D intensity by only one or two tenths of 1 percent).

A distinctive feature of the study by Gellman Research Associates (1976) is the use of an output measure covering a broad spectrum of industries, a count of some 500 innovations judged by experts to be among the major innovations introduced in the United States between 1953 and 1973. They found that the share of innovations introduced by the largest firms was barely greater than their share of employment. This is roughly consistent with much of the regression literature. Contrary to the Schumpeterian hypothesis, but consistent with the findings of Bound et al. (1984) concerning R&D intensity, they also found that companies with fewer than 1000 employees accounted for 47.3 percent of the important innovations, although their share of employment was only 41.2 percent in 1963, the sample period midpoint. Scherer (1984b) suggested that small firms may be a more important source of innovation in the United States than elsewhere; he noted that in a methodologically similar study using data on significant innovations in the United Kingdom between 1945 and 1980 [Pavitt (1983)] the largest firms were found to have the highest ratio of innovations per employee. Pavitt et al. (1987), however, using an updated version of the same British data set, found that both very small and very large firms were responsible for a disproportionate share of innovations.

The most notable feature of this considerable body of empirical research on the relationship between firm size and innovation is its inconclusiveness. Apart from the measurement problems we have identified, there are at least two reasons for this apparent disarray. First, most of the samples used in the regression studies are highly non-random, and with a few exceptions [Bound et al. (1984), Cohen et al. (1987)], no attempt has been made to study the presence or the effects of sample selection bias. Many of the earlier firm-level studies confined attention to the 500 or 1000 largest firms in the manufacturing sector, and, quite typically, firms that reported no R&D were excluded from the sample.

Second, the studies vary in the degree to which they control for characteristics of firms (other than size) and industries, despite the demonstrated importance of firm and industry effects [Scott (1984)], and the likely collinearity between them and firm size.[10] A few studies controlled for industry effects with separate regressions for each industry [e.g. Mansfield (1968), Scherer (1984b)]; others used fixed industry effects [e.g. Bound et al. (1984), Scott (1984), Cohen et al. (1987)]. It is not, however, a simple matter to control properly for industry effects in a

[10]The size distribution of firms varies markedly across industries, in part because of differences in the degree of scale economies in production and distribution. Thus, there is good reason to believe that fixed industry effects are correlated with firm size and that the omission of such effects will bias estimates of the effects of size on innovation. Similarly, firm characteristics such as diversification and some measures of financial capability are correlated with firm size.

sample of data at the level of the firm, because most larger firms are aggregations of business units engaged in a variety of industries.

Most scholars who have attempted to control for industry effects have assigned each sample firm to a primary industry and then used either a fixed effects model or specific industry characteristics as covariates. Such assignments are typically made at the two-digit SIC level, a procedure that introduces measurement error to the extent that relevant industry characteristics exhibit substantial variance across the constituent four-digit industries. On the other hand, when industry assignments are made at the three- or four-digit level, there is also systematic mismeasurement, because many firms (and most large ones) conduct the bulk of their business outside their designated primary industry.

It is useful to reconsider briefly the Schumpeterian hypothesis in light of the fact that most large firms operate business units in numerous industries. Although some arguments advanced to rationalize Schumpeter's hypothesis refer to the overall size of the firm (e.g. the ability to overcome capital market imperfections), others are more plausible at the level of the business unit (e.g. cost spreading). Moreover, scale economies in R&D may be relevant to the firm as a whole or to the firm's activities in particular industries. Although the great majority of the studies we have discussed examine the effect of firm size on firm-level R&D, the Federal Trade Commission's Line of Business data make it possible to separate the effects of business unit and firm size. Scherer (1984b) and Scott (1984) studied the effects of business unit size on business unit R&D, while Cohen et al. (1987) examined the effects of both business unit and firm size on business unit R&D.

A methodological problem common to almost all the studies of the relationship between size and innovation is that they overlook the effect of innovation on firm growth (and hence, ultimately, firm size).[11] It is curious that the endogeneity of firm size, central to Schumpeter's notion of creative destruction, has been neglected, while the simultaneity associated with creative destruction has been recognized in some studies of the relationship between innovation and market concentration. This lacuna probably reflects the profession's primitive understanding of the determination of the size and growth of firms, an area of research that has just recently been revived.[12]

Two other critiques of the literature under review derive from exegesis of Schumpeter. Fisher and Temin (1973) argued that to the extent that Schumpeter's hypothesis can be given a clear formulation, it must refer to a relationship

[11]An exception is Mowery (1983b), who found that R&D contributed to firm survival over the period 1921 through 1946.

[12]Although some effort was devoted to this question decades ago [Simon and Bonini (1958), Mansfield (1962), Scherer (1965c)], relatively little work has been done until recently [e.g. Gort and Klepper (1982), Klepper and Graddy (1986), Evans (1987a, 1987b), Hall (1987), and Pakes and Ericson (1987)].

between innovative output and firm size, not to a relationship between R&D (an innovative input) and firm size, which is the one most commonly tested in the literature. They demonstrated, among other things, that an elasticity of R&D with respect to size in excess of one does not necessarily imply an elasticity of innovative output with respect to size greater than one. Kohn and Scott (1982) established the conditions under which the existence of the former relationship does imply the latter.

More fundamentally, Markham (1965) and Nelson et al. (1967) suggested that most empirical studies tend to test a proposition that is quite different from Schumpeter's. They argued that Schumpeter did not postulate a continuous effect of firm size on innovation. Rather, by the time he wrote *Capitalism, Socialism, and Democracy*, he believed that industrial research no longer depended upon the initiative and genius of independent entrepreneurs; it had become the province of professional R&D laboratories run by large, bureaucratic corporations. Neither Schumpeter nor Galbraith (1952), who elaborated the argument, indicated that inventive activity should increase more than proportionately with firm size. The proposition was a weaker one, suggesting that formally organized R&D labs administered by large corporations are the source of most innovation in modern capitalist society.[13]

Even in this weaker form, Schumpeter's proposition is controversial. There is little doubt that large firms account for most of the R&D undertaken. For example, Scherer (1980), using NSF data, found that in 1972 U.S. firms with 5000 or more employees accounted for 89 percent of all R&D expenditures, but only 53 percent of manufacturing employment. It is much less clear that large firms are the source of most innovations. Indeed, Scherer found that a sample of 463 of the 500 largest manufacturing firms in 1955 contributed a share of the U.S. patents that was barely greater than their share of employment.

Recent work by Acs and Audretsch (1987) and Dorfman (1987) has indicated that the relative contributions of small and large firms to innovation may depend on industry conditions, and in particular on market structure. Acs and Audretsch found that large firms are more innovative in concentrated industries with high barriers to entry, while smaller firms are more innovative in less concentrated industries that are less mature. In a comparative study of four electronics industries, Dorfman (1987) reached a similar conclusion.

Some of the arguments rationalizing the hypothesized relationship between innovation and size suggest the existence of a direct relationship between innovation and other attributes of firms that are typically correlated with size. For example, a link between innovation and a firm's internally-generated funds is suggested by the argument that large firms are favored by the availability of

[13]We thank Richard Nelson for urging us to distinguish between Schumpeter's views and the profession's interpretation of those views.

internal funds in a world of capital market imperfections. A link between diversification and innovation is suggested by the argument that large firms are better positioned to exploit complementarities among their diverse activities.

A number of scholars have studied the influence of these correlates of firm size.[14] Cash flow, a measure of internal financial capability, has been the most thoroughly examined [e.g. Mueller (1967), Grabowski (1968), Elliot (1971), Branch (1974), Teece and Armour (1977), Kamien and Schwartz (1978), Armour and Teece (1981), and Link (1981)]. Many, but not all, of the studies, have found that a firm's cash flow is associated with higher levels of R&D intensity. Scholars have disagreed over the interpretation of this finding. Some have argued that it is difficult to distinguish cash flow as a measure of liquidity from its possible function as a signal of the future profitability of R&D investment [Elliot (1971)]. Others question whether cash flow encourages R&D or whether it simply reflects the profitability of past R&D [Branch (1974)].[15]

The other widely studied corporate attribute is diversification. The influence of product diversification upon basic research spending was first suggested by Nelson (1959), who argued that, because the results of basic research are inherently unpredictable, the diversified firm possesses more opportunities for the internal use of new knowledge. This argument implicitly assumes what Arrow (1962) later enunciated clearly: the market for information is imperfect and appropriability is better achieved by the internal application of knowledge than by its sale.

The most frequently tested variant of the Nelson hypothesis is that a higher degree of diversification encourages R&D expenditures. Scherer (1965a) found that an index of diversification was highly significant and explained considerable variance when introduced into simple cross-section regressions of patents and R&D intensity on firm size. The effect of diversification, however, was barely discernible in separate regressions at the two-digit industry level, which suggests

[14] We focus here on work done by economists concerning traditional economic attributes of firms. There are extensive literatures concerned with the effects on innovative performance of numerous organizational, managerial, sociological, and social psychological attributes of firms. A notable study that assessed the firm characteristics favorable to innovations was the SAPPHO project. In a detailed study of 43 matched pairs of successful and unsuccessful innovations, Rothwell et al. (1974) found that the most important determinants of success were: (1) close attention to user needs, (2) effective marketing (3) efficient management of the development process, (4) ability to utilize outside technology and communicate with the external scientific community in areas specifically relevant to the innovation, and (5) project management in the hands of a relatively senior individual who could serve effectively as a "product champion" within the organization. Rothwell et al. found that measures of firm size did not distinguish successful from unsuccessful innovations. Additional discussion of the SAPPHO project and related research on innovation is found in Freeman (1982).

[15] There is reasonably robust evidence, from case studies [Mansfield et al. (1971)] and from econometric work [Ravenscraft and Scherer (1982)], that the mean lag in returns from R&D expenditure is on the order of four to six years.

that Scherer's diversification measure may have reflected the influence of omitted two-digit industry effects in the full cross-section.

Subsequent results have been mixed. For example, Grabowski (1968) found that diversification encouraged R&D spending in chemicals and drugs, but not in petroleum; McEachern and Romeo (1978) got precisely the opposite results. More recently, Scott and Pascoe (1987) examined the hypothesis that R&D expenditures depend on the particular pattern of a firm's diversification. They found that when a firm diversifies into technologically-related industries, its pattern of R&D expenditures differs from the case where diversification is not so "purposive". In particular, such a firm tends to allocate a large share of R&D to industries in which appropriability is high. MacDonald (1985) looked at the reverse direction of causation, attempting to explain a firm's direction of diversification as a consequence of accumulated intangible R&D capital in its primary industry.[16]

The absence of robust findings concerning the roles of diversification and cash flow is unsurprising, since this research is beset with many of the problems discussed in connection with studies of the influence of firm size. For example, with the exception of Doi (1985), little attention has been paid to the influence of industry-level variables. Also, measurement problems are pervasive. Accounting measures of cash flow are deceptive to the extent that R&D and other investments in intangible capital are expensed and not capitalized [Grabowski and Mueller (1978)], and diversification is often represented by crude measures, such as the number of industries in which the firm participates.

Most of the literature considered thus far focuses on attributes that are hypothesized to make an individual firm most innovative – size, liquidity, and diversification. In a remarkable collection of case histories of 61 innovations, Jewkes, Sawers and Stillerman (1958; 2nd edn. 1969) illustrated that the innovative process within industries is considerably more complex than this focus implies. They argued that innovation is realized through the interactions of firms that are distinguished by size, expertise, and other attributes. For example, large firms tend to buy out small ones to bring an innovation to market, and they often enter into contracts with small firms or independent inventors to acquire critical skills or knowledge. In a view subsequently echoed by Nelson, Peck and Kalachek (1967), Scherer (1980) and Dorfman (1987), Jewkes, Sawers and Stillerman suggested that, "It may well be that there is no optimum size of firm but merely an optimal pattern for any industry, such a distribution of firms by

[16]Among the other corporate characteristics that might influence innovative activity is a firm's degree of vertical integration. Little quantitative work has been done in this area, but some case studies suggest the presence of economies of scope to R&D in vertically-related industries. For example, Malerba's (1985) work on the semiconductor industry suggests that the advantages of vertical integration for innovative activity have varied over the life cycle of the technology.

size, character and outlook as to guarantee the most effective gathering together and commercially perfecting of the flow of new ideas" (1969, p. 168). This conjecture provides a subtle view of the innovative process that undermines the quest to identify any single type of firm that is most innovative.

The conjecture of Jewkes, Sawers and Stillerman should be interpreted as an invitation to pursue the inquiry begun by Nelson (1986, 1989) to explore the complementarities and relationships among firms and other institutions (e.g. universities, technical societies, government) that facilitate successful innovation. We need to consider the circumstances under which a division of labor between the institutions generating new knowledge and the firms engaged in its commercialization occurs and is efficient. We also need to consider the circumstances under which the generation of new knowledge requires the cooperation of firms within an industry or the cooperation of firms with their customers or suppliers. Some theoretical work has considered the first of these issues in the context of licensing [e.g. Katz and Shapiro (1985a), Shepard (1987), Farrell and Gallini (1988)] and the second of these issues in the context of cooperative R&D [e.g. Katz (1986)]. Economists have, however, contributed little empirical research on these subjects, although there has been some econometric work on licensing [Wilson (1977), Caves et al. (1983)] and cooperative R&D [Link and Bauer (1987, 1988)], as well as descriptive studies of cooperative R&D [Johnson (1973), Peck (1986), Mowery (1988)] and the role of users and suppliers in innovation [e.g. von Hippel (1988)].

To enrich further the vision of Jewkes, Sawers and Stillerman, it would be useful to know how the distribution of firms types and relationships varies with industry conditions, such as appropriability and technological opportunity. No research has yet addressed this daunting agenda of considering the effects of various combinations of firm, contractual, and industry characteristics on innovative acivity and performance.

3.2. *Monopoly and innovation*

In Schumpeter's discussion of the effects of market power on innovation, there are two distinct themes. First, Schumpeter recognized that firms required the expectation of some form of transient market power to have the incentive to invest in R&D. This is, of course, the principle underlying patent law; it associates the incentive to invent with the expectation of ex post market power. Second, Schumpeter argued that an ex ante oligopolistic market structure and the possession of ex ante market power also favored innovation. An oligopolistic market structure made rival behavior more stable and predictable, he claimed, and thereby reduced the uncertainty associated with excessive rivalry that tended to undermine the incentive to invent. He also suggested, implicitly assuming that capital markets are imperfect, that the profits derived from the possession of ex ante market power provided firms with the internal financial resources necessary to invest in innovative activity.

The empirical literature has focused principally on the effects of concentration on innovative behavior. The literature has thus directly tested Schumpeter's conjectures about the effects of ex ante market structure and only indirectly tested his claims about ex ante market power. In the empirical work that explores the effects of expected ex post market power on innovation, most of it quite recent, traditional measures of market structure have not usually been employed. Rather, the potential for achieving ex post market power through innovation has been characterized under the general heading of appropriability conditions and measured by specific indicators of appropriability, which are discussed in the next section.

Economists have offered an array of theoretical arguments yielding ambiguous predictions about the effects of market structure on innovation. Some have supported Schumpeter's position that firms in concentrated markets can more easily appropriate the returns from inventive activity. Others have demonstrated, under the assumption of perfect ex post appropriability, that a firm's gains from innovation at the margin are larger in an industry that is competitive ex ante than under monopoly conditions [Fellner (1951), Arrow (1962)]. Still others have argued that insulation from competitive pressures breeds bureaucratic inertia and discourages innovation [e.g. Scherer (1980)].

The majority of studies that examine the relationship between market concentration and R&D have found a positive relationship [first among many were Horowitz (1962), Hamberg (1964), Scherer (1967a), and Mansfield (1968)]. A few have found evidence that concentration has a negative effect on R&D [e.g. Williamson (1965), Bozeman and Link (1983), and Mukhopadhyay (1985)]. A finding that captured the imagination of numerous theorists was that of Scherer (1967a), who found evidence of a non-linear, "inverted-U" relationship between R&D intensity and concentration. Scherer found, using data from the Census of Population, that R&D employment as a share of total employment increased with industry concentration up to a four-firm concentration ratio between 50 and 55 percent, and it declined with concentration thereafter. This "inverted-U" result, in the context of a simple regression of R&D intensity against market concentration and a quadratic term, has been replicated by other scholars using the FTC Line of Business data [Scott (1984), and Levin et al. (1985)].

Phillips (1966) was among the first to propose that industrial organization economists should explore the possibility that causality might run from innovation to market structure, rather than in the reverse direction. Although Schumpeter envisioned that the market power accruing from successful innovation would be transitory, eroding as competitors entered the field, Phillips argued that, to the extent that "success breeds success", concentrated industrial structure would tend to emerge as a consequence of past innovation. Phillips' (1971) monograph on the manufacture of civilian aircraft provides a brilliant illustration of how market structure can evolve as a consequence of innovation, as well as how it can affect the conditions for subsequent innovation.

Theoretical support for the proposition that a rapid rate of innovation leads to concentration can be found in the literature on stochastic models of firm growth, notably in the simulation models of Nelson and Winter (1978, 1982b). Most analytic results concerning this and related propositions, however, are asymptotic [see Rothblum and Winter (1985)]. By contrast, in the short run, the presence of long-lived capital and costly adjustment by firms and consumers implies that innovation, even dramatic innovation, can make a market more or less concentrated, a proposition for which Mansfield (1983) finds empirical support. The short-run effect of innovation on market structure depends, in part, on whether established leaders or new entrants are the source of innovation.[17]

Recognizing the potential simultaneity between innovation and concentration, some investigators [Howe and McFetridge (1976), Levin et al. (1985)] have used instrumental variables for concentration in regression studies of the effects of market structure on innovative activity. Others [Farber (1981), Levin (1981), Wahlroos and Backstrom (1982), Connolly and Hirschey (1984), Levin and Reiss (1984, 1988)] have used industry-level data to estimate multi-equation models in which concentration and R&D are both treated as endogenous.[18] There is a suggestion that such techniques are appropriate. Levin (1981), Connolly and Hirschey (1984), Levin and Reiss (1984), and Levin et al. (1985) all find that Wu–Hausman tests reject the hypothesis (maintained in the OLS specification) that the concentration variables are orthogonal to the error term. This result, however, may well arise from misspecification or omitted variables. In any event, Howe and McFetridge (1976) found that, relative to ordinary least squares, two-stage least squares produced little change in the coefficient on the concentration term in the R&D equation.

Perhaps the most persistent finding concerning the effect of concentration on R&D intensity is that it depends upon other industry-level variables. Scherer (1967a) found that the statistical significance of concentration was attenuated

[17]Innovation can also affect market structure by increasing or decreasing the efficient scale of production. If technological change causes the efficient scale of a firm to grow more rapidly than demand, concentration tends to increase over time. For a theoretical treatment in which such changes in scale and concentration are both endogenous, see Levin (1978). For evidence that technical change has increased efficient scale in various industries, see Hughes (1971) on electric power generation, Levin (1977) on several chemical industries, and Scherer et al. (1975) on steel, cement, brewing, refrigerators, paints, and batteries.

[18]Data limitations have made it convenient to treat concentration and R&D intensity as *simultaneously* determined variables, but this is inconsistent with the underlying Schumpeterian theory, as interpreted by Phillips (1966, 1971). Contemporaneous concentration, in this view, should indeed influence R&D spending, but current concentration is the consequence of past innovative activity. Only Levin (1981) estimates a model in this form, where a distributed lag of past R&D investment, not the current R&D intensity, appears on the right-hand side of the concentration equation.

with the addition of dummy variables classifying the industry's technology (chemical, electrical, mechanical, and traditional) and its products (durable/non-durable, consumer/producer goods). The dummy variables, especially those representing technology classes, were highly significant, and they explained considerably more variance in the dependent variables than did concentration. Wilson (1977) attained similar results, and Lunn and Martin (1986), splitting their sample into two technology classes, found that concentration had a significant effect on R&D intensity only in "low opportunity" industries.

Among others who have found the validity of the Schumpeterian hypothesis to depend on industry characteristics, Comanor (1967) found that the degree of product differentiation conditioned the relationship between concentration and R&D intensity, but he used advertising intensity, a jointly determined decision variable, to represent what should more properly have been represented by a set of predetermined product characteristics. Somewhat more defensibly, Shrieves (1978) obtained a similar result by classifying industries according to the nature of the final product market.[19] Angelmar (1985) suggested that the effect of concentration on innovation might depend on the degree of technological uncertainty, but the appropriateness of his measure of uncertainty – the average lag between initiating the development of a new product and its market introduction – is subject to serious doubt. Mueller and Tilton (1969) offered some evidence that the role of market structure depends importantly upon the industry's stage in the technology life cycle.

Scott (1984) and Levin et al. (1985) provide strong evidence that results concerning the effect of concentration on innovation are sensitive to industry conditions. Using the FTC data on R&D intensity at the business unit level, Scott found that the addition of fixed company and two-digit industry effects rendered statistically insignificant the coefficients on concentration and its square. Using the FTC data at the line of business level (a level of aggregation between the three- and four-digit SIC level), Levin et al. found that the addition of a set of measures representing technological opportunity and appropriability conditions (at the line of business level) replicated Scott's result in equations for both R&D intensity and innovative performance. With the new variables added, the coefficient and the *t*-statistic on concentration dropped by an order of magnitude in the R&D equation.[20]

Moreover, concentration contributes little to an explanation of the variance in R&D intensity. Scott found that line of business concentration and its square explained only 1.5 percent of the variance in R&D intensity across 3388 business units, whereas fixed two-digit industry effects explained 32 percent of this

[19]Shrieves classified industries on the basis of a factor analysis that took account of the composition of industry demand and the durability of the product.

[20]Geroski (1987) obtained a similar result using the SPRU data on British innovations and controlling for various industry conditions.

variance. Similarly, our re-examination of the data used in Levin et. al. (1985) revealed that concentration and its square explained only 4 percent of the variance in R&D intensity across 127 lines of business, whereas Cohen et al. (1987) reported that demand, opportunity, and appropriability measures explained roughly half of the between-industry variance. Together, these results leave little support for the view that industrial concentration is an independent, significant, and important determinant of innovative behavior and performance.

The conclusion that market concentration may exercise no independent effect on R&D intensity suggests that there may be no Schumpeterian tradeoff between innovation and the ex ante market power conferred by concentration. Recall, however, that Schumpeter also argued that the expectation of ex post market power acquired by successful innovation provides an important incentive to undertake inventive activity. Indirect evidence that this latter tradeoff exists can be provided by a demonstration that the ability of the firms to appropriate the returns from innovation encourages R&D investment. Recent work using the Levin et al. (1987) survey data [e.g. Levin et al. (1985), Cohen et al. (1987)] has begun to generate such evidence.

3.3. Evaluation of empirical research in the Schumpeterian tradition

The empirical results concerning how firm size and market structure relate to innovation are perhaps most accurately described as fragile. The failure to obtain robust results seems to arise, at least in part, from the literature's inadequate attention to the dependence of these relationships on more fundamental conditions. This overview highlights the basic methodological lesson that the omission of important and potentially correlated variables that influence the dependent variable – in this case, some measure of innovative activity or performance – can lead to misleading inferences concerning the effects of explanatory variables of particular interest – in this case, firm size and concentration. A clear implication is that further evaluation of the Schumpeterian hypotheses should take place within the context of a more complete model of the determination of technological progress.

Obtaining a better understanding of the Schumpeterian hypotheses is only one reason to move toward more complete models of technological change. There are other good reasons to move the profession's agenda beyond the Schumpeterian hypotheses and to focus attention on more fundamental determinants of technological progress. First, the effects of firm size and concentration on innovation, if they exist at all, do not appear to be important. Second, the welfare gains associated with technological progress are likely to be large relative to the efficiency losses associated with imperfect market structure.[21] Third, we have, at present, only a limited understanding of the primary economic forces driving innovation and how they differ across industries.

We thus proceed to consider the present state of empirical research on those fundamental determinants of innovation that appear to vary substantially across industries.

4. Industry characteristics

In seeking to understand why industries differ in the degree to which they engage in innovative activity, empirical researchers have come to classify explanatory variables under three headings: product market demand, technological opportunity, and appropriability conditions. Although the importance of each of these classes of variables has been acknowledged and illustrated in the historical literature and in case studies, economists have made relatively little progress in specifying and quantifying their influence. As we have suggested, one reason for this relative neglect has been the profession's preoccupation with the effects of firm size and market structure. Another reason is the absence of a clear and precise understanding of how the forces classified under the headings of technological opportunity and appropriability should be conceptualized and given operational definitions. Finally, even where a particular variable is well defined and a clear hypothesis is formulated regarding its influence, the data necessary for empirical work are often unavailable or unreliable.[22]

In the subsections that follow, we summarize and interpret what is known about how demand, technological opportunity, and appropriability conditions vary across industries and how they contribute to an explanation of interindustry differences in innovative activity and performance. We also offer suggestions to guide further exploration of this still relatively uncharted terrain.

[21] For example, suppose an economy could eliminate all dead weight loss and experience a 2 percent growth rate of productivity or it could tolerate a 10 percent dead weight loss and experience a 3 percent growth rate of productivity. It can be shown that, for any real social discount rate below 12 percent, total welfare over an infinite horizon would be greater under the more dynamically efficient regime. If the dead weight loss were only 5 percent, the higher growth rate would be preferred for all social discount rates under 22 percent.

[22] For example, a straightforward implication of many models is that interindustry differences in R&D investment can be explained in part by the parameters of industry demand functions. The researcher who hopes to estimate such a model, however, must choose between two unpleasant alternatives: locating data of suitable quality to identify and estimate demand functions for each industry in the sample or extracting from the literature a set of previously estimated parameters that are likely to be internally inconsistent or unreliable.

4.1. Demand

In his seminal work on technological change in various capital goods industries, Schmookler (1962, 1966) demonstrated that cycles in the output of capital goods and in capital expenditures by downstream industries "led" cycles in the time series on relevant capital goods patents. He argued from these findings that demand, rather than the state of technological and scientific knowledge, determined the rate and direction of inventive activity. Schmookler's contribution sparked a lively debate among economic historians and other economists concerning whether "demand-pull" or "technology-push" was the primary force behind technological change. In the terminology that has since come into use in industrial organization, the debate was about the relative importance of demand and technological opportunity.[23]

In arguing for the primacy of demand, Schmookler claimed that scientific knowledge and technological capability were applicable to a wide range of industrial purposes. Although he recognized that generic knowledge and capability tend to grow, he argued that at any point in time a common pool was uniformly available for industrial application. The industries that made use of this common resource, that made their own complementary investments in applied research and in process and product development, were those induced to do so by large and growing markets. Though he presented an impressive array of data to support the view that demand matters, Schmookler never attempted to test the maintained hypothesis that the supply conditions for innovation (technological opportunities) were uniform across industries.

Schmookler's proposition that demand almost alone determines the rate and direction of technical change has not survived empirical scrutiny. The consensus, after dozens of case studies, is that the Marshallian scissors cuts with two blades. Perhaps the most persuasive refutation of Schmookler's proposition is offered by Parker (1972) and Rosenberg (1974), who document several important historical examples (e.g. the mechanization of hand operations in agriculture, the use of coal as an industrial fuel) in which the sequence of particular applications of a "generic" technological idea was determined not by demand, but by the state of knowledge and inherent technological complexity of particular industrial applications. More recently, Scherer (1982c) offered statistical evidence that both blades matter. He found that dummy variables classifying industries by technology (chemical, electrical, mechanical, etc.) and variables representing demand conditions were statistically significant in a regression analysis of line of business patenting activity, but the technology variables explained considerably more variance.

[23]The early debate has been thoroughly reviewed by Mowery and Rosenberg (1979) and does not require detailed attention here.

A particularly interesting perspective on the demand-pull/technology-push debate is offered by Walsh (1984), who combined the case study approach with the time series methods of Schmookler. Walsh found that in several chemical industries the production series does indeed lead the patent series, but growth in production tends to follow not large numbers of patents, but one or several major innovations. An interpretation of this pattern is that relatively exogenous major innovation induces growth in demand, which in turn creates the incentive for subsequent incremental innovation.

The suggestion that major technological innovations may induce changes in demand, obvious as it may seem to the historian, gives pause to the economist, who typically models tastes as given and immutable. No reasonable economist believes that tastes never change. When we claim that demand, technological opportunity, and appropriability are "more fundamental" than firm size or market concentration in determining interindustry differences in the rate and direction of technological change, we are not asserting that the former conditions are strictly exogenous and the latter endogenous. We are simply suggesting that the demand, technological opportunity, and appropriability conditions confronting an industry tend to change more slowly than firm size and market structure, and, therefore, these conditions are reasonably taken as given for purposes of analyzing interindustry differences in innovative activity and the evolution of market structure.

There are two principal respects in which interindustry differences in demand conditions might be expected to affect the incentives to engage in innovative activity. First, as Schmookler himself emphasized, there is the size of the market, which might be represented in static terms by a scale parameter and in dynamic terms by a rate of growth. The argument is straightforward. The (expected) investment required to produce a given reduction in unit cost or a given improvement in product quality is independent of the level of output that will be produced once the innovation is made. The benefits realized by such investment, however, are proportional to the size of the market in which the innovation is used. More inventive activity would therefore be expected in the larger of two markets, holding constant the cost of innovation; in two markets of equal size, more inventive activity would be expected in the market that is expected to grow more rapidly.

Second, Kamien and Schwartz (1970) suggested that the price elasticity of demand will also affect the marginal returns to investment in R&D. They demonstrated that the gains from reducing the cost of production (process innovation) are larger the more elastic is demand. On the other hand, Spence (1975) demonstrates that the gains from improvement in product quality (product innovation) will, under many circumstances, be larger the more inelastic is demand, since inelastic demand tends to magnify the gains from a rightward shift in the demand curve. Thus, the effect of price elasticity will be ambiguous in empirical studies that do not distinguish between process and product innovation.

The distinction between process and product innovation raises the subtle conceptual and operational question of how to characterize the demand conditions relevant to product innovation. In the case of intermediate products, such as those studied by Schmookler, there is no mystery. The demand function for inputs of higher quality can in principle be derived from estimates of final product demand and the downstream production technology. It is more difficult to characterize and estimate the demand for consumer product innovation. A variety of econometric techniques can be used to estimate the demand for routine improvements in some measurable dimension of product quality (e.g. hedonic price models, Lancasterian demand models, and discrete choice models, where applicable). Such techniques, though useful in particular applications, are unlikely to be fruitful in cross-industry analysis, since they require very detailed data and special modelling efforts for each specific product.[24] A vastly more difficult problem is posed by major innovations that introduce an entirely new product (e.g. the television, the automobile). In such cases, there is no straightforward way to characterize latent demand from data on existing products, particularly if one acknowledges that tastes themselves may change as a consequence of a major innovation.

In regression studies of R&D investment, demand conditions, although rarely featured, have often been considered. To capture market size and growth effects, sales and the rate of growth of sales are typically used, despite the obvious problem that these variables measure not demand conditions, but the endogenous interaction of demand and supply conditions. A variety of categorical variables have been used, presumably as proxies for interindustry differences in price elasticity. Most common are those distinguishing durables from non-durables, as well as those distinguishing consumer goods from material inputs or investment goods. Some researchers have used input–output data on the disposition of industry output (i.e. the shares of output destined for personal consumption, intermediate use, exports, the government sector, etc.). Although these categorical and input–output variables are sometimes statistically significant in regressions explaining a measure of innovative activity, there are no notably robust findings.

In an attempt to develop demand measures that conform more closely to the requirements of theory, Levin (1981) calculated, from a set of estimated constant elasticity demand functions for consumer goods and the input–output table,

[24]Economists have used such techniques in a variety of applications, notably in predicting demand for new transport alternatives, a problem for which discrete choice models are particularly well suited. Economists have done little, however, to estimate the demand for new consumer products, though a variety of techniques, using both market and consumer survey data, have been employed by scholars in the fields of marketing [e.g. Keeney and Lilien (1987)] and technological forecasting [e.g. Alexander and Mitchell (1985)].

three demand parameters for each four-digit industry: a price elasticity, an income elasticity, and an exponential shift parameter. Although these parameters were significant as explanatory variables in simple regressions of R&D intensity on size and other industry characteristics [Cohen et al. (1987)], their contamination with measurement error may have hampered their usefulness in the estimation of more complex specifications [Levin and Reiss (1984, 1988)].[25]

4.2. Technological opportunity

Much of the empirical literature takes for granted that innovation, at prevailing input prices, is "easier" (less costly) in some industries than in others. Although it is widely accepted that industries differ in the opportunities they face for technical advance, there is no consensus on how to make the concept of technological opportunity precise and empirically operational. In the framework of the standard neo-classical theory of production, technological opportunity can be regarded as the set of production possibilities for translating research resources into new techniques of production that employ conventional inputs. Some theoretical treatments have thus represented technological opportunity as one or more parameters in a production function relating research resources to increments in the stock of knowledge, with the stock of knowledge entering in turn as an argument, along with conventional inputs, in the production function for output [Griliches (1979), Pakes and Schankerman (1984)]. Related approaches treat technological opportunity as the elasticity of unit cost with respect to R&D spending [Dasgupta and Stiglitz (1980a), Spence (1984)], as a shift parameter determining the location of an innovation possibility frontier representing the tradeoffs in the direction of technical change [Levin (1978)], and as a shift parameter determining the location of a frontier describing the tradeoff between the time and cost of an R&D project [Scherer (1984b)].

These formulations lend themselves in principle to direct econometric estimation, if only adequate data were available to identify the technological opportunity parameter(s) and other relevant parameters for each industry. To date, only Pakes and Schankerman (1984) have attempted this type of structural estimation. The panel data they used did not permit identification of the parameter representing technological opportunity or its contribution to the explanation of variance in R&D intensity. They were, however, able to identify the fraction of

[25] The quality of industry-level price elasticities does not inspire confidence. Mueller (1986) could not reject the hypothesis that Levin's price elasticities were uncorrelated with another set of estimates provided by Ornstein and Intriligator.

variance explained jointly by opportunity and appropriability, which they found to be substantial.

Most other attempts to represent technological opportunity as a determinant of innovative activity in regression studies have followed the practice introduced by Scherer (1965a), who classified industries on the basis of the scientific or technological field with which each was most closely associated. Scherer's initial classificatory scheme (chemical, electrical, mechanical) was refined in his subsequent work (1967a, 1982c), and variants have been used by numerous investigators.[26] Although Scherer's intention was to capture interindustry differences in the vigor of advance of underlying scientific and technological knowledge, he recognized that statistical results obtained with the use of such crudely defined categorical variables might also reflect the influence of unspecified industry practices or demand effects not captured by other regressors. Nonetheless, the simple classification of industries into a small number of technology groups has powerful statistical consequences; it has explained a substantial fraction of variance in patenting activity [Scherer (1965a, 1982c)] and R&D intensity [Scott (1984)].

Several investigators have used proxy variables thought to be associated with technological opportunity to explain innovative activity. Shrieves (1978) performed factor analysis on the distribution of scientific and technological employees by field across 411 firms to develop several technology factors; these constructed variables fared poorly in a regression analysis of R&D expenditures. Jaffe (1986) used data on the distribution of patents across patent classes to assign firms to twenty "technological opportunity clusters". The vector of cluster dummies was statistically significant in regressions to explain interfirm differences in patents, profits, and Tobin's q. Jaffe found, however, that conventional industry dummy variables performed equally well.[27]

In the optimization model of Levin and Reiss (1984), specific parameters of the cost function were interpreted as unobservable measures of technological opportunity and appropriability conditions. Each parameter was then formally treated as a function of observable variables. To represent technological opportunity, Levin and Reiss augmented a set of technology class dummy variables with measures of industry age (intended to capture the effects of technological life cycles), the fraction of R&D devoted to basic research (intended to capture an industry's "closeness" to science), and government R&D (intended to capture

[26]Some scholars have attempted to represent technological opportunity by assigning industries to "high" and "low" technological opportunity groups [Wilson (1977), Link and Long (1981), Lunn and Martin (1986)]. This practice introduces considerable risk of selecting on the dependent variable.

[27]Waterson and Lopez (1983) attempted to explain interindustry differences in R&D intensity in the United Kingdom with two variables claimed to be closely related to technological opportunity: capital intensity and the contemporaneous rate of labor productivity growth. The justification for an association of opportunity with capital intensity is questionable, and it seems inappropriate to treat productivity growth as exogenous.

externally generated opportunities for privately-funded R&D). Each of these variables was statistically significant in an equation for R&D intensity.

The survey of R&D executives in 130 lines of business discussed by Levin et al. (1987) attempted to measure several variables thought to represent an industry's technological opportunity. Among these are measures of the contribution of various basic and applied sciences to each industry's technological advance and the contribution of several other external sources of technical knowledge – upstream suppliers of the industry's materials, production, and research equipment, downstream users of the industry's product, universities, government agencies and labs, professional and technical societies, and independent inventors. Although these survey variables, constructed from responses along a semantic scale, are contaminated with considerable measurement error, they have performed well in regression studies of innovative activity. Levin et al. (1985), Cohen et al. (1987), and Cohen and Levinthal (1988b) have all found opportunity variables representing closeness to science and the sources of extraindustry knowledge to be jointly significant and to explain a substantial fraction of interindustry variance in R&D intensity.[28] The survey variables performed less well in estimates of the more structured optimization model of Levin and Reiss (1988), reflecting no doubt the shortcomings of the highly stylized model as well as the imprecision of the data.

For a fuller account of the role of technological opportunity, it is useful to consider the rich institutional and historical literature, as well as a few interesting theoretical conjectures. Consider first the role of science. Among economists, Rosenberg (1974) has argued most strongly for a close link between scientific and technological advance. Although he gave a convincing account of why certain technological innovations could not have occurred without certain foundational scientific advances, he did not provide historical examples to support the stronger claim that advances in science lead to technological innovation.

In a case study of the invention of the transistor, Nelson (1962) demonstrated that the contribution of science to invention is by no means simple. He explained, first, that the essential scientific knowledge required and utilized by the inventors of the transistor was in place more than fifteen years before the invention. He also illustrated how scientific knowledge directed and structured the thinking of the Bell Labs' research team at various steps along the way to the

[28] To the extent that the relevance of science and the contribution of extraindustry knowledge sources reflect an industry's technological opportunity, one would expect a positive relationship between these variables and innovative output. Greater opportunity, however, need not imply greater expenditure on R&D. Thus, Levin et al. (1985) found that each measure of opportunity derived from the R&D survey had a positive coefficient in an equation to explain each industry's self-reported rate of innovation. Levin et al. (1985) and Cohen et al. (1987), however, found that an increase in the contribution of its equipment suppliers *reduced* an industry's own R&D intensity, while increased contributions from the users of the industry's product and from government agencies and laboratories increased own R&D intensity.

ultimate discovery. Most remarkably, however, the invention of the device itself preceded and actually triggered the inquiry leading to a full scientific understanding of how it worked.[29]

Rosenberg (1974) also suggested a simple mechanism by which the growth in scientific knowledge encourages innovation; he claimed that "as scientific knowledge grows, the cost of successfully undertaking any given, science-based invention declines..." (p. 107). Conceptualizing R&D as a stochastic search process, Evenson and Kislev (1976) and Nelson (1982a) suggested that "strong" science affects the cost of innovation by increasing the productivity of applied research. Nelson in particular argued that a "strong" science base narrows the set of research options and focuses attention on the most productive approaches. The consequence is that the research process is more efficient. There is less trial-and-error; fewer approaches need to be evaluated and pursued to achieve a given technological end. From this perspective, the contribution of science is that it provides a powerful heuristic to the search process associated with technological change.

The historical and case study literature also illustrate how the development of technology may follow a course that is relatively independent of market influences. At any given time, innovative efforts within an industry, or a complex of related industries, tend to be concentrated on a limited number of distinct, identifiable problems. A breakthrough in one area typically generates new technical problems, creating imbalances that require further innovative effort to realize fully the benefits of the initial breakthrough. Rosenberg (1969) identifies this phenomenon as a "compulsive sequence", citing examples from the history of technology in the machine tool industry. The development of high speed steel, for instance, improved cutting tools and thus stimulated the development of sturdier, more adaptable machines to drive them. Similar "bottleneck-breakthrough" sequences have been described in nineteenth-century textile manufacture, iron and steel, and coal and steam technology [Landes (1969)], in twentieth-century petroleum refining [Enos (1962)], and in other technologies [Ayres (1988)].

A related phenomenon is the tendency for technologies to develop along "natural trajectories".[30] The notion is that in certain instances technological development proceeds along a relatively clear path, as if moving toward some physical limit. Engineers do not move myopically from one bottleneck to the next; they repeatedly focus on a particular class of engineering problems, drawing upon and strengthening a familiar method of solution. A good example of a natural trajectory is the progressive extension of the range of output over which scale economies are attainable, which has been documented for electric

[29]Rosenberg (1982) elaborated the point that technological developments may stimulate and focus basic scientific research.

[30]The term is attributable to Nelson and Winter (1977); the idea has been further developed by Sahal (1981) and Dosi (1982).

power by Hughes (1971) and for several chemical industries by Levin (1977). For a period that lasted approximately twenty-five years in both cases, engineers understood that lower production costs were possible if they could solve the design problems associated with building bigger plants. Another example is the progressive miniaturization of semiconductor devices [Braun and Macdonald (1982), Levin (1982)]. In this instance, engineers have understood for more than three decades that a tighter packing of circuit elements would lead to higher speeds for performing logical or data storage operations, but a host of related technological problems – such as obtaining sufficiently pure materials and etching ever-finer lines in silicon – have required solution with each successive generation of devices.

Although the case study literature provides many examples, we know very little about the degree to which phenomena such as natural trajectories, compulsive sequences, and other "patterns" are representative of the manufacturing sector as a whole.[31] The presence of such identifiable "technological regimes" in at least some industries, however, suggests two potentially fruitful and complementary directions for empirical research. First, in such industries, the participants in the R&D process probably have a relatively clear idea about how to characterize technological opportunities and the constraints on technical advance. Thus, interview and questionnaire methods may be a particularly appropriate way to gather useful data. Second, where a particular natural trajectory or other technological regime is present, careful modelling on an industry-specific basis may permit identification and estimation of the technological opportunity parameters that have proven elusive in cross-industry econometric work. Indeed, within the context of particular, well-characterized technological regimes, questions concerning the optimal size of firms and the market organization most conducive to innovation might be re-examined.

Just as Nelson (1982a) argued that a strong science base narrows the set of approaches that a researcher must seriously evaluate to achieve a given techno-

[31]Another pattern, widely discussed in the institutional literature, is the idea that industries experience a life cycle over which the nature of innovation changes in a predictable manner [Abernathy and Utterback (1978) and Utterback (1979)]. In the early years of an industry's evolution, the emphasis is on product innovation, as numerous small firms compete to establish a market position. Radical new product ideas are tested, and eventually a "dominant design" emerges. With the dominant design comes product standardization and a new emphasis on process innovation. In this phase "natural trajectories" associated with process innovation are pursued; effort is concentrated on realizing the benefits of large-scale production, mechanization, improving production yields, etc. The industry becomes more concentrated, the potential for further process innovation is eventually exhausted, and the industry becomes subject to external threats from competing products that eschew the dominant design.

The life cycle model provides a coherent interpretation of the history of the U.S. automobile industry [Abernathy (1978)], but its generality may be limited. For example, the model fits the experience of some segments of the worldwide semiconductor industry (memory devices) but not the experience of others (logic devices and microprocessors).

logical objective, it might be argued that working within a particular technological regime narrows the set of objectives to be pursued, and hence the range of specific technological problems to be investigated. Linkages to science and natural trajectories can thus both be understood as ways of coping with, and reducing, the enormous uncertainty inherent in the complex decision problem of formulating an optimal R&D strategy.

Powerful heuristics are less readily available to guide firms at those historical moments when they face a choice among technological regimes. Such moments occur with some regularity, and they can have important consequences. In the transitions from steam to diesel locomotives, from propeller to jet aircraft engines, and from vacuum tubes to transistors, leading firms changed regimes too late or with too little commitment. In the spirit of creative destruction, established market structures were entirely overturned in each of these cases. Although economists have neither analyzed nor quantified the consequences of choosing among regimes when more than one is available (e.g. steam, electric, or gasoline engines for automobiles), they have considered the related issue of the impact of technical standards that permit the realization of external economies (e.g. a railroad gauge, a color television standard, a programming language). David (1985) has provided a fascinating account of how the QWERTY typewriter keyboard became "locked-in" despite the presence of a demonstrably superior alternative. Arthur (1985) has offered other examples and a theoretical explanation of why, in such cases, the hidden hand does not necessarily work its magic.[32]

Just as a close link to science and the availability of engineering heuristics affect an industry's technological opportunity, so does the contribution of technical knowledge from sources external to the industry: suppliers, customers, universities, technical societies, government, and independent inventors. A voluminous institutional literature documents the contribution of extraindustry spillovers to technological progress.[33] The case studies of Jewkes, Sawers and Stillerman (1958) contain instances of virtually every type of external influence. A notable example of institutional-empirical work on this subject is von Hippel's (1976, 1977, 1988) treatment of the contributions of users to technological development in a variety of industries, including scientific instruments and semiconductor process equipment. The contribution of universities to technological progress in industry, particularly in collaborative research ventures, has been the subject of numerous recent reports [e.g. Blumenthal et al. (1986)].

[32]Among others, Farrell and Saloner (1985, 1986) and Katz and Shapiro (1985b, 1986) have developed theoretical models in which the choice of a Pareto-inferior standard is possible. With appropriate modification, some of these models could be adapted to consider the selection of technological regimes.

[33]To cite just a few examples, Brock (1975) indicates that most of the computer industry's innovations could be traced to technological developments outside the industry. Peck (1962) makes the same point in his study of innovation in the aluminum industry.

By far the most extensively studied extraindustry influence on technological opportunity has been that of government. In numerous sectors – notably agriculture, aircraft, and electronics – government has contributed to reducing the cost of innovation by its own research, by subsidizing and sponsoring private sector research, and by disseminating or subsidizing the dissemination of technological knowledge developed in its own labs and elsewhere.[34] The distribution of government expenditures on R&D across industries is highly skewed, especially in the United States, where industries supplying the military are the principal recipients of R&D support.[35]

Although the government's influence on innovation through its direct role in the creation and dissemination of knowledge is substantial in some sectors, its indirect influence is also felt through a variety of other channels that have a differential impact across industries. Most important is the impact of government demand on the rate and direction of innovation.[36] Regulation has had an important impact on innovation in several industries by altering demand conditions, constraining legally permissible choices from the set of technological opportunities, and limiting appropriability.[37]

Just as spillovers from extraindustry sources may augment a recipient firm's technological opportunity, so may spillovers within an industry reduce the own R&D required to achieve a given level of technical performance. Within-industry spillovers, however, also reduce the incentive to engage in R&D, because a firm must share with its competitors the benefits of its investment. We defer further discussion of this incentive effect to the next subsection and focus here on what Spence (1984) calls the "efficiency effect" of spillovers – the extent to which they enhance technological opportunity.

There have been several recent econometric attempts to measure the efficiency effects of both extraindustry and intraindustry spillovers. Pursuing a method suggested by Griliches (1979), Jaffe (1986) used data on the distribution of patents by patent class to measure the technological relatedness of every pair of firms in a sample of over 500 firms. For each firm, he constructed a "spillover pool", defined as the sum of all other firms' R&D weighted by the measure of

[34] A good introduction to the role of government in the United States may be found in the collection of case studies edited and summarized by Nelson (1982b). For a survey of international differences in the contribution of government to technological development in the major OECD countries, see Nelson (1984). A modest econometric literature finds that government R&D and, particularly, government procurement expenditures have a significant impact on private R&D spending [Levy and Terleckyj (1983), Levin and Reiss (1984), Lichtenberg (1987, 1988)].

[35] Aircraft and missiles (SIC 372 and 376) received over 50 percent of the U.S. Federal government's total expenditures on industrial R&D in 1985. Electrical equipment (SIC 36) received over 25 percent [see National Science Board (1987)].

[36] See the case studies of semiconductors, computers, and aircraft in the Nelson (1982b) volume.

[37] See, for example, Temin (1979) and Grabowski and Vernon (1982) on pharmaceuticals, and Caves (1962) on civilian aircraft.

relatedness. He found that the size of the spillover pool had a powerful positive effect on a firm's patents.[38]

Bernstein and Nadiri (1988, 1989) took a more direct approach to estimating the magnitude of spillover effects, by including the R&D capital of other firms or industries in the cost function of the receiving firm or industry. They found evidence of large efficiency gains from both intraindustry and extraindustry spillovers.[39]

Most of the recent work on spillovers has presumed that knowledge acquired from both intraindustry and extraindustry sources is costless. In contrast, Evenson and Kislev (1973) and Mowery (1983a) observed that firms that invest in their own R&D are more capable of exploiting externally-generated knowledge. Extending this observation to a consideration of the incentives to engage in R&D, Cohen and Levinthal (1989b) formulated and tested a model in which firms deliberately invest in R&D with two purposes: to generate new knowledge and to develop "absorptive capacity" – the ability to recognize, assimilate, and exploit outside knowledge. In this model, to the extent that R&D is directed to the latter purpose, variables affecting the ease of learning influence R&D incentives. Using the FTC's Line of Business data and the Levin et al. (1987) survey data, they found evidence suggesting that one such variable – the degree to which outside knowledge is targeted to concerns of the firm – influences R&D spending. Their findings suggest that spillovers from input suppliers can be absorbed with less R&D effort than spillovers from government and university labs.

4.3. *Appropriability conditions*

To the extent that new knowledge is transmitted at relatively low cost from its creator to prospective competitors and particularly to the extent that such knowledge is embodied in new processes and products that may be copied or imitated at relatively low cost, appropriable rewards may be insufficient to justify innovative effort. Recognition of this problem of appropriability predates classical, let alone neo-classical, economics. Indeed, the notion that monopoly privileges were required to provide adequate economic incentives for inventive activity motivated the Statute of Monopolies, passed by the English Parliament in 1623

[38]Using survey data, Levin (1988) also found that measures of the extent of intraindustry spillovers had a positive and significant effect on an industry's self-reported rate of innovation, but no effect on R&D intensity.

[39]Bernstein and Nadiri (1989) found elasticities of average cost with respect to intraindustry spillovers to be approximately -0.1 in machinery and instruments and approximately -0.2 in chemicals and petroleum. Most of their interindustry elasticities (1988) fell in the range of -0.05 to -0.1.

[Penrose (1951)]. Later, the problem was explicitly recognized by the framers of the Constitution of the United States.[40]

In theory, patents provide a solution to the problem of imperfect appropriability; the exclusive right granted by society enhances the incentive to invent by sanctioning restriction of an invention's use. To the would-be inventor, the prospect of a patent represents the expectation of ex post market power that Schumpeter claimed was an essential spur to innovation. In fact, industries differ widely in the extent to which patents are effective. The evidence suggests that patents are regarded as a necessary incentive for innovation in only a few industries. In many industries, however, firms find other means of appropriation to be quite satisfactory. In some instances, imitation is costly despite the absence of strong patent protection. In others, investment in complementary assets such as marketing, sales efforts, and customer service can facilitate appropriation when neither strong patents nor technical barriers to imitation are present. In this subsection, we first review the growing body of evidence on interindustry differences in appropriability conditions. We then proceed to discuss the more limited evidence on how differences in appropriability conditions affect innovative activity and performance.

In an early investigation that revealed substantial interfirm differences in patenting behavior, Scherer et al. (1959) suggested that the value of patent protection might differ across industries. The suggestion was pursued by Taylor and Silberston (1973), who examined the use and effectiveness of patents with a sample of 27 firms in four British industries. They found that 60 percent of pharmaceutical R&D, 15 percent of chemical R&D, 5 percent of mechanical engineering R&D, and a negligible amount of electronics R&D was dependent upon patent protection. Mansfield et al. (1981), using data on 48 product innovations, found that 90 percent of pharmaceutical innovations and about 20 percent of chemical, electronics, and machinery innovations would not have been introduced without patents.

Recent work by Mansfield (1986) has provided more comprehensive evidence on the extent to which the value and effectiveness of patents differs across industries. Mansfield asked a random sample of 100 firms from 12 (mostly two-digit) industries to estimate the proportion of inventions developed in 1981–83 that would not have been developed in the absence of patent protection. Only pharmaceutical and chemical inventions emerged as substantially dependent on patents; 65 percent of pharmaceutical inventions and 30 percent of chemical inventions would not have been introduced without such protection. Patents were judged to be essential for 10–20 percent of commercially-introduced

[40] In empowering Congress to grant "for limited times to authors and inventors the exclusive rights to their respective writings and discoveries", the express purpose of the framers was "to promote the progress of science and useful arts" (Article I, Section 8).

inventions in three industries (petroleum, machinery, and metal products) and for less than 10 percent in the remaining seven industries (electrical equipment, instruments, primary metals, office equipment, motor vehicles, rubber, and textiles). The last four of these industries reported that patent protection was not essential for the introduction of any of their inventions during the period studied.

Mansfield's findings were reinforced by the results of the Levin et al. (1987) survey of firms in 130 more narrowly defined lines of business. As a means of appropriating returns, product patents were regarded as highly effective (scoring six or more on a seven-point semantic scale) in only five industries – including drugs, organic chemicals, and pesticides – and as moderately effective (five to six on the scale) in about 20 other industries, primarily those producing chemical products or relatively uncomplicated mechanical equipment. Only three industries, however, regarded process patents as even moderately effective. The principal reason cited for the limited effectiveness of patents was that competitors can legally "invent around" patents. Some relatively mature industries, concentrated in the food processing and fabricated metal products sectors, cited difficulties in upholding patent claims in the face of legal challenges to their validity.[41] Only a few industries reported that the information disclosed in patent documents was a significant constraint on patent effectiveness.[42]

The Levin et al. survey revealed, however, that firms in many industries tend to regard other mechanisms as quite effective in appropriating the returns from innovation. In contrast to the 4 percent of industries that regarded product patents as highly effective, 80 percent regarded investments in complementary sales and services efforts as highly effective in capturing competitive advantage from their R&D activities.[43] In numerous lines of business outside the chemical and pharmaceutical industries, firms reported that the advantages of a head start

[41] Levin et al. (1987) suggested that the most probable explanation for the robust finding that patents are particularly effective in chemical industries is that comparatively clear standards can be applied to assess a chemical patent's validity and to defend against infringement. The uniqueness of a specific molecule is more easily demonstrated than the novelty of, for example, a new component of a complex electrical or mechanical system. Similarly, it is easy to determine whether an allegedly infringing molecule is physically identical to a patented molecule; it is more difficult to determine whether comparable components of two complex systems, in the language of the patent case law, "do the same work in substantially the same way". To the extent that simple mechanical inventions approximate molecules in their discreteness and easy differentiability, it is understandable that industries producing such machinery ranked just after chemical industries in the perceived effectiveness of patent protection.

[42] It is argued that firms sometimes refrain from patenting process innovations to avoid disclosing either the fact or the details of the innovation. See Horstmann et al. (1985) for a theoretical treatment of the issue.

[43] Teece (1986) has emphasized the importance of investments in "co-specialized assets" for appropriating the returns from R&D, providing details of several specific cases. Flaherty (1983) has noted that exploitation of a technological leadership position in particular segments of the semiconductor industry requires substantial investments in marketing and customer service.

and the ability to move quickly down the learning curve were more effective means of appropriation than patents. Most industries viewed secrecy as more effective than patents in protecting process innovations, with the notable exception of petroleum refining. Only 11 of 130 industries, all drawn from the food processing and metal-working sectors, reported that no mechanism of appropriating the returns from product innovation was even moderately effective.[44]

More quantitative evidence that patents are not essential instruments of appropriation outside the chemical industries comes from work on the cost and time required to imitate an innovation.[45] Both Mansfield et al. (1981) and Levin et al. (1987) found that patents raise imitation cost substantially in the chemical and petroleum industries but only slightly in electronics. Moreover, Levin et al. identified several industries, concentrated in the aerospace and industrial machinery sectors, that reported very high imitation costs and imitation time lags despite very weak patent protection. In these instances, the relative complexity of the products presumably makes reverse engineering difficult even in the absence of patent protection.[46]

Most empirical work on appropriability has focused on the mechanisms facilitating and constraining the ability of firms to capture the returns from new technology as it is embodied in specific industrial processes or products. It is misleading, however, to think that the only spillovers that reduce appropriability are those that lead to the direct imitation of an innovative process or product. Spillovers of technical knowledge can lead to the development of products that are not direct imitations but that nonetheless compete (perhaps even in different markets) with products of the firm in which the knowledge originated. More generally, spillovers of knowledge can enhance the overall technological capability of the receiving firm, rendering it a more potent rival in the long-run competitive dynamics of an industry. It has been claimed that Japanese firms have a decisive advantage over international rivals in effectively utilizing techno-

[44] Despite the relative inefficacy of patents outside the chemical industry, Mansfield (1986) found that all twelve of his sample industries patented at least half of their patentable inventions during the 1981–83 period. This implies that the benefits of patenting exceed the cost in most cases, but Levin et al. (1987) found some evidence that firms patent for reasons other than protecting their inventions from imitation, such as monitoring the performance of R&D employees and gaining access to foreign markets where licensing to host-country firms is a condition of entry.

[45] More than 85 percent of the industries covered by the Levin et al. (1987) survey reported that the cost of imitating an unpatented major innovation was at least 50 percent of the innovator's R&D cost. More than 40 percent of the responding industries indicated that imitation costs were in excess of 75 percent of innovation costs.

[46] Evidence that imitation (a non-cooperative endeavor) is quite costly even in the absence of patent protection is reinforced by findings in the literature on technology transfer (a cooperative endeavor), where it has been found that firms must make substantial investments to utilize technology licensed from other firms, or even technology transferred from another plant operated by the same firm [see, for example, the studies contained in Mansfield et al. (1982)].

logical knowledge developed externally [see, for example, Mansfield (1988) and Rosenberg and Steinmueller (1988)].[47]

Despite a growing body of evidence on interindustry differences in appropriability conditions, there is no clear empirical consensus about whether greater appropriability encourages innovative activity. This reflects, in part, the difficulties of finding suitable data and formulating precise tests to distinguish among competing hypotheses concerning the expected effects of appropriability. The simplest hypothesis, derived from the standard argument supporting the patent system, is that innovative activity will increase monotonically with appropriability, because spillovers create a disincentive to innovative effort. By this argument, the more effective are the means of appropriation, or the less extensive are intraindustry spillovers, the greater will be industry R&D investment. When the "efficiency effect" of spillovers is considered, however, some simple models [e.g. Spence (1984)] predict that although industry R&D intensity will rise with appropriability (fall with spillovers), innovative output may decrease with appropriability (increase with spillovers).

In the more fully developed model of Cohen and Levinthal (1989a,1989b), the simple "disincentive effect" of spillovers remains, but there is an offsetting incentive to invest in "absorptive capacity" to make use of them. In this case, an increase in spillovers (decrease in appropriability) has an ambiguous effect on industry R&D. We conjecture that a similar result could be derived in a model that distinguished innovative from imitative R&D in the spirit of the Nelson and Winter (1982a) simulation models; under appropriate assumptions, an increase in the ease of imitation would discourage innovative R&D and encourage imitative R&D, with an ambiguous effect on total R&D. Finally, Levin and Reiss (1988) have suggested yet another countervailing incentive effect. To the extent that own and rival R&D are heterogeneous, the knowledge produced by a firm's competitor may be complementary to that produced by the firm's own investment, raising the marginal product of own R&D.

The empirical findings to date do not establish whether the net effect of appropriability on R&D incentives is positive or negative, nor do we yet know the extent to which the net effect varies across industries. Although Bernstein and Nadiri (1989) found that intraindustry spillovers have a negative effect on R&D in each of four U.S. industries, Bernstein (1988) found a positive effect in three

[47]A related consideration is that the knowledge that spills out is not necessarily detailed knowledge of how a product or process works. Mansfield (1985) has shown that decisions to develop a new product are typically known to competitors within 12 to 18 months (somewhat sooner in electrical equipment and primary metals). Our conversations with R&D managers suggest that they find it very valuable to know what technical problem a competitor is trying to solve, what technical approach has been adopted, or what approach has succeeded. This suggests, curiously, that the problem of appropriability is not limited to protecting successful innovations. Knowledge that a project has failed may save a competitor money or help a competitor succeed.

R&D intensive industries in Canada. Levin et al. (1985) and Levin (1988) found that various survey-based measures of appropriability were individually and jointly insignificant in regressions that explain R&D intensity at the industry level. Using business unit data, however, Cohen et al. (1987) found some of these measures to have positive and significant effects on R&D intensity in pooled regressions, although the results were not robust across separate two-digit industry regressions. For example, they found a negative effect of appropriability within the electrical equipment sector, a result that Cohen and Levinthal (1989b) replicated and interpreted tentatively as reflecting a high payoff to investment in absorptive capacity. A fuller understanding of the empirical consequences of imperfect appropriability will require tests that distinguish more sharply among the various mechanisms by which spillovers affect the incentives for R&D directed toward innovation, imitation, and investment in underlying technological capability.

Although most of the literature has focused on how appropriability conditions within a single industry affect the volume of its innovative activity, von Hippel (1982) suggested that appropriability conditions in vertically-related industries affect the locus of innovative effort. In an attempt to specify the conditions under which process machinery is developed by machinery manufacturers rather than users of the machinery, von Hippel emphasized considerations such as the extent to which new knowledge is embodied in the machinery, the relative efficacy of patents or secrecy, whether the machinery is used in one industry or many, and the market structures of the manufacturing and using industries. These factors, hypothesized to determine the locus of innovation in vertically-related industries, may also affect the amount of innovation. Although these issues have not yet been thoroughly explored in the econometric literature, Farber (1981) introduced and found some support for the hypothesis that concentration on the buyer's side of the market influences R&D spending on the seller's side.

5. Conclusion

A central theme of this survey has been to emphasize the already perceptible movement of empirical scholars from a narrow concern with the role of firm size and market concentration toward a broader consideration of the fundamental determinants of technical change in industry. Although tastes, technological opportunity, and appropriability conditions themselves are subject to change over time, particularly in response to radical innovations that alter the technological regime, these conditions are reasonably assumed to determine interindustry differences in innovative activity over relatively long periods.

Although a substantial body of descriptive evidence has begun to accumulate on how the nature and effects of demand, opportunity, and appropriability differ across industries, the absence of suitable data constrains progress in many areas. Moreover, understanding could be advanced by a greater interaction between developments in the theoretical and empirical literatures. Some potentially valuable ideas, widely discussed in the theoretical literature, have been neglected by empiricists, while theorists in turn have paid insufficient attention to rationalizing and making coherent what is known empirically.

One neglected issue in the empirical literature is the role of strategic interaction, which has been the major preoccupation of theorists concerned with R&D investment and technical change. Curiously, this issue was given greater attention by empiricists in the 1960s and early 1970s than in more recent years. Although none of the early empirical studies provided rigorous tests of theoretical models, several used theoretical arguments concerning the nature of oligopolistic interaction to justify empirical findings.[48] Scherer (1967b) himself developed one of the first detailed theoretical models of R&D rivalry; its implications, like those deduced by Kamien and Schwartz (1976), were consistent with the empirical finding that an "inverted-U" characterized the relationship between R&D investment and market concentration.

One difficulty with testing the implications of recent game-theoretic models of R&D rivalry is that they analyze behavior in highly stylized and counterfactual settings. For example, many models focus on the interaction of a single incumbent and a single prospective entrant. Moreover, many of the results obtained in this literature, surveyed by Reinganum in Chapter 14 in this Handbook, depend upon typically unverifiable assumptions concerning the distribution of information, the identity of the decision variables, and the sequence of moves.[49] Nonetheless, empirical effort on the effect and importance of strategic behavior is warranted. Inspiration might be drawn from Lieberman's (1987) empirical examination of the role of strategic entry deterrence in affecting capacity expansion in a sample of chemical and metals industries. He concluded that strategic considerations were not paramount in most industries, but he identified several specific instances in which strategic considerations may have been important.[50]

[48]Grabowski and Baxter (1973) found evidence suggesting that firms in the chemical industry engage in "competitive matching" of R&D investment. Wilson (1977) used strategic considerations to rationalize several of the findings in his study of licensing behavior. For example, observing that cross-licensing is more prevalent the smaller the number of rivals, he argued that smaller numbers made a cooperative solution more likely.

[49]See Reinganum (1984) for a discussion of the contrasting propositions of Dasgupta and Stiglitz (1980b) and Loury (1979), on the one hand, and Lee and Wilde (1980), on the other.

[50]A reasonable conjecture, arising from perusal of the case study literature and the trade press, is that the relative importance of strategic considerations in R&D decisions varies across industries. For example, in airframes and some segments of the computer industry, firms appear to monitor rival behavior closely and to modify their own behavior in response. Strategic considerations appear to be less prominent in industries producing relatively homogeneous products, such as basic metals and commodity chemicals.

Another gap in the empirical literature is the absence of a satisfactory explanation for interfirm differences in innovative activity and performance. The variance in business unit R&D explained by fixed firm effects was approximately as large as the variance explained by fixed industry effects. While available measures of industry characteristics (demand, opportunity, and appropriability) account for about 50 percent of the variance explained by industry effects, the most widely used measures of firm characteristics, cash flow and the degree of diversification, jointly explain less than 10 percent of the variance explained by firm effects.

The theoretical literature may provide some guidance in identifying the sources of interfirm differences in innovative activity and performance. The line of inquiry explored by Williamson (1985) has suggested that – in the presence of asset specificity, uncertainty, and opportunistic behavior – differences in internal organization and interfirm contractual relationships may have substantial implications for innovative behavior and performance. Organizational and contractual issues have been given prominence in the literature concerned with management strategy [e.g. Teece (1986), Rumelt (1987)], but they have only begun to appear in econometric studies of R&D behavior or technological performance. The recent study by Clark et al. (1987) – examining how the organization of product development projects affects engineering performance – represents a promising beginning.

The work of Nelson and Winter (1982a) suggests another possibility: in a world of bounded rationality, differences among firms in idiosyncratic technological capabilities, accumulated in part by experience and in part by good "draws" from a stochastic environment, may also be sources of interfirm differences in behavior and performance. Despite recent efforts by Winter (1987) to suggest dimensions of technological capability that are observable in principle, the construction of measures suitable for econometric purposes remains a formidable challenge.[51]

Just as the empirical literature may benefit from importing ideas that have originated in theoretical work, it may also benefit from exporting puzzling results to the theorists for later re-importation in the form of new testable hypotheses. We have already offered one such challenge suggested by anomalous econometric results: can the disincentive and efficiency effects of spillovers on investment in innovation, imitation, and building technical capability be sufficiently disentangled to permit their empirical identification? Another is: How do the effects of opportunity and appropriability on innovation and industry structure differ when

[51]An alternative strategy for explaining interfirm variation in technological activity and performance would take seriously the proposition that much interfirm variation within a given industrial environment is a result of the past history of success and failure in the stochastic process of R&D competition. Such an approach would seek operational measures of the parameters of such a stochastic process (e.g. the degree of technological risk, barriers to market penetration) that might explain how the interfirm variance in R&D intensity, for example, varies across industries.

technologies are discrete rather than cumulative, in the sense that innovation depends upon prior innovation?[52]

One issue to which theorists and empiricists alike have devoted too little attention is the dynamics of innovation and market structure: the Schumpeterian process of "creative destruction". Robust analytical results in dynamic, stochastic models of populations of firms are not easily obtained, although there have been a few impressive attempts [e.g. Futia (1980), Iwai (1984a, 1984b)]. To date, the simulation models of Nelson and Winter (1982a) have provided the most illuminating theoretical treatment of the issues. Serious efforts to formulate dynamic, stochastic models that are empirically testable are just beginning.[53]

We close with the observation that much of our empirical understanding of innovation derives not from the estimation of econometric models, but from the use of other empirical methods. As we have illustrated with examples, the case study literature provides a rich array of insights and factual information. More strikingly, many of the most credible empirical regularities have been established, not by estimating and testing elaborate optimization models with published data, but by the painstaking collection of original data, usually in the form of responses to relatively simple questions. Even as econometric methods advance and the quality of published data improves, it will be important to remain catholic in the application of empirical techniques. Case studies will remain a valuable source of information and a source of inspiration for more rigorous approaches. It would, in addition, be worthwhile to refine the simulation techniques employed by Nelson and Winter, using models calibrated to permit simulation of specific industries, as was recently attempted by Grabowski and Vernon (1987). Finally, given the limitations of available data, advances in our understanding of innovation and market structure will depend importantly on the development of new data sources.

References

Abernathy, W.J. (1978) *The productivity dilemma*. Baltimore: Johns Hopkins University Press.

Abernathy, W.J. and Utterback, J.M. (1978) 'Patterns of industrial innovation', *Technology Review*, 41–47.

Acs, Z.J. and Audretsch, D.B. (1987) 'Innovation, market structure, and firm size', *The Review of Economics and Statistics*, 71:567–574.

[52]Industries with strong natural trajectories have technologies that are cumulative in the sense described here; solving the next problem along a trajectory requires knowledge of how the last problem was solved. Semiconductor technology is clearly cumulative [see Levin (1982) for a detailed explanation]; pharmaceutical technology, at least prior to recent developments in genetics and molecular biology, is not. Finding a new chemical entity with good therapeutic properties does not typically require knowledge of how the last drug was found.

[53]One such effort is the "active learning" model developed and tested by Pakes and Ericson (1987), which may be interpreted as a stylized model of innovative activity.

Alexander, A.J. and Mitchell, B.M. (1985) 'Measuring technological change of heterogeneous products', *Technological Forecasting and Social Change*, 27:161–195.

Angelmar, R. (1985) 'Market structure and research intensity in high-technological-opportunity industries', *Journal of Industrial Economics*, 34:69–79.

Armour, H.O. and Teece, D.J. (1981) 'Vertical integration and technological innovation', *Review of Economics and Statistics*, 62:470–474.

Arrow, K.J. (1962) 'Economic welfare and the allocation of resources for invention', in: Universities – National Bureau Committee for Economic Research, *The rate and direction of inventive activity*. Princeton: Princeton University Press.

Arthur, W.B. (1985) 'Competing technologies and lock-in by historical small events: The dynamics of allocation under increasing returns', CEPR publication no. 43, Stanford University.

Ayres, R.U. (1988) 'Barriers and breakthroughs: An "expanding frontiers" model of the technology-industry life cycle', *Technovation*, 7:87–115.

Baily, M.N. (1972) 'Research and development costs and returns: The U.S. pharmaceutical industry', *Journal of Political Economy*, 80:70–85.

Baldwin, W.L. and Scott, J.T. (1987) *Market structure and technological change*. Chichester: Harwood.

Basberg, B.L. (1987) 'Patents and the measurement of technological change: A survey of the literature', *Research Policy*, 16:131–140.

Bernstein, J.I. (1988) 'Costs of production, intra- and inter-industry R&D spillovers: Canadian evidence', *Canadian Journal of Economics*, 21:324–347.

Bernstein, J.I. and Nadiri, M.I. (1988) 'Interindustry R&D spillovers, rates of return, and production in high-tech industries', *American Economic Review Proceedings*, 78:429–439.

Bernstein, J.I. and Nadiri, M.I. (1989) 'Research and development and intraindustry spillovers: An empirical application of dynamic duality', *Review of Economic Studies*, forthcoming.

Blumenthal, D., Gluck, M., Louis, K. and Wise, D. (1986) 'Industrial support of university research in biotechnology', *Science*, 231:242–246.

Bound, J., Cummins, C., Griliches, Z., Hall, B.H. and Jaffe, A. (1984) 'Who does R&D and who patents?', in: Z. Griliches, ed., *R&D patents, and productivity*. Chicago: University of Chicago Press for the National Bureau of Economic Research.

Bozeman, B. and Link, A.N. (1983) *Investments in technology: Corporate strategies and public policy alternatives*. New York: Praeger.

Branch, B. (1974) 'Research and development activity and profitability: A distributed lag analysis', *Journal of Political Economy*, 82:999–1011.

Braun, E. and MacDonald, S. (1982) *Revolution in miniature*. Cambridge: Cambridge University Press.

Brock, G.W. (1975) *The U.S. computer industry*. Cambridge, Mass.: Ballinger.

Caves, R. (1962) *Air transport and its regulators*. Cambridge, Mass.: Harvard University Press.

Caves, R., Crookell, H. and Killing, P.J. (1983) 'The imperfect market for technology licenses', *Oxford Bulletin of Economics and Statistics*, 45:223–248.

Clark, K.B., Chew, W.B. and Fujimoto, T. (1987) 'Product development in the world auto industry', *Brookings Papers on Economic Activity*, 729–771.

Cockburn, I. and Griliches, Z. (1988) 'Industry effects and appropriability measures in the stock market's valuation of R&D and patents', *American Economic Review Proceedings*, 78:419–423.

Cohen, W.M. and Levinthal, D.A. (1989a) 'The implications of spillovers for R&D investment and welfare: A new perspective', in: A. Link and K. Smith, eds., *Advances in applied micro-economics, vol. 5: The factors affecting technological change*. Greenwich, Conn.: JAI Press.

Cohen, W.M. and Levinthal, D.A. (1989b) 'Innovation and learning: The two faces of R&D–Implications for the analysis of R&D investment', *Economic Journal*, forthcoming.

Cohen, W.M. and Mowery, D.C. (1984) 'The internal characteristics of the firm and the level and composition of research & development spending: Interim report, NSF grant PRA 83-10664', Carnegie-Mellon University, mimeo.

Cohen, W.M., Levin, R.C. and Mowery, D.C. (1987) 'Firm size and R&D intensity: A re-examination', *Journal of Industrial Economics*, 35:543–563.

Comanor, W.S. (1967) 'Market structure, product differentiation, and industrial research', *Quarterly Journal of Economics*, 81:639–657.

Connolly, R.A. and Hirschey, M. (1984) 'R&D, market structure, and profits: a value-based approach', *Review of Economics and Statistics*, 66:682–686.

Cowling, K. and Mueller, D.C. (1978) 'The social costs of monopoly power', *Economic Journal*, 88:724–748.

Cremer, J. and Sirbu, M. (1978) 'Une analyse econometrique de l'effort de recherche et developpement de l'industrie Française', *Revue Economique*, 29:940–954.

Dasgupta, P. and Stiglitz, J.E. (1980a) 'Industrial structure and the nature of innovative activity', *Economic Journal*, 90:266–293.

Dasgupta, P. and Stiglitz, J.E. (1980b) 'Uncertainty, industrial structure and the speed of R&D', *Bell Journal of Economics*, 11:1–28.

David, P.A. (1985) 'Clio and the economics of QWERTY', *American Economic Review Proceedings*, 75:332–337.

Doi, N. (1985) 'Diversification and R&D activity in Japanese manufacturing firms', *Managerial and Decision Economics*, 6:47–52.

Dorfman, N.S. (1987) *Innovation and market structure: Lessons from the computer and semiconductor industries*. Cambridge, Mass.: Ballinger.

Dosi, G. (1982) 'Technological paradigms and technological trajectories: A suggested interpretation of the determinants and directions of technical change', *Research Policy*, 11:147–162.

Dosi, G. (1988) 'Sources, procedures and microeconomic effects of innovation', *Journal of Economic Literature*, 36:1120–1171.

Elliott, J.W. (1971)'Funds flow versus expectational theories of research and development expenditures in the firm', *Southern Economic Journal*, 37:409–422.

Enos, J.L. (1962) *Petroleum progress and profits*. Cambridge, Mass.: MIT Press.

Evans, D. (1987a) 'The relationship between firm growth, size, and age: Estimates for 100 manufacturing industries', *Journal of Industrial Economics*, 35:567–581.

Evans, D. (1987b) 'Tests of alternative theories of firm growth', *Journal of Political Economy*, 95:657–674.

Evenson, R.E. and Kislev, Y. (1973) 'Research and productivity in wheat and maize', *Journal of Political Economy*, 81:1309–1329.

Evenson, R.E. and Kislev, Y. (1976) 'A stochastic model of applied research', *Journal of Political Economy*, 84:265–281.

Farber, S. (1981) 'Buyer market structure and R&D effort: A simultaneous equations model', *Review of Economics and Statistics*, 62:336–345.

Farrell, J. and Gallini, N. (1988) 'Second-sourcing as commitment: Monopoly incentives to attract competition', *Quarterly Journal of Economics*, forthcoming.

Farrell, J. and Saloner, G. (1985) 'Standardization, compatibility, and innovation', *Rand Journal of Economics*, 16:70–83.

Farrell, J. and Saloner, G. (1986) 'Installed base and compatibility: Innovation, product preannouncements, and predation', *American Economic Review*, 76:940–955.

Fellner, W. (1951) 'The influence of market structure on technological progress', *Quarterly Journal of Economics*, 65:556–577.

Fisher, F.M. and Temin, P. (1973) 'Returns to scale in research and development: What does the Schumpeterian hypothesis imply?', *Journal of Political Economy*, 81:56–70.

Flaherty, M.T. (1983) 'Market share, technology leadership, and competition in international semiconductor markets', in: Richard S. Rosenbloom, ed., *Research in technological innovation, management and policy*, vol. 1. Greenwich, Conn.: JAI Press, 1983.

Freeman, C. (1982) *The economics of industrial innovation*, 2nd edn. Cambridge, Mass.: MIT Press.

Futia, C. (1980) 'Schumpeterian competition', *Quarterly Journal of Economics*, 94:675–695.

Galbraith, J.K. (1952) *American capitalism: The concept of countervailing power*. Boston: Houghton Mifflin.

Gellman Research Associates (1976) *Indicators of international trends in technological innovation*, Final report to the National Science Foundation, NTIS document PB-263-738, Jenkintown, Penn: Gellman Research Associates.

Geroski, P.A. (1987) 'Innovation, technological opportunity and market structure', University of Southampton, mimeo.

Gort, M. and Klepper S. (1982) 'Time paths in the diffusion of product innovations', *Economic Journal*, 92:630–653.

Grabowski, H.G. (1968) 'The determinants of industrial research and development: A study of the chemical, drug, and petroleum industries', *Journal of Political Economy*, 76:292–306.

Grabowski, H.G. and Baxter, N.D. (1973) 'Rivalry in industrial research and development: An empirical study', *Journal of Industrial Economics*, 21:209–235.

Grabowski, H.G. and Mueller, D.C. (1978) 'Industrial research and development, intangible capital stocks, and firm profit rates', *Bell Journal of Economics*, 9:328–343.

Grabowski, H.G. and Vernon, J.M. (1982) 'The pharmaceutical industry', in: R.R. Nelson, ed., *Government and technical progress: A cross-industry analysis*. New York: Pergamon Press.

Grabowski, H.G. and Vernon, J.M. (1987) 'Pioneers, imitators, and generics – A simulation model of Schumpeterian competition', *The Quarterly Journal of Economics*, 102:491–525.

Griliches, Z. (1979) 'Issues in assessing the contribution of research and development to productivity growth', *Bell Journal of Economics*, 10:92–116.

Griliches, Z. (1981) 'Market value, R&D and patents', *Economic Letters*, 7:183–187.

Griliches, Z., Hall, B. and Pakes, A. (1987) 'The value of patents as indicators of inventive activity', in P. Dasgupta and P. Stoneman, eds., *Economic policy and technological performance*. Cambridge: Cambridge University Press.

Hall, B. (1987) 'The relationship between firm size and firm growth in the U.S. manufacturing sector', *Journal of Industrial Economics*, 35:583–606.

Hamberg, D. (1964) 'Size of firm, oligopoly, and research: The evidence', *Canadian Journal of Economics and Political Science*, 30:62–75.

Harberger, A.C. (1954) 'Monopoly and resource allocation', *American Economic Review*, 44:77–87.

Hausman, J., Hall, B.H. and Griliches, Z. (1984) 'Econometric models for count data with an application to the patents – R&D relationship', *Econometrica*, 52:909–938.

Hirsch, W.Z. (1952) 'Manufacturing progress functions', *Review of Economics and Statistics*, 34:143–155.

Hollander, S. (1965) *The sources of increased efficiency: A study of Dupont rayon plants*. Cambridge, Mass.: MIT Press.

Horowitz, I. (1962) 'Firm size and research activity', *Southern Economic Journal*, 28:298–301.

Horstmann, I., MacDonald, G.M. and Slivinski, A. (1985) 'Patents as information transfer mechanisms: To patent or (maybe) not to patent', *Journal of Political Economy*, 93:837–858.

Howe, J.D. and McFetridge, D.G. (1976) 'The determinants of R&D expenditures', *Canadian Journal of Economics*, 9:57–61.

Hughes, W.R. (1971) 'Scale frontiers in electric power', in: W.M. Capron, ed., *Technological change in regulated industries*. Washington: Brookings Institution.

Iwai, K. (1984a) 'Schumpeterian dynamics: An evolutionary model of innovation and imitation', *Journal of Economic Behavior and Organization*, 5:159–190.

Iwai, K. (1984b) 'Schumpeterian dynamics, part II: Technological Progress, firm growth, and economic selection', *Journal of Economic Behavior and Organization*, 5:321–355.

Jaffe, A.B. (1986) 'Technological opportunity and spillovers of R&D', *American Economic Review*, 76:984–1001.

Jewkes, J. Sawers, D. and Stillerman, R. (1958) *The sources of invention*. London: Macmillan.

Johnson, P.S. (1973) *Cooperative research in industry*. New York: Wiley.

Kamien, M.I. and Schwartz, N.L. (1970) 'Market structure, elasticity of demand, and incentive to invent', *Journal of Law and Economics*, 13:241–252.

Kamien, M.I. and Schwartz, N.L. (1976) 'On the degree of rivalry for maximum innovative activity', *Quarterly Journal of Economics*, 90:245–260.

Kamien, M.I. and Schwartz, N.L. (1978) 'Self-financing of an R&D project', *American Economic Review*, 68:252–261.

Kamien, M.I. and Schwartz, N.L. (1982) *Market structure and innovation*. Cambridge: Cambridge University Press.

Katz, M.L. (1986) 'An analysis of cooperative research and development', *Rand Journal of Economics*, 17:527–543.

Katz, M.L. and Shapiro, C. (1985a) 'On the licensing of innovations', *Rand Journal of Economics*, 16:504–520.

Katz, M.L. and Shapiro, C. (1985b) 'Network externalities, competition, and compatibility', *American Economic Review*, 75:424–440.

Katz, M.L. and Shapiro, C. (1986) 'Technology adoption in the presence of network externalities', *Journal of Political Economy*, 94:822–841.

Keeney, R.L. and Lilien G.L. (1987) 'New industrial product design and evaluation using multiattribute value analysis', *Journal of Product Innovation Management*, 4:185–198.

Kleinknecht, A. (1987) 'Measuring R&D in small firms: How much are we missing?', *Journal of Industrial Economics*, 36:253–256.

Klepper, S. and Graddy, E. (1986) 'Industry evolution and the determinants of market structure', Carnegie-Mellon University, mimeo.

Kohn, M.G. and Scott, J.T. (1982) 'Scale economies in research and development: The Schumpeterian hypothesis', *Journal of Industrial Economics*, 30:239–249.

Kuznets, S. (1962) 'Inventive activity: Problems of definition and measurement', in: Universities – National Bureau Committee for Economic Research, *The rate and direction of inventive activity*. Princeton: Princeton University Press.

Landes, D.S. (1969) *The unbound Prometheus: Technological change and industrial development in Western Europe from* 1750 *to the present*. Cambridge: Cambridge University Press.

Lee, T. and Wilde, L.L. (1980) 'Market structure and innovation: A reformulation', *Quarterly Journal of Economics*, 94:429–436.

Levin, R.C. (1977) 'Technical change and optimal scale: Some evidence and implications', *Southern Economic Journal*, 44:208–221.

Levin, R.C. (1978) 'Technical change, barriers to entry, and market structure', *Economica*, 45:347–361.

Levin, R.C. (1981) 'Toward an empirical model of Schumpeterian competition', working paper series A, no. 43, Yale School of Organization and Management.

Levin, R.C. (1982) 'The semiconductor industry', in: R.R. Nelson, ed., *Government and technical progress: A cross-industry analysis*. New York: Pergamon Press.

Levin, R.C. (1988) 'Appropriability, R&D spending and technological performance', *American Economic Review Proceedings*, 78:424–428.

Levin, R.C. and Reiss, P.C. (1984) 'Tests of a Schumpeterian model of R&D and market structure', in: Z. Griliches, ed., *R&D, patents, and productivity*. Chicago: University of Chicago Press for the National Bureau of Economic Research.

Levin, R.C. and Reiss, P.C. (1988) 'Cost-reducing and demand-creating R&D with spillovers', *Rand Journal of Economics*, forthcoming.

Levin, R.C., Cohen, W.M. and Mowery, D.C. (1985) 'R&D appropriability, opportunity, and market structure: New evidence on some Schumpeterian hypotheses', *American Economic Review Proceedings*, 75:20–24.

Levin, R.C., Klevorick, A.K., Nelson, R.R. and Winter, S.G. (1987) 'Appropriating the returns from industrial R&D', *Brookings Papers on Economic Activity*, 783–820.

Levy, D. and Terleckyj, N. (1983) 'The effects of government R&D on private R&D and productivity: A macroeconomic analysis, *Bell Journal of Economics*, 14:551–561.

Lichtenberg, F. (1987) 'The effect of government funding on private industrial research and development: A reassessment, *Journal of Industrial Economics*, 36:97–104.

Lichtenberg, F. (1988) 'The private R&D investment response to federal design and technical competitions', *American Economic Review*, 78:550–559.

Lieberman, M.B. (1984) 'The learning curve and pricing in the chemical processing industries', *Rand Journal of Economics*, 15:213–228.

Lieberman, M.B. (1987) 'Excess capacity as a barrier to entry: An empirical appraisal', *Journal of Industrial Economics*, 35:607–627.

Link, A.N. (1980) 'Firm size and efficient entrepreneurial activity: A reformulation of the Schumpeter hypothesis', *Journal of Political Economy*, 88:771–782.

Link, A.N. (1981) *Research and development in U.S. manufacturing*. New York: Praeger.

Link, A.N. (1982) 'An analysis of the composition of R&D spending', *Southern Economic Journal*, 49:342–349.

Link, A.N. (1985) 'The changing composition of R&D', *Managerial and Decision Economics*, 6:125–128.

Link, A.N. (1987) *Technological change and productivity growth*. Chichester: Harwood.

Link, A.N. and Bauer, L.L. (1987) 'An economic analysis of cooperative research', *Technovation*, 6:247–261.

Link, A.N. and Bauer, L.L. (1988) *Cooperative research and U.S. manufacturing: Assessing policy initiatives and corporate strategies*. Lexington, Mass.: Lexington Books.

Link, A.N. and Long, J.E. (1981) 'The simple economics of basic scientific research: A test of Nelson's diversification hypothesis', *Journal of Industrial Economics*, 30:105–109.

Loeb, P.D. (1983) 'Further evidence of the determinants of industrial research and development using single and simultaneous equation models', *Empirical Economics*, 8:203–214.

Loury, G.C. (1979) 'Market structure and innovation', *Quarterly Journal of Economics*, 93:395–410.

Lunn, J. (1986) 'An empirical analysis of process and product patenting: A simultaneous equation framework', *Journal of Industrial Economics*, 34:319–330.

Lunn, J. and Martin, S. (1986) 'Market structure, firm structure, and research and development', *Quarterly Review of Economics and Business*, 26:31–44.

MacDonald, J.M. (1985) 'R&D and the direction of diversification', *Review of Economics and Statistics*, 47:583–590.

Malecki, E.J. (1980) 'Firm size, location, and industrial R&D: A disaggregated analysis', *Review of Business and Economic Research*, 16:29–42.

Malerba, F. (1985) *The semiconductor business: The economics of rapid growth and decline*. Madison: University of Wisconsin Press.

Mansfield, E. (1962) 'Entry, Gibrat's law, innovation, and the growth of firms', *American Economic Review*, 52:1023–1051.

Mansfield, E. (1963) 'Size of firm, market structure, and innovation', *Journal of Political Economy*, 71:556–576.

Mansfield, E. (1964) 'Industrial research and development expenditures: Determinants, prospects, and relation of size of firm and inventive output', *Journal of Political Economy*, 72:319–340.

Mansfield, E. (1968) *Industrial research and technological innovation: An econometric analysis*. New York: Norton.

Mansfield, E. (1981) 'Composition of R and D expenditures: Relationship to size, concentration, and innovation output', *Review of Economics and Statistics*, 62:610–614.

Mansfield, E. (1983) 'Technological change and market structure: An empirical study', *American Economic Review Proceedings*, 73:205–209.

Mansfield, E. (1985) 'How rapidly does new industrial technology leak out?', *Journal of Industrial Economics*, 34:217–223.

Mansfield, E. (1986) 'Patents and innovation: An empirical study', *Management Science*, 32:173–181.

Mansfield, E. (1988) 'The speed and cost of industrial innovation in Japan and the United States: A comparison', *Management Science*, forthcoming.

Mansfield, E., Schwartz, M. and Wagner, S. (1981) 'Imitation costs and patents: An empirical study', *Economic Journal*, 91:907–918

Mansfield, E., Rapoport, J., Schnee, J., Wagner, S. and Hamburger, M. (1971) *Research and innovation in the modern corporation*. New York: Norton.

Mansfield, E., Romeo, A., Schwartz, M., Teece, D., Wagner, S. and Brach, P. (1982) *Technology transfer, productivity, and economic policy*. New York: Norton.

Markham, J.W. (1965) 'Market structure, business conduct, and innovation', *American Economic Review Proceedings*, 55:323–332.

Mason, E.S. (1951) 'Schumpeter on monopoly and the large firm', *Review of Economics and Statistics*, 33:139–144.

McEachern, W.A. and Romeo, A. (1978) 'Stockholder control, uncertainty, and the allocation of resources to research and development', *Journal of Industrial Economics*, 26:349–361.

Meisel, J.B. and Lin, S.A.Y. (1983) 'The impact of market structure on the firm's allocation of resources to research and development', *Quarterly Review of Economics and Business*, 23:28–43.

Mowery, D.C. (1983a) 'The relationship between intrafirm and contractual forms of industrial research in American manufacturing, 1900–1940', *Explorations in Economic History*, 20:351–374.

Mowery, D.C. (1983b) 'Industrial research and firm size, survival, and growth in American manufacturing, 1921–46: An assessment', *Journal of Economic History*, 43:953–980.

Mowery, D.C., ed. (1988) *International collaborative ventures in U.S. manufacturing*. Cambridge, Mass.: Ballinger.

Mowery, D.C. and Rosenberg, N. (1979) 'The influence of market demand upon innovation: A critical review of some recent empirical studies', *Research Policy*, 8:102–153.
Mueller, D.C. (1967) 'The firm's decision process: An econometric investigation', *Quarterly Journal of Economics*, 81:58–87.
Mueller, D.C. (1986) *Profits in the long run*. New York: Cambridge University Press.
Mueller, D.C. and Tilton, J.E. (1969) 'Research and development costs as a barrier to entry', *Canadian Journal of Economics*, 2:570–579.
Mukhopadhyay, A.K. (1985) 'Technological progress and change in market concentration in the U.S., 1963-77', *Southern Economic Journal*, 52:141–149.
National Science Board (1987) *Science and engineering indicators–1987*. Washington: U.S. Government Printing Office.
National Science Foundation (1983) *The process of technological innovation: Reviewing the literature*. Washington: Productivity Improvement Research Section, National Science Foundation.
Nelson, R.R. (1959) 'The simple economics of basic scientific research', *Journal of Political Economy*, 67:297–306.
Nelson, R.R. (1962) 'The link between science and invention: The case of the transistor', in: Universities–National Bureau Committee for Economic Research, *The rate and direction of inventive activity*. Princeton: Princeton University Press.
Nelson, R.R. (1982a) 'The role of knowledge in R&D efficiency', *Quarterly Journal of Economics*, 97:453–470.
Nelson, R.R., ed. (1982b) *Government and technical progress: A cross-industry analysis*. New York: Pergamon Press.
Nelson, R.R. (1984) *High-technology policies: A five-nation comparison*. Washington: American Enterprise Institute.
Nelson, R.R. (1986) 'Institutions supporting technical advance in industry', American Economic Review Proceedings, 76:186–189.
Nelson, R.R. (1989) 'Capitalism as an engine of progress', Columbia University, mimeo.
Nelson, R.R. and Winter, S.G. (1977) 'In search of useful theory of innovation', *Research Policy*, 6:36–76.
Nelson, R.R. and Winter, S.G. (1978) 'Forces generating and limiting concentration under Schumpeterian competition', *Bell Journal of Economics*, 9:524–548.
Nelson, R.R. and Winter, S.G. (1982a) *An evolutionary theory of economic change*. Cambridge, Mass.: Harvard University Press.
Nelson, R.R. and Winter, S.G. (1982b) 'The Schumpeterian tradeoff revisited', *American Economic Review*, 72:114–132.
Nelson, R.R., Peck, M.J. and Kalachek, E.D. (1967) *Technology, economic growth, and public policy*. Washington: Brookings Institution.
Pakes, A. (1985) 'On patents, R&D and the stock market rate of return', *Journal of Political Economy*, 93:390–409.
Pakes, A. (1986) 'Patents as options: Some estimates of the value of holding European patent stocks', *Econometrica*, 54:755–784.
Pakes, A. and Ericson, R. (1987) 'Empirical implications of alternative models of firm dynamics', Social Systems Research Institute Workshop series, University of Wisconsin.
Pakes, A. and Schankerman, M. (1984) 'An exploration into the determinants of research intensity', in: Z. Griliches, ed., *R&D, patents, and productivity*. Chicago: University of Chicago Press for the National Bureau of Economic Research.
Parker, W.N. (1972) 'Agriculture', in: L.E. Davis, R.A. Easterlin and W.N. Parker, eds., *American economic growth: An economist's history of the United States*. New York: Harper and Row.
Pavitt, K. (1983) 'Characteristics of innovative activities in British industry', *Omega*, 11:113–130.
Pavitt, K. (1984) 'Sectoral patterns of technical change: Towards a taxonomy and a theory', *Research Policy*, 13:343–373.
Pavitt, K. (1985) 'Patent statistics as indicators of innovative activities: Possibilities and prospects', *Scientometrics*, 7:77–99.
Pavitt, K., Robson, M. and Townsend, J. (1987) 'The size distribution of innovating firms in the UK: 1945–1983', *Journal of Industrial Economics*, 35:297–316.

Peck, M.J. (1962) 'Inventions in the postwar American aluminum industry', in: Universities–National Bureau Committee for Economic Research, *The rate and direction of inventive activity*. Princeton: Princeton University Press.

Peck, M.J. (1986) 'Joint R&D: The case of Microelectronics and Computer Technology Corporation, *Research Policy*, 15:219–232.

Peltzman, S. (1973) 'An evaluation of consumer legislation: The 1962 drug amendment', *Journal of Political Economy*, 81:1049–1091.

Penrose, E. (1951) *The economics of the international patent system*. Baltimore: Johns Hopkins University Press.

Phillips, A. (1966) 'Patents, potential competition, and technical progress', *American Economic Review*, 56:301–310.

Phillips, A. (1971) *Technology and market structure*. Lexington, Mass.: D.C. Heath.

Phlips, L. (1971) *Effects of industrial concentration: A cross-section analysis for the Common Market*. Amsterdam: North-Holland.

Ravenscraft, D. and Scherer, F.M. (1982) 'The lag structure of returns to research and development', *Applied Economics*, 14:603–620.

Reinganum, J.F. (1984) 'Practical implications of game theoretic models of R&D', *American Economic Review Proceedings*, 74:61–67.

Robson, M. and Townsend, J. (1984) 'Users manual for ESRC archive file on innovations in Britain since 1945: 1984 update', Science Policy Research Unit, University of Sussex, mimeo.

Robson, M., Townsend, J. and Pavitt, K. (1988) 'Sectoral patterns of production and use of innovations in the U.K.: 1945-1983', *Research Policy*, 17:1–14.

Rosenberg, N. (1969) 'The direction of technological change: Inducement mechanisms and focusing devices', *Economic Development and Cultural Change*, 18:1–24.

Rosenberg, N. (1974) 'Science, invention, and economic growth', *Economic Journal*, 84:90–108.

Rosenberg, N. (1982) *Inside the black box: Technology and economics*. New York: Cambridge University Press.

Rosenberg, N. and Steinmueller, W.E. (1988) 'Why are Americans such poor imitators?', *American Economic Review Proceedings*, 78:229–234.

Rothblum, U.G. and Winter, S.G. (1985) 'Asymptotic behavior of market shares for a stochastic growth model', *Journal of Economic Theory*, 36:352–366.

Rothwell, R., Freeman, C., Horsley, A., Jervis, V.T.P., Robertson, A.B. and Townsend, J. (1974) 'SAPPHO updated–Project SAPPHO phase II', *Research Policy*, 3:258–291.

Rumelt, R.P. (1987) 'Theory, strategy, and entrepreneurship', in: D.J. Teece, ed., *The competitive challenge: Strategies for industrial innovation and renewal*. Cambridge, Mass.: Ballinger.

Sahal, D. (1981) *Patterns of technological innovation*. New York: Addison Wesley.

Schankerman, M. and Pakes, A. (1986) 'Estimates of the value of patent rights in European countries during the post-1950 period', *Economic Journal*, 96:1052–1077.

Scherer, F.M. (1965a) 'Firm size, market structure, opportunity, and the output of patented inventions', *American Economic Review*, 55:1097–1125.

Scherer, F.M. (1965b) 'Size of firm, oligopoly, and research: A comment', *Canadian Journal of Economics and Political Science*, 31:256–266.

Scherer, F.M. (1965c) 'Corporate inventive output, profits, and growth', *Journal of Political Economy*, 73:290–297.

Scherer, F.M. (1967a) 'Market structure and the employment of scientists and engineers', *American Economic Review*, 57:524–531.

Scherer, F.M. (1967b) 'Research and development resource allocation under rivalry', *Quarterly Journal of Economics*, 81:359–394.

Scherer, F.M. (1980) *Industrial market structure and economic performance*, 2nd edn. Chicago: Rand McNally.

Scherer, F.M. (1982a) 'Inter-industry technology flows in the United States', *Research Policy*, 11:227–245.

Scherer, F.M. (1982b) 'Inter-industry technology flows and productivity growth', *Review of Economics and Statistics*, 44:627–634.

Scherer, F.M. (1982c) 'Demand-pull and technological innovation: Schmookler revisited', *Journal of Industrial Economics*, 30:225–237.

Scherer, F.M. (1983a) 'Concentration, R&D, and productivity change', *Southern Economic Journal*, 50:221–225.

Scherer, F.M. (1983b) 'The propensity to patent', *International Journal of Industrial Organization*, 1:107–128.

Scherer, F.M. (1984a) 'Using linked patent and R&D data to measure interindustry technology flows', in: Z. Griliches, ed., *R&D, patents, and productivity. Chicago: University of Chicago Press for the National Bureau of Economic Research.*

Scherer, F.M. (1984b) *Innovation and growth: Schumpeterian perspectives*. Cambridge, Mass.: MIT Press.

Scherer, F.M., et al. (1959) *Patents and the corporation*, 2nd edn. Boston: privately published.

Scherer, F.M., Beckenstein, A., Kaufer, E. and Murphy, R.D. (1975) *The economics of multi-plant operation*. Cambridge, Mass.: Harvard University Press.

Schmookler, J. (1962) 'Economic sources of inventive activity', *Journal of Economic History*, 22:1–10.

Schmookler, J. (1966) *Invention and economic growth*. Cambridge, Mass.: Harvard University Press.

Schumpeter, J.A. (1942) *Capitalism, socialism, and democracy*. New York: Harper.

Schwartzman, D. (1976) *Innovation in the pharmaceutical industry*. Baltimore: Johns Hopkins University Press.

Scott, J.T. (1984) 'Firm versus industry variability in R&D intensity', in: Z. Griliches, ed., *R&D, patents, and productivity*. Chicago: University of Chicago Press for the National Bureau of Economic Research.

Scott, J.T. and Pascoe, G. (1987) 'Purposive diversification of R&D in manufacturing', *Journal of Industrial Economics*, 36:193–206.

Shepard, A. (1987) 'Licensing to enhance demand for new technologies', *Rand Journal of Economics*, 18:360–368.

Shrieves, R.E. (1978) 'Market structure and innovation: A new perspective', *Journal of Industrial Economics*, 26:329–347.

Simon, H.A. and Bonini, C.P. (1958) 'The size distribution of business firms', *American Economic Review*, 48:607–617.

Soete, L.L.G. (1979) 'Firm size and innovative activity: The evidence reconsidered', *European Economic Review*, 12:319–340.

Spence, A.M. (1975) 'Monopoly, quality, and regulation', *Bell Journal of Economics*, 6:417–429.

Spence, A.M. (1984) 'Cost reduction, competition, and industry performance', *Econometrica*, 52:101–121.

Taylor, C.T. and Silberston, Z.A. (1973) *The economic impact of the patent system: A study of the British experience. Cambridge: Cambridge University Press.*

Teece, D.J. (1986) 'Profiting from technological innovation: Implications for integration, collaboration, licensing and public policy', *Research Policy*, 15:286–305.

Teece, D.J. and Armour, H.O. (1977) 'Innovation and divestiture in the U.S. oil industry', in D.J. Teece, ed., *R&D in energy – Implications of petroleum industry reorganization*. Stanford: Institute for Energy Studies.

Temin, P. (1979) 'Technology, regulation, and market structure in the modern pharmaceutical industry', *Bell Journal of Economics*, 10:429–446.

Thirtle, C.G. and Ruttan, V.W. (1987) *The role of demand and supply in the generation and diffusion of technical change*. Chichester: Harwood Academic Publishers.

Tilton, J. (1971) *International diffusion of technology: The case of semiconductors*. Washington: Brookings Institution.

Townsend, J., Henwood, F., Thomas, G., Pavitt, K. and Wyatt, S. (1981) 'Innovations in Britain since 1945', occasional paper no. 16, Science Policy Research Unit, University of Sussex.

Trajtenberg, M. (1987) 'Patents, citations and innovations: Tracing the links', working paper no. 2457, National Bureau of Economic Research.

Utterback, J.M. (1979) 'The dynamics of product and process innovation in industry,' in: Christopher T. Hill and James M. Utterback, eds., *Technological innovation for a dynamic economy*. New York: Pergamon Press.

von Hippel, E. (1976) 'The dominant role of the user in the scientific instrument innovation process', *Research Policy*, 5:212–239.

von Hippel, E. (1977) 'The dominant role of the user in semiconductor and electronic subassembly process innovation', *IEEE Transactions on Engineering Management*, EM-24:60–71.

von Hippel, E. (1982) 'Appropriability of innovation benefit as a predictor of the source of innovation', *Research Policy*, 11:95–115.

von Hippel, E. (1988) *The sources of innovation*. New York: Oxford University Press.

Wahlroos, B. and Backstrom, M. (1982) 'R&D intensity with endogenous concentration: Evidence for Finland', *Empirical Economics*, 7:13–22.

Walsh, V. (1984) 'Invention and innovation in the chemical industry: Demand-pull or discovery-push?', *Research Policy*, 13:211–234.

Waterson, M. and Lopez, A. (1983) 'The determinants of research and development intensity in the UK', *Applied Economics*, 15:379–391.

Williamson, O.E. (1965) 'Innovation and market structure', *Journal of Political Economy*, 73:67–73.

Williamson, O.E. (1985) *The economic institutions of capitalism: Firms, markets, relational contracting*. New York: Free Press.

Wilson, R.W. (1977) 'The effect of technological environment and product rivalry on R&D effort and licensing of innovations, *Review of Economics and Statistics*, 59:171–178.

Wilson, R.W., Ashton, P.K. and Egan, T.P. (1980) *Innovation, competition, and government policy in the semiconductor industry*. Lexington, Mass.: Lexington Books.

Winter, S.G. (1987) 'Knowledge and competence as strategic assets', in: D.J. Teece, ed., *The competitive challenge: Strategies for industrial innovation and renewal*. Cambridge, Mass.: Ballinger.

Chapter 19

AN UPDATED REVIEW OF INDUSTRIAL ORGANIZATION: APPLICATIONS OF EXPERIMENTAL METHODS

CHARLES R. PLOTT*

California Institute of Technology

Contents

*The general methodological discussions of this paper found in Sections 2, 6, and 7 are taken from an earlier review by the author [Plott (1982)]. At additional points, when describing the literature prior to 1980, this review also draws heavily on the earlier paper. The financial support of the National Science Foundation is gratefully acknowledged.

Handbook of Industrial Organization, Volume II, Edited by R. Schmalensee and R.D. Willig

1. Introduction

From the very beginning laboratory experiments in economics were motivated by theories of industrial organization. The first published market experiments were those of Chamberlin (1948) who explored the behavioral characteristics of markets he described as being "purely" but not "perfectly" competitive. He thought that the principles of monopolistic competition would be more useful than the theory of competitive demand and supply in explaining the observed behavior. Hoggatt (1959) and Sauermann and Selten (1959) independently provided the first experimental evidence that the Cournot model might be a reasonably accurate description of oligopolistic behavior. Oligopoly and bilateral monopoly motivated the classic work of Fouraker and Siegel (1963) which introduced several of the experimental techniques still used today. Smith's (1962) sensitivity to the organization of the floor of the stock exchanges led him to the fundamental discovery that the law of competitive demand and supply can be observed operating in an experimental environment. The field of experimental economics has experienced substantial evolution during the intervening twenty-eight years.

The chapter is organized as follows. Section 2 outlines some of the step-by-step details of laboratory procedures. Sections 3–5 summarize experimental results; Sections 6 and 7 are methodological in nature. In Section 3 markets with several participants are analyzed and compared to the competitive model. Section 4 summarizes imperfect competition results. Section 5 deals with product quality. This organization of the material is natural from the point of view of traditional theory, but the organization is not necessarily natural from the point of view of results. As will become evident from the following pages, market institutions have a substantial influence on performance and this influence sometimes outweighs the importance of market concentration and relative firm size, which have been the traditional center of attention for industrial organization theorists. Consequently, on occasion it is easier to organize and summarize results according to market institutional variables as opposed to numbers, size, or other economic parameters.

Section 6 addresses the obvious question regarding the relevance of laboratory methods. Several common criticisms of experimental methods are outlined. The section defines both the limitations and the qualifications that must accompany conclusions drawn from experimental evidence, and discusses them in terms of results. The recent explosion of professional interest in experimental methods reflects, in part, a recognition that experimental methods provide a source of shared experience for scholars who are developing and evaluating theories about complicated, naturally occurring processes. While laboratory processes are simple in comparison to naturally occurring processes, they are real processes in the sense that real people participate for real and substantial profits and follow real rules in doing so. It is precisely because they are real that they are interesting. General theories must apply to special cases, so models believed to be applicable to complicated naturally occurring processes should certainly be expected to help explain what occurs in simple, special-case laboratory markets.

Theories which do not apply to the special cases are not general theories and thus cannot be advocated as such. Critics who claim that laboratory markets are artificial have missed this fundamental point. They confuse simplicity with reality and fail to realize that they are grappling with a problem that accompanies experimental methods in general and not just in economics. Experiments in every branch of science are simple and special cases of the general and more complex phenomenon about which researchers are curious. The question that such critics wish to raise, and it is a question that must be answered in any experimental science, is whether or not anything is learned from the study of special cases. The answer to that more penetrating question depends upon the power and generality of our theories. Theory is the machine used to project us from the known special cases back to the unknown and more complex.

2. Laboratory market details

Real markets are easy to create. The difficult part is creating a market that demonstrates a point which remains valid upon replication in other subject pools and by other experimenters. Because market behavior is sensitive to both individual preferences and to the details of the structure of the institutional arrangements, the experimenter must avoid contaminating these variables with poorly developed experimental procedures. If the experimental procedures do not control these variables adequately, attempts to replicate the results may fail because the experimenter has unknowingly failed to conduct the same experiment. The section is a brief outline of the procedures, methods, and measurements.

2.1. Market creation

The key economic variables in all markets are the value individuals place on the object being transacted, and the form of the market organization within which buyers and sellers interact. Preferences are induced by a special application of derived demand theory called induced preference theory [Smith (1976b), Plott (1979)]. The theory takes advantage of the fact that principles of economics apply to all commodities and that otherwise neutral commodities receive value from the value of ultimate uses, i.e. derived demand. In an experimental market subjects normally trade a commodity (e.g. a paper transaction) that has no intrinsic or use value. The commodity is given value by the experimental rules governing the redemption values of buyers and the terms on which sellers can acquire the units they wish to sell. Buyers make money by buying units from sellers and reselling to the experimenter according to a predetermined redemption value schedule. The difference between the purchase price and redemption value is profit, which is the buyer's to keep. Sellers make a profit by purchasing units from the experimenter at a predetermined cost schedule and selling to the buyers. The difference is a profit which the seller keeps.

The idea is deceptively simple. An important property is that the profits are real and sufficiently high to be comparable to the probable opportunity cost of the subject. The key assumptions are that an individual prefers more money to less, has no attitude toward the commodity or situation other than the advantages created by potential resale, and that the individual fully understands the terms of resale. If these conditions hold, the redemption and cost schedules are measures of the limit price schedules for the subjects. The first column of Figure 19.1 contains an example of what buyers typically see. Row 1 shows the redemption value of the first unit this individual purchases during a period. The purchase price is entered in row 2, and the profit is entered in rows 3 and 4, respectively. As can be seen, these entries are made for each purchase during a period.

The incentives of individual i can be represented by a total revenue function $R^i(x_i)$ indicating the revenue generated by a quantity of purchases x_i. The magnitude $R^i(x_i) - R^i(x_i - 1)$, the redemption value for the x_ith unit can be seen as a limit price function. In the example shown in Figure 19.1 it is negatively sloped, but of course the slope as well as the pattern of such redemption value functions across agents are parameters under the control of the experimenter. Under competitive assumptions this redemption value schedule is the individual's inverse demand schedule. Thus, the experimenter, by varying these parameters, can control demand elasticity, market concentration, and other magnitudes of economic interest.

Incentives to suppliers are induced in a similar manner. The second column in Figure 19.1 demonstrates the technique for a typical individual supplier. Row 2 contains the cost of the first unit sold. This cost is incurred at the time of the sale. When the sale is made, the seller enters the selling price in the first row and then calculates the profits as directed by row 3. The profit from other sales made during this period is similarly calculated. Thus, individual i has a cost function $C^i(x_i)$, and the marginal cost, $\Delta C^i(x_i) = C^i(x_i) - C^i(x_i - 1)$, has already been calculated for the individual as shown on the forms. The shapes of the cost functions across sellers determine supply elasticity, concentration and entry, and are controlled by the experimenter.

At the top of Figure 19.1 you will notice a period indicator. Experimental markets are usually conducted over a series of periods of "trading days". The

REDEMPTION VALUES
INDIVIDUAL BUYER NUMBER ______
PERIOD ______

UNIT	ROW		VALUE
	1	1st UNIT REDEMPTION VALUE	$2.10
1	2	PURCHASE PRICE	
	3	PROFIT	
	4	2nd UNIT REDEMPTION VALUE	$1.60
2	5	PURCHASE PRICE	
	6	PROFIT	
	7	3rd UNIT REDEMPTION VALUE	$1.10
3	8	PURCHASE PRICE	
	9	PROFIT	
	10	4th UNIT REDEMPTION VALUE	$ .85
4	11	PURCHASE PRICE	
	12	PROFIT	
	13	5th UNIT REDEMPTION VALUE	$ .35
5	14	PURCHASE PRICE	
	15	PROFIT	
		TOTAL PERIOD EARNINGS	

COST
INDIVIDUAL SELLER NUMBER ______
PERIOD ______

UNIT	ROW		VALUE
	1	SELLING PRICE	
1	2	COST OF 1st UNIT	$.15
	3	PROFIT	
	4	SELLING PRICE	
2	5	COST OF 2nd UNIT	$ .65
	6	PROFIT	
	7	SELLING PRICE	
3	8	COST OF 3rd UNIT	$ .90
	9	PROFIT	
	10	SELLING PRICE	
4	11	COST OF 4th UNIT	$1.15
	12	PROFIT	
	13	SELLING PRICE	
5	14	COST OF 5th UNIT	$1.65
	15	PROFIT	
		TOTAL PERIOD EARNINGS	

Figure 19.1. Redemption and cost incentive forms.

length of a period is normally from 5 to 15 minutes depending upon the volume of activity anticipated. Unless the commodity has some explicit properties of an asset which has a life over time [Forsythe, Palfrey and Plott (1982)], each period is like an independent trading day with demands, supplies, profit potential, etc. independent of (but possibly identical with) those of previous periods. It is well established that trading patterns change as the market days are replicated. No good model of this dynamic exists but, as will be demonstrated below, the market equilibration process occurs with the replication of market periods.

Whether an individual is shown the redemption value for all periods at one time or just for one period at a time varies according to the purpose of the experiment. In many cases the individual knows his/her own redemption values for all periods at the beginning of the experiment, but there are important exceptions. If individual costs or redemption values are changing each period, for example, these would be revealed one at a time just before a period began. In almost all experiments the individual knows only his/her redemption value and nothing about the redemption value of others.[1] The procedures and instructions are designed to keep this type of information private.

In early experiments agents were given a small "commission" ranging from 5 to 15 cents for each trade. It is known that individuals tend not to trade units unless there is some advantage for doing so. The function of the commission was thus to induce marginal trades by overcoming what seems to be a small transactions cost [Plott and Smith (1978)]. More recent experimentation has dropped the use of commission and avoided the "marginal trade" problem by adjusting the market parameters to allow for some gains from trade at the margin. This practice is reflected in Figure 19.2.

The institutional organization of a market has been an important treatment variable. The mechanics of how buyers and sellers get together can substantially influence market performance. That is, for the same underlying incentives, the market performance is affected by a change of institutions. For example, the original experiments by Chamberlin (1948) had the agents circulating in a room and privately negotiating price when a buyer or seller was contacted. In some of these markets terms of trade were publicly displayed on the blackboard as they were consummated, while in others they were not. This market behaves much differently than, say, an oral double auction. In an oral double auction all bids and asks are orally tendered and publicly displayed, and only one outstanding (the last, the best, etc.) bid and ask is open at any time. Sellers (buyers) are free to accept an outstanding bid (ask) by a public, verbal indication. Thus, in the oral double auction, all bids, asks, and contracts are public information. Joyce (1983) demonstrates that the better information associated with the oral double auction as opposed to the Chamberlin process leads to a lower price variance, better convergence, and higher efficiencies.

Much of traditional industrial organization theory was developed to meet a need for understanding economic processes in which the market institutions themselves are endogenous. Questions regarding market conduct, market practices, cartel development, and evolution are all of primary importance, but they have not yet been addressed by experimentalists who, with very few exceptions, have tended to treat institutional variables as exogenous. Such decisions by experimentalists reflect in part, a need for more theory about the creation and evolution of market institutions. As theory and experimental techniques improve,

[1]Only one market experiment has allowed such complete information and it did not converge as expected [Smith (1981)]. Bargaining experiments reported in Roth, Malauf and Murnigham (1981) also suggest that models must be modified in the presence of an informational environment in which all monetary values are known by all agents.

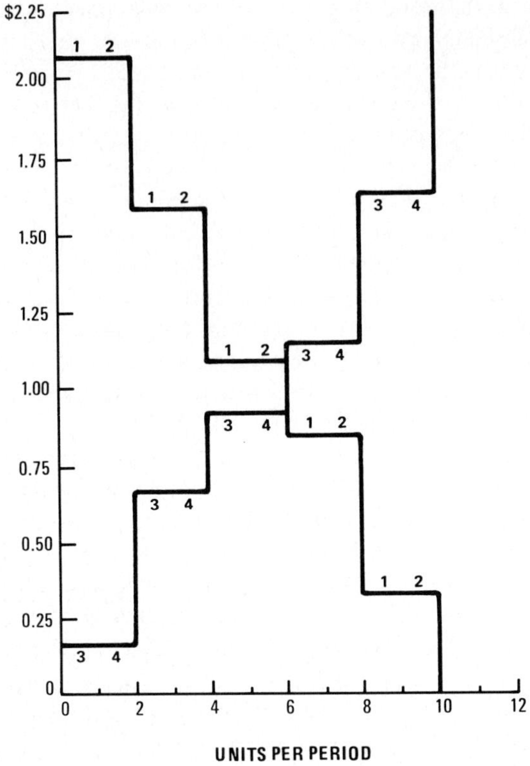

Figure 19.2. Aggregated limit values.

questions about the endogenous development of institutions and organization will be investigated.

Six prominent forms of market institutions have been studied in the experimental literature: (a) open outcry markets, (b) one-price mechanisms, (c) one-sided auctions, (d) posted-bid (offer) markets, (e) negotiated-price (telephone) markets, and (f) markets with "facilitating" devices.

Actually, the listing of only six different types involves an oversimplification. Each of these types can be subdivided further into special types. Auction markets, for example, can be either English or Dutch according to whether the prices start low and are bid up by competition or start high and are reduced until some competitor accepts. English auctions can be "oral double" or "one-sided". Markets differ according to whether or not the terms of contracts are public and the sequence in which bids, offers, and terms become known. The possibilities are so numerous that it sometimes seems more appropriate to think in terms of a continuum rather than fixed classes. For example, posted-price auctions look very similar to "sealed-bid" auctions if sellers must post prices without the knowledge of the prices of other sellers and without the ability to immediately "adjust" prices in light of the competition.

2.2. Laboratory procedures

The experimental procedures are one of the most important aspects of an experiment. The wording and the format of the instructions in most experiments have evolved so that very little about them is arbitrary or has escaped careful scrutiny. This extreme care is dictated by two overriding concerns. First, the procedures must be formulated so that other researchers, when following them, will be able to replicate reported results. The heart of the experimental method is replication and the procedures embody the operational content of many of the parameters and experimental conditions which, if changed may induce different results. If results are to replicate with different subject pools and different experimenters, then the procedures must be carefully considered. Secondly, there is a widespread belief that experimenters will or can influence the behavior of subjects by subtle suggestion about what the experimenter wants to demonstrate. Whether this belief is well founded is open to question,[2] but regardless of the answer the procedures must minimize the potential for such influences if the results are to be taken seriously by a large number of people.

Each of the procedural steps is subject to experimental control. Typically, subjects are recruited by announcements in class, bulletin boards, or newspapers.[3] Once subjects are assembled, the instructions are read and questions answered. Sometimes a practice period, or period zero in which no money is at stake, is conducted.

The technology used during the experiment is dictated by many considerations. Many experiments simply utilize a classroom with a chalkboard to record trades. Faculty offices and the connecting telephone system, the word processing system from typing pools, special electronic equipment designed for the experiment, and even citizens' band radios have been used. The most fully automated experiments are those using an interactive computer system.

The appendix contains sample instructions for posted-price markets and for oral auctions. Notice that subjects are not told to maximize or to make as much money as possible. Furthermore, words like "competition", "maximizing", "col-

[2]A possible example within the framework reviewed in this paper is explored in Cohen, Levine and Plott (1978). The case is one in which the subjects in a committee experiment evidently thought they were to provide insights for marketing strategies and ignored the incentive system in an attempt to do so.

[3]Sample announcements can be found in Hoffman and Plott (1983).

lusion", "coalition", etc. or other words which might suggest to the subject some theory or expectation on the part of the experimenter, have been carefully omitted. The examples used to illustrate accounting conventions and profit computations are standard across many different experiments. In fact, attempts are made to maintain – across vastly different types of experiments (e.g. committees vs. markets) – much of the wording and examples as possible in order to minimize the latitude for theories which seek to explain the results of a particular experimental series in terms of the language used in the instructions for that series. The instructions make clear the opportunities available to the subjects, but the motivation is supplied by the people.

The procedures can differ according to the purposes of the experiment. For example, marginal values are displayed in Figure 19.1 as opposed to total values so subjects need not compute the former in making decisions. It was done for them. The individuals take tests at the end of the instruction period to see if they can read these tables as hypothesized. After each of the first several periods, each individual's accounting is checked to see if there is any misunderstanding about the reward structure. Questions about the mechanics of calculating profits are welcomed and answered fully and openly. Yet, if someone asks, "What am I supposed to do?", the experimenter rereads the relevant portion of the instructions: "The experimenters do not care whether or how you participate so long as you stay within the confines of the rules". Presumably, if the capacity of an individual to understand or to recognize a reward structure was a variable to be studied as part of the market, then all of these procedures should possibly be changed, but for most of the experiments reviewed here this was not an objective.

Some of the procedures are adopted to allow individuals as much "independence" from the social situation as possible. Social security numbers and names (both of which are used as receipts for the monetary payments) are collected after the experiment is over. Individuals are paid in private so others need never know their earnings. When individuals are obviously confused or are having difficulty with the instructions, efforts are made to avoid any embarrassment. Commodity names or references to "similar" types of natural situations (stock markets, automobile industry, etc.) are usually not used in order to avoid giving some impression about how individuals are expected to act.

The level of incentives is typically somewhat above the hourly wage for the subject pool. For upper class undergraduate or graduate students the expected earnings are in the \$8–10 per hour range if the models are reasonably accurate. Employed adults participating at night or on weekends would earn more. Sometimes a flat payment, promised as a minimum in order to attract subjects, is paid at the beginning of the experiment in addition to money earned during the experiment.

From a pragmatic point of view experimentalists realize that their experiments will be checked by other researchers. Such researchers may have a vested interest in having the results *not* replicate. This is especially true in fields like industrial organization in which the data can become part of an adversary process. An unambiguous and complete set of experimental procedures is an important source of protection.

2.3. Performance measures

Price patterns, product quality, volume, distribution, and market efficiency are variables of obvious interest. Usually price is measured as the average of contract prices during a period but sometimes it means the last contract in a period. Volume and income distribution are easily observed. Product quality is observable in the sense that different quality items can be identified as different commodities in multicommodity experiments.

Efficiency as introduced by Plott and Smith (1978) is more subtle than the other performance measures, but the reader should note that it is exactly the traditional consumers' plus producers' surplus notion. In market experiments the system attains an efficient (Pareto optimal) allocation if and only if the subjects as a group maximize the total monetary payments from the experimenter. Thus, the relative efficiency of systems is determined by comparing the total payment to subjects with the maximum possible total payment. When uncertainty exists, the efficiency measure usually assumes no risk aversion and is thus based upon the maximum expected payment conditional on all the information that exists in the market.

In order to demonstrate how the measure of efficiency is related to ideas of consumers' plus producers' surplus, consider Figure 19.2. Assume the economy has two demanders, numbered 1 and 2, and two suppliers, numbered 3 and 4. The demanders are identical and each has the redemption values shown in Figure 19.1. The environment contains no random events. The suppliers are also identical and each has the marginal cost schedule in Figure 19.1. The market demand function is obtained by adding the (inverted) individual limit price functions, and the market supply is obtained by adding the (inverted) individual marginal cost functions. As can be seen, consumer plus producer surplus is maximized at six units with each buyer (seller) buying (selling) three (three) units. A quick check indicates that this allocation also maximizes total subject profits from the experiment. If, for example, another unit was purchased, the subjects' payment to the experimenter (marginal cost) would exceed experimenter payment to the subjects (redemption value) on this unit. Total profits would thus be decreased.

A typical market inefficiency would be of the following sort. Individual 3 from Figure 19.2 sells four units and individual 4 sells one. Exactly why and how this might occur is, of course, material for the field of industrial organization. From Figure 19.2 one can see that individual 3's fourth unit should have been excluded from the market because its cost is greater than the marginal benefit. Furthermore, individual 4's second and perhaps third unit should have been included in the market because the marginal social benefit was no less than the cost of these units.

The efficiency measure must be interpreted with some care when commissions are used. In some studies the commissions are included as part of the measure while in the other studies they are not. Including them makes the measure sensitive to whether or not the marginal (zero profit) trades are made, thereby capturing one aspect of efficiency. On the other hand, the commission seems to have no natural economic interpretation. Of course, in the example used here no commissions are used because the parameters are fixed to permit gains from marginal unit trades. Consequently, the problem does not arise.

The efficiency measure is also sensitive to the shapes of the curves as are all surplus measures. Suppose, for example, the first unit redemption values are increased by a factor of ten and the first unit marginal costs are reduced to zero. Because these units will almost surely trade and constitute a large proportion of the surplus, the system efficiency would increase for any expected pattern of trading. Thus, by adjusting the level of the base profit potential with intramarginal units that will almost surely trade and will constitute a large proportion of the surplus, the system efficiency would increase for any expected pattern of trading. Thus, by adjusting the level of the base profit potential with intramarginal units that will almost certainly trade, the absolute efficiency levels can be influenced.

A similar possibility exists with the allocation of redemption values across individuals. Suppose the two redemption values of $0.85 were held by a third and fourth individual who have the right to buy only the one unit. If either of these two individuals make a trade, efficiency drops. Since they have only one (inefficient) unit to trade, they stand ready to trade and will trade should the price *ever* "wander" down in that range. Thus, these units seem to have more opportunity to be traded than when they are held as the fourth unit by the original two traders. In the latter case, inefficient trading can occur only if the price wanders low enough *after* an individual has traded three units.

Other special problems with efficiency measures occur in the case of uncertainty. Thus far, experiments involving risk have had only a limited relevance to the industrial organization literature and will not be reviewed here [Plott and Sunder (1982)]. The important point is that comparisons of efficiencies across markets with different economic parameters must be treated with care. If the underlying economic parameters are held constant and the institutions alone are changed, the efficiency comparison has a more solid basis.

3. Competitive market models

This section reviews markets that have several agents who participate without benefit of collusion or market institutions that might facilitate collusive behavior. The principal forms of market organization reviewed are the open outcry markets, one-price processes, one-sided auctions, negotiated prices, and posted prices.

The influences of market organization can be subtle. The competitive law of supply and demand captures much of the long run tendencies better than any competing model. Experimental studies attempt to identify the influences of differences in market mechanisms in terms of convergence speed, distribution of income, and market efficiency.

The discussion begins with open outcry markets and in particular the oral double auction mechanism because of its major role in the development of experimental methods. The oral double auction is the most efficient of known mechanisms. It is also, in a sense, the most complicated. Many of the other mechanisms can be understood as placing emphasis on some subset of the features of the oral double auction (ODA). That is, the ODA seems to be constructed from the other mechanisms that are reviewed in this section. Thus, the study of the other mechanisms can be interpreted as a study of the different "parts" of the ODA. These relationships will be described along with the description of the ODA.

3.1. Open outcry markets: The oral double auction

Open outcry markets characterize the trading floors of stock exchanges and commodity exchanges. To observers these floors appear chaotic and disorganized. Yet the experimental research uncovers a remarkable system of order. The oral double auction, which is a type of open outcry market, was first studied by Vernon Smith who observed the rather remarkable equilibrating power of the mechanism [Smith (1962)]. His amazement is reflected in a series of experiments designed to explore the possibility that the equilibration first observed was due to the shapes of the curves. He also explored ideas about the dynamics of the convergence process [Smith (1965)].

The oral double auction mechanism (for single-unit trades) works as follows. Each buyer is free at any time during a period to tender a bid to buy one unit at a specified price. Likewise, each seller is free to tender an ask.[4] If the bid or ask is the first after a contract, then the amounts are unrestricted. If the bid is not the

[4] The language here differs among experimenters. The word "offer" is frequently used in place of the word "ask".

first after a contract, then it must be strictly higher than the previous bid[5] and it automatically cancels the previous bid. Elements of the English auction or "ascending" auction are evident in the oral double auction as the competition among buyers forces the bids upward until a contract occurs. The rule governing sellers is symmetric with that for buyers. If an ask is not the first after a contract, then the ask must be strictly lower than the previous ask. As competition among sellers brings the prices down in an attempt to get a buyer to accept, a process similar to the descending price clock[6] of the Dutch auction can be seen. Any buyer (seller) is free to accept an ask (bid) at any time to form a binding contract for one unit at the specified ask (bid). The resulting interplay allows elements of a third type of market mechanism, negotiated prices, to be seen as a single buyer repeatedly increases the bid and a single seller repeatedly lowers the ask, each "bargaining" in hope that the other will accept. Elements of sealed bids are present to the extent that reservation prices privately held by buyers and sellers, the prices at which they are willing to accept a contract, are equivalent to the privately determined bids in sealed-bid mechanisms. Similarly the reservation prices could be related to the prices posted in posted-price markets.

The oral double auction can be conducted by "hand" but several computerized versions now exist.[7] The overwhelming result is that these markets converge to the competitive equilibrium even with very few traders. Figure 19.3 contains the results of four experiments. The price of every sale in the order in which it occurred is shown. Each period represents a market day with a given demand and supply. The competitive equilibrium is slightly above $2 with a volume per period of eight contracts. As market days are replicated under identical conditions, prices tend to converge to the competitive equilibrium. Efficiency levels tend to converge to near 100 percent. This tendency is shown in all four experiments. If a change in parameters occurs, such as a shift in demand or supply, the prices converge to the new equilibrium after three or four periods.

As long as the industrial structure has a few buyers and sellers, these equilibrating and efficiency properties appear to be independent of the basic economic conditions. Different shapes of demands and supplies as systematically examined by Smith (1962, 1965, 1976a) yield no substantial differences in the overall conclusion concerning equilibrium. The variations explored covered various cases of demand elasticity and nonlinearity. Except for some special examples to be covered later, shape seems irrelevant to the question of equilibrium.

[5]This improvement requirement is called the New York Rule.

[6]In the Dutch auction a price "clock" starts at a high price and decreases until the descent is stopped by a buyer. The buyer who stopped the clock purchases the item at the price on the clock.

[7]The original computerized experimental market was developed by A. Williams (1980) for PLATO. Programs now exist for HP (Tom Copeland, GSM, UCLA), and IBM pc net [Johnson, Lee and Plott (1988)].

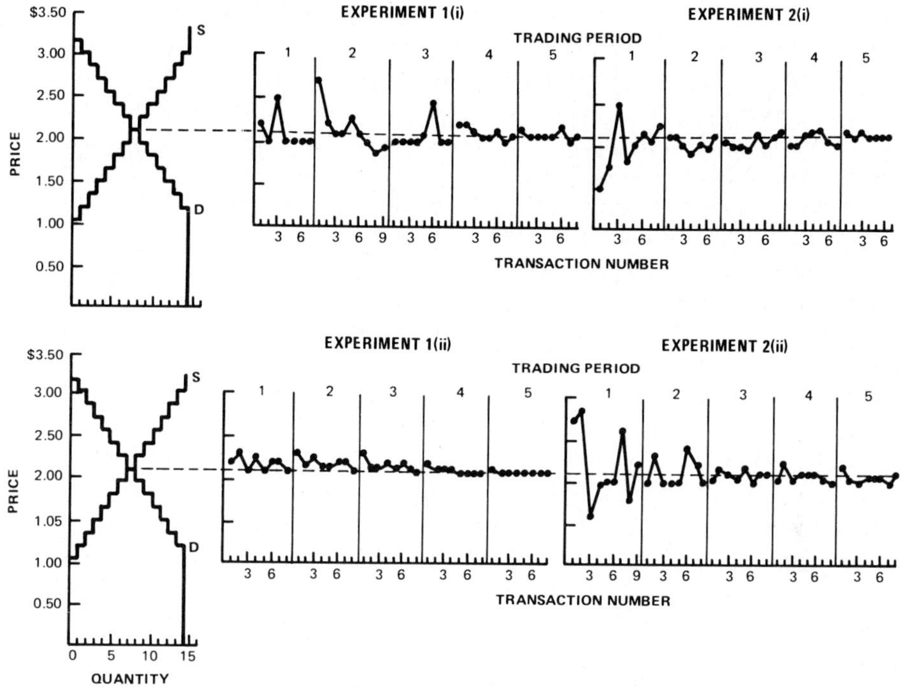

Figure 19.3. Oral double auction markets. *Source*: Smith (© 1976a, New York University, Chart 6, p. 53. Reprinted by permission of New York University Press).

Basic economic conditions do seem to influence the direction of convergence to equilibrium, and thus the distribution of income and profit. The path to equilibrium seems to be from above (below) if consumer's (producer's) surplus is greater than producer's (consumer's) surplus [Smith and Williams (1982a)]. Thus, one might expect that markets with relatively steep demands and reasonably flat supplies, record somewhat elevated profits for the sellers relative to the competitive equilibrium. These profits would accrue at disequilibrium trades and so the phenomenon would also be accompanied by falling prices. If the industry has been characterized by unanticipated demand or supply shifts, prices and profits can be affected by shape. Adjustment to a new equilibrium takes time, and profits or losses can certainly reflect disequilibrium trades. To date two studies have attempted to characterize the dynamic adjustment path [Smith (1965)], Daniels and Plott (1988)]. The conclusions from the Smith study are clouded by the fact that the choice of the estimation technique affects the conclusion regarding which dynamic adjustment theory Smith's data support [Nelson (1980)]. The Daniels and Plott study simply uses exponential adjustment as a maintained hypothesis

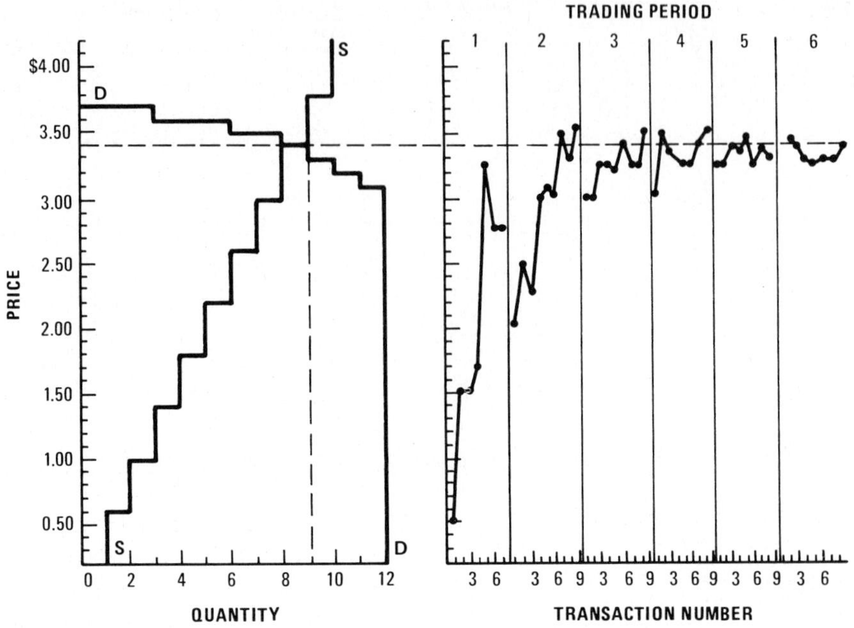

Figure 19.4. Oral double auction market. *Source*: Smith (© 1976a, New York University, Chart 3, p. 50. Reprinted by permission of New York University Press).

to demonstrate that markets with a constant percentage change in the competitive equilibrium equilibrate more slowly than stationary markets. No compelling theory of dynamic adjustment exists, and experimental studies have not yet explored the influence of basic economic conditions on adjustment paths sufficiently to provide any further generalizations.

Figure 19.4 has been added to show a typical adjustment path for an oral double auction when producer's surplus is greater than consumer's surplus. The path is from below. If the relative surpluses were reversed, the approach, according to currently accepted hypotheses, would be from above. The key parameter is the surpluses, however, and not demand or supply slopes, although in the case of linear functions these are obviously closely related.

Exactly why the convergence process occurs is unknown. Two theories have been advanced: Easley and Ledyard (1986) and Friedman (1984), but neither is a full explanation and neither has been systematically explored experimentally. Some general empirical properties are known. Computerized markets do not converge as rapidly as do those conducted orally. Expectations clearly play an important role in the convergence process. Both A.W. Williams (1987) and Daniels and Plott (1988) demonstrate that expectations in the oral double auction are near rational in the sense that the average of price forecasts are near the actual average price. The relationship between the forecasts and price is not clear because the bids and asks clearly contain information [Plott and Sunder (1982), Daniels and Plott (1988)]. Some insight about the dynamics of market adjustments are also provided by studies of the effects of price controls. Isaac and Plott (1981b) discovered that *nonbinding* controls could affect the adjustment path. A price ceiling slightly above the equilibrium path will cause the market to converge from below. Removal of a binding or nonbinding price ceiling causes a discontinuous jump in prices. The phenomenon is documented and explored extensively by Smith and Williams (1981b). In a most interesting demonstration Coursey and Smith (1983) find that the properties of nonbinding price controls carry over to posted-price markets discussed later in this review. Insights about price dynamics are also revealed in experiments with rules regarding price changes in security markets [Coursey and Dyl (1986)], but generally speaking models that have attempted to capture the dynamics of the equilibration of the oral double auction have not successfully captured the data from these markets in which some sort of nonbinding control exists.

There exists one major exception to the convergence to the competitive equilibrium. Holt, Langan and Villamil (1986) studied markets with five buyers and five sellers. Figure 19.5 contains the results typical of the markets they created. As can be seen the market does not converge and the key to the reason is in the demand and supply parameters. The five buyers are about equally sized and the market demand is very steep at the competitive equilibrium quantity. Only a single unit of excess supply exists. Furthermore, this unit is held by a "relatively large" seller with inframarginal units who can benefit from withholding the unit and thereby increasing the price. The individual holds some market power in this theoretical sense. Four of the six markets they created failed to converge to the competitive equilibrium.

The results support the model used by Holt, Langan and Villamil that market power will cause the oral double auction to generate prices other than the competitive equilibrium. However, the conclusion remains open to an alternative explanation because the results are also consistent with the model of convergence developed by Easley and Ledyard (1986). With one unit excess supply the Easley and Ledyard model predicts that the competitive equilibrium need not occur. Because both of the models are consistent with the data, additional experiments are necessary to remove any ambiguity associated with the explanation offered by Holt and Villamil.

Several variations of the oral double auction have been studied. The rules developed above included a "New York improvement provision", which calls for any bid or ask to be an improvement over the previous bid or ask. Many early experiments did not utilize the improvement provision. Some markets have dropped the provision that only one bid and ask be outstanding [R. Miller and Plott (1985), Lynch, R. Miller, Plott and Porter (1986)]. Markets with a specialist's book have been studied [Smith and Williams (1982a)]. The mechanism has been

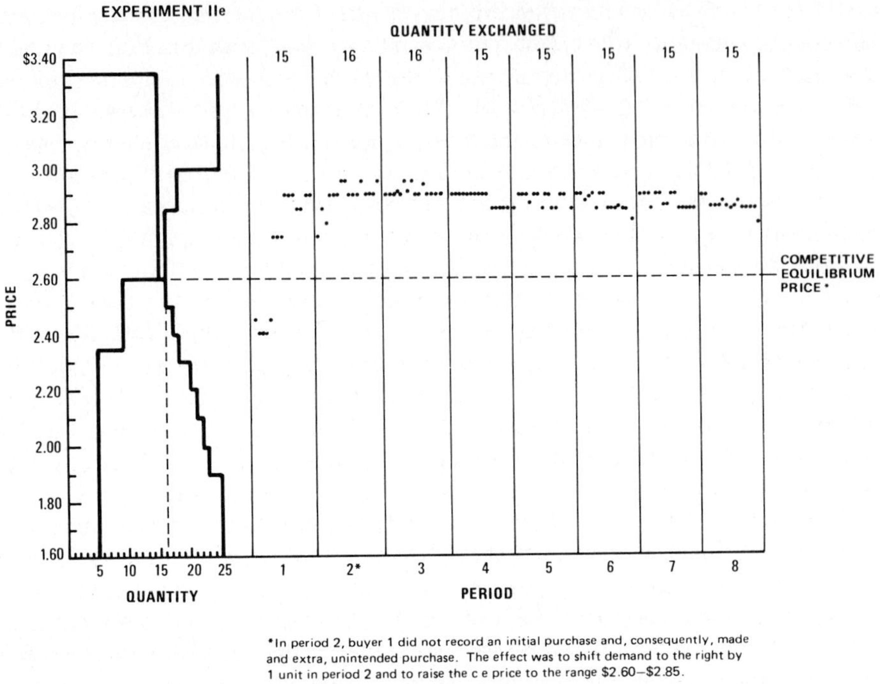

Figure 19.5. Oral double auction market. *Source*: Holt et al. (1986, p. 115).

generalized to accommodate multiple unit transactions [Plott and Gray (1988)]. While differences in these variations of the oral double auction mechanism have been observed, the overall convergence property has always been present.

It was once believed that one-sided oral auctions had special convergence properties. For example, it was thought that oral bid markets in which only bids and no asks could be tendered would converge from above [Plott and Smith (1978), Smith (1982), Plott (1982)]. Further research has demonstrated that the belief was formulated on an insufficient sample size [Walker and A.W. Williams (forthcoming)] and that the direction of convergence from one-sided oral auctions is no different from the double oral auctions.

3.2. *One-price mechanisms*

Trading in the oral double auction takes place at many different prices. With time and repetition the variance of prices decreases but the existence of trades at "disequilibrium" prices is a fundamental property of the process. By contrast one-price mechanisms attempt to find a single price at which the market "clears" and all trading takes place at that price. If the mechanism finds the competitive equilibrium price and facilitates all trades there, then the process would be 100 percent efficient. And if the competitive equilibrium price was obtained sufficiently quickly, the mechanism would outperform the oral double auction.

Two one-price mechanisms have been studied; a tâtonnement mechanism and a sealed bid-offer mechanism. The tâtonnement mechanism operated as follows [Joyce (1984)]. An auctioneer announced an arbitrary price. Buyers would each indicate on a card the amount they were willing to purchase at that price and the sellers would each hold up a card indicating the quantity they wished to sell. Subjects were not informed of the excess demand or supply at a price. They only knew if the price changed. Price changed according to the rule ΔP = 5¢ (revealed excess demand). If excess demand was small or flipped from positive to negative, the price changes became small with the exact amount "judiciously chosen" by the auctioneer. When the market cleared exactly the process stopped. Clearly, this stopping rule is important for the manipulability and observed efficiency of the mechanism. The exact rules for price changes were not told to the subjects so the latitude for manipulability was narrow.

Six markets were conducted with ten buyers and ten sellers who were able to trade one unit each. Trading in all markets was near the competitive equilibrium but prices did not settle down at the competitive equilibrium price and quantity. Only eighteen periods of a total of fifty-three periods were at the competitive equilibrium price and thirteen of the eighteen were at the competitive equilibrium volume. The marginal units tended to not trade. Consequently, efficiency of this mechanism might prove to be below that of the oral double auction in which marginal units do tend to trade,[8] but comparison experiments with the oral double auction were not conducted. Joyce did experiment with segregated buyers and sellers in a manner that placed each group in a separate room and made revealed demand public to buyers and revealed supply public to sellers. Some systematic underevaluation of quantities (relative to the competitive response) appears to be due to the segregation and related information changes. The important lesson seems to be that strategic behavior can be detected within a tâtonnement mechanism so it need not perform as competitive theory suggests.

Sealed bid-offer mechanisms were studied by Smith et al. (1982). Buyers submitted sealed bids and sellers submitted sealed asks. The bids were arranged in a market demand function and the asks were arranged in a supply function. Price was determined by the intersection of demand and supply. If the price so

[8] The efficiency numbers that Joyce reports are a little misleading. Commissions are paid by Joyce but are not included in the efficiency measure. Thus the numbers he reports do not reflect untraded marginal units.

determined was not unique, then the market price was the midpoint of the set of prices such that excess demand was zero.

Two different sealed bid-offer mechanisms were studied. In the first, termed PQ, buyers (sellers) could submit only a single price and maximum quantity they wished to purchase (sell). That is, only rectangular individual demand (supply) functions could be submitted. In the second mechanism, called $P(Q)$, there were no restrictions on the individual demand and supply functions that can be submitted. A separate price could be bid (ask) for each unit.

The two basic mechanisms were studied with and without the existence of a voting procedure. When the voting procedure was in place, these who had positive purchases or sales at the market-determined price were allowed to vote on whether or not the process would iterate thereby letting agents submit new demand and supply functions. Thus, in reality, four one-price processes were studied: PQ, $P(Q)$, and when votes were added, these mechanisms became two new mechanisms, PQv and $P(Q)v$.

The "best" mechanisms in terms of efficiency were the oral double auction and $P(Q)$. The next ordered by efficiency was $P(Q)$. The worst were PQ and PQv. Both of these latter suffered because of phenomena that Smith interprets as the strategic behavior reminiscent of monopoly vs. monopsony, which appears to be encouraged by the mechanism.

3.3. *Auction markets (sale of a fixed supply)*

The study of auctions is central to the study of industrial organization because auction processes seem to be the building blocks from which more complicated markets are constructed. All markets have features that are formalized in auctions. In a sense auctions embody the pure form of institutional arrangements.

A natural question turns on the degree to which the broadest of tools, the law of supply and demand, can be relied upon to predict the results of auctions. The demand and supply model is easy to apply. A fixed supply is auctioned so the supply function is vertical. The demand curve is dictated by the limit prices. A second natural question to ask is whether or not the market behavior is influenced by the type of auction. Of course a third question is what deeper principles dictate the answer to the first two questions. Those three questions are at the heart of the research.

Almost everyone is familiar with the English auction. According to the English auction rules (sometimes called a progressive auction) each unit is sold to the highest bidder. Each unit is auctioned separately with prices bid up in increments determined by the bidders themselves perhaps with the aid of an auctioneer. The unit is sold when the ascent stops or is stationary for a predetermined length of time.

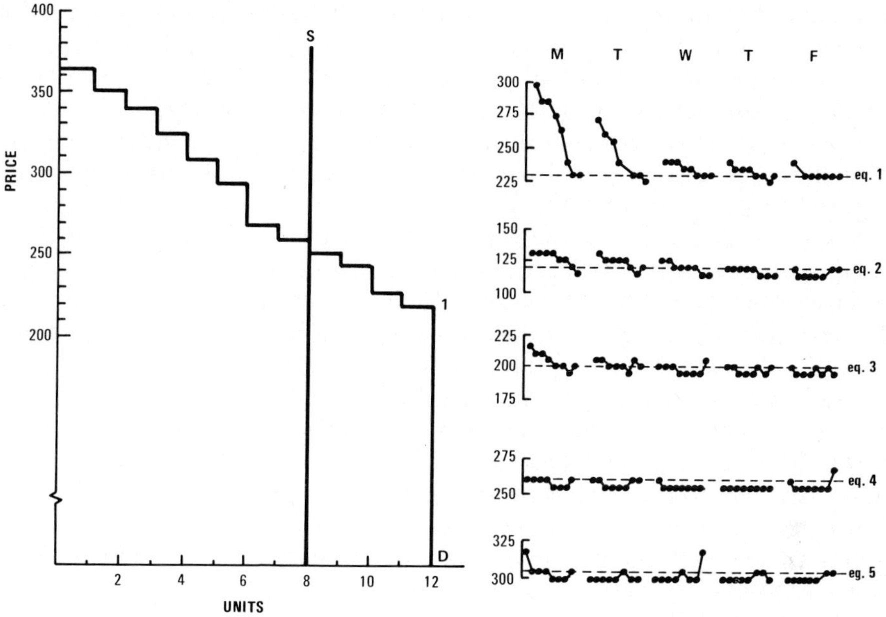

Figure 19.6. *Source*: P. Burns (1985, Fig. 1, p. 280, and Fig. B.1C., p. 297).

The convergence property of a multiple unit English auction under stable demand and supply conditions has been demonstrated[9] by Burns (1985). Figure 19.6 contains an example market from the series she reports. Each period a supply of eight units was sold. The demand curve was induced by the techniques described above. It was stationary as shown in the figure for five periods. Each trader knew only his/her own redemption values. As can be seen the first trades tend to be above equilibrium as high valued buyers compete with one another for the first units. With repetition the prices tend to equilibrate with low variances near the competitive equilibrium. Does the English auction always come into the equilibrium from above? Is the direction of convergence influenced by the shape of the curve? The answers to these questions are currently unknown.

Sealed-bid auctions are also common. The first sealed-bid experiments with many bidders were conducted by Smith (1967). The possible convergence to the competitive equilibrium was not the question posed by the early Smith experiments. Instead, his experiments were motivated by a controversy about the

[9]In an earlier work the English auction was studied by Frahm and Schrader (1969) who compared the English with a Dutch auction.

marketing of United States Treasury bonds. The Treasury uses a sealed-bid discriminative auction. If Q units are to be sold, they are sold to the Q highest bidders at prices equal to the bids. Critics of the Treasury believed that a sealed-bid, one-price auction would generate more money. In the one-price auction the Q units are sold to the Q highest bidders, but all bidders would pay the same price and this price would equal the Qth highest bid or the $(Q + 1)$th highest depending upon the rules.

Smith examined a market in which lotteries were auctioned. Belovicz (1979), using this same type of market, explored extensively the principal belief that emerged from the Smith study that the relative revenue-generating capabilities of the two auction institutions depended critically upon the magnitude of excess demand. The results emerging from the Belovicz study are mixed.

The question about the revenue-generating capacities of the two auctions was pursued further by G.J. Miller and Plott (1985) who also studied the behavior of repeated auctions under conditions of stationary demand and supply. This allowed the equilibrating properties to be observed and checked to see if the law of supply and demand applied. In the Miller and Plott study the personal value of the object was known with certainty but the values of other bidders was unknown. Bidders could purchase more than one unit. Individual demands were rotated each period in a manner which preserved aggregate demand but changed each individual demand.

The principal result of the study suggests that the relative revenue-generating capabilities of the two types of auctions depend upon demand elasticity with discriminative auctions generating more revenue when demand is relatively inelastic and one-price auctions generating more revenue when demand is relatively elastic. In part, this is due to the weight of "disequilibrium" auctions. Convergence is near the competitive equilibrium, and after convergence takes place, these two types of auction generate about the same revenue. A conjecture about the Smith–Belovicz conjecture also emerges from the study. In order to increase excess demand, Smith and Belovicz increased the number of demanders. If this increase in numbers also resulted in an increase in the slope, as from a population in which risk aversion was normally distributed could do, the latter and not the excess demand would account for differential revenues observed by Smith and Belovicz.

Figure 19.7, taken from G.J. Miller and Plott (1985), illustrates the point. The limit price function is the curve *LOL*. The Nash equilibrium bidding curve is the line *POL* for the discriminative auction and it is *LOL* for the one-price auction when there is some uncertainty. The actual bids for the first period under a discriminative auction are as shown by *dd*. Under one-price auctions the distribution of bids is about the same for the first period. Under the one-price auction the distribution of bids approaches the limit price function *LOL* after several periods so the price is *P*. The distribution of actual bids under the discriminative

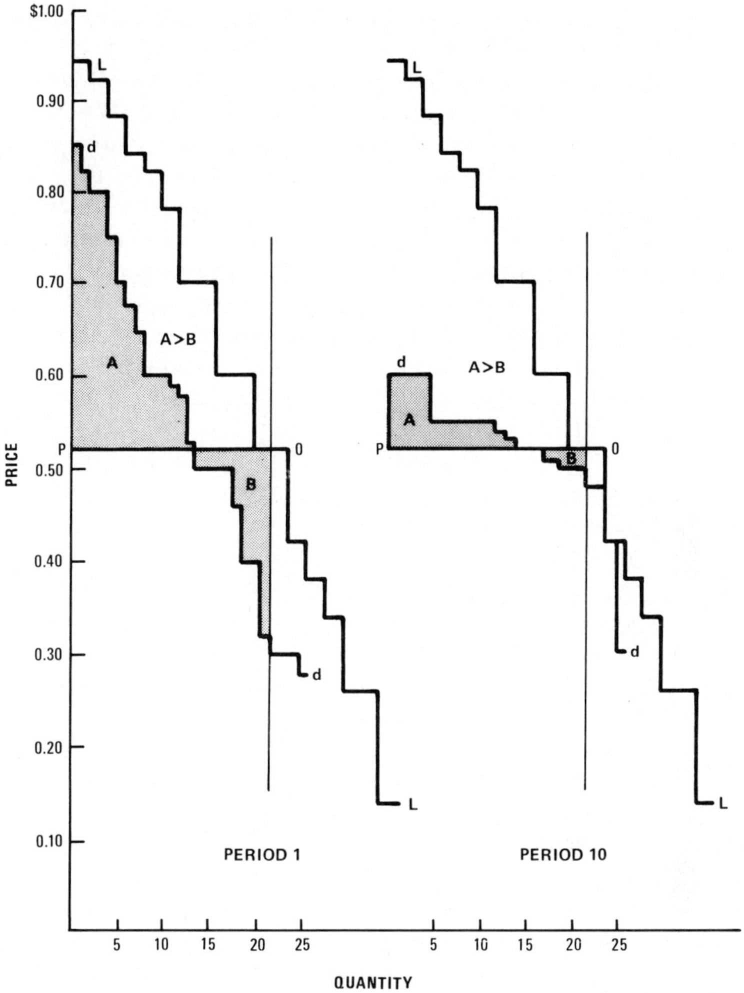

Figure 19.7. Demand and revealed demand in a discriminative auction. *Source*: G. Miller and Plott (1985, pp. 172, 173) and Plott (1982, p. 1506).

auction in the tenth period is shown. Since the area A is greater than the area B, the revenue under the discriminative auction is greater in this period.

Exactly why these auctions converge to the competitive equilibrium (or Nash equilibrium) is not fully understood. Intuitive explanations are not hard to generate but an explanation based upon first principles is something else. In fact, there exists no formal model of the convergence process shown in the two figures.

Formal models of bidding have been developed in a different environment. Assume that only one unit per period is sold. Assume further that individual valuations are drawn at random each period from a distribution that is public information. Thus, market demand as well as individual demands are not stationary from period to period. Modern auction theories based on such environments were tested by Coppinger, Smith and Titus (1980). The market institutions they examined there are the English auction, the Dutch auction,[10] first-price sealed-bid auction, and the second-price sealed-bid auction. Theoretically (Nash bidding hypothesis) the English and the second-price auction are equivalent and the Dutch and the first-price auction are equivalent in terms of prices and efficiency. Revenue from the Dutch auction and first-price auction should exceed that of the English auction and the second-price auction. Many experiments with these auctions indicate that the English and second-price auctions behave substantially the same, and prices and efficiencies of these two exceed those of the other two. The Dutch and first-price auction are not the same, with prices and efficiency of the latter greater. The models capture some of the data but paradoxes and contradictions exist.

The theory was explored even further in Cox, Roberson and Smith (1982) which investigates the general reliability of the Nash equilibrium hypothesis. For purposes of exposition we will report only on the single-unit case in which individual values v_i are independently drawn from a constant density on $[0, 1]$. By expressing bids as a fraction of the largest possible value the results generalize to any interval. Each agent knows his own value before bidding but not the value of others. The above facts are public knowledge and can be controlled for experimental purposes; that is, auctions can actually be created that objectively have the requisite properties.

The auction theory literature suggests that the system will behave *as if* the following are true.

(a) Agents choose in accord with the expected utility hypothesis. In order to obtain a model that can be solved we will assume each player has a utility function of wealth $U_i(y) = y^{r_i}$, where r is distributed across the population by a publicly known probability distribution ϕ on $[0, 1]$. The constant r is a risk aversion factor. This assumption will be treated as a maintained hypothesis for purposes of analyzing the data and testing the theory.

(b) At the time of choice each agent, i, knows (v_i, r_i), his own value and risk parameter, but knows only the probability distribution from which those of others were drawn.

(c) Each individual follows Bayes's law in forming expectations.

(d) Each individual will choose a Nash equilibrium bidding function.

(e) There are N agents.

[10] Prices start high and move downward in fixed intervals. The bidder who first stops the downward price movement purchases the object at the price.

Table 19.1
Theoretical predictions and means and variances pooled over n markets

		First		Second	
N	Statistics	Observed price	Risk neutral ($r = 1$) theoretical	Observed price	Theoretical
3	Mean	2.44 ($n = 70$)	2.5	1.97	2.5
	Variance	0.589	0.384	0.759	0.96
4	Mean	5.64 ($n = 60$)	4.9		
	Variance	1.80	0.96		
5	Mean	9.14 ($n = 60$)	8.1		
	Variance	1.37	1.83		
6	Mean	13.22 ($n = 60$)	12.1	11.21	12.1
	Variance	4.31	3.0	8.20	6.4
9	Mean	31.02 ($n = 30$)	28.9	27.02	28.9
	Variance	4.91	8.38	18.66	18.85

Source: Cox, Roberson and Smith (1982).

Under all of the above assumptions the symmetric Nash equilibrium bidding functions are:

$$b_i = \begin{cases} v_i, & \text{for all } i \text{ if the second-price auction is used,} \\ \dfrac{(N-1)v_i}{N-1+r_i}, & \text{for all } i \text{ if the first-price auction is used.} \end{cases}$$

The comparative institutional prediction is that the expected price under the first-price auction is greater than the expected price under the second-price auction. Table 19.1 reproduces the results of some of the Smith et al. experiments. The range of the support function $[0, \bar{V}]$ was varied with N to keep expected profits, as calculated by the model, the same as N increased. Notice first that the model is very accurate when applied to the second-price auction for $N > 3$. For example, if $N = 6$ the model predicts a mean price of 12.1 and the actual price averaged 11.21. The predicted variances are also close to those observed. As predicted by the model, people tend to bid their value when they participate in the second-price auction. Secondly, notice that the prediction about the *market* treatment variable is also correct. The average price for the second-price auctions is below the average price of the first-price auctions for every value of N. The first-price auction generates more revenue as predicted.

The risk neutral model ($r = 1$) tends to develop inaccuracies when applied to the magnitude of first-price auction bids. Of course, the risk neutrality parameter was not controlled in these experiments. In any case, prices in the first-price auction are higher than those predicted by the model if we assume $r = 1$. If the data are tested against the risk averse model, which predicts that observed prices will be above the risk neutral prediction, for every value of N the model cannot be rejected for $N > 3$. Cox, Smith and Walker (1985) report on examinations of individual bidding behavior that test more directly the existence of the constant relative risk aversion utility used in the model. Their data continues to support the model but some rather sharp contradictions were observed when they attempted to apply incentive methods that might control for risk aversion [Berg et al. (1986)].

The support for the Nash equilibrium-based models has continued [Cox, Smith and Walker (1984)] as research has expanded to a study of the multiple units case although the model has encountered difficulties for some values of N. For the single-unit case, however, the full Nash equilibrium model with all of its implicit and explicit rationality assumptions is the most accurate model that exists. To the extent that the model places restrictions on data it is consistent with the facts in an absolute sense.

Recently the study of experimental sealed-bid auctions has been extended to the more general class of common-value auctions in which a "winner's curse" can occur [Kagel and Levin (1986)]. The winner's curse involves a type of systematic overbidding for an item with an uncertain value, thereby causing the winners to lose money on average. A prominent theory is that the phenomenon exists because of a systematic and special type of judgment failure of the bidders as opposed to a more general failure of rationality or a more general failure of the Nash equilibrium model. The research centers around two fundamental questions: (a) Can a winner's curse be observed, and (b) does it occur because of the particular theoretical reasons? The answers to both questions are the same – yes.

The experimental auctions used in the Kagel and Levin study each consisted of the sale of a single item to the highest bidder. The redemption value of the item was the same, unknown value to all bidders. The value of the item, V, was determined prior to the auction by a draw from a uniform distribution over the internal $[\underline{V}, \overline{V}]$. Typically the internal was [\$15, \$100] or [\$25, \$225]. Once the value, V, of the item was determined, each agent was given a private signal x_i about the value. The variables, x_i, were drawn from a distribution uniform on the interval $[V - \varepsilon, V + \varepsilon]$, e.g. $[V - \$12, V + \$12]$.

Now the expected value of the item given a signal is

$$E(V|x_i) = x_i. \tag{1}$$

However, the relevant expected value for purposes of bidding is the expected value given that the agent won the item, which intuition correctly suggests, is the expected value given that the agent's private signal is the highest. Because an order statistic is involved, the formula becomes:

$$E(V|x_i = \text{highest}) = x_i - \varepsilon\frac{(N-1)}{(N+1)}. \tag{2}$$

The potential irrationality can now be seen. If competitors use the second, correct formula in computing a bid function, the risk neutral Nash equilibrium bid function is

$$b(x_i) = x_i - \varepsilon + y \quad \text{(RNNE)}, \tag{3}$$

where $y = [2\varepsilon/N + 1]\exp[-(N/2\varepsilon)(x_i - \bar{V} - \varepsilon)]$. Suppose agents use the expected value neglecting the order statistic property. Then the bid function becomes the bounded rational function:

$$b(x_i) = x_i - (2\varepsilon/N) + Y/N \quad \text{(BR)}. \tag{4}$$

If $N > 3$ the bounded rational function (BR), equation (4), produces a winner's curse. That is, $b(x_i) > E(V|x_i = \text{highest})$. So the function (BR) of equation (4) becomes a model to be compared with (RNNE) of equation (3).

The experimental data provide no support for the winner's curse in groups of size 3 and 4. The RNNE model did better than the zero (to negative) profit prediction of winner's curse model. The bids were somewhat higher than predicted by the model with profits averaging 0.68 of predicted profits. In groups of size 6 or 7 the picture differs. Negative expected profits occurred regularly. Furthermore, the mechanism by which the losses occurred was substantially as outlined by the bounded rationality theory. The agents with the highest signals tended to win the auctions. The bids tendered by the winners were closer to the BR model than to the RNNE model.

The winner's curse experiments are particularly interesting. The data continue to generate support for Nash equilibrium behavior. However, the Nash equilibrium operative in these markets is derived from individual decision rules that contain a systematic statistical error on the part of agents. Agents behave strategically but they do not adjust for the order statistic property of the winning bid and they do not behave as if other agents will make the same error. The errors appear to be transitory in the sense that trial and error with the accompanying losses appears to discipline participants into "rational" behavior, but the data suggests that the learning is situation specific. That is interpreted to mean that the reasons for the error, as captured by the order statistic property is not automatically incorporated into the cognitive aspects of the decision and is therefore not carried over to unfamiliar bidding situations. In other words, the learning is not rational in a cognitive sense.

Experimental auction research has not been restricted to basic science. Grether, Isaac and Plott (1981, forthcoming) used the results of experimental auction markets as the tool for exploring proposed reform of methods of determining air-carrier access to the four major airports. At the time, 1979, airport access was determined by committees of carriers certificated to operate at the airport. These committees operated under unanimity. The Grether, Isaac and Plott report was based on a direct study of these committees; a study of experiments with committees operating under the same rules; and a study of experiments with auction processes that were designed to do the same allocation job as the committees.

The report concluded that the committees should be replaced by one-price auctions with an aftermarket. It also recommended either lotteries with an aftermarket or grandfathered rights with an aftermarket as alternatives. After several years of politics an alternative process involving grandfathered rights to land and markets for these rights was adopted.[11] The landing right problem is especially interesting because of the complementarities among items to be sold at different auctions. A carrier might not want the right to take off at O'Hare unless it had the right to land at Washington National. Yet the rights were to be sold at different auctions. The obvious coordination problem has been addressed by a new type of computer assisted auction, created by Rassenti, Smith and Bulfin (1982) that ties these markets together.

The exploration of sealed-bid institutions is initiated along a different dimension by Palfrey (1983, 1985). The question is whether a monopolist who has several different objects to sell by a first-price sealed-bid auction is better off by selling them separately or by bundling them together and selling the packages. With few bidders, bundling is profitable, but as the number of bidders increases, the advantage of bundling over separate auctions decreases.

3.4. Negotiated prices

A large and diverse literature addresses two-person bargaining [Roth (1987)]. One approach to the analysis of markets with negotiated prices would be to build principles of market behavior from models of two person interactions. Currently that is not possible. An alternative approach is to study the market aggregates without a full understanding of the activities at the levels of pairs of bargainers. Studies that adopt this alternative approach are reviewed here.

Market mechanisms in which price negotiations take place have two prominent features that have been explored. The first is the fact that the price setting process is negotiated, which appears to involve much more complicated strategy spaces than mechanisms like the oral double auction. If negotiation is face to face or involves verbal communication, the potential sources of information, signals, etc. are so numerous that no real attempt exists to completely characterize the

[11] Correspondence between Charles Plott and Chris deMuth in *Aviation Daily*, Washington, D.C., 25 July, 1983, back of pages 124 and 127.

mechanism. The second feature is the potential private nature of negotiations. Negotiation strategies, positive final contract prices, opportunities, etc. may be known only to the contracting parties so shopping and searching for better deals may be costly in terms of time and forgone opportunities.

The very first market experiments, those reported by Chamberlin (1948) were negotiated price markets. Agents circulated in a room making contracts which were made public depending upon the treatment. The second study of negotiated price markets was reported by Hong and Plott (1982) in which the market was made through bilateral telephone conversations. Agents were located in separate offices. Buyers and sellers could call each other and discuss terms and/or agree on a contract price. Contact among buyers or among sellers was prevented so information about prices was limited. Buyers could shop at the cost of a (free) phone call.

The distribution of prices from Hong and Plott experiments is shown in Figure 19.8. As can be seen, the system begins with a wide variance in prices. Evidently some buyers are just better negotiators than others but the source of this (dis)advantage, whether they shop more (less), or make more (less) credible promises or threats, etc., is unknown.

With time the variance of contract prices shrinks. The mean price approaches the competitive equilibrium. When demand shifts (periods 5 and 9) the prices approach the new equilibrium. Efficiency in these markets is in the 80–90 percent range as shown in the figure. Volume in the Hong and Plott experiments is greater than the competitive equilibrium volume. This result, when combined with those of Chamberlin (1948) and Joyce (1983), suggests that poor information may result in sales exceeding the competitive equilibrium.

Only two different industrial structures have been explored within this market institution. The Hong and Plott study had eleven buyers of about equal size. The twenty-two sellers ranged from relatively large (the five largest firms had 60 percent of the market) to relatively small sellers, some of whom should not be able to make transactions according to the competitive model because their costs were above the competitive equilibrium price. The price time series shows that the competitive model is a reasonably accurate predictor of equilibrium, but some marginal sellers were able to sell at prices above the competitive equilibrium price to buyers who were evidently poorly informed or did not choose to shop.

The second study, by Grether and Plott (1984), examined telephone markets with two large sellers (each with 35 percent of the market) and two small sellers (15 percent each). Sellers in the experiment even had accurate knowledge of the market demand functions. The average prices, shown in Figure 19.9, are typical of the general results. Similar to the Hong and Plott results, prices initially have a high variance. With time, variance is reduced and the competitive equilibrium is approached.

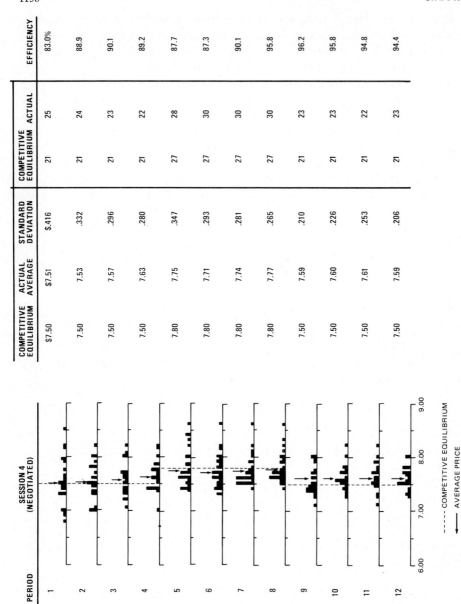

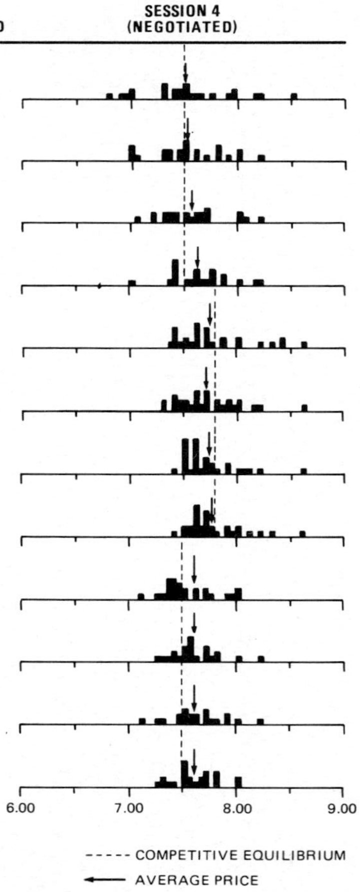

PERIOD	COMPETITIVE EQUILIBRIUM	ACTUAL AVERAGE	STANDARD DEVIATION	COMPETITIVE EQUILIBRIUM	ACTUAL	EFFICIENCY
1	$7.50	$7.51	$.416	21	25	83.0%
2	7.50	7.53	.332	21	24	88.9
3	7.50	7.57	.296	21	23	90.1
4	7.50	7.63	.280	21	22	89.2
5	7.80	7.75	.347	27	28	87.7
6	7.80	7.71	.293	27	30	87.3
7	7.80	7.74	.281	27	30	90.1
8	7.80	7.77	.265	27	30	95.8
9	7.50	7.59	.210	21	23	96.2
10	7.50	7.60	.226	21	23	95.8
11	7.50	7.61	.253	21	22	94.8
12	7.50	7.59	.206	21	23	94.4

Figure 19.8. Telephone market. *Source*: Plott (1982, p. 1497).

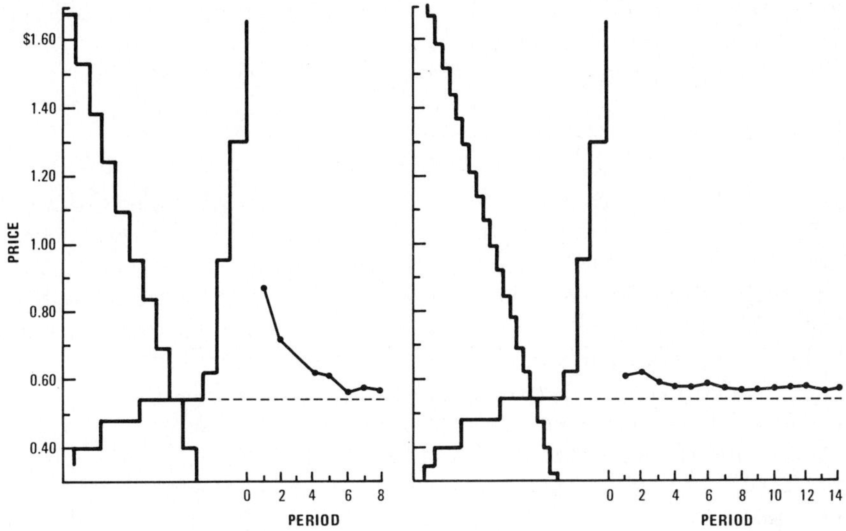

Figure 19.9. Average price per period for all periods in two markets. *Source*: Plott (1982, p. 1498).

A third study by Crössman (1982) was not a telephone market. Individual negotiations took place in private booths. Prices and other terms of contracts were strictly private information, so information was less available than in telephone markets in which several shopping calls could be made easily. Multiple-unit or block trades were possible. Sellers were required to make binding quantity decisions prior to the opening of a market period. On average, prices were near the competitive equilibrium relative to the predictions of other static models. In these cobweb, unstable markets there exist no pronounced cycles.

The fourth and most recent study was by Joyce (1983). The Chamberlin mechanism of privately negotiated prices was compared to the oral double auction. Both of these mechanisms were further refined according to whether or not transactions were written on the chalkboard.[12] Three markets were conducted under each of the four market organizations giving a total of twelve markets. Average prices in all markets were close to the competitive equilibrium. The price variance was much higher in the negotiated price markets. Volume in the negotiated price markets was also higher. These findings are consistent with the other studies in which possible restrictions of information about alternative prices was a variable. Better information reduces price variance and tends to exclude extra marginal agents. The efficiency values of all four markets is high

[12]The exact timing of this public announcement is unclear for the Chamberlin mechanism conducted by Joyce. Presumably the announcement was made as soon as the deal was made during a period.

due, perhaps, to Joyce's choice of experimental parameters.[13] No substantial differences in efficiency are reported.

3.5. *Posted prices*

Posted-price research has tended to concentrate on mechanisms in which prices are privately posted and then made public. Once the prices are public, no discounting from published prices is permitted and prices cannot be changed for some suitable period of time. The process resembles a rate bureau more than an auction. In a posted offer (as opposed to posted bid) experiment, each seller submits a price, presumably in a sealed-bid fashion without benefit of consultation with other sellers. All prices are publicly posted, typically on a chalkboard, and cannot be changed by the seller for some fixed period. Buyers first approach the lowest priced seller, who can sell only at the posted price and who sells units until he wishes to sell no more at that price. As the low price sellers run out of stock, buyers move to the higher priced sellers. Since buyers will seek the low price advantages of the first buyer, a random device is usually applied to determine orderly access. After all buyers have had an opportunity to purchase, the period ends and sellers make pricing decisions for the next period.

The results of two experimental oral double auction markets are shown in Figure 19.10 in the upper right corner and the results of two experimental posted-offer markets are shown in the lower right. Each market consisted of four buyers and four sellers. The graph in the left of the figure is the market supply and demand model constructed from the parameters. The parameters of all markets were the same, but the participants differed. In the oral double auction markets, the average price during the first period is shown as the first dot and the average price during the second period is shown as the second dot. The price range during the period is the shaded area. Similar data are shown for the two posted-offer markets. The results are typical of data that have been generated by many replications.

Two aspects of the results are of interest. First, with repetition under fixed conditions, the market prices are near those predicted by the model, and efficiencies approach 90–100 percent. Second, prices tend to be higher for posted-price markets than for oral double auctions (about 10 cents higher in these markets) and efficiencies are lower. The efficiencies for the posted-price markets are in the low 90s, compared to 100 percent for the oral double auction markets.

The posted-price institution induces an upward pressure on prices. It also exerts a downward pressure on efficiency. This result signals a potential delicacy

[13] The markets had only one extramarginal unit. Furthermore, the "steps" in the functions were large ($0.20) so it was easy for extramarginal units to be excluded from trades.

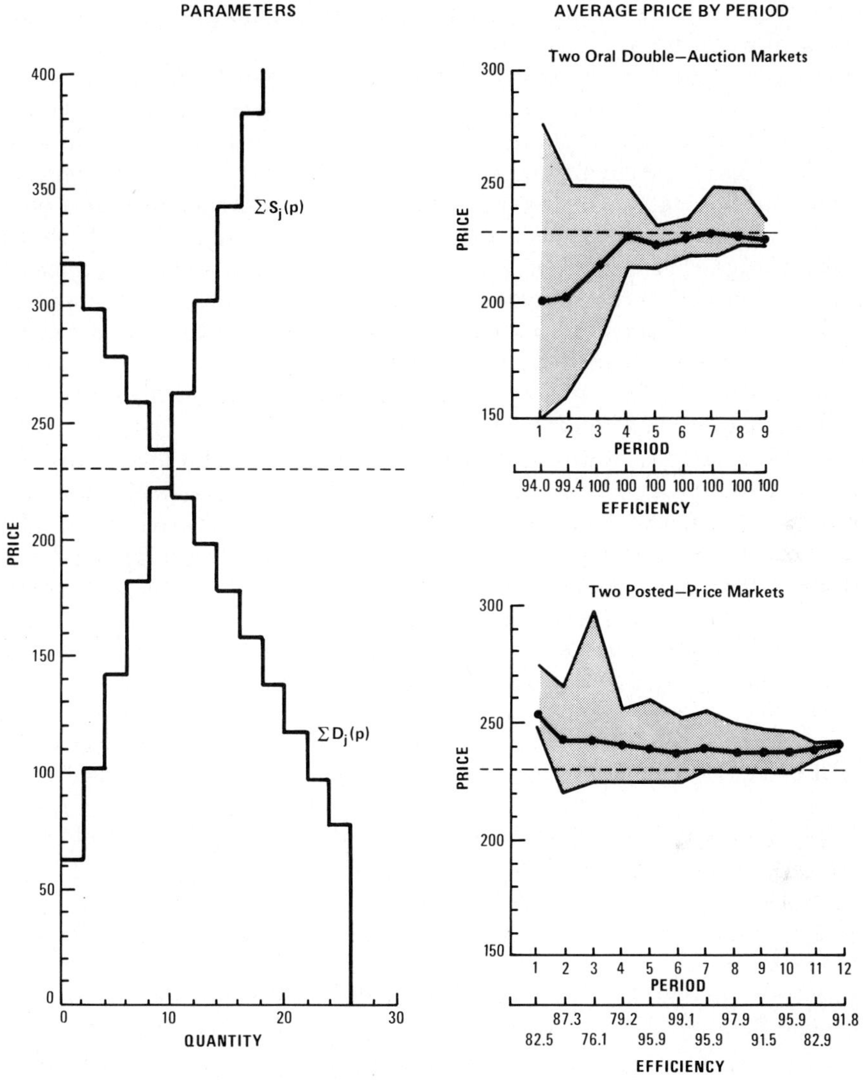

Figure 19.10. Parameters and average price per period for oral double auction and posted-price markets. *Source*: Plott (1986, p. 734).

in the market's performance by showing how it can be influenced by subtle features of organization.

The relative effect of the posted prices was first demonstrated by Plott and Smith (1978) in comparison experiments. The phenomenon had been observed earlier by F.E. Williams (1973) who believed that it was due to the fact that individuals could trade multiple units. Cook and Veendorp (1975) also observed the phenomenon and attributed it to asymmetries in information. Even now no theory about the influence of the posted-price institution has been published to my knowledge, but the effect has persisted under a variety of parametric situations. Extensive replications were made by Ketcham, Smith and A.W. Williams (1984). Markets with speculators were investigated by Hoffman and Plott (1981). Markets with a relatively large number of sellers were studied by Hong and Plott (1982). A variety of supply and demand configurations and asymmetries were studied by Davis and A.W. Williams (1984). The higher prices and lower efficiencies of posted-price markets, relative to the oral double auctions, have held up so far. In a more recent study Mestelman and Welland (1986) summarize the results of a series of projects [Mestelman, Welland and Welland (forthcoming), Mestelman and Welland (1987)] in which the production or supply decision was made prior to the opening of a market period. Thus, sellers were at risk. Under these conditions for the parameters they consider[14] the price differences between the double auction and the posted offer were not so evident. However the efficiency of the oral double auction is higher.

4. Imperfect competition

This section begins with a discussion of monopoly. A perfectly functioning cartel behaves as a monopoly, so in a sense monopoly is the polar case of oligopoly theory. Theories of imperfect competition must deal with the coordination of decisions among competitors, but the theory must also deal with the behavior of buyers. The buyers are not neutral in a market. Their actions tend to exacerbate the problems experienced by cartels, so the monopoly problem, where the natural coordination problem of oligopolists is absent, is a good place to begin.

4.1. Monopoly

Experiments with monopoly can be used to emphasize a fundamental theme that runs through experimental studies: the details of market organizations are

[14]Consumer surplus was greater than producer surplus which ordinarily places upward pressure on initial prices in the convergence process under the oral double auction. Of course, with advanced production the supply function in a period changes when the production decision is made. Cost becomes zero up to the supply, which creates a relative surplus that differs from the original parameters.

important to market performance. If organization matters, then can it be used to protect consumers against the natural advantages that are believed to characterize the position of a monopolist? Does the organization need to be in the form of direct regulation or will some sort of decentralized process do? The section reviews experiments with unregulated monopoly, regulated monopoly, and contested markets.

The difference in market performance when there exists several sellers under oral auctions, as opposed to posted prices, leads naturally to an inquiry about whether or not the behavior carries over to the case of a single seller. Monopoly experiments under both institutions [Smith (1981), Smith and A.W. Williams (1981a)] provide a dramatic demonstration of the importance of both market structure and the institutional environment in determining market performance.

Monopoly can definitely cause prices to diverge from the competitive equilibrium. However, when the market is organized as a single unit oral double auction, the standard monopoly model does not do so well. There is a strong tendency for prices to erode away from the monopoly equilibrium price. On occasion, in Smith's experiments the prices actually approached the competitive equilibrium. The data are sufficiently mixed and the number of observations are so small that we cannot determine which model, the monopoly model or the pure competitive model, will be the easiest to modify to capture the behavior for monopolized oral double auctions. Figure 19.11 reproduces the time series from a particularly interesting experiment. It illustrates the difficulty of reaching any

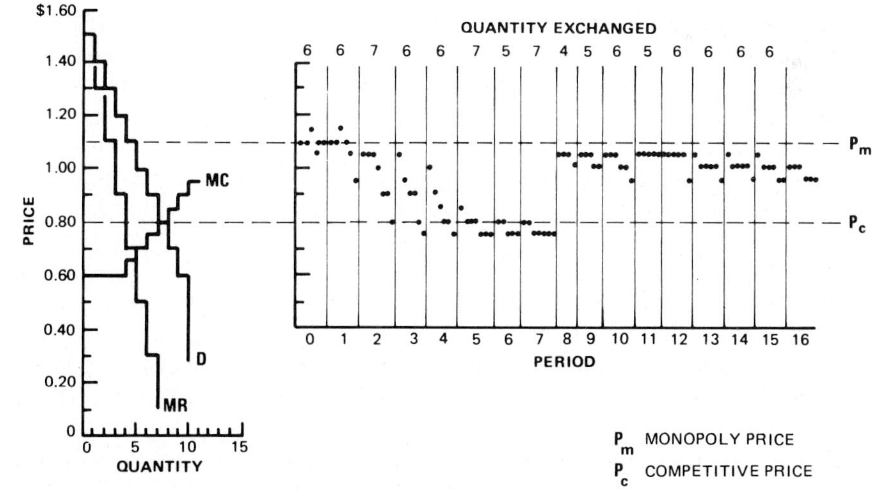

Figure 19.11. Double auction monopoly, where P_m = monopoly price, P_c = competitive price. *Source*: Smith (© 1981, Purdue Research Foundation, Chart 3, p. 91).

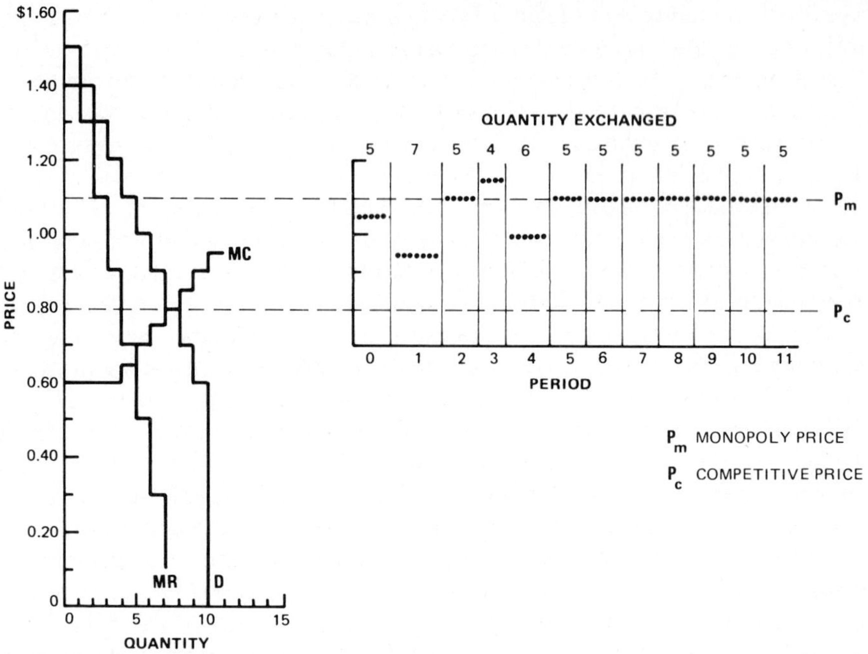

Figure 19.12. Posted offer monopoly, where P_m = monopoly price, P_c = competitive price. *Source*: Smith (© 1981, Purdue Research Foundation, Chart 5, p. 93).

general conclusions about the comparative accuracy of the models. Prices start high near the monopoly price, erode to the competitive equilibrium, return to the high levels, and begin to erode again. For the most part volume is closer to the monopoly level of five than to the competitive level of eight units. This interesting behavior seems to be attributable to the considerable power of buyers in this institution. Perhaps by "counterspeculation" they tend to withhold purchases and force prices down when facing a monopolist. Exactly what coordinates this action is unknown (these buyers cannot communicate except through bids and asks) but, as will be shown below, certain institutions seem to prevent it and therefore help the monopolist.

In contrast, in posted-price (offer) markets a different picture emerges in the case of monopoly. When the monopolists post prices, market behavior is more accurately captured by monopoly theory. The results of one experiment are in Figure 19.12. This monopolist adjusts prices to measure demand. The measurements are accurate because under the posted prices the effects of buyer "counterspeculation" seem not so severe and so demand gets revealed at each price.[15] The

[15]"Counterspeculation" may be present but in these markets it was not sufficiently pronounced to be measurable.

monopolist ascertains the profit at each price, sets price at the monopoly level, and leaves it there. Volume stays at the monopoly level.

Compared to the oral auction, the posted-offer markets tend to be mechanical. These data suggest that monopolists have a vested interest in having some variant of posted-offer institutions. Of course the dual is that customers would prefer the single unit oral double auction or the posted-bid institution, both of which result in lower prices in experimental markets. Obviously such results are not sufficiently well understood to serve as the sole basis for public utility regulation reform but they certainly suggest some hitherto unappreciated potential for market institutions in this regard.

A study of natural monopolies has been initiated by Coursey, Isaac and Smith (1984) and Coursey, Isaac, Luke and Smith (1984). The focus of the two studies has been the possibility that "contestable" markets might provide a form of market control of monopoly. Between the two studies a total of twenty-two markets have been studied. In each market there were either one or two potential firms with identical declining average costs sufficient for the emergence of natural monopolies. Cost conditions at the individual firm level were such that marginal and average costs declined for ten units, after which further increases in supply were impossible. That is, marginal cost became infinite at the eleventh unit.

Demand price was above the average variable cost through the tenth unit when it was $0.15 above the average variable cost of a firm producing ten units and $1.00 below the average cost of a firm producing one unit.[16] A monopolist would theoretically sell six units[17] at a price of $2.25 ($1.15 above minimum average cost and exactly equal to the marginal variable cost of producing the first unit). The competitive outcome was ten units at $1.25 ($0.15 above minimum average variable cost) as will be described below.

In four control markets only one firm existed, which was an uncontested monopolist. For an additional six markets, two firms existed and entry costs (fixed costs) were zero. These markets thus provide an opportunity to study contestability in the absence of entry costs. For an additional twelve markets entry costs were $2. This entry fee or fixed cost allowed a firm to operate for five periods without additional fixed costs. Firms that entered and paid the entry fee faced only variable costs. Firms "bid" for the market by submitting a price and a maximum quantity. In an order determined randomly buyers would then purchase from the seller of their choice.

A check of the parameters will reveal that the market can maintain two firms operating at two units each. However, the declining marginal costs place two firms in an unstable situation according to competitive theory. The competitive

[16] The continuous approximation of the variable cost function is $C(x) = \$2.50x - (\$0.125)x^2$ for $x \leq 10$ and $C(x) = \infty$ for $x > 10$. The continuous approximation of the demand function is $P = \$3.50 - \$0.25x$.

[17] Discontinuities in the functions dictated by practicalities of experimentation are responsible for the discrepancy between this number and the one produced by the continuous approximation.

equilibrium price, P_c, is the price that clears the market for the largest quantity that can be profitably sustained. Given the actual parameters the ten units capacity limitation is the maximum number that can be profitably sustained. If there are no fixed costs, then P_c is any price in the interval [1.10, 1.25]. In the experiments with entry costs the cost of entry was $2.00 for a five-period term, so if ten units were sold per period, the entry cost is $0.04 averaged over the units sold in the term. When entry costs are present, P_c is in the interval [1.14, 1.25].

Interest in the design stems from the fact that a plausible story can be made for any of several outcomes. Fear of a price war and resulting losses in the case of costly entry might prevent entry and allow a single firm to occupy the market and change monopoly prices. At the other end of the spectrum any profit of the existing firm might attract entry so prices are forced to stay in the competitive range. Or, prices might fluctuate wildly as entry and exit occurs. Or, in the case of the entry fee, neither firm might enter because of a fear of wars and losses or simply because of a lack of coordination. Of course, the market can hold both firms simultaneously if something like a "kinked demand curve" will keep prices up. The question posed by the experiments is which of the many competing ideas best capture the experience in these simple markets. If any model does well, the next natural question is to ask why?

The markets were organized as posted offer markets. Research reviewed above suggests that markets organized along these lines are most favorable to models of imperfect competition. However, even with the posted-offer institution buyers are not completely passive so in order to isolate the effects of contestability from other strategic features of market interaction, the demand side was simulated by a computer in most of the markets. The separation of the real buyers from simulated buyers was such that no confusion of results occurs.

The results are in Table 19.2. Without contestability the monopoly model best describes the data. Contestability with and without such costs does help control the monopolist. Furthermore, these markets showed no tendency to collapse in the sense that all firms withdrew from the market out of the fear of losses due to uneconomical entry. With sunk costs some unstable pricing was observed as firms attempted to change a monopoly price and attracted entry. Some limit pricing was observed with prices at or near the competitive range. In most periods the market was contested with two firms paying the fixed cost but one not producing because competition had lowered prices to the point of no profit from potential production and competition.

These results are only an initial probe into the behavior of contestable markets. The basic behavioral model is evolving toward those found successful in sealed-bid research. The fact that few players exist has implications that simply have not been touched by experiments. Clearly, the contestants would have an interest in mechanisms which would restrict the quantity that each offered to the market. Perhaps institutions or practices, which make the quantities offered public, along

Table 19.2
Number of experiments which on the eighteenth period were closer to the designated hypothesis

Hypothesis	Uncontested monopoly (total number of experiments = 4)	Contested market with entry cost = 0 (total number of experiments = 6)	Contested market with entry cost = \$2 (total number of experiments = 12)
Monopoly: $P > \frac{P_c + P_m}{2}$	4	0	0
Weak contestable: $P \leq \frac{P_c + P_m}{2}$	0	6	12
Strong contestable: $P \leq P_c$	0	4	6

Source: Coursey, Isaac, Luke and Smith (1984).

with the market demand functions and individual sales volumes, would help sellers coordinate decisions in a tacit collusion. Obviously such speculations can be addressed by further experiments.

While contestable markets constitute one form of organization that shifts the gains from exchange from the monopolist to consumers, other ideas exist. Theories of incentive regulation are just beginning to appear in the literature and experiments are being used to explore implementations of the theoretical ideas. Experimental work is continuously demonstrating that arguments that are simple in formal and mathematical terms can be very complicated or contradictory when made operational. The creation of simple types of otherwise abstract mechanisms involves such checks. Harrison and McKee (1985) began by investigating a regulatory scheme proposed by Loeb and Magat (1979). The scheme requires that regulators know the demand curve but not necessarily the cost curve of the monopolist. While the mechanism requires less information than, say, marginal cost pricing, it has the property (presumably undesirable) of requiring a large subsidy to be granted to the monopolist. The implementation chosen and tested by Harrison and McKee seemed to generate no surprises in that the processes worked approximately as advertised by the theory.[18] The mechanism guided

[18] Harrison and McKee called attention to an unusual aspect of their data. Subjects placed in the position of an uncontested monopoly, without regulatory complications, without random variables, and with simulated buyers who did not behave strategically, did not settle on the exact monopoly price. Because no subject ever chose the monopoly price, there must have been something complicated about the experimental environment that cannot be detected by simply reading the instructions used in the experiments. The existence of such inexplicable behavior compounds the usual problems encountered in attempts to generalize about experimental results.

choices in a manner that would protect consumers as was predicted by the theory, but substantial subsidies were required as indicated by the model. In order to avoid the subsidy problem Harrison and McKee devised a process that involves bidding for a franchise for the regulated monopoly thereby utilizing potential competition in a manner similar to the way it is used in the contestability literature. The franchise bidding scheme compares well to the performance of contested markets but of course it requires that the market demand function be known to the regulator.

Regulatory strategies were studied further by Cox and Isaac (1986) who were investigating alternatives to rate of return regulation for the Arizona Corporations Commission. They studied a proposal suggested by Finsinger and Vogelsang (1981) which does not require that the regulator know either the market demand function or the firm's cost function. In the markets Cox and Isaac created, the Finsinger and Vogelsang (FV) process demonstrated a potential for very perverse behavior. They describe the results as follows:

> The results of our FV series are a perfect example of how laboratory experimental tests of proposed regulatory institutions can be invaluable in public policy analysis. The theory states that this mechanism's optimal path will converge to the efficient outcome (in this case, an output of 12 units). But what happens if the firm errs, and gets off the optimal path? As Seagraves (1984) has noted, there is the possibility of such "cycles" adversely affecting the firm's profits. In fact, subject bankruptcy was a robust occurrence in our tests of the FV mechanism. [For example, in the second experiment]. ... the seller raised his price to \$4.80 and then dropped it too quickly, becoming bankrupt. At this point, we cancelled his debts and went over with him step-by-step the path to his bankruptcy. Then, we told him that we would not cancel his debts again, but that we would be happy at any point to explain in advance the consequences of any decision he might want to make. Nevertheless, this seller again went bankrupt with a "Seagraves-cycle" in periods 10–11... .
>
> ... even though the FV mechanism has theoretically desirable optimal convergence properties, it is a mechanism which is permanently "unforgiving" of errors. In our laboratory markets, this feature proved to be important, with three of four sellers going bankrupt because of errors off the theoretically optimal path (p. 133).

This behavioral problem led Cox and Isaac to recommend against further consideration of the FV mechanism as a practical regulatory process. Unless an improved process can be found they did not think that the investigation would produce a process that they could comfortably recommend for a field trial.

4.2. *Oligopoly*

If monopoly, which is a perfectly coordinated cartel, has difficulty in attaining the monopoly profit position under the oral double auction, it should not be surprising that duopolists do much worse. After a brief review of the behavior of oligopolists' behavior in the absence of any type of facilitating device, the section turns to features of markets other than numbers that might make monopolizing behavior easier.

The analysis begins with the possibility that a harmony of interest is not easily recognizable by participants untrained to look for one. Perhaps agents automatically treat competitive situations as zero-sum games so the collusive predictions of some oligopoly theories never occur.

As it turns out, market participants almost always recognize a harmony of interest and this recognition can be identified in the market signals which occur almost constantly in oral double auctions. After a contract, when the market is open for bids or asks, the bidding will sometimes start with a clearly unacceptable bid or ask (e.g. a bid of 1 cent or something far below any previously accepted price, or an ask from two to ten times higher than any previously accepted price). Such bids (asks) are often followed by similar bids (asks) from other buyers (sellers) who are indicating a willingness to keep offers low (high). When this happens, the other side of the market tends not be passive. Such "outrageous" terms are frequently answered by equally ridiculous terms from the other side which is indicating that it too has that strategy available. Even when there is no answer, the terms of such high bids or offers are not accepted, as the other side simply waits (counterspeculates). Competition slowly works the terms into the previously accepted range. Signals such as these never seem to work to affect prices in the double auction institution or if they do the effectiveness is not immediately obvious.

In some experiments a harmony of interest is easily recognizable. In studies by R.M. Miller, Plott and Smith (1977), F.E. Williams (1973) and Hoffman and Plott (1981) the markets had two speculators who could purchase units in one period (period A) and sell them in the next period (period B). These two individuals were the only agents who had the ability to buy units and carry them forward. They had a clear interest in maintaining a low price in period A and a high price in period B. In spite of this recognizable interest and the fact that only two agents had such powers, the market behavior is modeled well by an intertemporal competitive equilibrium.

The point is made somewhat more forcefully in Plott and Uhl (1981). In these markets four middlemen had the capacity to buy in one market in which they were the only buyers and sell in a physically separated market in which they were the only sellers. Unlike the speculation experiments in which all participants heard all bids, asks, and contracts, in the Plott and Uhl markets the initial sellers were one group of people who saw the action in the primary market and the final purchasers were a different group of people who saw only the action in the secondary market which was physically removed from the first. Both the harmony of interest and the collective power of the middlemen were obvious, but explicit conspiracy was not possible since middlemen were never allowed to speak directly to each other. Nevertheless, the competitive model fits the data closely.

In two studies, focal points were given the opportunity to operate as collusive devices. In Isaac and Plott (1981b) and in Smith and A.W. Williams (1981b) price ceilings (floors) were imposed slightly above (below) the equilibrium. A theory is sometimes advanced [Scherer (1970, pp. 179–182)] that such controls act as a focal point and thereby facilitate tacit collusion. In the oral double auction markets reported in these studies there is absolutely no support at all for the theory that nonbinding controls operate that way. If anything, the *opposite* is true. A ceiling (floor) that is nonbinding according to competitive theory tends to lower (increase) prices.

Private, preperiod meetings by one side of the market were studied by Isaac and Plott (1981a) as a facilitating practice under the oral double auction institution. Four sellers (buyers) were allowed to talk freely between periods, while the buyers (sellers) left the room to get the next period's demand (cost) functions. Side payments and profit sharing were not allowed and discussions of such schemes were prohibited.

The study asked the following questions: Do traders discuss collusion when given the opportunity? Can the traders formulate some sort of agreement? Once formulated, do they stick to it? Can the consequences of the conspiracy be detected in the market performance?

The answer to the first two questions is yes. These traders discussed conspiracy almost immediately and they had no difficulty in articulating an agreement. The answers to the second two are not without qualification. Data in Figure 19.13 provide a comparison with the oral double auction when no collusion is present (the first three experiments, I.P.I., I.P.II, and I.P.III) with those in which there is a seller's conspiracy (the fourth and fifth indexed as I and II) and a buyer's conspiracy (the sixth and seventh indexed as III and IV). The top charts are the average prices each period. The middle charts are the per period volumes, and the bottom charts are the efficiencies.

In order to see the effects, it is important to notice the near monotone convergence of *all three* measures in the first three nonconspiratorial markets. Prices, volume, and efficiency—all three move monotonically to the competitive equilibrium levels. This does not happen in the conspiracy markets. In each of the four experiments with conspiracy, with the possible exception of experiment III, at least one of these measures exhibits some erratic behavior in the sense of a "pronounced" movement away from competitive equilibrium. In this sense the

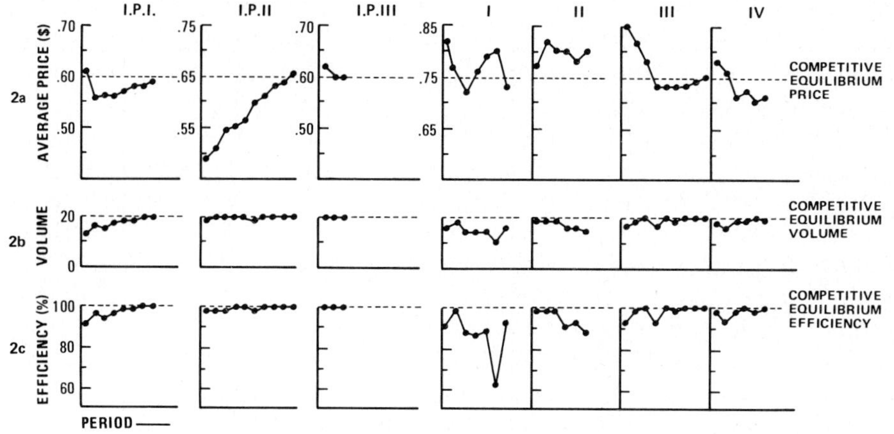

Figure 19.13. Average price, volume, and efficiency per period. *Source:* Isaac and Plott (1981a, Fig. 2, p. 10).

conspiracy might be detectable from market data, but experiment III indicates the difficulty. Notice in experiment III there is a strong tendency toward the competitive levels even though there is an active conspiracy.

Figure 19.14 will help explain what is happening. Shown there is the sequence of bids, offers, and contracts from experiment III. This experiment involved the dramatic reduction in prices in period 4 as a result of a successful buyer's conspiracy.

> Some general discussion began after period 3. Note that, unlike period 3, the buyers in period 4 did not rush to accept high seller offers. In period 3, five of the first six trades were offers between 83 cents and 88 cents. In period 4, no offers were accepted until they reached 73 cents. In period 5, the tenth bid was at 72 cents. Between periods 5 and 6 the [buyers][19] agreed to try to hold the price at 71 cents. In period 6, the first twenty-seven bids were all either at 70 cents or 71 cents, with several intervening offers at 72 cents ignored. The twenty-eighth bid broke the agreement, and there were ten immediate trades at 72 cents [Isaac and Plott (1981a, p. 18)].

Of particular interest in this context are the high offers in period 5. These are interpreted as signals by sellers as an attempt to get other sellers to hold out. Frequently, however, they are made by sellers who have already sold and now

[19]This corrects an error in the original paper [Isaac and Plott (1981a)] in which the word "sellers" was used instead of the correct word, "buyers".

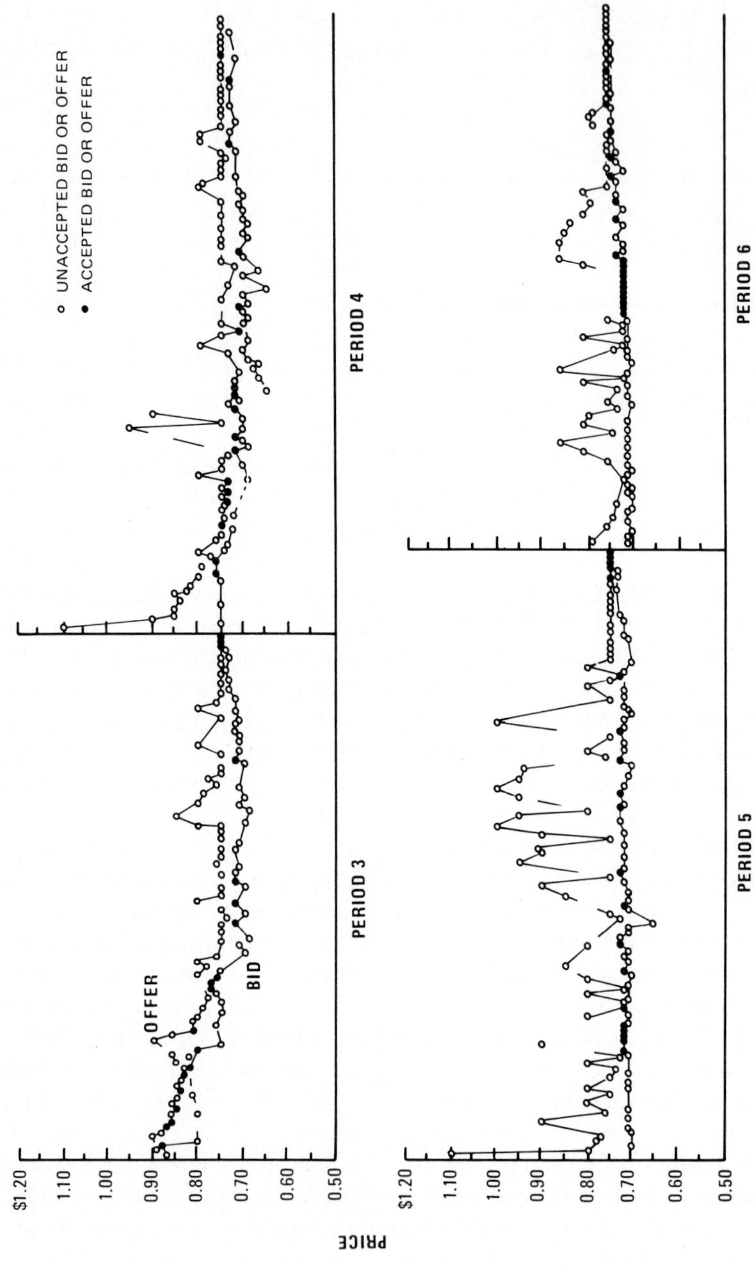

Figure 19.14. Experiment III – periods 3, 4, 5, and 6, all bids and offers. *Source:* Isaac and Plott (1981a, Fig. 11, p. 20).

have only high cost units which they do not expect to sell. The cost of signaling to them is low. Nevertheless, the fact that the nonconspirators are not simply passive is obvious.

The difficulty these conspirators have in substantially affecting market conduct seems to be related to the market institutional environment. As the Smith results reviewed above demonstrate, even a perfect conspiracy (monopoly) has difficulty in the double auction. When one adds this property of auction markets to the fact that oligopolists can have difficulty in achieving coordination even under the most favorable conditions, perhaps it is not surprising that the market structure in the Isaac and Plott experiments (four buyers and four sellers) would make successful conspiracy difficult.

The properties of the oral double auction seem to carry over to negotiated price markets in which information is not as good. However, very little data exist currently. The only nonconspiratorial oligopoly markets that have been studied experimentally in which prices are privately negotiated are those in the Grether and Plott (1984) study. In these markets each buyer and seller was located in a private office. Buyers had the phone numbers of sellers but not other buyers, and sellers had the phone numbers of buyers and not other sellers. Thus there was no possibility of conspiracy. In addition, phone calls were privately monitored through a master switchboard in a secretarial pool as a further control. Subjects were told that side payments or discussions of side payments in any form (e.g. physical threats) were prohibited and that if any were detected, the experiment would be terminated immediately.

In all other respects these markets were similar to those conducted under oral auction institutions. The time periods were longer (10–15 minutes). As might be expected, the volume in a telephone market moves more slowly because of the time involved with dialing, negotiating, etc.

Results typical of these experiments are shown in Figure 19.9. Variance in price is high at first but begins to shrink over time. Prices, as can be seen, hang slightly above the competitive equilibrium. Nevertheless, the market behavior is still more closely approximated by the competitive equilibrium model than any other "standard" theory.

Conspiracy was allowed in a study by Selten (1970). Negotiations took place privately in booths. The four sellers each made supply quantity decisions before a period opened. The number of buyers varied between nine and twelve in the ten markets studied. Side payments, cartels, buyers and/or sellers conversations, futures contracts, etc. were all permitted since one of the purposes was to see what practices emerged from the marketplace. Convergence to the competitive equilibrium can be read into many of the price patterns but abrupt movements away from equilibrium exist. On average the results are the competitive equilibrium.

4.3. Oligopoly and price posting

Most experiments with oligopoly that have been conducted over a twenty-five year period can be interpreted as having (unknowingly) implemented the posted-price institution. Early experimenters [Hoggatt (1959), Fouraker and Siegel (1963)] gave subjects a profit table or its functional equivalent. The table contained the agents' profits expressed as a function of his/her own price and the price of a competitor. Sometimes the profit tables of both agents were public information. Such an experimental procedure removes from the picture all strategic behavior of the buyers and it reveals to the seller demand data that is privately held by buyers. It removes all price variance and it removes the opportunity to change strategies while market information is being generated. Since these are many of the behavioral features of posted price markets, most of the research that followed and that used profit tables to describe opportunities to subjects can be discussed in the context of price posting.

The resulting experimental literature is extensive and it has been reviewed in the paper from which this paper is developed [Plott (1982)] so it will not be reviewed again here. Instead, three of the prominent features will be listed. The chief results are that

(1) When there is imperfect information about actions or payoffs, prices converge to near the competitive equilibrium. When products were not "homogeneous", the Cournot model is the best of those examined.

(2) Full information about payoffs, symmetric payoffs, full information about opponents' choices, and very long periods of interaction tend to facilitate collusive behavior.

(3) The higher than competitive prices that is now known to be typical of posted prices in general seem to be observed in these early experiments.

More recent experiments that have utilized the same methodology with the market institutional framework simulated by a profit table have provided a deeper insight for the previously observed tendencies. Holt (1985) considered the possibility that the consistent equilibrium and not the Cournot equilibrium is the principle that lies behind the observed behavior. He noticed that almost all previous results could be interpreted in terms of the consistent-conjectures hypothesis as opposed to the Nash (Cournot) equilibrium model that had been used to interpret the results. He also felt that problems existed with the instructions used in early experiments and that special payoffs had biased the experiments against the consistent-conjectures equilibrium in those cases when the outcomes were not nearest to the consistent-conjectures equilibrium.

In a new series of experiments Holt adjusted the instructions and payoffs to correct for what he perceived to be biases against the consistent conjectures hypothesis. He chose parameters that clearly separated consistent-conjectures equilibria from the Nash (Cournot) equilibria and he conducted the experiments with experienced subjects.

His results strongly support the Nash (Cournot) model over the consistent-conjectures equilibrium. He also observed some collusive behavior as had been observed in previous experiments with public and symmetric payoffs. The Holt experiments when added to previous work indicates that the Nash (Cournot) equilibrium is reasonably reliable in such environments and that the previous results strongly supporting the Nash model are not due to an accidental coincidence with the consistent-conjectures equilibrium.

A recent paper by Alger (1987) provides useful insights about the nature and importance of repeated game models. Alger, whose primary interest was in definitions of equilibrium and associated tests of equilibrium, designed experiments that push the limits of competitive equilibrium behavior. Given what is known about conditions under which monopoly results are likely, his parameters are a priori very favorable to monopoly behavior. Almost all of the markets were duopoly. Posted prices are used. Costs are identical. Costs are constant except for the first unit in a few cases. No commissions are paid so there is no incentive to trade marginal units at the competitive equilibrium prices. The experiments are conducted for as many as 160 periods.

The results after many periods appear to be bimodal (assuming that markets that attained a stable pattern of prices early at or near the Cournot equilibrium monopoly price would have sustained that price for the long term). Experiments were terminated after sufficient stationarity was observed. Most markets do not settle down to perfectly constant prices. Those that do so tend to be near the Cournot equilibrium, which in the Alger parameters is also near the monopoly level. Those that do not tend to be nearer the competitive equilibrium. The time path of competition is U-shaped. Prices tend to be high and converge downward. Once down near the competitive equilibrium, frequent attempts to get prices up are apparent. If prices ever gravitate up near the Cournot equilibrium or the monopoly price, the prices stick at a consistent level (on average but not universally). However, many never turn up and remain at relatively low levels with perfect stationarity of prices never occurring.

The upward bias of price posting occurs even when a "large" number of competitors exist. The upward pressure does not necessarily result in an edging of prices to the monopoly level as compared to the Cournot equilibrium even in very favorable underlying structural circumstances and many repeated trials. Posted prices facilitate the maintenance of prices at higher than competitive equilibrium levels but do not guarantee it.

A signal such as a nonbinding price control is not sufficient to coordinate competitors to move posted prices to monopoly levels. However, conspiracy in the presence of price posting appears to do the trick. Two papers begin the documentation needed. Sealed-bid markets are studied in Isaac and Walker

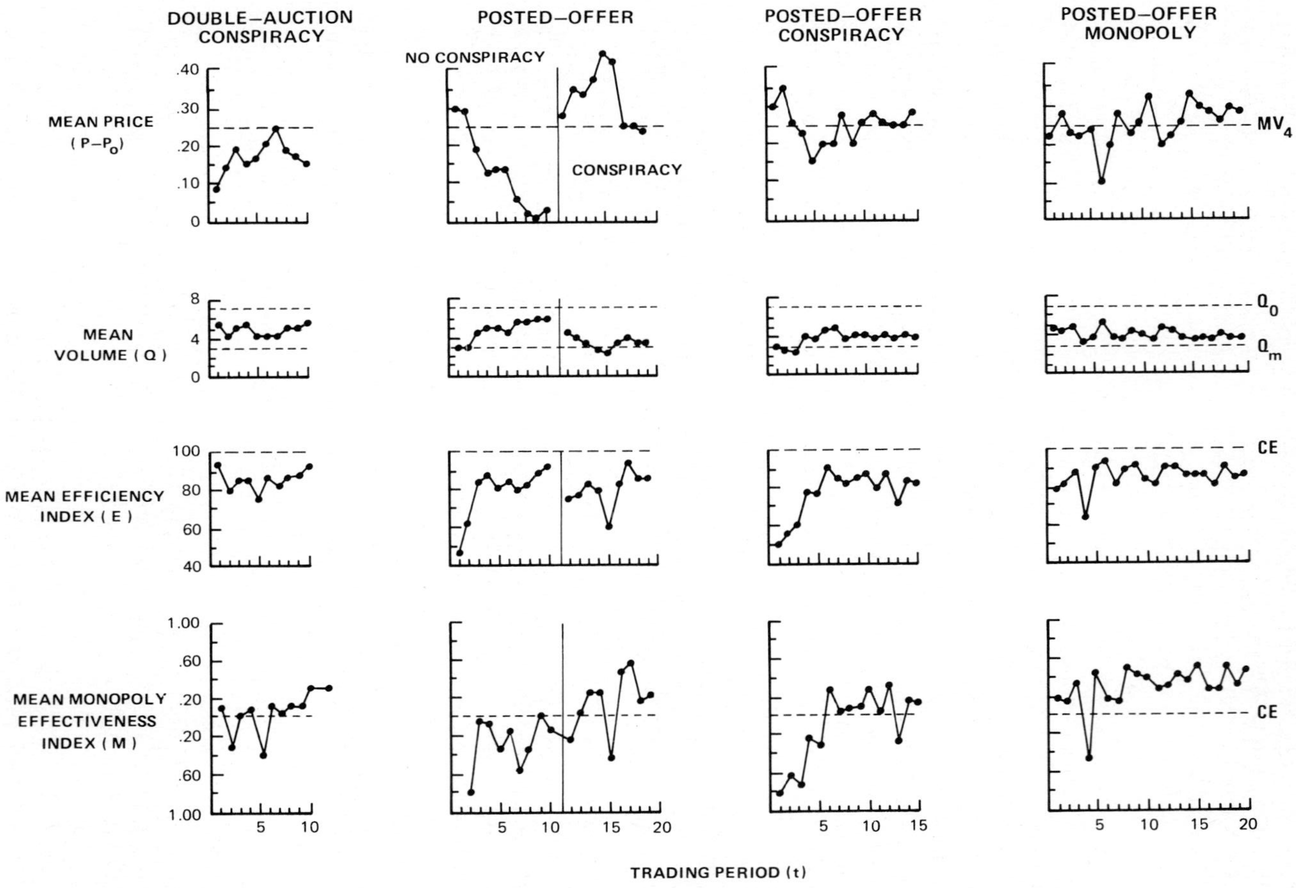

Figure 19.15. Comparison of market performance criteria. *Source:* Isaac, Ramey and Williams (1984, p. 217).

(1985). Conspiracies work to get prices to monopsony levels but the stability is fragile. Conspiracies in posted-offer markets are studied in Isaac, Ramey and Williams (1984). Figure 19.15 shows comparison experiments between double auction conspiracy and posted-offer conspiracy. Posted-offer monopoly and posted-offer no-conspiracy are controls. Double auction no-conspiracy controls are unnecessary since it is known that the behavior is captured adequately by the competitive model.

The conspiracies could fix prices but no side payments were permitted. The price P_m is the monopoly price but at this price one of the sellers would be excluded from the market with zero profit. The price MV_4 is the highest price that keeps all sellers in the market. The figure shows the average of the four experiments conducted under each treatment.[20] The index of monopoly effectiveness is the difference between actual sellers' profit and the profits they would have made at the competitive equilibrium taken as a percentage of the maximum possible difference.

The behavior of conspiracy with posted prices was substantially the same as was the behavior of the monopolists under posted prices. However, both forms of organization fell short of achieving the full monopoly price. On the other hand posted-price conspiracies are more effective than are double auction conspiracies.

The results of these experiments add more data to answer the questions about conspiracy originally posed by Isaac and Plott (1981a). Do trades recognize a harmony of interest? Will they attempt to collude when given the opportunity? Can they formulate an agreement? The answer to those three questions is clearly yes, but the answer to the next two questions depends upon the nature of facilitating devices. Once an agreement is formulated, do they try to implement it in the market? Does the attempted implementation affect the market? If the institution is posted prices, the answer is clearly yes.

4.4. Markets with advance notification and price protection

The recent actions taken by the Federal Trade Commission[21] have drawn attention to the market institution in the antiknock compound industry.[22] Four industrial practices were in dispute. First, customers were assured of a thirty-day advance notice of price changes (increases). Secondly, prices were quoted in terms of delivered prices with the same price prevailing regardless of transportation costs. The last two were in contracts which typically included a "price

[20] The no-conspiracy treatment under posted offer involved only two experiments. The behavior of these two is typical of the many others that have been conducted.

[21] The Federal Trade Commission complaint against Ethyl, DePont, PPG and Nalco Chemical Company (Ethyl Corporation et al. FTC Docket No. 9128. Complaint issued 31 May, 1979).

[22] The product is added to gasoline by refiners to reduce knock and raise gasoline octane rating.

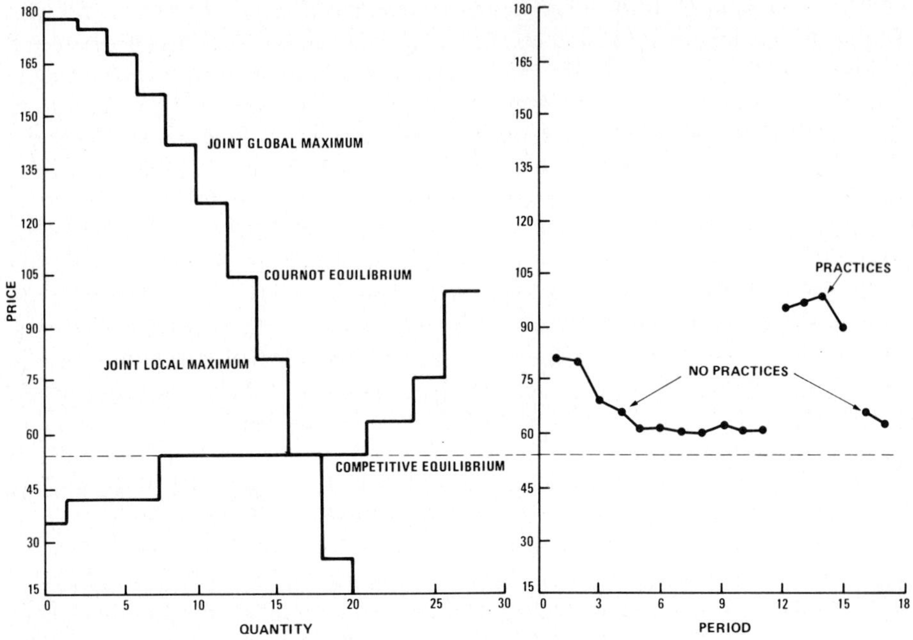

Figure 19.16. Parameters and average price per period. *Source:* Plott (1982, p. 1519).

protection" clause which guarantees (i) that the seller will sell to no one at a price less than the price quoted the buyer, and (ii) the seller will meet any lower price in the market or release the buyer from the contract.

The market structure is characterized by two large sellers of equal size (approximately 35 percent of the market each) and two small sellers of about equal size. A long-run declining demand (due to a reduction in lead use in gasoline) and existing excess capacity discourages entry. Eight large buyers account for about 60 percent of the sales and many very small buyers account for the rest.

Grether and Plott (1979, 1981) have explored markets with these properties. Each agent was assigned an office. Sellers were able to post prices by means of a digital electronic display system such that price announcements were made known immediately to all market agents. Orders were placed through the telephone system. Price increases required advance notice and all transactions were made at advertised prices (the buyer protection clause which precludes all discounts). The market structure was as described above with the market demand and supply functions as shown in Figure 19.16.

The major conclusion of this study is that these practices and market structure cause prices to be above those that would otherwise exist if either variable were appropriately changed. Figure 19.16 gives the average prices during each of seventeen trading periods. Market institutions were a simple telephone market during the first twelve periods. As can be seen, the prices begin to decay toward the competitive equilibrium. The four disputed practices were imposed beginning in period 13 and remained through period 15. As can be seen, prices jump immediately to near those which exist at the Cournot equilibrium. When the practices were removed (periods 16 and 17) prices immediately fell. These data are representative of the pattern of findings from ten experimental markets.

The theoretical explanation of this phenomenon has some support. Advance notice given sufficiently in advance of the deadline for advance notification provides a signal to other sellers. If the notice involves a price sufficiently far in the future, it induces no current business loss. Only a single price is involved, so the signal is uncomplicated with minimal dimensions over which disagreement can occur. Other sellers know that if they do not increase prices before the deadline, the original firm will rescind the proposed price increase. Thus other sellers do not have the option of "underselling" and acquiring a larger market share. The Nash strategy for such firms is simply to match the proposed price if a uniform industry price at the higher level will increase the firm's profits and do nothing otherwise. On the downside, due to the homogeneous nature of the product, if not the buyer's protection, price cuts will be matched, so the incentive to cut prices depends upon the anticipated share of demand increase due to lower price levels. This model predicts that prices will certainly be at Cournot levels if not higher.

These institutions seem to have an effect on buyers similar to the posted-price institutions. Buyers do not anticipate discounts because the institutions prevent them. Furthermore, since any price concessions must be offered to all, buyers can see that price concessions can be costly to the seller and thus have less expectation of winning them. As a result, the buyers seem to have less "counterspeculation" than in, say, the telephone markets alone. Thus these institutions appear to remove one source of buyer pressure for reduced prices while at the same time easing the problem of price coordination for the seller and eliminating the advantages of price cuts.

5. Product quality

Only recently have studies of product quality begun to appear in the experimental literature. The delay reflects the fact that markets with variable product quality are actually multiple markets. Each level of quality is in essence a separate commodity so experimentation requires an extension of the methodology to (potential) multimarket processes. As experiments with the operation of multimarket systems began to grow,[23] markets with variable product qualities began to appear.

One of the primary objectives of some of the early experiments was to create markets that would reliably fail. Failure means only one quality product would be supplied even though social efficiency calls for a different quality to be supplied. The research strategy was clear. Perhaps by studying markets that fail, better insight about the behavioral principles that lead to failure could be gained. More importantly, observed market failures must be available if policies intended to correct failures are to be studied. In other words the research has been an attempt to create something that was broken in order to study the reliability of broad policies intended to get things fixed.

A key feature of markets with quality variability is asymmetric information between the buyers and sellers. Generally the seller knows something that the buyer would like to know and the seller also has a self-interest in the buyer's decisions. Plott and Wilde (1982) explored this type of relationship within experimental markets that had some of the prominent features of markets in which professional diagnosis plays a special role. The study was commissioned by the Federal Trade Commission (FTC) which reviews the behavior of such markets and from time to time considers regulatory actions. The idea was to create a market that failed in the theoretical sense and use it as a baseline to study tools used by the FTC to detect failures and as a baseline for additional experiments with policies under consideration by the FTC. The interesting result from this study is that markets which were designed to fail according to guidelines provided by existing theory actually failed to fail. The markets worked very well even though they were not supposed to work well according to accepted theory.

Buyers were given redemption values of the form $V^i(x_i, \theta_i)$, where $x_i \in \{X, Y\}$ and $\theta_i \in \{A, B\}$.[24] For each agent the probability that θ_i took value A and B was respectively $1/3$ and $2/3$. In addition, for each i a clue was available. It was a sample of twelve independent observations of a random variable $s_i \in \{0, I\}$ with $\text{prob}(0|A) = 1/4$ and $\text{prob}(0|B = 1/3)$.

[23]Multiple market experiments began with R. Miller, Plott and Smith (1977) in which the economy had two markets separated in time. Speculators could buy in one market and sell in the other. Many studies in the field of finance have extended the multimarket research. Four markets with complements were studied in Grether, Isaac and Plott (1981, forthcoming). The basic technology for studying multimarket systems is in place but the dynamics and other features of equilibration remain open questions.

[24]$V^i(X, A) = V^i(X, B) = \$1.55 = V^i(Y, B)$; $V^i(Y, A) = \$9.45$. These values reflect the idea that X will always "help" a problem and so is a valuable thing to purchase. However, if the individual is in state A, commodity Y is of much greater value than is X.

Under one condition, the professional diagnosis condition, the functions prob(θ_i) and prob($s_i|\theta_i$) were known only to the seller and the sample of twelve observations was known only to the seller.[25] Thus, the seller was in a position to evaluate the posterior probability of θ_i given s_i and had been trained in earlier sessions to make guesses about θ given the sample information s. Each period a draw of θ was determined for each buyer. The clue was issued and the buyer would purchase either an X or a Y after having sought the advice of one or more sellers. The accuracy of the advice was not learned by buyers until the end of the entire experiment which consisted of several periods and associated purchases.

Under a second condition, the self-diagnosis condition, buyers were trained with the probabilistic mechanism used to determine θ and s. Buyers had the training and practice in guessing θ_i given s_i. Buyers also had the information contained in the signal s_i. So in the self-diagnosis case buyers relied on sellers for nothing other than the units that sellers sold.

Prices were determined competitively.[26] The rents were greater for the Y at prices near competitive levels so sellers had an interest in selling the Y commodity.

The condition of professional diagnosis involves an obvious conflict of interest on the part of sellers. Buyers have no direct information on which to assess the professional abilities of the seller. One might reasonably expect sellers to recommend Y, the most profitable item. They could do this by diagnosing the state of the individual customer to be A, which makes Y the most desired item from the buyer's point of view. The "big lie" hypothesis was that sellers would recommend the most profitable item. Buyers unable to ever directly check the quality of the diagnosis would be induced to buy an expensive item that was unneeded. According to the "big lie" hypothesis, Y sales under the professional-diagnosis condition would exceed Y sales under the self-diagnosis condition.

The surprising result was that the "big lie" hypothesis was rejected. The "market failure" that was expected and the resulting flood of "lemons" that was expected did not occur. In fact, the markets in which buyers made their own diagnoses performed worse in an expected value of surplus sense than did markets in which the buyers were forced to rely on information provided by the sellers. The result was summarized by Plott and Wilde (1982, p. 97) as follows:

> Seller advice seems to be governed by systematic competitive principles similar to those which govern price competition. In particular, there seems to emerge a "uniform recommendation" depending strictly upon the clue (or symptoms) similar to the principle of "one price" in a market. The intuition behind the

[25] Each period each buyer was given a card that could only be seen by the seller. The card contained the sample of twelve observations of s_i.

[26] The market organization was not the oral double auction. The paper should be consulted for the details.

conjecture stems from the apparent low variance of advice across sellers and the possible tendency for buyers to avoid purchasing from sellers who deviated far from the "mean recommendation". Thus sellers who wish to make sales *at all* (of either the low-profit item or the high-profit item) must give advice similar to other sellers, and in the absence of collusion the best strategy is the "truth" as seen by the seller. This proposed principle of "truthful, uniform recommendations" is subject to at least the three qualifications listed below. This general thesis (along with the qualifications) can be explored by further experimentation.

Markets with lemons have been successfully created by Lynch, Miller, Plott and Porter (1986). The conditions were similar to "experience" goods whose quality was endogenously determined. Buyer and seller identifications were unknown to transacting parties.[27] Sellers had a total capacity limitation of two units to sell per period. After a sale and prior to delivery, sellers would choose the grade of the unit to be either regular or super. Costs to the seller were constant with the cost of supers being higher than the cost of regulars. The grade of all units delivered was public. Buyers preferred supers to regulars. The market was conducted for several periods.

Figure 19.17 tells much of the story. Market demands and supplies for supers and regulars are drawn as they would be if only one grade was offered for sale. The lemons' allocation is that all units are regulars and the equilibrium is a price just below 165. The efficient allocation, which is preferred to the lemons' allocation by all buyers and all sellers, is that all units be supers. The equilibrium price would be just below 300. The time series of trades shows that prices start high and the low-grade lemons are delivered. (Regulars are indicated by a dot and supers are indicated by an X.) Prices fall reflecting the fact that buyers fully anticipate the low quality. The quality is poor but buyers are not being misled.[28] In period 7 a costlessly enforceable warranty is made available to sellers. When this instrument exists, competition forces its use and as can be seen the equilibrium almost immediately shifts to the sale of supers. Efficiency jumps to near 100 percent. Buyers avoid units without the warranty even when low priced, and if they purchase such a unit, they expect the low quality. The power of costlessly enforced warranties is clear.[29] It removes uncertainty and the economy functions as a general equilibrium system might be expected to.

When seller identifications were known so reputations were possible, market quality improved. The backward induction hypothesis, which theoretically leads

[27]Buyers were in one room and sellers were in another. Bids and asks, which were unrestricted and remained open until accepted or canceled, were transmitted by a citizen's band radio.

[28]In some experiments false advertising was allowed. Most sellers falsely advertised but buyers were not misled in the sense that prices stayed near the lemons' equilibrium.

[29]In the experiment the instrument was an express warranty.

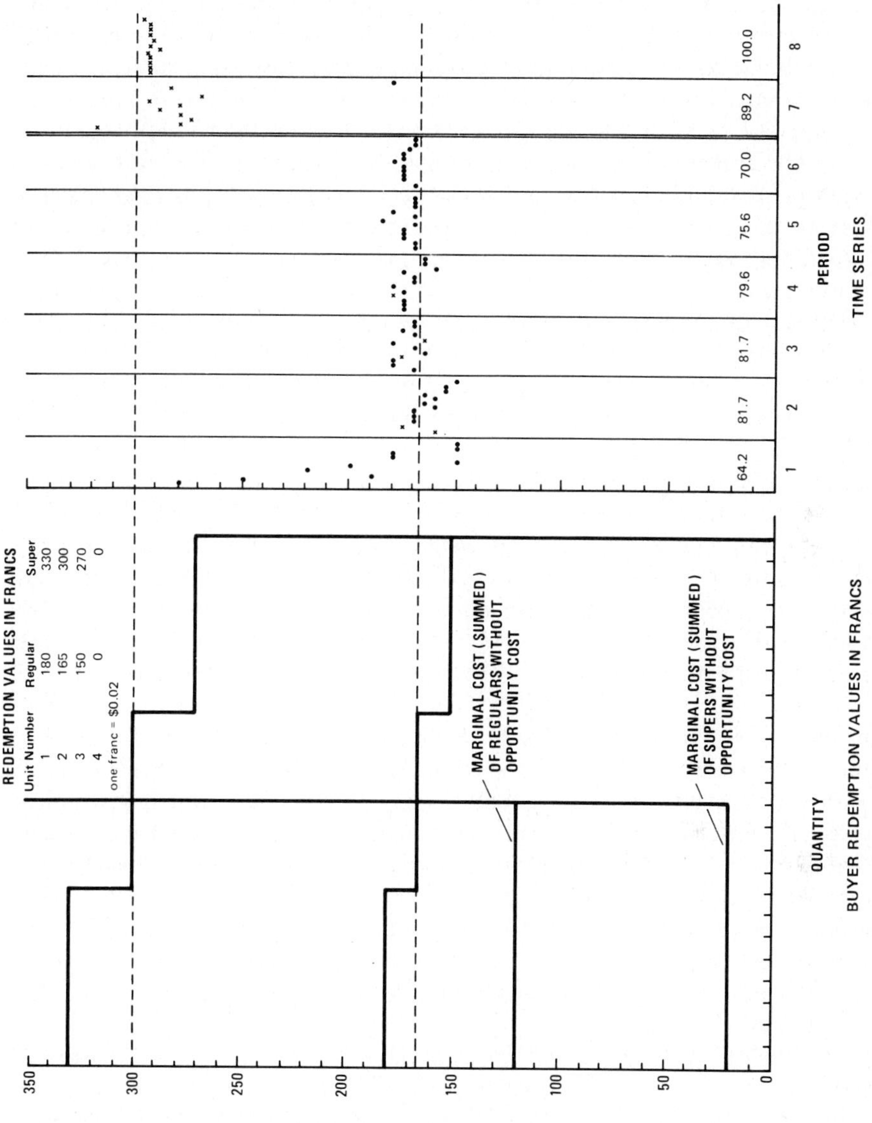

Figure 19.17. *Source:* Lynch et al. (1986, Fig. 1, p. 254, and Fig. 11, p. 275).

to lemons in these finite period markets (because of the repeated prisoner's dilemma nature of the situation), does not work. Attempts to establish reputations can be seen, but many things make reputation formation difficult in the absence of instruments like warranties. Sellers who wish reputations must first deliver quality units at low prices and thus suffer the (hopefully) temporary losses.[30] The magnitude of loss depends upon the speed of market adjustment to the high prices necessary to support high quality. Once quality is established at high prices, the price itself serves as a signal, thereby allowing competitors to free ride on the reputation building investments of the high-quality sellers. Sellers who decide to "cash in" on reputations and deliver lemons at high prices create an external diseconomy on sellers who are attempting to maintain a reputation as buyers shy away from all high-priced sellers for fear of being burned. Briefly put, reputation development can be important but the dynamics by which this occurs in the laboratory environments involves many aspects not captured by current theory.

Markets in which special product characteristics (e.g. the terms of warranties) are endogenously determined in response to asymmetric information about quality features that are exogenously determined have been the focus of three additional studies. In the first study, by Palfrey and Romer (1986), sellers were able to choose one of three types of warranties that covered the units.[31] A commodity thus became an underlying grade that was exogenously determined by an underlying randomness and a warranty package that protected the buyer in various ways. The study also implemented dispute resolution mechanisms that differed according to the party that bore the cost of the mechanism. The study is useful as an attempt to construct a laboratory environment with a variety of warranty instruments and as an initial study to determine which instrument survived. An insufficient amount of experimentation prevents solid conclusions but the warranty offerings differed from predictions. According to the model, one type of warranty should drive out the other type. As it turns out, both types of warranties survived. Palfrey and Romer remain somewhat perplexed by the results and initiated some tests of "subrational" models. The price data support a Bayesian equilibrium model as opposed to a "myopic" learning model. No definitive results are offered.

In the second study, Holt and Sherman (1986) study bundling decisions in response to uncertainty. Under certain cost and uncertainty conditions, bundling of commodities by sellers in a "take it all or leave it all" unit can be the most efficient base for transactions as opposed to selling each unit separately. The average quality can be provided more reliably for a bundle than for an individual

[30]If prices are not near the cost of the low-quality units then the profitability of high-quality production may be insufficient to make reputation development worthwhile.

[31]In some experiments only two types of warranties were available.

unit. The bundling is a response to an underlying randomness. A total of four experiments were conducted. The efficient commodity type tended to emerge in all four.

The third study, by R. Miller and Plott (1985), also involved units of exogenously determined grade. Sellers observed the underlying grade (regular or super) but buyers could not. Sellers could make units more valuable by adding amounts of "quality". Since the amount of quality added could vary from 0 to 1000, a very large number of potential commodities existed in the market. The marginal cost of adding quality was higher for units of grade regular than for units of grade super. Demand and cost conditions were such that signaling equilibria existed in appropriately applied signaling models. The general tendency in the markets studied was for the quality added to serve as a signal for the underlying grade. Several markets approached the most efficient signaling equilibrium. The approach to equilibrium was from the direction of excess quality.

6. Defense of experiments[32]

Many of the studies reviewed above were designed and executed to answer reasonably specific questions related primarily to basic science. Sometimes applied scientists dismiss the experimental results and methods as being irrelevant and inapplicable. Needless to say, most questions cannot be answered by applying experimental methods. The theme of this section is on the art of posing questions which can.

The relevance of experimental methods rests on the proposition that laboratory markets are "real" markets in the sense that principles of economics apply there as well as elsewhere. Real people purse real profits within the context of real rules. The simplicity of laboratory markets in comparison with naturally occurring markets must not be confused with questions about their reality as markets.[33]

If the reality of laboratory markets as markets is accepted, then the art of posing questions rests on an ability to make the study of simple special cases relevant to an understanding of the complex. General theories and models by definition apply to all special cases. Therefore, general theories and models should be expected to work in the special cases of laboratory markets. As models fail to capture what is observed in the special cases, they can be modified or rejected in light of experience. The relevance of experimental methods is thereby established.

Several different research strategies are apparent in the research reviewed in this paper but five will be identified here.

[32]This section of the paper is reproduced from Plott (1982, pp. 1519–1523).
[33]See Plott (1979, 1987) and Smith (1980, 1982) for a detailed discussion.

6.1. *Theory rejection*

A model may be so poor at capturing observed behavior that it may be best to consider it no further or to use it even if no alternative model is available. The original experiments by Smith could be viewed as a potential basis for rejecting the ideas of demand and supply. If the model had not been at all accurate when applied to a simple market designed explicitly to give the model its "best chance", if, for example, the data were rectangularly distributed over the trading range in all periods, then it could be rejected as capturing none of the phenomena. However, the model worked extraordinarily well and as a result the original experiments were essentially ignored by the economics profession. Those who had a strong belief in principles of demand and supply said the results were "obvious". Critics of demand and supply dismissed the results saying that the markets were "rigged" so that demand and supply would work. When the approach is one of "model rejection", negative results instead of positive results are "interesting".

6.2. *Theory competition*

In most cases competing models exist and existing data are not an adequate basis for rejecting one in favor of the other. The idea, then, is to create simple laboratory markets which are special cases of markets in which the models are generally applied. The experiments will, hopefully, indicate which is more accurate in the simple cases. While relative accuracy in a simple case does not prove that the model will continue to be relatively accurate when applied to the complex case, it does provide some experiences with the models. More importantly, it places the burden of proof squarely on those who continue to advocate the "losing" model to establish why the model they prefer would do relatively poorly in simple cases but perform relatively accurately in the complex. Presumably the arguments they advance in an attempt to establish this result can themselves be examined by application of additional theory and more complicated experiments.

6.3. *Model robustness*

We have seen that changes in the market institutional environment can change market performance. These facts were discovered as experimenters inquired about the accuracy of the competitive model under alternative institutional regimes. These were checks on the robustness of the model under institutional perturbations. Similarly, some studies have checked the robustness of the model under parametric perturbations such as number of competitors, demand elasticity, etc. Even though no formal theory (or any theory at all) exists about the influence of these factors, it is only natural to check. Then, once an important variable is found which was not anticipated by existing theory, the data from the experiments serve as a motivation for the development of extensions of the theory to cover the new facts. The influence of the posted price is a good example. No formal theory exists yet which completely explains the properties of this institution.

6.4. *Measurement*

When most scholars think of experiments, they have measurement in mind (e.g. What is the probability of tacit collusion? What is the speed of adjustment to equilibrium?). Laboratory experimental methods can be applied to these ends but none of the experiments above were predicated on the hypothesis that they were measuring numerical constants of nature. Questions of this type would seem to require elaborate sampling procedures and explicit definitions of the populations to which the measurement is to be applied. The studies above all involved hypotheses about *relative* behavior as opposed to numerical constants.

6.5. *Simulation*

Another popular preconception about the function of experiments is simulation. In circumstances in which a policy is going to be imposed on a social system, simulation objectives involve an attempt to recreate the situation on a smaller scale in order to provide decisionmakers with some experience with how the situation might evolve.

If there is no theory to indicate which variables are important, the complexity of the small situation must mirror the complexity of the large as closely as is possible. Furthermore, without theory to unify the observations, the experiments must be conducted enough times to assure the "statistical validity" of any asserted pattern in the results. Thus theory, even in the case of simulation, serves importantly to simplify the experimental process. The more that accepted theory can be invoked, the less the experimental process needs to "mirror" the natural analog. The tendency of scholars to reject experimental methods as irrelevant may be because they are fundamentally interested in simulation while being unaware of the role of theory on the one hand and being very aware of the complexities of the situation (and the impossibility of recreating it) on the other hand.

The arguments above are straightforward, but it is easy to be pulled off track. Sometimes scholars use the term "real world" to refer to nonlaboratory processes and the term "artificial market" or "simulated market" to refer to laboratory markets. Such language invites criticism by failing to acknowledge the argument above about laboratory markets being real markets. In addition, the language suggests that the primary test of relevance for laboratory market results is how closely the laboratory market approximates some naturally occurring market thus implying that the purpose is simulation. This test neglects all of the other modes of learning from experiments. The laboratory environments provide an arena within which the relative accuracy of competing general theories can be evaluated and the poorer models rejected. Recall that general theories and models of markets must apply to all special cases independently of how those special cases compare with some other complicated special case which could itself be the result of several accidents of history. In essence, a demand that laboratory experiments designed to test general theories should simulate some naturally occurring case in its full complexity denies the relevance of a study of special cases, and such a requirement would pose just as many problems for experimental methods in the physical science as it would for experimental economics.

The problem of relevance can surface in many different forms. In the remaining paragraphs four of the most common sources of skepticism will be discussed.

The first argument is a claim that "real" businessmen do not behave as do the subjects in these experiments. Stated like this the argument is not a criticism of experimental methods, it is a hypothesis about behavior in different subject pools and is thus a call for more experiments (with businessmen subjects). Similarly, arguments that the monetary amounts involved were too little (or too much) are simply demands for more experiments. The fact of the matter is, however, that a variety of subjects and payment levels have been used. The Hong and Plott (1982) study, for example, used employed adults. To date, no subject pool differences which bear on the reliability of economic theory have been reported.

The next three arguments derive from the fact that naturally occurring phenomena are inherently more complex than are laboratory processes. The first argument is that the laboratory environment is *artificial*. Exactly why is not articulated, but with this argument the word is used many times and preferably loudly. It probably results from a gestalt view that there are so many important variables that they cannot be enumerated and that they interact in ways that are necessarily precluded in the laboratory.

This argument, notice, is not an argument against experimental methods in economics, it is an argument against experimental methods in general. Physical scientists must deal with it and so must economists. Since the assertion cannot be falsified, the only answer lies in experimental work that has been helpful in generating successful models and points of view regarding more complex processes. As applied researchers find the data from experiments useful in shaping their own hypotheses and beliefs, this argument becomes less important.

The second argument is more specific in that it notes that naturally occurring processes do not occur in isolation. Industries are embedded in a larger social context. Businessmen have social relationships and friendships. They also know that their decisions, while with one firm, may affect their possibilities for changing firms.

This argument suggests the behavior in very complex environments may follow different laws than those which govern behavior in relatively simple situations. This is an excellent reason for being careful in any attempt to extrapolate behavior from a laboratory to a complex industry. Notice, however, that it is not an argument against experimental methods. It is an argument for a particular type of experiment – one in which the complexity of the experimental environment is gradually increased to make its characteristics more nearly similar to those of a given industry. If complications destroy the applicability of models, it might be possible to identify the precise complications which cause the problem and adjust the model accordingly. In a sense this program of increasing complexity is exactly how experiments are proceeding.

The final criticism also relies on the complexity of naturally occurring processes. How is one to know if the elasticity of demand and costs used in an experiment or if the particular market institution are those of the industry? If the results of the laboratory experiments are to be applied, should not these magnitudes be "right"? The answer to these types of criticisms are still more experiments under varying parameters. With a wide range of parameters explored, the question collapses into a judgment about parameters and not the experimental methods.

All of these arguments should make one cautious about extrapolating results generated from laboratory processes to naturally occurring processes. This type of extension must be dealt with artfully in the physical sciences as well as in economics. It is the most difficult task that any researcher faces. Experiments are simply an additional source of data and experience that one adds to other sources in making judgments about how the word works.

An easier task, involving a somewhat negative approach, places the burden of proof on those who advocate theories. General theories apply in special cases. They should therefore be expected to work in the simple laboratory environments and if they do not, or if a competing theory works better, the burden of proof is on the advocate to tell us exactly why we should not judge him to be wrong. By adopting this point of view, researchers can use data from laboratory economics to reduce the size of the set of competing ideas.

7. Closing remarks[34]

Experimental studies demonstrate clearly that market institutions and practices can influence market performance. Variables traditionally classified as aspects of market structure are also of demonstrable importance. Furthermore, rather

[34]This section is reproduced from Plott (1982, pp. 1523–1524).

standard mathematical models are able to capture much of what can be observed behaviorally.

Three models do well in predicting market prices and quantity: the competitive equilibrium, the Cournot model, and monopoly (joint maximization) model. Experiments help define the conditions under which each of these alternative models apply. Some tendency exists for the error of a model when applied to data to be sensitive to structural and institutional variables (e.g. posted prices tend to be higher than prices under oral double auctions) but, generally speaking, when a model applies, it does so with reasonable accuracy.

Interestingly enough, while experimental studies demonstrate that it is possible to model economic processes, they have also uncovered a problem in determining the conditions under which a model will be applicable. There is an interaction between variables which has not been fully explained. It is *not* the case that competitors are capable of collusive activity when merely recognizing a harmony of interests. It is also *not* the case that competitors *cannot* collude in the absence of direct communication and the enforcement of agreements. Competitors seem to be willing to collude (so the rivalistic hypotheses[35] advanced in the early experimental studies can be safely dropped) but some market structures and institutions make it easy while others make it almost impossible (in the sense that successful collusion has *never* been observed). Even a monopolist has difficulty within certain market institutions. Existing theory does not tell us exactly why this occurs, but the data suggest that one key is the behavior of the buyers. The data also suggest that market performance is very fragile (or "nonlinear") with respect to underlying structural and institutional variables and that "slight" changes (from four to two firms, or from price posting to some other institution can switch a market from "competitive" to "collusive" or vice versa.

No doubt the ultimate usefulness of experimental work will be determined by demonstrations that experiments provide insights about what one finds upon close examination of industries. Prosecutors and regulators must choose which cases to prosecute and what reliefs to purse, and frequently the choices must be based on very thin data and controversial economic theories. The facts which might falsify the theory are often impossible to obtain without undertaking the long and expensive process of litigation. Experiments are an alternative, relatively inexpensive, and quick source of data. How these data will be regarded by the courts is yet to be determined [Kirkwood (1981)] but there seems to be no substantial difference between data from experimental markets and data from other types of experiments. Of course, this source of data has one more substantial advantage. The fact that experiments can always be rerun and the validity of

[35]This hypothesis maintained that competitors will attempt to maximize relative profits, thereby transforming the market into a zero-sum game.

claims checks places severe veracity constraints upon those who might enter such data as evidence in a court proceeding.

Appendix: Instructions

A.1. General

This is an experiment in the economics of market decisionmaking. The instructions are simple and if you follow them carefully and make good decisions you might earn money which will be paid to you in cash.

In this experiment we are going to conduct a market in which some of you will be buyers and some of you will be sellers in a sequence of market days or trading periods. Attached to the instructions you will find a sheet labeled Buyer or Seller, which describes the value to you of any decisions you might make. **You are not to reveal this information to anyone.** It is your own private information.

The currency in these markets is francs. Each franc is worth _____ dollars to you.

A.2. Specific instructions to buyers

During each market period you are free to purchase from any seller or sellers as many units as you might want. For the first unit that you buy *during a trading period* you will receive the amount listed in row (1) marked *1st unit redemption value*; if you buy a second unit you will receive the additional amount listed in row (4) marked *2nd unit redemption value*, etc. The profits from each purchase (which are yours to keep) are computed by taking the difference between the redemption value and purchase price of the unit bought. That is,

$$[\text{your earnings} = (\text{redemption value}) - (\text{purchase price})].$$

Suppose, for example, that you buy two units and that your redemption value for the first unit is 200 and for the second unit is 180. If you pay 150 for your first unit and 160 for the second unit, your earnings are:

$$\begin{aligned} \text{earnings from first} &= 200 - 150 = 50 \\ \text{earnings from second} &= 180 - 160 = 20 \\ \text{total earnings} &= \ \ 50 + \ \ 20 = 70 \end{aligned}$$

The blanks on the table will help you record your profits. The purchase price of the first unit you buy during the first period should be recorded on row (2) *at the time of purchase*. You should then record the profits on this purchase as directed on row (3). At the end of the period record the total of profits on the last row on the page. Subsequent periods should be recorded similarly.

A.3. Specific instructions to sellers

During each market period you are free to sell to any buyer or buyers as many units as you might want. The first unit that you sell *during a trading period* you obtain at a cost of the amount listed on the attached sheet in row (2) marked *cost of 1st unit*; if you sell a second unit you incur the cost listed in row (5) marked *cost of 2nd unit*; etc. The profits from each sale (which are yours to keep) are computed by taking the difference between the price at which you sold the unit and the cost of the unit. That is,

$$[\text{your earnings} = (\text{sale price of unit}) - (\text{cost of unit})].$$

Suppose, for example, your cost of the first unit is 140 and your cost of the second unit is 160. For illustrative purposes we will consider only a two-unit case. If you sell the first unit at 200 and the second unit at 190, your earnings are:

$$\text{earnings from first} = 200 - 140 = 60$$

$$\text{earnings from second} = 190 - 160 = 30$$

$$\text{total earnings} = 60 + 30 = 90$$

The blanks on the table will help you record your profits. The sale price of the first unit you sell during the first period should be recorded on row (1) *at the time of sale*. You should then record the profits on this sale as directed on row (3). At the end of the period, record the total of profits on the last row on the page. Subsequent periods should be recorded similarly.

A.4. Market organization (multiple unit ODA)

The market for units is organized as follows. The trading period is open for_____minutes. Any person is free to bid, to buy (ask to sell) at any time that recognition is gained from the auctioneer. The bid (ask) is tendered by giving the sequence: name, bid price per unit (ask price per unit), quantity. The bid (ask) will be written on the chalkboard and will remain there until accepted, canceled or replaced by a higher (lower) bid (ask). Anyone is free to accept any part of a standing bid (ask) and the remainder continues to stand. If a person accepts all or part of a bid (ask), a binding contract has been closed and both parties must record the transaction.

References

Alger, D.R. (1987) 'Laboratory tests of equilibrium predictions with disequilibrium data', *Review of Economic Studies*, 54:105–146.

Aviation Daily, 25 July, 1983.

Belovicz, M.W. (1979) 'Sealed-bid auctions experimental results and application', in: V.L. Smith, ed., *Research in experimental economics*, vol. 1. Greenwich, Conn.: JAI Press, 279–238.

Berg, J.E., Daley, L.A., Dickhaut and O'Brien J.R. (1986) 'Controlling preferences for lotteries on units of experimental exchange', *Quarterly Journal of Economics*, 101:281–306.

Burns, P. (1985) 'Market structure and buyer behavior: Price adjustment in a multi-object progressive oral auction', *Journal of Economic Behavior and Organization*, 6:275–300.

Chamberlin, E.H. (1948) 'An experimental imperfect market', *Journal of Political economy*, 56:95–108.

Cohen, L., Levine, M.E. and Plott, C.R. (1978) 'Communication and agenda influence: The chocolate pizza design', in: H. Sauermann, ed., *Coalition forming behavior: Contributions to experimental economics*, vol. 8. Tübingen, Germany: J.C.B. Mohr (Paul Siebeck), 329–357.

Cook, W.D. and Veendorp, E.C.H. (1975) 'Six markets in search of an auctioneer', *Canadian Journal of Economics*, 8:238–257.

Coppinger, V.M., Smith, V.L. and Titus, J.A. (1980) 'Incentives and behavior in English, Dutch and sealed-bid auctions', *Economic Inquiry*, 18:1–22.

Coursey, D. and Dyl, E.A. (1986) 'Trading suspensions, daily price limits, and information efficiency: A laboratory examination', in: S. Moriarity, ed., *Laboratory market research*. Norman, Oklahoma: University of Oklahoma, Center for Econometrics and Management Research, 153–168.

Coursey, D. and Smith. V.L. (1983) 'Price controls in a posted offer market', *American Economic Review*, 73:218–221.

Coursey, D., Isaac, R.M. and Smith, V.L. (1984) 'Natural monopoly and contested markets: Some experimental results', *Journal of Law and Economics*, 27:91–114.

Coursey, D., Isaac, R.M., Luke, M. and Smith, V.L. (1984) 'Market contestability in the presence of sunk (entry) cost', *Rand Journal of Economics*, 15:69–84.

Cox, J.C. and Isaac, R.M. (1986) 'Incentive regulation: A case study in the use of experimental analysis in economics', in: S. Moriarity, ed., *Laboratory market research*. Norman, Oklahoma: University of Oklahoma, Center for Econometrics and Management Research.

Cox, J.C., Roberson, B. and Smith, V.L. (1982) 'Theory and behavior of single object auctions', in: V.L. Smith, ed., *Research in experimental economics*, vol. 2. Greenwich, Conn.: JAI Press.

Cox, J.C., Smith, V.L. and Walker, J.M. (1984) 'The theory and behavior of multiple unit discriminative auctions', *Journal of Finance*, 39:983–1010.

Cox, J.C., Smith, V.L. and Walker, J.M. (1985) 'Experimental development of sealed-bid auction theory; calibrating controls for risk aversion', *American Economic Review*, 75:160–165.

Crössman, H.J. (1982) *Entscheidungsverhalten auf unvollkommenen mäkten*. Frankfurt am Main, Germany: Barudio and Hes Verlag.

Daniels, B. and Plott, C.R. (1988) 'Inflation and expectations in experimental markets', in: R. Tietz, W. Albers and R. Selten, eds., *Bounded rational behavior in experimental games and markets. Lecture Notes in Economics and Mathematical Systems no. 314*. Berlin/Heidelberg: Springer-Verlag.

Davis, D.D. and Williams, A.W. (1984) 'The effects of rent asymmetrics in posted offer markets', mimeo.

Easley, D. and Ledyard, J.O. (1986) 'Theories of price formation and exchange in double oral auctions, Social Science working paper no. 611, California Institute of Technology, Pasadena.

Finsinger, J. and Vogelsang, J. (1981) 'Alternative institutional frameworks for price incentive mechanisms', *Kyklos*, 388–404.

Forsythe, R., Palfrey, T.R. and Plott, C.R. (1982) 'Asset valuation in an experimental market', *Econometrica*, 50:537–567.

Fouraker, L.E. and Siegel, S. (1963) *Bargaining behavior*. New York: McGraw-Hill.

Frahm, D. and Schrader, L.F. (1969) 'An experimental comparison of pricing in two auction systems', *American Journal of Agricultural Economics*, 52:528–535.

Friedman, D. (1984) 'On the efficiency of experimental double auction markets', *American Economic Review*, 74:60–72.

Friedman, D., Harrison, G.W. and Salmon, J.W. (1984) 'The informational efficiency of experimental asset markets', *Journal of Political Economy*, 92:349–408.

Grether, D.M. and Plott, C.R. (1984) 'The effects of market practices in oligopolistic markets: An experimental examination of the ethyl case', *Economic Inquiry*, 22:479–507.

Grether, D.M., Isaac, R.M. and Plott, C.R. (1981) 'The allocation of landing rights by unanimity among competitors', *American Economic Review*, *71*:166–171.

Grether, D.M., Isaac, R.M. and Plott, C.R. (forthcoming) *The allocation of scarce resources: Experimental economics and the problem of allocating airport slots. Underground Classics in Economics.* Boulder, CO: Westview Press.

Harrison, G.W. and McKee, M. (1985) Monopoly behavior, decentralized regulation, and contestable markets: An experimental evaluation', *Rand Journal of Economics*, 16:51–69.

Hoffman, E. and Plott, C.R. (1981) 'The effect of intertemporal speculation on the outcomes in seller posted offer auction markets', *Quarterly Journal of Economics*, 96:233–241.

Hoffman, E. and Plott, C.R. (1983) 'Pre-meeting discussions and the possibility of coalition-breaking procedures in majority rule committees', *Public Choice*, 40:21–39.

Hoggatt, A.C. (1959) 'An experimental business game', *Behavioral Science*, 4:192–203.

Holt, C.A. (1985) 'An experimental test of the consistent conjectures hypothesis', *American Economic Review*, 75:314–325.

Holt, C.A. and Sherman, R. (1986) 'Quality uncertainty and bundling', in: P.M. Ippolito and D.T. Scheffman, eds., *Empirical approaches to consumer protection economics*. Federal Trade Commission, 221–250.

Holt, C.A., Langan, L.W. and Villamil, A.P. (1986) 'Market power in oral double auctions', *Economic Inquiry*, 24:107–123.

Hong, J.T. and Plott, C.R. (1982) 'Rate filing policies for inland water transportation: An experimental approach'. *Bell Journal of Economics*, 13:11–19.

Isaac, R.M. and Plott, C.R. (1981a) 'The opportunity for conspiracy in restraint of trade: An experimental study', *Journal of Economic Behavior and Organization*, 2:1–30.

Isaac, R.M. and Plott, C.R. (1981b) 'Price controls and the behavior of auction markets: An experimental examination', *American Economic Review*, 71:448–459.

Isaac, R.M. and Walker, J. (1985) 'Information and conspiracy in sealed bid auctions', *Journal of Economic Behavior and Organization*, 6:193–260.

Isaac, R.M., Ramey, V. and Williams, A.W. (1984) 'The effects of market organization on conspiracies in restraint of trade', *Journal of Economic Behavior and Organization*, 5:191–222.

Johnson, A., Lee, H.Y. and Plott, C.R. (1988) 'Multiple unit double auction user's manual', Social Science working paper no. 676, California Institute of Technology, Pasadena.

Joyce, P. (1983) 'Information and behavior in experimental markets', *Journal of Economic Behavior and Organization*, 4:411–424.

Joyce, P. (1984) 'The Walrasian tâtonnement mechanism and information', *Rand Journal of Economics*, 15:416–425.

Kagel, J.H. and Levin, D. (1986) 'The winner's curse and public information in common value auctions', *American Economic Review*, 76:894–920.

Ketcham, J., Smith, V.L. and Williams, A.W. (1984) 'A comparison of posted-offer and double-auction pricing institutions', *Review of Economic Studies*, 51:595–614.

Kirkwood, J.B. (1981) 'Antitrust implications of the recent experimental literature on collusion', in: S.C. Salop, ed., *Strategy, predation and antitrust analysis*. Washington, D.C.: U.S. Federal Trade Commission, Bureau of Economics, Bureau of Competition, 605–621.

Loeb, M. and Magat, W.A. (1979) 'A decentralized method for utility regulation', *Journal of Law and Economics*, 22:399–404.

Lynch, M., Miller, R.M., Plott, C.R. and Porter, R. (1986) 'Product quality, consumer information and 'lemons' in experimental markets', in: P.M. Ippolito and D.T. Scheffman, eds., *Empirical approaches to consumer protection economics*. Federal Trade Commission, 251–306.

Mestelman, S. and Welland, D. (1986) 'Advance production in experimental markets', QSEP research report no. 172, McMaster University, Hamilton, Canada.

Mestelman, S. and Welland, D. (1987) 'Advance production in oral double auction markets', *Economic Letters*, 23:43–48.

Mestelman, S., Welland, D. and Welland, D. 'Advance production in posted offer markets', *Journal of Economic Behavior and Organization*, forthcoming.

Miller, G.J. and Plott, C.R. (1985) 'Revenue generating properties of sealed-bid auctions: An experimental analysis of one-price and discriminative processes', in: V.L. Smith, eds., *Research in experimental economics*, vol. 3. Greenwich, Conn.: JAI Press, 31–72.

Miller, R.M. and Plott, C.R. (1985) 'Product quality signaling in experimental markets', *Econometrica*, 53:837–872.

Miller, R.M., Plott, C.R. and Smith, V.L. (1977) 'Intertemporal competitive equilibrium: An empirical study of speculation', *Quarterly Journal of Economics*, 91:599–624.

Nelson, F.D. (1980) 'A note on 'experimental auction markets and the Walrasian hypotheses', Social Science working paper no. 307, California Institute of Technology, Pasadena.

Palfrey, T.R. (1983) 'Bundling decision by a multiproduct monopolist with incomplete information', *Econometrica*, 51:463–483.

Palfrey, T.R. (1985) 'Buyer behavior and welfare effects of bundling by a multiproduct monopolist: A laboratory test', in: V.L. Smith, ed., *Research in experimental economics*, vol. 3. Greenwich, Conn. JAI Press.

Palfrey, T.R. and Romer, T. (1986) 'An experimental study of warranty coverage and dispute resolution in competitive markets', in: P.M. Ippolito and D.T. Scheffman, eds., *Empirical approaches to consumer protection economics*. Federal Trade Commission, 307–372.

Plott, C.R. (1979) 'The application of laboratory experimental methods to public choice', in: C.S. Russell, eds., *Collective decision making: Applications from public choice theory*. Baltimore, Md.: Johns Hopkins University Press for Resources for the Future, 137–160.

Plott, C.R. (1982) 'Industrial organization theory and experimental economics', *Journal of Economic Literature*, 20:1484–1527.

Plott, C.R. (1987) 'Dimensions of parallelism: Some policy applications of experimental methods', in: A.E. Roth, ed., *Laboratory experimentation in economics: Six points of view*. New York: Cambridge University Press.

Plott, C.R. and Agha, G. (1983) 'Intertemporal speculation with a random demand in an experimental market', in: R. Tietz, ed., *Aspiration levels in bargaining and economic decision making. Lecture Notes in Economics and Mathematical Systems*, no. 213. New York: Springer.

Plott, C.R. and Gray, P. (1988) 'Multiple unit double auction', Social Science working paper no. 625, California Institute of Technology, Pasadena.

Plott, C.R. and Smith, V.L. (1978) 'An experimental examination of two exchange institutions', *Review of Economic Studies*, 45:133–153.

Plott, C.R. and Sunder, S. (1982) 'Efficiency of experimental security markets with insider information: An application of rational expectations models', *Journal of Political Economy*, 90:663–698.

Plott, C.R. and Uhl, J.T. (1981) 'Competitive equilibrium with middlemen: An empirical study', *Southern Economic Journal*, 47:1063–1071.

Plott, C.R. and Wilde, L.L. (1982) 'Professional diagnosis versus self-diagnosis: An experimental examination of some special features of markets with uncertainty', in: V.L. Smith, ed., *Research in experimental economics*, vol. 2. Greenwich, Conn.: JAI Press.

Rassenti, S.J., Smith, V.L. and Bulfin, R.L. (1982) 'A combinatorial auction mechanism for airport time slot allocation', *Bell Journal of Economics*, 13:402–417.

Roth, A.E., ed. (1987) *Laboratory experimentation in economics: Six points of view*. New York: Cambridge University Press.

Roth, A.E., Malauf, M.W.K. and Murnigham, J.P. (1981) 'Sociological versus strategic factors in bargaining', *Journal of Economic Behavior and Organization*, 2:153–178.

Sauermann, H. and Selten, R. (1960) 'An experiment in oligopoly', in: L. von Bertalanffy and A. Rapoport, eds., *General systems yearbook of the society for general systems research*, vol. 5. [Translation of 'Ein Oligopolexperiment', *Zeitschrift für die Gesante Staatswissenschaft* (1959) 115:427–471.] Ann Arbor, Mich.: Society for General Systems Research.

Scherer, F.M. (1970) *Industrial market structure and economic performance*. Chicago: Rand McNally.

Seagraves, J. (1984) 'Regulating utilities with efficiency incentives', *Public Utilities Fortnightly*, 18–23.

Selten, R. (1970) 'Ein marktexperiment', in: H. Sauermann, ed., *Beiträge zur experimentellen wirtschaftsforschung* (*Contributions to experimental economics*), vol. 2. Tübingen, Germany: J.C.B. Mohr (Paul Siebeck), 33–98.

Smith, V.L. (1962) 'An experimental study of competitive market behavior', *Journal of Political Economy*, 70:111–137.

Smith, V.L. (1965) 'Experimental auction markets and the Walrasian hypotheses', *Journal of Polotical Economy*, 73:387–393.

Smith, V.L. (1967) 'Experimental studies of discrimination versus competition in sealed-bid auction markets', *Journal of Business*, 40:56–84.

Smith, V.L. (1976) 'Bidding and auctioning institutions: Experimental results', in: Y. Amihud, ed., *Bidding and auctioning for procurement and allocation*. New York: New York University Press, 43–63.

Smith, V.L. (1976) 'Experimental economics: Induced value theory', *American Economic Review*, 66:274–279.

Smith, V.L. (1980) 'Relevance of laboratory experiments to testing resource allocation theory', in: J. Kmenta and J. Ramsey, eds., *Evaluation of econometric models*. New York: Academic.

Smith, V.L. (1981) 'An empirical study of decentralized institutions of monopoly restraint', in: G. Horwich and J.P. Quirk, eds., *Essays in contemporary fields of economics in honor of Emanuel T. Weiler* (1914–1979). West Lafayette, Ind.: Purdue University Press.

Smith, V.L. (1982) 'Microeconomic systems as an experimental science', *American Economic Review*, 72:923–955.

Smith, V.L. and Williams, A.W. (1981a) 'The boundaries of competitive price theory: Convergence, expectations and transaction cost', paper presented at Public Choice Society Meetings, New Orleans.

Smith, V.L. and Williams, A.W. (1981b) 'On nonbinding price controls in a competitive market', *American Economic Review*, 71:467–474.

Smith, V.L. and Williams, A.W. (1982a) 'The effects of rent asymmetries in experimental auction markets', *Journal of Economic Behavior and Organization*, 3:99–116.

Smith, V.L. and Williams, A.W. (1982b) 'An experimental comparison of alternative rules for competitive market exchange', in: M. Shubik, ed., *Auctions, bidding and contracting: Uses and theory*. New York: New York University Press.

Smith, V.L., Williams, A.W., Bratton, W.K. and Vannoni, M.G. (1982) 'Competitive market institutions: Double auctions vs. sealed bid-offer auctions', *American Economic Review*, 72:58–77.

Walker, J.M. and Williams, A.W. (forthcoming) 'Market behavior in the bid, offer and double auctions', *Journal of Economic Behavior and Organization*.

Williams, A.W. 'Computerized double-auction markets: Some initial experimental results', *Journal of Business*, 53:235–258.

Williams, A.W. (1987) 'The formation of price forecasts in experimental markets', *Journal of Money, Credit, and Banking*, 19:1–18.

Williams, F.E. (1973) 'The effect of market organization on competitive equilibrium: The multiunit case', *Review of Economic Studies*, 40:97–113.

PART 4

INTERNATIONAL ISSUES AND COMPARISONS

Chapter 20

INDUSTRIAL ORGANIZATION AND INTERNATIONAL TRADE

PAUL R. KRUGMAN

Massachusetts Institute of Technology

Contents

Handbook of Industrial Organization, Volume II, Edited by R. Schmalensee and R.D. Willig

1. Introduction

In retrospect, it seems obvious that the theory of international trade should draw heavily on models of industrial organization. Most of world trade is in the products of industries that we have no hesitation in classifying as oligopolies when we see them in their domestic aspect. Yet until quite recently only a handful of papers had attempted to apply models of imperfect competition to international trade issues. Indeed, in 1974 Richard Caves still felt that a lecture on the relationship between trade and industrial organization needed to begin with an apology for the novelty of the idea.

Only in the last decade have we seen the emergence of a sizeable literature that links trade theory and industrial organization. This new literature has two main strands. One is fundamentally concerned with modelling the role of economies of scale as a cause of trade. To introduce economies of scale into the model requires that the impact of increasing returns on market structure be somehow taken into account, but in this literature the main concern is usually to get the issue of market structure out of the way as simply as possible – which turns out to be most easily done by assuming that markets are characterized by Chamberlinian monopolistic competition. The first section of this chapter summarizes the main insights from this approach.

Since this chapter is aimed primarily at an audience of industrial organization (IO) researchers rather than trade theorists, however, most of it will be devoted to the second strand in recent literature, which views imperfect competition as the core of the story rather than an unavoidable nuisance issue raised by the attempt to discuss increasing returns. Here there are four main themes, each represented by a section of the chapter. First is the relation between trade policy and the market power of domestic firms. Second is the role of price discrimination and "dumping" in international markets. Third is the possibility that government action can serve a "strategic" role in giving domestic firms an advantage in oligopolistic competition. Fourth, there is the question of whether industrial organization gives us new arguments in favor of protectionism. A final section of the chapter will review some recent attempts at quantifying these theoretical models.

Generality in models of imperfect competition is never easy to come by, and usually turns out to be illusory in any case. In this survey I will not even make the attempt. Whatever is necessary for easy exposition will be assumed: specific functional forms, constant marginal cost, specific parameters where that helps. And at least one part of the tradition of international trade theory will be retained: much of the exposition will be diagrammatic rather than algebraic.

2. The monopolistic competition trade model

2.1. Origins of the model

The monopolistic competition model of trade began with an empirical observation: neither the pattern of trade nor its results seem to accord very well with what traditional trade models would lead us to expect. The most influential of trade models is the Heckscher–Ohlin–Samuelson model, which tells us that trade reflects an interaction between the characteristics of countries and the characteristics of the production technology of different goods. Specifically, countries will export goods whose production is intensive in the factors with which they are abundantly endowed – e.g. countries with a high capital–labor ratio will export capital-intensive goods. This model leads us to expect three things. First, trade should typically be between complementary countries – capital-abundant countries should trade with labor-abundant. Second, the composition of trade should reflect the sources of comparative advantage. Third, since trade is in effect an indirect way for countries to trade factors of production, it should have strong effects on income distribution – when a country trades capital-intensive exports for labor-intensive imports, its workers should end up worse off.

What empirical workers noticed in the 1960s was that trends in world trade did not seem to accord with these expectations. The largest and rapidly growing part of world trade was trade among the industrial countries, which seemed fairly similar in their factor endowments and were clearly becoming more similar over time. The trade between industrial countries was largely composed of two-way exchanges of fairly similar goods – so-called "intra-industry" trade. Finally, in several important episodes of rapid growth in trade – notably formation of the European Economic Community and the Canadian–U.S. auto pact – the distributional effects turned out to be much less noticeable than had been feared.

From the mid-1960s on, a number of researchers proposed a simple explanation of these observations. Trade among the industrial countries, they argued, was due not to comparative advantage but to economies of scale. Because of the scale economies, there was an essentially arbitrary specialization by similar countries in the production of different goods, often of goods produced with the same factor intensities. This explained both why similar countries traded with each other and why they exchanged similar products. At the same time, trade based on increasing returns rather than indirect exchange of factors need not have large income distribution effects. Thus, introducing economies of scale as a determinant of trade seemed to resolve the puzzles uncovered by empirical work.

The problem, of course, was that at the time there was no good way to introduce economies of scale into a general equilibrium trade model. Without being embedded in a formal model, the theory of intra-industry trade could not become part of mainstream international economies. The crucial theoretical development thus came in the late 1970s, when new models of monopolistic competition were seen to allow a remarkably simple and elegant theory of trade in the presence of increasing returns. This marriage of industrial organization and trade was first proposed independently in papers by Dixit and Norman (1980), Krugman (1979), and Lancaster (1980). It was further extended by Helpman (1981), Krugman (1980, 1981), Ethier (1982), and others. Now that a number of years have gone into distilling the essentials of this approach, it is possible to describe in very compact form a basic monopolistic competition model of trade.

2.2. *The basic model*

Consider a world economy in which all countries share a common technology. There are two factors of production, capital and labor. These factors are employed in two sectors, Manufactures and Food.

Food we will take to be a homogeneous product, with a constant returns technology and thus a perfectly competitive market structure. Manufactures, however, we assume to consist of many differentiated products, subject to product-specific economies of scale. There is assumed to be a suitable choice of units such that all of the potential products can be made to look symmetric, with identical cost and demand functions. Furthermore, the set of potential products is assumed to be sufficiently large, and the individual products sufficiently small, that there exists a free-entry noncooperative equilibrium with zero profits.

Much effort has gone into the precise formulation of product differentiation. Some authors, including Dixit and Norman (1980), Krugman (1979, 1980, 1981), and Ethier (1982) follow the Spence (1976) and Dixit–Stiglitz (1977) assumption that all products are demanded by each individual, and thus build product differentiation into the utility function. Others, including Lancaster (1980) and Helpman (1981), follow the Hotelling–Lancaster approach in which the demand for variety arises from diversity of tastes. The Hotelling–Lancaster formulation has the advantage of greater realism, and leads to somewhat more plausible formulation of the nature of the gains from trade. However, it is quite difficult to work with. The Spence–Dixit–Stiglitz approach, by contrast, while less convincing, lends itself quite easily to modelling. (A "rock-bottom" model of trade along these lines is given in the Appendix.) Fortunately, it turns out that for the purposes of describing trade it does not matter at all which approach we take. All we need is the result that equilibrium in the Manufactures sector involves the production of a large number of differentiated products, and that all profits are competed away.

Now under certain circumstances, which will become clear shortly, international trade allows the world economy to become perfectly integrated, that is, to

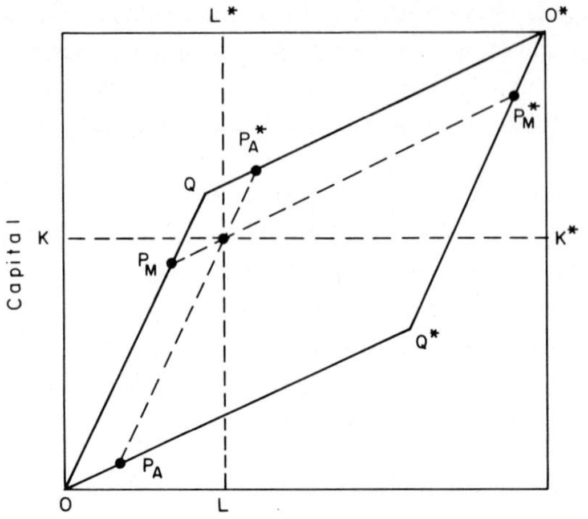

Figure 20.1

achieve the same outcome that would occur if all factors of production could work with each other freely. Associated with this integrated equilibrium outcome would be a set of resource allocations to the two sectors, goods prices, factor prices, and so on. Figure 20.1 represents some key features of such an equilibrium. The combined factor endowments of two trading countries are shown as the sides of a box. With full employment this endowment will be exhausted by the resources used in the two sectors. We let OQ be the resources used in Manufactures, and QO^* be the resources used in Food. Thus, Manufactures is assumed to be capital-intensive.

Will trade actually lead to this integrated economy outcome? As Dixit and Norman (1980) have shown, the answer depends on whether it is possible to allocate the integrated economy's production among the trading countries in such a way as to fully employ all factors of production while each country produces non-negative amounts of every good. This has a simple geometric interpretation. Suppose that there are two countries, Home and Foreign. Let us measure Home's resources from the point O, and Foreign's from O^*. Then the division of the world's resources among countries can be represented by a point in the box. If the endowment point is E, for example, this means that Home has a capital stock OK and a labor force OL, while Foreign has a capital stock O^*K^* and a labor force O^*L^*. Since E is above the diagonal, Home is capital-abundant, Foreign labor-abundant.

What can we now say about the world's production? The answer is that as long as the resources are not divided too unequally – specifically, as long as E lies inside the parallelogram OQO^*Q^* – it is possible to reproduce the production of the integrated economy without moving resources from one country to the other. We can determine the allocation of production between the countries by completing parallelograms. Thus, Home will devote resources OP_{M} to Manufactures, OP_{A} to Food; Foreign will devote $O^*P^*_{\mathrm{M}}$ and $O^*P^*_{\mathrm{A}}$ to Manufactures and Food, respectively.

Now it is immediately apparent that a redistribution of resources from one country to another will have a strongly biased effect on the distribution of world production. Suppose, for example, that Home were to have more capital and Foreign less. Then it is clear that Home would produce more Manufactures and *less* Food – a familiar result for trade theorists. It follows, given identical demand patterns, that capital-abundant Home will be a net exporter of Manufactures and a net importer of Food. Thus, at the level of *interindustry* trade flows conventional comparative advantage continues to apply.

Where economies of scale and monopolistic competition enter the story is in *intra*industry specialization. When production of Manufactures is split between Home and Foreign, economies of scale will imply that output of each individual differentiated product is concentrated in one country or the other. Which country produces which products is indeterminate (in a fundamental sense – see the Appendix), but the important point is that within the Manufactures sector each country will be producing a different set of goods. Since each country is assumed to have diverse demand, the result will be that even a country that is a *net* exporter of Manufactures will still demand some imports of the manufactures produced abroad.

The resulting pattern of trade is illustrated in Figure 20.2. There will be two-way "intraindustry" trade within the manufacturing sector, as well as conventional interindustry trade. The former will in effect reflect scale economies and product differentiation, while the latter reflects comparative advantage. We can notice two points about this pattern of trade. First, even if the countries had identical resource mixes (i.e. if point E in Figure 20.1 were on the diagonal) there will still be trade in Manufactures, because of intraindustry specialization.

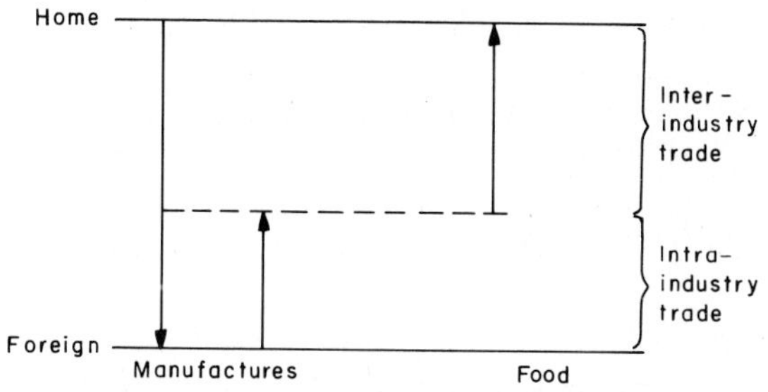

Figure 20.2

Second, the more similar the countries are in their factor endowments, the more they will engage in intra- as opposed to interindustry trade.

2.3. Extensions of the model

A number of authors have applied the monopolistic competition approach to models that attempt to capture more complex insights than the one we have just described. Many of these extensions are treated in Helpman and Krugman (1985); here I describe a few of the extensions briefly.

Intermediate goods: Ethier (1982) has emphasized that much intraindustry trade is in reality in intermediate goods. Models that reflect this are Ethier (1982), Helpman (1984) and Helpman and Krugman (1985, ch. 11). As it turns out, this extension makes little difference.

Nontraded goods: Helpman and Razin (1984) and Helpman and Krugman (1985, ch. 10) introduce nontraded goods into the model. Again, this does not make much difference. The major new implication is that differences in the size of national markets can give rise to new incentives for factor mobility.

Market size effects: Krugman (1980), Helpman and Krugman (1985), and Venables (1985b) develop models in which transport costs make the size of the domestic market an important determinant of trade. Specifically, countries tend other things equal to export the products of industries for which they have large domestic markets.

Multinational firms: Helpman (1985) and Helpman and Krugman (1985) develop models in which it is assumed that economies of scope and/or vertical integration lead to the emergence of multi-activity firms. Within the monopolistic competition framework it is then possible to let comparative advantage determine the location of activities, allowing models that describe both trade and the extent of multinational enterprise.

Alternative market structures: Helpman and Krugman contains some efforts to extend the insights of the monopolistic competition model beyond the highly special Chamberlinian large-group market structure. The insights survive essentially intact when the structure is instead assumed to be one of "contestable markets" in the manner of Baumol, Panzar and Willig (1982). [Helpman and Krugman (1985, ch. 4).] A much more qualified set of results occurs when the structure is instead assumed to be one of small-group oligopoly. [Helpman and Krugman (1985, chs. 5 and 7).]

2.4. Evaluation

The monopolistic competition model has had a major impact on research into international trade. By showing that increasing returns and imperfect competition can make a fundamental difference to the way we think about trade, this approach was crucial in making work that applies industrial organization concepts to trade respectable. In effect, the monopolistic competition model was the thin end of the IO/trade wedge.

From the point of view of IO theorists, however, the monopolistic competition trade model may be the least interesting part of the new trade theory. In essence, theorists in this area have viewed imperfect competition as a nuisance variable in a story that is fundamentally about increasing returns. Thus, the theory has little to teach us about industrial organization itself. By contrast, the other strand of the new trade theory is interested in increasing returns primarily as a cause of imperfect competition, and it is this imperfect competition that is the main story. Thus, it is this second strand which will occupy the rest of this survey.

3. Protection and domestic market power

Many economists have noted that international trade reduces the market power of domestic firms, and argued that conversely protection increases domestic market power. The interest of trade theorists has been centered on two extensions of this argument. First is the proposition that the effects of protection depend on the form it takes – specifically, that quantitative restrictions such as import quotas create more domestic market power than tariffs. This proposition was first demonstrated by Bhagwati (1965) in a model in which a domestic monopolist faces competitive foreign suppliers; only with recent work by Krishna (1984) has the analysis been extended to the case where both domestic and foreign firms are large agents. More recently still, Rotemberg and Saloner (1986) have argued that when collusive behavior is backed by the threat of a breakdown of that collusion, import quotas may actually perversely increase competition.

The second proposition is that protection, by initially generating monopoly rents, generates excessive entry and thus leads to inefficiently small scale production. This proposition, originally proposed by Eastman and Stykolt (1960), is backed by substantial evidence, and has been modelled by Dixit and Norman (1980).

3.1. Bhagwati's model

Consider an industry in which one firm has a monopoly on domestic production, but is subject to competition from price-taking foreign suppliers. Why the domestic market structure should differ from that in the rest of the world is left unexplained; presumably there are unspecified economies of scale that are large relative to the domestic market but not relative to the world market. Although

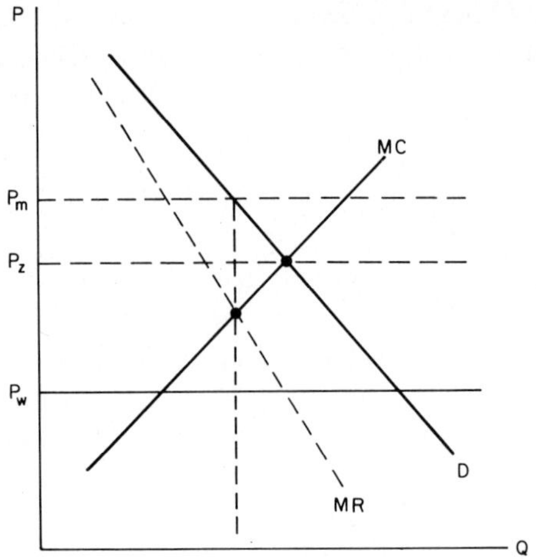

Figure 20.3

economies of scale may explain the existence of the monopoly, however, the marginal cost curve is assumed to slope upward. Foreign supply is assumed for simplicity to be perfectly elastic. [This differs slightly from Bhagwati, who allowed for upward-sloping foreign supply; nothing crucial hinges on the difference. Also, Corden (1967) analyzed the case when domestic marginal cost is downward sloping. In this case any tariff sufficient to establish the domestic firm also eliminates imports.]

Figure 20.3 can be used to analyze the effects of tariffs in this model. In the figure, D is the domestic demand curve facing the monopolist, MC the monopolist's marginal cost curve. P_w is the world price, i.e. the price at which imports are supplied to the domestic market. P_z is the price that would obtain if all domestic demand were supplied by the monopolist but the monopolist were to behave as a price taker. P_m is the price the monopolist would charge if there were no import competition.

Consider first the case of free trade. The domestic firm cannot raise the price above P_w, so the profit-maximizing strategy is to set marginal cost equal to P_w, producing Q_0. In this case the monopolist has no monopoly power.

Now suppose the government imposes a tariff. The effect is to raise the price at which imports will come into the market. As long as the tariff-inclusive import price lies between P_w and P_z, however, it remains true that the domestic firm acts like a price-taker, setting output where price equals marginal cost.

In a competitive industry, a tariff that raised the import price to P_z would be prohibitive, and any increase in the tariff beyond that level would have no effect – there would be "water in the tariff". Here the monopoly position of the

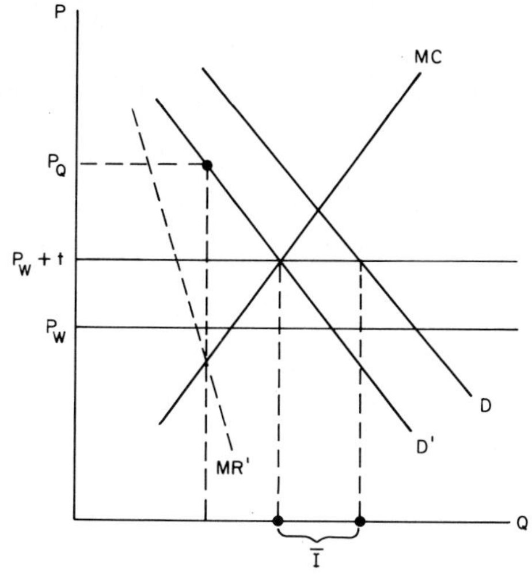

Figure 20.4

domestic firm matters. A tariff that raises the price above P_z allows the firm to raise its own price to the same level, something that will be profitable as long as the tariff price is below P_m. That is, even when no imports actually occur, the *threat* of imports keeps the monopolist from exercising its monopoly power fully, and raising an already prohibitive tariff therefore leads to domestic price increases. It also follows that such tariff increases actually *reduce* domestic output.

Now consider the effects of an import quota. In perfectly competitive models a quota is equivalent in its effects to a tariff that limits imports to the same level. Once we have domestic market power, however, an important difference emerges. A monopolist protected by a tariff cannot raise its price above the tariff-inclusive import price without losing the domestic market to imports. By contrast, a firm sheltered by quantitative restrictions need not fear increased imports, and is free to exercise its market power. The result is that an import quota will lead to a higher domestic price and lower domestic output than an "equivalent" tariff, defined as a tariff that leads to the same level of imports.

Figure 20.4 illustrates the nonequivalence of tariffs and quotas. As before, D is the domestic demand curve, MC marginal cost, P_w the world price. We compare a tariff t that reduces imports to $\bar{I}$, and an import quota that restricts imports to the same level.

With a tariff, the domestic firm simply sets marginal cost equal to $P_w + t$. With the equivalent quota, however, the firm now faces the demand curve D', derived by subtracting $\bar{I}$ from the domestic demand curve D. Corresponding to D^1 is a marginal revenue curve MR'. The profit-maximizing price with the quota is therefore P_Q; the quota leads to a higher price and lower output than the tariff.

Bhagwati's model produces a clear and compelling result. Better still, it yields a clear policy message: if you must protect, use a tariff rather than a quota. There are, however, two troubling features of the model. One is the asymmetry between domestic and foreign firms; we would like foreigners also to be modelled as imperfectly competitive. The other is the lack of any model of the process of entry that leads to imperfect competition. Both features have been the subject of recent research, the first most notably by Krishna (1984), the second by Dixit and Norman (1980).

3.2. *Krishna's model*

To get away from an arbitrary asymmetry between a domestic monopolist and price-taking foreign firms, it seems natural to examine a duopoly. We can let there be a single domestic firm that supplies the market with local production, and a single foreign firm that exports to the market. Collusion is of course possible, but as a modelling device we would prefer to assume noncooperative behavior. (For some possible implications of collusion, however, see below.)

In modelling noncooperative oligopolies, the choice of strategy variables is crucial. The two main alternatives are of course the Cournot approach, in which firms take each others' outputs as given, and the Bertrand approach, in which prices are taken as given. In analyzing the effects of protection, both approaches turn out to be problematic. The Cournot assumption fails to capture Bhagwati's insight regarding the difference between quotas and tariffs; the Bertrand assumption fails to yield a pure strategy equilibrium.

The problem with the Cournot approach may be simply stated. Bhagwati's model argued that a quota creates more market power than a tariff because the domestic firm knows that an increase in its price will lead to an increase in imports. In the Cournot approach, however, the domestic firm is assumed to take the level of imports as given in any case; so a quota and a tariff that leads to the same level of imports once again have equivalent effects on the domestic firm's behavior.

If Bhagwati's argument for a lack of equivalence between tariffs and quotas is right, however – and most international economists feel that it is – then this approach is missing an important insight. The alternative is a Bertrand approach. What Krishna shows is that this leads to unexpected complexities.

Krishna considers a market in which a domestic and foreign firm produce imperfect substitutes (an assumption that is necessary if Bertrand competition is not to collapse to marginal cost pricing). In the absence of quantitative trade restrictions, that is, either under free trade or with a tariff, Bertrand competition can be treated in a straightforward fashion. Each firm determines a profit-maximizing price given the other firm's price; given reasonable restrictions, we can draw two upward-sloping reaction functions whose intersection determines equilibrium.

But suppose that an import quota is imposed. This creates an immediate conceptual problem, which in turn leads to a problem in the understanding of equilibrium.

The conceptual problem is how to handle the possibility of excess demand. Suppose that at the prices set by the domestic and foreign firms, domestic consumers demand more foreign goods than the import quota allows. What happens? Krishna assumes, plausibly, that an unspecified group of middlemen collects the difference between the price charged by the foreign firm and the market-clearing consumer price. That is, incipient excess demand is reflected in an increased "dealer markup" rather than in rationing.

This now raises the next question, which is how to interpret Bertrand competition in this case. Which price does the domestic firm take as given, the foreign factory price or the dealer price? Here Krishna assumes, again sensibly, that the domestic firm takes the foreign factory price rather than the dealer price as given. This means that the domestic firm recognizes its ability to affect the consumer price of foreign substitutes when the import quota is binding.

But this seemingly innocuous assumption turns out to imply a basic discontinuity in the domestic firm's response function. The domestic firm in effect has two discrete pricing options: an "aggressive" option of charging a low price that limits imports to less than the quota, or a "timid" option of retreating behind the

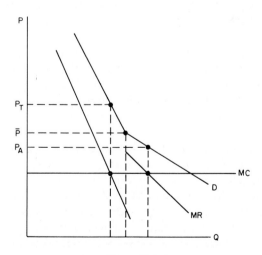

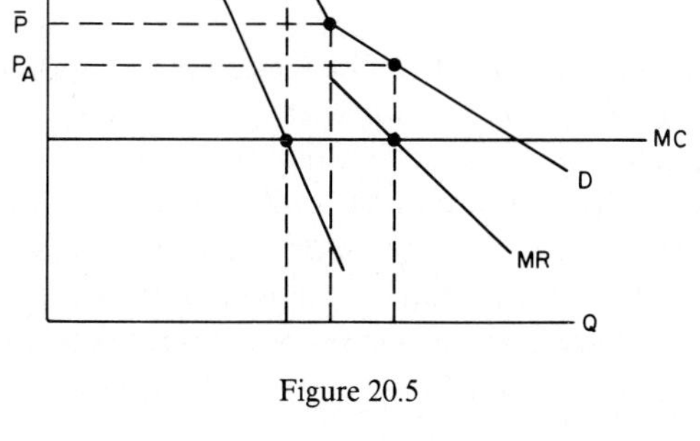

Figure 20.5

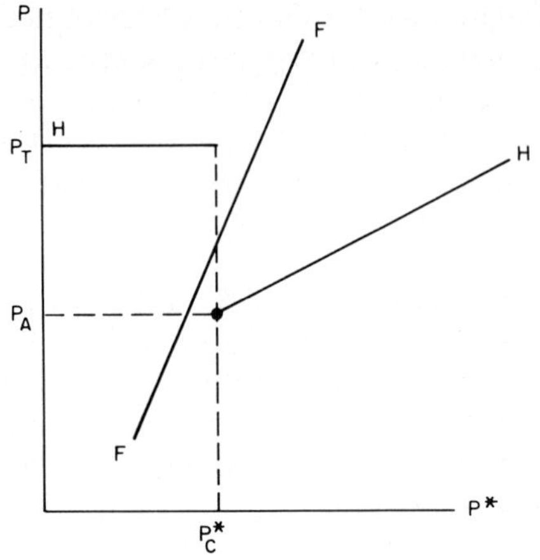

Figure 20.6

quota and charging a high price. A small rise in the foreign firm's price can shift the domestic firm's optimal response from "timid" to "aggressive".

Figure 20.5 illustrates the point. It shows the demand curve and the associated marginal revenue curve facing the domestic firm for a given foreign firm factory price. The price $\bar{P}$ is the price at which the quota becomes binding. That is, at a domestic firm price above $\bar{P}$ there is an incipient excess demand for imports, which is reflected in dealer markups that the domestic firm knows it can affect. By contrast, at prices below $\bar{P}$ the dealer price of imports is taken as given. That is, at prices below $\bar{P}$ the domestic firm takes the prices of the imported substitute as given, while at prices above $\bar{P}$ it believes that increases in its own price will increase the prices of the substitutes as well. The result is a discontinuity in the slope of the perceived demand curve, which is steeper just above $\bar{P}$ than it is just below; and hence a discontinuity in the *level* of the marginal revenue curve, which jumps up at the quantity corresponding to $\bar{P}$.

What is clear from the figure is that there are two locally profit-maximizing domestic prices: the "timid" maximum P_T, and the "aggressive" maximum P_A. Which maximum is global depends on the price charged by the foreign firm. The profitability of the timid option is unaffected by what the foreign firm does, but the higher the foreign price, the more profitable the aggressive option.

The result is a home reaction function looking like *HH* in Figure 20.6. At low levels of the foreign price P^*, the domestic firm retreats behind the quota and therefore chooses a price locally independent of P^*. At a sufficiently high P^*, however, the domestic firm abruptly sallies out from behind the quota with a cut in its price.

The foreign best response function *FF* has no such discontinuity. However, if the quota matters at all, *FF* must, as shown, pass right through the hole in *HH*! Thus, no pure strategy equilibrium exists.

A mixed strategy equilibrium does exist. If the foreign firm charges P_C^*, the home firm is indifferent between P_T and P_A; by randomizing its choice of P_A and P_T with the right probabilities, the home firm can induce its competitor to choose P_C^*.

In this mixed strategy equilibrium, we notice that the foreign firm, despite its monopoly power, does not always raise its price enough to capture all of the quota rents, a result in contrast to conventional wisdom. We can also note that with some probability the quota will fail to be binding, in the sense that imports are strictly less than the quota – yet both domestic and foreign prices are unambiguously higher even in this case than under free trade.

A point stressed by Krishna is that in this duopoly case a quota can easily raise the profits of *both* firms. Consider, for example, a quota that only restricts imports not to exceed their free trade level. Clearly, if the domestic firm charges P_T, it is because this is more profitable than the free trade price, while the foreign firm will sell the same output as under free trade, yet at a higher price. On the other hand, if the domestic firm charges P_A, this "aggressive" price is still above the free trade price, so the foreign firm must be earning higher profits. (The domestic firm of course earns the same in both states.) So profitability of both firms increases unambiguously.

3.3. *Protection vs. collusion*

Almost all theoretical work on industrial organization/trade issues assumes that firms act noncooperatively. In industrial organization theory itself, however, there has recently been a drift toward taking the possibility of collusive behavior more seriously. The key to this drift has been the recognition that collusive behavior may be individually rational in an indefinitely repeated game, where each player believes that his failure to play cooperatively today will lead to noncooperative behavior by others tomorrow. The influential experimental work of Axelrod (1983) suggests that reasonable strategies by individuals will indeed lead to cooperative outcomes in a variety of circumstances.

Recently Davidson (1984) and Rotemberg and Saloner (1986) have proposed analyses of the effects of protection on collusion that seem to stand Bhagwati on his head. They argue that precisely because protection tends to raise profitability in the absence of collusion, it reduces the penalty for cheating on a collusive agreement. By thus reducing the prospects for collusion, the protection actually increases competition.

The case is clearest for an import quota, analyzed by Rotemberg and Saloner. To understand their argument, consider Krishna's model again, but now suppose that the two firms attempt to agree on prices higher than the noncooperative level. Suppose also that the only enforcement mechanism for their agreement is the belief of each firm that if it cheats this period, the other firm will thenceforth play noncooperatively. Then collusion will succeed only if the extra profits gained by cheating now are more than offset by the present discounted value of the profits that will subsequently be lost by the collapse of collusion. A viable price-fixing agreement must therefore set prices low enough to make cheating unappealing.

But as we saw in our discussion of Krishna's model, a quota can actually raise the profitability of both firms in noncooperative equilibrium. This paradoxically makes collusion more difficult to sustain, by reducing the penalty for cheating. If the firms manage to collude nonetheless, they may be forced to agree on lower prices in order to make their collusion sustainable. So in this case an import quota actually leads to more competition and lower prices than free trade!

Davidson considers the case of a tariff, which raises the noncooperative profits of the domestic firm but lowers that of the foreign competitor. If the result is to encourage the domestic firm to cheat, the tariff will likewise increase competition.

It remains to be seen whether this argument will shake the orthodox presumption that protection is bad for competition. The modelling of collusive behavior is still in its infancy. To me, at least, the approach taken in this new line of work seems an odd mix of ad hoc assumptions about retaliation with hyper-rational calculations by firms about the consequences of such retaliation. Yet the argument is profoundly unsettling, which means that it must be valuable (though not that it must be right!).

3.4. *Protection and excessive entry*

In the 1950s, during the honeymoon period of import-substituting industrialization strategies, it was often argued that economies of scale in production provided an argument for protection – a view with a lineage going back to Frank Graham. At first, the point seems obvious: protection raises the sales of domestic firms, and thus allows them to slide down their average cost curves. In an influential paper, however, Eastman and Stykolt (1960) argued that often the reverse is true. In their view, bolstered by an appeal to Canadian experience, protection typically leads to a smaller scale of production and thus reduced efficiency.

The Eastman–Stykolt view was not couched in terms of an explicit model. Basically, however, they considered the typical case to be that where the number of firms permitted by economies of scale is more than one but small enough to allow effective collusion. Such a collusive industry will seek to raise its price to monopoly levels unless constrained by foreign competition. A tariff or quota will thus lead initially to higher prices and profits. The long-run result, however, will be entry of new firms into the industry. If integer constraints do not bind too much, this entry will eliminate profits by driving scale down and average cost up. Thus, the effect of protection is to create a proliferation of inefficiently small producers. Such proliferation is indeed one of the favorite horror stories of critics of protection in less-developed countries, with the history of the Latin American auto industry the classic case.

This original version of the inefficient entry problem depended on the assumption of collusion among domestic producers. The problem could, however, arise even with noncooperative behavior, as is clear from a model offered by Dixit and Norman (1980). They show that in a Cournot market with free entry, expanding the size of the market leads to a less than proportional increase in the number of firms, and to a fall in average cost. Since international trade in effect links together national markets into a larger world market, it would have the same result. Protection, on the other hand, fragments the world market and hence leads to a proliferation of firms and a rise in costs.

We will return to the inefficient entry problem below. It plays a key role in the debate over "strategic" trade policy, and is also central to some attempts to quantify the effects of trade policy.

3.5. Evaluation

The basic Bhagwati model of protection and market power is admirably clear and simple, and has been in circulation for long enough to have percolated into practical policy analysis. Market power analysis along Bhagwati's lines has become part of the book of analytical recipes used by the International Trade Commission [Rousslang and Suomela (1985)]. Market power considerations have now and then helped dictate the form taken by protection; for example, the trigger price mechanism on steel during the Carter Administration was deliberately designed to minimize the effect of protection on the monopoly power of both domestic and foreign firms. And perceptions of the impact of trade policy on market power seem to be playing a role in antitrust decisions: in the steel industry, for example, it appears that the Justice Department appreciates that foreign competition is less effective a discipline than import penetration would suggest thanks to import quotas and voluntary export restraints.

More sophisticated models have yet to find application. It is at this point hard to see how Krishna's model might be made operational, let alone the inverted logic of the collusion models. The one exception is the excess entry story, which as we will see is the central element in Harris and Cox's (1984) effort to quantify the effect of protection on Canada's economy.

4. Price discrimination and dumping

The phenomenon of "dumping" – selling exports at less than the domestic price – has long been a major concern of trade legislation. It is also self-evidently an imperfect competition issue. It is therefore not surprising that the new literature on trade and IO sheds some further light on dumping as a particular case of price discrimination. More surprising, perhaps, is the fact that the new literature on dumping actually identifies a new explanation of international trade, distinct from both comparative advantage and economies of scale.

Much as in the case of protection and market power, the initial insight here comes from an asymmetric model in which a domestic monopolist confronts price-taking foreign firms. This insight becomes both enlarged and transformed when rival oligopolists are introduced. Finally, the welfare effects of trade based on dumping are of some interest.

4.1. An asymmetric model

An extremely simple model of dumping is presented by Caves and Jones (1985) and illustrated in Figure 20.7. As in the case of protection and market power, a single domestic monopolist is assumed to face a given world price P_w. We now, however, reverse the assumptions about the possibilities for trade. Before, we let the firm face import competition while disregarding the possibility of exports. Now we assume that the domestic market is somehow closed to imports, while allowing the domestic firm to export.

In the figure I have drawn a particular case, where with a price-taking domestic firm there would be neither imports nor exports. If the domestic firm acts as a monopolist, however, it will want to set marginal revenue equal to marginal cost in both the domestic and the foreign markets. Marginal revenue on the foreign market is however just P_w, so the profit-maximizing solution is the one illustrated. The firm sets a domestic price above P_w, yet it exports, "dumping" on the world market where additional sales do not depress the price received on inframarginal units.

Three points should be noted about this example. The first is that while for simplicity it has been assumed that P_w is given, this is not essential. What is important is that the firm perceives itself as facing a higher elasticity of demand on exports than on domestic sales. That is, dumping is simply international price discrimination.

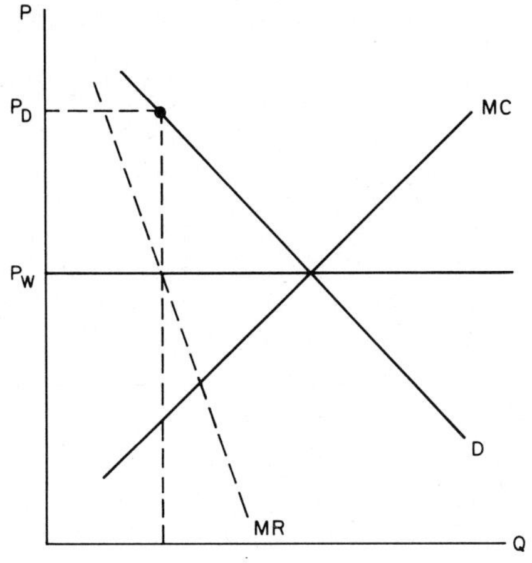

Figure 20.7

Second, the figure illustrates a case in which a price-taking domestic firm would not export – in the usual sense of the term, the domestic industry has neither a comparative advantage nor a comparative disadvantage. Yet the firm does in fact export. Clearly, we could have an industry which has at least some comparative *disadvantage*, and yet dumps in the export market. In other words, dumping can make trade run "uphill" against conventional determinants of its direction.

Third, the difference between the domestic and foreign markets remains unexplained. Why should the domestic firm be a price-setter at home, a price-taker abroad (or more generally, face more elastic demand for exports)? We would like to have a model in which this asymmetry is derived, rather than built in by assumption. In the new IO trade literature, such models have finally emerged.

4.2. Brander's model

A duopoly model of dumping was developed by Brander (1981) and elaborated on by Brander and Krugman (1983). This model goes to the opposite extreme from the asymmetrical model we just described, by postulating instead a perfectly symmetrical situation. We assume that some good is consumed in two countries, each of which has the same demand; and we assume that there is a single firm in each country, and that the two firms have identical costs. There is some positive cost of transporting the good internationally, so that in a perfect competition setting there would be no trade.

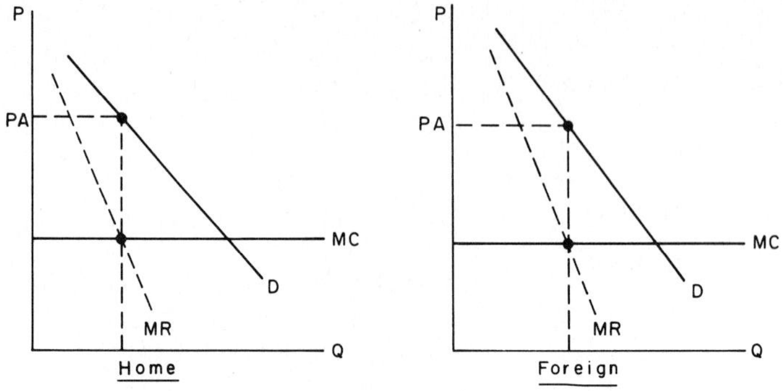

Figure 20.8

If the transport costs are not too large, however, and if the firms behave in a Cournot fashion, trade will nevertheless result. To see why, consider Figure 20.8, which illustrates what would happen in the absence of trade. We see each firm acting as a monopolist, and thus each country having a price that exceeds marginal costs. The firms do not expand their output, however, because this would depress the price on inframarginal units.

But suppose that the markup over marginal cost exceeds the transport cost between the markets. In this case each firm will have an incentive to absorb the transport cost so as to export to the other's home market. The reason is that an extra unit sold abroad, even though it yields a price net of transportation less than a unit sold domestically, does not depress the price of inframarginal sales (it depresses the price the other firm receives instead). So as long as price less transportation exceeds marginal cost, it is worth exporting.

The result is a mutual interpenetration of markets, described by Brander and Krugman as "reciprocal dumping". With Cournot behavior, equilibrium will take the following form: each firm will have a larger share of its home market than the foreign market, and will thus perceive itself as facing a higher elasticity of demand abroad than at home. The difference in perceived elasticity of demand will be just enough to induce firms to absorb transport costs. The result will therefore be a determinate volume of "cross-hauling": two-way trade in the same product. In the symmetric example considered, this pointless trade will be balanced.

From a trade theorist's point of view, this result is startling: here we have international trade occurring despite a complete absence of comparative advantage and without even any direct role for economies of scale (although an indirect role can be introduced if we support that increasing returns is the explanation of oligopoly). From an industrial organization point of view, the result may not seem quite so outlandish, since it bears a family resemblance to the theory of basing-point pricing [Smithies (1942)]. Nonetheless, the trade-theorist's approach offers the new possibility of an explicit welfare analysis.

4.3. Reciprocal dumping and welfare

Reciprocal dumping is a totally pointless form of trade – the same good is shipped in both directions, and real resources are wasted in its transportation. Nonetheless, the trade is not necessarily harmful. International competition reduces the monopoly distortion in each market, and the pro-competitive effect can outweigh the resource waste.

The welfare effects of reciprocal dumping are illustrated in Figure 20.9. Since the countries are assumed to be symmetric, looking at only one market will do. We note two effects. First, some of the exports that are dumped in each country are a net addition to consumption. In the figure this is represented as an increase of total deliveries from an initial level z to the level $x + y$. Since the initial price P_A exceeds marginal cost c plus transportation cost t, this represents a net gain, and can be equated with the pro-competitive effect. On the other side, some of the imports displace domestic production for the domestic market. This is represented as a fall of deliveries from the domestic firm to its own market from z to x, with the quantity y both imported and exported. Since this involves a waste of resources on transportation, this constitutes a loss. From the diagram it seems impossible to tell whether the net effect is a gain or a loss.

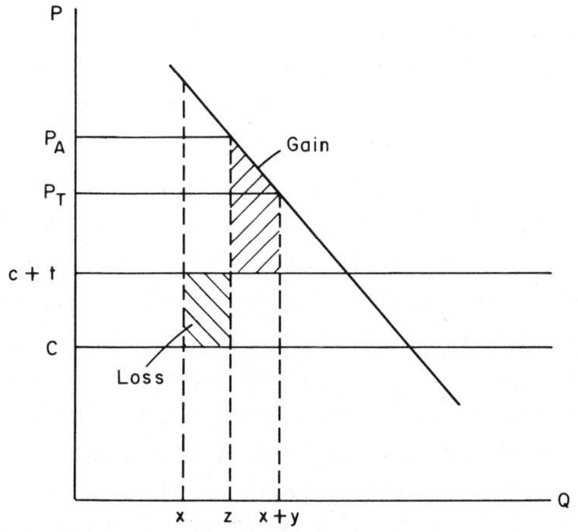

Figure 20.9

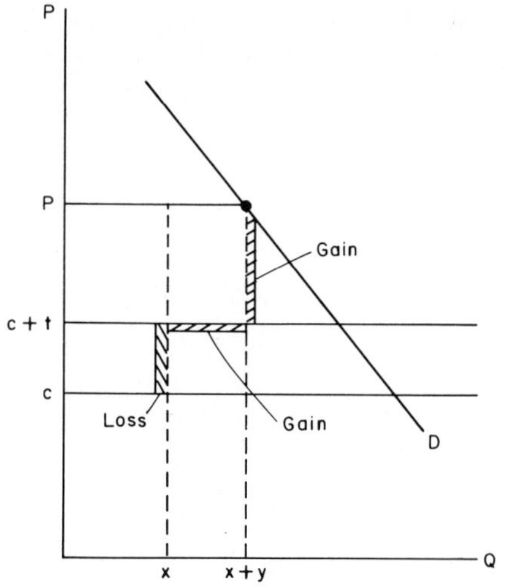

Figure 20.10

We know, however, that in one case at least there must be a gain. If transport costs are zero, cross-hauling may be pointless but it is also costless, and the pro-competitive effect yields gains. Presumably this remains true for transport costs sufficiently low.

This suggests that we examine how welfare changes as we vary transport costs. Consider the effects of a small reduction in transport costs, illustrated in Figure 20.10. There will be three effects. First, there will be a direct reduction in the cost of transporting the initial level of shipments – a clear gain. Second, there will be an increase in consumption, which will be a gain to the extent that the initial price exceeds marginal cost plus transportation cost. Third, there will be a displacement of local production by imports, which will be a loss by the change times the initial transport cost.

Can we sign the total effect? We can do so in two cases. First, suppose that transport costs are near zero. Then the last effect is negligible, and a reduction in transport is clearly beneficial.

More interestingly, suppose that initially transport costs are almost large enough to prohibit trade. Recalling our discussion above, this will be a situation where price is only slightly above marginal cost plus transport, and where the volume of trade is very small. This means that when transport costs are near the prohibitive level, the two sources of gain from a small decline in these costs become negligible, and a decline in transport costs thus reduces welfare.

Putting these results together, what we see is the relationship illustrated in Figure 20.11. If transport costs are high, but not high enough to prevent trade, trade based solely on dumping leads to losses. If they are low, trade is beneficial.

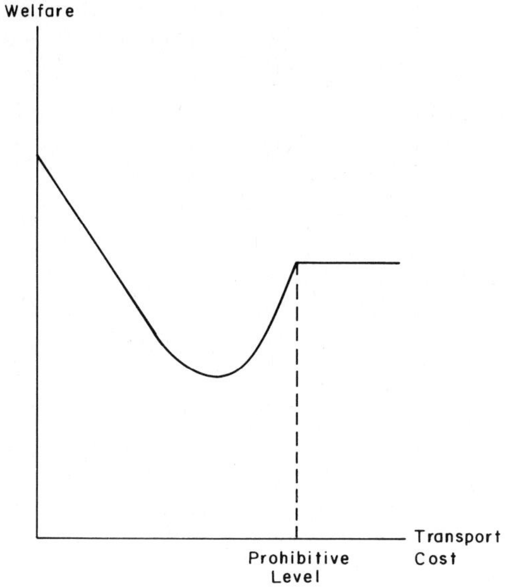

Figure 20.11

4.4. Evaluation

The new literature on dumping has so far been resolutely nonpolicy and nonempirical. Still, nothing that suggests a previously unsuspected explanation of international trade can be dismissed as without importance. Furthermore, the modelling techniques developed in the dumping literature are beginning to find at least some application. As we will see, attempts to calibrate models to actual data have so far relied on assumptions that bear a clear family resemblance to those introduced by Brander, and Brander and Krugman.

5. Strategic trade policy

One of the most controversial ideas of the new IO/trade literature has been the suggestion that government intervention can raise national welfare by shifting oligopoly rents from foreign to domestic firms. The starting point of this debate was several papers by Brander and Spencer (1983, 1985), who showed that in principle government policies such as export subsidies can serve the same purpose as, for example, investment in excess capacity in the IO literature on entry deterrence. That is, government policies can serve the "strategic" purpose of altering the subsequent incentives of firms, acting as a deterrent to foreign competitors. The "strategic" analysis seems to offer a possible rationale for trade policies, such as export subsidies, that have been almost universally condemned by international economists in the past.

The Brander–Spencer analysis, coming at a time of heated debate over U.S. international competitiveness, appears dangerously topical, and other economists have been quick to challenge the robustness of their results. The critiques are themselves of considerable analytic interest. In this survey I consider four important lines of research suggested by the critique of Brander–Spencer strategic trade policy. First is the dependence of trade policy recommendations on the nature of competition between firms, analyzed by Eaton and Grossman (1986). Second is the general equilibrium issue raised by the fact that industries must compete for resources within a country, analyzed by Dixit and Grossman (1984). Third is the question of entry, studied by Horstmann and Markusen (1986) and Dixit (forthcoming b). Finally is the question of who is behaving strategically with respect to whom, analyzed by Dixit and Kyle (1985).

5.1. The Brander–Spencer analysis

As is often the case in the IO/trade literature, the initial insight in strategic trade policy was obtained by subtraction rather than addition: by simplifying a trade issue to a form where a familiar model of imperfect competition can be easily applied.

Consider an industry in which there are only two firms, each in one country. The clever simplification that Spencer and Brander suggest is to assume that neither country has any domestic demand for the industry's products. Instead, both countries export to a third market. Also, distortions other than the presence of monopoly power in this industry are ruled out – i.e. the marginal cost of each firm is also the social cost of the resources it uses. The result is that for each country national welfare can be identified with the profits earned by its firm.

Since the firms are themselves attempting to maximize profits, one might imagine that there is no case for government intervention. However, this is not necessarily the case. To see why, we assume for now that the two firms compete in Cournot fashion, and illustrate their competition with Figure 20.12.

Each firm's reaction function will, for reasonable restrictions on cost and demand, slope down, and the Home firm's reaction function will be steeper than its competitor's. Point N is the Nash equilibrium. Drawn through point N is one of the Home firm's iso-profit curves. Given that the reaction function is constructed by maximizing Home's profits at each level of Foreign output, the iso-profit curve is flat at point N.

Now it is apparent that the Home firm could do better than at point N if it could only somehow commit itself to produce more than its Cournot output.

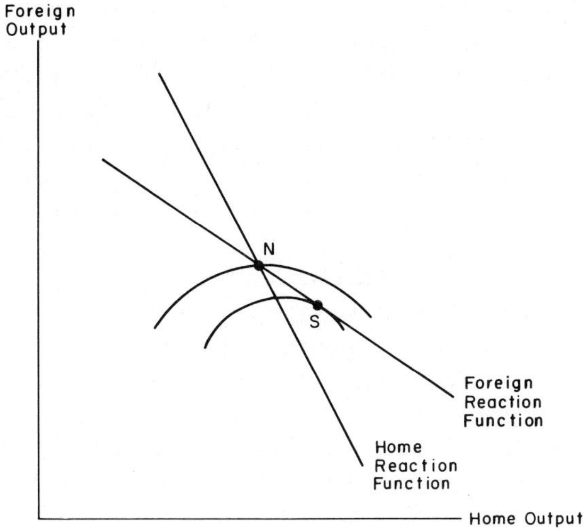

Figure 20.12

Indeed, if the Home firm could pre-commit itself to any level of output, while knowing that the Foreign firm would revise its own plans optimally, the outcome could be driven to the Stackleberg point S. The problem is that there is no good reason to assign the leadership role to either firm. If no way to establish a commitment exists, the Nash outcome is what will emerge.

What Spencer and Brander pointed out was that a government policy could serve the purpose of making a commitment credible. Suppose that the Home government establishes an export subsidy for this industry. This subsidy will shift the Home reaction function to the right, and thus the outcome will shift southeast along the Foreign reaction function. Because the subsidy has the deterrent effect of reducing Foreign exports, the profits of the Home firm will rise by *more* than the amount of the subsidy. Thus Home national income will rise. The optimal export subsidy is of course one that shifts the reaction function out just enough to achieve the Stackleberg point S.

It is possible to elaborate considerably on this basic model. Most notably, we can imagine a multi-stage competitive process, in which firms themselves attempt to establish commitments through investment in capital or R&D. In these models, considered in Brander and Spencer (1983), optimal policies typically involve subsidies to investment as well as exports. The basic point remains the same, however. Government policy "works" in these models for the same reason that investing in excess capacity works in entry deterrence models, because it alters the subsequent game in a way that benefits the domestic firm.

5.2. The nature of competition

Eaton and Grossman (1986) have argued forcefully that the argument for strategic trade policy is of limited use, because the particular policy recommendation depends critically on details of the model. In particular, they show that the Brander–Spencer case for export subsidies depends on the assumption of Cournot competition. With other assumptions, the result may go away or even be reversed.

To see this, suppose instead that we have Bertrand competition, with firms taking each others' prices as given. (As in our discussion of import quotas above, we must assume the two firms are producing differentiated products if the model is not to collapse to perfect competition.) Then the reaction function diagram must be drawn in price space.

Figure 20.13 shows the essentials. Each firm's best responses describe a reaction function that is upward sloping. With reasonable restrictions, Home's curve is steeper than Foreign's. The Nash equilibrium is at N, and the Home iso-profit curve passing through N is flat at that point.

The crucial point is that now Home can increase its profits only by moving northeast along the Foreign reaction function. That is, it must persuade Foreign to charge a *higher* price than at the Nash equilibrium. To do this, it must commit to a higher price than will ex post be optimal. To achieve this, what the government must do is impose, not an export subsidy, but an export *tax*!

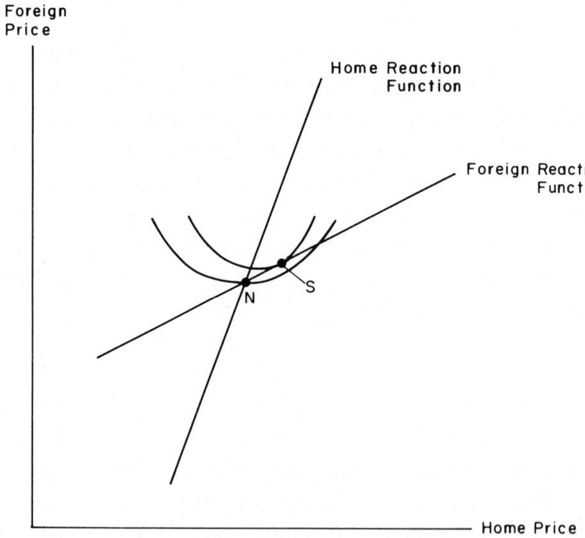

Figure 20.13

So what Eaton and Grossman show is that replacing the Cournot with a Bertrand assumption reverses the policy recommendation. Given the shakiness of any characterization of oligopoly behavior, this is not reassuring.

Eaton and Grossman go further by embedding both Cournot and Bertrand in a general conjectural variations formulation. The result is of course that anything can happen. One case that these authors emphasize is that of "rational" conjectures, where the conjectures actually match the slope of the reaction functions (a case that I do not find particularly interesting, given the problems of the conjectural variation approach in general). In this case, not too surprisingly, free trade turns out to be the optimal policy.

5.3. Competition for resources

Dixit and Grossman (1984) offer a further critique of the case for strategic trade policy based on the partial equilibrium character of the models. Their point may be made as follows: an export subsidy works in the Brander–Spencer model essentially by lowering the marginal cost faced by the domestic exporter. Foreign firms, seeing this reduced marginal cost, are deterred from exporting as much as they otherwise would have, and this is what leads to a shifting of profits. But in general equilibrium, an export industry can expand only by bidding resources away from other domestic industries. An export subsidy, while it lowers marginal cost in the targeted industry, will therefore raise marginal cost in other sectors. Thus, in industries that are not targeted the effect will be the reverse of deterrence.

Dixit and Grossman construct a particular tractable example where a group of industries must compete for a single common factor, "scientists". An export subsidy to one of these sectors necessarily forces a contraction in all the others. As we might expect, such a subsidy raises national income only if the deterrent effect on foreign competition is higher in the subsidized sector than in the sectors that are crowded out. As the authors show, to evaluate the desirability of a subsidy now requires detailed knowledge not only of the industry in question but of all the industries with which it competes for resources. Their conclusion is that the likelihood that sufficient information will be available is small.

5.4. Entry

The strategic trade policy argument hinges on the presence of supernormal profits over which countries can compete. Yet one might expect that the possibility of entry will limit and perhaps eliminate these profits. If so, then even in oligopolistic industries the bone of contention may be too small to matter.

Horstmann and Markusen (1986) have analyzed the Brander–Spencer argument when there is free entry by firms. The number of firms in equilibrium is limited by fixed costs, but they abstract from the integer problem. The result of allowing entry is to restore the orthodox argument against export subsidy, in a strong form: *all* of a subsidy is absorbed either by reduced scale or worsened terms of trade, and thus constitutes a loss from the point of view of the subsidizing country.

Dixit (forthcoming b) is concerned with a more dynamic version of the same problem. He notes that in industries characterized by technological uncertainty, there will be winners and losers. The winners – who will actually make up the industry – will appear to earn supernormal profits, but this will not really indicate the presence of excess returns. Ex ante, an investment, say in R&D, may be either a winner or a loser, so that the costs of those who did not make it should also be counted. Dixit develops a technology race model of international competition in a single industry, and shows that in such an industry high profits among the winners of the race do not offer the possibility of successful strategic trade policy.

5.5. A larger game?

The Brander–Spencer analysis assumes that the government in effect can commit itself to a trade policy before firms make their decisions. They also leave aside the possible reactions of foreign governments. Yet a realistic analysis would surely recognize that firms also make strategic moves designed to affect government decisions, and that governments must contend with the possibility of foreign reactions. Many of the ramifications of these larger games have been explored by Dixit and Kyle (1985).

To see what difference this extension makes, consider two cases. First, suppose that there is a firm that faces the following situation: it can commit itself to produce by making an irreversible investment. Once this cost is sunk, it will be socially optimal to provide the Brander–Spencer export subsidy, and with this subsidy the firm will find that its entry was justified. From a social point of view, however, it would have been preferable for the firm not to have entered at all.

In this case, what is clear is that if the firm can move first, the government will find itself obliged to provide the subsidy. Yet it would have been better off if it could have committed itself not to provide the subsidy, and thus deterred the undesirable entry. The possibility of an export subsidy, though it raises welfare *given* entry, in the end is counterproductive. The government would have been better off if it had never heard of Brander and Spencer, or had a constitutional prohibition against listening to them.

Alternatively, consider the case of two countries, both able to pursue Brander–Spencer policies. It is certainly possible that both countries may be worse off as the result of a subsidy war, yet they will find themselves trapped in a prisoner's dilemma.

The point of the extended game analysis, then, is that even though interventionist policies may be shown to be locally desirable, it may still be in the country's interest that the use of such policies be ruled out.

5.6. Evaluation

Strategic trade policy is without doubt a clever insight. From the beginning, however, it has been clear that the attention received by that insight has been driven by forces beyond the idea's intellectual importance. The simple fact is that there is a huge external market for challenges to the orthodoxy of free trade. Any intellectually respectable case for interventionist trade policies, however honestly proposed – and the honesty of Brander and Spencer is not in question – will quickly find support for the wrong reasons. At the same time, the profession of international economics has a well-developed immune system designed precisely to cope with these outside pressures. This immune system takes the form of an immediate intensely critical scrutiny of any idea that seems to favor protectionism. So Brander–Spencer attracted both more attention and more critical review than would normally have been the case.

That said, *does* the marriage of trade and IO offer an important new case for protectionism? To answer this we must go beyond the Brander–Spencer analysis of export competition to consider a wider range of models.

6. A new case for protection?

To the extent that the IO/trade linkage offers any new comfort to protectionists, it takes the form of four not wholly distinct arguments. First is the possibility that trade policy can be used to extract rent from foreign monopolists. Second is the potential for shifting rent from foreign to domestic firms. Third is the possible use of protectionist policies as a way to get firms further down their average cost curves. Last is the use of protection to promote additional entry, where this is desirable.

6.1. Extracting rent from foreigners

The possibility of using a tariff to extract gains from a foreign monopolist has been emphasized in two papers by Brander and Spencer (1981, 1984). In its simplest version, their analysis considers a foreign monopolist selling to the domestic market without any domestic competition. They point out that under a variety of circumstances a tariff will be partly absorbed by the foreign firm rather than passed on to domestic consumers. For example, suppose that demand is linear and that a specific tariff is imposed: then only half of the tariff will be passed on in prices, with the rest coming out of the firm's markup.

This observation suggests a terms-of-trade justification for tariffs similar to the traditional optimum tariff argument. The difference is that there is no requirement that the tariff-imposing country be large relative to world markets. As long as the foreign seller is charging a price above marginal cost, and as long as it is able to discriminate between the domestic market and other markets, it will be possible for a tariff to lower prices.

In one extension of their analysis, Brander and Spencer go on to consider the case where the foreign firm is attempting to deter entry by a potential domestic competitor. They follow an early Dixit model in which the incumbent firm does this by setting a limit output high enough that if it were to be maintained post-entry this entry would be unprofitable. (In Dixit's model the potential entrant is assumed to believe that the incumbent firm will maintain its pre-entry output, even though it would not be profit-maximizing to carry out this threat ex post. Such ad hoc entry deterrence models are now unfashionable, but this paper was written before Dixit acquired enlightenment and became (subgame) perfect.) The result in this case is that any tariff low enough that the limit pricing strategy is maintained will be wholly absorbed by the foreign firm.

6.2. *Rent-shifting*

Clearly, a tariff can give domestic firms a strategic advantage in the domestic market, in the same way that export subsidies can give them an advantage in foreign markets. Welfare assessment of strategic tariff policy is however complicated by the need to worry about domestic consumers. What Brander and Spencer (1984) point out, however, is that rent-shifting will generally reinforce rent extraction. That is, if in the absence of domestic competitors a tariff would be partly absorbed by foreign firms, the presence of domestic competitors will reinforce the case for a tariff.

6.3. *Reducing marginal cost*

In Krugman (1984a) it is pointed out that protection of the domestic market can serve as a form of export promotion. The model is a variant of Brander and Krugman (1983), where two firms interpenetrate each others' home markets through reciprocal dumping. Instead of constant marginal cost, however, each firm has downward-sloping marginal cost. Suppose now that one firm receives protection in its Home market. The immediate result will be that it sells more and the other firm less. This will reduce the Home firm's marginal cost, while raising its competitor's cost; this will in turn have the indirect effect of increasing the Home firm's sales in the unprotected foreign market. In the end, "import protection is export promotion": protection of the Home market actually leads to a rise in exports. The same results obtain when the economies of scale are dynamic rather than static, arising for example from R&D or a learning curve.

Is this policy desirable from the point of view of the protecting country? We can surmise that it might be, because it is in effect a strategic export policy of the kind with which we are now familiar. A numerical example in Krugman (1984b) shows at least that such a policy could be worth carrying out – if there is no retaliation.

6.4. *Promoting entry*

Venables (1985a) considers another variant of the Brander–Krugman model in which marginal cost is constant, but there are fixed costs. This time, however, he allows free entry and waives integer constraints on the number of firms. He now asks what the effects of a small tariff imposed by one country would be.

It is immediately apparent that such a tariff would raise the profitability of domestic firms and lower the profitability of foreign, leading to entry on one side and exit on the other. This makes the Home market more competitive, and the Foreign market less competitive. What Venables is able to show, surprisingly, is that for a small tariff this indirect effect on competition has a stronger effect on prices than the direct effect of the tariff itself. The price of the protected good will *fall* in the country that imposes the tariff, while rising in the rest of the world!

To understand this result, first note the first-order condition for a firm's deliveries to each market:

$$p + x(\mathrm{d}p/\mathrm{d}x) = c,$$

where x is the firm's deliveries to the market and c is the marginal cost. In a Cournot model $\mathrm{d}p/\mathrm{d}x$ as perceived by the firm will be the slope of the market demand curve, and thus will itself be a function of the market price p. Thus, x will be a function of p, as will the revenues earned by the firm in that market.

Since everything is a function of p, we can write the zero-profit condition that must hold with free entry as a function of p and of p^*, the price in the foreign market. In Figure 20.14, the schedule HH represents the combinations of P and P^* consistent with zero profits for a representative firm producing in Home, FF

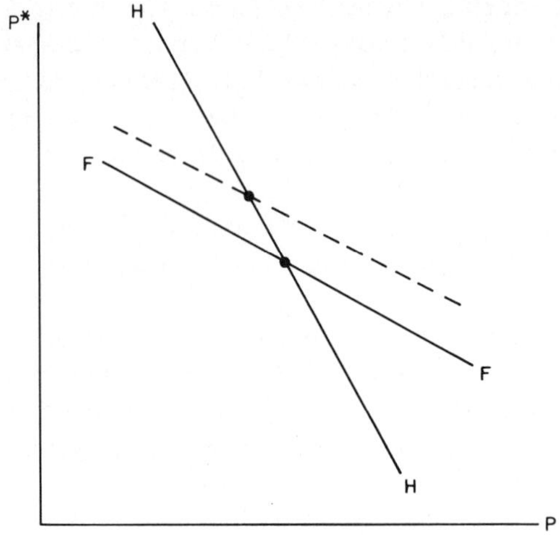

Figure 20.14

the zero-profit locus for a firm producing in Foreign. In the presence of transport costs it will ordinarily be true that *HH* is steeper than *FF*, i.e. Home firms are relatively more affected by the Home price than Foreign firms. A free entry equilibrium will occur when both zero-profit conditions are satisfied.

Now suppose that a tariff is imposed by Home. The zero-profit locus for Home firms will not be affected, but Foreign firms will face increased costs on shipment to Home. They will have to receive a higher price in at least one market to make up for this, so *FF* shifts out. We now see Venables' result: the price in Home must actually fall, while that in Foreign rises.

The welfare calculation is now straightforward. Profits are not an issue, because of free entry. Consumers are better off in the protecting country. And there is additional government revenue as well.

6.5. *Evaluation*

The new literature on IO and trade certainly calls into question the traditional presumption that free trade is optimal. Whether it is a practical guide to productive protectionism is another matter. The models described here are all quite special cases; small variations in assumptions can no doubt reverse the conclusions, as was the case in the Brander–Spencer model of export competition.

It may be questioned whether our understanding of how imperfectly competitive industries actually behave will ever be good enough for us to make policy prescriptions with confidence. What is certain is that purely theoretical analyses will not be enough. Until very recently, there was essentially no quantification of the new ideas in trade theory. In the last two years, however, there have been a handful of preliminary attempts to put numbers into the models. I conclude the chapter with a discussion of these efforts.

7. Quantification

Efforts to quantify the new theoretical models have been of three kinds. First have been econometric studies of some of the aggregate predictions of the intraindustry trade model described in Section 2 of this chapter. Second, and most recent, have been efforts to "calibrate" theoretical models to fit the facts of particular industries. Finally, and most ambitiously, Harris and Cox have attempted to introduce industrial organization considerations into a general equilibrium model of the Canadian economy.

7.1. Testing the intraindustry trade model

The empirical analysis of intraindustry trade, in such studies as that by Grubel and Lloyd (1975), long predates the monopolistic competition theory described in this survey. Without a theoretical base, however, discussion of intraindustry trade often seemed confused. Only once formal models became available was it possible for empirical workers to concentrate on propositions derived from these models.

Two studies focus on the most direct proposition, that the proportion of intraindustry as opposed to interindustry trade should be positively correlated with the degree of similarity between countries' capital–labor ratios. Loertscher and Wolter (1980) use differences in per capita income as a proxy for differences in resource endowments, and confirm the correlation using a cross-section for a single year. Helpman (1985) uses a more extended data set to confirm the proposition over a number of years; he also shows that as the industrial countries became more similar over time the relative importance of intraindustry trade grew, just as the model would suggest.

Havrylyshyn and Civan (1984) study a proposition that is less clearly implied by the model, but in the same spirit: namely, that intraindustry trade is likely to be more prevalent in the trade between advanced countries than in trade among LDCs, on the presumption that advanced countries produce more differentiated products. They find that this is, indeed, the case.

These regression studies suffer from a common problem of lack of congruence between the data and the concepts in the theoretical model. In the theory, an "industry" is a group of products produced with similar factor intensities, so that trade within an industry cannot be explained by conventional comparative advantage. Whether this concept of an industry has anything to do with a three-digit Standard International Trade Classification category – the unit to which the analysis is in each case applied – is anybody's guess. What is clear is that the data does not provide a very good correspondence to the theoretical concept.

7.2. Calibrated models

The newest development in the IO/trade field is the attempt to quantify models by calibrating them to data from actual industries. This style of analysis seems likely to grow, and needs a name; for now we may call these studies Industrial Policy Exercises Calibrated to Actual Cases (IPECACs).

The pioneering work here is Dixit's (forthcoming a) model of the auto industry. The U.S. auto market is represented as a noncooperative oligopoly, with foreign autos differentiated from domestic. Demand functions are derived from other published studies; constant terms and cost parameters are derived from actual industry data. In order to make the model fit, Dixit is also obliged to adopt a conjectural variations approach, with the conjectures derived in the process of calibrating the model.

Once the model is calibrated, it is possible to perform policy experiments on it. In particular, Dixit calculates the optimal trade policy when a tariff is the only available instrument, and the optimal trade-cum-industrial policy when a production subsidy is also available. He finds that a modest tariff is in fact justified, for the reasons we described above. The gains from this optimal tariff are however fairly small. When a production subsidy is allowed, the additional role for a tariff is greatly reduced, with the gains from adding tariffs as an instrument extremely small.

A model similar in spirit but quite different in detail is Baldwin and Krugman (forthcoming), which studies the competition in 16K Random Access Memories. The model is a variant of Krugman (1984a), with strong learning-by-doing providing the increasing returns. As in the Dixit analysis, the model's parameters are partly drawn from other published studies, partly estimated by calibrating the model to actual data. Also, as in Dixit's study, it proves necessary to adopt a conjectural variations approach in order to match the observed industry structure.

In the Baldwin–Krugman analysis, the policy experiment is a historical counterfactual. How would the competition in 16K RAMs have been different if the Japanese market, which appears to have been de facto closed to imports, had been open? The model yields a striking result: instead of being substantial net exporters, the Japanese firms would not even have been able to compete in their own home market. Thus, import protection was export promotion with a vengeance.

The welfare implications of this counterfactual can also be computed. According to the model, Japanese market closure, although it successfully promoted exports, did not benefit Japan. Because Japanese firms appear to have had inherently higher costs than their U.S. rivals, market closure was a costly policy that hurt both the United States and Japan.

At the time of writing, the only other IPECAC is a study by Venables and Smith (1986). They apply methods that combine those of the Dixit and Baldwin–Krugman papers, as well as an interesting formulation of multi-model competition, to study the U.K. refrigerator and footwear industries. The results are also reminiscent to some degree of both other studies: modest tariffs are welfare-improving, and protection has strong export-promoting effects.

The calibrated trade models are all at this point rather awkward constructs. They rely on ad hoc assumptions to close gaps in the data, and they rely to an uncomfortable degree on conjectural variations – an approach that each of the papers denounces even as it is adopted. To some extent the results of this literature so far might best be regarded as numerical examples informed by the data rather than as studies that are seriously meant to capture the behavior of particular industries. Nonetheless, the confrontation with data does lend a new sense of realism and empirical discipline to the IO/trade literature.

7.3. *General equilibrium*

The most ambitious attempt to apply industrial organization to trade policy analysis is the attempt by Harris and Cox to develop a general equilibrium model of Canada with increasing returns and imperfect competition built in. This effort, reported in Harris (1984) and Harris and Cox (1984), stands somewhat apart from much of the other literature reviewed here. Although some elements of the monopolistic competition model are present, the key to the results is the adoption of the Eastman–Stykolt pricing assumption, that firms are able to collude well enough to raise the domestic price to the foreign price plus tariff.

Given this assumption, it is naturally true that Canadian import-competing industries are found to have excessive entry and inefficiently small scale. The authors also offer a fairly complex analysis of pricing and entry in export markets, which leads them to believe that inefficient scale in Canadian export industries results from U.S. protection. Combining these effects, the authors find that the costs to Canada from its partial isolation from the U.S. market are several times higher than those estimated using conventional computable general equilibrium models. Thus, the Harris–Cox analysis makes a strong case for free trade between the United States and Canada.

The Harris–Cox study has not yet been followed by a body of work that would enable us to evaluate the robustness of its conclusion. It is unclear, in particular, how much the assumption of collusion-cum-free entry is driving the results; would a noncooperative market structure still imply comparably large costs from protection? It is a fairly safe bet, however, that over the next few years workers in this area will attempt to fill in the space between Harris–Cox and the calibrated models, building more or less general equilibrium models that also have some detailing of the process of competition in individual industries.

7.4. Evaluation

The attempts at quantification described here are obviously primitive and preliminary. However, the same could be said of attempts to apply industrial organization theory to purely domestic issues. The problem is that the sophistication of our models in general seems to have outrun our ability to match them up with data or evidence. The first efforts in this direction in international IO are therefore welcome. One might hope that this effort will be aided by an interchange with conventional IO research that poses similar issues, such as the analysis of the effects of mergers.

8. Concluding comments

The rapid growth in the application of industrial organization concepts to international trade seems to be remaking trade theory in IO's image. Traditional trade theory was, by the late 1970s, a powerful monolithic structure in which all issues were analyzed using variants of a single model. The new literature has successfully broken the grip of that single approach. Increasingly, international economics, like industrial organization, is becoming a field where many models are taught and research is an eclectic mix of approaches.

This transformation of the subject has been extremely valuable in several ways. First of all, the fundamental insight is right – markets are often not perfectly competitive, and returns to scale are often not constant. Beyond this, the new approaches have brought excitement and creativity to an area that had begun to lose some of its intellectual drive.

At this point, however, the central problem of international trade is how to go beyond the proliferation of models to some kind of new synthesis. Probably, trade theory will never be as unified as it was a decade ago, but it would be desirable to see empirical work begin to narrow the range of things that we regard as plausible outcomes.

Appendix: Some basic models

Applications of industrial organization to international trade so far rely on fairly simple models, so that it is still possible to describe most research in this field verbally and graphically. For completeness, however, this Appendix offers formal presentations of simple versions of the two "workhorse" models of the new field: the monopolistic competition model of international trade resulting from economies of scale, and the homogeneous-product duopoly model.

A.1. Monopolistic competition

The simplest version of the monopolistic competition model of trade is one in which there is only one factor of production and countries have identical technologies, so that economies of scale are the only reason for trade. We further assume that product differentiation takes the Spence–Dixit–Stiglitz form in which each individual has a taste for variety, rather than letting the demand for variety arise from differences between consumers. The model can be further simplified by assuming particular forms for both production and utility functions. The result is a "rock-bottom" model which reveals the essentials of the approach in the simplest possible form.

Let us assume, then, that there is a very large number of potential products N (it would be more rigorous to assume a continuum of products, but this would complicate the exposition with no gain in insight). These products enter symmetrically into the utility of all consumers, with the utility function taking the specific convenient form:

$$U = \sum_{i=1}^{N} c_i^{\theta}, \quad 0 < \theta < 1, \tag{1}$$

where c_i is an individual's consumption of good i, and θ measures the degree of substitution between varieties; note that (1) can be monotonically transformed into a CES function with elasticity of substitution $1/(1-\theta)$.

There is only one factor of production, labor. Not all goods will in general be produced. For any good that is produced the labor employed is:

$$l_i = \alpha + \beta x_i, \quad \alpha, \beta > 0, \tag{2}$$

where x_i is output of good i. The presence of the fixed cost α introduces economies of scale into the model. As we will see, it is this fixed cost that limits the number of varieties that any one country actually produces, and therefore leads to both trade and gains from trade.

Let L be an economy's total labor force. Then full employment requires that

$$L = \sum_{i=1}^{n} (\alpha + \beta x_i), \tag{3}$$

where n is the number of goods actually produced.

A.1.1. A closed economy

First we consider equilibrium in a single economy that does not trade with the rest of the world. Each consumer will maximize welfare subject to his budget constraint; the first-order conditions from that maximization problem will take the form:

$$\theta c_i^{\theta-1} = \lambda p_i, \tag{4}$$

where λ is the marginal utility of income. This may be rewritten in the form:

$$c_i = [(\lambda/\theta) p_i]^{-1/(1-\theta)}. \tag{4'}$$

If the number of available products is sufficiently large, the marginal utility of income of each will be negligibly affected by changes in its price, so that the demand for each good will have a constant elasticity $1/(1-\theta)$.

Next we turn to the problem of firms. We begin by noting that as long as there are more potential varieties than are actually produced, there will be no reason for more than one firm to produce any given variety; since the varieties are symmetrical, a firm will always prefer to switch to a different variety rather than compete with another firm head to head. Thus, each good will be produced by a monopolist. Since the monopolist faces demand with an elasticity $1/(1-\theta)$, her optimal price is:

$$p = (\beta/\theta) w, \tag{5}$$

where w is the wage rate. Notice that there is no subscript. Given the symmetry assumed among the goods, they will all have the same price p. We can choose labor as the numeraire and write the price equation as:

$$p/w = \beta/\theta. \tag{5'}$$

Next we introduce the possibility of entry and exit. If firms are free to enter and exit, and we ignore integer constraints, then profits will be driven to zero. But the profits of a representative firm are:

$$\pi = (p - \beta w)x - \alpha w$$

or

$$\pi/w = p/w - \beta x - \alpha = 0. \tag{6}$$

This implies that the output of a representative firm is:

$$x = \alpha\theta/[\beta(1-\theta)]. \tag{7}$$

Using the full-employment condition we can then conclude that the number of firms, which is also the number of goods actually produced, is:

$$n = L/[\alpha + \beta x] = L(1-\theta)/\alpha. \tag{8}$$

Note that it is the fixed cost α that limits the number of goods produced. If there were no fixed cost, or the fixed cost were very small, the product space would become saturated and our assumption that each good is produced by a single firm would break down.

Also note that while we can determine the *number* of goods n that is produced, we cannot determine *which* n goods are produced. This indeterminacy cannot be eliminated without spoiling the simplicity of the model. It arises precisely because of the assumed symmetry of the goods, which in turn is what allows us to find a zero-profit equilibrium.

Finally, we can determine the utility of a representative household. Let us assume that each household owns one unit of labor. Then it has an income w, which it will divide equally among all available products. Utility is therefore:

$$U = n(w/np)^{\theta} = (w/p)^{\theta} n^{1-\theta} = (\theta/\beta)^{\theta} n^{1-\theta}. \tag{9}$$

Welfare is therefore increasing in the number of goods available.

A.1.2. A trading world

Now consider a world of two countries: Home, with a labor force L, and Foreign, with a labor force L^*. In the absence of trade each of these countries would be described by the analysis just developed. Suppose, however, that the countries are able to trade with each other at zero cost. Then wages will be equalized, and the countries will in effect constitute a single larger economy with a labor force $L + L^*$. Home will produce $n = L\alpha/(1-\theta)$ goods, Foreign $n^* = L^*\alpha/(1-\theta)$ goods. Since firms will still never compete over a market, these will be different goods – i.e. each good that is produced will be produced in only one country. Thus, the countries will be specialized in producing different ranges of goods, and will trade with each other.

There are three important points to note about this trade. First, since it is indeterminate who produces what, the pattern of trade is indeterminate. We know that the countries specialize, but not in what. This indeterminacy is at first disturbing, but it is characteristic of models with increasing returns.

Second, while the pattern of trade is indeterminate, the volume of trade is fully determined. Each household will spend the same share of income on each good, and each household will spend a share $n/(n + n^*)$ on Home-produced goods, $n^*/(n + n^*)$ on Foreign goods. The total income of Home is wL, the total income of Foreign wL^*. Thus, the value of Home's imports from Foreign is $wLL^*/(L + L^*)$, which is also the value of Foreign's imports from Home. Trade is balanced, as it must be in a model with no saving.

Finally, trade is mutually beneficial. In the absence of trade Home households would have had only n products available; as a result of trade the number available increases to $(n + n^*)$. Letting U_A be welfare in the absence of trade and U_T be welfare with trade, we have:

$$U_T/U_A = [(n + n^*)/n]^{1-\theta} > 1. \tag{10}$$

Foreign households similarly gain. Note that the gain from trade is larger, the smaller is θ, i.e. the greater the gains from variety.

A.2. Homogeneous-product duopoly

The other most widely used model in applications of industrial organization to international economics is the simple model of homogeneous product duopoly. This model can be used to demonstrate the pro-competitive effect of trade; the motivations behind dumping; the potential for strategic trade policy; and the possibility that protection promotes exports. I present here a simple linear version, then indicate how it can be extended.

Suppose that there are two countries, Home and Foreign, that both demand some product. For simplicity they will be assumed to have identical, linear demand curves, which we write in inverse form as:

$$p = A - Bz, \tag{11}$$

$$p^* = A - Bz^*, \tag{12}$$

where z, z^* are total deliveries to the Home and Foreign markets, respectively.

Each of the countries is also the base of a single firm producing the good. Each firm can deliver to either country; we let x be the Home firm's deliveries to its own market, x^* its deliveries to the Foreign market. Then its costs will depend on its shipments:

$$C = F + cx + (c + t)x^*, \tag{13}$$

where marginal cost is for the moment assumed constant, and t may be interpreted as transport cost. Also, let y be the Foreign firm's deliveries to the Home market and y^* its deliveries to its own market; if the firms have identical costs we then have:

$$C^* = F + cy^* + (c + t)y. \tag{14}$$

In the absence of trade each firm would be a monopolist, and we would have $z = x$, $z^* = y^*$. In that case it is straightforward to see that the price in each market would be:

$$p = c + (A - c)/2. \tag{15}$$

If the markup $(A - c)/2$ exceeds the transport cost t, however, each firm will have an incentive to ship into the other firm's market, since it will be able to sell goods there at above its marginal cost of delivery. Thus, we need to analyze an equilibrium in which each firm may ship to both markets, and therefore

$$z = x + y, \tag{16}$$

$$z^* = x^* + y^*. \tag{17}$$

Each firm must choose its levels of shipments to each market based on its beliefs about the other firm's actions. The simplest assumption is that each firm takes the other firm's deliveries to *each* market as given – the Home firm maximizes profits taking y and y^* as given, and vice versa. Then the model breaks into two separate Cournot games in the two markets. Since these games are symmetric, it is sufficient to examine only what happens in the Home market. The Home firm's reaction function is:

$$x = (A - c)/2B - y/2, \tag{18}$$

while the Foreign firm's reaction function is:

$$y = (A - c - t)/2B - x/2. \tag{19}$$

These reaction functions are shown in Figure 20.15. Note that there is a positive intersection if and only if $(A - c)/2 > t$ – that is, if the monopoly markup in the absence of trade would have exceeded the transport cost.

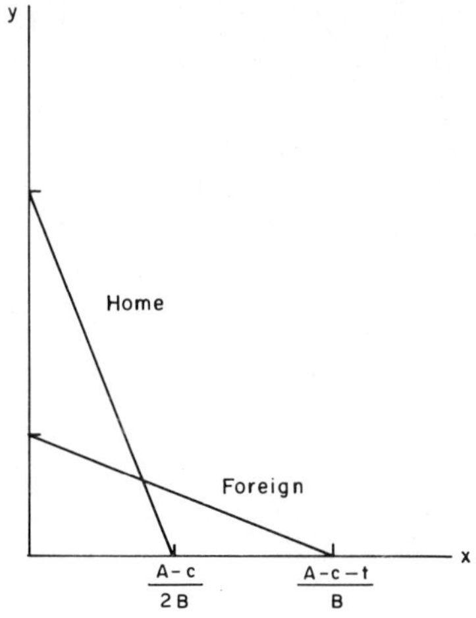

Figure 20.15

If there is a positive intersection, there will be trade. That is, the Foreign firm will have positive sales in the Home market. Given the symmetry of the markets, furthermore, this will be two-way trade in the same product: the Home firm will ship the same product to the Foreign market.

A.2.1. Interpretation and effects of trade

We have described this trade as "reciprocal dumping". In what sense is this dumping? The point is that the price that each firm receives on its export sales is the same that it receives on domestic sales, and therefore does not compensate for transport cost. Equivalently, we can observe that if the firm simply sold all its output at a fixed price at the factory gate, private shippers would not find it profitable to export. It is only because the firm is willing to absorb the transport cost, receiving a lower net price on export sales than on domestic sales, that trade takes place.

Why are firms willing to do this? *Price* net of transport cost is lower on export sales than on domestic sales. In equilibrium, however, each firm will have a smaller share of its export market than of its domestic market, and will therefore perceive itself as facing a higher elasticity of demand abroad than at home. This is what makes the marginal revenue on export sales equal that on domestic sales, despite the lower net price.

What are the effects of this seemingly pointless trade? First, it unambiguously lowers the price in both markets, and hence raises consumer surplus. This pro-competitive effect is strongest in the case of zero transport costs, in which the markup over marginal cost falls from $(A - c)/2$ to $(A - c)/4$ as a result of trade.

Second, trade leads to a waste of resources in seemingly pointless cross-hauling of an identical product – except in the case where transport costs are zero.

Finally, trade leads to a fall in profits both because the price falls and because firms incur transport expenses.

The net welfare effect is ambiguous, except in the case of zero transport cost. The pro-competitive effect reduces the monopoly distortion, but against this must be set the waste of resources in transportation. For this linear model it is possible to show that trade leads to gains if t is close to zero, but to losses if t is close to $(A - c)/2$, the monopoly markup in the absence of trade.

A.2.2. Extensions

One extension is to add government policy to the model, in the form of a tax on imports, a subsidy on exports, etc. The simplest Brander–Spencer model takes this basic framework but assumes that instead of selling to each other both countries sell to a third market. This means that each country's welfare can be identified with the profits earned from these exports. It is then straightforward to show that an export subsidy will raise profits at the expense of the other country.

A second extension is to vary the linear cost function. Specifically, assume that each firm's costs take the form:

$$C = C(x + x^*) + tx^*, \tag{20}$$

with $C'' < 0$, declining marginal costs. This now introduces an interdependence between the two markets: the more the Home firms sells in one market, the lower its marginal costs of shipment to the other market. In this case protection of the domestic market has the effect of increasing exports. A tariff or import quota increases the protected firm's sales in its domestic market, while lowering the sales of its rival. This in turn lowers the marginal cost of the protected firm, raises the marginal cost of the other firm, and thus leads to a rise in sales abroad as well as at home.

References

Axelrod, R. (1983) *The evolution of cooperation*. New York: Basic Books.

Baldwin, R. and Krugman, P.R. 'Market access and international competition: A simulation study of 16K random access memories', in: R. Feenstra, ed., *Empirical research in international trade*. Cambridge: MIT Press, forthcoming.

Baumol, W.J., Panzar, J.C., and Willig, R.D. (1982) *Contestable markets and the theory of industry structure*. New York: Harcourt Brace Jovanovitch.

Bhagwati, J. (1965) 'On the equivalence of tariffs and quotas', in: R.E. Baldwin, ed., *Trade, growth, and the balance of payments*. Amsterdam: North-Holland.

Brander, J.A. (1981) 'Intra-industry trade in identical commodities', *Journal of International Economics*, 11:1–14.

Brander, J.A. and Krugman, P.R. (1983) 'A reciprocal dumping model of international trade', *Journal of International Economics*, 15:313–321.

Brander, J.A. and Spencer, B.J. (1981) 'Tariffs and the extraction of foreign monopoly rents under potential entry', *Canadian Journal of Economics*, 14:371–389.

Brander, J.A. and Spencer, B.J. (1983) 'International R&D rivalry and industrial strategy', *Review of Economic Studies*, 50:707–722.

Brander, J.A. and Spencer, B.J. (1984) 'Tariff protection and imperfect competition', in: H. Kierzkowski, ed., *Monopolistic competition and international trade*. Oxford: Oxford University Press.

Brander, J.A. and Spencer, B.J. (1985) 'Export subsidies and international market share rivalry', *Journal of International Economics*, 18:83–100.

Caves, R.E. and Jones, R.W. (1985) *World trade and payments*. Boston: Little, Brown.

Corden, W.M. (1967) 'Monopoly, tariffs, and subsidies', *Economica*, 34:59–68.

Davidson, C. (1984) 'Cartel stability and trade policy', *Journal of International Economics*, 17:219–237.

Dixit, A.K. (1984) 'International trade policy for oligopolistic industries', *Economic Journal (Supplement)*, 1–16.

Dixit, A.K. 'Optimal trade and industrial policy for the U.S. automobile industry', in: R. Feenstra, ed., *Empirical research in international trade*. Cambridge: MIT Press, forthcoming (a).

Dixit, A.K. 'The cutting edge of international technological competition', *American Economic Review*, forthcoming (b).

Dixit, A.K. and Grossman, G.M. (1984) 'Targeted export promotion with several oligopolistic industries', discussion paper in economics no. 71, Woodrow Wilson School, Princeton University.

Dixit, A.K. and Kyle, A.S. (1985) 'The use of protection and subsidies for entry promotion and deterrence', *American Economic Review*, 75:139–152.

Dixit, A.K. and Norman, V. (1980) *Theory of international trade*. Cambridge: Cambridge University Press.

Dixit, A.K. and Stiglitz, J.E. (1977) 'Monopolistic competition and optimum product diversity', *American Economic Review*, 67:297–308.

Eastman, H. and Stykolt, S. (1960) 'A model for the study of protected oligopolies', *Economic Journal*, 70:336–347.

Eaton, J. and Grossman, G.M. (1986) 'Optimal trade and industrial policy under oligopoly', *Quarterly Journal of Economics*, 101:383–406.

Ethier, W. (1982) 'National and international returns to scale in the modern theory of international trade', *American Economic Review*, 72:389–405.

Grubel, H.G. and Lloyd, P.J. (1975) *Intra-industry trade*. New York: Wiley.

Harris, R. (1984) 'Applied general equilibrium analysis of small open economies with scale economies and imperfect competition', *American Economic Review*, 74:1016–1033.

Harris, R. and Cox, D. (1984) *Trade, industrial policy and Canadian manufacturing*. Toronto: University of Toronto Press.

Havrylyshyn, O. and Civan, E. (1984) 'Intra-industry trade and the state of development', in: P.K.M. Tharakan, ed., *The economics of intra-industry trade*. Amsterdam: North-Holland.

Helpman, E. (1981) 'International trade in the presence of product differentiation, economies of scale, and monopolistic competition: A Chamberlinian–Heckscher–Ohlin approach', *Journal of International Economics*, 11:305–340.

Helpman, E. (1984) 'A simple theory of international trade with multinational corporations', *Journal of Political Economy*, 92:451–472.

Helpman, E. (1985) 'Imperfect competition and international trade: Evidence from fourteen industrial countries', mimeo.

Helpman, E. and Krugman P. (1985) *Market structure and foreign trade: Increasing returns, imperfect competition, and the international economy*. Cambridge: MIT Press.

Helpman, E. and Razin, A. (1984) 'Increasing returns, monopolistic competition, and factor movements: A welfare analysis', in: H. Kierzkowski, ed., *Monopolistic competition and international trade*. Oxford: Oxford University Press.

Horstmann, I. and Markusen, J.R. (1986) 'Up your average cost curve: Inefficient entry and the new protectionism', *Journal of International Economics*, 20:225–249.

Kierzkowski, H., ed. (1984) *Monopolistic competition and international trade*. Oxford: Oxford University Press.

Krishna, K. (1984) 'Trade restrictions as facilitating practices', discussion paper in economics no. 55, Woodrow Wilson School, Princeton University.

Krugman, P.R. (1979) 'Increasing returns, monopolistic competition, and international trade', *Journal of International Economics*, 9:469–479.

Krugman, P.R. (1980) 'Scale economies, product differentiation, and the pattern of trade', *American Economic Review*, 70:950–959.

Krugman, P.R. (1981) 'Intraindustry specialization and the gains from trade', *Journal of Political Economy*, 89:959–973.

Krugman, P.R. (1984a) 'Import protection as export promotion: International competition in the presence of oligopolies and economies of scale', in: H. Kierzkowski, ed., *Monopolistic competition and international trade*. Oxford: Oxford University Press.

Krugman, P.R. (1984b) 'The US response to foreign industrial targeting', *Brookings Papers on Economic Activity*, 1984 (1):77–131.

Lancaster, K. (1980) 'Intra-industry trade under perfect monopolistic competition', *Journal of International Economics*, 10:151–175.

Loertscher, R. and Wolter, F. (1980) 'Determinants of intra-industry trade: Among countries and across industries', *Weltwirtschaftliches Archiv*, 8:280–293.

Rotemberg, J.J. and Saloner, G. (1986) 'Quotas and the stability of implicit collusion', MIT, mimeo.

Rousslang, D.J. and Suomela, J.W. (1985) 'Calculating the consumer and net welfare costs of import relief', U.S. International Trade Commission Staff research study no. 15.

Smithies, A. (1942) 'An economic analysis of the basing-point system', *American Economic Review*, 32:705–726.

Spence, A.M. (1976) 'Product selection, fixed costs, and monopolistic competition', *Review of Economic Studies*, 43:217–235.

Venables, A.J. (1985a) 'Trade and trade policy with imperfect competition: The case of identical products and free entry', *Journal of International Economics*, 19:1–19.

Venables, A.J. (1985b) 'Trade and trade policy with differentiated products: A Chamberlinian–Ricardian model', Sussex, mimeo.

Venables, A.J. and Smith, A. (1986) 'Trade and industrial policy under imperfect competition', *Economic Policy*, 1:621–660.

Chapter 21

INTERNATIONAL DIFFERENCES IN INDUSTRIAL ORGANIZATION

RICHARD E. CAVES*

Harvard University

Contents

*Helpful comments and suggestions from W.J. Adams, C. Antonelli, B. Carlsson, H. Daems, S.W. Davies, P. Ghemawat, A.P. Jacquemin, and H. Yamawaki are gratefully acknowledged.

Handbook of Industrial Organization, Volume II, Edited by R. Schmalensee and R.D. Willig
© Elsevier Science Publishers B.V., 1989

1. Introduction

This chapter focuses not on a body of theory or its empirical testing but on a method of inference: international differences in industrial organization, behavior, and performance as bases for testing hypotheses or as sources of new ones. Such a focus can make a substantial although indirect contribution to the ongoing dialogue between the formulation and testing of theories. It provides the intellectual analog of Winter's (1971) "innovating remnant" – an inductive check into the possibility that important phenomena or behavior patterns may be missed by both those who formulate and those who test theoretical models. Thanks to its successes, modern analytical economics is treated by its practitioners as institution-free – exposing the consequences of fundamental human motives and technological opportunities unclouded by any detritus of law, culture, language, custom, or history. Institutions can be dismissed with a wave of the hand: they would not emerge, were they not efficient.

Yet this transparency of the institutional context of economic behavior is an assumption, not a tested hypothesis. Paying attention to international differences is particularly warranted, because much of industrial organization's formal development has taken place in the English-speaking countries, with the United States serving as the dominant firm (if not the monopolist). As a result, the search for interesting questions has focused on the industrial sector of the United States and on the normative issues that have been defined or emphasized by U.S. public policy. One goal of this chapter accordingly is to identify analytically significant differences among national institutions.

As a corollary, the distribution of research effort – both theoretical and applied – might have looked substantially different if the institutional structures of other countries had been generating the agenda. We may hope, therefore, that a review of lines of research on questions arising outside the anglocentric core, or of comparative research involving the industrial sectors of differently situated countries, can reveal analytical possibilities that will otherwise elude the professional research agenda. This chapter seeks to provide a selective survey of these lines of research. Both for exposing variations in the structural influences on market decision-makers and for controlling unwanted variance in their environments, international differences hold promise that has been only lightly realized. A review of the empirical leverage that international differences have yielded may prime the pump for new lines of inquiry – especially as data grow more abundant and training in modern research methods more widespread. Another goal of this chapter is to survey research that has utilized this strategy.

It is important to stipulate what is *not* being attempted in this chapter. Traditions of research in industrial organization exist outside of the English-speaking area. For example, in continental Europe considerable interest attaches to informal analyses of dynamic processes or "life cycles" of industries, and to competition as a process rather than a structural condition or equilibrium state. That this tradition of research responds to institutional features specific to the European economies seems doubtful. In any case, it will not be addressed here.[1] There is also a good deal of empirical research dealing with economies other than the United States that takes the form of replications or near-replications of research that has originated in the anglocentric tradition. These studies are important but will be neglected except insofar as they ring analytical changes on the original designs:[2] this chapter addresses differences, not similarities.

The goals of testing for institutional influences and revealing the leverage of international or comparative research designs lead us into a number of substantive areas of industrial organization. These are taken up selectively, with the following discussion grouped around three questions: (1) What determines the boundaries of the firm, and indeed are the firm's boundaries equally well-defined in all industrial countries? (2) What are the effective boundaries of the market, and what consequences do they have in economies smaller and generally more open to international influences than that of the United States? (3) What insights do international differences provide concerning the determinants of market performance?

2. Agency and organization of enterprise

Some of the most conspicuous and intriguing international differences in institutions lie in the control, ownership, and integration of enterprises. It is widely accepted that Coase's classic question – Why does the boundary between the firm and the market fall where it does? – is answered by identifying the transaction-cost advantages that may attach to either the market or the firm as allocators of resources. The actual boundaries are drawn in a Darwinian process by which the more efficient institution displaces the less efficient one. If this Darwinian competition worked the same way in every country and the transaction-cost efficiencies of firms and markets were independent of laws, cultural traits, and other distinguishing traits of nationhood, then we should expect the allocation between firms and markets to differ only inessentially from country to country.

[1] This research tradition has been surveyed elsewhere [de Jong (1986)].

[2] Selective reports on these replications can be found in Caves and Uekusa (1976), Jacquemin and de Jong (1977), and Curry and George (1983).

Yet one's eye falls upon certain national institutions that seem quite distinctive – the close control of industrial enterprises by banks in Germany, the extensive linkages effected through holding companies in Belgium and enterprise groups in France, the enterprise clubs found in Japan, and the networks of subcontracting relationships observed in Japan and France. Each of these institutions calls into question an assumption that is standard in much of our theoretical and empirical work: that a clean boundary separates the purely administrative allocations made within the firm from purely market transactions that the firm undertakes with other agents. Rather, these institutions imply that the firm's internal allocations can be shaped by important forms of quasi-integration with ostensibly independent legal entities.

A certain amount of analytical research is now available on these institutions, and it tends to show that they represent parallel organizational responses to common underlying problems with the organization of transactions through spot markets. For example, Encaoua and Jacquemin (1982) investigated the incidence in French industry of corporate groupings that resemble diversified firms, yet the subsidiaries (separate legal entities) are only partially owned by the parent and controlled through loose links such as interlocking directorates rather than strict administrative hierarchies. The prevalence of group-affiliated firms in French manufacturing industries increases, they found, with the extent of plant scale economies and multiplant operations, the scale of the firm's fixed capital, and the importance of research and development outlays. The groups are more prevalent among intermediate- and capital-good industries, where transaction-specific capital is likely to be shared among firms. They do not appear to serve the function of coordinating direct market competitors.

Somewhat resembling the French groups in both incidence and organization are the Japanese *keiretsu*, loose groupings that are in part the descendents of pre-World War II *zaibatsu* holding companies. In their present-day form their member companies are linked through regular contacts among executives, limited intercorporate shareholdings (insufficient to convey control), and stable patterns of lender–borrower arrangements and other transactions. No systematic study of their incidence parallels Encaoua and Jacquemin, but casual evidence suggests a close resemblance: Large-scale, heavily capitalized producer-good industries with a substantial research orientation [Caves and Uekusa (1976, pp. 59–68), Goto (1982)]. The groups' principal activities seem associated with the mutual pursuit of opportunities (e.g. mobilizing resources to overcome barriers to entry into an industry) or assistance in the face of unexpected reverses. They might seem merely to substitute for the highly diversified large firms found in the United States. However, Japanese firms do diversify in response to the same structural opportunities as U.S. firms, if not so extensively [Yoshihara et al. (1981)]. Corporate organizational structures have also been adjusted to the requirements of the diversified formal business organization. The Japanese groups clearly are not just substitutes for the practice of corporate diversification found in other nations [Imai and Itami (1984)].

Yet another distinctive intercorporate institution is the holding companies that control about 24 percent of Belgian operating companies' share capital [Daems (1978)]. Also prevalent in producers' and intermediate goods sectors and capital-intensive industries, they similarly effect lender–borrower links and loose forms of coordination through interlocking directorates and interchanged personnel; but they lack close administrative coordination.[3]

These findings about the incidence and behavior of French, Japanese, and Belgian enterprise groupings suggest both their similarity to each other and their affinity for the factors that explain diversification. In both Canada [Lemelin (1982)] and the United States [MacDonald (1985)], researchers have found interindustry patterns of corporate diversification to depend on similar factors – notably the importance of research and other intangibles and the role of large-scale or "lumpy" facilities that are usable in several industries. However, diversified corporations are at least capable of substantially higher levels of internal coordination than the Japanese or European groups can attain. The question that stands unanswered is whether the latter forgo some economies of coordination or (instead) large, diversified firms exist only in part to mitigate transaction costs.

If industrial groups' roles are related to diversification and internalization, they also show affinity for the problem of agency in the ownership and control of firms. The concept of agency provides the tool needed to analyze the "split between ownership and control" in the large, public corporation, and it suggests the sort of device that might be expected to emerge in order to avert the slippage in diffuse agency relationships. Again, selected evidence identifies significant institutions in several countries. In a careful examination of large industrial holding companies in Belgium, Daems (1978), after ruling out several other possible explanations, marked their role as centralizing control over operating companies that would otherwise have been subject to diffuse ownership of equity shares. Implicitly, the ultimate owners of Belgian industrial shares pay the net cost of the intervening holding companies (which Daems estimated to be 1.46 percent of their portfolio revenues) in order to enjoy the gains from averting the agency problem associated with diffuse shareholding.[4]

The close relationships between banks and industrial firms in the Federal Republic of Germany support an interpretation similar to the one that Daems offered for Belgium's holding companies. German banks, voting shares that they

[3]Relevant to these intercountry differences in the institutions of corporate control is Adams' (1977) finding that liabilities structures differ systematically among large firms based in different countries, but their production structures and profitability tend not to differ significantly.

[4]Daems (1978, ch. 6) emphasized not the problem of agency but rather the potential ex ante gains from forming controlling coalitions when shareholders have divergent expectations.

own or hold in custody, account for 36 percent of the shares of the top 100 industrial companies and thus a substantial consolidation of control. Cable (1985) tested the influence on these companies' profits of several links through which banks (individually or jointly) may be able to monitor and shape their policies – shareholdings, direct lending, and representation on supervisory boards. His data reject none of these as without effect. Nor do they reject the hypothesis that the profit increments could be monopoly rents, although they are inconsistent with that as the sole explanation.

As a corollary of this analysis, the superior performance of owner-controlled over manager-controlled firms found in some U.S. studies should fail to appear where other institutions of control are dominant. This corollary confirmed by Thonet and Poensgen (1979) for Germany and Cable and Yasuki (1985) for Japan. In the Japanese case profits are also unrelated to group affiliation, although some evidence suggests that rents pass to financial institutions within the group, whose holdings of affiliates' debt conveys more control than it would in Western countries. As another corollary, the close influence exerted by debt-holders on nonfinancial corporations in these countries may account for the high debt–equity ratios that prevail there. As Adams (1985) pointed out, in countries whose tax systems create a preference for debt over equity, a privately efficient solution is high debt–equity ratios coupled with close supervision by concentrated debt-holders to prevent companies from undertaking risky investments that would transfer wealth from debt- to equity-holders.

That enterprise groupings apparently represent responses to transaction costs and agency problems whets one's appetite for additional data points. For example, what about developing countries, in which imperfections of both financial and commodity markets might amplify the motive to internalize transactions through industrial groupings? White (1974) noted the inclusion of banks and insurance companies in Pakistan's family-based industrial groups and suggested an important role for arbitraging around an underdeveloped capital market. However, his other evidence (chapters 6, 7) associates pecuniary gains to these groups largely with successful rent-seeking through the public sector.[5] Leff (1978), drawing on various studies, urged that groups function to allocate inputs such as "honesty and trustworthy competence on the part of high-level managers" that are otherwise poorly allocated in some LDCs.

3. Sizes of markets, plants, and firms

Economies of scale pose the question whether efficient-scale production trades off against numbers of competitors adequate to align price with marginal cost. Empirical research on scale economies in the United States has emphasized the

[5] Also see Lindsay (1979) on the Philippines and Jones and Sakong (1980, chs. 6, 8) on Korea.

excess of actual concentration over the minimum needed to satisfy the constraint. In the smaller industrial economies, where this trade-off may be tightly constraining, the problem for public policy is often regarded as the likely failure of market processes to assure plant and company scales large enough to minimize costs. A number of theoretical and empirical questions arise. If minimum efficient scale is indeed large relative to the market's size, under what conditions will profit-maximizing producers select suboptimal scales? Does the empirical evidence confirm that national market size constrains the scales of plants and firms? Is it indeed appropriate to assume, as the conjecture does, that the national boundary is the operative perimeter for determining the effective size of the market?

Scherer et al. (1975) provided much of the foundation for analyzing the relation between market sizes and sizes of plants and firms. Assuming that plant-cost curves show increasing returns up to some minimum efficient scale, followed by constant returns, they modeled the dependence of actual plant-size distributions on outbound transportation costs interacted with the density of demand, the cost penalties of suboptimal scale, and other factors (including the structural differentiation of the product). Their empirical analysis [Scherer et al. (1975, ch. 3)] of a panel of twelve industries observed in six countries both confirmed that the basic model could explain the variance of actual plant sizes relative to minimum efficient scale and concluded that the mechanism seems to operate the same way in the European countries in the panel as in North America.[6]

Scherer et al. also investigated the complementary question of how much the sizes of leading firms diverge from the sizes of efficient plants due to multiplant operation. Again, the size of the market (relative to the capacity of the minimum-efficient-scale plant) appears in the model, which also embraces controls for multiplant economies of coordinating production and distribution in geographically fragmented markets or of a heterogeneous line of related products. They expected its positive influence to stem from an "opportunity to multiply plants" or the pursuit of monopoly via horizontal mergers. However, it could be looked at more broadly as limiting the attainment of advantages of size to the firm – both nonproduction scale economies and pecuniary benefits from market dominance. Whatever the causal mechanism, they found domestic disappearance in the national market strongly to influence the extent of multiplant operations. Although they concluded that North America and the sampled European nations could be regarded statistically as a homogeneous population, the elasticity of multiplant operations with respect to market size proved about twice as large in the United States as in the other countries. The interpretation of this difference seems problematical, because differences in public policy toward

[6]The analysis of Scherer et al. (1975) has substantial antecedents in Eastman and Stykolt (1967) and Bain (1966). However, Eastman and Stykolt employed a less complete model, and some of Bain's findings are qualified by an unfortunate choice in research procedure (as Scherer et al. pointed out).

horizontal mergers and the marginal advantages of multiplant operations to obtain nonproduction scale economies to the firm would both point to stronger effects outside the United States. However, the difference is consistent with a random-process model: the firm that obtains a favorable random drawing while operating in a large market finds its expansion less constrained by diminishing marginal net revenue.[7]

Scherer et al. (1975) and Eastman and Stykolt (1967) held an advantage over many other studies touching on these questions in that they employed explicit estimates of minimum efficient plant scales rather than proxies. However, other investigators have reported qualitatively very similar findings concerning the sensitivity of both plant and firm sizes to national market size. Saving's (1961) demonstration that plant sizes vary with market sizes among industries in the United States was picked up by Gorecki (n.d., pp. 43–44), who pointed out that the same relation holds in Canada and that the estimated elasticities of typical plant size to market size seem to land in the same range (roughly 0.5) regardless of the country studied. Broadly consistent results for other countries can be found in other papers that were summarized by Curry and George (1983). Because industries' technologies are free to vary in these interindustry analyses (compare Scherer's intercountry dimension), the thought arises that technologies themselves are devised with an eye to market size, and that the stock of usable technologies may thus depend on market size (and perhaps other economic characteristics).[8] Pryor (1972b) confirmed the intercountry correlation of plant size with market size in a sample of 23 nations, and the coefficients of his different plant-size indexes suggest that absolutely large plants increase more than proportionately with market size – another hint of random processes at work.

One link between plant and market size has been explored in research on Canadian manufacturing. Plant scale economies presumably depend partly on the technology of the particular product, partly on the overhead of plant and its general-purpose systems. If the market for a particular product limits a specialized plant to suboptimal scale, a possible response for the manager is to diversify the plant's output mix. Thus, producers respond to market-size constraints partly by selecting smaller plant sizes, partly by including more product lines in a plant of any given size. Caves (1975) found evidence of this mechanism in a comparison of scales and degrees of output diversity of Canadian and U.S. plants. Baldwin and Gorecki (1986) pursued the relation farther, showing that Canadian plants are larger relative to minimum efficient scale in industries that afford greater scope for the in-plant diversification of outputs.

[7]For empirical evidence of the explanatory value of a random-process model for the size distributions of firms that are larger than minimum efficient scale, see Mansfield (1962) on the United States and Davies and Lyons (1982) on the United Kingdom.

[8]Scherer et al. (1975) concluded, however, that effective minimum efficient production scale does not vary among industrial countries for manufacturing industries in their sample.

The relation between the size of a company and the market it serves has been explored in several international contexts, notably in the comparison of concentration ratios. Any standard measure of concentration reflects the number and relative sizes of firms in some combination. If firm sizes increased proportionally with market sizes, then the concentration ratio for a given industry should be independent of the size of the country in which we observe it. With firm size responsive to market size but inelastic, concentration should decrease with market size but less than proportionally – if also firm-size distributions are uncorrelated with market size. However, the latter condition is unlikely to hold. Rosenbluth (1957, ch. 4) first established that the concentration of Canadian industries regularly exceeds their U.S. counterparts. The smaller Canadian market makes room for substantially fewer firms, but their sizes are less unequal, and Canadian concentration thus appears higher because the former effect outweighs the latter. Caves, Porter and Spence (1980, ch. 3) confirmed this finding and showed that both plant- and firm-size inequalities increase with market size.[9]

The concept of market size has been used loosely in its relation to the scale of the national economy. The central idea is simply that the position of the national-market demand curve facing a selling industry depends on gross national product or some related parameter of the scale of the national economy. Connections between the size of the national economy and the production units it contains are not, however, confined to the demand side. The scales of business organizations may depend on the relative cost of labor, and thus on national income per capita. In Lucas's (1978) formulation, any person can be either an employee or a manager, but managerial talent is distributed unevenly among individuals. As the price of labor services rises, the opportunity cost of using labor services in the entrepreneurial rather than the employee role increases, and the implication follows that the sizes of production units (both plants and firms, presumably) should be larger in countries with higher incomes per capita. Caves and Uekusa (1976, pp. 101–106) confirmed this in a simple cross-country statistical analysis and also showed that the substantial small-enterprise population remaining in Japan is consistent with this model on the assumption that the process of enterprise consolidation proceeds with a lag in fast-growing countries, where the rising opportunity cost of labor services has not yet had its full effect of reallocating marginal entrepreneurs. Kirkpatrick, Lee and Nixson (1984, ch. 3) reviewed the data on small-enterprise populations in developing countries,[10] and some interesting evidence on the role of small business in Italy's modernization is summarized by Brusco (1982) and Fua (1983).

The broadest treatment of international differences in concentration was provided by Pryor (1972a), who found that concentration levels of given in-

[9] Also see Hart and Clarke (1980, ch. 4) on Great Britain.

[10] Banerji (1978) demonstrated that plant sizes are pervasively smaller in developing countries, but he did not distinguish between the two obvious causes – small market sizes and underdevelopment per se.

dustries do not differ significantly among the larger industrial countries, but they do increase as one proceeds to smaller and smaller industrial markets.[11] Pryor emphasized how well an industry's concentration in one country predicts that same industry's concentration in another country, which implies that the factors determining an industry's concentration are strongly rooted in its production technology and the use of its product, and relatively independent of influences specific to the nation [see also Horowitz (1970) and Meller (1978)]. Caves and Uekusa (1976, pp. 19–26) showed that the shapes of cumulative concentration curves of matched Japanese and U.S. manufacturing industries tend to be very similar, so that marginal concentration ratios of the U.S. industries are good predictors for their Japanese counterparts.

These findings about the role of national market size and the similarity of given industries' concentration patterns from country to country seem to ignore the role of international trade. While these findings clearly indicate that the nation is a good first approximation to the geographic span of "the market" in manufacturing industries, however small and open its economy, they leave to be established the role of international commerce in shaping the structures as well as the overall scales of various national producer groups. We take up this issue in the following section.

A further influence on market structures revealed in international studies is that of competition policy, particularly policies toward cartel agreements and horizontal mergers. Particularly striking is the experience of the United Kingdom after horizontal price-fixing and similar collusive arrangements became illegal in the late 1950s. What changes should ensue depends on how collusion is modeled and what consequences are imputed to it. Elliott and Gribbin (1977) noted the conclusion of Swann et al. (1974, ch. 4) that the abandonment of restrictive practices was typically followed by substantial removals of capacity from the industries in question. Given that prices declined substantially and demand presumably increased, excess capacity under collusion must have been substantial indeed. Apparently collusion either attracted inefficient entrants who could earn normal profits at collusion-inflated margins or induced incumbents to maintain excess capacity in order to capture high-margin sales at times when (stochastic) demand was strong. Either way, the abandonment of collusion should have been associated with the removal of capacity and a reduction in the number of firms, and Elliott and Gribbin concluded that it did.[12]

[11] Phlips (1971, p. 148) found median concentration to be higher in smaller nations, and George and Ward (1975, p. 56) reported the excess of company over plant concentration to increase with the size of the national market. That concentration does not vary more sensitively with country size suggests that the sizes of companies also vary with that of the national market, as we shall see below.

[12] Scherer et al. (1975, pp. 110–112) obtained an incidental result that was interpretable as indicating a greater mutual respect for market shares in concentrated European industries than in their U.S. counterparts – consistent with the findings about the consequences of explicit collusive arrangements in Britain.

Horizontal mergers are strongly discouraged by U.S. antitrust laws but lightly restricted under the competition policies of most other countries. Whatever the motives for such mergers (market control or efficiency), we would accordingly expect them to account for more of changes in producer concentration outside the United States. Utton (1971) among others [see Curry and George (1983, pp. 238–247)][13] confirmed this hypothesis for Britain, as did Müller (1976) for West Germany.

4. International trade and market structure

The research summarized so far has been surprisingly unanimous in assigning a significant role to national market size in determining the structure and performance of industrial markets.[14] Apparently, no nation is so small and open that we may simply regard it as a corner of a competitive world market. But that leaves the question of how strongly international links do influence the market's structure and performance – one appropriately investigated by comparing countries that differ in size and openness.

Theory deals rather awkwardly with the effect of international influences on market structure and performance unless that influence takes an all-or-nothing form. Assume that a country is "small" relative to the world market, but that national producers can obtain access to export markets (comparative advantage permitting) only by incurring substantial transaction costs; assume also that similar access costs significantly insulate domestic producers by elevating the delivered price of imports above their world price. Then domestic disappearance (production minus exports plus imports) becomes an appropriate primary measure of the market's size, but with its influence cancelled where substantial export opportunities are seized or import competition is effective. (Product differentiation complicates the picture, especially for import-competing sectors.)

The empirical evidence from several countries confirms the distinction between trade-exposed and trade-sheltered sectors. In their six-country sample Scherer et al. (1975) found sizes of plants relative to minimum efficient scale to increase significantly with industries' access to export markets. Gorecki (n.d.) obtained the same result for Canada. Prais (1981, ch. 3) noticed a strong correlation between

[13] Hart and Clarke (1980, ch. 5) concluded that mergers had been responsible for half of the U.K.'s increase in concentration over 1958–68. They did not confirm the tendency found in the United States for much larger increases in concentration to occur in those consumer-good industries that (in the United States) make heavy use of network television as an advertising medium.

[14] A substantial number of studies have found the incidence of excess profits in small, open economies to depend on national market structures in the same way as in larger and more self-sufficient ones – so long as the model controls properly for industries' international linkages. Notable in this regard is the research on Belgium, such as Jacquemin, de Ghellinck and Huveneers (1980).

plant size and exporting activity in a sample of 33 industries observed in Britain, West Germany, and the United States. Caves, Porter and Spence (1980, ch. 3) found that concentration in Canadian manufacturing industries with significant exports bore no net relation to the size of the Canadian market itself.

If export markets affect entrepreneurial decisions about plants' and firms' scales, then micro data should indicate an association between the sizes of production units and the extent to which their outputs flow to foreign buyers. That exporting tends to be concentrated in the larger production units in an industry has been found for several countries – Japan [Rapp (1976)], Belgium [Glejser, Jacquemin and Petit (1980)], France [Auquier (1980)], Great Britain [Hannah and Kay (1977, pp. 21–22), Utton and Morgan (1983, pp. 8–9), compare Kumar (1984, chs. 8, 9)], and Austria [Stankovsky (1982)], as well as the United States [Caves (1986)]. These studies suggest and selectively confirm several mechanisms that may be at work. The obvious one is that access to export markets increases the chances that producers will fully attain the available economies of scale (which constraints of demand and rivals' reactions in the domestic market might otherwise deter). The existence of high fixed costs of exporting is confirmed by the evidence that smaller units, if they export at all, tend to export large proportions of their outputs.

The differential effect of export markets on scales of production has been exposed in the formation of the European Community – an experiment in the effective enlargement of market sizes through the permanent elimination of intra-Community tariffs. In a hypothetical long run, reduced trade barriers increase producers' preferred scales of plants or firms by increasing the elasticity of the derived demands that they face (derived on Cournot assumptions, for example). In the short run, with plant costs of both domestic and foreign competitors sunk in place, the question becomes whether a given suboptimal-scale producer can profitably expand to or replace with an efficient-scale facility. To utilize an efficient-scale unit, output must be expanded, depressing price until a sufficient number of inefficient-scale producers exit. Enlarging a market through, say, forming a customs union brings a larger number of inefficient producers under the gun of the entrepreneur who expands capacity, lowering the present value of negative cash-flow components due to the competing down of incumbent capacity [Scitovsky (1958, ch. 3), Owen (1983, ch. 2)].

Empirically, Owen (1983, ch. 3) found a positive correlation across industries in three pairs of Community nations between plant sizes and relative net-export positions. The direction of causality in this relation, however, is unclear, and his industry case studies (chs. 4–6) give the impression that product or process innovations were also strongly involved: national producer groups in the Community that substantially increased their scales and exports were typically riding on successful innovations as well as claiming previously unutilized economies of scale. Similarly, Müller and Owen (1985) concluded that due to increasing exposure to trade plant sizes were enlarged relative to MES by more than 100 percent in a sample of German industries between 1965 and 1978.

If the product is homogeneous, the effect of import competition on domestic market structure should be symmetrical with that of export opportunities. The same holds for a differentiated product with all of its varieties subject to the same production technology and entering symmetrically into demand, and some corollaries of the Chamberlinian models of international trade are confirmed by research on the determinants of intraindustry trade and of the distribution of exporting activities among an industry's producers.[15] However, empirical research on import competition in countries with highly exposed manufacturing sectors has tended to reject both sets of theoretical considerations and to emphasize two different sets of conditions. First, not all varieties of a product have equally large minimum efficient scales of production, so that an improvement in an import-competing industry's comparative advantage or an increase in its tariff protection can actually lower the average scales of its production units.[16] Second, where import-competing producers can collude effectively, the world price plus the domestic tariff becomes a natural focal point for price-setting, and (depending on entry barriers) domestic producers "crowd in" to the market at suboptimal scales until further entry produces negative profits. Evidence confirming the performance implications of this model is summarized in the next section.

Market structures depend on international transactions other than merchandise trade – foreign direct investment and arm's length transactions in proprietary information (licenses of technologies, patents, trademarks, designs, etc.). The extensive research on the bases for multinational enterprises (MNEs) has been able to explain their interindustry distributions in most settings by the importance of the industry's investments in or holdings of intangible assets – research and development, media advertising outlays, managerial skills.[17] The prevalence of MNEs is highly correlated with industries' levels of producer concentration, because the factors just mentioned are sources of scale economies or first-mover advantages to the firm and thus of barriers to entry. Some observers have inferred one causality or the other from this correlation, but joint dependence on common underlying factors seems the more prudent conclusion to draw. The force of the

[15]Caves (1981) confirmed the positive association between product differentiation and intraindustry trade, while Carlson (1974) found that structural differentiation also affects the speeds of adjustment in international trade. Regarding differentiation's effect on the relation between firms' sizes and exporting activities, evidence for France [Auquier (1980)] and the United States [Caves (1985)] supports different hypotheses.

[16]Perhaps for this reason, investigations of the relation between import competition and production-unit scale (mainly for Canada) have found no significant relationship.

[17]These conclusions flow from studies that control for the choice made by the firm possessing the intangibles between exporting the services of its intangibles and exporting goods that embody them. For surveys see Dunning (1981) and Caves (1982).

relation for industrial structures is illustrated by some research findings on Canada. Multinationals serve as favored potential entrants, as reflected in concentration levels of Canadian producers (relative to U.S. counterpart industries) that are lower in sectors strongly prone to foreign investment. Also, Canadian concentration levels are more highly correlated with those of their U.S. counterparts in these industries, consistent with the hypothesis that the intangible assets utilized through a company's foreign investments will command for it similar shares in different national markets [Caves, Porter and Spence (1980, pp. 53–54)].[18]

5. International differences in efficiency

A line of research that has gained substantially from international and transnational comparative research is the analysis of efficiency. The concept of efficiency is used here in an omnibus way. We shall refer both to specific failures of cost minimization within the national industry – usually called technical inefficiency or "X-inefficiency" – and to efficiency in the sense of comparative advantage taken from the field of international economics. Although theoretically we distinguish between an industry that suffers a comparative disadvantage due to the national factor endowment and input costs and one that fails to attain minimum costs, a disadvantaged industry that we actually observe may be suffering from any combination of these.[19]

We start with a line of research that is distinguished by a strategy of experimental design rather than a model or hypothesis. Suppose that one wishes to test a hypothesis about determinants of productivity or efficiency in some national economy. If that national economy is a unique entity, there is no way to perform a direct test. However, if the hypothesized factor affects productivity or efficiency differently in that economy's various industries, then a feasible strategy is to express each industry's efficiency level relative to some external standard and test the hypothesis on the resulting interindustry differences in relative efficiency. The external efficiency standard may be an empirical one: for coun-

[18]Two related conclusions are interesting but may be specific to the close propinquity and common culture of the Canadian and U.S. economies. Meredith (1984) showed that Canadian industries with large populations of foreign subsidiaries seem to economize on media advertising, consistent with the MNEs benefiting from spillovers from the United States. Also, U.S. foreign investment in Canada is significantly related to economies of coordinating multiplant operation (reflected by its extent among leading U.S. firms), whereas foreign investment in distant and insular Britain is not [Caves (1974a)].

[19]Accordingly, empirical investigations of the determinants of countries' patterns of international trade have found the core general-equilibrium models based on national factor endowments to possess rather limited explanatory power and have turned instead to hypotheses and explanatory variables that are more the province of industrial organization. See, for example, Hufbauer (1970) and Baumann (1976).

tries with productivity levels below those of the United States, productivity in the counterpart U.S. industry has been assumed to fill this reference function. Or a standard may be inferred from best practice within the national industry using the measures of technical efficiency that have evolved following Farrell (1957).

The international-comparative line of research comprises a number of studies that have used the United States as a reference point for evaluating the efficiency (or productivity growth) in counterpart industries of such countries as Canada, Japan, Australia, Great Britain, and France.[20] Their diverse hypotheses have devolved from constraints on efficiency observed directly in the respective economies. Investigators of both Canada [West (1971), Bloch (1974), Caves, Porter and Spence (1980, ch. 10), Saunders (1980), Bernhardt (1981)] and Australia [Caves (1984)] have been principally concerned with the response of domestic import-competing producers to a conjunction of small-size domestic market and substantial protection from foreign competitors and its implications for industry structures and productivity levels. Bloch (1974) observed that those Canadian industries charging high prices (relative to their U.S. counterparts) were marked by a conjunction of high concentration and substantial tariff protection. Yet these industries did not report correspondingly abnormal profits, implying that the elevation of prices was due to some systematic form of inefficiency. The later Canadian studies imputed this pattern to a conjunction of scale economies in production, tariff protection, and cost disadvantages to suboptimal-scale production that were not large enough to preclude the survival of many inefficient-scale producers behind the tariff wall. In Australia [Caves (1984)] as well as Canada [Caves, Porter and Spence (1980)], this conjunction of forces was found to reduce the scales of domestic production units as well as the productivity of their resource inputs.[21]

In the case of Great Britain [Davies and Caves (1987)], the emphasis of the hypotheses was shifted from specific market equilibria to the consequences of social attitudes and priorities, apparently reflected in a highly suboptimal effort bargain within the plant or firm – in plain language, the consequences of bloody-minded labor interacting with inept management. Because the complexity of

[20] Davies and Caves (1987, ch. 2) discussed the methodology in some detail and set forth a way to base the research design on a consistent model of production functions. At best the studies cited rest on comparisons of total factor productivity with corrections for factor-quality differences and some allowance for interindustry differences in production functions; some studies lack some of these refinements.

[21] Baldwin and Gorecki (1983a, 1983b) closely investigated the constraining influence of market size on Canadian plant scales, the exacerbation of the market-size constraint when tariffs are high and domestic producers concentrated, and the way in which plant-level output diversity (lengths of production runs) adjust jointly with plant scales in response to these factors. They showed that import-competing Canadian producers responded to trade liberalization by more specialized production rather than more efficient plant scales. On the other hand, de Melo and Urata (1986) concluded that Chilean trade liberalization, which led to concentration rising just as profits fell, resulted in substantial closings of small production units.

managerial tasks and the environment of the workplace (scale, skill mix, etc.) both vary substantially from one manufacturing industry to the next, it was possible to test these hypotheses on a matched panel of British and U.S. industries studied in cross-section for 1968 and 1977. The hypotheses were broadly confirmed: although blame for low relative productivity cannot be neatly apportioned between management and labor, their interaction in large-size plants clearly is an important negative effect on productivity. Although the core hypotheses may lie outside of industrial organization, Davies and Caves showed that the effect of Britain's managerial capacity and the effort bargain with labor interact strongly with economic elements of market structure.[22]

The rates of productivity growth in British industries (relative to their U.S. counterparts) were also affected – increased by Britain's managerial input (despite the managerial drag on the historic level) but retarded by trade-union organization. Also, the interindustry variance of productivity growth rates proved greater in Britain than in the United States, with the improvement of productivity strongly curbed where it would involve the reduction in an industry's labor force.[23] This finding touches on a larger issue that could be investigated with this methodology. European industrial countries are said to exhibit large interindustry differences in total factor productivity due to policy constraints on plant closings, industrial subsidies, large intersectoral wage differentials, and similar factors that inhibit the equalization of returns to factors among sectors [Carlsson (1983)]. These factors should enlarge the variance of a country's sectoral productivity levels, a hypothesis that could be tested using transnational comparisons of productivity in matched industries.

This method of analyzing relative productivity might find application to developing countries, where the determinants of industrial productivity are a major concern of policy. Indeed, a great deal of emphasis has been given to productivity-depressing but rational responses of producers to various restrictive and protective policies. Only a few researchers have made use comparative productivity analyses in this research. Diaz-Alejandro (1965) and Clague (1967) concluded that the efficiency of Argentine and Peruvian industries (respectively) is higher relative to the United States the more capital-intensive are the U.S.

[22]Because the studies of industrial productivity in Canada and Australia (on the one hand) and Britain (on the other) have emphasized such different interindustry determinants, we should note evidence that warrants this disjoint treatment. The extensive case studies developed by Prais (1981) on matched industries in Germany, Britain, and America assigned plant-scale differences a surprisingly small role in explaining productivity differences, which seemed due to much more diverse organizational factors. The result calls into question the normative importance of the relationship between production-unit size and market size summarized above.

[23]We note Houseman's (1985) analysis of job security as an acknowledgement of nonmarketed satisfactions that employees obtain as adjuncts of their jobs or job locations. She showed that the European Community's plans for rationalizing its various integrated steel mills were influenced both by the differing relative efficiencies of these mills and the varying degrees to which their closures would have impaired job property rights.

counterparts, confirming the maintained hypothesis that in the setting of a less-developed economy frontier levels of productivity are more easily attained in machine-paced than in operator-paced technologies [also see Arrow et al. (1961) on Japan]. White (1976) concluded that manufacturing industries in Pakistan exhibit inefficiently high levels of capital-intensity in the presence of high concentration and absence of exporting opportunities.

Perhaps the most thorough application of this research strategy to a developing economy is Lee's (1986) study of technical and allocative efficiency in Korea. He found that Korean industries' productivity levels (adjusted to world prices) increase with their attained scale efficiencies and exporting successes and decrease with Korea's rates of effective protection and an indicator of the extent of rent-seeking activities; technical and allocative efficiency are related in the expected way (technical inefficiency dissipates the profits that market structures might otherwise permit).[24]

Research on technical efficiency has also employed Farrell-type efficiency measures that evaluate the efficiency of the average plant in an industry against "best practice" observed within the country. Such measurements have been made using linear programming techniques [Carlsson (1972)] and, more recently, stochastic frontier production functions.[25] Once again, interest attaches to those traits of an industry that serve to predict its level of technical efficiency. Carlsson (1972) found the technical efficiency of Swedish industries to be depressed by tariff protection and to increase with the concentration of domestic producers and (not quite significantly) with actual exposure to international trade. Meller (1976), proceeding less formally with his interindustry analysis, concluded that public-sector protectionism contributes to inefficiency in Chilean manufacturing. Several single-sector studies [for example, Albach (1980)] concluded that the identities of efficient and inefficient firms tend to remain stable over time, although they did not identify the conditions that preserve the dispersion.

Other investigations of technical efficiency have pursued particular experiments of public policy, such as the abrupt outlawing of price-fixing and related cartel activities in Britain in the late 1950s. Downie (1958), using a simple measure of the dispersion of price–cost margins of firms within individual U.K. manufacturing industries, had found that firms' efficiency levels were previously more scattered in industries that maintained price-fixing agreements and were sufficiently concentrated to make the collusive agreements effective. As mentioned above, Swann et al. (1974, ch. 4) found that abandonment of these agreements was followed by substantial exit of excess capacity, despite price reductions on the order of 20 percent that should have raised the utilization of capacity;

[24] Technical inefficiency, he found, also impairs industries' responses to export incentives.

[25] We neglect here a number of interesting applications of stochastic frontier production functions to individual industries [for example, Førsund and Hjalmarsson (1979)].

therefore, incomplete collusive arrangements must have promoted the holding or retention of excess capacity and depressed technical efficiency.

6. Determinants of profitability

A final area of research in industrial organization that has benefited from international and comparative study is the determinants of allocative efficiency (measured inversely by profitability) and the effects of policies seeking to improve it. Many investigators apply roughly the same cross-section model of the determinants of allocative efficiency without reference to distinctive national institutional conditions or use of international leverage. However, a number of exceptions do shed light on this central question of research on industrial organization. Schwartzman (1959) early confirmed that industries which are unconcentrated in the United States but concentrated in Canada (and not heavily involved in export markets) exhibit significantly higher price–cost margins in Canada than in the United States. This method of testing the standard hypotheses about allocative efficiency offers a way to control for structural differences among industries that are otherwise difficult to handle, and has been used in a few other investigations. Khalilzadeh-Shirazi (1976) evaluated the statistical similarity of the interindustry models of allocative efficiency that have been fitted for different countries. He accepted the hypothesis that the same regression plane overall applies to his sample of matched British and American manufacturing industries. We are left uncertain whether to rejoice because the model's power is unaffected by the major economic, cultural, and legal differences between the two countries, or to despair because it fails to indicate any of the effects that we might expect them to have.

A few national studies of allocative inefficiency have nonetheless indicated roles for specific national differences. Adams (1976) argued that differences in the concentration–profits relationship for large firms based in different industrial countries were roughly consistent with differences in those countries' competition policies. Caves and Uekusa (1976, pp. 92–96) noted that, relative to other countries, producer concentration has much more power to explain monopoly rents in Japan and structural entry barriers much less. They attributed this to the relatively unsolidified state of entry barriers in the fast-growing Japanese economy and to the presence of institutions that get around capital-cost barriers.[26] Caves, Porter and Spence (1980, ch. 9) concluded that domestic research and development yields no systematic rents to Canadian manufacturing industries but that R & D in the United States does generate rents counted in the profits of

[26] However, other (later) studies of profit determinants in Japan such as Yamawaki (1986) get results more in line with those for Western industrial countries.

foreign subsidiaries operating in Canada. Williamson (1984) was able to investigate the effect of foreign subsidiaries on the pricing of domestic output and competing imports in Australia; as expected, extensive foreign control reduces the sensitivity of the domestic price markup over costs to import prices because of the role of captive imports and perhaps other effects.

An international difference commonly conjectured is the "softer" competition alleged to prevail in industrial markets outside the United States. Although tests of technical efficiency (reviewed above) give some support to the conjecture, investigations of allocative efficiency have not grappled with it directly. Suggestive results appear in an international investigation of the persistence of large firms' profits directed by Dennis Mueller [see Odagiri and Yamawaki (1986)]. It concludes that rent differentials among large manufacturing firms are persistent in all countries studied; implied steady-state profit rates are actually more dispersed for the United States than for France, Germany, or Japan – not less, as "hard competition" would imply. However, the typical U.S. firm's profits track its estimated steady-state profit rate less closely (i.e. converge on its steady state less rapidly), leaving one doubtful that "conventional wisdom" has been upended.[27]

Although international competition significantly affects allocative efficiency in all countries that have been studied closely, interesting variations appear for some nations. Williamson (1984)[28] broke with the tradition of characterizing imports as a competitive excess supply to any given country, showing that the pricing response to disturbances of Australian imports is affected by producer concentration in the regions that are leading exporters to Australia.[29] Yamawaki (1986) uncovered specific evidence of the interdependence of Japanese and U.S. producers, in that the profit margin on Japanese exports increases with the structural bases for monopoly rents in the corresponding U.S. industry. And Auquier (1977, ch. 3) concluded that the margins of French manufacturing industries were affected more sensitively by rival imports from neighboring Economic Community countries than by those from other sources. And Sleuwaegen, Weiss, and Yamawaki (1986) showed that, over the period of the Common Market's formation (1963–78), Community-wide producer concentration came to have more influence on national price–cost margins and national concentration correspondingly less. Overseas studies have shed much light on the sensitivity of the determinants of allocative efficiency to macroeconomic disturbances. Studies of allocative efficiency in Japan fail to confirm the usual

[27]Another study of indirect relevance is Encaoua (1983), whose investigation of short-run price adjustments found contrasts between (e.g.) Japan and Britain that are consistent with softer competition in the latter.

[28]Reported in Caves and Williamson (1985).

[29]Several statistical tests of the "law of one price" suggest the presence of strategic behavior in pricing imports in the face of short-run impediments to trade. See Norman (1975) on British imports.

mechanism during periods of explosive growth,[30] and Neumann, Böbel and Haid (1985) found the determinants of German industries' price–cost margins to vary over the business cycle in ways consistent with the breakdown of oligopolistic consensus in recessions.

7. The want list

One could extend this survey to cover scattered contributions addressed to other issues in industrial organization. At this point, however, it seems appropriate to turn from collecting what exists to contemplating what might be. In this concluding section we list a short selection of topics that might benefit from substantially more use of the modes of international and comparative analysis surveyed above.

7.1. International oligopoly

Much concern has been expressed in the realm of public policy about the ability of national firms to "stand up" to foreign competition, and theoretical research has revealed many possibilities for governments to deploy profit-shifting policies in order to manoeuvre global oligopoly rents into the pockets of its citizens. Discussions in the field of business strategy have focused on "global competition" in which international rivals pursue strategies that treat the world's submarkets as interdependent. Yet systematic empirical research on international oligopolistic behavior is quite limited. Could the international recognition of mutual dependence be an empty box? Case studies (many musty with age) and Yamawaki (1986) assert that it is not. Yet economists' current interest in tightly formulated empirical models of strategic interaction has not penetrated strongly into the international sphere. One possibility is the study of market-value changes for international competitors to determine whether oligopolistic disturbances redistribute value among rivals as one might expect [Luehrman (1986)]. The many studies of short-run adjustments of trade to restrictions and exchange-rate changes have never given serious attention to the role of oligopolistic rivalry.

7.2. Advertising and market power

A vigorous debate has proceeded in the United States over the question whether high levels of advertising expenditures, chiefly on television, have given rise to entry barriers in some industries. The industrial countries have employed very different policies on advertisers' access to television, limiting it in different

[30] The relevant papers were summarized by Caves and Uekusa (1976, pp. 35–37, 88–89).

degrees and permitting its introduction at different times. International comparisons therefore provide controlled experiments that might resolve this debate.

7.3. Research and international diffusion of technology

A major gap is the international diffusion and appropriation of technological knowledge. Most research on the determinants of research and development spending and of productivity growth assumes that the technology that the nation uses is what it produces. This assumption is dubious for the United States and wrong for the rest of the world. A few studies of R & D determinants in countries that are heavy importers of technology have observed the influence of this openness [Caves, Porter and Spence (1980, ch. 7), Antonelli (1985)]. The multinational corporation has been identified as one conduit for the international transfer of technology [Caves (1974b), Globerman (1979)], and national competitors have been found to imitate or match the multinational's innovations [Mansfield and Romeo (1980)]. The little systematic evidence on the international market for technology licenses confirms the expected imperfections but suggests that it is nonetheless large and important. How closely rates of technical progress of the various national branches of a given industry are kept in line by international diffusion and what channels contribute most to the alignment are largely unknown. We do have evidence, though, that process innovations diffuse more rapidly within the country of their discovery than internationally [Nabseth and Ray (1974), Benvignati (1982)].[31] The shortcomings of research here extend to its normative side: the classic market failures in the production of knowledge interact with discrepancies between national and global interests in ways that have been little explored.

7.4. Effects of public policies

Industrial countries have made diverse choices about the scope and intensity of their public policies toward market structure and behavior. Vertical restraints between manufacturers and distributors, horizontal mergers, and various collusive arrangements have been legal in some countries but illegal or lightly restricted in others.[32] Some case studies [Bianchi (1982)] are suggestive of the

[31] The case studies in Nabseth and Ray also suggest that determinants of international diffusion generally match those (such as extent of the cost saving) found significant in statistical studies of diffusion within national economies. Davidson and McFetridge (1984) found that newer and less routine technologies tend to be transferred within multinational firms rather than through arm's length licensing.

[32] Mueller (1980) paid some attention to the prevalence of horizontal mergers. They were more common abroad, but their prevalence did not mitigate the uniformly poor post-merger profit performance of acquiring firms found in all the countries studied.

consequences, and the effects of diverse tolerances of horizontal mergers have gained some attention. Differing access of advertisers to large-scale sales promotion through nationwide television seems a natural way to approach the issue of policy toward seller-supplied information.

7.5. *State-owned enterprises*

Countries have embraced the state-owned enterprise (SOE) as a policy device to sharply differing degrees and have embedded it in diverse market structures. The net effects of SOEs' operations on market performance is another question susceptible to empirical treatment through international differences. We know that the sectoral distribution of SOEs is quite similar among the industrial countries, where it seems to cluster in "heavy industries" that are highly capital-intensive, potentially monopolistic, and subject to extensive forward linkages [Pryor (1976), Levy (1988)]. Some approaches have been made to applying the theory of public choice in order to formulate objective functions for SOEs [Baldwin (1975)]. A great deal of descriptive material addresses the SOEs' relationship to the general national government and the shifting mixture of particular SOEs' objectives. But systematic research on SOEs' net effect on market performance is lacking.

References

Adams, W.J. (1976) 'International differences in corporate profitability', *Economica*, 43:367–379.

Adams, W.J. (1977) 'Large industrial firms in the Atlantic community: Production methods, asset finance, profitability, and growth', in: A.P. Jacquemin and H.W. de Jong, eds., *Welfare aspects of industrial markets*. Leiden: Martinus Nijhoff.

Adams, W.J. (1985) 'Explaining the differences in financial leverage between French and American corporations', working paper, University of Michigan.

Albach, H. (1980) 'Average and best-practice production functions in German industry', *Journal of Industrial Economics*, 29:55–70.

Antonelli, C. (1985) 'A failure inducement model of research and development expenditures: The Italian evidence', Centre for European Policy Studies, mimeo.

Arrow, K.J., et al. (1961) 'Capital–labor substitution and economic efficiency', *Review of Economics and Statistics*, 43:225–250.

Auquier, A.A. (1977) 'Industrial organization in an open economy: French industry and the formation of the European Common Market', Ph.D. dissertation, Harvard University.

Auquier, A.A. (1980) 'Sizes of firms, exporting behavior, and the structure of French industry', *Journal of Industrial Economics*, 29:203–218.

Bain, J.S. (1966) *International differences in industrial structure: Eight nations in the 1950s*. New Haven, Yale University Press.

Baldwin, J.R. (1975) *The regulatory agency and the public corporation: The Canadian air transport industry*. Cambridge: Ballinger.

Baldwin, J.R. and Gorecki, P.K. (1983a) 'Trade, tariffs and relative plant scale in Canadian manufacturing industries', discussion paper no. 232, Economic Council of Canada.

Baldwin, J.R. and Gorecki, P.K. (1983b) 'Trade, tariffs, product diversity and length of production run in Canadian manufacturing industries: 1970–1979', discussion paper no. 247, Economic Council of Canada.

Baldwin, J.R. and Gorecki, P.K. (1986) 'The relationship between plant scale and product diversity in Canadian manufacturing industries', *Journal of Industrial Economics*, 34:373–388.

Banerji, R. (1978) 'Average size of plants in manufacturing and capital intensity: Across-country analysis by industry', *Journal of Development Economics*, 5:155–166.

Baumann, H.G. (1976) 'Structural characteristics of Canada's pattern of trade', *Canadian Journal of Economics*, 9:208–224.

Benvignati, A.M. (1982) 'The relationship between the origin and diffusion of industrial innovation', *Economica*, 49:313–323.

Bernhardt, I. (1981) 'Sources of productivity differences among Canadian manufacturing industries', *Review of Economics and Statistics*, 63:503–512.

Bianchi, P. (1982) *Public and private control in mass product industry: The cement industry cases*. Studies in Industrial Organization no. 3. The Hague: Martinus Nijhoff.

Bloch, H. (1974) 'Prices, costs, and profits in Canadian manufacturing: The influence of tariffs and concentration', *Canadian Journal of Economics*, 7:594–610.

Brusco, S. (1982) 'The Emilian model: Productive decentralisation and social integration', *Cambridge Journal of Economics*, 6:167–184.

Cable, J. (1985) 'Capital market information and industrial performance: The role of West German banks', *Economic Journal*, 95:118–132.

Cable, J. and Yasuki, H. (1985) 'Internal organisation, business groups and corporate performance', *International Journal of Industrial Organization*, 3:401–420.

Carlson, S. (1974) 'Market information, selling intensity and the dynamics of international economic integration', *De Economist*, 122;502–520.

Carlsson, B. (1972) 'The measurement of efficiency in production: An application to Swedish manufacturing industries, 1968', *Swedish Journal of Economics*, 74:468–485.

Carlsson, B. (1983) 'Industrial subsidies in Sweden: Macro-economic effects and an international comparison', *Journal of Industrial Economics*, 32:1–23.

Caves, R.E. (1974a) 'Causes of direct investment: Foreign firms' shares in Canadian and United Kingdom manufacturing industries', *Review of Economics and Statistics*, 56:279–293.

Caves, R.E. (1974b) 'Multinational firms, competition, and productivity in host-country industries', *Economica*, 41:176–193.

Caves, R.E. (1975) *Diversification, foreign investment, and scale in North American manufacturing industries*. Ottawa: Economic Council of Canada.

Caves, R.E. (1981) 'Intraindustry trade and market structure in the industrial countries', *Oxford Economic Papers*, 33:203–223.

Caves, R.E. (1982) *Multinational enterprise and economic analysis*. New York: Cambridge University Press.

Caves, R.E. (1984) 'Scale, openness, and productivity in manufacturing', in: R.E. Caves and L.B. Krause, eds., *The Australian economy: A view from the North*. Washington, D.C.: Brookings Institution.

Caves, R.E. (1986) 'Exporting behavior and market structure: Evidence from the United States', in: H.W. de Jong and W.G. Shepherd, eds., *Mainstreams in industrial organization*. Dordrecht: Martinus Nijhoff.

Caves, R.E. and Uekusa, M. (1976) *Industrial organization in Japan*. Washington, D.C.: Brookings Institution.

Caves, R.E. and Williamson, P.J. (1985) 'What is product differentiation, *really*?', *Journal of Industrial Economics*, 34:113–132.

Caves, R.E., Porter, M.E., and Spence, A.M. (1980) *Competition in the open economy: A model applied to Canada*. Cambridge: Harvard University Press.

Clague, C.S. (1967) 'An international comparison of industrial efficiency: Peru and the United States', *Review of Economics and Statistics*, 49:487–493.

Curry, B. and George, K.D. (1983) 'Industrial concentration: A survey', *Journal of Industrial Economics*, 31:203–255.

Daems, H. (1978) *The holding company and corporate control*. Leiden: Martinus Nijhoff.

Davidson, W.H. and McFetridge, D.G. (1984) 'International technology transactions and the theory of the firm', *Journal of Industrial Economics*, 32:253–264.
Davies, S.W. and Caves, R.E. (1987) *Britain's productivity gap: A study based on British and American industries*, 1968–77. Cambridge: Cambridge University Press.
Davies, W. and Lyons, B.R. (1982) 'Seller concentration: The technological explanation and demand uncertainty', *Economic Journal*, 92:903–919.
de Jong, H.W. (1986) 'European industrial organization: Entrepreneurial economics in an organizational setting', in: H.W. de Jong and W.G. Shepherd, eds., *Mainstreams in industrial organization*. Dordrecht: Martinus Nijhoff.
de Melo, J. and Urata, S. (1986) 'The influence of increased foreign competition on industrial concentration and profitability', *International Journal of Industrial Organization*, 4:287–306.
Diaz Alejandro, C.F. (1965) 'Industrialization and labor productivity differentials', *Review of Economics and Statistics*, 47:207–214.
Downie, J. (1958) *The competitive process*. London: Butterworth.
Dunning, J.H. (1981) *International production and the multinational enterprise*. London: Allen and Unwin.
Eastman, H.C. and Stykolt, S. (1967) *The tariff and competition in Canada*. New York: St. Martin's Press.
Elliott, D.C. and Gribbin, J.D. (1977) 'The abolition of cartels and structural change in the United Kingdom', in: A.P. Jacquemin and H.W. de Jong, eds., *Welfare aspects of industrial markets*. Leiden: Martinus Nijhoff.
Encaoua, D. (1983) 'Price dynamics and industrial structure: A theoretical and econometric analysis', working paper no. 10, OECD Economics and Statistics Department.
Encaoua, D. and Jacquemin, A. (1982) 'Organizational efficiency and monopoly power: The case of French industrial groups', *European Economic Review*, 19:25–51.
Farrell, M.J. (1957) 'The measurement of productive efficiency', *Journal of the Royal Statistical Society*, 120:253–282.
Førsund, R. and Hjalmarsson, L. (1979) 'Frontier production functions and technical progress: A study of general milk processing in Swedish dairy plants', *Econometrica*, 47:883–900.
Fua, G. (1983) 'Rural industrialization in later developed countries: The case of northeast and central Italy', *Banca Nazionale del Lavoro Quarterly Review*, 147:351–378.
George, K.D. and Ward, T.S. (1975) *The structure of industry in the EEC*. Cambridge: Cambridge University Press.
Glejser, H., Jacquemin, A. and Petit, J. (1980) 'Exports in an imperfect competition framework: An analysis of 1,446 exporters', *Quarterly Journal of Economics*, 94:507–524.
Globerman, S. (1979) 'Foreign direct investment and 'spillover' efficiency benefits in Canadian manufacturing industries', *Canadian Journal of Economics*, 12:42–56.
Gorecki, P.K. 'Economies of scale and efficient plant size in Canadian manufacturing industries', research monograph no. 1, Department of Consumer and Corporate Affairs, Ottawa.
Goto, A. (1982) 'Business groups in a market economy', *European Economic Review*, 19:53–70.
Hannah, L. and Kay, J.A. (1977) *Concentration in modern industry: Theory, measurement, and the U.K. experience*. London: Macmillan.
Hart, P. and Clarke, R. (1980) 'Concentration in British industry, 1935–75', occasional paper no. 32, National Institute of Economic and Social Research. Cambridge University Press, Cambridge.
Horowitz, I. (1970) 'Employment and concentration in the Common Market', *Journal of the Royal Statistical Society*, 133:463–479.
Houseman, S.N. (1985) 'Job security and industrial restructuring in the European Community steel industry', Ph.D. dissertation, Harvard University.
Hufbauer, G.C. (1970) 'The impact of national characteristics and technology on the commodity composition of trade in manufactured goods', in: R. Vernon, ed., *The technology factor in international trade*. New York: National Bureau of Economic Research.
Imai, K. and Itami, H. (1984) 'Interpenetration of organization and market: Japan's firm and market in comparison with the U.S.', *International Journal of Industrial Organization*, 2:285–310.
Jacquemin, A.P. and de Jong, H.W. (1977) *European industrial organization*. New York: Wiley.
Jacquemin, A.P., de Ghellinck, E. and Huveneers, C. (1980) 'Concentration and profitability in a small open economy', *Journal of Industrial Economics*, 29:131–144.

Jones, L.P. and Sakong, I. (1980) *Government, business and entrepreneurship in economic development: The Korean case*. Cambridge: Harvard University Press.

Khalilzadeh-Shirazi, J. (1976) 'Market structure and price–cost margins: A comparative analysis of U.K. and U.S. manufacturing industries', *Economic Inquiry*, 14:116–128.

Kirkpatrick, C.H., Lee, N. and Nixson, F.I. (1984) *Industrial structure and policy in less developed countries*. London: Allen and Unwin.

Kumar, M.S. (1984) *Growth, acquisition and investment: An analysis of the growth of industrial firms and their overseas activities*. Cambridge: Cambridge University Press.

Lee, J. (1986) 'Market performance in an open developing economy: Technical and allocative efficiencies of Korean industries', *Journal of Industrial Economics*, 35:81–96.

Leff, N. (1978) 'Industrial organisation and entrepreneurship in the developing countries: The economic groups', *Economic Development and Cultural Change*, 26:661–675.

Lemelin, A. (1982) 'Relatedness in patterns of interindustry diversification', *Review of Economics and Statistics*, 64:646–657.

Levy, B. (1988) 'The determinants of manufacturing ownership in less developed countries', *Journal of Development Economics*, 28:217–231.

Lindsay, C.W. (1979) 'Size structure, turnover, and mobility of the largest manufacturing firms in a developing country: The case of the Philippines', *Journal of Industrial Economics*, 28:189–200.

Lucas, Jr., R.E. (1978) 'On the size distribution of business firms', *Bell Journal of Economics*, 9:508–523.

Luehrman, T.A. (1986) 'Firm value, real exchange rate changes, and competitiveness', Ph.D. dissertation, Harvard University.

MacDonald, J.M. (1985) 'R&D and the directions of diversification', *Review of Economics and Statistics*, 67:583–590.

Mansfield, E. (1962) 'Entry, Gibrat's law, innovation, and the growth of firms', *American Economic Review*, 52:1023–1051.

Mansfield, E. and Romeo, A. (1980) 'Technology transfer to overseas subsidiaries by U.S.-based firms', *Quarterly Journal of Economics*, 95:737–750.

Meller, P. (1976) 'Allocative frontiers for industrial establishments of different sizes', *Explorations in Economic Research*, 3:379–407.

Meller, P. (1978) 'The pattern of industrial concentration in Latin America', *Journal of Industrial Economics*, 27:41–47.

Meredith, L. (1984) 'U.S. multinational investment in Canadian manufacturing industries', *Review of Economics and Statistics*, 66:111–119.

Mueller, D.C., ed. (1980) *The determinants and effects of mergers: An international comparison*. Cambridge: Oelgeschlager, Gunn and Hain.

Müller, J. (1976) 'The impact of mergers on concentration: A study of eleven West German industries', *Journal of Industrial Economics*, 25:113–132.

Müller, J. and Owen, N. (1985) 'The effect of trade on plant size', in: J. Schwalbach, ed., *Industry structure and performance*. Berlin: Edition Sigma.

Nabseth, L. and Ray, G.F., eds. (1974) 'The diffusion of new industrial processes: An international study', Economic and social studies no. 29, National Institute of Economic and Social Research, Cambridge University Press, Cambridge.

Neumann, J., Böbel, I. and Haid, A. (1985) 'Domestic concentration, foreign trade, and economic performance', *International Journal of Industrial Organization*, 3:1–19.

Norman, N.R. (1975) 'On the relationship between prices of home-produced and foreign commodities', *Oxford Economic Papers*, 27:426–439.

Odagiri, H. and Yamawaki, H. (1986) 'A study of company profit-rate time series', *International Journal of Industrial Organization*, 4:1–23.

Owen, N. (1983) *Economies of scale, competitiveness, and trade patterns within the European Community*. Oxford: Clarendon Press.

Phlips, L. (1971) *Effects of industrial concentration: A cross-section analysis for the Common Market*. Amsterdam: North-Holland.

Prais, S.J. (1981) *Productivity and industrial structure: A statistical study of manufacturing industry in Britain, Germany and the United States*. Cambridge: Cambridge University Press.

Pryor, F.L. (1972a) 'An international comparison of concentration ratios', *Review of Economics and Statistics*, 54:130–140.

Pryor, F.L. (1972b) 'The size of production establishments in manufacturing', *Economic Journal*, 82:547–566.

Pryor, F.L. (1976) 'Public ownership: Some quantitative dimensions', in: W.G. Shepherd, et al., eds., *Public enterprise: Economic analysis of theory and practice*. Lexington: Lexington Books.

Rapp, W.V. (1976) 'Firm size and Japan's export structure: A microview of Japan's changing export competitiveness since Meiji', in: H. Patrick, ed., *Japanese industrialization and its social consequences*. Berkeley: University of California Press.

Rosenbluth, G. (1957) *Concentration in Canadian manufacturing industries*. Princeton: Princeton University Press for National Bureau of Economic Research.

Saunders, R. (1980) 'The determinants of productivity in Canadian manufacturing industries', *Journal of Industrial Economics*, 29:167–184.

Saving, T.R. (1961) 'Estimation of optimum size of plant by the survivor technique', *Quarterly Journal of Economics*, 75:569–607.

Scherer, F.M., et al. (1975) *The economics of multi-plant operation: An international comparisons study*. Cambridge: Harvard University Press.

Schwartzman, D. (1959) 'The effect of monopoly on price', *Journal of Political Economy*, 67:352–362.

Scitovsky, T. (1958) *Economic theory and Western European integration*. London: Allen and Unwin.

Sleuwaegen, L., Weiss, L.W. and Yamawaki, H. (1986) 'Industry competition and the formation of the European Common Market', mimeo.

Stankovsky, J. (1982) 'Erweiterte Exportkennzahlen der österreichischen Wirtschaft', *Monatsberichte des osterreichischen Instituts fürr Wirtschaftsforschung*, 4:245–258.

Swann, D., et al. (1974) *Competition in British industry: Restrictive practices legislation in theory and practice*. London: Allen and Unwin.

Thonet, P.J. and Poensgen, O.H. (1979) 'Management control and economic performance in Western Germany', *Journal of Industrial Economics*, 28:23–38.

Utton, M. (1971) 'The effect of mergers on concentration: U.K. manufacturing industry, 1954–65', *Journal of Industrial Economics*, 20:42–59.

Utton, M.A. and Morgan, A.D. (1983) 'Concentration and foreign trade', occasional paper no. 35, National Institute of Economic and Social Research. Cambridge University Press, Cambridge.

West, E.C. (1971) *Canada–United States price and productivity differences in manufacturing industries*, 1963. Ottawa: Information Canada.

White, L.J. (1974) *Industrial concentration and economic power in Pakistan*. Princeton: Princeton University Press.

White, L.J. (1976) 'Appropriate technology, *X*-inefficiency, and a competitive environment: Some evidence from Pakistan', *Quarterly Journal of Economics*, 90:575–589.

Williamson, P.J. (1984) 'Import penetration in imperfectly competitive markets: A study of firm and industry behaviour under import threat', Ph.D. dissertation, Harvard University.

Winter, S.G. (1971) 'Satisficing, selection, and the innovating remnant', *Quarterly Journal of Economics*, 85:237–261.

Yamawaki, H. (1986) 'Exporting, foreign market structure, and profitability: Japanese and U.S. manufacturing', *Review of Economics and Statistics*, 68:618–627.

Yoshihara, H. et al. (1981) *Diversification strategies of Japanese firms*. Tokyo: Nihon Keizai Shinbunsha [in Japanese].

PART 5

GOVERNMENT INTERVENTION IN THE MARKETPLACE

Chapter 22

ECONOMIC PERSPECTIVES ON THE POLITICS OF REGULATION

ROGER G. NOLL*

Stanford University

Contents

*I am especially indebted to Paul Joskow, except for whose modesty would be a co-author, and Richard Schmalensee for help in preparing this chapter.

Handbook of Industrial Organization, Volume II, Edited by R. Schmalensee and R.D. Willig
© *Elsevier Science Publishers B.V., 1989*

1. Introduction

Economics research on regulation has three main themes. The first and oldest deals with market failures and the corrective actions that government can undertake to ameliorate them. The second examines the effects of regulatory policies, and asks whether government intervention is efficient (an easy question) or more efficient than doing nothing (often a very hard question). The spread of mathematical modeling to applied fields of economics and the development of econometrics and computers greatly facilitated this research, and it has been the predominant form since the late 1950s. The third, which became an important part of the literature only in the 1970s,[1] investigates the political causes of regulatory policy. The motivation arises from the disjointness in the first two areas of research: regulation as practiced commonly was found to be inefficient and to adopt methods that do not appear to be the best choices for tackling their associated market failures.[2]

The purpose of this chapter is to provide an interpretative survey of the third category of research. The focus is on research that employs the conceptual model and methods of economics, i.e. that assumes rational, goal-directed behavior by all relevant agents (consumers, firms, voters, politicians, input suppliers, etc.), that uses economic theoretic (though not always mathematical) arguments to make predictions about political behavior, and, where relevant, that employs methods of testing theoretical hypotheses that economists commonly employ. Hence, our coverage includes work done in disciplines other than economics, and especially by lawyers and political scientists.

The logical place to begin an analysis of the politics of regulation is the so-called "public interest" theory, which in the context of this chapter refers to the view that, as a matter of positive theory, the normative goal of curing market failures animates the choice of regulatory policies. In a limited but complex sense, normative welfare economics constitutes a positive theory of government if the conditions of the Coase Theorem [Coase (1960)] are true: information is perfect and costless, and the political process is free of its counterparts to transactions costs. Section 2 is devoted to the development of this argument.

[1] The watershed event is the publication of Stigler's (1971) highly influential paper, which was referenced approvingly when Professor Stigler deservedly was awarded the Nobel Prize. Notable antecedents of Stigler's work are Bernstein (1955), Downs (1957), Caves (1962), Kolko (1965), MacAvoy (1965), Olson (1965), and Buchanan and Tullock (1962).

[2] The economic effects of regulation are discussed in the chapters by Joskow and Rose (Chapter 25) and Gruenspecht and Lave (Chapter 26) in this Handbook.

Section 3 addresses the next logical step: why might the Coase Theorem not apply, and what are the implications if it does not? The key point here is that imperfect information and transactions costs provide an entering wedge for political theories as to why regulation can be inefficient: capture by interest groups for the purpose of acquiring monopoly rents, or otherwise redistributing wealth to themselves in ways that also create inefficiency [Stigler (1971)].

Regardless of the motives of political actors, an essential ingredient to a theory of regulatory policy when the Coase Theorem fails is how political officials control agencies. Whether the aim of regulation is to maximize efficiency or to transfer wealth to a special interest, politicians face a principal–agent problem in trying to assure reasonable bureaucratic compliance with the objectives behind a legislative mandate. Section 4 addresses these issues.

2. Welfare economics and positive political theory

The theory of market failure consists of a littany of ways in which the conditions for competitive equilibrium may fail to be satisfied. For our purposes, it is useful to think of the market failure rationale for regulation as having three distinct components: a positive theory of conditions under which a market produces an inefficient outcome, a normative theory that government ought to undertake actions to improve the efficiency of poorly functioning markets, and finally a positive theory that, in the presence of important market failures, government will attempt to ameliorate them through regulation.

2.1. Market failure rationales

The importance of the first component is that in literally every circumstance the adoption or extension of regulation has been defended by its proponents on the basis of allegations (sometimes implausible) of market failure.[3] In the United States, the first examples of regulatory programs were justified on the basis of natural monopoly: a specific good or service (in this case, grain elevators, water supply, and railroads)[4] could be produced at lowest cost only if supplied by a single firm,[5] but this would give rise to monopolistic abuse and dead-weight loss

[3] A comprehensive list of the sources of market failure and their relationship to regulation can be found in Breyer (1981).

[4] For useful summaries of the important early court decisions which permitted regulation of these industries, see Weiss and Stickland (1982).

[5] For a comprehensive statement of the definition of natural monopoly and the method for detecting it, see Baumol (1977).

in an unregulated market. Regulation was proposed as a means to capture the efficiency advantages of monopoly while eliminating some of the potential for monopolistic abuse.

A second form of market failure, imperfect information, has been the rationale for regulating consumer products and workplaces, beginning with the Pure Food and Drug Act of 1906. Complex, costly information can lead to poorly informed and sometimes potentially hazardous decisions about goods, services, and jobs. It can also lead suppliers to provide either too much or too little quality, and industries to adopt inefficient technical compatibility standards.[6] In principle, regulation can provide two types of efficiency gains. First, by increasing the supply of information, it can reduce uncertainties about the consequences of market decisions, thereby causing the market to make a better match between suppliers and demanders. Second, by setting minimum standards, it can protect uninformed participants against bad outcomes, including a "market for lemons" equilibrium in which quality is supplied at inefficiently low levels.

The third form of market failure is the presence of external effects and public goods. These arise when economic agents impose costs on, or deliver benefits to, others who are not parties to their transaction. This form of market failure has been used most notably to justify environmental regulation,[7] regulatory allocation of the use of the electromagnetic spectrum,[8] and the "universal service" doctrine in communications.[9] For example, regulation of the electromagnetic spectrum, by assigning frequencies within a geographic area to particular users, could prevent mutually interfering transmissions. Zoning and emissions standards could force industry to make location decisions and adopt production processes that produce fewer external diseconomies. Optimal pricing of telephones might require price regulation that causes subsidies for basic subscription, financed by an implicit tax on other telecommunications services that produce no external benefits.

Two additional rationales for regulation, while commonly defended in political discourse, are nonetheless of more debatable economic validity. These are scarcity rent and destructive competition.

Scarcity rent is the producers' surplus that arises in otherwise competitive and efficient markets with rising industry supply curves. Examples are easy to find in resource economics and in urban location theory. Since the very beginnings of

[6]See Akerloff (1974), Oi (1973), Spence (1977), Shapiro (1983), Schwartz and Wilde (1985), and Milgrom and Roberts (1986).

[7]For an excellent survey, see Fisher and Peterson (1976).

[8]A comprehensive treatment of rationales for regulating broadcasting on the basis of externalities, whether interference or social spillovers from broadcast messages, can be found in Spitzer (1987).

[9]If another customer is added to a telephone or mail delivery system, the value of the system to other users is enhanced by the possibility of communicating with the new customer.

the oil and gas industries, regulation has been proposed – and periodically enforced – as a means of stripping scarcity rents from especially low-cost producers [Sanders (1981)]. And residential rent controls have occasionally been imposed for the same purpose, most notably in New York City [Olsen (1972)]. The core of the pro-regulatory argument here is that scarcity rents are socially undesirable. Usually the argument is based on the effects of scarcity rents on income distribution, but in some cases a kind of externality/efficiency argument is made as well. For example, rising land values in an urban area can lead to eviction of low-income people from their residences. Decisions to upgrade the use of land normally do not take into account the costs imposed on the forced relocation of these people. Even if the conversion of the use of the land is efficient, compensation is rarely sufficient to cover the losses of the displaced. The fact that the dispossessed cannot pay land owners enough to prevent their eviction is not fully dispositive that their replacement is economically efficient, for if they were fully compensated the income effect could, in principle, change the outcome of the compensation test [Chipman and Moore (1973)]. That this may be a serious issue is suggested by research by anthropologists, which shows that morbidity, mortality, and socially deviant behavior are substantially greater after forced relocation, especially among elderly and less educated populations [Scudder and Colson (1982)]. Lawyers have argued that a value of regulation can be that it avoids these "demoralization costs" [Michelman (1967)] by protecting "dignitary" human values [Mashaw (1985)].

Destructive competition is the circumstance in which an industry that is not a natural monopoly nonetheless lacks a stable competitive equilibrium. It was used to support the argument for regulation of truck and airline transportation in the 1930s, but subsequently has been almost unanimously rejected in economics research.[10] The destructive competition rationale for regulation is that in its absence the instability of such an industry would require that producers and consumers assume unnecessarily high risks, thereby producing an inefficient market outcome. The most respectable economic theoretic example of such a circumstance is the theory of the core, which demonstrates the nonexistence of competitive equilibrium in an industry in which capacity is lumpy and firms are myopic in making investment commitments.[11]

Finally, regulation may be regarded as a necessary byproduct of other government policies that are justified on other grounds. For example, distributional considerations could lead a nation to subsidize medical care, but this could leave the government vulnerable to a moral hazard problem with respect to both

[10]For good early treatments, see Meyer, Peck, Stenason and Zwick (1959), Caves (1962), Friedlaender (1969), and Eads (1972).

[11]Telser (1972).

patients and medical professionals.[12] Government then might seek to regulate medical care prices, and/or to regulate health hazards in order to avoid the pecuniary externality of hazards that is created by the subsidization policy.

2.2. Regulation as the best policy instrument

The second component of the public interest theory of regulation is that government ought to adopt regulatory strategies that cope with these market failures. The preceding rationales are only part of such a theory. If economic analysis does demonstrate that a market has failed and that additional economic welfare is available if the failure is cured, only the necessary condition for government regulation has been satisfied. In addition, it must also be demonstrated that a regulatory policy is the most effective remedy.

The economics literature contains a rich array of alternatives to regulation as a means of coping with market failures.[13] For example, instead of regulating the prices charged by a natural monopoly, the government could assist in the formation of customer cooperatives for providing the same service, or could use competitive bidding and contracting for awarding monopoly franchises of limited duration [Demsetz (1968)]. Or, as initially analyzed by Pigou (1920), clever uses of taxes and subsidies could be used to cope with a variety of market-failure issues, ranging from environmental externalities to scarcity rents. Or, as especially emphasized since Coase (1960), some market failures are amenable to solution simply by redefining property rights and creating a market in them.[14]

The positive theory of public interest regulation posits that the regulatory policies which are adopted will be the most effective remedy for a market failure. The essence of any such theory must rest in the fact that a market imperfection creates a dead-weight loss (e.g. greater costs than benefits), so that (in principle) those suffering its adverse consequences can bid more to cure the problem than its beneficiaries can bid to maintain the status quo.

Of course, if the conditions for the Coase Theorem are not met, the normative link in the three-link chain of argument in the public interest theory is broken. Specifically, the Coase Theorem holds only with perfect information and no

[12] The "moral hazard" problem in medical care arises from two sources. First, consumers generally do not pay for the medical care services they consume, and so have an incentive to consume too much relative to an efficiency standard. Second, payors – government, insurance companies, employees – cannot prevent this effectively, for they cannot costlessly observe how much medical care would be most efficient for any given patient. For an excellent statement of the issue, see Arrow (1963).

[13] These are presented comprehensively in Breyer (1981).

[14] See Dales (1968) on environmental policy and Spitzer (1987) on spectrum allocation.

transactions costs.[15] If this is the case, the sufferers from a market failure simply can buy out its beneficiaries and cure the market failure themselves. Regulation is then at best an equally attractive means of solving the problem.

By moderately relaxing the assumptions that give rise to the Coase Theorem, a far more serious public interest theory of political action can be constructed [see, for example, Levine (1981) and Becker (1983, 1985)]. One direction of modification is to relax the assumption of zero transactions costs. Instead, assume that in order to negotiate the amelioration of a market failure, all participants would face significant transactions costs. If transactions costs are lower to secure government action against the market failure, regulation can be a superior alternative to a negotiated settlement. This might occur if passing a bill is cheaper than negotiating a contract, or if a political leader can effectively overcome the costs of organizing an interest group by becoming its spokesperson in government, presumably in return for its political support. Alternatively, because the state has coercive powers, government regulation may permit the sufferers from a market failure to avoid paying off those who cause it. Even here, however, the transactions costs of government action must not be significantly higher than direct negotiation, or else the beneficiaries of the market failure, rationally expecting their bonanza to be terminated through coercion, could offer the sufferers a better bargain than the political solution.

A second direction of modification is to relax the assumption of perfect information on behalf of the sufferers from the market failure. In this case, political entrepreneurs can play the role of market perfectors, identifying failures and reporting them to those harmed. As long as the costs of collecting and disseminating the information are low in comparison with the magnitude of the efficiency loss from the market failure, the opportunity exists for a mutually beneficial transaction among the sufferers, the beneficiaries, and the political entrepreneur.[16] Once again, however, a further detail is required to explain why the outcome is political entrepreneurship, rather than a private transaction orchestrated by a broker possessing superior information. An example of such detail is the argument that information pertinent to identifying market failures is most cheaply acquired and disseminated by government. Government alone can compel private parties to provide it, and relevant information is a byproduct of other government activities. Moreover, government officials, because of their

[15]Here "transactions cost" takes its most general meaning. It includes not only the costs of negotiating a deal, but also the costs each side must bear to prepare itself for negotiations, and, afterwards, to make sure the other party complies. In the case of, say, environmental externalities, the former would include the costs of organizing the group of sufferers from pollution to negotiate as a unit with a source of pollution. Organization costs are discussed in detail in the next section.

[16]For a discussion of how Senator Edward Kennedy played this role with respect to airline deregulation, see Breyer (1981).

importance and recognizability, can more readily access the public through the media to announce the information they acquire.

In this form, the public interest theory is compatible with the presence of organized interest groups – so-called "special interests" – that participate actively in the political process. These groups are manifestations of transactions costs, of course, but the decision of, say, environmentalists and the electric power industry to fight their battles before regulators, rather than simply to merge, would reflect lower transactions costs for government action. Each party has a willingness-to-pay for favorable political action that is the difference between its stake in a market imperfection and the transactions costs involved in the process of implementing policy. If policy is for sale to the highest bidder, the outcome will be the action that can command the greatest aggregate willingness to pay, which, ceteris paribus, is favorable to the elimination of market failures.

This line of analysis leads to a number of predictions about regulation. First, if a market failure is increasingly important as time passes, the likelihood of political action increases. The reason is that transactions costs, being independent of the scope of the market failure (and instead dependent on the difficulties of organizing affected parties and reaching an agreement), will remain constant, whereas the benefits of agreement and the likelihood that the imperfection will be detected will both increase.

Second, transactions costs and information imperfections limit the extent to which regulation can depart from efficiency with respect to anyone affected by it. Specifically, no group can experience losses under regulation that fall short of compensating gains to other groups by more than the amount necessary (a) to overcome transactions costs or (b) to reach the threshold at which the information imperfection is overcome, whichever implies a larger departure from efficiency. Thus, if the most efficient form of pricing for a natural monopoly is to employ Ramsey prices, no price can depart from the Ramsey optimum in a manner that generates an efficiency loss of more than the transactions cost of pointing out that fact to the government (unless the magnitude of that departure is too small to be observed by the parties that suffer the attendant efficiency loss).

Third, deregulation occurs when the costs of regulation exceed the transactions cost of repealing it plus the costs of the remaining market failure. Thus, if outward shifts in demand and technological change continue to erode the position of a natural monopoly, at some point (short of perfect competition) both the monopolist and its customers can be made better off by deregulation if the transactions costs of repeal and the inefficiency of the remaining market power of the monopolist are less than the cost of maintaining the regulatory system.

Fourth, the theory predicts that when regulation is adopted, it is the most effective means for dealing with the market failure, but it may persist after that is the case. Obviously, once the transactions costs for political action are paid, the greatest amount of wealth is available for political distribution if the most efficient policy is adopted. But once regulation is in place, it can depart from the optimum policy if the departure is unknown to those harmed by it, or the inefficiency is small compared to the transactions cost of changing the policy instrument.

As posed above, the public interest theory of regulation does not require that regulation be perfectly efficient. As pointed out by Levine (1981), a proponent of a weakened form of the public interest theory, the job of political actors and analysts alike would be considerably less interesting if either markets or public policies worked perfectly. But the theory does require that regulation is adopted only in the presence of a genuine market failure, that at the time regulation is the best available policy instrument, and that it not persist once it begins to impose sufficiently large costs. It also implies a rather pluralist view about the regulatory process: the broader the spectrum of interests that are actively participating in regulatory policymaking, the more efficient should be the performance of the regulated market. Thus, liberal rules of standing and subsidies to assist the participation of some interests are likely to be warranted on efficiency grounds [Stewart (1975)], although they may cause an offsetting social waste in the cost of participation in the regulatory process [Posner (1975), Rogerson (1982)]. Finally, the sophisticated version of the public interest theory implies that political leaders ought to favor simple, open decision processes and the widespread dissemination of information about market performance and the effects of regulatory rules. To do so reduces the transactions costs of regulatory policy and increases the likelihood that a constituency will acquire the necessary information about an inefficiency to trigger a political response. Both thereby increase the demand for political action and raise the price that political actors can charge for market-enhancing regulatory policies.

The key insight on which this analysis is built is a close cousin of Adam Smith's invisible hand. Self-interested actors who view regulatory policy as a means of capturing wealth may conflict over the distribution of the rents available in a market, but they have a common interest in minimizing inefficiency. Competition among them for the favorable attention of self-interested political actors creates an incentive on behalf of the latter to find the most efficient policy response to this competition, for greater efficiency confers upon political actors a greater amount of economic wealth to allocate among political supporters.

One tough hurdle for the theory is to provide a convincing explanation of why the state is involved at all. The relevant hypothesis here is that the coercive power of the state causes transactions costs and information imperfections to be lower for government action than for private negotiations. An important feature of some alternative theories of regulation is that they take issue with this hypothesis.

Another controversial aspect of the sophisticated public interest theory is the implicit supposition that institutional arrangements in government are not an especially important object of study. They are simply selected, and evolve, to serve the end of maximizing efficiency. The maintained hypothesis is closely related to Samuelson's famous dichotomy between efficiency and equity [see Samuelson (1954, 1955)], wherein issues regarding income redistribution were to be resolved by rearranging endowments, whereas specific public policies were to be implemented so as to be economically efficient. The difficulty with this proposition is that government may not have available policy instruments that can achieve distributional objectives without causing inefficiencies. If so, public officials are likely to be forced into compromises between efficiency and distributional goals [Okun (1975)]. Much of the work on alternative theories of regulation focuses on the details of political and economic institutions and how they affect both distributional and efficiency consequences of policies.

3. How regulation can make matters worse

Numerous avenues of attack on the public interest theory can and have been traveled. Most fundamentally, many scholars in law, philosophy, political science, and psychology reject welfare economics as having interesting normative content and microeconomic theory as a relevant scientific approach to studying political behavior.[17] The scope of this chapter, however, is more narrowly concerned with the microeconomic foundations of political behavior and regulatory policy. Consequently, the focus here is on arguments fought on basically the same ground as the arguments presented in the previous section.

Because the essence of the economic theory of policymaking (including regulation) is tied up in the concepts of transactions costs and information imperfections as they apply to political phenomena, it is natural to exposit this theory in the framework of the principal–agent problem. Regulatory policy is promulgated through a complex set of agency relationships, each of which typically involves multiple principals and multiple agents. First, elected political officials act as agents for their constituents. The re-election process and the career path through the hierarchy of political offices provide the means by which citizens enforce compliance by an elected official with their policy preferences. Citizens, in turn, vote for or otherwise support numerous elected officials. Second, regulatory agencies act as agents for elected political officials in both the legislative and executive branches of government. In this relationship, legislation, executive orders, appointments of agency leaders, the budgetory process, and direct intervention in decisions all are available to elected officials as means for enforcing

[17]For a comprehensive statement of these objections, see Rhoads (1985); for a specific discussion of the relevance of microeconomic theory in the setting of safety regulation, see Slovic, Fischhoff and Lichtenstein (1985). Both contain numerous additional references.

compliance with their policy preferences. Third, within legislative bodies, internal delegation of responsibility takes place. Legislatures normally delegate day-to-day policy oversight, annual budget review, and responsibility for initiating legislation to committees.[18] Because members of a committee are largely self-selected, they tend to be atypically intense in their interests in the program, often because of close connections to organized groups which are especially affected by a committee's policy decisions [Shepsle (1979)].

The result of this institutional structure is a very complex set of agency relationships that mediate the relationship between the policy preferences of citizens and the policy outcomes of agencies. At each stage, the degree to which agents comply with the preferences of principals depends on several important factors: (1) the extent to which principals and agents have conflicts of interest; (2) the costs and accuracy of methods for principals to monitor the performance of agents; and (3) the power of the principals' enforcement mechanisms for redirecting the incentives of the agent. To the extent that monitoring and enforcement are imperfect, agents can carry out policies that do not reflect the interests of their principals. To the extent that the costs and benefits of monitoring and enforcement differ systematically among principals, policy outcomes will not only be bent toward the preferences of agents, but will be biased in favor of some principals at the expense of others. In order to understand how both sources of policy drift can occur requires some further development of the theory of these various agency relationships. The rest of this section focuses on relationships between citizens and elected officials, and specifically on the role of interest groups. The next section focuses on relationships among government officials, and especially on the role of administrative law in the political control of regulatory agencies.

The central problem of a citizen in dealing with government is powerlessness. A single vote is inconsequential, and does not permit revelation of the intensity of preferences. Moreover, candidates embody a complex array of policy preferences and personal attributes which cannot be unpacked. Voters cannot selectively express preferences on each issue, but must send a simple signal of acceptance or rejection of an entire platform. The implication is that voters face relatively high costs but low expected benefits from engaging in sophisticated evaluations of political candidates [Downs (1957)]. Hence, voters are likely to be poorly informed, and their evaluations are likely to be based on a few especially important issues on which they have become at least partly informed through other aspects of their daily lives, such as their experiences in factor and product

[18] In parliamentary systems, these responsibilities are usually given to ministers and sub-ministerial members of parliament who also have executive responsibilities, so that the second and third agency relationships are combined: however, this is not a necessary feature of parliamentary systems. New Zealand, for example, has a parliamentary system that also has a committee structure which is similar to that of the U.S. Congress.

markets or as consumers of the mass media [Campbell, Converse, Miller and Stokes (1960), Key (1966), Fiorina (1987)].

A second aspect of the political system is the difficulty of assigning responsibility for the performance of the public sector [Fiorina (1981)]. Elected officials, the courts, and the bureaucracy all play a role in shaping policy, and even within a controlling party the assignment of individual responsibility for a change in policy is problematic.

The appeal of organized interest groups in democratic political systems is that they simultaneously attack the problems of powerlessness and informational imperfections [Olson (1965), Moe (1980)]. Citizens of like mind can pay to create an organization that will monitor political activities, inform members about a politician's performance in office, and influence policy by virtue of its status as a representative of a significant number of voters. The last can occur through directly influencing the voting behavior of group members, or by providing resources (contributions, volunteers) to favored politicians. Thus, all else equal, organized citizens are more likely to be influential in controlling the decisions of political actors than are unorganized ones.

Most Western democracies rely upon decentralized parties or even decentralized legislatures to protect against the obvious potential abuse of organized interests.[19] Decentralization allows a large number of different interests to be represented in policy decisions, thereby protecting against oligarchical control [Madison (1961)]. But even this is an imperfect protection, for a number of additional factors affect which types of interests are likely to be organized at all, regardless of the structure of governmental institutions.

Interest group organizations constitute an important part of the transactions costs of government actions, and these transactions costs depend on the nature of the interest group.[20] First, because effective organization requires coordination and communication among group members, transactions costs are larger for larger groups, although there are likely to be economies of scale for very small groups owing to the fixed cost of acquiring and preparing relevant information. Second, the degree of homogeneity of the preferences of the group affects its ability to reach a stable consensus. In general, groups are more likely to be successful politically if they have a relatively narrow political focus on an issue about which there is little disagreement among their members. Thus, groups of people with the same or very similar source of income (a labor organization, a trade association) can easily find common ground on improving their collective bargaining power, whereas groups organized around consumption activities face

[19] Usually, decentralization is achieved by constructing numerous legislative districts, each of which contains a very small proportion of the population. Typically the basis of legislative decentralization is geographic, but sometimes it is ethnic or cultural.

[20] For a more complete development the points in this and the next paragraph, see Moe (1980) and Noll (1983).

more serious costs of finding consensus owing to differences in tastes. Third, groups organized for other purposes, having already paid the fixed costs of formation, have an advantage over interests that would have to become organized to take effective political action. This is especially important if the political activities of a group are susceptible to the "free rider" problem. If an organization achieves a desired political outcome, but cannot limit the beneficiaries to its membership, it will have a more difficult time organizing in the first place than a group which is already organized for the purpose of providing private or team goods to its members. This favors groups organized around production (unions, trade associations) and social organizations (churches) in relation to interests with nothing in common other than a similar policy objective.

The implications of these and other similar arguments about organized political participation are as follows. First, not all policy positions face the same transactions costs for effective political participation. They will differ according to the difficulty they face in organizing, and the degree to which the organization can obtain financial backing at or near its members' willingness to pay for effective policy representation. In general, large, heterogeneous groups with relatively small per capita stakes and which are otherwise unlikely to organize will be disadvantaged relative to small, homogeneous groups with high per capita stakes that are already organized. Second, because political organizations themselves are a means for reducing the informational imperfections in political processes, unorganized groups will be further disadvantaged. They are less likely to detect a policy change that harms them and to assign responsibility accurately when it is detected.

In the context of the public interest theory, the key implication is that the trigger threshold of costs that can be imposed on any group differs systematically according to how effectively it is organized. Unions, trade associations, religious organizations, and large businesses are likely to be systematically favored. So, too, when relevant, are other political entities, e.g. city governments when dealing with a national government.

In the domain of regulatory policy, the way in which policy departs from an efficient outcome is complex, and dependent on the specific circumstances of the industry and market failure in question. Generally, represented groups should favor actions that maximize the rents available for distribution among them [Becker (1985)]. If all interests affected by a regulatory decision were represented with roughly equal effectiveness, circumstances would favor a relatively efficient outcome [Becker (1983)]. If not, circumstances favor a policy which creates monopoly rents, but then dissipates them among the represented interests [Posner (1971)] approximately in proportion to their stakes (net of organization costs) in the regulatory policy [Peltzman (1976)]. The resulting policy will be efficient only if an efficient arrangement is available which maximizes the joint rents of the represented interests.

In the extreme, where only a single interest is effectively organized, the result is Stigler's simple "capture" – the one organized group will tend to be a monopoly or cartel that is protected by regulators. It will adopt efficient monopoly pricing – e.g. perfect discrimination, optimal two-part tariffs, Ramsey rules – only if the costs of enforcing them, such as by preventing arbitrage, are sufficiently low. The more normal circumstance is that several groups are represented, including some suppliers and some customers as well as multiple firms in an industry.[21] Regulation then becomes a forum among them for creating and dividing rents. Indeed, the groups that are represented initially may even endogenize the extent to which others are represented by deciding whether to threaten sufficiently costly actions against a given interest that it triggers their participation. The cost of bringing in another interest is the share of rents that a newly represented group will be able to acquire; the potential benefit is that the new group may open new opportunities for extracting more rents. The logic behind such an action is essentially the same as the logic of certain types of mergers, such as vertical integration by an upstream monopolist to cause more efficient as well as joint profit-enhancing operations by downstream firms [Warren–Boulton (1974) and Perry (1978)]. Thus, to Williamson's (1975) "markets and hierarchies", we can add regulatory processes as an alternative institutional arrangement among firms for maximizing joint profits.

Regulated businesses and their employees are likely participants in the formation and execution of regulatory policy, and especially in decisions that directly and immediately affect them. All else equal, this implies an outcome that first creates monopoly rents, and then engages in rent-sharing between management and labor of the benefits thereby attained. Although this is most easily detected in economic regulation, where a disorganized group may face monopoly prices, similar outcomes can also arise in environmental, health, and safety regulation, in which standards can be written so as to reduce competition. One prediction from this analysis is that a relaxation of regulation, should it occur, ought to cause some combination of lower wages and harder financial times for regulated (or formerly regulated) firms. Regulated firms are likely to face higher than competitive costs because of rent-sharing with input suppliers, and may have specialized investments to supply some customers at a subsidy.

A second prediction is that all forms of regulation are likely to retard entry by new firms either directly by franchising [Stigler (1971)] or indirectly by imposing higher costs on potential entrants. Entrants are likely to be less effectively represented in the political process. The employees and customers of a potential entrant are unlikely to know in advance who they are, and to be organized to offset the influence of groups associated with established firms who stand to lose

[21] See Wilson (1980) and Noll and Owen (1983) for several case examples of how different patterns of representation arose to influence several areas of regulatory policy.

if entry is permitted. As a result, they are vulnerable to being disadvantaged by onerous entry requirements, such as more rigorous standards to comply with environmental, health, and safety regulations [Ackerman and Hassler (1981)]. Note that if regulation divides rents among the existing represented groups, the dissipation of those rents through competition is likely to be opposed by literally all those represented. Even represented customer groups can be brought into the fold of opposing entry if the existing regulatory arrangement cuts them into the rent-sharing. In economic regulation, this is done by cross-subsidizing them [Posner (1971)], and in social regulation by providing special, targeted benefits, such as environmental regulations that differentially protect a particular industry or geographic area [Crandall (1983), Pashighian (1985)].

The last observation leads to a third prediction, which is the systematic nature of departures from an efficient regulatory policy: regulation will depart from efficiency only when it is necessary to create and divide rents among represented interests [Becker (1985)]. In economic regulation, represented interests favor efficient pricing as long as it can be implemented in ways favorable to them. Thus, multipart tariffs, for example, are attractive as long as they do not interfere with rent-sharing and the maximal extraction of rent from unrepresented constituencies. Moreover, to the extent efficient pricing is adopted, it will be based on "cost" calculations that contain the rents accruing to labor and management through gold-plating, excessive capitalization, and above-market wages. (Note that the mechanics of how labor or management would be favored relate to the stringency of cost review, not manipulation of the price structure.)

Other than triggering more representation through attempts to extract too much rent, the departure of regulation from efficiency is constrained by two other phenomena. First, political entrepreneurs (rather than those harmed by a policy) can effectively pay the organization costs of an unrepresented group [Wilson (1980)], as argued in the public interest theory. Second, technological change and rising incomes can cause previously unrepresented interests eventually to have sufficient stakes in a particular domain of regulation to become represented in it. Eventually, this can make the problem of creating rents and allocating them among the interests so difficult that the represented groups themselves become divided about the desirability of regulation, thereby causing it to be radically restructured or to collapse [Weingast (1981)].

The role of political entrepreneurs is limited by the context in which they must find political support. Unrepresented interests, as argued above, are likely to have relatively low individual stakes in any given regulatory issue, and to differ in the details of how regulation affects them. The former makes it difficult for political actors to interest constituents who are harmed by a regulatory policy in focusing on that policy rather than one which is more directly important to them. The latter makes it difficult to identify a concrete policy action on which a significant amount of political support can be based, even if the first hurdle is overcome.

Thus, the most likely form of political entrepreneurship in regulatory policy is to try to obtain a cut in the regulatory rents for a specific interest that is in any case on the threshold of representation. This may or may not make regulation more efficient, depending on the circumstances. Special provisions, such as a targeted price cut or a partial exemption from a costly requirement, reduce the net rent extracted from the favored group, but may be more distortionary from the perspective of efficiency.

In the long run, a series of such acts of political entrepreneurship systematically reduces the value of regulation to its beneficiaries, while raising its costs as more groups participate and so decisions become more complex. Hence, it can lead to the internal destruction of the process as described above. In addition, as regulation becomes more complex with more groups receiving favors, the opportunity arises for reform at the higher level of the overall business policy of the government. In a sense, each regulatory policy suffers from a form of common property resource problem. Within the narrow confines of a given policy, extracting rents from unrepresented groups may not trigger an adverse political reaction. But eventually, as the summation of further attempts to cut more groups into any given process grows, the gross effect of all regulatory policies can itself become an issue, perhaps expressed in ideological terms [Derthick and Quirk (1985)]. Externally imposed general reform (rather than internal to the specific regulatory policy) arises owing to the cumulative impact of two phenomena: generally excluded groups who bear the costs of regulation are triggered to take effective political action not by any specific policy, but by their cumulative effects, and some represented groups perceive that their share of the rents from regulation have dwindled sufficiently that their net returns from the system as a whole are negative.

The last political factor that can influence regulatory policy is the arrangements by which organized interests or unorganized constituencies can influence political outcomes. The mechanics of representation presume that blocks of voters, either organized around interests or available for political entrepreneurs, can credibly threaten an adverse electoral outcome if they are not dealt with by policymakers. This means not only that they have the franchise, but that they could alter the probability that a political party or candidate for office will retain or acquire power. If parties/candidates are motivated by the desire to win elections, they will consider entreaties only from groups that potentially could be part of a winning political coalition. In nearly every democratic society, electoral institutions fall short of granting all interests this form of effective political power. Groups that do not vote or that have preferences far from the political mainstream have no prospect for influencing policies through the electoral process, even if they are organized and informed. Moreover, because different parties/candidates have different support coalitions, at any given time the distribution of rents through regulatory policies will depend in part on who is in power as well as how well the various interests are organized. In general, coalitions for dividing rents are unstable, although risk-averse legislators may devise practices within the legislature (so-called "norms") that stabilize these divisions so that they will not be dramatically affected by changes in the distribution of power within the legislature [Weingast (1979)].

Tests of interest-group theories

A large and growing literature attempts to test interest-group theories of regulatory policy. Initially, tests of interest-group influence on regulatory policy simply made inferences from the observable effects of regulation on prices, costs, and income distribution. Recently, more direct tests use statistical models of the voting behavior of members of the U.S. Congress on regulatory policy measures.

The first generation of sophisticated studies of the effects of regulation focused primarily on economic regulation, especially in the transportation sector. The latter was a ripe target because not only had it appeared to be at least somewhat competitive before regulation, but also it remained structurally (if not behaviorally) competitive after regulation. Economic theory led scholars to be skeptical that in such circumstances regulation could provide economic benefits. Indeed, the early studies found regulation to be inefficient, to protect the interests of regulated firms, and to use the price system to engage in tax-subsidy schemes among customer groups.[22] Because this conflicted with the traditional historical account, which accorded with the standard "market failure" interpretation of regulatory origins, it gave rise to a series of revisionist historical studies of the oldest national regulatory institution, the Interstate Commerce Commission (ICC).

The standard account of the formation of the ICC was that railroads, while competing for shipments between major transportation hubs, exercised monopoly power for shipments to and from the small towns along each route. The ICC was said to be formed to eliminate monopoly pricing in the "short-haul" routes from small towns to the nearest hub. In the 1950s, students of the ICC concluded that its actual post-war behavior reflected its "capture" by regulated interests who had succeeded in deflecting the agency from its original purpose [Bernstein (1955)]. Typically, observers blamed this capture on the political unimportance and invisibility of regulatory agencies, the failure of politicians to engage in active oversight and to give them sufficient resources, and the flawed, overly broad character of their legislative mandate.[23] Beginning with Kolko (1965) and MacAvoy (1965), revisionist historical studies examined the early effects of ICC regulation, and concluded that the ICC, rather than being captured long after its

[22] Meyer, Peck, Stanason and Zwick (1959), Caves (1962), Harbeson (1969), MacAvoy and Sloss (1967), Friedlaender (1969).

[23] See, for example, Cary (1967) and Friendly (1962). For a summary of these arguments, see Noll (1971, ch. 3).

origins, was in fact created to facilitate the operation of only a partially successful railroad cartel.[24] Rather than eliminate monopoly pricing on short-haul routes, the ICC was seen as helping railroads make their cartel more effective on long-haul routes.

While the origins of other regulatory policies have not been as exhaustively studied, the extensive literature on the current effects of regulation contains numerous studies which reach the same general conclusions as the research on transportation regulation.[25] The importance of this literature with respect to the study of the politics of regulation is that it documents the claim that regulatory policy has a widespread tendency to protect certain well-organized economic interests, most commonly the industries that are regulated. But this literature cannot be regarded as a valid test of the political theory of regulation outlined here. The reason is that these studies were not based on a comprehensive political theory of why government would decide to deliver benefits to regulated firms (and *not* to unregulated firms). Indeed, this literature was not intended to test a political theory, but to disprove the traditional, benign view of regulation as a cure for market failure. Nevertheless, the first generation of these studies was the antecedent of the political theory of regulation. Stigler's (1971) influential study, containing as examples truck regulation and occupational licensing, used the general idea of organized interests to produce an explanation of why regulation worked to cartelize regulated industries.

While the findings of the studies of the economic effects of regulation are consistent with interest-group theories, their scope is too narrow to constitute a test of them. The reason is that they do not link the effects of regulation to the causal variables that are the focus of the political theories – the elements of transactions costs and information imperfections that would permit an inefficient political equilibrium that delivered distributive benefits in ways that are predicted by the nature and sources of these factors. More recent studies have attempted to test these theories by explicitly measuring the sources of interest-group influence on votes on regulatory legislation in the U.S. Congress. Because the U.S. legislature is decentralized and has relatively weak parties, members exercise considerable independence in casting floor votes on legislation. The question addressed in this literature is whether these votes can be explained in part by measures of the interests of a legislator's constituency.

Numerous difficulties plague such a statistical analysis. A major problem is to measure a legislator's relevant constituency. Legislative districts are heterogenous, and legislators represent only some of their constituents [Fenno (1978)]. Relatively little is known about the relationship between interest-group participa-

[24]See Also Spann and Erickson (1970), Ulen (1982), Zerbe (1980), and Porter (1983).

[25]See, for example, the case studies in Capron (1971), Phillips (1975), and Weiss and Klass (1981, 1986), and the references therein.

tion and voting behavior in legislative elections. Hence, the statistical studies normally rely upon relatively broad socioeconomic measures of the entire constituency, not the relevant support constituency, which normally would be only somewhat more than half of the whole. Usually the composition of the support coalition can be indirectly measured by such things as the legislator's party membership or ratings by political organizations. Ratings are provided by two general types of organizations: "issue" groups (like environmentalists or labor organizations) and "ideological" groups that attempt to measure the degree of conservatism or liberalism of a representative by considering a broad range of legislative issues. In fact, the line is very blurry between the types: both form part of the support coalition of elected officials, and there is a high statistical correlation among the ratings of all groups. This makes it very difficult to separate interest-group influence from general ideological tendencies.

A final serious problem with this literature is that it normally cannot distinguish between two quite different bases for political action by an interest group: the desire to cure a market failure that falls especially heavily on members of the group, and the desire to redistribute rents in their favor. Are environmental groups, for example, motivated more by the desire to make polluting industries more efficient, or to finance their atypically strong tastes for environmental cleanliness by a tax on firms and their customers?

Numerous studies do find some important relationships between the characteristics of constituencies and the policies advocated by their representatives. Members of Congress from districts with high union membership are more likely to support increases in the minimum wage,[26] an especially interesting finding because of its relatively pure distributional character. Members representing districts with a relatively large number of people who belong to environmental organizations were more likely to support various environmental programs.[27] Coal mining areas in the eastern United States and industrial areas that used their coal or the electricity generated from it were more likely to support legislation that imposed high environmental costs on western coal, even though the latter is less harmful to the environment.[28] The latter is more convincing than the former, of course, because it more clearly separates the "interest-group" and

[26]Silberman and Durden (1976); however, Kau and Rubin (1978) found the unionization variable to have the right sign but to be insignificant when average hourly earnings were also included in the model.

[27]Kalt and Zupan (1984), Pashigian (1985). The former argue that their results, which accord most of the explanatory power of the estimation to scores by ideological groups, indicate "shirking" by legislators who, they argue, should be adhering more closely to interests of the home constituency. The implied hypothesis is that constitutents do not also have ideologies which legislators try to represent. Another interpretation of these results is that liberal (conservative) legislators represent the 60 percent or so most liberal (conservative) constituents, not the entire constituency [Fenno (1978)], so that the results cannot be clearly distinguished from faithful representation based on issues.

[28]Crandall (1983), Pashigian (1985); a similar observation, without statistical analysis, was also made by Ackerman and Hassler (1981).

"public-interest" theories. Another study found that legislators representing districts containing pulp or paper mills were more likely to vote against water pollution abatement bills.[29] Again, the study does not deal directly with whether the costs at stake to the industry were excessive or an efficient correction of a market failure.

Several studies have attempted to disentangle the distributive aspects of energy regulation during the 1970s,[30] and in general they find that the state of energy supply and demand in an area – whether it is a net importer or exporter of energy resources, and what resources, if any, it holds – affects votes on energy regulation bills. Another study finds that the pattern of support for the various forms of the original Act to Regulate Commerce (which introduced the regulation of the railroads) depended on the economic structure of legislative districts.[31] In these cases as well, efficiency gains and expropriation of rent are not comprehensively measured, so the role of market failures, and the trade-off between efficiency and distributive politics, cannot be treated in a definitive fashion.

Some studies have attempted to use differences in economic structure (and therefore, interest-group influence) among states to explain interstate differences in regulation. Consumer and business characteristics are found to be related to the nature and extent of consumer protection regulation,[32] and the extent of competition and demand for power is related to the date at which states adopted regulation of electric utilities.[33] Once again, the models do not measure the extent to which these tendencies were driven by efficiency or redistribution, or, in the latter case, underlying cost differences.

The impression left by all of this literature is that interests directly affected by a proposed regulatory policy do influence floor votes in the legislature, but that these variables contribute less to explaining voting behavior than do party and ideological scores. In essence, these studies confirm the coalitional basis of government, and the role of organized interests in shaping government policy. But without explicit measures of the magnitude and nature of the net stakes of groups at risk in the vote, they cannot distinguish among alternative theories that are based on interest-group analysis. An idealistic pluralist, believing that majority rule always converges to efficient policy outcomes in the end as long as a substantial number of conflicting interests are represented, would not find this pattern of results to be uncongenial.

[29] Leone and Jackson (1981).

[30] Bernstein and Horn (1981), Kalt (1981, 1982), Riddlesperger and King (1982), and Wayman and Kutler (1985). In most cases the effects of energy interests were detected, but were weaker than party and ideology.

[31] Gilligan, Marshall and Weingast (1987).

[32] Oster (1980).

[33] Jarrell (1978).

The key empirical question is whether the distribution of rents in the regulatory process accords with the principles of interest-group theory, and in particular whether regulation seeks to maximize the rents available for distribution to the represented groups. Thus, empirical studies of the effects of regulation – inefficiencies and obvious redistributional practices – play a central role in testing political theories of regulatory policy.

In a remarkably rich and detailed study of water pollution regulation by the Environmental Protection Agency (EPA), Magat, Krupnick and Harrington (1986) examined industry-specific standards for total suspended solids and biological oxygen demand to detect the extent to which efficiency and distributional objectives were traded off by the agency. One of their key findings is that the EPA systematically departs from maximizing efficiency of water-pollution control in order to distribute abatement costs more equally across industries and firms. They also find that weaker standards are applied to industries that have higher profits and better-financed trade associations. In a manner equaled by no previous work, these authors document the importance of all three conflicting forces in regulatory decisions: efficiency, equity in the form of equalizing costs, and a bias in favor of industries that have the greatest financial resources behind their representation in the process.

One clearly distinctive difference between public interest and interest-group theories is that the former requires efficient pricing and use of labor, whereas the latter predicts that labor, as an organized group, will benefit from regulation. The few studies that exist indicate that the latter is correct.[34] Anecdotally, U.S. deregulation in transportation, communications, and financial markets has been disruptive of labor markets, leading simultaneously to greater employment and lower wages in some cases (most notably airlines), but in every case at least to lower wages. Another study finds that the stringency of regulations for total suspended solids was weaker in industries where regulation caused unemployment, but no similar effect was detected for standards regarding biological oxygen demand [Magat, Krupnick and Harrington (1986)].

Another prediction of interest-group theories is that large businesses should benefit at the expense of small businesses unless the latter are organized into an effective trade association that is active in regulatory policy. Again, both statistical and anecdotal information confirm this prediction in environmental, health, and safety regulation.[35] The key point, of course, is not just that small business

[34]Rose (1985), Bailey (1986).

[35]Cornell, Noll and Weingast (1976), Linneman (1980), Bartel and Thomas (1985), Maloney and McCormick (1982), Neuman and Nelson (1982), Pashigian (1984); Magat, Krupnick and Harrington (1986), however, did not find a bias against small firms in EPA's water pollution control program, although they found that industries with well-financed trade associations did have less costly standards.

faces higher costs of compliance per unit output; the important issue is whether these costs are warranted on the basis of differences in the degree to which small or large firms create market failures requiring regulatory intervention. While not all of these studies address this question, some do, and the consensus is that the cost differences are unwarranted by performance differences.

Entry controls provide another basis for testing the implications of political theory. Established interests generally will prefer to retard entry by new firms. Of course, entry is a phenomenon that takes place in markets; hence, theory predicts that when entry does occur, it will be from established firms. Moreover, the allocation of entry rights will be based in part on political considerations – a politically determined division of the rents – as well as economic efficiency. If firm structure affects efficiency, the result will be a compromise of efficiency to maintain relative stakes in the regulatory process.

An illustration of this hypothesis is the route structure and number of firms in transportation before and after deregulation.[36] Airline deregulation has caused almost a complete restructuring of the U.S. airline industry. The old "local service" or regional carriers have been virtually eliminated through merger or expansion. A "hub and spoke" route structure has replaced the criss-cross pattern under regulation. A similar reorganization has taken place in trucking. In both cases, the change has been accompanied by reductions in costs as well as wages of employees in the industry.

Broadcasting regulation provides another example of inefficient allocation. The allocation of spectrum rights and power limitations in radio and, especially, television regulation were based on the "local service doctrine": maximize the number of communities with broadcasting outlets, rather than the number of outlets received by a consumer. The result was a relatively small number of stations in nearly all cities. In television, these few outlets became immensely profitable because of protections against entry in the face of rapidly growing demand. The result was far less competition and fewer national networks than were economically feasible, coupled with almost exclusive reliance on national sources of programs by the "local" outlets.[37] Only with the entry of cable television in areas with poor reception was the opportunity created for expanded competition, and here technology managed to create a new organized interest that, after a decade of legal and political battles, finally was cut in on the distribution of regulatory rents in the 1970s.

While much of regulation seems superficially, at least, to reflect the fundamental properties of interest-group politics, there are some anomalous puzzles. State regulation of local public utilities – electricity, gas, telephones – has not been as extensively studied as federal regulation, but on the surface raises some serious

[36] Eads (1972), Bailey, Graham and Kaplan (1985).
[37] Noll, Peck and McGowan (1973), Park (1975).

questions about regulatory politics. In general, residential customers are charged less for service than are businesses, although one would expect the opposite. Consider the case of telephones.[38] The monthly telephone bill is a tiny fraction of household costs, and consumers are unlikely to become organized to cast votes on the basis of telephone rates. Yet residential rates are half or less of business rates. Moreover, residential demand is almost perfectly inelastic, so the difference is unlikely to reflect rational price discrimination by the regulated firm. Indeed, in recent years, local telephone companies have tried in vain to convince regulators to permit significant increases in residential prices. The interpretation of this phenomenon is still a matter of controversy. Perhaps residences are receiving service roughly at cost, and regulation is serving the public interest. Perhaps residences are being subsidized by business. Or, perhaps telephone pricing is a mechanism for providing subsidies generally to rural areas, where telephone costs are especially high, and reflects the historical success of rural organizations at attaining all forms of governmental benefits. As a scientific matter, the details of the cost and subsidy flows in local telephone service are only beginning to emerge, and the nature of regulatory politics at the state level is now only a matter of crude speculation.

Another troubling issue is whether regulation is necessarily the most effective means for achieving a given political objective. Perhaps the clearest example here is in environmental regulation, where a substantial literature has developed in support of the superior efficiency of marketable emissions permits compared to source-specific regulatory standards. If emissions permits are distributed on the basis of present emissions under existing standards, the efficiency gains of marketable permits will accrue to polluters. However, implementing change redistributes wealth in another way that may be harmful to polluters by reallocating the risks of changes in regulatory policy and of the consequences of energy shortages.[39] Moreover, polluters may be wary of the durability of emissions permits, fearing that efficiency gains may be expropriated by regulators through tougher standards. Environmentalists have mixed views; some worry that tradable permits represent backsliding from environmental goals, although this has not been the experience to date with the minor degree of tradability that has been permitted.[40] Nevertheless, none of these objections seems insurmountable, raising the question why regulators, environmentalists, and polluting firms have not successfully negotiated a way to implement a clearly superior method of environmental regulation.

Another potentially interesting improvement in methods is the possibility of using bidding processes to award utility franchises and set prices. Demsetz (1968)

[38] Noll (1986).
[39] Hahn and Noll (1983).
[40] Liroff (1986).

introduced the concept by proposing that utilities be granted franchises on the basis of competitive bidding over prices and service quality. The more recent literature on cost-revelation processes, surveyed by Baron in Chapter 24 of this Handbook, attempts to construct regulatory decision rules about prices, output, and whether a utility will keep its franchise which yield efficient operation at least in the second-best sense. Others have argued that contracting problems are too difficult to expect such processes to substitute for regulation.[41] One key issue is whether political agents can credibly commit to durable, long-term arrangements with utilities which, even if optimal ex ante, could produce supracompetitive profits ex post. Such an outcome would leave the architects of a bidding or cost-revelation mechanism vulnerable to attack by political entrepreneurs seeking elective office. But even if this problem could be solved, interest-group theory suggests that such mechanisms are extremely unlikely to be politically acceptable because they reduce to formula the politically relevant act of creating and distributing rents. Only upon the collapse of an economic regulatory process when too many interests are being cut in, combined with natural monopoly, would the political process be likely to consider such a mechanism. These circumstances have taken place in railroads, and may be under way in electricity and local telephone networks. An interesting issue is whether this type of method is therefore on the verge of serious consideration in these areas.

Recent deregulation in the United States represents another challenge to the interest-group theory, and indeed its occurrence gave rise to a rebirth of the more sophisticated version of the public interest theory in the late 1970s. One recent account proposes that deregulation came about because of the intellectual force of economists' arguments against it.[42] Yet, in each case technology seems to have created severe problems for retaining regulation in its old form, and a plausible argument can be made that technology created new organized interests, which in turn either divided the old interests or created impossible management problems for regulators.[43] Moreover, during the 1970s some political leaders did manage to make overall regulatory policy an issue in the general political debate. Regulatory horror stories were part of campaigns against intrusive government waged first by Jimmy Carter and then by Ronald Reagan. Thus, Derthick and Quirk, in illustrating the connection between economic studies showing inefficiencies of regulation and regulatory reform, may have been observing only a manifestation of a more fundamental political phenomenon.

Taken together, the empirical studies surveyed here are broadly consistent with, but do not really prove, the political theory of regulation set forth at the outset of this section. Organized interests not only seem to succeed, but usually

[41] Williamson (1976), Goldberg (1976), Zupan (1986).
[42] Derthick and Quirk (1985), who are political scientists, not economists.
[43] See the case studies in Noll and Owen (1983).

they do so at the cost of economic efficiency, at least as far as the data can tell us. Yet the evidence is still far from fully conclusive. One major weakness is that, except for simple cases involving one or two interest groups, the relationship between the stakes of groups and their political strengths remains a mystery, largely because in nearly all studies neither stakes nor gains in regulation are directly measured. The second weakness is the lurking danger of tautology, i.e. of attributing causality to an inevitable consequence of any public policy action. It is impossible to imagine that regulation could be imposed without redistributing income. Hence, a look for winners in the process – and organizations that represent them – is virtually certain to succeed. Until fundamental measurement problems about stakes, power, and gains are overcome, analysts will not be able fully to predict and to explain the details of regulatory policy. Only when they do can it reasonably be argued that interest group theories of regulation have been fully tested.

4. The politician's agency problem

For several decades, a recurring theme in the literature on regulation – especially as written by legal scholars and the popular press – has been the difficulties faced by political leaders in controlling the behavior of regulatory agencies. The essence of the argument is as follows. Regulatory agencies (and other bureaus) possess superior information about the effects of their policies [Wildavsky (1964), Schultze (1968)], and can change policies in subtle ways without political overseers being fully cognizant until the deed is done. Monitoring the behavior of an agency is costly, as is subsequent legislative or executive action to undo an agency's misdeed, the latter because the policy surprise tends to create a new constituency to defend its continuation [Noll and Owen (1983)]. Hence, agencies have an opportunity to engage in "shirking" – consciously failing to pursue the policy objectives that elected political leaders would desire.

The ways in which agencies could engage in shirking are several. First, to comport with the normal definition of the term, agencies may simply under-supply policymaking effort, thereby failing to carry out with precision the policy objectives of political overseers [Niskanen (1971)]. The motive for such behavior would be the desire to avoid investigative work or intense conflict with the parties that appear before it. As to the latter, an agency can avoid the effort of subsequent appeals to its decisions by placating the parties who participate in the agency's decisions, even if pleasing them is contrary to the intent of the agency's legislative mandate [Noll (1971)].

Second, agency officials may have their own political agenda. The legislative mandate of an agency normally represents a compromise among a broad coalition of interests within a party or a legislature. The personal political preferences of the handful of leaders of an agency may differ from the consensus of the coalition. The result is a form of capture, in that agency decisions systematically favor one of the several interests whose welfare is at stake in the agency's decisions.

Third, agency personnel may be motivated by personal career objectives. One form that careerism might take, emphasized by much of the scholarly literature on bureaucracy [e.g. Wildavsky (1964), Niskanen (1971)], is to promote the growth and power of the agency as an end itself, perhaps by attempting to extend the agency's jurisdiction into activities not fully contemplated in its legislative mandate, but not ruled out, either. Another form of excessive careerism is to use regulatory processes as vehicles to demonstrate managerial talent as well as a particular policy slant in order to curry favor with prospective future employers. Once again, the consequence, should this be significant, is interpreted as capture by a subset of the interests whose welfare is at stake in agency decisions.[44]

Fourth, agencies may be populated by professionals that genuinely attempt to pursue public interest objectives, but who have a narrow or uninformed perception of where that interest lies. One potential problem is an overemphasis of a particular bias in the methods of a professional group, such as the emphasis of economists on theoretical efficiency, lawyers on procedural equity, or medical care professionals on risks to health [see Perrow (1961)]. Another problem is that analysts may be forced to rely on selective information that is controlled by interest groups, and face selective likelihood of appeal and reversal through the courts owing to the unequal participation of interest groups in their decision process. In either case, decisions, on balance, can reflect capture by the interests represented before them [Noll (1985)].

While these arguments give plausible reasons why an agency might be prone to stray from the positions most desired by their political overseers, the question remains whether and to what extent these forms of shirking occur in reality. Theoretically, there are several reasons to believe that agencies do not stray far from the range of policies acceptable to the supporting political coalition of the statutory policy.

First, the purpose of enacting a regulatory statue containing elaborate fact-finding procedures for solving market failures may well be to remove hard decisions from the direct control of political officials [Fiorina (1985)]. Faced by divided represented interests and irresolvable conflict, politicians may decide to

[44]A detailed analysis of the representativeness of high-level regulatory officials, containing a mix of arguments and evidence about (a) the narrow perspective of regulators and (b) their careerism, can be found in the studies published by the Senate Government Operations Committee in connection with their investigation into regulatory reform during the late 1970s. See also Gormley (1979) and Eckert (1972).

"shift the responsibility" to bureaucratic officials for the purpose of attenuating specific political accountability for the results. Hence, the coalition enacting a statue may have no clear policy preference, other than that the issue be resolved in an adversarial, evidentiary process that is constructed to reach some sort of compromise. The only way in which an agency can shirk such a mandate is not to provide the forum for resolving the issue.

Second, the details of the procedures established by political officials for making regulatory decisions govern who will be represented in the process. To the extent that participation matters in terms of outcomes, the ability to shape it confers a means of political control – albeit indirect – on the decisions of the agency. In fact, by assuring participation by the members of the enacting political coalition, legislators "mirror" the politics of enactment in the procedures of the agency [McCubbins, Noll and Weingast (1987)]. This gives agencies an early signal concerning the political environment facing their elected overseers. Moreover, it creates the opportunity for "fire alarm" oversight of the agency [McCubbins and Schwartz (1984)], whereby disaffected participants in the process warn political overseers of impending decisions that are inconsistent with the coalition agreement. This enables political overseers to intervene informally in agency policymaking before decisions are rendered, new interests and wealth positions are established, and hence the costs of reversal are increased by an unsatisfactory fait accompli by the agency.

Third, the extent of information dependence and professional bias in an agency is also to some degree under the control of political overseers. The magnitude of the agency's budget in relationship to the scope and complexity of its responsibilities affects the extent to which the agency can assure itself of multiple and independent sources of information [Noll (1983)], and the professional composition of an agency can be controlled by legislation, executive order, or the appointments to leadership positions.

To illustrate some mechanics of procedural details as means of political control, consider the following examples. In 1970, the U.S. Congress enacted the National Environmental Protection Act, which required that all agencies formally consider the environmental consequences of their decisions, and, if those consequences were potentially significant, undertake an environmental impact statement as part of their decision criteria. NEPA did not require that these considerations actually change outcomes, but it profoundly changed agency decisions nonetheless [Taylor (1984)]. First, it gave standing to people representing environmental interests, and thereby caused agencies to confront the facts and arguments raised by these groups. Second, it caused agencies to acquire staff to review environmental arguments and perform EIS studies. Third, it forced agencies to consider EIS information in reaching decisions, and to state reasons for overriding environmental issues, or face a significant chance that the courts would overturn their decisions. The result was a profound change in a variety of agencies that had previously ignored environmental concerns.[45]

The importance of staffing is illustrated by the history of safety and health regulation in the 1970s. The legislation establishing the new safety and health agencies oriented them to be sensitive to well-represented interests, and to pay little attention to economic efficiency [Cornell, Noll and Weingast (1976)]. For example, the Occupational Safety and Health Act virtually forced the agency it created, OSHA, to adopt voluntary industry safety standards as mandatory regulations, to delegate priority setting to labor and industry organizations, and to ignore benefit–cost analysis. The Consumer Product Safety Commission was given essentially no staff, and was required to use "offerors" – largely unpaid volunteers, usually trade associations – to write its standards. By the mid-1970s, however, economic analysis began to be forced upon these processes by the creation of the Council on Wage and Price Stability through a series of Executive Orders. COWPS was created to be a group of independent economist-gadflies, one of whose major tasks was to participate in the regulatory processes of the environmental, health and safety agencies. [For some examples of economic interventions from the Executive Office of the President, see Miller and Yandle (1979) and White (1981).]

Another example is the choice between case-by-case decisions and broad rulemaking as the primary means of making economically relevant decisions. Specific cases – the price of a shipment of a specific commodity between two cities, the award of a franchise to serve a specific market, an emissions control standard for a particular plant – generally are of great interest to the regulated firm whose business is at stake. But most case decisions will have very little effect on overall policy. Hence, relatively little attention will be paid to the case by anyone other than the firms with a direct interest, such as customer groups, labor unions, environmentalists, etc. General rules, such as a formula for setting all prices in an industry, an emissions standard to apply to all sources of a given pollutant, or a set of criteria to be followed in future cases, have much greater policy significance, and hence will draw more attention from a wide spectrum of interests. The expected consequence is that processes based on case-by-case decisions are most likely to favor regulated firms, whereas regulatory processes that emphasize rulemaking are more likely to reach some sort of policy balance. Because the extent to which an agency relies on such procedures can be controlled by statute, political leaders thereby can control the particular distributive orientation of the policy.

Empirical studies of regulatory processes bear out the general argument that political actors have influence on agency decisions. For example, the National

[45]See Cohen (1979) regarding the regulation of nuclear power and Taylor (1984) with respect to federal construction projects.

Labor Relations Board (which regulates labor–management disputes in the United States) has been shown to vary the degree of pro-business or pro-labor slant in its decisions according to the preferences of congressional oversight committees[46] and the orientation of the President [Scher (1960) and Moe (1985)]. Weingast and Moran (1983) have shown that shifts in the composition of legislative oversight committees are reflected in the decisions of the Federal Trade Commission, the agency charged with protecting against product misinformation, consumer fraud, and, in part, antitrust policy. Weingast (1984) has found similar results for the Securities and Exchange Commission.

Moe (1985) also shows that staff recommendations have considerable weight, implying that the magnitude of the agency's budget (and hence the size of its staff) is another potential control variable [see also Weingast (1981)]. Magat, Krupnick and Harrington (1986) find that the quality of background studies and the continuity of staff affect the stringency of water pollution regulations.

State regulatory proceedings provide another source of evidence. Generally, state regulation of utilities takes the form of broad reviews of all aspects of a given utility's operations, from cost estimation through review of the prudency of its expenditures to setting overall revenue requirements and their distribution among all services and customer classes. This maximizes the saliency of rate hearings, and hence participation in them as well as their political and public visibility. And, the behavior of the commissions appears to be to seek compromise and consensus among the represented parties [Joskow (1972, 1974)].

As in the previous section, these studies do not prove that political control of regulatory decisions through manipulation of process is a perfect solution to the agency problem faced by political actors. Instead, they are broadly consistent with the view that (a) decisions are responsive to changes in underlying political circumstances, even in the absence of explicit directives from political overseers, and (b) process matters in determining the policy orientation of an agency. The primary lesson from this literature is that the absence of direct political oversight – with public hearings, explicit directions through legislation or executive order, and occasionally punishment of agency miscreants – does not imply a lack of political control and an opportunity for runaway bureaucracy.

5. Conclusions

The literature on the politics of regulation provides few concrete, quantitative predictions about how regulatory policy will affect efficiency and the distribution

[46]Concern about the preference of committees, rather than Congress as a whole, follows from the tendency of Congress to delegate much of its policy responsibilities to committees. This gives committees considerable autonomy in directing agencies. For a thorough treatment of the relationship between Congress and its committees, see Weingast and Marshall (1986).

of rents. The theory is ahead of the empirical work, containing a number of interesting predictions about which interests will be represented, to what extent the intensities of their stakes will be translated into effective political participation, and the relative allocation of rents by the regulatory process. None of these qualitative predictions about relative shares has been convincingly demonstrated empirically, but the empirical literature is broadly consistent with the view that representation matters, and that regulation may or may not be more efficient than its absence, depending on the political and economic circumstances.

Nevertheless, the field is in its infancy. Serious attempts to deal with the political control of regulatory policy date only from approximately 1970. Moreover, the underlying more general theory of the political process – the way voters, politicians, and bureaucrats interact to formulate policy – is progressing very rapidly, constantly raising new questions in its application to regulatory policy.

The future research agenda certainly contains two obvious priorities. One is more theoretical insight about the role of citizens acting as heterogeneous, numerous, but marginally interested consumers, and how political entrepreneurs mobilize their support for regulatory reform, or even for day-to-day management of a regulatory institution in a manner that protects their perceived interests (e.g local telephone rates). The other is empirical: How can more meaty tests of interest-group theories be devised? In part, the solution is hard work – real effort, as exhibited in a handful of the best studies, to measure the stakes of groups, their effectiveness of organization and participation, and their relevance to the support constituencies of elected officials. A similar observation is apt for studies of the way elected political officials influence agency decisions, directly or by controlling the information available to agencies and the participants in their decision processes. Again, detailed studies that trace the influence of political leaders on the development of policies in an agency are necessary to resolve the question of the relative importance of political factors (interest groups, political entrepreneurs) and bureaucratic discretion in determining regulatory outcomes.

References

Ackerman, B.A, and Hassler, W.T. (1981) *Clean air/dirty coal*. New Haven: Yale University Press.

Akerloff, G.A. (1974) 'The market for "lemons": Quality uncertainty and the market mechanism', *Quarterly Journal of Economics*, 84:488–500.

Arrow, K.J. (1963) 'Uncertainty and the welfare economics of medical care", *American Economic Review*, 53:941–973.

Bailey, E.E. (1986) 'Deregulation: Causes and consequences", *Science*, 234:1211–1216.

Bailey, E.E., Graham, D.R. and Kaplan, D.P. (1985) *Deregulating the airlines*. Cambridge: MIT Press.

Bartel, A.P. and Thomas, L.G. (1985) 'Direct and indirect effects of regulation: A new look at OSHA's impact', *Journal of Law and Economics*, 28:1–25.

Baumol, W.J. (1977) 'On the proper cost test for natural monopoly in a multiproduct industry', *American Economic Review*, 67:809–822.

Becker, G.S. (1983) 'A theory of competition among pressure groups for political influence', *Quarterly Journal of Economics*, 98:371–400.

Becker, G.S. (1985) 'Public policies, pressure groups, and dead weight costs', *Journal of Public Economics*, 28:329–347.

Bernstein, M.S. (1955) *Regulating business by independent commission*. Princeton: Princeton University Press.

Bernstein, R.A. and Horn, S.R. (1981) 'Explaining house voting on energy policy: Ideology and the conditional effects of party and district economic interests', *Western Political Quarterly*, 34:235–245.

Breyer, S.G. (1981) *Regulation and its reform*. Cambridge: Harvard University Press.

Buchanan, J.G. and Tullock, G. (1962) *The calculus of consent*. Ann Arbor: University of Michigan Press.

Campbell, A., Converse, P.E., Miller, W.E. and Stokes, D.E. (1960) *The American Voter*. New York: Wiley.

Capron, William M., ed. (1971) *Technological change in regulated industries*. Washington, D.C.: Brookings Institution.

Cary, W.E. (1967) *Politics and the regulatory agencies*. New York: McGraw-Hill.

Caves, R.E. (1962) *Air transport and its regulators*. Cambridge: Harvard University Press.

Chipman, J.S., and Moore, J.C. (1973) 'Aggregate demand, real national income, and the compensation principle', *International Economic Review*, 14:153–181.

Coase, R.H. (1960) 'The problem of social cost', *Journal of Law and Economics*, 3:1–44.

Cohen, L.R. (1979) 'Innovation and atomic energy: Nuclear power regulation, 1966–present', *Journal of Law and Contemporary Problems*, 43:67–97.

Cornell, N.W., Noll, R.G. and Weingast, B.R. (1976) 'Safety regulation', in: H. Owen and C.L. Schultze, eds., *Setting national priorities: The next ten years*. Washington, D.C.: Brookings Institution.

Crandall, R.W. (1983) *Controlling industrial pollution: The economics and politics of clean air*. Washington, D.C.: Brookings Institution.

Dales, J.H. (1968) *Pollution, property and prices*. Toronto: Toronto University Press.

Demsetz, H. (1968) 'Why regulate utilities?', *Journal of Law and Economics*, 11:55–65.

Derthick, M. and Quirk, P.J. (1985) *The politics of deregulation*. Washington, D.C.: Brookings Institution.

Downs, A. (1957) *An economic theory of democracy*. New York: Harper and Row.

Eads, G.C. (1978) *The local service airline experiment*. Washington, D.C.: Brookings Institution.

Eckert, R.D. (1972) 'Spectrum allocation and regulatory incentives', in: *Conference on communications policy research: Papers and proceedings*. Washington: Office of Telecommunications Policy.

Fenno, R.F. (1978) *Home style*. Boston: Little, Brown.

Fiorina, M.P. (1981) *Retrospective voting in American national elections*. New Haven: Yale University Press.

Fiorina, M.P. (1985) 'Group concentration and the delegation of legislative authority', in: R.G. Noll, ed., *Regulatory policy and the social sciences*. Berkeley: University of California Press.

Fiorina, M.P. (1987) 'Information and rationality in elections', in: J.A. Ferejohn and J. Kuklinski, eds., *Information and democratic processes*. Champaign: University of Illinois Press.

Fisher, A.C. and Peterson, F.M. (1976) 'The environment in economics: A survey', *Journal of Economic Literature*, 14:1–33.

Friedlaender, A.F. (1969) *The dilemma of freight transport regulation*. Washington, D.C.: Brookings Institution.

Friendly, H.J. (1962) *The federal administrative agencies: The need for better definition of standards*. Cambridge: Harvard University Press.

Gilligan, T.W., Marshall, W.J. and Weingast, B.R. (1987) 'The economic incidence of the interstate commerce act of 1887', social science working paper no. 629, California Institute of Technology.

Goldberg, V.P. (1976) 'Regulation and administered contracts', *Bell Journal of Economics*, 7:426–448.

Gormley, Jr., W.T. (1979) 'A test of the revolving door hypothesis at the FCC', *American Journal of Political Science*, 23:665–683.

Harbeson, R.W. (1969) 'Toward better resource allocation in transportation', *Journal of Law and Economics*, 12:231–338.

Hahn, R.W. and Noll, R.G. (1983) 'Barriers to implementing tradable air pollution permits: Problems of regulatory interactions', *Yale Journal on Regulation*, 1:63–91.
Jarrell, G.A. (1978) 'The demand for state regulation of the electric utility industry', *Journal of Law and Economics*, 21:269–295.
Joskow, P.L. (1972) 'The determination of the allowed rate of return in a formal regulatory hearing', *Bell Journal of Economics and Management Science*, 3:632–644.
Joskow, P.L. (1974) 'Inflation and environmental concern: Structural change in the process of public utility price regulation', *Journal of Law and Economics*, 17:291–327.
Kalt, J.P. (1981) *The economics and politics of oil price regulation*. Cambridge: MIT Press.
Kalt, J.P. (1982) 'Oil and ideology in the United States Senate', *Energy Journal*, 3:141–166.
Kalt, J.P. and Zupan, M.A. (1984) 'Capture and ideology in the economic theory of politics', *American Economic Review*, 74:279–300.
Kau, J.B. and Rubin, P.H. (1978) 'Voting on minimum wages: A time-series analysis', *Journal of Political Economy*, 86:337–342.
Key, Jr., V.O. (1966) *The responsible electorate*. Cambridge: Harvard University Press.
Kolko, G. (1965) *Railroads and regulation, 1877–1916*. New York: Norton.
Leone, R.A. and Jackson, J.E. (1981) 'The political economy of federal regulatory activity: The case of water-pollution controls', in: G. Fromm, ed., *Studies in public regulation*. Cambridge: MIT Press.
Levine, M.E. (1981) 'Revisionism revisited? Airline deregulation and the public interest', *Journal of Law and Contemporary Problems*, 44:179–195.
Linneman, P. (1980) 'The effects of consumer safety standards: The 1973 mattress flammability standard', *Journal of Law and Economics*, 23:461–479.
Liroff, R.A. (1986) *Reforming air pollution regulation: The toil and trouble of EPA's bubble*. Washington: The Conservation Foundation.
MacAvoy, P.W. (1965) *The economic effects of regulation: The trunkline railroad cartels and the ICC before 1900*. Cambridge: MIT Press.
MacAvoy, P.W. and Sloss, J. (1967) *Regulation of transport innovation*. New York: Random House.
Madison, J. (1961) 'The federalist no. 10', in: *The federalist papers*. New York: Mentor.
Magat, W.A., Krupnick, A.J. and Harrington, W. (1986) *Rules in the making*. Washington, D.C.: Resources for the Future.
Maloney, M.T. and McCormick, R.E. (1982) 'A positive theory of environmental quality regulation', *Journal of Law and Economics*, 25:99–123.
Mashaw, J.L. (1985) *Due process in the administrative state*. New Haven: Yale University Press.
McCubbins, M.D. (1985) 'The legislative design of regulatory structure', *American Journal of Political Science*, 29:721–748.
McCubbins, M.D. and Schwartz, T. (1984) 'Congressional oversight overlooked: Police patrols vs. fire alarms', *American Journal of Political Science*, 28:165–179.
McCubbins, M.D., Noll, R.G. and Weingast, B.R. (1987) 'Administrative procedures as instruments of political control', *Journal of Law, Economics and Organization*, 3:243–277.
Meyer, J.R., Peck, M.J., Stenason, J. and Zwick, G. (1959) *The economics of competition in the transportation industries*. Cambridge: Harvard University Press.
Michelman, F.I. (1967) 'Property, utility and fairness: Comments on the ethical foundations of 'just compensation' laws', *Harvard Law Review*, 80:1165–1258.
Milgrom, P.R. and Roberts, D.J. (1986) 'Price and advertising signals of product quality', *Journal of Political Economy*, 94:796–821.
Miller, III, J.C. and Yandle, B., eds. (1979) *Benefit–cost analyses of social regulation*. Washington: American Enterprise Institute.
Moe, T. (1980) *The organization of interest*. Chicago: University of Chicago Press.
Moe, T. (1985) 'Control and feedback in economic regulation: The case of the NLRB', *American Political Science Review*, 79:1094–1117.
Moore, T.G. (1978) 'The beneficiaries of trucking regulation', *Journal of Law Economics*, 21:327–343.
Neumann, G.R. and Nelson, J.P. (1982) 'Safety regulation and firm size: Effects of the coal mine health and safety act of 1969', *Journal of Law and Economics*, 25:183–199.
Niskanen, W. (1971) *Bureaucracy and representative government*. Chicago: Aldine–Atherton.
Noll, R.G. (1971) *Reforming regulation*. Washington, D.C.: Brookings Institution.

Noll, R.G. (1983) 'The political foundations of regulatory policy', *Zeitschrift für die gesamte Staatswissenschaft*, 139:377–404.

Noll, R.G. (1985) 'Government regulatory behavior: A multidisciplinary survey and synthesis', in: R.G. Noll, ed., *Regulatory policy and the social sciences*. Berkeley: University of California Press.

Noll, R.G. (1986) 'State regulatory responses to competition and divestiture in the telecommunications industry', in: R.E. Grieson, ed., *Antitrust and regulation*. Lexington: Lexington.

Noll, R.G. and Owen, B.M. (1983) *The political economy of deregulation*. Washington: American Enterprise Institute.

Noll, R.G., Peck, M.J. and McGowan, J.J. (1973) *Economic aspects of television regulation*. Washington, D.C.: Brookings Institution.

Oi, W.Y. (1973) 'The economics of product safety', *Bell Journal of Economics*, 4:3–28.

Okun, A.M. (1975) *Equality and efficiency: The big trade-off*. Washington, D.C.: Brookings Institution.

Olsen, E.O. (1972) 'An economic analysis of rent control', *Journal of Political Economy*, 80:1081–1100.

Olson, M. (1965) *The logic of collective action*. Cambridge: Harvard University Press.

Oster, S.M. (1980) 'An analysis of some causes of interstate differences in consumer regulations', *Economic Inquiry*, 18:39–54.

Park, R.E. (1975) 'New television networks', *Bell Journal of Economics*, 6:607–620.

Park, R.E. (1980) 'New television networks: An update', in: Network Inquiry Special Staff, *New television networks: Entry, jurisdiction, ownership and regulation*. Washington, D.C.: Federal Communications Commission.

Pashighian, B.P. (1984) 'The effects of environmental regulation on optimal plant size and factor shares', *Journal of Law and Economics*, 27:1–28.

Pashighian, B.P. (1985) 'Environmental regulation: Whose self-interests are being protected?', *Economic Inquiry*, 23:551–584.

Peltzman, S. (1976) 'Toward a more general theory of regulation', *Journal of Law and Economics*, 19:211–240.

Perrow, C. (1961) 'The analysis of goals in complex organizations', *American Sociological Review*, 26:854–866.

Perry, M.K. (1978) 'Vertical integration: The monopsony case', *American Economic Review*, 66:267–277.

Phillips, A.E., ed. (1975) *Promoting competition in regulated industries*. Washington, D.C.: Brookings Institution.

Pigou, A.C. (1920) *The economics of welfare*. London: MacMillan.

Porter, R.H. (1983) 'A study of cartel stability: The joint executive committee, 1880–86', *Bell Journal of Economics*, 14:301–314.

Posner, R.A. (1971) 'Taxation by regulation', *Bell Journal of Economics*, 2:22–50.

Posner, R.A. (1975) 'The social cost of monopoly and regulation', *Journal of Political Economy*, 83:807–827.

Rhoads, S.E. (1985) *The economist's view of the world: Government, markets, and public policy*. Cambridge: Cambridge University Press.

Riddlesperger, Jr., J.W. and King, J.D. (1982) 'Energy votes in the U.S. Senate', *Journal of Politics*, 44:838–847.

Rogerson, W.P. (1982) 'The social costs of monopoly and regulation', *Bell Journal of Economics*, 13:391–401.

Rose, N.L. (1985) 'The incidence of regulatory rents in the motor carrier industry', *Rand Journal of Economics*, 16:299–318.

Samuelson, P.A. (1954) 'The pure theory of public expenditure', *Review of Economics and Statistics*, 36:387–389.

Samuelson, P.A. (1955) 'Diagrammatic exposition of a theory of public expenditure', *Review of Economics and Statistics*, 37:350–356.

Sanders, M.E. (1981) *The regulation of natural gas: Policy and politics*. Philadelphia: Temple University Press.

Scher, S. (1960) 'Congressional committee members as independent agency overseers: A case study', *American Political Science Review*, 54:911–920.

Schultze, C.L. (1968) *The politics and economics of public spending*. Washington, D.C.: Brookings Institution.
Schwartz, A. and Wilde, L.L. (1985) 'Product quality and imperfect information', *Review of Economic Studies*, 52:251–262.
Scudder, T. and Colson, E. (1982) 'From welfare to development: A conceptual framework for the analysis of dislocated people', in: A. Hansen and A. Oliver-Smith, eds., *Involuntary migration and resettlement: The problems and responses of dislocated people*. Boulder: Westview Press.
Shapiro, C. (1983) 'Premiums for high quality products as returns to reputation', *Quarterly Journal of Economics*, 98:659–680.
Shepsle, K.A. (1979) 'Institutional arrangements and equilibrium in multidimensional voting models', *American Journal of Political Science*, 23:27–59.
Shepsle, K.A. and Weingast, B.R. (1981) 'Structure induced equilibrium and legislative choice', *Public Choice*, 37:503–520.
Silberman, J.I. and Durden, G.C. (1976) 'Determining legislative preferences on the minimum wage: An economic approach', *Journal of Political Economy*, 84:317–329.
Slovic, P., Fischhoff, B. and Lichtenstein, S. (1985) 'Regulation of risk: A psychological perspective', in R.G. Noll, ed., *Regulatory policy and the social sciences*. Berkeley: University of California Press.
Spann, R. and Erickson, E.W. (1970) 'The economics of railroading: The beginning of cartelization and regulation', *Bell Journal of Economics*, 1:227–244.
Spence, A.M. (1977) 'Consumer misperceptions, product failure, and producer liability', *Review of Economic Studies*, 44:561–572.
Spitzer, M.L. (1987) *Seven dirty words and six other stories*. New Haven: Yale University Press.
Stewart, R.B. (1975) 'The reformation of administrative law', *Harvard Law Review*, 88:1669–1813.
Stigler, G.J. (1971) 'The theory of economic regulation', *Bell Journal of Economic and Management Science*, 2:3–21.
Taylor, S. (1984) *Making bureaucracies think: The environmental impact statement strategy of administrative reform*. Palo Alto: Stanford University Press.
Telser, L.G. (1972) *Competition, collusion and game theory*. Chicago: Aldine–Atherton.
Ulen, T. (1982) 'Railroad cartels before 1887: The effectiveness of private enforcement of collusion', *Research in Economic History*, 8:125–144.
Warren-Boulton, F.R. (1974) 'Vertical control with variable proportions', *Journal of Political Economy*, 82:783–802.
Wayman, F.W. and Kutler, E. (1985) 'The changing politics of oil and gas deregulation: Ideology, campaign contributions, and economic interests, 1973–82', presented at Annual Meetings of the American Political Science Association.
Weingast, B.R. (1979) 'A rationale choice perspective on congressional norms', *American Journal of Political Science*, 24:245–263.
Weingast, B.R. (1980) 'Congress, regulation, and the decline of nuclear power', *Public Policy*, 28:231–255.
Weingast, B.R. (1981) 'Regulation, reregulation and deregulation: The foundations of agency–clientele relationships', *Law and Contemporary Problems*, 44:147–177.
Weingast, B.R. (1984) 'The congressional-bureaucratic system: A principal–agent perspective', *Public Choice*, 44:147–192.
Weingast, B.R. and Marshall, W.J. (1986) 'The industrial organization of Congress (or why legislatures, like firms, are not organized as markets)', working paper in political science P-86-10, Hoover Institution.
Weingast, B.R. and Moran, M. (1983) 'Bureaucratic discretion or congressional control: Regulatory policymaking by the Federal Trade Commission', *Journal of Political Economy*, 91:765–800.
Weiss, L.W. and Klass, M.W. eds. (1981) *Case studies in regulation*. Boston: Little, Brown.
Weiss, L.W. and Klass, M.W. eds. (1986) *Regulatory reform: What actually happened*. Boston: Little, Brown.
Weiss, L.W. and Strickland, A.D. (1982) *Regulation: A case approach*. New York: McGraw-Hill.
White, L.J. (1981) *Reforming regulation: Processes and problems*. Englewood Cliffs, N.J.: Prentice-Hall.
Wildavsky, A. (1964) *The politics of the budgetary process*. Boston: Little, Brown.

Williamson, O.E. (1975) *Markets and hierarchies*. New York: Free Press.
Williamson, O.E. (1976) 'Franchise bidding for natural monopoly – in general and with respect to CATV', *Bell Journal of Economics*, 7:73–104.
Wilson, J.Q., ed. (1980) *The politics of regulation*. New York: Basic Books.
Zerbe, R.O. (1980) 'The costs and benefits of early railroad regulation', *Bell Journal of Economics*, 11:343–350.
Zupan, Mark A. (1986) 'Franchising and bidding competition: How well do they promote efficiency in cable tv markets?', working paper, USC Department of Finance and Business Economics.

Chapter 23

OPTIMAL POLICIES FOR NATURAL MONOPOLIES

RONALD R. BRAEUTIGAM*

Northwestern University

Contents

*The author would like to express appreciation to the two editors of this Handbook, and to John Panzar and Tai-Yeong Chung for a number of helpful comments and suggestions.

Handbook of Industrial Organization, Volume II, Edited by R. Schmalensee and R.D. Willig

1. Introduction

Over the past decade there has been substantial reform in many industries historically operating under heavy governmental control, both in the United States and abroad. In the United States, where such governmental control typically takes the form of regulation of privately owned enterprises when policy-makers believe that competition will not work well to allocate resources, remarkable changes have occurred in all or parts of the airline, railroad, motor carrier, telephone, cable television, natural gas and oil industries, among others.[1] Many other countries, including those in which such governmental intervention takes the form of nationalization, have recently been reconsidering the role of such governmental intervention as well.[2]

In many cases the basis for regulation has itself been at issue in the policy debates surrounding regulatory reform, often leading to a removal of or a reduction in the extent of governmental control of traditionally regulated industries. In other cases reform has had some effect even when the hand of regulation has not been retracted. For firms such as local electric and gas utilities, local telephone operating companies, and oil and gas pipelines (to name just a few), heavy regulation persists. Still, regulatory reform in these industries has led to a reassessment of the kinds of controls that might be utilized under regulation.

The primary purpose of this chapter is to examine some of the optimal policies that might be used to control a "natural monopoly". At the outset we must define just what a natural monopoly is from an economic perspective, and why it poses a problem that might warrant government intervention. Section 2 begins by examining these issues from a traditional perspective, which argues for regulation when there are pervasive economies of scale in a market. It then offers a more contemporary characterization of natural monopoly based on the concept of subadditivity of costs rather than on economies of scale.

Section 3 re-examines the natural monopoly problem with a thoughtful eye on the question: To regulate or not to regulate? Although the traditional view suggests that government intervention and natural monopoly go hand in hand, economic analysis since the late 1960s has suggested rather forcefully that there may be ways to introduce competition for a market, even if a natural monopoly structure exists within a market. Thus, one of the themes of this chapter is that

[1] See Weiss and Klass (1986) for a discussion of the nature and effects of regulatory reform in a number of these industries.

[2] Examples include the possible "privatization" of some railroads in Japan, the debate surrounding the sale of part of the ownership of the telephone system to the private sector in Great Britain, and the liberalized rules for interconnecting privately owned equipment to the telephone network in West Germany, among many others.

regulation is only one of several possible ways of dealing with a natural monopoly. Section 3 then provides an overview of possible competitive approaches to the natural monopoly problem.

As Section 3 will make clear, there will be circumstances when competition as a policy toward natural monopoly is not feasible or, even if feasible, may lead to a market outcome which is quite inefficient. Section 4 summarizes a number of ways in which one might improve the efficiency of resource allocation with government intervention, including external subsidies to the firm, and the regulation of tariffs with price discrimination (or "differential pricing") or the introduction of nonlinear outlay schedules (nonlinear tariffs). The concepts are introduced in the context of the single product firm. The section then discusses some of the problems encountered in the case of the multiproduct firm, including the common cost problem, i.e. the problem of pricing individual services when there are costs of production that are shared in the production of more than one output, and therefore cannot clearly be attributed to individual services.

The chapter then turns to some of the major concepts in optimal (economically efficient) pricing in regulated industries. These include peak load pricing (Section 5), Ramsey pricing (Section 6), and nonlinear outlay schedules (Section 7). Finally, Section 8 addresses a set of issues related to the "fairness" of regulated prices, often discussed in the context of "cross subsidy" or "interservice subsidy". After presenting and discussing the implications of some of the possible notions of subsidy, the section concludes by relating the concepts of subsidy free and economically efficient prices.

A chapter of this kind necessarily relies on (in fact focuses on) the work of many other researchers. Any attempt to cite the literature exhaustively would be futile, and another author attempting the same task would no doubt include a set of references somewhat different from those used here. My hope is that glaring omissions have been minimized and that readers will be understanding on this point. At the same time the author would like to acknowledge two references especially useful in the preparation of this manuscript. These are Baumol, Panzar and Willig (1982) and Brown and Sibley (1986).

2. The natural monopoly problem: A "traditional" view

The central economic argument for regulation of an industry is that the industry is characterized by "natural monopoly". The concept of natural monopoly has been refined over the years, particularly during the last decade. In this section we will first discuss a rather traditional view of natural monopoly and its importance with respect to the role of regulation as it might have been presented before the 1970s. We will then summarize a more recent perspective on these same issues.

In his classic treatise Kahn (1971, p. 2) describes the concept of natural monopoly to mean "that the technology of certain industries or the character of the service is such that the customer can be served at least cost or greatest net benefit only by a single firm (in the extreme case) or by a limited number of 'chosen instruments' ".[3] In Kahn's extreme case average cost declines as output increases throughout the range of production in the market; thus a single large firm serving the entire market would have a lower average cost than any smaller rival. In that case it will not be possible to have more than one firm operating in the market if the lowest possible average cost is to be achieved.

> This view is also presented by Scherer (1980, p. 482) who writes: "The most traditional economic case for regulation assumes the existence of natural monopoly – that is – where economies of scale are so persistent that a single firm can serve the market at a lower unit cost than two or more firms. Reasonably clear examples include electric power and gas distribution, local telephone service, railroading between pairs of small to medium-sized metropolitan areas, and the long-distance transportation of petroleum and gas in pipelines."[4]

The traditional story thus hinges on the existence of *economies of scale* (or *increasing returns to scale*) in an industry.

Strictly speaking, of course, the concept of economies of scale is one based on the technology of the firm.[5] In a single product production process with constant prices for factors of production, the notion of economies of scale means that the average cost schedule for the firm declines as market output increases. This can be illustrated as in Figure 23.1. The figure represents a market being served by a single firm producing a single, nonstorable output (or service), whose level is denoted by y. The (inverse) demand schedule for this product is shown as $p(y)$, where p refers to the price of the output. The firm produces any given y at the

[3]For good references on many of the topics addressed in this chapter, see Schmalensee (1978) and Crew and Kleindorfer (1986), which deal with alternatives in controlling a natural monopoly. See also "State Regulation of Public Utilities and Marginal Cost Pricing", by L.W. Weiss, Chapter 9 in Weiss and Klass (1981, p. 263).

[4]Scherer (1980, p. 482) also points out that regulation may be implemented in industries for a variety of reasons other than the existence of natural monopoly. For example, regulation might occur even in an efficiently operating market if those who hold political power are displeased with the market outcome. It might also be imposed if well organized political interest groups are able to "manipulate political levers" to realize political or economic gains that would not be achieved in an unregulated market. Because these reasons for regulation are based on political economy rather than on "natural monopoly", they are not treated further in this article. For more on these topics, see, for example, Hughes (1977), Posner (1974), and Peltzman (1976).

[5]See J.C. Panzar's contribution in Chapter 1 of this Handbook for an extensive overview of the production and cost concepts we will be using throughout this chapter.

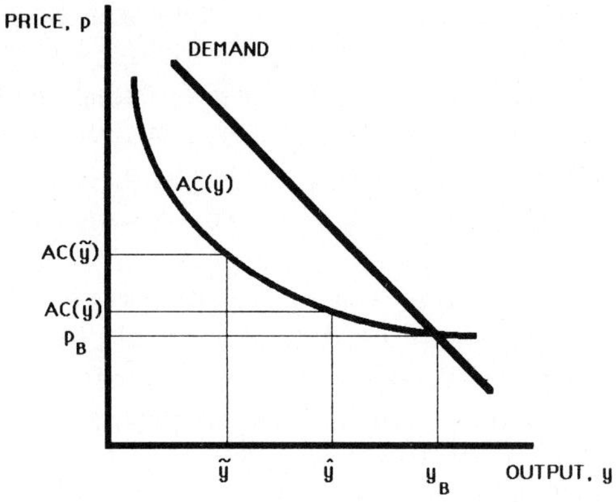

Figure 23.1. The "classic" natural monopoly problem.

minimum possible total cost, $C(y)$, and the average cost of production is denoted by the schedule $AC(y) = C(y)/y$.[6]

For the moment, assume that the firm receives no subsidy from external sources (including the government), and that it is not possible for the firm to price discriminate, so that a single, uniform price prevails in the market. The producer will need to generate total revenues that are at least as large as total costs to remain economically viable. Thus, the price charged by any firm will need to be at least as large as the average cost of production for that firm. As is clear from Figure 23.1, no firm can enter and produce $y > y_B$, since the output cannot be stored and profits would be negative for such a level of production. Furthermore, if any firm with the same technology enters the market and produces $\tilde{y} < y_B$, another firm could enter and produce $\hat{y}$, where $\tilde{y} < \hat{y} \le y_B$; this second firm could charge a price p in the range $AC(\hat{y}) \le p < AC(\tilde{y})$, and drive the first firm from the market while remaining economically viable itself. The only production level that would preclude profitable entry by another firm charging a lower price is $y = y_B$, with $p = p_B$. In the traditional view the market is said to be characterized by a natural monopoly, since competition *within* the market is not possible.

The natural monopoly problem takes on added complexity when entry and exit are not costless and a temporal dimension is added to the problem. Firms might have incentives to enter the market, charge a price in excess of average cost to earn supernormal profits, and threaten to reduce price to a very low level (even

[6]More completely, the cost function is also a function of a vector of factor prices, w, $C(y, w)$. However, factor prices will be assumed constant throughout this chapter, so references to them will be suppressed to simplify notation as much as possible.

less than average cost) in the short run if any other firm should attempt to enter. As Kahn (1971, p. 2) states: "In such circumstances, so the argument runs, unrestricted entry will be wasteful... with cycles of excessive investment followed by destructive rivalry (spurred by the wide spread between marginal and average costs)". The potential for this so-called "destructive competition" has often been cited as a basis for regulating markets served by firms with substantial scale economies.

In short, the traditional notion of natural monopoly is based on the existence of economies of scale throughout the relevant range of production on the market. Such scale economies were typically taken to mean that competition might lead to greatly inefficient and even wildly fluctuating, unstable prices, so that government intervention of some sort was necessary.

What has happened to change the traditional view about natural monopoly? First, much of the regulatory experience of the past thirty years has made it clear that in many circumstances appropriate models of regulation must focus on the multiproduct nature of regulated firms. For example, during the 1960s the Federal Communications Commission began to open up so-called private line telephone service to competition, while leaving much of the intercity long distance telephone service regulated as a monopoly. Many researchers realized that the standard single product treatment of regulation in the literature was inadequate. Relatively recent research has shown that the appropriate definition of natural monopoly is one that rests on the concept of subadditivity of costs (discussed below) rather than on the more traditional notion of economies of scale; the two are related but not identical, and the difference between the two becomes particularly important when the production process involves multiple products.

To see this, first observe that a natural monopoly need not exhibit economies of scale throughout the range of production in the market. The simple single product example provided in Figure 23.2 makes this point clearly. Assume all firms that might like to provide the service in question have identical cost structures. In the figure each firm's average cost curve declines up to the production level y^1, and then increases (so that there are decreasing returns to scale) thereafter. The market demand schedule intersects the average cost curve at the output level $y_{\mathrm{B}} > y^1$. Given the shapes of the curves in Figure 23.2, it is clear that a single supplier could serve the entire market at a lower unit cost than any industry configuration with two or more firms. In this sense the industry is therefore a natural monopoly, even though economies of scale do not exist for all levels of output up to y_{B}.

How then does subadditivity provide a better basis than economies of scale for determining when a natural monopoly exists? Consider the case in which there are n different products and k different firms. Each firm may produce any or all of the n products. Let y_r^i be the amount of output r produced by firm i $(i = 1,\ldots, k)$ and $(r = 1,\ldots, n)$. Also let the vector y^i be the vector of outputs

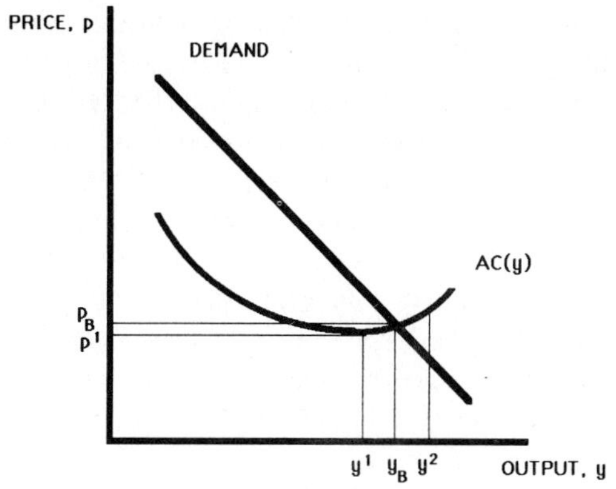

Figure 23.2. Subadditivity without global economies of scale.

$(y_1^i, y_2^i, \ldots, y_n^i)$ produced by the ith firm. Then, using the definition of Baumol, Panzar and Willig (1982, p. 17) a "cost function $C(\mathbf{y})$ is *strictly subadditive* at $\mathbf{y}$ if for any and all quantities of outputs $\mathbf{y}^1, \ldots, \mathbf{y}^k$, $\mathbf{y}^j \neq \mathbf{y}$, $j = 1, \ldots, k$, such that

$$\sum_{j=1}^{k} \mathbf{y}^j = \mathbf{y} \quad \text{we have} \quad C(\mathbf{y}) < \sum_{j=1}^{k} C(\mathbf{y}^j)." \tag{1}$$

As (1) indicates, the vector $\mathbf{y}$ represents the industry output. The basic question here is whether $\mathbf{y}$ can be produced more cheaply by one firm producing $\mathbf{y}$ all alone than it would be for a collection of two or more firms whose individual output vectors sum to the same industry output $\mathbf{y}$.

Since costs may be subadditive at some values of $\mathbf{y}$ but not at others, the next step toward defining a natural monopoly is to examine whether costs are subadditive at all of the "relevant" industry output vectors $\mathbf{y}$ that might be produced; the demand for each of the outputs will help to define this relevant range of outputs. Baumol, Panzar and Willig go on to define a natural monopoly (still on p. 17) as follows: "An industry is said to be a natural monopoly if, over the entire relevant range of outputs, the firms' cost function is subadditive".

The example of Figure 23.2 illustrates that a subadditive cost structure need not exhibit economies of scale "over the entire relevant range of outputs". The example is constructed so that the output level associated with minimum cost, y^1, is slightly less than y_B, the output level at which the demand schedule intersects the average cost schedule. The average cost schedule has the typical "U" shape, and it is subadditive for $0 < y < y^2$ although economies of scale exist only over the (smaller) range of output $0 < y < y_B$. Thus, even in the single product case subadditivity does not imply economies of scale.

In the single product case it is clear that economies of scale imply subadditivity. However, it turns out that economies of scale need not imply subadditivity in the multiproduct case; this should not be a great surprise since, "given the crucial role of various forms of cost complementarity and economies of joint production, it is to be expected that economies of scale cannot tell the whole story in the multiproduce case".[7]

A comparison of Figure 23.1 with Figure 23.2 leads to another concept (sustainability) which is useful in appreciating difficulties that might be associated with the natural monopoly problem. Let us assume entry and exit are costless, that entrants will provide exactly the same service as the incumbent, and that all firms (the incumbent and all potential entrants) operate with access to the same technology, and therefore with the same cost functions. In the first graph, which depicts the traditional view of natural monopoly, it would be possible for the firm to find a price which deters entry by any other firm seeking to take away the incumbent's market by charging a lower price than the incumbent. In particular, if the extant firm charges a price p_B, then any entrant charging a lower price will not be able to break even. In other words, if the incumbent charges p_B, it can sustain its monopoly position against entry.

However, Panzar and Willig (1977) have pointed out that it will not always be the case that a natural monopoly can sustain itself against entry. They show that, contrary to conventional wisdom, a regulated monopolist may be vulnerable to entry, even if the incumbent produces efficiently, earns only a normal return on investment, and is confronted by an entrant operating with the same technology as its own.

Figure 23.2 presents such a case. Suppose that in serving the whole market the incumbent charges p_B. Then it would be possible for an entrant to charge a lower price (say, $p = p^1$), provide y^1 units of service, and avoid a deficit. This is a case in which the market is unstable, and in which the natural monopoly is "unsustainable". If the whole market is to be served, it would therefore require two or more firms (since the entrant will produce only y^1 in the example). Furthermore, since the cost structure is subadditive in Figure 23.2, entry would be socially inefficient; yet, such entry is a real possibility, even though entrants might provide no new services and operate with no better productive technique.

Panzar and Willig have defined the concept of sustainability in a framework allowing for multiple products. Briefly, suppose that the monopolist produces n different products in a product set N, and allow S to be any subset of that

[7]See Baumol, Panzar and Willig (1982, pp. 173). For example, equation 7C1 on p. 172 represents a cost function that has globally increasing returns to scale, but is not subadditive everywhere. The cost function for that example is $C(y_1, y_2) = y_1^a + y_1^k y_2^k + y_2^a$, with $0 < a < 1$ and $0 < k < 1/2$. Sections 7C–7E of that book outline some proper tests of natural monopoly and sufficient conditions for subadditivity. See also J.C. Panzar's contribution in Chapter 1 of this Handbook for a more extensive discussion of several important concepts regarding market structure, including among others economies of scale and scope, the degrees of economies of scale and scope and product specific economies of scale.

product set ($S \subseteq N$). Let $\boldsymbol{p}^{\mathrm{m}}$ be a price vector charged by the monopolist over its product set N, let $\boldsymbol{p}_S^{\mathrm{e}}$ be the price vector charged by an entrant providing the product set S, and let the price vector charged by the monopolist over S and over the services not provided by the entrant $[S]$ respectively be $\boldsymbol{p}_S^{\mathrm{m}}$ and $\boldsymbol{p}_{[S]}^{\mathrm{m}}$. Finally, denote by $\boldsymbol{Q}(\boldsymbol{p}^{\mathrm{m}})$ the vector of quantities that would be demanded if only the monopolist served the market, and let $\boldsymbol{Q}^S(\boldsymbol{p}_S^{\mathrm{e}}, \boldsymbol{p}_{[S]}^{\mathrm{m}})$ be the quantities of the product set S demanded when the entrant appears. Then the price vector $\boldsymbol{p}^{\mathrm{m}}$ is sustainable if and only if (i) the monopolist earns non-negative profits at $\boldsymbol{p}^{\mathrm{m}}$, and (ii) $\boldsymbol{p}_S^{\mathrm{e}} \cdot \boldsymbol{y}_S^{\mathrm{e}} - C(\boldsymbol{y}_S^{\mathrm{e}}) < 0$ (entrants earn negative profits) for all $S \subseteq N$, with $\boldsymbol{p}_S^{\mathrm{e}} \leq \boldsymbol{p}_S^{\mathrm{m}}$, $\boldsymbol{y}_S^{\mathrm{e}} \leq \boldsymbol{Q}^S(\boldsymbol{p}_S^{\mathrm{e}}, \boldsymbol{p}_{[S]}^{\mathrm{m}})$ and $\boldsymbol{y}_S^{\mathrm{e}} \neq \boldsymbol{Q}(\boldsymbol{p}^{\mathrm{m}})$ (which excludes the trivial possibility that the entrant will exactly duplicate the entire operation of the incumbent). Then a natural monopoly is said to be sustainable if and only if there is at least one sustainable price vector.

Panzar and Willig (1977) have set forth a number of necessary conditions under which a regulated monopoly would be sustainable in a world with frictionless entry and exit. Among these are that the natural monopoly must produce $\boldsymbol{y}^{\mathrm{m}}$, the output vector associated with $\boldsymbol{p}^{\mathrm{m}}$, at least cost, earn only a normal return on its investment, and operate with a production structure that is subadditive. One further necessary condition requires the following definition:

Definition (undominated price vector)

Let $\boldsymbol{p} = (p_1, p_2, \ldots, p_n)$ and $\hat{\boldsymbol{p}} = (\hat{p}_1, \hat{p}_2, \ldots, \hat{p}_n)$ be vectors yielding zero profits for a monopoly. The vector $\boldsymbol{p}$ is *undominated* if there exists no $\hat{\boldsymbol{p}} \neq \boldsymbol{p}$ with $\hat{p}_i \leq p_i$, $\forall i$, and $\hat{p}_i < p_i$ for at least one i.

In the single product example of Figure 23.1 there will be only one undominated vector (here a scalar), p_{B}. However, in the multiproduct case there may be an infinite number of such vectors. The two product case is illustrated in Figure 23.3. Here the vectors $\boldsymbol{p}^1$ and $\boldsymbol{p}^2$ are undominated, while $\boldsymbol{p}^3$ is dominated (by $\boldsymbol{p}^1$, for example).

The price vector $\boldsymbol{p}^{\mathrm{m}}$ must also be undominated if it is sustainable. There are other necessary conditions for sustainability regarding economic efficiency and cross subsidy, concepts that will be introduced in subsequent sections. We therefore postpone comments on these until a more appropriate time.[8]

[8]Among other conclusions of Panzar and Willig are some that we will address no further other than to mention them here. First, there is no way to transform an unsustainable monopoly into a sustainable oligopoly by some regulatory act splitting the market among a number of oligopolists. Second, strong demand substitutability among the products offered by the monopolist and product specific economies of scale make it more difficult for a monopoly to be sustainable. As a related point, although it is relatively easy to identify a number of necessary conditions for sustainability, it is also relatively difficult to find rather general sufficient conditions. Vertical integration also introduces a set of interesting problems for sustainability of a natural monopoly; for an analysis of this see Panzar (1980). For another good general reference on sustainability, see Sharkey (1981).

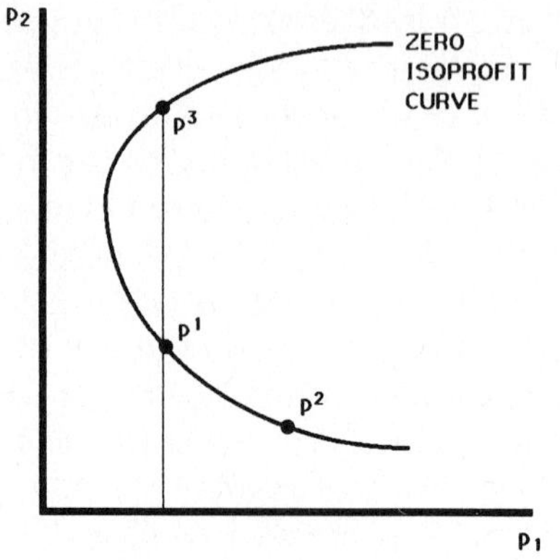

Figure 23.3. Undominated price vector.

Recent research in the characterization of natural monopoly has yielded a number of interesting results on the empirical front as well as theoretically. Much empirical work utilizing modern production and econometric theory has been directed at traditionally regulated industries in the last decade; no small part of this work casts doubt on whether some of the industries historically regulated in the United States do in fact have the structural characteristics of a natural monopoly.[9]

Finally, recent economic research has increasingly emphasized that a structure of "natural monopoly" is *not* sufficient as a basis for regulation. As the next section shows, even if an industry is characterized by natural monopoly in the sense that there is not room for competition *within* a market, under some circumstances competition *for* the market may succeed in allocating resources quite efficiently in the absence of regulation. The theoretical and empirical research on natural monopoly has contributed many economic arguments in support of deregulation and other measures of regulatory reform in a number of American industries since 1970.[10]

[9]See, for example Spady and Friedlaender (1978) and Friedlaender and Spady (1982), who reject the conclusions of earlier studies that show the motor carrier industry to have economies of scale; they show that, when empirical studies of the costs of motor carriers control for the effects of regulation, the structure of the industry is one with essentially constant returns to scale. See also Caves, Christensen and Tretheway (1983) regarding the structure of the airlines industry. For an example of an empirical test of subadditivity (as opposed to economies of scale), see Evans and Heckman (1984).

[10]For a summary of the developments in several recently deregulated industries, see Weiss and Klass (1986).

3. Why regulate?

Regulation is a political act. In any particular case there may be a host of possible political and economic answers to the question: Why regulate? Answers are offered by both positive and normative research. In this chapter we will focus on the latter. This is not to diminish the importance of the positive analyses of regulation; that is treated elsewhere in this Handbook.[11] On the contrary, from a political view, perhaps the most significant feature of regulation is that it redistributes income, creating winners and losers, thereby shaping interest groups and coalitions. Thus, it is not surprising that there is a large positive literature on regulation, both in economics and political science, addressing reasons for regulation far broader than natural monopoly. These writings deal both with the creation of regulatory agencies by Congress and with the behavior of regulatory bodies once they are in place.[12]

In focusing instead on normative issues from an economic perspective, we ask a narrower question in this section: When should a natural monopoly be regulated at all? In assessing the effects of regulation, and later in comparing various options for public utility pricing, we need to employ a clear measure of economic benefits to consumers and producers. While such measures do exist, they are often difficult to apply given the kinds of market data that are usually available. The work of Willig (1976) has suggested that the well-known measure of consumer and producer surplus is an adequate approximation in most circumstances, and that is the notion that is adopted in this chapter.[13]

[11]See the chapters of this Handbook by Noll (Chapter 22) and by Joskow and Rose (Chapter 25) for a discussion of many hypotheses about the reasons for and effects of regulation.

[12]See also Joskow and Noll (1981), and Noll and Owen (1983) for excellent discussions of the political economy of regulation. Stigler (1971) describes how regulatory bodies may redistribute income with activities that have effects as powerful as taxation itself. Posner (1974) and Stigler (1975) describe how organized interest groups may "capture" a regulatory agency, either by the initial design of the regulatory process or by other means as time passes. Peltzman (1976) casts the theory of regulation into a supply and demand framework, the supply of regulation being provided by politicians and agencies desiring to maximize vote margins, and the demand from interest groups who would benefit under various regulatory outcomes. Fiorina and Noll (1978) begin with the voters' demand for Congressional facilitation services to explain the congressional demand for administrative activity. Goldberg (1976) suggests that regulation may be viewed as a contract between a regulatory agency (acting as the agent of consumer groups) and regulated firms. Owen and Braeutigam (1978) describe strategies by which the regulatory process may be used to attenuate the rate at which changes in market and technological forces affect individual economic agents, effectively giving agents legal rights to the status quo. See also Hughes (1977) for an interesting historical perspective on the impetus for and transition of regulation from colonial times in the United States (and even earlier in England) until the present.

[13]As a technical point, the use of the usual Marshallian demand schedule observed from market data to measure consumer surplus will be an exact measure of the welfare change associated with a price change for an individual if there are zero income effects. However, Willig (1976) has shown that even if there are nonzero income effects, the measure of consumer surplus obtained from a Marshallian demand schedule may serve to approximate the actual welfare change quite closely.

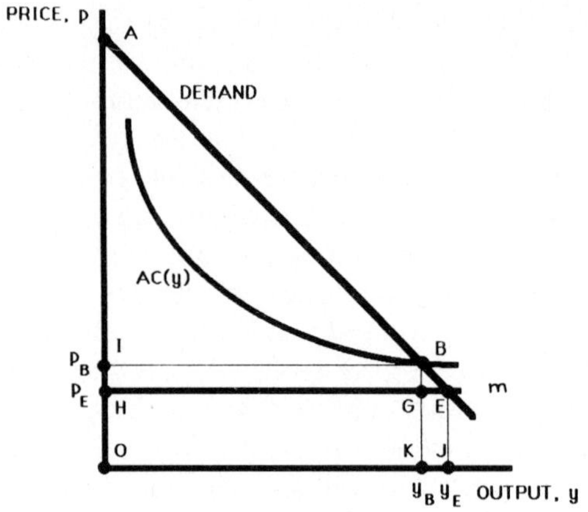

Figure 23.4. First and second best.

Consider now the case of the single product firm operating with economies of scale throughout the operating range of production as in Figure 23.4. For illustrative purposes, assume the cost structure is affine, with a positive fixed cost F and constant marginal cost m, so that $C(y) = F + my$. In this example the average cost schedule declines everywhere since marginal cost is less than average cost.

Assume that the firm must charge a uniform tariff (i.e. the same price) to all customers, and that we seek that price that maximizes net economic benefit (alternatively, to maximize economic efficiency) as measured by the standard concept of consumer plus producer surplus.[14] Standard economic principles indicate that net economic benefit will be maximized when the level of output $y = y_E$, with service provided to all customers (and *only* to those customers) who are willing to pay at least as much as the marginal cost of producing y_E.[15] In that case the total surplus is represented by the area AEH less the fixed cost F.[16] Since this is the maximum surplus that can be generated in the market, a pricing policy that leads to this allocation of resources is termed "first best".[17]

[14] There are a number of classic references dealing with the connection between economic efficiency and regulation. See, among others, Hotelling (1938), Pigou (1920), Taussig (1913), and Turvey (1969). More recent work which summarizes modern developments in the economic theory of regulation include Brown and Sibley (1986), Rees (1984), Sharkey (1982b), and Zajac (1978), all of which are excellent references in the field.

[15] See Turvey (1968, 1969) on the economics of marginal cost pricing.

[16] The fixed cost can be represented in many ways in Figure 23.4; one such measure is the area $IBGH$, so that with marginal cost pricing the total surplus is represented by the area AEH less the area $IBGH$.

[17] In the example here we have assumed that the firm must charge the same price for each unit sold in the market. It may be possible to achieve first best without incurring a deficit if the firm can charge different prices to different users (price discrimination) or if different units of output can be sold at different prices (nonlinear tariffs). Both of these alternatives will be addressed below.

However, in the example the firm will not break even with marginal cost pricing. In fact, given the affine cost function $C = F + my$, the profits of the firm are $\pi = -F < 0$. Thus, in order for the firm to remain economically viable, it will have to receive a subsidy of F.[18]

Since regulators (particularly in the United States) are not typically endowed with the powers of taxation, they may find themselves faced with a need to find a pricing policy that avoids a deficit for the firm. Without price discrimination or external subsidies to the firm, the regulator might attempt to direct the firm to set that price which maximizes net economic benefit while allowing the firm to remain viable. Since profits are negative at the first best price, there will be a net benefit loss associated with the need to satisfy a breakeven constraint for the firm (i.e. $\pi \geq 0$). Any price higher than p_B will reduce total surplus below the level attainable when $p = p_B$ (the area ABI). Thus, the breakeven-constrained optimum (which is termed "second best") occurs at the price $p = p_B$.[19] The welfare loss associated with second best (as opposed to first best) is therefore the area BGE in Figure 23.4. Such an efficiency loss is often called a "deadweight loss".

The point of this discussion is to suggest that in many circumstances it may not be possible to achieve first best without government intervention (e.g. with an external subsidy to the firm), and a program for government intervention may be quite costly. Yet, as we shall show now, it may often be possible to achieve an economic performance near second best without government intervention (even if costs are subadditive over the relevant range of outputs so that it might not be possible to have many firms competing simultaneously within a given market). *Thus, policy-makers may wish to ask whether the deadweight loss at second best is large enough to warrant intervention, especially if some form of competition can be introduced into the market that would lead to second best.*

How might there be an alternative form of competition for such a market? One answer was suggested in a classic article by Demsetz (1968). The focus of Demsetz's article is on competition *for* the market rather than *within* the market. Demsetz pointed out that much of traditional economics is directed at the notion of competition within the marketplace, which may not be possible if there are substantial economies of scale. He suggests that even if competition within the market is not possible, one might still have competition for the right to operate in the market. In other words one could envision bidding among prospective

[18]If the subsidy is provided by the government, then one must take into account not only the welfare effects in the market for y, but also the possible welfare losses in other markets that will be taxed in order to provide revenues for the external subsidy provided to keep the firm viable. If the taxes are levied in markets with totally inelastic demands, then the welfare loss from the tax will be zero and $p = m$ in the market for y will be first best. However, if welfare losses occur as a result of the taxation, then $p = m$ may not be optimal.

[19]For more on the theory of second best and optimal taxation see Atkinson and Stiglitz (1980), Diamond and Mirlees (1971), Mirlees (1976), Lipsey and Lancaster (1956–57), and Bohm (1967). Some of these articles deal rather explicitly with the distributional issues that are central to the political debate in taxation.

entrants for the franchise rights to serve the market; this form of rivalry is often called "Demsetz competition", which may be possible if two conditions are satisfied. First, inputs must be available to all bidders in open markets at competitively determined prices. Second, the cost of collusion among bidding rivals must be prohibitively high, so that competitive bidding is in fact the outcome of the bidding process.

Demsetz competition could occur in a variety of circumstances. A relatively simple environment would be the local collection of refuse. In this example companies could bid for the right to collect refuse for a specified period of time, where the "bid" would be the price that the prospective franchisee would charge customers for the collection service, and the company with the lowest bid would win the competition. In this example, the municipal authority need not own the facilities used by the refuse collection company.

A more complicated scenario might involve the right to operate a cable television franchise for a specified time period [see Williamson (1976)]. Here the government might own the facility, but auction off the right to operate the system. The government might charge a fee to the operating company to reflect the social cost of the use of the government-owned facilities.

In the single product environment with a uniform price, Demsetz competition would lead to average cost pricing, since all excess profits would be bid away. Suppose all producers have access to the same technology and could produce efficiently, and that p^* is the lowest price that would allow the firm to break even. One would expect to see bids of $p \geq p^*$, since a lower bid would leave a bidder with negative profits. If the number of bidders is large enough so that the bidding process is in fact competitive, one would expect to see a winning bid of p^*, since at that price a producer would earn only normal profits. As noted in the previous section, this is a second best (rather than a first best) outcome.

Demsetz competition is appealing because it suggests competition may be possible even where there are substantial economies of scale, and it is free of the usual regulatory apparatus and regulation-related incentives for firms to behave in an economically inefficient manner.[20] However, the approach is not entirely free of concern. To begin with, while it does lead to second best, there may still be substantial welfare losses relative to first best.

The outcome of Demsetz competition is in effect a contract between a franchisor (e.g. a governmental authority) and a franchisee. Since the franchisee might well adopt the short run strategy of providing the lowest quality service possible once it has won the right to serve, the franchisor may have to specify minimum quality standards for the service to be provided. The question arises:

[20]See, for example, Chapter 24 by David Baron in this Handbook which deals with the design of regulatory institutions and incentives under various regulatory mechanisms, and Chapter 25 (by Paul Joskow and Nancy Rose) which assesses the evidence on the effects of regulation. See also Owen and Braeutigam (1978) and Joskow and Noll (1981).

How does the government set the quality standards? How such standards are set is a problem common to Demsetz competition as well as to traditional regulation; neither approach resolves the problem of specification of quality.

The terms of the contract may be difficult to specify for other reasons. Since the contract may be in force over a period of years, it may be necessary to include procedures to allow for adjustments in terms of service, such as price and quality of service, as conditions in the market change. Some of these contingencies may be relatively easy to incorporate in a written contract, while others may be both unknown and unknowable at the time the franchise is established. The difficulty in writing a contract that includes all sets of possible contingencies is well known. In the context of Demsetz competition this means that a firm that wins the bidding today may attempt to renegotiate its contract tomorrow. The franchisor may then find itself deciding whether to attempt to force compliance, renegotiate, or initiate a new bidding process to find another franchisee. None of these alternatives will be costless.

Another potential difficulty with the use of Demsetz competition arises when the enterprise provides more than one service to its customers. As mentioned earlier, in the single product case the winner might be chosen on the basis of the tariff that franchisee would charge to customers, and that tariff would be second best. However, this selection criterion does not naturally generalize to the case of multiple products. Demsetz competition may lead to a number of different bids which are undominated; recall, for example, that $\boldsymbol{p}^1$ and $\boldsymbol{p}^2$ in Figure 23.3 both yield no excess profits and are undominated. Demsetz competition offers no obvious basis for choice among a number of undominated prices, even though some of these may be quite inefficient relative to others.

A second way in which it may be possible to introduce competition for the marketplace has been formalized with the concept of "contestability" [see Baumol, Panzar and Willig (1982), and also Panzar's Chapter 1 in this Handbook]. Although contestability and Demsetz competition are similar to one another, they are not identical. They key idea in contestability is that competition for the market can lead to second best, even if the cost structure is subadditive over the relevant range of market outputs, *as long as there are no "sunk" costs*. The assumption that there are no sunk costs is one not required by Demsetz competition, but if the additional assumption is satisfied, second best may be achieved through competition for the market *without* the need for a government supervised auction of the sort required in Demsetz competition.

To see how this works, consider first the notions of fixed cost and sunk cost. As defined by Baumol, Panzar and Willig,[21] fixed costs are those that do not vary with output *as long as output is positive*. Let $\boldsymbol{y}$ and $\boldsymbol{w}$ represent respectively

[21]Equations (2) and (3) in the text are respectively contained in Definitions 10A1 and 10A2 of Baumol, Panzar and Willig (1982, pp. 280–281).

vectors of outputs and factor prices, and let C_L be the long run cost of production in (2):

$$C_L(y, w) = \delta F(w) + V(y, w), \quad \text{with } \delta = \begin{cases} 0, & \text{if } y = 0, \\ 1, & \text{if } y > 0. \end{cases} \tag{2}$$

This definition permits fixed costs to exist even in the long run, and $F(w)$ is the magnitude of that fixed cost. Fixed costs are *not* incurred if the firm ceases production.

As the usual argument goes, the long run is long enough for all costs to be avoided if the firm ceases production. However, in the shorter run, say a production period projected s years into the future, a firm may have to make precommitments to incur some costs even if production ceases. If $C(y, w, s)$ is the short run cost function given the production horizon of s years, then $K(w, s)$ are costs sunk for at least s years, if

$$C(y, w, s) = K(w, s) + G(y, w, s), \quad \text{with } G(\mathbf{0}, w, s) = 0. \tag{3}$$

Since a sunk cost cannot be eliminated or avoided for some period of time, even if an enterprise ceases production altogether, during that period sunk costs cannot be viewed as an opportunity cost of the firm.[22]

The idea behind contestability in the single product case is as follows. If no costs are sunk, then firms operating with identical technologies and products would be free to enter the market as they please, charging whatever prices they wished. Any firm charging a price higher than average cost would find itself driven from the market by another firm charging a lower price. The consequence of competition for the market would thus be average cost pricing (and hence second best performance in the market).[23]

[22] In the long run, the usual notion that no costs are sunk means that

$$\lim_{s \to \infty} K(w, s) = 0.$$

[23] In recent years an extended discussion has developed about the meaning of contestability and the extent to which it may be appropriate to employ this concept in connection with real world markets. For example, the theory of contestability (using the notion of sustainability) focuses on prices as decision variables and models potential entrants as evaluating the profitability of entry at the incumbent's pre-entry prices. Some authors have suggested that more complicated forms of the game between entrants and incumbents might be appropriate. Alternative models might include more complicated dynamic aspects of the interactions among potential entrants and the incumbent and the use of quantities as well as prices as decision variables. A detailed discussion of this literature is well beyond the scope of this chapter. For interesting formulations of the rivalry between an incumbent and a potential entrant, see Brock (1983) for suggestions of alternative possible strategies, Dixit (1982) for a treatment of the dynamics of rivalry, Knieps and Vogelsang (1982) for an interpretation of a sustainable industry configuration as a Bertrand equilibrium, and Brock and Scheinkman (1983) for an extension of the traditional Sylos postulate to a multiproduct setting. See also Baumol (1982), Weitzman (1983), Shephard (1984), Schwartz and Reynolds (1984), and Baumol, Panzar and Willig (1984) for further discussions of strategic behavior and the role of fixed and sunk costs as barriers to entry.

Why is a lack of sunk costs critical if competition for the market is to lead to second best? If a firm incurs sunk costs, then $K(w, s) > 0$ in (3). In order for the firm to be willing to enter the market, it must charge a price that generates revenues that cover the variable costs $G(y, w, s)$ as well as the sunk costs. If the firm were assured of the right to operate in the market for s years (a time period long enough to allow it to recover its sunk costs), then it could charge a price equal to average cost $(C(y, w, s)/y)$, and second best could be achieved. But under contestability the firm is not granted a franchise as it would be under Demsetz competition. The firm does not know how long it will be in the market until another firm comes along and tries to undercut its own price, and it therefore would have to charge a price higher than $C(y, w, s)/y$ to protect against the possibility that entry may occur before s years have passed. Consequently, second best pricing will not be achieved under contestability if there are sunk costs.

Furthermore, the sunk costs of the incumbent would be a bygone in the event of entry by a new firm. A prospective entrant would have to contend with rivalry from a firm (the incumbent) with relatively low opportunity costs. Knowing this, an entrant might not sink its own costs in response to relatively high prices charged by an incumbent.

One might expect industries with large capital requirements, especially where the capital cannot easily be moved from one location or one use to another, to have substantial sunk costs. For example, in the railroad industry there are substantial costs associated with way and structure, including the roadbed, which might typically be regarded as sunk. The same might be said for much of the pipeline industry. Industries such as these are therefore not likely to be contestable, although one could still conceivably introduce competition for the market through some other means, such as Demsetz competition.

On the other hand, industries in which capital is highly mobile may be contestable. An example is the airlines industry. Here research has suggested that there may be "economies of density," which means that average costs will decline as more traffic is passed through a given airline network [see Caves, Christensen and Tretheway (1983)]. On the surface, this suggests that it may be efficient for only one firm (or a few firms) to operate *within* some city-pair markets. However, this is not sufficient to conclude that prices and entry in airline markets need be regulated. On the contrary, it has been argued that airline markets are contestable since entry and exit is quite easy, and that there are virtually no sunk costs in the industry [see, for example, Bailey, Graham and Kaplan (1985), and Bailey and Panzar (1981)]. These articles rely on contestability to suggest why deregulation for the airlines was an appropriate policy on economic grounds.[24]

[24]For a further discussion of the role of contestability in public policy concerning antitrust as well as regulation, see Bailey (1981).

Beyond Demsetz competition and contestability, competition can also be introduced in a third way, through Chamberlinian monopolistic competition [see Chamberlin (1962)]. For example, in the transportation sector of the economy monopolistic competition among various modes of transport is often referred to as "intermodel competition". This term is employed to describe the rivalry between railroads, motor carriers, pipelines, and water carriers, all of whom compete for freight traffic. If intermodal competition is strong enough, it might be cited as a basis for deregulation even if one or more of the modes of transport appears to have the structure of a natural monopoly.

Consider a simple example of freight transportation between two points. Suppose that a railroad and a competitive motor carrier industry can provide the required point to point service, and suppose the railroad has the cost structure of a natural monopoly.[25] If the intermodal competition between the railroad and the motor carriers is strong enough to prevent the railroad from earning supernormal profits (even when the railroad acts as an unconstrained profit-maximizer), then the unregulated market outcome may be very nearly second best in the absence of regulation.[26] In recent years the move toward deregulation of the railroad industry no doubt partially results from pervasive intermodal competition among the railroads and other modes. In fact deregulation of the motor carrier industry in 1980 has led to declining rates in that industry, which further strengthens the extent of the intermodal competition faced by the railroads [see Moore (1986)].

In other industries similar types of competition have occurred. For example, cable television, a once heavily regulated industry, has largely been deregulated, no doubt in part because of heavy competition from over-the-air broadcasting. Currently, there is much discussion over whether oil pipelines should be deregulated. The proponents of deregulation rely on the argument that there is much competition from other transport modes, including, for example, the railroads, that would keep the pipeline industry from earning large excess profits in the absence of price regulation.

In sum, the views of conditions under which it is appropriate to regulate (or deregulate) have changed considerably during the last two decades. A (no doubt highly) simplified comparison of the older and newer views is shown in Figures 23.5 and 23.6. The more traditional view is depicted in Figure 23.5; there the existence of "natural monopoly" (as characterized by economies of scale) was the

[25]This assumption is for the sake of example in the text. A review of the literature on railroad costs is beyond the scope of the current chapter; suffice it to say here that there is mixed evidence on whether railroads operate with economies of scale, although most papers that have addressed the issue of economies of density (which, for a single product railroad, means that average costs will decline as more traffic is passed through a given network) have found evidence that they exist.

[26]For more on the theory of second best with intermodal competition, see Braeutigam (1979). Of course, if railroads have no scale economies in this example, then the unregulated outcome would be first best instead of second best.

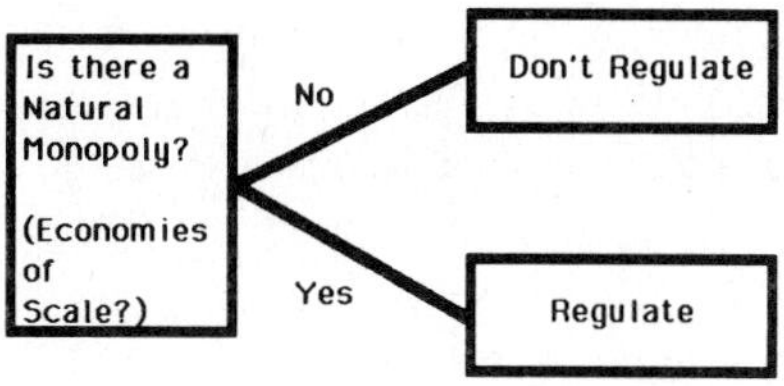

Figure 23.5. Regulation of prices and entry: "traditional" economic justification.

critical factor in determining whether an industry should be regulated. Natural monopoly was taken to preclude competition within the market, and there was very little emphasis on competition for the market as an alternative to regulation.

Although the more current view might be represented in a number of ways, the presentation of Figure 23.6 allows a convenient comparison with the more traditional view. The question of whether a natural monopoly exists is now based on the concept of subadditivity rather than on economies of scale. If there is no natural monopoly and competition within the market is possible (i.e. minimum optimal scale is small relative to the market demand), then a policy of no regulation may be used to reach first best without government intervention.

If a natural monopoly exists, then regulation may still not be warranted. Competition for the market may be possible even if competition within the market is not. If competition for the market is not possible, then some form of government intervention may be required. If competition for the market *is* possible, then performance close to second best might be reached without regulation (through Demsetz competition, contestability, or some form of monopolistic (or intermodal) competition).

It may also be possible to achieve a level of performance better than second best (perhaps even as good as first best) with regulation. One might then compare the deadweight loss at second best with the deadweight loss under a regulatory regime designed to improve performance under government intervention (including an external subsidy, some form of price discrimination, or the use of nonlinear tariffs), keeping in mind the fact that a program of government intervention is not costless.[27] If the deadweight loss at second best is intolerably large (and this requires a value judgment on the part of policy-makers), then government intervention may be warranted. To reiterate, the main point of this exercise is to indicate that even where a natural monopoly exists, government intervention may not be required to achieve economic efficiency for a number of reasons, in contrast with the more traditional view of regulation.

[27]The costs of maintaining a regulatory commission and staff, together with all of the attendant administrative support, can be quite large, as Wiedenbaum (1978) has suggested.

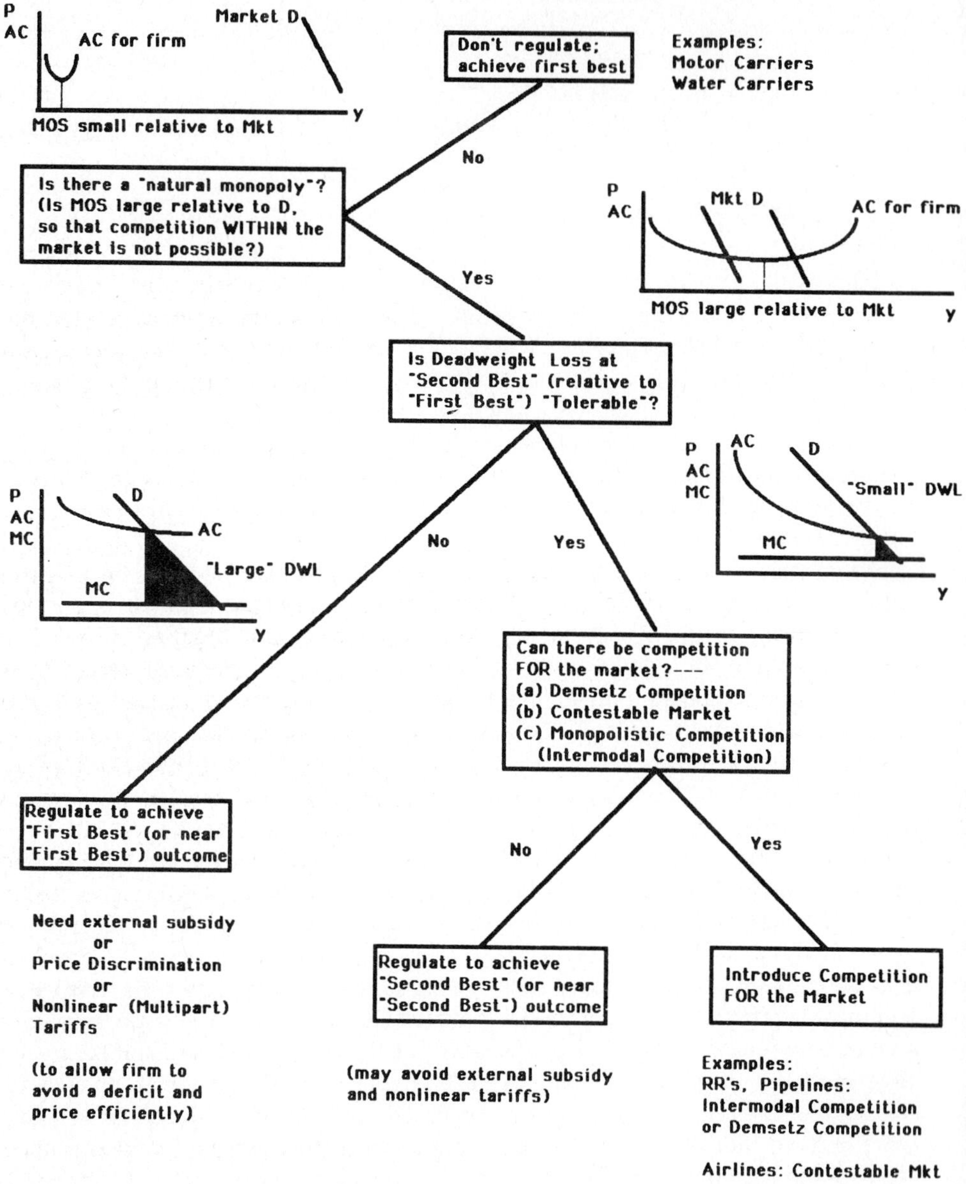

Figure 23.6. Policy "roadmap" for regulation.

To this point we have addressed one facet of the optimal policy toward natural monopoly, namely whether to regulate at all or rely on some form of competition instead. We now turn to optimal strategies where regulation is selected as the appropriate policy. The menu of possible regulatory controls over price and entry is a rich one. The balance of this chapter will discuss some of those controls.

4. Pricing alternatives: Basic concepts

If regulation is undertaken as a response to the natural monopoly problem, there are several courses of action that might be followed by the regulator with respect to pricing. Of course, changes in prices have both distributive and allocative effects. In this section we will focus on the latter, that is, pricing policies designed to achieve economic efficiency.

As Figure 23.6 indicates, regulation might be implemented for a variety of reasons related to economic efficiency. For example, a natural monopoly might be regulated because no form of competition for the market is viable; here prices might be regulated to reduce the deadweight loss associated with the unregulated monopoly price, perhaps to a level associated with either second best or first best. Or, even if second best could be achieved through competition for the market, policy-makers might determine that the deadweight loss associated with second best is intolerably large, in which case regulation might be introduced to increase efficiency (perhaps even to reach first best).

Section 3 presented the basic dilemma of marginal cost pricing with a natural monopoly. In particular Figure 23.4 illustrated why marginal cost pricing will lead to a deficit for a firm operating with economies of scale if all units of output are sold at marginal cost.[28] In this case the firm will not be "revenue adequate", and would therefore require an externally provided subsidy to cover the deficit if it is to continue production. With economies of scale and a single price charged for all units of output, one can achieve first best only if an external subsidy is provided, and avoid such a subsidy only by incurring a deadweight loss. This tension between economic efficiency and revenue adequacy provides a focus for much of the literature on regulated industries.

However, it turns out that there may be other ways to achieve greater efficiency than at second best (perhaps even reach first best) without an external subsidy when there are economies of scale throughout the relevant operating range. To see this, recall that the earlier discussion of Figure 23.4 assumed that the same price is charged for all units of output sold in the market. Restated, this means

[28]Here one should keep in mind the distinction between economies of scale and subadditivity. If natural monopoly were characterized by a subadditive cost structure, but not by economies of scale over the relevant operating range, as in Figure 23.2, then marginal cost (i.e. first best) pricing would allow the firm to breakeven or even to earn some extranormal profit.

that (1) each unit purchased by an individual customer is sold at the same (i.e. uniform) price and that (2) the price per unit is the same for all customers (i.e. there is no price discrimination over customers).

4.1. Price discrimination (differential pricing)

The foregoing discussion suggests that there are two ways one might further improve economic efficiency by departing from the rather restrictive assumption that the same price is charged for all units of output sold in the market. One way would be to engage in some form of *price discrimination*, sometimes referred to as *differential pricing*. As these terms suggest, a regulator could charge different prices to different customers in the market, even if each customer pays the same price for all of the units he purchases. In the simplest instance, suppose that customer i must pay p_i for every unit of service he purchases, and that customer j must pay p_j for every unit of service he purchases. Differential pricing means that $p_i \neq p_j$ for some customers i and j. Peak load pricing and Ramsey pricing schemes fall into this category and will be discussed in greater detail in Sections 5 and 6.

Price discrimination is, of course, a subject that has received much attention in both regulated and unregulated industries. Much of that discussion surrounds the legality of the practice [see, for example, Scherer (1980, chs. 11 and 12)]. A discussion of the legality of price discrimination is not our focus here. We should observe that even if regulators wish to allow or impose price discrimination, it still may not be possible for economic reasons. As is well known, in order for differential pricing to be feasible the seller must be able to identify the price each customer (or at least different groups of customers) would be willing to pay for the service. Furthermore, resale must not be possible for either legal or technological reasons, so that a customer could not purchase the service at a low price and then sell it to another customer at a higher price. If resale is possible, arbitrage will work to eliminate price discrimination so that all customers would face the same price in the market.

To see how differential pricing might be used to improve economic efficiency while allowing the firm to avoid a deficit, consider again Figure 23.4, where the firm operates with the affine cost structure $C = F + my$. Suppose the firm knows how much each consumer is willing to pay for the service, and that resale is impossible. Now let the firm charge a price equal to p_{B} to all customers who would be willing to pay a price greater than or equal to p_{B}, i.e. to all customers located to the left of point B on the demand schedule. Call these "type I customers". Then let the firm charge a price equal to p_{E} to each of the customers who would be willing to pay a price greater than or equal to p_{E}, but not more than p_{B}. Call these "type II customers".

What would be the consequences of such a schedule? The revenues generated by the type I customers would cover not only the variable costs of producing y_B units, but also all of the fixed costs F. [Observe that $p_B = C(y_B)/y_B$, which means that $y_B p_B = F + my_B$.] The revenues generated by the type II customers would then cover just the variable costs from providing $(y_E - y_B)$ units of service. Therefore, one consequence of the suggested schedule is that total costs would then cover total revenues, and there would be no need for an external subsidy to keep the firm viable. Also note that every customer who is willing to pay an amount at least equal to the marginal cost of producing the service receives it, while service is not provided to customers who are not willing to pay at least the marginal cost of production. Thus, a second consequence of the suggested schedule is that it is "first best" or economically efficient. It should also be noted that the proposed schedule leaves the firm with no extranormal profits (producer surplus), since total revenues exactly equal total costs in the example, while consumer surplus would be equal to the sum of the areas ABI and BGE.

One could envision many other possible discriminatory tariff schedules that would accomplish the same objectives (achieving first best without an external subsidy). As a simple example, suppose each customer desires only one unit, and suppose the firm is allowed and able to price discriminate perfectly so that it charges each customer a price equal to the maximum amount that customer is willing to pay for the unit purchased. Consumer surplus is zero under this pricing schedule since each consumer is paying the maximum amount he is willing to pay in order to get the service. In the example of Figure 23.4, the firm's revenues would then equal the area represented by $AEJO$, while the costs of production would be the sum of the areas $IBKO$ and $GEJK$. Again, the firm remains viable (and in fact earns a producer surplus equal to the sum of the areas ABI and BGE). Thus, total surplus (the sum of consumer and producer surplus) is as great as it was under the imperfectly discriminating tariff schedule that charged p_B to type I customers and p_E to type II customers, and once again first best is achieved for the same reasons as given in that earlier example. Of course, the division of the total surplus is strikingly different under the two schedules, with consumers receiving it all in the first example and producers receiving it all in the second. With still other forms of price discrimination it would be possible to achieve other distributions of the total surplus under a first best pricing structure.

4.2. *Nonlinear outlay schedules (nonlinear tariffs)*

The second way of departing from the assumption that the same price is charged for all units of output sold would be to charge an individual customer an amount per unit purchased that varies with the total quantity he purchases. This kind of pricing is often referred to as a *nonlinear outlay schedule*, or sometimes a *nonlinear tariff*. The difference between a linear and a nonlinear outlay schedule can be illustrated easily. Suppose that customer i must pay p_i for every unit of service he purchases, and that he purchases y_i units. His total outlay (expenditure) is $p_i y_i$, so that *the average outlay per unit purchases is constant*. By direct analogy, a *nonlinear outlay schedule* is one in which *the average outlay is not constant as the number of units purchased varies*.[29]

One might suspect that there are many possible ways of structuring nonlinear tariff schedules. Indeed this is so, as will be discussed in greater length in Section 7. For now we offer only a simple example of such a tariff. Consider the so-called two-part tariff; as the name suggests, the tariff has two parts here, a "fixed" and a "variable" component. Suppose, for example, there are N identical consumers in the market, and that the firm operates with the affine cost structure $C = F + my$. One could envision a tariff structure that would assess each customer a fixed charge e (per month), where $e = F/N$ is to be paid regardless of the number of units actually purchased. In addition customers would be required to pay a variable charge equal to m for each unit actually purchased. Thus, the total expenditure by a customer would be $e + my$, which is an affine tariff schedule. First best is achieved since each additional unit consumed is priced at marginal cost. In addition the firm would remain financially viable since the total revenues would be $N(e + my) = F + Nmy$.

The reader may (correctly) suspect that income effects may introduce complexities in the way such tariffs are structured if economic efficiency is to be achieved; we address these effects in Section 7. In fact, nonlinear tariffs may involve more than two parts as in the previous example. The main point of the examples in this section is to illustrate that nonlinear tariff structures can be useful as a means of achieving greater efficiency without external subsidies.[30]

4.3. *The common cost problem in the multiproduct firm*

We have now suggested several ways in which one might improve economic efficiency by departing from a single price for all units of output sold in the market. The problems discussed thus far are simplified in one very important respect: the firm has been assumed to produce only one product. The problem of pricing becomes even more difficult when there is more than one output produced by the firm.

[29]One possible source of confusion in the taxonomy here should be pointed out. Since a linear outlay schedule is defined as one in which average outlay is constant, it follows trivially that total outlay is linear in output. However, a nonlinear outlay structure may also be linear in output; in particular, with the affine structure referenced in the text expenditures are linear in output. The important point is that *average* (not total) outly is not constant with respect to output purchased.

[30]As will be indicated in Section 7, nonlinear tariffs may not always lead to first best, but nonlinear tariffs can be used to increase economic efficiency relative to second best even when first best is not achieved.

To see this consider a firm which produces two products whose levels of output are respectively y_1 and y_2. Let the marginal costs of production for the services be constant and respectively m_1 and m_2, and suppose there is a fixed cost of production F. This describes a simple multiproduct affine cost function where the total costs are $C = F + m_1 y_1 + m_2 y_2$.

The fixed cost is said to be "common" to both services. In other words, it is a cost shared in the production of y_1 and y_2. The presence of such a common cost poses a particularly difficult problem for regulators trying to set prices so that the firm can break even. Assume that the firm must price each service uniformly, so that purchasers of service i will all pay a price per unit equal to p_i for that service. As in the single product affine cost case, it is clear that the firm cannot break even with marginal cost pricing. If $p_1 = m_1$ and $p_2 = m_2$, the profits of the firm will be negative (in fact, profits are $\pi = -F$).

The question then becomes: How might the regulator set rates so that the firm breaks even? This is an age-old question that has been examined in many contexts in the economic literature as well as in regulatory proceedings [see, for example, Taussig (1913), Pigou (1920) and Clark (1923) for excellent early treatises on this subject].[31]

For many years regulators had relatively little in terms of economic theory to guide their decisions in ratemaking in the face of common costs. In practice regulatory authorities such as the Interstate Commerce Commission and the Federal Communications Commission historically have determined tariffs (rates) using so-called fully distributed (fully allocated) costs, which we shall refer to here as FDC pricing. We discuss this briefly here to contrast this often used regulatory approach with those based on economic efficiency to be discussed in subsequent sections.

Under FDC pricing, as a first step regulators do (somehow) allocate the common costs among the individual services. In other words, each service is assigned a fraction f_i of the common costs, so that the share of common costs for service i is $f_i F$. (The fractions f_i must add to 1 if the costs are fully allocated; in our example $f_1 + f_2 = 1$.) Each service is then priced so that the revenues generated from that service will cover all of the costs directly attributable to that service plus the assigned portion of the common costs (again, in the example $p_i y_i = f_i F + m_i y_i$ for $i = 1, 2$).

The issue of pricing then critically depends on the way in which the allocators (f_i) are set. In principle, of course, there are an infinite number of ways one can allocate the common costs since there are an infinite number of ways one select f_1 and f_2 to sum to unity. In practice regulators have sometimes allocated common costs in proportion to (1) gross revenues (so that $f_1/f_2 = p_1 y_1 / p_2 y_2$), or

[31]See also Kahn (1970), Baumol, Panzar and Willig (1982), Brown and Sibley (1986), Faulhaber (1975), Faulhaber and Levinson (1981), Owen and Braeutigam (1978), Sharkey (1982a, 1982b), Weil (1968) and Zajac (1978) for a few among many references on the subject of the common cost problem. Some of these will be discussed further below.

(2) physical output levels (so that $f_1/f_2 = y_1/y_2$) or (3) directly attributable costs (so that $f_1/f_2 = m_1y_1/m_2y_2$).[32]

Without extending the discussion of this practice, it is rather immediately apparent that there are many potential problems with FDC pricing.[33] Regarding the arbitrariness of the method, Friedlaender (1969) notes: "Various means of prorating the common or joint costs can be used, but all of them have an arbitrary element and hence are dangerous to use in prescribing rates." It may involve circular reasoning since prices, revenues or output levels are used to determine the allocators which are used in turn to set prices. It may also lead to prices which are dominated in the sense defined in Section 2.[34] And, with respect to a point that is central to this chapter, FDC pricing will lead to prices which are in general economically inefficient, which is not surprising given the fact that the practice focuses heavily on cost and little on conditions of demand (including demand elasticities) which are important in determining the size of the deadweight losses from any pricing policy.

In connection with the common cost problem it is worthwhile to comment on a relatively new line of research called the "axiomatic" approach to common cost allocation. This work is not based on economic efficiency in its treatment of the problem (as is Ramsey pricing, discussed in Section 6); neither does it stem from an attempt to find prices which are free of cross subsidy (various notions of which are covered in Section 8). Instead, it begins with a set of features desired in a cost allocation scheme, represents them axiomatically, and derives pricing rules consistent with these desiderata. The exact specification of the axioms depends on the cost structure, and in particular whether there are fixed costs or not.

Mirman, Samet and Tauman (1983) have presented six axioms for the allocation of common costs, and analyzed pricing rules that satisfy these axioms for the case in which the firm may be operating with fixed costs. The cost function may be written $C = F + V(y)$, where F is a fixed cost and V is a variable cost function dependent on the level of outputs $y = (y_1, y_2, \ldots, y_n)$.[35] (This allows for the possibility that the relevant horizon for the firm or the regulator is the

[32]Friedlaender (1969, p. 32) noted that the ICC had often allocated common costs between freight and passenger services "on the basis of revenues derived from each source", and (p. 133) "the most usual basis of prorating [costs among freight services] is on the basis of ton-miles" (brackets added); of course, in this case the outputs must have a common measure of output, such as ton-miles of various types of freight (this practice would make no sense for allocating common costs among, for example, passenger service and freight service). Kahn (1970, p. 151) notes that allocation according to attributable costs has been used to some extent in the transportation industry.

[33]See Braeutigam (1980) for a more detailed analysis of FDC pricing.

[34]Sweeney (1982) considers the case of a multiproduct firm which provides some of its services in a competitive market and others in a regulated monopolistic setting. Sweeney shows that for FDC pricing rules with allocators that monotonically increase in output, prices will be on a dominated part of the isoprofit locus.

[35]As is the normal case in this chapter, factor prices are suppressed in the representation of the cost function since they are assumed constant.

short run, during which it may not be possible to adjust all factors of production to the levels that would be efficient in the long run.)

Briefly the six axioms require that (1) the prices resulting from the allocation mechanism generate revenues sufficient to cover total costs; (2) if the units of measurement for the commodities are rescaled, the prices measured with the new dimensions should be rescaled accordingly; (3) if for some subset S of outputs total cost depends only on the sum of the levels of the outputs in S, then the prices of any two outputs in S should be the same (this implies that outputs with the same marginal costs should have equal prices);[36] (4) if C and $\hat{C}$ are two different cost structures with $C(\mathbf{0}) \geq \hat{C}(\mathbf{0})$ and $(C - \hat{C})$ increasing as outputs increase, then prices should be higher under C than under $\hat{C}$; (5) if $V(y)$ can be written as a sum of the variable costs from $k = 1, \ldots, K$ stages of production so that $V(y) = V_1(y) + V_2(y) + \cdots + V_K(y)$, then the mechanism should allocate a fraction of the common cost $f_k F$ to each stage k, with $\sum f_k = 1$ so that all of the common costs are allocated; and (6) if for any two stages i and j described in (5) it is true that $V_i(y) > V_j(y)$, then $f_i > f_j$, so that the size of the allocation is higher when variable costs are higher.[37]

Mirman, Samet and Tauman show that the only pricing rule consistent with the six axioms is one based on the Aumann–Shapley price for each service. In the case of a general cost function, there is no obvious interpretation of this price, and we do not present a detailed statement of the pricing rule here. However, there is a case of special interest worth noting. If the cost structure can be written in an additively separable fashion $C = F + \sum_i V_i(y_i)$, then the only price rule satisfying the axioms is the allocation of common costs in proportion to directly attributable costs, which happens to be one of the fully distributed cost mechanisms discussed earlier in this section.[38] This finding is of particular interest. While the additively separable cost structure is simplistic, it has been used by some regulatory commissions in the past.[39]

We now focus on economically efficient pricing schemes that might be used where shared costs exist. The next section considers a set of pricing policies that rely on differential pricing, commonly known as peak load pricing.

[36]The third axiom makes it clear that the "axiomatic approach" bears no necessary relationship to pricing which is economically efficient. As will be clear from the discussion of Ramsey pricing in section 6, if two services have identical marginal costs, an economically efficient price will be greater for the product with the more inelastic demand.

[37]Under some circumstances a single axiom of additivity can replace the last two listed in the text (i.e. axioms (5) and (6) in the text) if the firm is operating on its long run cost function; see Mirman and Tauman (1982) and Samet and Tauman (1982) for more on this point.

[38]Braeutigam (1980) has shown that when the regulated firm operates at zero profit, two of the FDC mechanisms discussed above are equivalent. These are the allocation of common costs (1) in proportion to directly attributable costs and (2) in proportion to gross revenues.

[39]For example, Friedlaender (1969) has discussed the use of such a cost structure (Rail Form A) by the Interstate Commerce Commission in setting railroad rates.

5. Peak load pricing

The term "peak load" suggests a problem faced by many utilities, and one which has been treated widely in the literature. There are three essential features of the traditional peak load problem: (1) the firm must provide service over a number of time periods having perhaps greatly different demand schedules, (2) the firm must choose a single plant size (capacity) to be in place during all of the time periods over which production takes place, and (3) output is nonstorable.[40] A large number of formal models have been developed in the literature to characterize economically efficient prices for the peak load problem, all of which have led to prices that vary across time in some way. Thus, peak load pricing schemes are a form of price discrimination across time periods.

In regulatory settings the issue of peak load pricing often revolves around the fact that the plant is shared by users of all time periods. The question to be resolved is: What share of the cost of the plant should be borne by users in the various time periods? The most famous classical economic model of the peak load problem is that of Steiner (1957).[41] That work generated optimal pricing rules that are commonly known even to regulatory commissioners today, including the widely cited principle that all of the plant costs should be loaded on to the peak load period. But as we shall see, the latter conclusion is one which is very sensitive to the nature of the technology and demands.

To compare a few of the basic peak load formulations in the literature, consider the following framework. Assume the production period (e.g. a day) is divided into T equal parts, indexed by $t = 1, \ldots, T$.[42] Assume that x_t units of a single variable input are used in period t, and that k represents the amount of the capital input which is chosen for all periods. Let $y_t = f(x_t, k)$ be the production function for period t, relating the output in that period y_t to the inputs. The nature of this production function will be crucial to the form of the peak load pricing rules, and will be specified in detail in the models discussed below. Finally, let $p_t = p_t(y_t)$ represent the (inverse) demand schedule in period t. The demand schedule is downward sloping, so that $p_t'(y_t) < 0$.[43]

[40] If output is storable without cost, then a firm could produce and store more than is demanded in an off peak period, and then use the stored output to serve the higher demand in the peak period. This would allow the firm to pool production over all of the time periods, effectively eliminating the peak load problem. Of course, one could introduce storage costs which are positive, and still retain the essence of the peak load problem examined in this section.

[41] This classical formulation of the peak load problem is also discussed at length in Kahn (1970, ch. 5).

[42] The assumption that the production period is divided into equal parts is not necessary, but does facilitate exposition.

[43] The prime symbol will be used to denote derivatives where that can be done unambiguously in the text; thus $p_t'(y_t) \equiv \partial p_t / \partial y_t$.

Consider first the traditional formulation of Steiner. The production function has a Leontief structure, so that $y_t = f(x_t, k) = \min(x_t/a, k)$, with the constant $a > 0$. One can represent this production structure in terms of a cost function. Let $\tilde{b}$ be the cost of a unit of the variable factor, which is assumed here to be the same in each period. Then the total variable cost incurred in period t will be $\tilde{b}x_t = \tilde{b}ay_t$. For simplicity in notation, let $b = \tilde{b}a$, so that the period t variable cost is by_t. Let β be the (rental) cost of a unit of capital over all time periods $t+1,\dots,T$. Assume the firm must meet all demand, so that capital must be chosen to be $k = \max_t y_t$. Then the total cost for the firm will be

$$C = b\sum_{t=1}^{T} y_t + \beta \max{}_j y_j. \tag{4}$$

Suppose that gross economic benefit can be represented as $A(y_1, y_2,\dots, y_T)$.[44] Then net economic benefit, W, can be written as (5):

$$W = A(y_1, y_2,\dots, y_T) - C. \tag{5}$$

In *off peak* periods (in which $y_t < \max_j y_j$) the first order necessary conditions for an interior optimum (in which $y_t > 0$) of (5) would be

$$\partial W/\partial y_t = p_t - b = 0, \quad \text{for } y_t < \max{}_j y_j, \tag{6}$$

which implies that $p_t = b$. In other words, in off peak periods, users will be required to pay only for the variable costs of production, with no revenues being contributed toward the costs of capacity for the enterprise. In the *peak* period (in which $y_t = \max_j y_j$) the first order condition for an interior optimum of (5) would be

$$\partial W/\partial y_t = p_t - b + \beta = 0, \quad \text{for } y_t = \max{}_j y_j, \tag{7}$$

which implies that $p_t = b + \beta$. In other words, in peak periods, users will be required to pay for the variable costs of production *plus* the capacity costs of the enterprise.

An example using the peak load pricing principles with this Leontief technology is depicted in Figure 23.7. In the figure, the day is divided into three time

[44] One could write A in terms of the usual consumer surplus integrals:

$$A(y_1, y_2,\dots, y_T) \equiv \sum_{t=1}^{T}\int_0^{y_t} p_t(\xi)\,\mathrm{d}\xi.$$

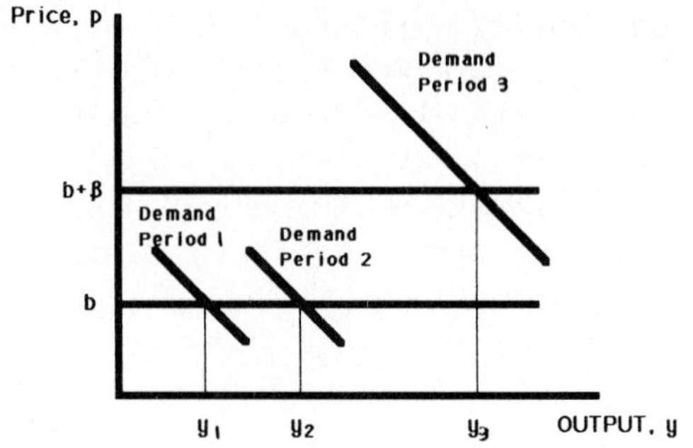

Figure 23.7. Peak load pricing with a Leontief technology.

periods, daytime (y_3), evening (y_2), and night (y_1). The daytime period is the peak period, with the other two being off peak periods. The Steiner model would indicate that the off peak users would pay a price of b, while the daytime users would pay $b + \beta$, since revenues generated from daytime service would have to cover variable costs and plant costs.

Note that in this example all of the costs of the enterprise are covered by revenues generated by the three classes of users. Revenues from the daytime users are $y_3(b + \beta)$; for evening and night users the revenues are respectively by_2 and by_1, so that all of the costs in (4) are covered. Furthermore, each class of users is paying a price equal to the marginal cost of production, since $\partial C/\partial y_1 = b$, $\partial C/\partial y_2 = b$, and $\partial C/\partial y_3 = b + \beta$, which includes the marginal cost of capacity expansion if the peak period production is increased. Therefore first best and revenue adequacy can be achieved simultaneously with this peak load pricing scheme.[45]

The peak load pricing problem can also be formulated in terms of a neoclassical production function instead of a Leontief technology. As Panzar (1976) has shown, somewhat different results follow. Again let the production function for period t be $y_t = f(x_t, k)$, where, as before, k is fixed across all time periods. Let f be twice differentiable and quasiconcave in x_t and k, with the partial derivatives $\partial f/\partial x_t > 0$, $\partial f/\partial k > 0$, $\partial^2 f/\partial x_t^2 < 0$, and $\partial^2 f/\partial k^2 < 0$, so that the marginal products of capital and the variable factor are positive and decreasing.

One can write the variable cost function associated with f, which minimizes the variable cost of producing any specified y_t given the level of k in place. Let the variable cost function in period t be denoted by $V(y_t, b, k)$, where b is the (parametric) price of a unit of the variable factor, and assume the variable cost

[45]In this example, of course, the production structure exhibits constant returns to scale, since a doubling of outputs will lead to a doubling of total production costs. Thus, it is not surprising that marginal cost pricing will lead to revenue adequacy.

function has the standard derivative properties $\partial V/\partial y_t > 0$ (marginal variable cost is positive), $\partial V/\partial k < 0$ (k and x_t are substitutes in production), and $\partial^2 V/\partial y_t^2 > 0$ (for fixed k the marginal cost is increasing in output). In addition let $V(0, b, k) = 0$ (variable costs are zero when output is zero).

Then with the same demand structure as used in the Leontief model, net economic benefit, W, can be written as (8):

$$W = A(y_1, y_2, \ldots, y_T) - \sum_{t=1}^{T} V(y_t, b, k) - \beta k. \tag{8}$$

Let the output levels (or, equivalently, prices) and the level of capital be chosen to maximize W. At an interior optimum ($y_t > 0$ and $k > 0$), first order conditions require that (1) $p_t = \partial V/\partial y_t$, and (2) $\sum_t \partial V(y_t, b, k)/\partial k = -\beta$. The second condition shows that capital is employed until the total variable cost savings from an added unit of capital equals the cost of that added unit of capital. The first condition indicates that the price equals the marginal variable cost in each period. Here, too, with constant returns to scale, marginal cost pricing will lead to revenue adequacy.

Finally, recall that $\partial^2 V/\partial y_t^2 > 0$, which means that marginal costs are rising for any given size of plant. Consider any two periods, and denote them by $t = 1$ and $t = 2$ without loss of generality. Suppose $y_2 > y_1$. Then $p_1 = \partial V/\partial y_1 < p_2 = \partial V/\partial y_2$. Thus, prices will not be equal in periods with different demands; in fact price will be higher in the period with the higher demand.

Still a third possible technology, having elements of both the Leontief and the neoclassical production structure, is examined by Waverman (1975), with some interesting conclusions. Assume that *any* output-variable factor ratio can be chosen, but that once the ratio is chosen, it is then applicable in all periods. (By contrast, the Leontief technology assumes that the ratio y_t/x_t is fixed and not freely chosen, while the neoclassical structure allows the ratio to be chosen at different levels in different time periods.) To illustrate this formulation, consider a three period model, with period three having the peak demand. As before, assume there is a single variable factor, whose levels are x_1, x_2, and x_3 in the three periods respectively, and whose unit price is $\tilde{b}$. With the same demand structure as used previously, assume the firm chooses y_t, x_t, and k to maximize net economic benefit, W, as follows:

$$\max_{(y_t, x_t, k)} W = A(y_1, y_2, y_3) - \tilde{b} \sum_{t=1}^{T} x_t - \beta k \tag{9}$$

$$\text{subject to } \quad x_1/y_1 = x_2/y_2 = x_3/y_3$$

$$\text{and } f(x_3, k) \geq y_3.$$

Waverman's analysis indicates that in the two off peak periods prices will be equal to one another and equal to the (marginal) variable cost of production, a conclusion much like that of the Steiner model. Furthermore, the ratio of the peak price to the off peak price does depend on the distribution of outputs across time periods in the Waverman model, whereas in the Steiner model that ratio does not depend on the distribution of output.

Without belaboring these models further, it can be concluded that the optimal pricing policy does depend on the nature of the underlying technology, as suggested earlier. This has an important implication for applications of economic theory to peak load problems; one might be advised to examine the properties of estimated cost or production functions to find out what kind of technology exists before advocating any particular optimal pricing rule.

Finally, there are a number of other articles that address other problems related to peak load pricing. For example, Bailey and White (1974) show that a peak period price can actually be less than the price in an off peak period under a variety of circumstances. Among others these include pricing for a welfare maximizing firm operating with a decreasing average cost in production. Here the firm needs to satisfy a breakeven constraint while maximizing welfare over all periods. For example, a higher off peak price might result in the off peak period if the demand in the off peak period is inelastic relative to the elasticity of demand in the peak period.[46] One must also be careful when trying to identify which period is a peak period; when one moves from a high price to a lower price, demand schedules for two periods may intersect one another, so that the peak period may change. Carlton (1977) has addressed the problem of peak load pricing when demands are stochastic, in contrast to the survey of this section in which demands are known with certainty. Crew and Kleindorfer (1976) have introduced the possibility that firms may operate with diverse technologies, including several types of plants, as is often observed in industries such as the electric utility industry. Additional discussions of peak load pricing models can be found in Littlechild (1970), which applies the theory to the telephone industry, in Brown and Sibley (1986) and in Rees (1984).

6. Ramsey pricing

The discussion of peak load pricing in the previous section indicated how differential pricing might be used to improve economic efficiency when a single plant size must be chosen to provide service over more than one time period. The nonstorability of the service and the variation in demand across time periods were identified as crucial aspects of the peak load problem. In the standard

[46] The addition of the breakeven constraint in the face of increasing returns to scale is a problem that will be discussed below in greater detail in the section on Ramsey pricing, where economically efficient prices depend on the elasticities of demand as in Bailey and White (1974).

presentation of the peak load problem, returns to scale are constant; thus optimal pricing schemes lead to first best while allowing the firm to break even.

Let us now turn to the case in which the firm is unable to break even when a uniform price is set equal to marginal cost for each of the services offered by the firm. The outputs of the firm might be essentially the same product provided in different periods (as with electricity in the peak load case), or, unlike the peak load problem, they might be services which are entirely different from one another (e.g. passenger and freight transportation services). Suppose the regulator has determined that the firm (1) charge a uniform price for each of its services, and (2) price its services so that it breaks even without an external subsidy, i.e. the firm must remain viable with no subsidy from the government or from some other source outside the firm. Under these circumstances the firm will need to charge prices that deviate from marginal costs in some or all of its markets in order to avoid a deficit.

In Section 3 we indicated how a single product monopoly would set the price in order to maximize economic efficiency while allowing the firm to avoid negative profits. We showed that this problem of second best was solved by pricing at average cost for the single product firm because no greater net economic benefit can be achieved if the breakeven constraint for the firm is to be satisfied. Recall that for any price less than average cost, the firm will incur a deficit, which violates the breakeven constraint. For any price greater than average cost, the firm will remain profitable, but the size of the deadweight loss will be larger than when price equals average cost. As suggested in Section 3, the second best price can be viewed as simultaneously maximizing net economic benefits (total surplus) and minimizing the deadweight loss given the constraint on non-negativity of profits for the firm.

The notion of second best pricing becomes more complicated for the case of the multiproduct firm. In general the concept of average cost will not be well defined for a multiproduct technology; if there are shared costs of production, in the sense defined in Section 4, then there is no unambiguous way to allocate the common costs. Thus, there is no clear way to determine an economically meaningful measure of the average cost associated with each service.

The name "Ramsey pricing" stems from the work of the English economist Frank Ramsey, who developed the concept in the context of optimal taxation in 1927 [see Ramsey (1927)]. It was later extended to the problem of public monopolies by Boiteux [see the original version in French, Boiteux (1956) and the English language version, Boiteux (1971)], and further developed by Baumol and Bradford (1970).[47]

To facilitate the exposition, we adopt the following notation. Consider the case of the N product firm, where y_i is the level of output of the ith service produced by the firm, $i = 1, \ldots, N$. Let p_i be the price of the ith output, $\mathbf{y}$ the vector of

[47]See also Sorenson, Tschirhart and Winston (1978).

outputs $(y_1, y_2, \ldots, y_N)$, and $\boldsymbol{p}$ the vector $(p_1, p_2, \ldots, p_N)$. Let $y_i(\boldsymbol{p})$ be the demand schedule for the ith service, $i = 1, \ldots, N$, and $\psi(\boldsymbol{p})$ be the consumer surplus at the price vector $\boldsymbol{p}$.[48] Let w_i be the factor price of the ith input employed by the firm, $i = 1, \ldots, l$, $\boldsymbol{w}$ be the vector factor prices $(w_1, w_2, \ldots, w_l)$, and $C(\boldsymbol{y}, \boldsymbol{w})$ represent the firm's long run cost function. Finally, note that $\pi = \boldsymbol{p} \cdot \boldsymbol{y} - C(\boldsymbol{y}, \boldsymbol{w})$ corresponds to the economic profit of the firm.

Formally one can represent the Ramsey pricing problem as follows. Ramsey optimal (second best) prices will maximize the sum of consumer and producer surplus, T, subject to a constraint on the non-negativity of profits, $\pi \geq 0$:

$$\max_{\boldsymbol{p}} T = \psi(\boldsymbol{y}) + \boldsymbol{p} \cdot \boldsymbol{y} - C(\boldsymbol{y}, \boldsymbol{w}) \tag{11}$$

$$\text{subject to} \quad \pi = \boldsymbol{p} \cdot \boldsymbol{y} - C(\boldsymbol{y}, \boldsymbol{w}) \geq 0. \tag{12}$$

Let λ be the non-negative Lagrange multiplier associated with the profit constraint (12). At an interior optimum (in which $p_i > 0$), the constraint will be binding when marginal cost pricing for all outputs would lead to a deficit; thus $\lambda > 0$. In addition the following conditions must hold:

$$\partial T / \partial p_i + \lambda \, \partial \pi / \partial p_i = 0, \quad \forall i, \tag{13}$$

which can be rewritten as:

$$-\lambda y_i = (1 + \lambda) \sum_{j=1}^{n} \left[p_j - \partial C / \partial y_j \right] \left(\partial y_j / \partial p_i \right), \quad \forall i. \tag{14}$$

In general, of course, the terms $\partial y_j / \partial p_i$ need not be zero for $i \neq j$. In fact, this cross derivative will be positive when products i and j are substitutes, negative when they are complements, and zero when the demands are independent. For simplicity, consider the special (and most famous) case in which all demands are independent, and let the price elasticity of demand for output i with respect to price p_j be denoted by ε_{ij} and defined in the usual way as $(\partial y_i / \partial p_j)(p_j / y_i)$. Then after some algebra the conditions for optimality can be expressed in the following form:

$$\left\{ \frac{p_i - \partial C / \partial y_i}{p_i} \right\} \varepsilon_{ii} = \left\{ \frac{p_j - \partial C / \partial y_j}{p_j} \right\} \varepsilon_{jj} = -\frac{\lambda}{1 + \lambda}, \quad \forall i, j. \tag{15}$$

[48] The consumer surplus measure was discussed in Section 3; here one could represent it in terms of the familiar integral form as

$$\psi(\boldsymbol{p}) = \int_{\boldsymbol{p}}^{\infty} y(\hat{\boldsymbol{p}}) \, \mathrm{d}\hat{\boldsymbol{p}}.$$

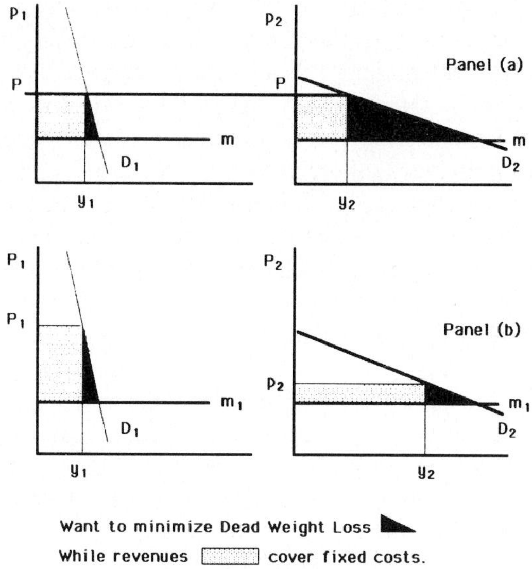

Figure 23.8. Ramsey pricing.

This relationship is the most well-known form of the Ramsey pricing rule. The terms in brackets in (15) represent the extent to which price deviates from marginal cost in the indicated (subscripted) markets, and is often referred to as the "markup" of price over marginal cost. The product of this markup and the corresponding elasticity of demand is known as the "Ramsey number"; for example, $(p_i - \partial C/\partial y_i)\varepsilon_{ii}/p_i$ is the Ramsey number for market i. The Ramsey number will be negative at an optimum in which the breakeven constraint is binding ($\lambda > 0$), since its numerical value is $-\lambda/(1+\lambda)$, which lies between zero and minus one; it will be zero when the breakeven constraint is not binding ($\lambda = 0$). When the demands are independent, the second best price in each market will be above marginal cost (i.e. the markup is positive) when the breakeven constraint is binding, and equal to marginal cost (i.e. first best) when the breakeven constraint is not binding.

Equation (15) indicates that the Ramsey number in each market must be equal. This relationship represents the famous "inverse elasticity rule", since it indicates that a lower markup must be associated with a more elastic demand when the breakeven constraint is binding. For an intuitive explanation of this result, consider the example illustrated in Figure 23.8. In this example the cost structure is affine, with equal marginal costs in each of the two markets served by the firm. Let the cost function be $C(y) = F + m(y_1 + y_2)$, and suppose the demands are independent.

Suppose first that the markups in the two markets are identical, instead of being based on the inverse elasticity rule. Since the marginal costs in the two markets are equal, equal markups mean equal prices in the two markets. This situation is depicted in panel (a) of Figure 23.8 (the top panel). The lightly shaded area in each market represents the revenues in excess of variable costs in that market; in each market that area can be thought of as a contribution toward covering the firm's fixed cost (F). The idea in panel (a) is to have equal markups (at a price p) which are large enough to have the dollar sum represented by the lightly shaded areas just equal to F. The demand in market 2 is drawn to be more elastic than the demand in market 1 when the price in each market is equal to p. Since the price in each market exceeds marginal cost, there is a deadweight loss, in each market represented by the black triangle. The sum of the areas of these triangles will be the dollar measure of the total economic inefficiency introduced by charging the prices $p_1 = p_2 = p$ instead of the first best prices $p_1 = p_2 = m$.[49]

The approach of requiring equal markups is but one of many possible ways of achieving non-negative profits. The question is: Is there another set of prices that would leave the firm without a deficit and make the sum of the deadweight losses smaller than the one indicated in panel (a), and in fact smaller than any other possible set of prices (p_1, p_2)? The inverse elasticity rule suggests how one might go about the task of finding that set of second best prices. It shows that the markup in market 1, the one with the more inelastic market, should be higher than in the (more elastic) market 2. Therefore one could adjust the markups accordingly, as represented in panel (b) of Figure 23.8. In panel (b) the sum of the lightly shaded areas in the two markets is intended to be the same as in panel (a), so that the revenues generated from the two markets once again just cover the fixed costs F. At the Ramsey optimal prices (p_1, p_2) in panel (b), the sum of the areas of the black deadweight loss triangles is smaller than in panel (a), and in fact is as small as possible given that the firm must break even.

As the formulation of the Ramsey optimal problem (11)–(14) suggests, the inverse elasticity rule (15) is valid for much more general cost and demand structures than the linear ones illustrated in Figure 23.8. In fact the demands need not be independent, although the inverse elasticity rule (15) needs some modification in that case. Rohlfs (1979) has developed the Ramsey optimal rules in some detail for the case of interdependent demands.[50] The rule (15) must be altered to incorporate the effects of the cross partial derivatives $\partial y_i/\partial p_j$; this can be done in a straightforward fashion. For example, in the two product case, define Rohlfs' "superelasticity" as follows; $E_1 = \varepsilon_{11} - \varepsilon_{12} p_1 y_1 / p_2 y_2$ and $E_2 = \varepsilon_{22} - \varepsilon_{21} p_2 y_2 / p_1 y_1$, and then restate (15) to (16) to include the effects of demand

[49] The simple exercise of adding the welfare triangles in the two markets will not be valid if the demands in the two markets are interdependent. For more on welfare measurement in this case, see Braeutigam and Noll (1984).

[50] See also Zajac (1974).

interdependencies:

$$\left\{\frac{p_1 - \partial C/\partial y_1}{p_1}\right\}E_1 = \left\{\frac{p_2 - \partial C/\partial y_2}{p_2}\right\}E_2, \quad \forall i, j. \tag{16}$$

Observe that (16) simplifies to (15) when the cross elasticities of demand are zero.

The standard formulation of the Ramsey pricing problem [such as in the work of Baumol and Bradford (1970) and others cited above] assumes that the regulator operates with certainty about cost and demand relationships. That work is also typically developed in a static framework, and assumes that the regulated firm has a monopoly position in each of its markets. One might easily envision a host of additional modifications in the problem of second best in any particular industrial setting.[51] While we cannot hope to treat all of these extensions in detail, we do indicate the general nature of and provide selected references to some of this work.

Ramsey pricing principles have been developed for the case of uncertainty about the demand structure by Sherman and Visscher (1978).[52] Brock and Dechert (1983) and Braeutigam (1983) have shown how the principles can be extended to find optimal prices (and plant size) in a dynamic setting.[53]

The theory of Ramsey pricing has also been applied to cases in which the multiproduct firm does not have a monopoly in each of its markets. Braeutigam (1979) noted this problem in connection with the regulation of intermodal competition in surface freight transportation. Suppose one were interested in characterizing second best prices in the following setting. There are two modes of transport, each providing only a single service. Mode 1 is comprised of a single firm operating with economies of scale.[54] Mode 2 is comprised of a set of atomistic other firms which are competitive with one another.[55] All of the mode 2

[51]Examples of applications of second best pricing include among others Owen and Willig (1981), who apply Ramsey pricing to postal services, Willig and Bailey (1979), who examine AT & T's long distance rates by miles and time of day as well as postal rates, Willig (1979), who examines the problem of determining prices for access to a network (such as the telephone network), and Winston (1981), who examines the welfare losses from observed surface freight transportation rates relative to the losses that would have been observed at second best prices.

[52]The earlier work of Visscher (1973) is also of interest on this point.

[53]As one might suspect, there are interesting alternative ways of specifying both objective functions and constraints in these more complicated models. For example, in a dynamic formulation the exact form of optimal pricing rules will depend on whether the firm must break even at each point in time, or whether the firm must simply satisfy a constraint that requires the present value of profits over the relevant time horizon be non-negative.

[54]For example, mode 1 might be a railroad or a pipeline; this is stated here merely for illustration, and does not assert that any given railroad necessarily operates under economies of scale, since that is an empirical issue.

[55]An example of such a mode might be water carriers or motor carriers.

firms produce exactly the same service, and that service is an imperfect substitute for the service produced by mode 1. That paper shows that second best prices would in principle have to be set for *all* of the firms with interacting demands, not for just the mode with economies of scale. It also suggests why a Ramsey optimum might not be sustainable, since second best rates might typically be above marginal costs for mode 2.[56]

To be sure, each of these additional complexities leads to some modification in the exact form of the appropriate Ramsey rules. However, it seems fair to say that the essential principles of Ramsey pricing emerge in a robust fashion from the analysis, particularly as embodied in an inverse elasticity rule in some form.[57]

In closing this section, it is appropriate to point out that there is a fundamental difference between the approaches to pricing represented by Ramsey pricing and fully distributed cost pricing described in Section 4. As that earlier discussion indicated, FDC pricing proceeds with an ex ante allocation of common cost to all of the services, and then sets prices so that the revenues generated by each service will cover all of the costs allocated to that service. In other words, an allocation of common costs is the first step taken in a process that ultimately leads to a determination of prices.

Under Ramsey pricing, no allocation of common costs is made on the way to determining economically efficient prices. *After* the efficient prices are found, it may be possible to determine how the common costs would have to be allocated

[56]One could envision a kind of "third best" model in which the regulator allows the competitive mode 2 to clear its markets without regulation, thereby focusing only on the rates charged by the mode with economies of scale. This concept of regulation is called "partially regulated second best" (PRSB) in Braeutigam (1979), in contrast to "totally regulated second best" (TRSB) in which all rates for *all* competing modes are set by the regulator, a formidable task indeed. PRSB rates look very much like the Ramsey rules developed by Baumol and Bradford (1970), except that the elasticities of demand are those facing the firm instead of an industry (there is no well-defined industry demand since there are imperfect substitutes in the market).

This line of work has been extended still further. Baumol, Panzar and Willig (1982, ch. 11) suggest a concept of "viable firm Ramsey optimum" for Ramsey pricing in the case in which two or more firms, each operating with economies of scale, provide outputs which are perfect substitutes for one another. Braeutigam (1984) has developed Ramsey pricing rules for the case in which two or more firms, each operating with economies of scale, provide outputs which are *im*perfectly substitutable with one another.

[57]It turns out that, although it is not obvious, there is also a connection between prices that are sustainable and Ramsey optimal. Baumol, Bailey and Willig (1977) have stated a "Weak Invisible Hand Theorem" which points out that under a set of assumptions including a cost structure which exhibits both economies of scale and transray convexity (see Panzar's description of these concepts in Chapter 1 of this Handbook), Ramsey optimal prices are sufficient to guarantee sustainability. However, Faulhaber (1975) has generated a simple example in which a cost function not satisfying both economies of scale and transray convexity yields Ramsey optimal prices which are not sustainable; in fact a simple affine cost structure in which there are product specific fixed costs ($C = F_0 + F_1 + m_1 y_1 + F_2 + m_2 y_2$) is not transray convex if F_i can be avoided when $y_i = 0$, and thus the Weak Invisible Hand theorem will not generally hold with such a structure.

in order for the second best prices to be generated from an FDC process.[58] However, this is an ex post exercise in allocating common costs. Although an allocation that is entirely cost-based may be desirable from an accounting perspective, it is not useful in the determination of efficient prices.

7. Nonlinear outlay schedules

In the previous two sections we have examined ways of increasing economic efficiency by charging different prices to customers in different markets served by the firm. For example, with peak load prices, daytime customers of electricity might be charged a price different from that charged to users of electricity in the nighttime. With Ramsey pricing as discussed in Section 6, shippers of different kinds of freight might be charged different rates by a railroad. However, in each case (Ramsey and peak load), users are still paying uniform prices within each market. For example, in the peakload case, daytime users are all paying the same (average) amount per unit purchased. We now extend the analysis of pricing to allow for tariffs which are not uniform as a way of improving economic efficiency still further. There is a rich literature on nonlinear outlays [see, for example, Oi (1971), Leland and Meyer (1976), Mirman and Sibley (1980), Schmalensee (1981), Spence (1981a), and Stiglitz (1977)], to name only a few important contributions. A particularly useful reference on this topic is Brown and Sibley (1986).

As was suggested in Section 4, there are many possible ways of structuring nonlinear outlay schedules; there the two part tariff was considered as one example. Recall that this kind of tariff has a "fixed" component and a "variable" component, as is illustrated in Figure 23.9. Suppose the customer must pay a fixed charge (sometimes called an entry charge) of $\$e$ per month to have access to the service in question (e.g. electricity or telephone service), where e is to be paid regardless of the number of units actually purchased. In addition customers would be required to pay a variable charge equal to m for each unit actually purchased during the month. The customer's total outlay would be $E = e + my$, an affine tariff schedule which is illustrated in Figure 23.9. The marginal outlay schedule (i.e. the schedule showing the *additional* expenditure m incurred with the purchase of an *additional* unit of service) is constant; the average outlay schedule, which is nonlinear, is also shown in the second panel of Figure 23.9.

[58] Consider the simple case of a two product firm operating at a Ramsey optimum (with zero economic profits) under an affine cost structure, $C = F + m_1 y_1 + m_2 y_2$; let the Ramsey optimal prices be (p_1, p_2). Then the contribution of revenues above the attributable costs for services 1 and 2 respectively would be $(p_1 y_1 - m_1 y_1)$ and $(p_2 y_2 - m_2 y_2)$; these two contributions must sum to F, since the firm is earning zero economic profits. Thus, the decimal fraction of the common cost F allocated to service 1 is $(p_1 y_1 - m_1 y_1)/F$.

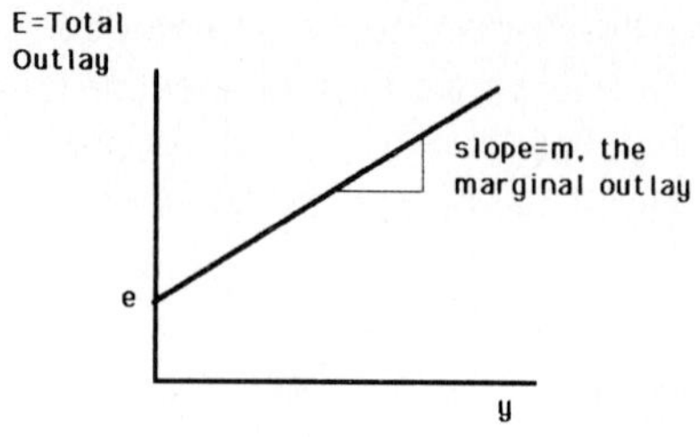

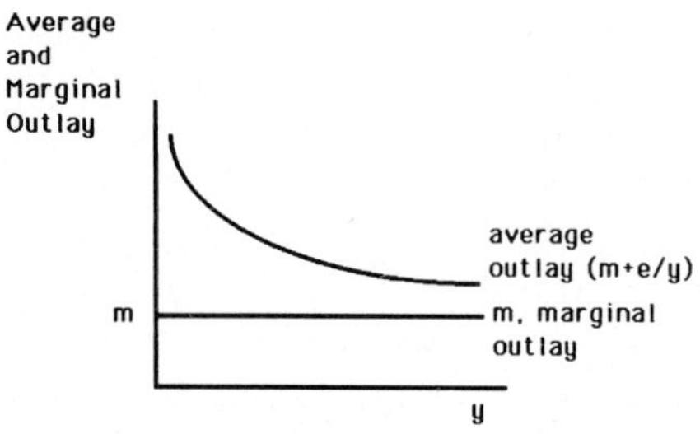

Figure 23.9. Affine tariff structure.

Note that a two part tariff with a zero fixed charge is therefore just a uniform tariff.

One could extend this approach to tariffs with more than two parts. For example, a four part tariff could be constructed with a fixed charge e, and three variable charges as follows:

$$E = \begin{cases} e + m_1 y, & \text{if } y \le y_1, \\ e + m_1 y_1 + m_2(y - y_1), & \text{if } y_1 \le y \le y_2, \\ e + m_1 y_1 + m_2(y_2 - y_1) + m_3(y - y_2), & \text{if } y_2 \le y. \end{cases} \tag{17}$$

This can be generalized to construct an "n part tariff", which consists of a fixed charge e and $(n - 1)$ variable charges, $m_1, m_2, \ldots, m_{n-1}$.

A nonlinear outlay schedule need not have a fixed charge. For example, suppose a tariff structure assesses each customer a charge of m_1 for each unit purchased up to some limit, y_1, and then a different amount per unit m_2 for each unit purchased in excess of y_1. Then the total outlay for the customer, E, would be as follows, where y is the number of units the customer purchases:

$$E = \begin{cases} m_1 y, & \text{if } y \le y_1, \\ m_1 y_1 + m_2(y - y_1), & \text{if } y > y_1. \end{cases} \tag{18}$$

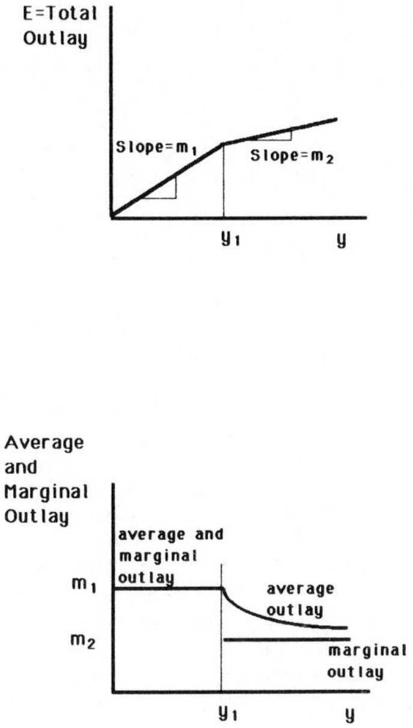

Figure 23.10. Nonlinear outlay structure.

The total, average and marginal outlay schedules for this tariff are shown in Figure 23.10. With this tariff, the average outlay is constant for output up to y_1, and declines thereafter, and is therefore nonlinear in y.

One could construct an n part tariff in which the number n becomes very large. In the limit, as n approaches infinity, the tariff schedule would result in a smooth nonlinear outlay schedule of the kind illustrated in Figure 23.11. This tariff involves a total outlay $E = e + G(y)$, where e is a fixed charge per month and $G(y)$ is the total variable charge per month. Here the slope of the total outlay schedule is continuously changing as output increases; since the slope of the total outlay schedule represents the value of the marginal outlay, the marginal outlay schedule is nonlinear everywhere in this example.

7.1. Pareto improving nonlinear outlay schedules

How might a nonlinear outlay schedule lead to improved economic efficiency over a uniform tariff? Willig (1978) has demonstrated that any uniform price not equal to marginal cost can be Pareto dominated by a nonlinear outlay schedule.

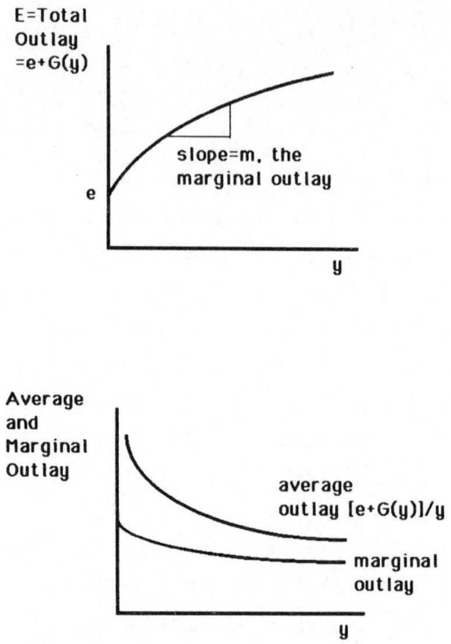

Figure 23.11. Nonlinear outlay schedule.

This important result can be illustrated with the aid of Figure 23.12.[59] Suppose a firm provides a product or service with an affine cost function, so that the marginal cost is constant. Consider the very simple example in which there are two consumers in the market, one with a "low" demand for the service, with a demand schedule D_L, and one with a "high" demand for the service, with a demand schedule D_H. If the firm must charge a uniform price to both consumers, the price must exceed marginal cost if the total revenues are to cover total costs

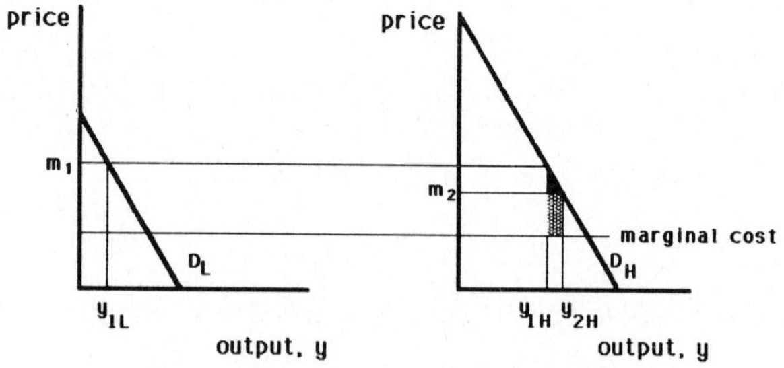

Figure 23.12. Pareto superior nonlinear outlay.

[59] This simple explanation was suggested to me in a conversation with John Panzar.

including the fixed cost of production; let the lowest uniform price that allows the firm to break even be m_1. At that price the quantities purchased by the low and high demand users will be y_{1L} and y_{1H} respectively, so that the total quantity demanded will be $(y_{1L} + y_{1H})$.

Now introduce some nonlinearity. Suppose that a tariff schedule like (18) were put in place. Figure 23.12 illustrates the demands of the two consumers, each demand being represented in a different panel of the figure. Suppose the tariff states that when consumer i purchases $y_i \leq y_{1H}$, his total outlay will be $m_1 y_i$. If the consumer purchases $y_i > y_{1H}$, then his total outlay will be $m_1 y_{1H} + m_2(y_i - y_{1H})$, where $m_2 < m_1$, and m_2 is assumed greater than marginal cost in the figure. Note that the large consumer will be better off, since his consumer surplus has increased by the amount represented by the area of the solid black triangle in Figure 23.12. The small consumer is unaffected by the change in the tariff schedule. Finally, the firm is strictly better off since its profits have increased by the amount represented by the area of the dotted rectangle in Figure 23.12. Thus, the large user and the firm are strictly better off and the small user is no worse off under the nonlinear tariff, and the new tariff is therefore Pareto superior to the uniform tariff. In fact the firm could take a portion of the excess profit it has generated with the nonlinear tariff and lower m_1 by some amount so that even the small users are better off.

In the example just considered, the nonlinear tariff constructed included no fixed charge. It is also possible that economic efficiency can be improved over the level achievable with a uniform tariff by introducing an n part tariff, which, as described earlier, has a fixed charge and $(n - 1)$ variable components.

To see how this might work, once again suppose a firm provides a product or service with an affine cost structure (with a fixed cost F) to a market with two consumers. Figure 23.13 illustrates the demands of the two consumers, with, as before, each demand being represented in a different panel. As before let the lowest uniform price that allows the firm to break even be m_1. Under this tariff low and high demand customers realize consumer surpluses represented respec-

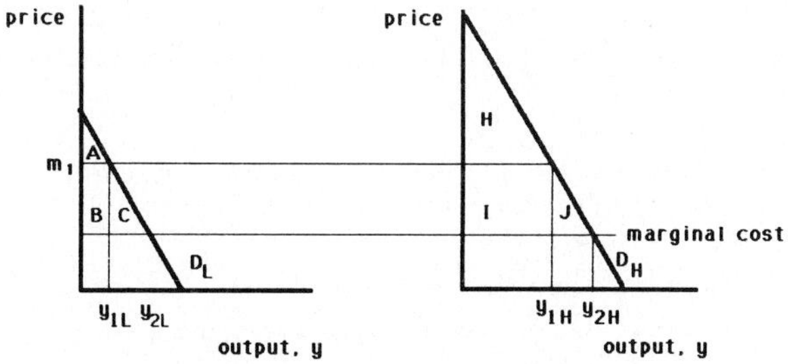

Figure 23.13. Pareto superior nonlinear outlay with entry fee.

tively by the areas A and H. The sum of the areas B and I will have the same magnitude as the fixed cost F since the firm is just breaking even when the tariff is m_1. The deadweight loss under m_1 is the sum of the areas C and J.

One possible way of introducing a two part tariff is to charge each customer a fixed charge $e = F/2$ and a variable component of the tariff equal to marginal cost.[60] As long as the area $(A + B + C)$ is greater than the fixed charge $F/2$, then both consumers will remain in the market.[61] Furthermore, the firm is still just breaking even under the two part tariff and the market is operating at first best since the deadweight loss $(C + J)$ has been eliminated.

As noted, this scheme is qualified by the condition that the area $(A + B + C)$ be greater than the fixed charge $F/2$. If this is not satisfied, then the smaller customer will drop out of the market since he would be better off with no service than with service under the two part tariff. One might be tempted to split the coverage of the fixed cost somewhat differently, perhaps assigning a smaller fixed component e_L to the smaller customer and a larger entry fee e_H to the larger user (still requiring that $e_L + e_H = F$). This may even be feasible if the firm can discriminate between the two users. However, in order to implement this discriminatory scheme, the firm must know the identity of the two customers (who is large and who is small) so that a large customer can not pretend to be small, thereby incurring only e_L, and leaving the firm with a deficit.[62] The problem arises here since the firm has established two different tariff schedules with the two entry fees, but has no way of forcing the high demand user to admit he is a high demand user in order to collect the higher entry fee from him.

The example illustrates that the limit on the efficiency of uniform entry fees is the elasticity of membership in the system with respect to the entry fee. Once users are recognized as being on the margin with respect to the entry fee, the entry fee becomes another price to be set with Ramsey pricing principles.

7.2. *Asymmetric information*

This brings us to one of the central ideas in the literature on nonlinear pricing: pricing under asymmetric information. Information is asymmetric here because the customer knows his own type, but in practice the firm often does not. If more

[60] This is the form of the two part tariff originally suggested by Coase (1946). The idea extends simply enough to the case of n consumers; each customer would pay a fixed fee equal to F/n, and a variable component equal to marginal cost.

[61] Since D_H is a "larger" demand than D_L (i.e. D_H would lie to the right of D_L if drawn on the same graph), the area $(H + I + J)$ exceeds the area $(A + B + C)$; if the low demand customer remains in the market under the two part tariff, so will the high demand customer.

[62] Even if the firm knows the identity of the two users, there is also a possible problem with entry fees since one user can resell the output to the other customer in a way that would make it more attractive than buying from the firm directly. This restriction on resale is a standard condition for price discrimination to be possible.

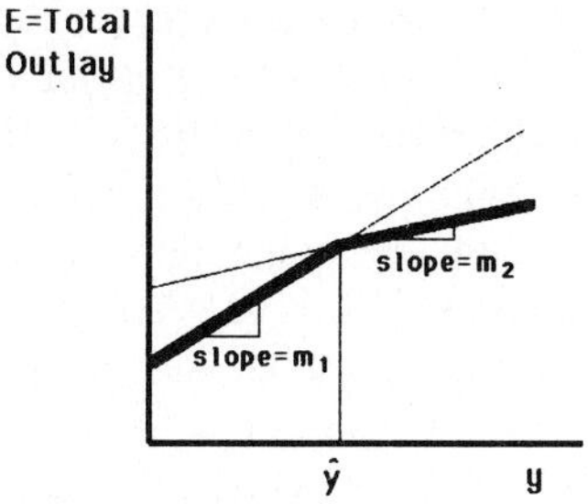

Figure 23.14. Self-selecting two part tariff.

than one tariff is announced by the firm, each consumer will choose ("self-select") that tariff schedule which is best for himself. In the case discussed above, each customer will find that the two part tariff with the lower entry fee dominates the one with the higher entry fee (since the variable components to the tariffs are identical), and no rational customer would ever pay the higher entry fee. It is therefore often not feasible to implement a pricing strategy which offers different tariff schedules to different customers.

Of course, this does not rule out a strategy of offering more than one tariff option to *all* customers. For example, the firm might announce two options that any customer may choose. The outlay schedules might take the form $E_i = e_i + m_i y$, where y is the amount purchased by an individual. Suppose there are two such options, with $e_1 < e_2$. Then in order for tariff schedule 1 not to be dominated by tariff schedule 2 for all customers, it must be the case that $m_1 > m_2$. Some customers (presumably the "high" demand users) may find their optimal consumption to be with a high entry fee and a low variable fee (schedule 2), while other customers (presumably the "low" demand users) might prefer a low entry fee and a high variable fee (schedule 1). Such an arrangement is sometimes referred to as a self-selecting two part tariff. This is illustrated in Figure 23.14. A customer planning on consuming $y < \hat{y}$ would find his total outlay lower under tariff schedule 1 than under schedule 2. If consumption is greater than $\hat{y}$, a customer would find it less expensive to purchase under schedule 2. The lower envelope of the outlay schedules (represented by the heavy line segments in Figure 23.14) indicates that outlay schedule that would be chosen by a rational consumer since it minimizes the outlay in purchasing any given quantity of the service.

In the example above, welfare was improved by offering a tariff with two options since there were two types of customers. In the example if three options were introduced, one of the options would not be utilized since there are only two types of customers. However, in general there may be many "types" of consumers, instead of just the "low" and "high" demand users considered in the examples above. With more types of customers one can improve welfare by allowing consumers to self-select among more options.

Consider an example in which there are $j = 1, \ldots, J$ consumer types. Assume that if a consumer of type j purchases service when confronted with an option (e_i, m_i), he will purchase $y^j(m_i)$. Assume the consumer types can be ordered from smallest to largest so that $y^1(m_i) < y^2(m_i) < \cdots y^J(m_i)$ for any m_i.[63] Now construct an n part tariff (with $n + 1 < J$) which is comprised of a collection of n two part tariffs $(e_1, m_1), (e_2, m_2), \ldots, (e_n, m_n)$ from which the consumer can select the one optimal for himself. Let the entry fees be ordered so that $e_1 < e_2 < \cdots e_n$, and the variable fees be ordered so that $m_1 > m_2 > \cdots m_n$, so that no option is always dominated by another for all customers. An extension of the reasoning of Willig (1978) leads to the conclusion that a Pareto improvement can be achieved by introducing still another option (e_{n+1}, m_{n+1}) with $m_{n+1} < m_n$ and m_{n+1} no less than marginal cost.[64] Although we do not treat it in detail here, the idea is as follows.

Consider a consumer of the highest demand type J, who is choosing the tariff whose parts are (e_n, m_n) under the n part tariff. Under the n part tariff, customer J's demand for the good was $y^J(m_n)$, and his total outlay was $e_n + m_n \cdot y^J(m_n)$. He will surely be induced to purchase under the new tariff option if his total outlay for $y^J(m_n)$ under (e_{n+1}, m_{n+1}) is less than it was under (e_n, m_n); in other words he will purchase under (e_{n+1}, m_{n+1}) if $e_{n+1} + m_{n+1} \cdot y^J(m_n) < e_n + m_n \cdot y^J(m_n)$. Restated, since the consumer's demand schedule is downward sloping, he will achieve new consumer surplus from the new units he will purchase at the new option (e_{n+1}, m_{n+1}).[65] The firm is no worse off since the total outlay on $y^J(m_{n+1})$ is as great as it was under the n part tariff, and the firm gets to keep any revenues above marginal cost on the new sales $y^J(m_{n+1}) - y^J(m_n)$. Thus, the $n + 1$ part schedule is Pareto superior to the n part tariff since both the firm and consumers of type J are better off under the new schedule, and consumers of other types are no worse off by having the new option available to them as well.

Although we have not yet addressed the optimality of a nonlinear outlay schedule, the arguments on Pareto superiority indicate that, at an optimum, the value of the variable component of the tariff (m_i) available to the largest class user will be equal to marginal cost. This important result follows from the fact that the Willig argument can be used to generate Pareto improvements whenever

[63] The assumption that demands can be ordered in the strongly monotonic fashion indicated by $y^1(m_i) < y^2(m_i) < \ldots < y^J(m_i)$ for any m_i is not innocuous, but it is the assumption utilized in most of the literature on nonlinear pricing. In particular it rules out the possibility that the demand schedules for any two types of consumers may intersect or cross one another at some price m_i.

[64] See chapter 4 of Brown and Sibley (1986) for an extended discussion of this point.

[65] The consumer gains from a lower m_{i+1} on the purchases of the $y^J(m_i)$ units he is already purchasing but those inframarginal gains are taxed away by the higher entry fee e_{m+1} under the new option. However, the consumer does get to keep the surplus on the additional units $[y^J(m_{i+1}) - y^J(m_i)]$ he purchases under (e_{n+1}, m_{n+1}).

m_i exceeds marginal cost, and therefore a value of m_i greater than marginal cost for the largest type user is not optimal.

One exception to the Pareto superiority arguments described in this section is worth noting. Ordover and Panzar (1980) have developed a model of a monopoly selling output to a single downstream industry. Thus, "consumers" of the product of the monopoly in this case are firms rather than direct end users, as we have considered above. Ordover and Panzar consider the case in which the downstream industry is competitive in its own product market, but that the firms in the industry differ with respect to their cost structure. Some of the firms produce with higher costs than others. Ordover and Panzar point out that if a nonlinear outlay schedule is introduced for the product of the monopoly, it may not be optimal to sell the final unit to the largest producer at marginal cost. This could occur since such a sale could lower the equilibrium price in the competitive downstream industry by enough so that "too many" higher cost firms are driven from the market, thereby eliminating a source of demand for the regulated product. They thereby demonstrate why it may be optimal for the final unit of the regulated product to be sold at a price greater than marginal cost.

7.3. Optimal nonlinear outlay schedules

Up to this point the discussion has addressed the Pareto superiority of nonlinear outlay schedules. The presentation has depended rather crucially on the ability to tailor nonlinear tariffs according to the desires of consumers of different types. It is worth stating that the results summarized so far do not depend on the distribution of consumer types. In other words, the Pareto superiority arguments depend on the existence of consumers of different types, they do not require information on the *number* of consumers of each type.

In the case of the determination of the exact values of the parameters of an optimal nonlinear outlay schedule, the distribution of consumer types (although not the identity of the type of any particular customer) must be known. The distribution may be discrete or continuous, and pricing formulations in the literature have treated both cases. [See, for example, Goldman, Leland and Sibley (1984) and Brown and Sibley (1986, chs. 4 and 5) for theoretical discussions of the problem of distribution of consumer types, and Mitchell (1978) for an empirical study of optimal pricing of local telephone service, which employs a lognormal distribution.]

In this subsection we briefly present one of the approaches that might be taken for the case in which consumers are distributed continuously. [This is treated in more detail in Brown and Sibley (1986, appendix to chapter 5).] Let θ be a parameter that indexes consumer type where observed types are bounded so that $\theta_L \leq \theta \leq \theta_U$, and let the (inverse) demand schedule for a type θ customer be

$p(y, \theta)$, with $p_y < 0$ and $p_\theta > 0$, the latter representing the strong monotonicity assumption that requires that demands of consumers of different types not cross one another. Denote the number of consumers of type θ by $g(\theta)$, with a cumulative measure $G(\theta)$. Also, assume the cost structure is affine with a fixed cost F and a constant marginal cost c.

Let the tariff schedule be $p(y)$. This schedule indicates the price a consumer must pay for the yth (marginal) unit; thus $p(y)$ is said to be the marginal price for any unit of output. For a given quantity y, there will be a critical value of θ, $\hat{\theta}$, such that a consumer of type $\hat{\theta}$ just has an incentive to purchase the yth unit under the tariff schedule $p(y)$. Thus, the marginal consumer type at y given $p(y)$ is defined by the self-selection condition $p(y) = p(y, \hat{\theta})$, since consumers of type $\theta > \hat{\theta}$ will purchase the unit while those of type $\theta < \hat{\theta}$ will not. The self-selection condition implies that $\partial\hat{\theta}/\partial p(y) = 1/[\partial p(y, \hat{\theta})/\partial\theta] > 0$, a fact that will be useful in a later substitution. The total consumer and producer surplus over all y can be written (ignoring the fixed cost F):

$$T = \int_0^\infty \left\{ \int_{\hat{\theta}}^{\theta_U} [p(y, \theta) - p(y)]\, g(\theta)\, d\theta + \left[1 - G(\hat{\theta})\right] \cdot [p(y) - c] \right\} dy, \tag{19}$$

where, for a differential (small) market dy around a given y, $\int [p(y, \theta) - p(y)] g(\theta)\, d\theta$ represents the consumer surplus for customers in the market (with $\theta \geq \hat{\theta}$) and $[1 - G(\hat{\theta})] \cdot [p(y) - c]$ represents producer surplus. Thus, integration over all y yields the total surplus associated with the schedule $p(y)$. The breakeven constraint for the firm (including the fixed cost F) is then:

$$\pi = \int_0^\infty \left\{ \left[1 - G(\hat{\theta})\right] \cdot [p(y) - c] \right\} dy - F \geq 0. \tag{20}$$

One can then characterize the outlay schedule $p(y)$ that maximizes (19) subject to (20). This leads to an expression of the following kind:

$$\frac{p(y) - c}{p(y)} = \frac{\lambda}{1 + \lambda} \cdot \frac{1 - G(\hat{\theta})}{p(y) g(\hat{\theta}) \partial\hat{\theta}/\partial p} = \frac{\lambda}{1 + \lambda} \cdot \frac{1}{\varepsilon(y, p(y))}, \tag{21}$$

where λ is the multiplier associated with the constraint (20), the quantity $[1 - G(\theta)]$ is the quantity demanded in the differential market dy, and $\varepsilon(y, p(y))$ is the absolute value of the price elasticity of demand in that differential market.[66]

[66] The second order conditions for an optimum require that the marginal price schedule $p(y)$ cut the willingness to pay schedule $p(y, \theta)$ from below [i.e. $p(y, \theta)$] must have a more negative slope in y than $p(y)$. For more on this see Goldman, Leland and Sibley (1984).

The relationship in (21) is of interest for several reasons. First, it is a kind of Ramsey rule now derived for a nonlinear outlay schedule instead of for the linear outlay schedules of Section 6. The deviation of price from marginal cost in each differential $\mathrm{d}y$ market is inversely related to the price elasticity of demand in that market. Although the actual calculation of optimal prices may be difficult, the notion of Ramsey optimality unifies the literature on linear and nonlinear outlays. Equation (21) also indicates that for the final unit purchased by the largest customer ($\theta = \theta^{\mathrm{U}}$), $G(\hat{\theta}) = 1$, so that price equals marginal cost. This verifies a principle of optimality suggested earlier in this section for the case in which all customers are end users (rather than businesses).

In addition to the points just noted, one can summarize some of the important ideas from the literature on nonlinear outlays as follows. If a firm cannot break even under uniform marginal cost pricing, nonuniform tariffs can be used to improve welfare in a Pareto superior fashion. Nonuniform prices do this by tailoring tariffs according to the preferences of various types of consumers. They are typically implemented in a setting of asymmetric information, since a consumer knows his type but the firm does not. If there are more types of consumers than two part options within a tariff structure, then a Pareto improvement is possible with the addition of still another two part option. Finally, an economically efficient nonlinear outlay schedule covers total costs by requiring consumers with the greatest demands to make larger contributions on the inframarginal units they purchase. An optimal pricing relationship can be interpreted as a kind of Ramsey pricing rule.

8. Interservice subsidy

The discussions of pricing in the last four sections have focused on the economic efficiency of various pricing alternatives under regulation. Yet it has often been argued that the historical emphasis in regulatory rate-making has been on the "fairness" of rates rather than whether rates are economically efficient. Parties to regulatory hearings as well as commissions themselves have often asked whether a proposed rate is "fair", even in cases in which a party argues that a rate is economically efficient. The frequent tension between pricing to achieve economic efficiency and pricing to avoid interservice subsidy have been effectively summarized by Zajac (1978).

In this section we discuss the concept of a fair rate. It is usually raised in connection with the prices charged by a multiproduct firm for its different services. It is also often cast in terms of a question as to whether a rate is free of "cross subsidy" or its synonym "interservice subsidy". Crudely speaking interservice subsidy is said to occur when some service (or group of services) is either (i) not generating revenues sufficient to cover its fair share of the costs or (ii) generating revenues that cover more than its fair share of the costs. The problem becomes particularly interesting and difficult when there are common costs of production in the sense defined in Section 4. Recall that common costs are those that are shared in the production of two or more services; it is therefore impossible to allocate these costs in an unambiguous fashion among the services of the firm. Since tests for cross subsidy typically relate revenues for a service (or group of services) to the costs of providing that service, attempts to base tests of subsidy on fully distributed costing methods are themselves fraught with ambiguity. Therefore in this section we will confine ourselves to tests of cross subsidy which avoid the allocations of common costs as a procedural matter.

One could still envision a number of tests. One possibility would be to require that a service be priced no lower than marginal cost if it is to avoid subsidy. This has the virtue of avoiding any allocation of common costs, but it is a rather weak test. To see this, suppose that the cost structure of the firm is affine with total costs $C = F + F_1 + m_1 y_1 + F_2 + m_2 y_2$, where $(F_i + m_i y_i)$ are costs unambiguously attributable to service i $(i = 1,2)$ and F is a common cost. In this simple case a service that is priced to pass the marginal cost test may not even generate revenues sufficient to cover the costs directly attributable to that service. For example, if $p_1 = m_1$ (which passes the marginal cost test for service 1), the revenues from service 1 will not cover any of the fixed cost F_1 directly attributable to that service. Furthermore, if the firm earns zero economic profits, the revenues from service 2 will have to cover the balance of the costs $(F + F_1 + F_2 + m_2 y_2)$; thus service 2 is generating revenues sufficient to cover not only all of its own attributable costs and all of the common costs F, but also all of the fixed cost F_1 directly attributable to service 1.

For these reasons the marginal cost test has not received widespread attention in the literature on regulation. Yet, if price were below marginal cost, one might well argue that at least the consumer of the marginal unit is being subsidized, since the price received for that unit would not cover the added costs of producing it. For that marginal unit the difference between price and marginal cost would have to be covered by revenues from other customers if the firm were to remain revenue adequate.

For a number of reasons discussed below the literature has focused on two other tests for subsidy. These are the *incremental cost test* and the *stand alone test*. To begin with, assume that the firm produces N products under a cost structure $C(y) = C(y_1, y_2, \ldots, y_N)$. Consider now any subset of these services $S \subseteq N$. Let $C(y_S)$ denote the cost of producing the given levels of products in the subset S, and let $C(y_{N-S})$ be the cost of providing the given levels of products other than those in the subset S.

The incremental cost test [as defined by Faulhaber (1975)] requires that the revenues from the subset S at least cover the increment to total cost that occurs when S is produced as opposed to not being produced at all, holding constant the levels of the outputs in y_{N-S}. Formally this test can be stated as follows:

$$\sum_{i \in S} p_i y_i \geq C(y) - C(y_{N-S}) \equiv IC_S, \tag{22}$$

where IC_S is the incremental cost of producing the product set S. If revenues from the product set S do not satisfy (22), then service S is said to be subsidized by revenues from other services.[67]

By contrast the stand alone test sets an upper (rather than a lower) bound on the revenues generated by services in the set S. The idea behind this test is that if the revenues generated by services in the subset S exceed the cost of providing those services alone, then users of the services in S are subsidizing users of other services. In other words suppose users of products in S are paying more revenues when S is provided in conjunction with other services not in S than they would have to pay if only the products in S are offered. Then the customers of S could in principle withdraw from the production process that generates S and the other services, form their own productive enterprise producing only S, and be better off, since the total revenues they would have to generate in a stand alone operation could be reduced relative to what they are currently paying. Formally the stand alone test can be represented as follows:

$$\sum_{i \in S} p_i y_i \leq C(y_S). \tag{23}$$

Several interesting observations can be made about these two tests. First, it can be shown that when profit for the firm is zero, then set S passes the incremental cost test if and only if the remaining product set $(N - S)$ passes the stand alone test. This can be demonstrated rather easily. Consider the condition that the firm is just breaking even:

$$\sum_{i \in N} p_i y_i = C(y). \tag{24}$$

Suppose S passes the incremental cost test, so that (22) is satisfied, and that the

[67]For example, under the affine cost structure

$$C = \begin{cases} F + F_1 + m_1 y_1 + F_2 + m_2 y_2, & y_1 > 0 \text{ and } y_2 > 0, \\ F + F_1 + m_1 y_1, & y_1 > 0 \text{ and } y_2 = 0, \\ F + F_2 + m_2 y_2, & y_1 = 0 \text{ and } y_2 > 0, \end{cases}$$

the incremental cost test on service 1 would require that $p_1 y_1 \geq F_1 + m_1 y_1$.

firm is just breaking even. Then subtracting (22) from (24) implies that

$$\sum_{i\in(N-S)} p_i y_i \leq C(y_{N-S}), \tag{25}$$

which is the condition that the stand alone test on $(N-S)$ is satisfied. This connection between the incremental cost test on S and the stand alone test on $(N-S)$ is valid for any partition of the product set N as long as the firm is earning zero economic profits.

A second observation about the subsidy tests is that it is not enough to test for subsidy only at the level of the individual services. In fact, when profits are zero either the incremental cost test or the stand alone test must be passed for *all* possible subsets S if subsidies are to be avoided [see Faulhaber (1975)].[68] With N services, this means that one would have to carry out $(2^N - 1)$ tests (including a test on all N services taken together) in order to be sure that all possible groups of services are free of subsidy.[69]

Third, in a contestable market, one would expect entry to occur if any of the subsidy tests (on any subset of services) were not satisfied. This follows directly from two observations. First, in a contestable market one would expect to see the firm just breaking even; otherwise entry would occur or service would disappear. Second, given zero economic profits, if any of the subsets of services fails one of the subsidy tests, there is some subset of products which is generating revenues in

[68] Faulhaber also contributed the important insight that for a multiproduct firm with a subadditive cost structure, there may be *no* prices that are subsidy free according to the incremental cost and stand alone cost tests for all subsets of services. Thus subsets of consumers might find it attractive to purchase from alternative suppliers, even though the natural monopoly structure indicates that it would be socially efficient to have only a single supplier. Panzar and Willig (1977) showed that cost complementarities eliminate this possibility.

[69] To see why this might be a problem, consider a three product affine cost structure as follows:

$$C = \begin{cases} F + F_{12} + F_1 + m_1 y_1 + F_2 + m_2 y_2 + F_3 + m_3 y_3, & y_1 > 0,\ y_2 > 0 \text{ and } y_3 > 0, \\ F + F_{12} + F_1 + m_1 y_1 + F_2 + m_2 y_2, & y_1 > 0,\ y_2 > 0 \text{ and } y_3 = 0, \\ F + F_{12} + F_1 + m_1 y_1 + F_3 + m_3 y_3, & y_1 > 0,\ y_2 = 0 \text{ and } y_3 > 0, \\ F + F_{12} + F_2 + m_2 y_2 + F_3 + m_3 y_3, & y_1 = 0,\ y_2 > 0 \text{ and } y_3 > 0, \\ F + F_{12} + F_1 + m_1 y_1, & y_1 > 0,\ y_2 = 0 \text{ and } y_3 = 0, \\ F + F_{12} + F_2 + m_2 y_2, & y_1 = 0,\ y_2 > 0 \text{ and } y_3 = 0, \\ F + F_3 + m_3 y_3, & y_1 = 0,\ y_2 = 0 \text{ and } y_3 > 0. \end{cases}$$

Then the incremental cost of producing y_1 is $C(y_1, y_2, y_3) - C(0, y_2, y_3) = F_1 + m_1 y_1$. Suppose that incremental cost test is just passed so that $p_1 y_1 = F_1 + m_1 y_1$. Similarly the incremental cost of producing y_2 is $C(y_1, y_2, y_3) - C(y_1, 0, y_3) = F_2 + m_2 y_2$. Suppose that incremental cost test is just passed so that $p_2 y_2 = F_2 + m_2 y_2$. Then the total revenues from services 1 and 2 will be $(F_1 + m_1 y_1 + F_2 + m_2 y_2)$; yet this falls short of the incremental costs of services 1 and 2 taken together by an amount F_{12}, since that incremental cost would be $C(y_1, y_2, y_3) - C(0, 0, y_3) = F_{12} + F_1 + m_1 y_1 + F_2 + m_2 y_2$. Therefore, passing the incremental cost test for individual services does not guarantee that the incremental cost test for a group of services collectively will be passed.

excess of stand alone costs. In a contestable market this subset of products would be a target for entrants who would be satisfied with normal returns on that subset.[70]

Finally, much has been written about the relationship between subsidy-free prices and economically efficient (particularly Ramsey optimal) prices. One important result is the Weak Invisible Hand Theorem of Baumol, Bailey and Willig (1977). These authors showed that, under a set of assumptions including (among others) economies of scale and transray convexity, Ramsey optimal price vectors are sufficient (but not necessary) for sustainability.[71] Since sustainable prices must be subsidy-free, then under the conditions of the Weak Invisible Hand Theorem, Ramsey optimal prices would be subsidy-free.

While the assumptions required for the Weak Invisible Hand Theorem may be plausible for many cases, they are not totally innocuous. Early on Zajac (1972) pointed out that Ramsey optimal prices need not be subsidy-free according to the incremental cost test. This is intuitively easy to understand. Consider a two product firm operating with an affine cost structure. One of the markets it serves has a demand that is highly elastic (call this market 1) and the other has a rather inelastic demand (market 2). Then the inverse elasticity rule (see Section 6) would indicate that the Ramsey optimal markup of price over marginal cost would be relatively small in market 1. However, suppose there are fixed costs that are directly attributable to service 1, and which are avoidable if that service is discontinued.[72] Then the incremental cost of service 1 would include that attributable fixed cost, which might not be covered by revenues under Ramsey optimal prices sufficiently close to marginal cost. An alternative characterization of the example just given is that the demand in market 2 is so inelastic that Ramsey optimal prices would yield a price in that market which violates the stand alone test in market 2.[73]

In a contestable market, such a price could not be sustained without entry since entry would occur in the market or set of markets that fail the stand alone test. In regulated markets which are not contestable, one could think of modify-

[70]This view of subsidy has been generalized to the industry level (as opposed to the level of the firm) in markets that are contestable. Faulhaber and Levinson (1981) point out that any (and all) groups of consumers will pay an amount at least equal to industry wide incremental cost and no more than their own stand alone cost, regardless of their identities or consumption choices; Faulhaber and Levinson therefore call this distributive property "anonymous equity".

[71]Among the other assumptions the Weak Invisible Hand Theorem in the form presented above does not apply when there are demand complementarities. The requirements of transray convexity and no demand complementarities can be relaxed to some extent [see appendix 11 to chapter 8 in Baumol, Panzar and Willig (1982)].

[72]The Weak Invisible Hand Theorem does not apply in this example because the cost function is not transray convex. This occurs because the directly attributable fixed cost for service 1 creates a discontinuity of the cost function when service 1 disappears.

[73]Concern over a situation like the one described here might occur if, for example, service 2 is essential to some group of users. If our two product firm is the sole supplier of this service, then the provision of the service might constitute a "bottleneck" to users who need this product.

ing the second best Ramsey optimal formulation of (11) and (12) in Section 6 by appending additional constraints to ensure that the resulting prices are as efficient as possible while both being subsidy-free and allowing the firm to break even. These additional constraints would contribute to dynamic efficiency by guiding prices to send appropriate signals on entry.

9. Conclusion

This chapter has examined a number of optimal policies that might be used to control a natural monopoly. It has indicated why the traditional view of natural monopoly, which argues for regulation when there are pervasive economies of scale in a market, has been extensively questioned and modified in the literature since the late 1960s. It provides a summary of the contemporary literature characterizing a natural monopoly and shows how economic analysis has suggested rather forcefully that there may be ways to introduce competition for a market, even if a natural monopoly structure exists within a market. Competition for the market in these instances will lead to economically efficient prices. The possible optimality of such competition (at least in the sense of second best) in dealing with a natural monopoly is one of the main themes pursued here.

The chapter has also indicated that there are circumstances under which competition as a policy toward natural monopoly may not be feasible, or, even if feasible, may not lead to an economically efficient market outcome. It has summarized a number of ways in which one might improve the allocation of scarce resources if price regulation is imposed. These included peak load, Ramsey, and nonlinear pricing schemes.

While most of the discussion has dealt with efficiency, the chapter has also addressed a set of issues related to the "fairness" of regulated prices. It presented and discussed a set of possible notions of "cross subsidy" or "interservice subsidy", and related these concepts and economically efficient prices to one another.

Research described in this chapter has no doubt contributed to the many economic arguments that have supported deregulation or other regulatory reform in a number of American industries since 1970. Examples include the deregulation of airlines, motor carriers and cable television. They also include the efforts of the postal service to eliminate cross subsidies among postal services, the Federal Communications Commission's use of peak load pricing principles for telephone services, changes in structure and pricing in the electric power industry under the Public Utility Regulatory Policy Act of 1978, and the decision of the Interstate Commerce Commission to use Ramsey pricing principles and interservice subsidy tests in the railroad industry. A better understanding of natural monopoly will no doubt lead to improved theoretical and empirical work in the future, and should contribute still more to enlightened policy.

References

Atkinson, A.B. and Stiglitz, J.E. (1980) *Lectures in public economics*. New York: McGraw-Hill.

Bailey, E.E. (1981) 'Contestability and the design of regulatory and antitrust policy', *American Economic Review*, 71:178–183.

Bailey, E.E. and Panzar, J.C. (1981) 'The contestability of airline markets during the transition to deregulation', *Law and Contemporary Problems*, 44:125–145.

Bailey, E.E. and White, L.J. (1974) 'Reversals in peak and off-peak prices', *Bell Journal of Economics*, 5:75–92.

Bailey, E.E., Graham, D.R. and Kaplan, D.P. (1985) *Deregulating the airlines*. Cambridge: MIT Press.

Baumol, W.J. (1982) 'Contestable markets: An uprising in the theory of industry structure', *American Economic Review*, 72:1–15.

Baumol, W.J. and Bradford, D.E. (1970) 'Optimal departures from marginal cost pricing', *American Economic Review*, 60:265–283.

Baumol, W.J. and Willig, R.D. (1981) 'Fixed cost, sunk cost, entry barriers and sustainability of monopoly', *Quarterly Journal of Economics*, 95:405–431.

Baumol, W.J., Bailey, E.E. and Willig, R.D. (1977) 'Weak invisible hand theorems on the sustainability of prices in a multiproduct monopoly', *American Economic Review*, 67:350–365.

Baumol, W.J., Panzar, J.C. and Willig, R.D. (1982) *Contestable markets and the theory of industry structure*. New York: Harcourt Brace Jovanovitch.

Baumol, W.J., Panzar, J.C. and Willig, R.D. (1984) 'Contestable markets: An uprising in the theory of industry structure: Reply', *American Economic Review*, 73:491–496.

Bohm, P. (1967) 'On the theory of 'second best',' *Review of Economic Studies*, 34:301–314.

Boiteux, M. (1956) 'Sur la gestion des monopoles publics astreint á l'équilibre budgetaire', *Econometrica*, 24:22–40.

Boiteux, M. (1971) 'On the management of public monopolies subject to budgetary constraints', *Journal of Economic Theory*, 3:219–240.

Braeutigam, R.R. (1979) 'Optimal pricing with intermodal competition', *American Economic Review*, 69:38–49.

Braeutigam, R.R. (1980) 'An analysis of fully distributed cost pricing in regulated industries', *Bell Journal of Economics*, 11:182–196.

Braeutigam, R.R. (1983) 'A dynamic analysis of second best pricing', in: J. Finsinger, ed., *Public sector economics*. London: Macmillan, 103–116.

Braeutigam, R.R. (1984) 'Socially optimal pricing with rivalry and economies of scale', *Rand Journal of Economics*, 15:124–131.

Braeutigam, R.R. and Noll, R.G. (1984) 'The regulation of surface freight transportation: The welfare effects revisited', *The Review of Economics and Statistics*, 56:80–87.

Brock, W.A. (1983) 'Contestable markets and the theory of industry structure', *Journal of Political Economy*, 91:1055–1066.

Brock, W.A. and Dechert, W. (1983) 'Dynamic Ramsey pricing', manuscript, Department of Economics, University of Wisconsin–Madison.

Brock, W.A. and Scheinkman, J.A. (1983) 'Free entry and the sustainability of natural monopoly: Bertrand revisited by Cournot', in: D.S. Evans, ed., *Breaking up Bell: Essays on industrial organization and regulation*. Amsterdam: North-Holland.

Brown, S.J. and Sibley, D.S. (1986) *The theory of public utility pricing*. Cambridge: Cambridge University Press.

Carlton, D. (1977) 'Peak load pricing with stochastic demands', *American Economic Review*, 67:1006–1010.

Caves, D., Christensen, L. and Tretheway, M. (1983) 'The structure of airline costs and prospects for the U.S. airline industry under deregulation', SSRI workshop series paper 8313, University of Wisconsin–Madison.

Chamberlin, E. (1962) *The theory of monopolistic competition*, 8th edn. Cambridge: Harvard University Press.

Clark, J.M. (1923) *Studies in the economics of overhead costs*. Chicago: University of Chicago Press.

Coase, R. (1946) 'The marginal cost controversy', *Economica*, 13:169–189.

Crew, M. and Kleindorfer, P. (1976) 'Peak load pricing with a diverse technology', *Bell Journal of Economics*, 7:207–231.
Crew, M. and Kleindorfer, P. (1986) *The economics of public utility regulation*. Cambridge: MIT Press.
Demsetz, H. (1968) 'Why regulate utilities?', *Journal of Law and Economics*, 11:55–65.
Diamond, P. and Mirlees, J. (1971) 'Optimal taxation and public regulation', *American Economic Review*, 61:261–278.
Dixit, A. (1982) 'Recent developments in oligopoly theory', *American Economic Review*, 72:12–17.
Evans, D.S. and Heckman, J.J. (1984) 'A test for subadditivity of the cost function with an application to the Bell system', *American Economic Review*, 74:615–623.
Faulhaber, G.R. (1975) 'Cross-subsidization: Pricing in public enterprises', *American Economic Review*, 65:966–977.
Faulhaber, G.R. and Levinson, S. (1981) 'Subsidy free prices and anonymous equity', *American Economic Review*, 71:1083–1091.
Fiorina, M.P. and Noll, R.G. (1978) 'Voters, bureaucrats and legislators: A rational choice perspective on the growth of bureaucracy', *Journal of Public Economics*, 9:239–254.
Friedlaender, A.F. (1969) *The dilemma of freight transport regulation*. Washington, D.C.: Brookings Institution.
Friedlaender, A.F. and Spady, R. (1982) *Freight transport regulation*. Cambridge: MIT Press.
Goldberg, V. (1976) 'Regulation and administered contracts', *Bell Journal of Economics*, 7:250–261.
Goldman, M.B., Leland, H.E. and Sibley, D.S. (1984) 'Optimal nonuniform prices', *Review of Economic Studies*, 51:305–319.
Hotelling, H. (1938) 'The general welfare in relation to problems of taxation and railway and utility rates', *Econometrica*, 6:242–269.
Hughes, J.R.T. (1977) *The governmental habit: Economic controls from colonial times to the present*. New York: Basic Books.
Joskow, P.L. and Noll, R.G. (1981) 'Regulation in theory and practice: An overview', in: G. Fromm, ed., *Studies in public regulation*. Cambridge: MIT Press, 1–65.
Joskow, P.L. and Schmalensee, R. (1981) *Markets for power: An analysis of electric utility deregulation*. Cambridge: MIT Press.
Kahn, A.E. (1970) *The economics of regulation: Principles and institutions*, vol. I. New York: Wiley.
Kahn, A.E. (1971) *The economics of regulation: Principles and institutions*, vol. II. New York: Wiley.
Knieps, G. and Vogelsang, I. (1982) 'The sustainability concept under alternative behavioral assumptions', *Bell Journal of Economics*, 13:234–241.
Leland, H. and Meyer, R. (1976) 'Monopoly pricing structure with imperfect discrimination', *Bell Journal of Economics*, 7:449–462.
Lipsey, R.G. and Lancaster, K. (1956–57) 'The general theory of second best', *Review of Economic Studies*, 24:11–32.
Littlechild, S.C. (1970) 'Peak-load pricing of telephone calls', *Bell Journal of Economics and Management Science*, 1:191–200.
Mirlees, J.M. (1976) 'Optimal tax theory: A synthesis', *Review of Economic Studies*, 38:175–208.
Mirman, L.J. and Sibley, D. (1980) 'Optimal nonlinear prices for multiproduct monopolies', *Bell Journal of Economics*, 11:659–670.
Mirman, L.J. and Tauman, Y. (1982) 'Demand compatible, equitable, cost sharing prices', *Mathematics of Operations Research*, 7:40–56.
Mirman, L., Samet, D. and Tauman, Y. (1983) 'Axiomatic approach to the allocation of a fixed cost through prices', *Bell Journal of Economics*, 14:139–151.
Mitchell, B.M. (1978) 'Optimal pricing of local telephone service', *American Economic Review*, 68:517–537.
Moore, T.G. (1986) 'Rail and trucking deregulation', in: L.W. Weiss and M.W. Klass, eds., *Regulatory reform: What actually happened*. Boston: Little, Brown, 14–39.
Noll, R.G. and Owen, B.M. (1983) *The political economy of deregulation: Interest groups in the regulatory process*. Washington, D.C.: American Enterprise Institute.
Oi, W.Y. (1971) 'A Disneyland dilemma: Two part tariffs for a Mickey Mouse monopoly', *Quarterly Journal of Economics*, 85:77–90.

Ordover, J.A. and Panzar, J.C. (1980) 'On the nonexistence of Pareto superior outlay schedules', *Bell Journal of Economics*, 11:351–354.

Owen, B.M. and Braeutigam, R.R. (1978) *The regulation game: Strategic use of the administrative process*. Cambridge: Ballinger.

Owen, B.M. and Willig, R.D. (1981) 'Economics and postal pricing policy', in: J. Fleishman, ed., *The future of the Postal Service*. New York: Praeger.

Panzar, J.C. (1976) 'A neoclassical approach to peak load pricing', *Bell Journal of Economics*, 7:521–530.

Panzar, J.C. (1980) 'Sustainability, efficiency and vertical integration', in: P. Kleindorfer and B.M. Mitchell, eds., *Regulated industries and public enterprise*. Lexington: Heath.

Panzar, J.C. and Willig, R.D. (1977) 'Free entry and the sustainability of natural monopoly', *Bell Journal of Economics*, 8:1–22.

Peltzman, S. (1976) 'Toward a more general theory of regulation', *Journal of Law and Economics*, 19:2111–2140.

Pigou, A.C. (1920) *The economics of welfare*. London: MacMillan.

Posner, R.A. (1974) 'Theories of economic regulation', *Bell Journal of Economics and Management Science*, 5:335–358.

Ramsey, F.P. (1927) 'A contribution to the theory of taxation', *Economic Journal*, 37:47–61.

Rees, R. (1984) *Public enterprise economics*. London: Weidenfeld and Nicolson.

Rohlfs, J.H. (1979) 'Economically efficient Bell system pricing', Bell Laboratories Economic Discussion Paper 138.

Samet, D. and Tauman, Y. (1982) 'A characterization of price mechanisms and the determination of marginal cost prices under a set of axioms', *Econometrica*, 50:895–910.

Scherer, F.M. (1980) *Industrial market structure and economic performance*. Chicago: Rand McNally.

Schmalensee, R. (1978) *The control of natural monopolies*. Lexington: Lexington Books.

Schmalensee, R. (1981) 'Monopolistic two-part pricing arrangement', *Bell Journal of Economics*, 12:445–466.

Schwartz, M. and Reynolds, R. (1984) 'Contestable markets: An uprising in the theory of industry structure', *American Economic Review*, 73:488–490.

Sharkey, W.W. (1981) 'Existence of sustainable prices for natural monopoly outputs', *Bell Journal of Economics*, 12: 144–154.

Sharkey, W.W. (1982a) 'Suggestions for a game theoretic approach to public utility pricing and cost allocation', *Bell Journal of Economics*, 13:57–68.

Sharkey, W.W. (1982b) *The theory of natural monopoly*. Cambridge: Cambridge University Press.

Shephard, W. (1984) '"Contestability" vs. competition', *American Economic Review*, 74:572–587.

Sherman, R. and Visscher, M. (1978) 'Second best pricing with stochastic demand', *American Economic Review*, 68:41–53.

Sorenson, J., Tschirhart, J. and Winston, A. (1978) 'A theory of pricing under decreasing costs', *American Economic Review*, 68:614–624.

Spady, R. and Friedlaender, A.F. (1978) 'Hedonic cost functions for the regulated trucking industry', *Bell Journal of Economics*, 9:159–179.

Spence, A.M. (1981a) 'Multi-product quantity dependent prices and profitability constraints', *Review of Economic Studies*, 47:821–841.

Spence, A.M. (1981b) 'Nonlinear prices and welfare', *Journal of Public Economics*, 8:1–18.

Steiner, P.O. (1957) 'Peak loads and efficient pricing', *Quarterly Journal of Economics*, 71:585–610.

Stigler, G. (1971) 'The theory of economic regulation', *Bell Journal of Economics and Management Science*, 2:3–21.

Stigler, G. (1975) *The citizen and the state: Essays on regulation*. Chicago: University of Chicago Press.

Stiglitz, J.E. (1977) 'Monopoly, nonlinear pricing and imperfect information', *Review of Economic Studies*, 44:407–430.

Sweeney, G. (1982) 'Welfare implications of fully distributed cost pricing applied to partially regulated firms', *Bell Journal of Economics*, 13:525–533.

Taussig, F.W. (1913) 'Railway rates and joint costs', *Quarterly Journal of Economics*, 27:692–694.

Turvey, R. (1968) *Optimal pricing and investment in electricity supply*. Cambridge: MIT Press.
Turvey, R. (1969) 'Marginal cost', *Economic Journal*, 79:282–299.
Visscher, M. (1973) 'Welfare maximizing price and output with stochastic demand: Comment', *American Economic Review*, 63:224–229.
Waverman, L. (1975) 'Peak-load pricing under regulatory constraint: A proof of inefficiency', *Journal of Political Economy*, 83:645–654.
Weil, Jr., R.L. (1968) 'Allocating joint costs', *American Economic Review*, 58:1342–1345.
Weiss, L.W. and Klass, M.W. (1981) *Case studies in regulation: Revolution and reform*. Boston: Little, Brown.
Weiss, L.W. and Klass, M.W. (1986) *Regulatory reform: What actually happened*. Boston: Little, Brown.
Weitzman, M. (1983) 'Contestable markets: An uprising in the theory of industry structure: Comment', *American Economic Review*, 73:486–487.
Wiedenbaum, M.W. (1978) *The cost of government regulation of business*. Washington, D.C.: U.S. Congress, Joint Economic Committee, Subcommittee on Economic Growth and Stabilization.
Williamson, O.E. (1966) 'Peak load pricing and optimal capacity under indivisibility constraints', *American Economic Review*, 56:810–827.
Williamson, O.E. (1976) 'Franchise bidding for natural monopolies – in general and with respect to CATV', *Bell Journal of Economics*, 7:73–104.
Willig, R.D. (1976) 'Consumer's surplus without apology', *American Economic Review*, 66:589–597.
Willig, R.D. (1978) 'Pareto superior nonlinear outlay schedules', *Bell Journal of Economics*, 9:56–59.
Willig, R.D. (1979) 'The theory of network access pricing', in: H.M. Trebing, ed., *Issues in public utility regulation*. East Lansing, Michigan: Michigan State Public Utilities Papers, 109–152.
Willig, R.D. and Bailey, E.E. (1979) 'The economic gradient method', *American Economic Review*, 69:96–101.
Winston, C. (1981) 'The welfare effects of ICC rate regulation revisited', *Bell Journal of Economics*, 12:232–244.
Zajac, E.E. (1972) 'Some preliminary thoughts on subsidization', presented at the Office of Telecommunications policy research conference on communication policy research, Washington, D.C.
Zajac, E.E. (1974) 'Note on an extension of the Ramsey inverse elasticity of demand pricing or taxation formula', *Journal of Public Economics*, 3:181–184.
Zajac, E.E. (1978) *Fairness or efficiency: An introduction to public utility pricing*. Cambridge: Ballinger.

Chapter 24

DESIGN OF REGULATORY MECHANISMS AND INSTITUTIONS

DAVID P. BARON*

Stanford University

Contents

*This research has been supported by NSF Grant No. IST-8606157. The author would like to thank Robert Gibbons, Michael Riordan, David Sappington, Robert Thomas, Jean Tirole, Barry Weingast, and Michael Whinston for their helpful suggestions.

Handbook of Industrial Organization, Volume II, Edited by R. Schmalensee and R.D. Willig

1. Introduction

Regulation involves government intervention in markets in response to some combination of normative objectives and private interests reflected through politics. Whatever objective regulation is intended to achieve, the regulator must choose policies tailored to the particular regulatory setting and to the characteristics of the firms subject to its authority. In choosing those policies, the regulator must take into account the strategies the firm might employ in response to those policies. The focus of this chapter is the design of regulatory policies that take into account the opportunities for strategic behavior provided by incomplete information and limited observability on the part of the regulator.

Dupuit (1952) was perhaps the first to address the regulatory design issue when he considered the pricing policy for a bridge that requires a fixed expenditure for its construction but has no incremental cost for a crossing. He concluded that the first-best pricing policy was to set a price of zero for each crossing and to levy a fixed charge to cover the costs of construction. Dupuit reached this conclusion under the assumptions that (1) the designer has complete information about the construction cost of the bridge, (2) the costs are not a function of actions taken during construction or operation, and (3) the costs remain the same over time. The design of regulatory mechanisms is straightforward, albeit complex, in such a case where the regulator or mechanism designer has the same information as the regulated firm, can observe the actions taken by the firm, and has the authority to exercise control.[1]

The focus of this chapter is the design of regulatory mechanisms and institutions in settings in which the regulator has incomplete information and limited ability to observe the actions of the firms under its jurisdiction. Incomplete information and limited observability create opportunities for strategic behavior on the part of both the regulator and the regulated. The mechanisms considered in this chapter are reflections of that strategic behavior and will be characterized as equilibria of a game whose structure corresponds to the authority granted to the regulator. Regulatory policies are thus viewed as endogenous responses to informational asymmetries and limited observability rather than as exogenously-specified mechanisms descriptive of actual regulatory arrangements. Although the mechanisms may thus be weak in their descriptive power, they reflect the incentives present in regulatory relationships and take into account how the parties involved respond to those incentives.

[1] The optimal regulatory policies for this setting are characterized in Chapter 23 of this Handbook.

This chapter is not intended to provide a complete survey of the many contributions to this literature but rather is intended to provide a unified approach to the design of mechanisms progressing from a simple setting such as that studied by Dupuit and to more complex settings involving dynamics and multiple parties. Surveys of this literature have recently been provided by Caillaud, Guesnerie, Rey and Tirole (1988), Sappington and Stiglitz (1986), and Besanko and Sappington (1987). In addition, Romer and Rosenthal (1985) have surveyed the political dimension of regulatory research, and Hart and Holmstrom (1987) present an overview of contracting theory under symmetric information with a focus on cases in which performance is not verifiable by the participants.

The context in which the theory of regulatory mechanisms will be developed in this chapter is the regulation of a franchise monopolist in an industry characterized by decreasing average costs. This simple setting permits a focus on mechanism design without the complication of strategic competition among suppliers. The approaches developed here are applicable to a variety of other regulatory and nonregulatory settings including defense procurement, the control of bureaucracies and government-owned firms, and labor-managed firms.[2]

To motivate the setting to be considered, it is useful to consider a number of features of regulation in the United States. In the United States regulation is applied to firms owned by private investors, so at least in principle regulated firms have the same objectives as any other firm.[3] The firms considered here will thus be represented as profit-maximizers and will be assumed to take whatever actions are permitted within the regulatory framework to maximize their profits. The regulator, however, has broader objectives, so the regulatory relationship involves a conflict of objectives that is resolved endogenously through the strategies chosen by the regulator and the firm.

The objective of the regulator is generally not unambiguous and depends on a variety of normative and positive factors. From a normative perspective the regulator might be charged with maximizing total surplus or might be assigned distributional objectives such as maximizing the surplus of consumers. From a positive perspective regulation may be a response to competing interests of consumers and firms as intermediated by a legislature. Although some regulatory commissions are publicly-elected and others are appointed, in either case the legislature is responsible for the budget of the regulator and for monitoring the

[2] The models presented here can be directly applied to the case of the provision of goods by public agencies either through procurement from privately-owned firms or through a bureaucracy. Niskanen (1971) was the first to pose formally the question of the control of a bureaucracy that has private information about the cost of production.

[3] An exception is cooperatives which, for a variety of reasons including favorable tax treatment and antitrust exemptions, have grown to some importance in the United States in certain regulated industries such as electricity. Cooperatives can be considered in the framework developed here using a model related to that of a labor-managed firm. Guesnerie and Laffont (1984) develop the theory of a labor-managed firm in the context of the information and observability problems considered here.

performance of the regulator. The electoral relationship, directly between voters and regulators or indirectly through executive officers and legislators, suggests the possibility, if not the likelihood, that regulatory objectives reflect interests manifested through an electoral connection. Consequently, the design of regulatory mechanisms will be parameterized by the weight assigned to various interests.

In furthering its objective the regulator is bound by the limits of the authority delegated to it.[4] In the case of a franchise monopoly, regulatory authority generally includes control over prices and profits and often extends to the approval of investment and financing plans. The regulator may also have the authority to command certain information from the firm and to monitor its performance. That authority, however, generally does not include the power to impose taxes on the firm or to subsidize it from public funds.[5] Consequently, the revenue received by the firm comes from consumers and not from the state. Since property rights must be respected, regulatory authority is also constrained by procedural requirements derived from constitutional protections including due process, just compensation in the form of a fair return on invested capital, administrative requirements specified in the Administrative Practices Act and in the regulator's mandating legislation, and procedures established by the regulatory body itself. The regulator may, however, be allowed to impose certain limited penalties on the firm.

To indicate the difference between exogenously-specified and endogenous regulatory mechanisms, a model, presented by Averch and Johnson (1962), of an exogenously-specified regulatory mechanism is considered in the next section. In Section 3 endogenous mechanisms are introduced, and an equilibrium mechanism is characterized in Section 4 for a static model in which the firm has private information about its marginal cost. The regulatory setting in that section is based on the assumption that the regulator is unable to observe the performance of the firm, so in Section 5 the regulator is assumed to be able to observe, perhaps imperfectly and at a cost, the actual cost incurred by the firm. In Section 6 the models are extended to a dynamic setting with an emphasis on the ability of the regulator to commit to a multiperiod policy. The models considered in these sections involve a regulator and firm that has already been selected to be the supplier, and in Section 7 mechanisms are introduced that incorporate both the selection of the firm and the policy to regulate the selected firm. The selection of the regulated firm is a form of ex ante competition that improves the efficiency of

[4]The capture theory of regulation as developed by political scientists argues that the regulators adopt the objectives of the firms they regulate either because the initial legislation establishing the regulation reflects those interests or because the firm induced the regulator to share its goals. Those political forces will not be considered here.

[5]The authority to impose taxes is generally restricted to representative bodies elected by the citizenry. In addition, regulatory agencies are seldom granted appropriations to be used to subsidize either the firm or consumers. Cross-subsidization among consumers, however, is a frequently observed characteristic of regulation.

regulation, and in Section 8 ex post competition is considered. Section 9 considers the case in which the regulator also has private information that may be revealed by the mechanism it chooses. The mechanisms considered in these sections are Bayesian in the sense that they are based on a probabilistic representation of the information available to the parties. In Section 10 non-Bayesian mechanisms are considered in which the regulator bases its policy in each period on the observation of performance in previous periods. Extensions are considered in Section 11, and directions for future research are considered in the final section.

2. Exogenous regulatory mechanisms: The Averch–Johnson model

Early research on regulatory mechanisms focused on models representing stylized descriptions of actual regulatory processes. For example, the regulation of public utilities can be viewed as a grant of a franchise monopoly to a firm and the subsequent setting of prices that generate sufficient revenue from customers to cover the total costs of the firm including a fair return on the capital employed. This "revenue requirements" perspective is characterized by Robichek (1978) and Breyer (1982) and may be thought of as focusing on cash and noncash costs. Since cash costs are measured by accounting systems that are audited on a regular basis, attention often centers on noncash costs such as the required return to equity capital.[6] The model formulated by Averch and Johnson thus ostensibly focuses on controlling monopoly profits with a regulatory mechanism that establishes the rate-of-return on equity that the firm is allowed to earn.[7]

An alternative interpretation of the Averch–Johnson model is as a mechanism employed in response to incomplete information about characteristics of the firm's costs or demand. Averch and Johnson assume that the profit, or the cash flow, and the capital stock of the firm are observable and thus base the regulatory mechanism on those two variables. With those observables, it is natural to view the regulator as directly controlling profit as a function of the capital the firm employs, or equivalently indirectly controlling profit through the rate-of-return the firm is allowed to earn. Both pricing and factor input decisions are thus delegated to the firm. A sufficient condition for the firm to participate in this regulatory arrangement is thus that the allowed rate-of-return is at least as great as the cost of capital to the firm.

The model is formulated with the firm choosing its capital κ and labor L inputs with the price set to equate demand to the resulting output q. The

[6]Regulation may also focus on cash costs as in the case of fuel adjustment clauses.

[7]Comprehensive analysis of the implications of the Averch–Johnson model are provided by Baumol and Klevorick (1970) and Bailey (1973). A number of models including Bailey and Coleman (1971) extend the Averch–Johnson framework to multiperiod settings to investigate the consequences of regulatory lag on the efficiency of input choices.

production function $q = G(\kappa, L, \theta)$ may be specified as incorporating a technology parameter θ about which the firm is informed and the regulator is not. The profit π of the firm is

$$\pi = R(q) - wL - r\kappa, \tag{2.1}$$

where $R(q)$ is the resulting revenue, w is the factor price of labor, and r is the cost of capital. In the Averch–Johnson formulation, the revenue is given by $R(q) = P(q)q$, where $P(q)$ is the inverse demand function. With this price structure, regulation cannot achieve first-best efficiency if the technology is characterized by increasing returns to scale. Second-best efficiency is thus the relevant efficiency standard for the Averch–Johnson model.

Regulation as represented in the Averch–Johnson model is equivalent to specifying an allowed rate-of-return s which is applied to the capital stock so as to restrict the profit of the firm, i.e.[8]

$$\pi = P(q)q - wL - r\kappa \leq (s - r)\kappa. \tag{2.2}$$

The right-hand side of (2.2) represents the excess return $(s > r)$ allowed by the regulator to enable the firm to access the capital markets.[9]

The incentives created by regulation in the Averch–Johnson model are evident from (2.2). Since the price (or output) and the factor input decisions are delegated to the firm, it will choose them to maximize its profits. To do so, the firm will choose the largest capital stock κ such that it can attain the allowed profit $s\kappa$. Intuitively, the firm would like (a) to have as low an output price as possible so that more capital can be employed and (b) to substitute capital for labor so that more capital can be employed for whatever output is produced. Such substitution increases costs, however, which requires a higher price and that reduces the capital that can be employed.

To determine the optimal factor inputs, it is convenient to rewrite the profit function in terms of the labor requirements function $L(q, \kappa, \theta)$ defined by

$$q \equiv G(\kappa, L(q, \kappa, \theta), \theta). \tag{2.3}$$

The Lagrangian $\mathscr{L}$ for the firm's problem of maximizing π in (2.1) subject

[8]The regulator is assumed to know the cost of capital or at least an upper bound on that cost.
[9]The constraint in (2.2) can be restated in terms of the cash flow $(P(q)q - wL)$ of the firm as

$$P(q)q - wL \leq s\kappa.$$

From this specification, it is clear that the regulator is assumed to be able to observe the cash flow and the capital stock of the firm.

to (2.2) is

$$\mathscr{L} = P(q)q - wL(q,\kappa,\theta) - r\kappa$$
$$+\lambda[(s-r)\kappa - (P(q)q - wL(q,\kappa,\theta) - r\kappa)],$$

where λ is a non-negative multiplier. The first-order condition for κ is

$$-(1+\lambda)(wL_\kappa + r) + \lambda(s-r) = 0, \tag{2.4}$$

where L_κ is the partial derivative of L with respect to κ. The multiplier λ is positive when s is below the monopoly rate of return, so

$$L_\kappa = -\frac{r}{w} + \frac{\lambda(s-r)}{1+\lambda} > -\frac{r}{w}. \tag{2.4a}$$

Efficiency requires that $L_\kappa = -r/w$, so the firm employs more capital relative to labor than is efficient given the quantity produced. This is Averch and Johnson's well-known overcapitalization result.

The quantity the firm chooses satisfies the first-order condition:

$$P'(q)q + P(q) - wL_q = 0. \tag{2.5}$$

Thus, q, κ, and λ are determined by (2.4), (2.5), and (2.2) as an equality.[10]

The Averch–Johnson model of regulation predicts both technical and allocative inefficiency. First, the firm employs too much capital relative to labor for the output it produces. Second, because production is inefficient, the required price is too high. These inefficiencies result because the regulator is assumed either only to be able to observe the profit and capital stock of the firm or only to have the authority to restrict profits.

These inefficiencies would not result under a variety of other assumptions. For example, if factor prices and the technology, including θ, were known to the regulator and the regulator had the authority to regulate the price, the regulator could simply specify the price corresponding to the efficient marginal cost. The regulator can determine the efficient marginal cost because it knows the factor prices and the technology. That is, if $L^*(q,\theta)$ and $\kappa^*(q,\theta)$ denote the efficient inputs given the quantity q and the parameter θ, the regulator's problem is

$$\max_q q$$

$$\text{subject to } \pi^*(q) \equiv P(q)q - wL^*(q,\theta) - r\kappa^*(q,\theta) = 0. \tag{2.6}$$

[10]The firm never has an incentive to waste capital or to gold plate, since waste is dominated by substituting capital for labor to reduce the marginal cost in (2.5).

The solution q^* is the quantity that maximizes total surplus subject to the constraint that $\pi^*(q) = 0$.

Since all regulators of public utilities have the authority to regulate prices, Baron and Taggart (1980) interpret the Averch–Johnson model as representing a naive regulator that in effect adjusts price as a function of the cost incurred by the firm. That is, the price can be viewed as a function $p(\kappa)$ chosen to generate revenue sufficient to cover cost. That is, $p(\kappa)$ is defined by

$$p(\kappa)Q(p(\kappa)) \equiv wL(Q(p(\kappa)), \kappa, \theta) + s\kappa,$$

where $Q(\cdot)$ denotes the demand function. The firm then maximizes profit with respect to κ subject to the constraint:

$$p(\kappa)Q(p(\kappa)) - wL(Q(p(\kappa)), \kappa, \theta) - s\kappa \geq 0,$$

which requires that the price $p(\kappa)$ be such that the allowed rate of return can be earned. Baron and Taggart show that this naive regulation results in the Averch–Johnson outcome. Regulatory behavior in the Averch–Johnson model is thus equivalent to the regulator setting the price for the output of the firm in response to the capital input the firm chooses.

As is evident from (2.6), the regulator can act in a sophisticated manner by setting a price p^S taking into account the firm's response to that price. For any price p^S, the firm will choose the efficient inputs $L^*(Q(p^S), \theta)$ and $\kappa^*(Q(p^S), \theta)$, so the regulator can achieve second-best efficiency by choosing the lowest price p^S such that total revenue covers total cost or $p^S = P(q^*)$. If second-best efficiency is not achieved, it thus must be due to incomplete information, limited observability, or restricted authority.

The Averch–Johnson model thus may be given two interpretations. One interpretation is that the regulator and the firm have symmetric information about demand and cost, and the regulator acts naively by regulating profit by controlling the rate of return. Since this interpretation provides no explanation for why the regulator does not regulate in a sophisticated manner, it is not very compelling. The second interpretation is that information is asymmetric and/or that the regulator has only a limited ability to observe the actions of the firm. For example, if the regulator does not know the parameter θ of the production function and is only able to observe the capital input and profit, the Averch–Johnson model represents one form that regulation could take. A more satisfactory approach, however, is to ask if the representation of regulation in the Averch–Johnson model would arise endogenously as the optimal form of regulation when information is either incomplete or observability is limited.[11] The approach taken in the following sections is thus not to focus on the properties of

[11] Besanko (1984) adopts this approach, and his model is considered in Subsection 4.7.

exogenously-specified mechanisms but to derive endogenously the regulatory mechanisms as a function of the information, observable variables, and authority present in the regulatory setting.

3. Asymmetric information and regulatory mechanisms

3.1. Introduction

The consideration of endogenous regulatory mechanisms will begin with the case in which the firm has private information about its costs. Suppose that the cost function $C(q, \theta)$ of the firm is a function of output q and a parameter $\theta \in \Theta \subset \Re^1$, which represents private information about its costs. The parameter θ will at times be referred to as the "type" of the firm. The parameter θ might, for example, represent as in the previous section a characteristic of the production function, or factor prices that are observable only to the firm because they involve opportunity costs, or managerial ability. The cost function will be assumed to be an increasing function of θ for all $q > 0$, so higher values of θ correspond to a less efficient firm. In addition, marginal cost C_q will be assumed to be increasing in θ. Higher θ thus correspond to higher average and marginal costs. The firm is assumed to know θ, but the regulator has only imperfect information about θ as represented by a density function $f(\theta)$ defined on the domain Θ of possible types. All other information is assumed to be common knowledge.

The regulator is assumed to have the authority to control certain aspects of the firm's operations, and in the case of public utilities, the most widespread authority is over prices. The authority to regulate prices is generally accompanied by the requirement that the firm satisfy all demand at the designated price.[12] The price is important for the efficiency of the regulatory mechanism, since if the price structure involves only a unit price so that revenue equals $pQ(p)$, the resulting mechanisms may be quite inefficient if, for example, production is characterized by increasing returns to scale.[13] Efficiency can be improved if a nonlinear price structure can be used. To simplify the analysis, the nonlinear price structure will be assumed to be two-part, composed of a unit price p and a fixed payment. The fixed payment could be a direct transfer from the state paid from taxes, or a fixed charge in a two-part pricing policy in which consumers pay a unit price p plus an amount independent of the quantity purchased. The two-part pricing policy interpretation will be used here. To simplify the analysis,

[12] The regulator need not monitor or police all the activities of the firm directly. For example, the regulator may post the price for the firm's output and let customers detect any deviations. McCubbins and Schwartz (1984) refer to this as fire alarm monitoring, since consumers can be relied upon to alert the regulator to any deviation from the established price or for failure to satisfy demand at that price.

[13] Baron (1985a) analyzes this case in the context of a simple model.

the demand of consumers will be assumed to depend only on the price p.[14] The analysis thus can be conducted in terms of the aggregate fixed charges T paid to the firm by consumers. The regulatory instruments thus are the price p (or equivalently the quantity q) and the aggregate fixed charges T transferred between consumers and the firm, where $T > (<) 0$ represents a transfer from (to) consumers to (from) the firm.

To represent the institutional structure of regulation in which the regulator has authority over aspects of the firm's operations, the regulator is assumed to move first by making a take-it-or-leave-it offer of a mechanism. The regulator, however, does not know θ, so it is unable to specify directly the first-best pricing policy. Instead, the regulator will prefer to offer a mechanism, a menu of price policies (p, T), to the firm and to let the firm select from the menu the policy that it prefers given its type. The task of the regulator is to design the mechanism in such a manner that the policy chosen by the firm is efficient given the incomplete information available to the regulator.[15]

The regulatory relationship may be modeled as a Bayesian game as defined by Harsanyi (1967–68). Formally, the players, the regulator and the firm, are assumed to have common knowledge about the distribution $f(\theta)$ of possible types, and Nature moves first by drawing a type θ for the firm. The regulator moves next by choosing a mechanism which is a set of pricing policies (p, T). The firm moves last, and its strategy is the selection of one of the policies. The regulatory policy to be studied is then the equilibrium of this game.

This regulatory game can be viewed in terms either of delegation or of revelation. In the delegation formulation, the regulator is viewed as delegating the price decision to the firm by specifying a mechanism $\{t(p), p \in [0, \infty)\}$, where $t(p)$ is the fixed charges expressed as a function of the price p the firm chooses. By making $t(p)$ a decreasing function of the price, the firm can be induced to choose a price below the monopoly price. In this formulation, a strategy of the firm is thus a mapping $p(\cdot)$: $\Theta \to [0, \infty)$. In the revelation approach, the price $p(\hat{\theta})$ and the fixed charges $T(\hat{\theta})$ can be viewed as functions of $\hat{\theta} \in \Theta$, where $\hat{\theta}$ denotes the choice made by the firm. That choice may be modeled as the firm choosing a report $\hat{\theta}$ to make to the regulator and the regulator then using the report to set the prices $(p(\hat{\theta}), T(\hat{\theta}))$. Thus, regulation involves a report about, or a revelation of, the firm's true type θ. A strategy of the firm thus is a response function $\hat{\theta}(\cdot)$: $\Theta \to \Theta$. The delegation and the revelation formulations are based on the principle of self-selection in which the regulator chooses a mechanism or menu of policies and the firm chooses a policy from that menu. Actual regulatory

[14] The total fixed charge may thus be thought of as apportioned among consumers in such a manner that no consumer is excluded from purchasing the good.

[15] This structure is closely related to that in the optimal taxation literature as initiated in the seminal work of Mirrlees (1971).

procedures may be thought of as having this feature, since pricing rules are generally responsive to the information about costs reported by the firm.

With either formulation of the regulatory game, the natural incentive of the firm is to choose too high a price, or equivalently, to overstate ($\hat{\theta} = \hat{\theta}(\theta) > \theta$) its cost, in order to obtain a higher price and thereby a higher profit. To illustrate this incentive, consider the case of constant marginal cost with the cost function specified as

$$C(q, \theta) = \theta q + K,$$

where θ is marginal cost and K is the fixed cost. Suppose that the regulator attempted to implement the first-best policy $p(\hat{\theta}) = \hat{\theta}$ and $T(\hat{\theta}) = K$. Given this policy, the profit $\pi(\hat{\theta}; \theta)$ of the firm when it reports $\hat{\theta}$ and its true marginal cost is θ, is

$$\pi(\hat{\theta}; \theta) = p(\hat{\theta})Q(p(\hat{\theta})) - \theta Q(p(\hat{\theta})) - K = (\hat{\theta} - \theta)Q(p(\hat{\theta})) - K.$$

The firm will choose its report $\hat{\theta}(\theta)$ to satisfy the first-order condition:

$$Q(\hat{\theta}(\theta)) + (\hat{\theta}(\theta) - \theta)Q'(\hat{\theta}(\theta)) = 0,$$

which implies that $\hat{\theta}(\theta) > \theta$. The firm thus has a natural incentive to overstate its cost to obtain a higher price and a higher profit. This is not to be thought of as something approaching fraud but instead might correspond to the selective presentation of data and choice of methodologies intended to achieve a more profitable policy.[16] To mitigate this incentive, the regulator can choose both a price function that differs from marginal cost and a fixed charges function that dampens the incentive to overstate costs. In the equilibrium to be characterized in Section 4, the regulator finds it optimal to choose a mechanism from the class of mechanisms which induce the firm to choose a truthful report $\hat{\theta}(\theta) = \theta$.

The next two subsections present the delegation and revelation approaches in more detail.

[16]Ruff (1981) describes a federal expenditure program that illustrates the information problem faced by the designers of institutions and procedures. The Federal Water Pollution Control Act of 1972 established a program under which federal funds would be allocated to build municipal sewage treatment facilities. In 1971 prior to enactment, the EPA had assessed the funds requirements of municipalities to be \$18 billion, but by 1974 the needs estimate had increased to \$342.3 billion. In part this was due to additional pollution control requirements included in the Act, but it also undoubtedly reflected "that municipalities are competing for federal funds by overstating their 'needs,'..." [Ruff (1981, p. 256)]. Although this expenditure program may be as much pork barrel as pollution control, the informational asymmetry between the municipalities and the program administrators undoubtedly limits the efficiency of the program.

3.2. The delegation approach

Consider the case in which the regulatory objective is the maximization of total surplus TS where

$$TS = CS + \Pi,$$

and

$$CS \equiv \int_p^\infty Q(p^0)\,\mathrm{d}p^0 - t(p) \tag{3.1}$$

is consumer surplus, and

$$\Pi = pQ(p) + t(p) - \theta Q(p) - K$$

is profit.[17] The optimal regulatory policy in this case has been given by Loeb and Magat (1979) who observed that if the transfer $t(p)$ equals consumer surplus plus the fixed cost K, the profit of the firm will equal total surplus. The firm then will choose to price at marginal cost.[18]

To demonstrate this, suppose that the regulator delegates the price (or equivalently, the output) decision to the firm and specifies the transfer $t(p)$ as

$$t(p) = \int_p^\infty Q(p^0)\,\mathrm{d}p^0 + K. \tag{3.2}$$

The profit $\Pi(\theta)$ of the firm with parameter θ then is

$$\Pi(\theta) = pQ(p) + \int_p^\infty Q(p^0)\,\mathrm{d}p^0 - \theta Q(p). \tag{3.3}$$

This equals total surplus, so by acting as a profit-maximizer the firm will find it in its interest to set $p(\theta)$ equal to marginal cost θ. To verify this, the first-order condition for the maximum of profit in (3.3) is

$$\frac{\mathrm{d}\Pi(\theta)}{\mathrm{d}p} = [p(\theta) - \theta]Q'(p(\theta)) = 0. \tag{3.4}$$

Whatever its type, the firm thus finds it in its interests to choose the welfare maximizing price.

[17]More general welfare functions could be used in the analysis, but the use of consumer surplus is convenient for relating regulatory policy to pricing.

[18]This result was also noted by Weitzman (1978, p. 685).

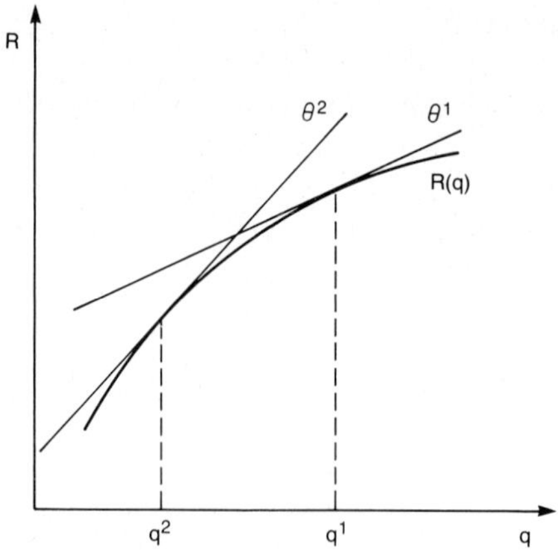

Figure 24.1. Self-selection.

This delegation approach relies on self-selection where a type θ is given the incentive to choose a price $p(\theta)$ that equals marginal cost thus yielding first-best efficiency. The self-selection nature of this mechanism may be illustrated graphically in quantity–revenue space. The quantity $q = Q(p)$ the firm chooses to produce under the regulatory policy corresponds to a revenue $R(q) \equiv P(q)q + t(P(q))$, so profit is $\Pi = R(q) - \theta q - K$. An indifference curve of the firm in R–q space thus has slope

$$\frac{\mathrm{d}R}{\mathrm{d}q} = \theta .$$

The revenue function $R(q)$, or offer curve, specified by the regulator has slope

$$R'(q) = P(q),$$

which is decreasing in q, as indicated in Figure 24.1. The optimality condition in (3.4) is equivalent to a firm of type θ choosing a quantity that equates the slope of its indifference curve to the slope of the regulator's offer curve. A firm with a low marginal cost θ^1 has a flatter indifference curve than a firm with a high marginal cost θ^2 ($\theta^2 > \theta^1$), so as indicated in Figure 24.1, a firm with type θ^1 will select a greater quantity q^1 than a firm with higher marginal cost θ^2 will select.[19] The regulatory mechanism thus induces the firm to choose the quantity appropriate for its type.

An important feature of this mechanism is that it has minimal information requirements, since the regulator only needs to know the demand function and

[19] This is the familiar "single-crossing" property employed in signalling models.

requires no information about the cost function. The regulator thus can use the same mechanism whatever is its prior information about θ. Furthermore, if the costs of the firm are random and realized after the firm has produced, first-best efficiency is still attained. The regulator thus has no need to monitor the activities of the firm and hence has no demand for observable measures of performance.

The firm will choose to participate in the regulatory relationship only if its profit is non-negative, and the profit $\Pi(\theta)$ is

$$\Pi(\theta) = p(\theta)Q(p(\theta)) + \int_{p(\theta)}^{\infty} Q(p^0)\,\mathrm{d}p^0 + K - \theta Q(p(\theta)) - K,$$

$$= \int_{p(\theta)}^{\infty} Q(p^0)\,\mathrm{d}p^0 \geq 0. \tag{3.5}$$

Profit is a strictly decreasing function of θ, since $p(\theta)$ is an increasing function of θ. A low-cost firm thus earns greater profit than does a high-cost firm.

Consumer surplus under the equilibrium mechanism is determined by substituting (3.2) into (3.1), which indicates that consumer surplus equals $-K$. In contrast, the profit of the firm equals total surplus plus K. This regulatory mechanism thus achieves first-best efficiency but leaves a distributional problem, since the firm captures all the surplus leaving none for consumers.[20] One response to this distributive problem is to auction the right to be the franchise monopolist and to distribute the proceeds to consumers in the form of lump-sum payments. This issue will be considered in more detail in Section 7.

3.3. The revelation approach

In the revelation approach, a regulatory policy is represented by a pair of functions $(p(\hat{\theta}), T(\hat{\theta}))$ that give the price and fixed charges as a function of the report $\hat{\theta}$ made by the firm. The resulting profit $\pi(\hat{\theta}; \theta)$ is

$$\pi(\hat{\theta}; \theta) = p(\hat{\theta})Q(p(\hat{\theta})) + T(\hat{\theta}) - \theta Q(p(\hat{\theta})) - K. \tag{3.6}$$

The transfer corresponding to $t(p)$ in (3.2) is

$$T(\hat{\theta}) = \int_{p(\hat{\theta})}^{\infty} Q(p^0)\,\mathrm{d}p^0 + K. \tag{3.7}$$

Assuming that $p(\hat{\theta})$ is differentiable, substitution of $T(\hat{\theta})$ into (3.6) and differ-

[20] Consumers, of course, receive profits in proportion to their ownership share.

entiation with respect to $\hat{\theta}$ yields the necessary optimality condition:

$$\frac{\partial \pi(\hat{\theta};\theta)}{\partial \hat{\theta}} = (p(\hat{\theta}) - \theta)Q'(p(\hat{\theta}))p'(\hat{\theta}) = 0. \tag{3.8}$$

If the price function is specified as $p(\hat{\theta}) = \hat{\theta}$, the firm will thus report truthfully, i.e. $\hat{\theta} = \theta$, and price then equals marginal cost. The first-best allocation is thus attained.

As with the delegation approach, this mechanism can be interpreted as a self-selection mechanism. In the revenue–quantity space in Figure 24.1, a firm reports a type which determines the quantity to be supplied and the revenue to be received. The mechanism induces a firm with a lower marginal cost θ^1 to choose a point on the offer curve corresponding to a greater output than that chosen by a firm with a higher marginal cost θ^2. The offer curve chosen by the regulator in equilibrium induces the firm to choose the pricing policy corresponding to its true marginal cost.

3.4. A generalized welfare measure

The mechanism characterized in the previous two subsections results in first-best efficiency because the objective of the regulator is the maximization of total surplus. Although this welfare function is consistent with normative principles, it does not appear to be descriptive of the actual objectives of regulators nor does it reflect the costs associated with implementing regulatory policies. Consequently, from a positive perspective the equilibrium may not be a good predictor of the efficiency consequences of implementing a regulatory mechanism when information is asymmetric. Laffont and Tirole (1986, 1988), for example, argue that transfers between a firm and either consumers or the state may involve administrative costs, tax distortions, or inefficiencies that must be taken into account in the design of the regulatory mechanism. Baron and Myerson (1982) consider a regulatory objective that is a weighted function of consumer and producer surplus. A rationale for this specification is that regulators are interested in serving the interests of the citizens in their jurisdiction, and since all the consumers reside in the regulatory's jurisdiction but not all of the owners of the firm do, state regulatory commissions adopt a perspective that favors consumer interests over producer interests. Both Bower (1981) and Bailey (1976), who have served on regulatory commissions, argue that this is descriptive of the approach of regulatory commissions.

A complete regulatory theory would explain how regulatory objectives arise in addition to characterizing the regulatory policy following from those objectives.

Baron (1988) presents a positive model of the choice of a regulatory objective based on the control of a regulatory commission by a legislature. Suppose, for example, that the institutional arrangement is hierarchical with a legislature choosing the regulatory objective and the regulatory commission choosing the mechanism optimal for that objective. If each legislator has (induced) preferences over the well-being of consumers and of the owners of the firm who reside in his or her jurisdiction, the preferences of the legislators will not be identical because of differences in constituencies and differences in the distributive consequences of policies. To simplify the analysis, suppose that the legislature is to choose the weight α, $\alpha \in [0,1]$, in the "welfare" function W^* or regulatory mandate given by

$$W^* = CS + \alpha\pi . \tag{3.9}$$

If the legislature is to choose α by majority rule and if induced preferences are single-peaked in α, the equilibrium α will be the ideal point of the median legislator.[21] This ideal point would be expected to be an $\alpha < 1$ if a majority of legislators favor consumer, and hence voter, interests over the interests of the owners of the firm.

With this specification, a transfer of a dollar from consumers to the firm would result in a "loss" of $(1 - \alpha)$ dollars. The Loeb and Magat mechanism is thus costly to implement, since it results in a loss equal to a $(1 - \alpha)$ proportion of the fixed charges in (3.7) transferred between consumers and the firm. In the remainder of this chapter the more general and descriptive specification of the regulatory objective in (3.9) will be employed. This specification, of course, includes when $\alpha = 1$ – the special case of total surplus.

An implication of the use of a total surplus specification of the regulatory objective is that the equilibrium mechanism is independent of the prior information $f(\theta)$ the regulator has about marginal cost θ. Consequently, if the regulator knows θ or if it has very imprecise information, the same mechanism would be employed. This is a result of the assumption that transfers between the firm and consumers are costless. For $\alpha < 1$ in (3.9), the equilibrium mechanism will depend on the information the regulator has about θ.

4. Asymmetric information: A general revelation approach

4.1. Feasible mechanisms

To characterize the equilibrium in this regulatory game, the approach of Baron and Myerson (1982) and Guesnerie and Laffont (1984) will be adopted. They

[21]See Black (1958) for the demonstration of this result.

view mechanism design as involving two stages. In the first, the class of implementable or feasible mechanisms is characterized, and in the second stage, the optimal or equilibrium mechanism is selected from that class. More formally, in the revelation approach the regulatory relationship is represented as a Bayesian game in which the regulator chooses a mechanism that is optimal given the optimal response of the firm, and given that mechanism the firm chooses an optimal strategy conditional on its private information. The game will be modeled as a direct revelation game in which a strategy of the firm is a mapping $\hat{\theta}(\theta)$ from the set Θ of possible types into itself or $\hat{\theta}(\cdot)$: $\Theta \to \Theta$. A strategy for the regulator is a collection of policies $(p(\hat{\theta}), T(\hat{\theta}))$ for each type $\hat{\theta}$ that the firm may report. Such a strategy is referred to as a mechanism and is denoted by $M = \{(p(\hat{\theta}), T(\hat{\theta})), \hat{\theta} \in \Theta\}$.[22] When the strategy set is the set of types, the game form is referred to as direct, and M is said to be a direct revelation mechanism.

In the Bayeisan approach, the regulator is assumed to have prior information about the parameter θ represented by a density function $f(\theta)$, which, to avoid technical problems, will be assumed to be positive on its support which will be specified as $\Theta = [\theta^-, \theta^+]$. A Bayesian Nash equilibrium of this game is (1) a mechanism $M^* = \{(p^*(\hat{\theta}), T^*(\hat{\theta})), \hat{\theta} \in \Theta\}$ that maximizes the regulator's objective given the strategy $\hat{\theta}^*(\cdot)$ of the firm, and (2) a strategy $\{\hat{\theta}^*(\theta), \theta \in \Theta\}$ that maximizes the firm's profit for each possible type given the mechanism M^*.

To determine an equilibrium of this game, it is useful to apply the *revelation principle* which states that, given any mechanism $M^+ = \{(p^+(\hat{\theta}), T^+(\hat{\theta})), \hat{\theta} \in \Theta\}$ such that the optimal response of the firm is $\hat{\theta}^+(\theta)$, there exists another mechanism $M = \{(p(\theta), T(\theta)), \theta \in \Theta\}$ that induces a response $\hat{\theta}(\theta) = \theta$, $\forall \theta \in \Theta$, and is at least as good in terms of the regulator's objective as is the mechanism M^+.[23] The revelation principle thus states that the regulator can restrict its attention to the class of mechanisms in response to which the firm reports its type truthfully. To demonstrate this, define the policies by

$$p(\cdot) \equiv p^+(\hat{\theta}^+(\cdot)) \quad \text{and} \quad T(\cdot) \equiv T^+(\hat{\theta}^+(\cdot)).$$

Given the mechanism $M = \{(p(\theta), T(\theta)), \theta \in \Theta\}$, the firm finds it optimal to report θ truthfully, since doing so yields the same outcome attained with the

[22] The firm can choose to participate in the game and will do so only if its profit is non-negative, but that decision will be suppressed to simplify the notation. Similarly, the regulator's strategy can be defined to include the decision of whether to allow the firm to produce as a function of $\hat{\theta}$. To simplify the notation, consumer surplus is assumed to be sufficiently great that the regulator prefers to have all types produce.

[23] The revelation principle is established in Myerson (1979), Dasgupta, Hammond and Maskin (1979), and Harris and Townsend (1981).

original, and optimal, response $\hat{\theta}^+(\theta)$ to the mechanism M^+. The revelation principle thus implies that the regulator can restrict its attention to the class of mechanisms such that the firm has no incentive to misrepresent its type. Such mechanisms are said to be incentive compatible.[24]

The advantage of the revelation approach is that it provides a means of characterizing the class of feasible mechanisms and allows the equilibrium to be computed from a programming problem. The first step in the characterization of the regulatory equilibrium is thus to determine the class of implementable incentive compatible mechanisms. A mechanism is implementable, or feasible, if it is incentive compatible and induces the firm to participate in the regulatory relationship.

The firm will choose a response function $\hat{\theta}(\theta) = \theta$ if its profit $\pi(\theta; \theta)$ is at least as great as the profit $\pi(\hat{\theta}; \theta)$ it could obtain for any report $\hat{\theta}$. Thus, the class of incentive compatible mechanisms is the set of mechanisms that satisfy the constraints:

$$\pi(\theta) \equiv \pi(\theta; \theta) \geq \pi(\hat{\theta}; \theta), \quad \forall \hat{\theta} \in [\theta^-, \theta^+], \quad \forall \theta \in [\theta^-, \theta^+]. \tag{4.1}$$

These constraints are *global* in the sense that for each θ, they must be satisfied for all reports $\hat{\theta} \in [\theta^-, \theta^+]$.

The firm is assumed to have the right not to participate in the regulatory relationship and will participate only if its profit $\pi(\theta)$ is at least as great as its reservation profit, which will be assumed to zero. A mechanism thus must satisfy:[25]

$$\pi(\theta) \geq 0, \quad \forall \theta \in [\theta^-, \theta^+]. \tag{4.2}$$

These constraints are referred to as individual rationality or participation constraints.

A mechanism $M = \{(p(\theta), T(\theta)), \ \theta \in [\theta^-, \theta^+]\}$ will be said to be implementable or *feasible* if it satisfies (4.1) and (4.2). The firm will respond to any feasible mechanism with a strategy $\hat{\theta}(\theta) = \theta$ for all $\theta \in [\theta^-, \theta^+]$. Characteriza-

[24] For the class of incentive compatible mechanisms, the firm has a dominant strategy of responding truthfully.

[25] To deal with the case in which the firm's cost is sufficiently high that the regulator's objective function is negative, the regulator can be viewed as denying the firm the franchise. In the formulation here, this can be modeled as the regulator specifying as a component of the mechanism a probability $r(\hat{\theta})$ that the firm will be granted a franchise when it reports $\hat{\theta}$. The equilibrium in this model specifies a $\theta^* \in [\theta^-, \theta^+]$ such that the probability equals zero for $\theta > \theta^*$ and equals one for $\theta \leq \theta^*$ as Baron and Myerson show. This specification is used in Subsection 4.3 for the case of asymmetric information about fixed costs.

tion of the class of feasible mechanisms will proceed in four steps based on the approach in Baron and Myerson. The first step is to determine a property of the profit function implied by the constraints in (4.1). The second step is to use that property to replace the set of individual rationality constraints in (4.2) by a single constraint. The third step is to specify the form of the fixed charges function $T(\theta)$ that implements "locally" any price function $p(\theta)$. The fourth step is to develop a necessary and sufficient condition on $p(\theta)$ for $\hat{\theta}(\theta)=\theta$ to be a globally optimal or equilibrium response of the firm to the mechanism $M = \{(p(\theta), T(\theta)),\ \theta \in [\theta^-, \theta^+]\}$. Once the class of feasible mechanisms has been characterized, the regulator can solve a programming program to determine the optimal, and thus equilibrium, mechanism.

For the first step, note that the profit $\pi(\hat{\theta}; \theta)$ of the firm of type θ that reports its type as $\hat{\theta}$ can be rewritten as

$$\pi(\hat{\theta}; \theta) = \pi(\hat{\theta}) + C\big(Q(p(\hat{\theta})), \hat{\theta}\big) - C\big(Q(p(\hat{\theta})), \theta\big). \tag{4.3}$$

For an incentive compatible mechanism the constraints in (4.1) imply, using (4.3):

$$\begin{aligned}\pi(\theta) &\geq \pi(\hat{\theta}; \theta)\\ &= \pi(\hat{\theta}) + C\big(Q(p(\hat{\theta})), \hat{\theta}\big) - C\big(Q(p(\hat{\theta})), \theta\big),\end{aligned} \tag{4.1a}$$

which implies that

$$\pi(\theta) - \pi(\hat{\theta}) \geq C\big(Q(p(\hat{\theta})), \hat{\theta}\big) - C\big(Q(p(\hat{\theta})), \theta\big). \tag{4.4}$$

Reversing the roles of θ and $\hat{\theta}$ in (4.3) and (4.1a) implies that

$$\pi(\theta) - \pi(\hat{\theta}) \leq C\big(Q(p(\theta)), \hat{\theta}\big) - C\big(Q(p(\theta)), \theta\big). \tag{4.5}$$

Combining (4.4) and (4.5) yields for all $\hat{\theta}$ and θ:

$$\begin{aligned}C\big(Q(p(\theta)), \hat{\theta}\big) - C\big(Q(p(\theta)), \theta\big) \geq \pi(\theta) - \pi(\hat{\theta}) \geq\ & C\big(Q(p(\hat{\theta})), \hat{\theta}\big)\\ & - C\big(Q(p(\hat{\theta})), \theta\big).\end{aligned} \tag{4.6}$$

Dividing the inequalities in (4.6) by $\hat{\theta} - \theta$ for $\hat{\theta} > \theta$, and taking the limit as

$\hat{\theta} \rightarrow \theta$ yields:[26]

$$\frac{\mathrm{d}\pi(\theta)}{\mathrm{d}\theta} = -C_\theta(Q(p(\theta)), \theta), \tag{4.7}$$

almost everywhere. Viewing the profit function $\pi(\theta)$ as a state variable, its derivative is thus equal to the negative of the derivative of the cost function with respect to the type θ. Since a derivative is a local property of a function, (4.7) is a local condition that indicates that for any incentive compatible mechanism the profit of the firm viewed across the possible types is a decreasing function of θ since $C_\theta > 0$. The profit of a high-cost firm (high θ) is thus less than the profit of a low-cost firm (low θ) for any incentive compatible mechanism. The condition in (4.7) may be integrated to obtain an equivalent local condition on the profit function:[27]

$$\pi(\theta) = \int_\theta^{\theta^+} C_\theta(Q(p(\theta^0)), \theta^0)\,\mathrm{d}\theta^0 + \pi(\theta^+), \tag{4.8}$$

where $\pi(\theta^+)$ is the profit of a firm with the highest possible marginal cost. This condition completes the first step of the characterization. Note that from (4.8) that profit is a decreasing function of θ.

Since the profit function $\pi(\theta)$ is a decreasing function of the parameter θ for any incentive compatible policy, the individual rationality constraints in (4.2) will be satisfied if the profit of the highest cost type θ^+ is non-negative. The continuum of constraints in (4.2) can thus be replaced by the single constraint:

$$\pi(\theta^+) \geq 0. \tag{4.9}$$

[26]Given differentiable policies $p(\theta)$ and $T(\theta)$, this condition can also be derived by differentiating the profit $\pi(\theta)$ which yields:

$$\begin{aligned}
\frac{\mathrm{d}\pi(\theta)}{\mathrm{d}\theta} &= \left.\frac{\mathrm{d}\pi(\hat{\theta}(\theta);\theta)}{\mathrm{d}\theta}\right|_{\hat{\theta}=\theta} \\
&= \left.\frac{\partial\pi(\hat{\theta}(\theta);\theta)}{\partial\hat{\theta}}\frac{\mathrm{d}\hat{\theta}(\theta)}{\mathrm{d}\theta}\right|_{\hat{\theta}=\theta} + \left.\frac{\partial\pi(\hat{\theta}(\theta);\theta)}{\partial\theta}\right|_{\hat{\theta}=\theta} \\
&= \left.\frac{\partial\pi(\hat{\theta}(\theta);\theta)}{\partial\theta}\right|_{\hat{\theta}=\theta} \\
&= -C_\theta(Q(p(\theta)), \theta).
\end{aligned}$$

The third equality follows from the first-order condition for the firm's optimal choice of its response function $\hat{\theta}(\theta)$.

[27]This is the same condition developed in (3.5).

The second step in the characterization has thus been completed.

The third step involves demonstrating that a price function $p(\theta)$ can be implemented locally by choosing the fixed charges $T(\theta)$ to induce the firm to choose the strategy $\hat{\theta}(\theta) = \theta$. To determine $T(\theta)$, equate the representation of the profit function in (4.8) with the definition of $\pi(\theta)$, which is

$$\pi(\theta) = p(\theta)Q(p(\theta)) + T(\theta) - C(Q(p(\theta)), \theta). \tag{4.10}$$

Solving for $T(\theta)$ yields:

$$T(\theta) = \int_{\theta}^{\theta^+} C_\theta\big(Q(p(\theta^0)), \theta^0\big)\,\mathrm{d}\theta^0 - p(\theta)Q(p(\theta))$$
$$+ C(Q(p(\theta)), \theta) + \pi(\theta^+). \tag{4.11}$$

Substituting $T(\hat{\theta})$ into $\pi(\hat{\theta}; \theta)$ in (4.3), and differentiating with respect to $\hat{\theta}$ indicates that $\hat{\theta}(\theta) = \theta$ satisfies the first-order condition for all θ. Consequently, $T(\theta)$ given in (4.11) induces the firm to prefer locally to report truthfully.[28]

For the fourth step, a necessary and sufficient condition on the price function $p(\theta)$ for the firm to report $\hat{\theta}(\theta) = \theta$ for all $\theta \in [\theta^-, \theta^+]$ will be presented. To develop this condition, note that from (4.6) incentive compatibility requires that the price function $p(\cdot)$ satisfy

$$C(Q(p(\theta)), \hat{\theta}) - C(Q(p(\theta)), \theta) \geq C\big(Q(p(\hat{\theta})), \hat{\theta}\big) - C\big(Q(p(\hat{\theta})), \theta\big),$$
$$\forall \hat{\theta}, \theta \in [\theta^-, \theta^+]. \tag{4.12}$$

The necessary and sufficient condition will be developed for the case in which the marginal cost is constant and equal to θ or

$$C(q, \theta) = \theta q + K. \tag{4.13}$$

The condition in (4.12) then is

$$(\hat{\theta} - \theta)Q(p(\theta)) \geq (\hat{\theta} - \theta)Q\big(p(\hat{\theta})\big), \quad \forall \hat{\theta}, \theta \in [\theta^-, \theta^+]. \tag{4.14}$$

If $\hat{\theta} > \theta$, then (4.14) requires that $Q(p(\theta)) \geq Q(p(\hat{\theta}))$. Consequently, for this specification of the cost function a necessary condition for the price function $p(\theta)$ to be implementable, or to be globally incentive compatible, is that it be a nondecreasing function of θ. This corresponds to the intuitive notion that the price should be (weakly) higher the higher is the marginal cost of the firm.

[28] A sufficient condition is developed in (4.15) below.

For the specification in (4.13), the necessary condition that the price function $p(\theta)$ is a nondecreasing function can be shown also to be sufficient for the policy to be incentive compatible. Substituting $\pi(\hat{\theta})$ from (4.8) for $\hat{\theta} = \theta$ into (4.3) yields:

$$\pi(\hat{\theta}; \theta) = \pi(\theta^{+}) + \int_{\hat{\theta}}^{\theta^{+}} Q(p(\theta^{0}))\, d\theta^{0} + (\hat{\theta} - \theta)Q(p(\hat{\theta})).$$

Substituting $\pi(\hat{\theta})$ from (4.8) yields:

$$\pi(\hat{\theta}; \theta) = \pi(\theta) - \int_{\theta}^{\hat{\theta}} Q(p(\theta^{0}))\, d\theta^{0} + (\hat{\theta} - \theta)Q(p(\hat{\theta})).$$

Combining terms yields:

$$\pi(\hat{\theta}; \theta) = \pi(\theta) - \int_{\theta}^{\hat{\theta}} [Q(p(\theta^{0})) - Q(p(\hat{\theta}))]\, d\theta^{0}. \tag{4.15}$$

Consequently, global incentive compatibility, i.e. $\pi(\theta) \geq \pi(\hat{\theta}; \theta)$ for all $\hat{\theta}$ and all θ, is satisfied if the integral in (4.15) is non-negative. That integral is non-negative if the price function $p(\theta)$ is nondecreasing. To see this, note that if $\hat{\theta} > \theta$, the integrand is non-negative, and if $\hat{\theta} < \theta$, the integrand is nonpositive but the direction of the integral is reversed, so the integral is non-negative. Consequently, if the price function $p(\theta)$ is nondecreasing, the regulatory policy that induces a response function $\hat{\theta}(\theta) = \theta$ is incentive compatible.[29] The class of feasible, i.e. incentive compatible mechanisms that satisfy the individual rationality constraints in (4.2) and can be implemented by the regulator, is thus composed of those policies in which the price function is nondecreasing in θ and the corresponding fixed charges $T(\theta)$ satisfy (4.11). This completes the characterization of the class of mechanisms from which the regulator will choose.

4.2. The equilibrium

The characterization of the class of feasible mechanisms provides the basis for a method to determine the regulatory equilibrium. Any mechanism with a nondecreasing price function is feasible and thus can be implemented, so the firm's strategic behavior can be captured by the regulator taking the report $\hat{\theta}$ to be the

[29] Note that this necessary and sufficient condition is independent of the demand function. This is due to the assumption of constant marginal cost. If the cost function is not linear in θ, the necessary condition for $p(\theta)$ to be implementable is that $C(Q(p(\theta)), \theta)$ be a nondecreasing function of θ. The sufficient condition is that the integral in (4.15) be non-negative. The condition required on $p(\theta)$ then depends on the properties of the demand function.

firm's true type θ. This allows the game to be converted to a programming problem incorporating the constraints in (4.1) and (4.2) and the constraint that $p(\theta)$ be nondecreasing. As indicated above, the regulator can replace the individual rationality constraints by the single constraint in (4.9). Similarly, the constraints in (4.1) are satisfied by choosing $T(\theta)$ to satisfy (4.11) when $p(\theta)$ is nondecreasing, and then the condition in (4.8) can be used to replace (4.1). The constraint that $p(\theta)$ is nondecreasing is difficult to incorporate into a mathmatical program without assuming that $p(\theta)$ is differentiable. The approach taken here is to ignore this constraint and then to check if the solution obtained has the required property. If it does not, then the regulator's program has to be "convexified" as in Maskin and Riley (1984), Baron and Myerson, and Guesnerie and Laffont. The technical details of this convexification will not be addressed here.

The objective or welfare function W of the regulator is the maximization of the ex ante, or expected, weighted sum W^* of consumer and producer surplus in (3.9) using the prior information $f(\theta)$ of the regulator regarding θ or

$$W = \int_{\theta^-}^{\theta^+} \left\{ \int_{p(\theta)}^{\infty} Q(p^0)\,\mathrm{d}p^0 - T(\theta) + \alpha\pi(\theta) \right\} f(\theta)\,\mathrm{d}\theta. \tag{4.16}$$

Appendix A presents a control theoretic solution of the regulator's program of maximizing this objective function subject to the constraints in (4.2), (4.7), and (4.10). The approach taken here is to derive a less constrained formulation of the program that can solved with simpler methods. To develop this approach, first note that the welfare measure in (4.16) can be rewritten by substituting $T(\theta)$ from (4.10) into (4.16) to yield:

$$W = \int_{\theta^-}^{\theta^+} \left\{ \int_{p(\theta)}^{\infty} Q(p^0)\,\mathrm{d}p^0 + p(\theta)Q(p(\theta)) - \theta Q(p(\theta)) \right.$$
$$\left. -K - (1-\alpha)\pi(\theta) \right\} f(\theta)\,\mathrm{d}\theta. \tag{4.17}$$

This representation of the regulator's objective is the expectation of the social surplus from the firm's output less the "loss" $(1-\alpha)\pi(\theta)$ from the portion of the firm's profits that is not counted in the regulatory objective.

The profit $\pi(\theta)$ of the firm is a state variable in (4.17), which for an incentive compatible policy has the form given in (4.8). The state variable can replace its representation in (4.8), which incorporates the local representation of the incentive compatibility constraints. This eliminates the local constraint in (4.7). This also expresses welfare solely in terms of the control $p(\theta)$. Since the expression for W in (4.17) involves the expectation of $\pi(\theta)$, so the expectation of (4.8) will be substituted into (4.17). Taking the expectation of $\pi(\theta)$ and integrating by parts yields:

$$\int_{\theta^-}^{\theta^+} \pi(\theta) f(\theta)\,\mathrm{d}\theta = \int_{\theta^-}^{\theta^+} Q(p(\theta))F(\theta)\,\mathrm{d}\theta + \pi(\theta^+),$$

where $F(\theta)$ is the distribution function corresponding to $f(\theta)$. Substituting this into (4.17) and collecting terms yields:

$$W = \int_{\theta^-}^{\theta^+} \left\{ \int_{p(\theta)}^{\infty} Q(p^0)\,\mathrm{d}p^0 + p(\theta)Q(p(\theta)) - \left(\theta + (1-\alpha)\frac{F(\theta)}{f(\theta)}\right) Q(p(\theta)) - K \right\} f(\theta)\,\mathrm{d}\theta - (1-\alpha)\pi(\theta^+). \tag{4.18}$$

The regulator's "relaxed" or "unconstrained" programming program is thus to maximize W in (4.18) with respect to $p(\theta)$ and $\pi(\theta^+)$ subject to the single constraint in (4.9). Since W is decreasing in $\pi(\theta^+)$, it is immediate that $\pi(\theta^+) = 0$ is optimal. Consequently, the firm with the highest cost has zero profit under an optimal mechanism.

The necessary condition for the optimal price function $p(\theta)$ is obtained by pointwise differentiation of W which yields:

$$\frac{\partial W}{\partial p(\theta)} = \left[p(\theta) - \left(\theta + (1-\alpha)\frac{F(\theta)}{f(\theta)}\right)\right] Q'(p(\theta))f(\theta) = 0,$$

so the optimal price is

$$p(\theta) = y_\alpha(\theta) \equiv \theta + (1-\alpha)\frac{F(\theta)}{f(\theta)}. \tag{4.19}$$

Because marginal cost is constant, the optimal price is independent of the demand function and depends only on the marginal cost, the prior information of the regulator, and α.

The price function satisfying (4.19) maximizes the regulator's welfare function when the constraint that $p(\theta)$ is nondecreasing is ignored. To determine if that constraint is binding, note from (4.19) that the price function will be nondecreasing in θ if and only if $y_\alpha(\theta)$ is nondecreasing. A sufficient condition is $F(\theta)/f(\theta)$ nondecreasing, and since $F(\theta)$ is an increasing function, this condition will be satisfied if the density function does not increase too rapidly. The term $F(\theta)/f(\theta)$ is nondecreasing for the uniform, normal, exponential, and other frequently used distributions, so throughout the remainder of this chapter, the assumption that $y_\alpha(\theta)$ is nondecreasing in θ will be maintained. If this condition is not satisfied, the regulator's program must be convexified.

The equilibrium mechanism is thus composed of the price function given in (4.19) and a fixed charges function given in (4.11). To interpret the equilibrium, first note that price exceeds marginal cost θ when $\alpha < 1$ for all θ other than θ^-. The type with the lowest marginal cost receives a price equal to its marginal cost, and all higher cost types receive a price that is greater than their marginal cost. The price is a decreasing function of α, so the more weight the regulator gives to the profit of the firm the lower is the price. To see why the price is set above marginal cost, the profit of the firm must be interpreted.

The profit of the firm is due solely to the private information of the firm, since if information were symmetric the regulator would set price equal to marginal cost and the fixed payments would equal the fixed cost. The profit is thus a rent to the private information of the firm. That rent is given in (4.8), which for a constant marginal cost is

$$\pi(\theta) = \int_\theta^{\theta^+} Q(p(\theta^0))\,\mathrm{d}\theta^0. \tag{4.8a}$$

The rent is greater the lower is the firm's marginal cost and the greater is the quantity resulting from the price function $p(\theta)$. Since the price function is a decreasing function of α, the more weight given to profit in the regulator's objective, and hence the smaller the loss $(1-\alpha)\pi(\theta)$, the lower is the price and the greater the rent.

The information rents result because, as indicated in Section 3.1, a firm with marginal cost θ has a natural incentive to report its costs as $\theta + \Delta\theta$, $\Delta\theta > 0$ in order to obtain higher profits. The gain from such a report is approximately $\Delta\theta Q(p(\theta + \Delta\theta))$, and thus the rents are the sum of these increments as indicated in (4.8a). To eliminate this incentive, the regulator must offer the firm with marginal cost θ rents sufficient to negate that incentive. This is accomplished by structuring the fixed charges function appropriately as is evident by comparing (4.8a) and (4.11) for the specification in (4.13). As is evident from the welfare measure in (4.17), the information rents represent a reduction in welfare when $\alpha < 1$, so the regulator prefers that those rents be as small as possible. The regulator cannot eliminate the rents, however, because they arise from the need to induce the firm with marginal cost θ to choose the pricing policy designed for it.

Since the information rents in (4.8a) depend on the quantity produced, and hence the price $p(\theta)$, the regulator can reduce those rents by increasing the price. The gains from reducing the information rents by raising the price, of course, come at the expense of a reduction in consumer surplus. The optimal tradeoff between these two involves a reduction in consumer surplus equal to $Q'(p(\theta))p(\theta)$ and a reduction in ex ante or expected rents given by $(\theta + (1-\alpha)[F(\theta)/f(\theta)]Q'(p(\theta)))$. The optimal tradeoff is reflected in the distortion indicated in (4.19) of price from marginal costs. The term $((1-\alpha)[F(\theta)/f(\theta)])$ represents the marginal information rents, and thus the equilibrium mechanism establishes a price equal to the sum of the marginal cost θ and the marginal information rents. The regulator thus finds it optimal to distort price from marginal cost for all but the most efficient type of firm when $\alpha < 1$. For higher α price is distorted less from marginal cost because the rents represent a smaller loss in the regulator's welfare function. For $\alpha = 1$ the price equals marginal cost, and the resulting regulatory policy is the same as that obtained by Loeb and Magat.

As an example, if $f(\theta)$ is uniform on $[0, \theta^+]$, the price is

$$p(\theta) = (2-\alpha)\theta,$$

since the marginal information rent is $(1-\alpha)\theta$. The corresponding fixed charges function $T(\theta)$ is then

$$\begin{aligned} T(\theta) &= -(p(\theta)-\theta)Q(p(\theta)) + K + \int_{\theta}^{\theta^+} Q(p(\theta^0))\,\mathrm{d}\theta^0 \\ &= -(1-\alpha)\theta Q((2-\alpha)\theta) + K + \int_{\theta}^{\theta^+} Q((2-\alpha)\theta^0)\,\mathrm{d}\theta^0. \end{aligned}$$

The mechanism derived here is ex ante optimal for the regulator in the sense that it maximizes expected welfare given the prior information of the regulator. The mechanism, however, is not ex post efficient, or perfect, because price is distorted from marginal cost. Consequently, once the firm has made its report, both the regulator and the firm have an incentive to revise the regulatory policy and to share the efficiency gains. If the firm knew that this would occur, however, it would have an ex ante incentive to report a different $\hat{\theta}$. The regulator then would have to take this strategy into account and thus would be faced with a game similar to that addressed above. The equilibrium when this renegotiation cannot be precluded is a price function $p(\theta) = \theta$ and fixed charges given in (3.7). Because of the loss $(1-\alpha)\pi(\theta)$, the welfare function W is lower than when price is distorted from marginal cost as in (4.19). The regulator thus prefers to sacrifice ex post efficiency for ex ante efficiency whenever it has an objective other than the maximization of total surplus. The equilibrium mechanism characterized here thus requires that the regulator be able to commit credibly not to renegotiate the policy once the firm has reported its marginal cost.

The model presented in this section has been interpreted as pertaining to the case in which the firm takes no actions and the regulator has no opportunity to observe the actual cost of the firm. The model, however, can be given other interpretations. For example, the model is analogous to a model in which the firm has private information about its marginal costs, costs can be observed ex post by the regulator, and the firm takes an unobservable effort decision. To demonstrate this, suppose that the cost function of the firm is $c(q;\theta,a) = (\theta - a)q$, where a denotes the effort expended by the manager of the firm. Effort is assumed to have a disutility given by $\psi(a)$, which is strictly increasing and strictly convex. A policy specifies a price $p(\hat{\theta})$, a cost target $C(\hat{\theta})$, and fixed charges $T(\hat{\theta})$. Since the actual cost realized equals $(\theta - a)Q(p(\hat{\theta}))$, the fixed charges can be chosen so that the firm is severely penalized if its actual cost differs from the cost target. Consequently, the firm must choose its effort $a(\hat{\theta};\theta)$ to satisfy the restriction:

$$(\theta - a(\hat{\theta};\theta))Q(p(\hat{\theta})) + K = C(\hat{\theta}) = (\hat{\theta} - a(\hat{\theta};\hat{\theta}))Q(p(\hat{\theta})) + K.$$

This condition can be solved for $a(\hat{\theta};\theta)$ which expresses the effort in terms of the true θ and the report $\hat{\theta}$. The profit of the firm is then $\pi^*(\hat{\theta}, a(\hat{\theta};\theta);\theta)$, which can be written as

$$\pi^*(\hat{\theta}, a(\hat{\theta};\theta);\theta) = p(\hat{\theta})Q(p(\hat{\theta})) + T(\hat{\theta}) - \psi(\hat{\theta} - \theta + a(\hat{\theta};\hat{\theta}))$$
$$- (\hat{\theta} - a(\hat{\theta};\hat{\theta}))Q(p(\hat{\theta})) - K.$$

This formulation is analogous to that considered above with $\pi(\hat{\theta};\theta) \equiv \pi^*(\hat{\theta}, a(\hat{\theta};\theta);\theta)$. The formulation considered in this subsection thus also pertains to the case of the regulator observing the actual cost of the firm when the firm has private information and takes an unobservable effort decision. This formulation will be considered in more detail in Section 5.

4.3. *Private information about fixed costs*

The model in the previous subsection can be directly applied to the case in which the private information θ affects fixed rather than marginal costs. To illustrate the features of the equilibrium mechanism, consider the case in which marginal cost c is common knowledge and the fixed cost θ is known only to the firm. In this case the mechanism problem must deal with the possibility that the fixed cost may be sufficiently high that the regulator prefers that certain types not produce.

Using the same approach presented above, the welfare function analogous to (4.18) is

$$W = \int_{\theta^-}^{\theta^+} \left[\int_{p(\theta)}^{\infty} Q(p^0)\,\mathrm{d}p^0 + p(\theta)Q(p(\theta)) \right.$$
$$\left. - cQ(p(\theta)) - \theta - (1-\alpha)\frac{F(\theta)}{f(\theta)} \right] f(\theta)\,\mathrm{d}\theta. \tag{4.20}$$

Since the regulator knows the marginal cost c, the optimal price is

$$p(\theta) = c, \quad \forall \theta \in [\theta^-, \theta^+].$$

The welfare $W(\theta)$ conditional on θ is the integrand in (4.20) and is equal to

$$W(\theta) = \int_c^{\infty} Q(p^0)\,\mathrm{d}p^0 - y_\alpha(\theta). \tag{4.21}$$

Letting $r(\theta) = 1$ indicate that the firm is allowed to produce and $r(\theta) = 0$ indicate that the firm is not allowed to produce, the optimal policy is to allow the firm to produce if and only if consumer surplus is at least as great as $y_\alpha(\theta)$ or

$$r(\theta) = \begin{cases} 1, & \text{if } \int_c^{\infty} Q(p^0)\,\mathrm{d}p^0 \geq y_\alpha(\theta), \\ 0, & \text{if } \int_c^{\infty} Q(p^0)\,\mathrm{d}p^0 < y_\alpha(\theta). \end{cases}$$

Since $y_\alpha(\theta)$ is a strictly increasing function of θ, the policy may be restated as

$$r(\theta) = \begin{cases} 1, & \text{if } \theta \leq \theta_c, \\ 0, & \text{if } \theta > \theta_c, \end{cases} \tag{4.22}$$

where θ_c is defined by $y_\alpha(\theta_c) \equiv \int_c^{\infty} Q(p^0)\,\mathrm{d}p^0$. If $\theta_c \geq \theta^+$, all types of the firm produce, but if $\theta_c \in [\theta^-, \theta^+)$, the optimal regulatory mechanism will result in some types not producing even though it is ex post efficient for them to produce. This ex post inefficiency is desirable because it reduces the rents of the firm.[30] The rent under the optimal mechanism is given by

$$\pi(\theta) = \begin{cases} \theta_c - \theta, & \text{if } \theta \le \theta_c, \\ 0, & \text{if } \theta > \theta_c. \end{cases}$$

This optimal regulatory mechanism can be implemented by the regulator announcing that it will pay θ_c to the firm if it will produce the quantity $Q(c)$ and sell it at the price c. If the firm has a fixed cost less than or equal to θ_c, it will accept the offer, and if it has a higher fixed cost, it will decline the offer.

4.4. Multiple information parameters

An important limitation of the theory presented above is that it is based on the assumption that the private information of the firm has only one dimension. That is, the private information pertains only to marginal cost or to fixed cost or to both in a perfectly correlated manner. If, for example, the marginal cost and the fixed cost are private information and are not perfectly correlated, the mechanism design is considerably complicated.[31] Rochet (1984) has characterized the optimal mechanism for the case in which the marginal cost θ and the fixed cost ϕ are not perfectly correlated. He shows that the optimal mechanism may involve randomization between allowing the firm to produce and not.[32] He also shows that the optimal price function may depend on the properties of the demand function even though marginal cost is constant.

Rochet provides an explicit solution for the case in which θ and ϕ are independent and uniformly distributed and the demand function is linear. He demonstrates that on the subset of the support of (θ, ϕ) for which the firm is allowed to produce with probability one, the price is independent of the demand function and equals $y_\alpha(\theta)$. On the subset on which the regulator randomizes between production and no production, the price depends on both marginal and fixed costs. On the other subsets the firm is either not allowed to produce, produces a quantity of zero, or earns no profit.

The difficulty in extending to the theory developed in the previous subsections to multiple information parameters constitutes a significant limitation to the application of the theory of mechanism design with asymmetric information.

[30] Since $y_\alpha(\theta)$ is decreasing in α, the higher is α, the more likely it is that the firm will produce when it is ex post efficient for it to produce.

[31] The principal technical difficulty is that the conditions analogous to (4.7) represent partial differential equations the solution to which is difficult to characterize.

[32] Baron and Myerson (1982) provide a discrete example with this property.

4.5. Multiple outputs

The model analyzed in this section has only one output, but the extension to multiple outputs is straightforward as long as there is only one information parameter. Sappington (1983a) considers the case of a firm with multiple products produced with a technology conditioned on a parameter θ known to the firm but not known to the regulator. The regulator can choose a two-part pricing system with a unit price for each output and fixed charges paid by consumers to the firm. Although it is feasible for the regulator to induce the firm to choose an efficient technology for all θ, Sappington shows that the regulator adopts a pricing policy that induces the firm to choose an inefficient technology at least for some θ. As in the single-output case, the regulator chooses to distort the price from marginal cost in order to reduce the information rents and to distort the technology as well to control more efficiently the rents.

4.6. Unobservable actions

In the above models the only action of the firm is to select a regulatory policy from the menu of policies offered. The firm, however, may have actions that can be taken that affect the cost it will incur in satisfying demand at the price specified in the regulatory policy. These decisions can be considered in the context of either a value maximization or a managerial model. In a value maximization model, the firm is typically represented as having a choice among technologies or factor inputs. In a managerial model, the manager of the firm is typically represented as making an unobservable effort decision. Managerial models are based on the separation of ownership and control and represent the manager as pursuing his own interests rather than those of the owners. When the actions of the manager are only imperfectly observable to the owners, the manager has an opportunity to serve his own interests rather than those of the owners. The owners then will structure the incentives of the manager so that they are more closely aligned with the interests of the owners. A simple version of such a managerial model is considered in the following subsection and more complex models are considered in Subsections 5.3 and 5.4.

Consistent with the models considered above in this section, these cases will be considered under the assumption that the regulator observes no ex post measure of performance.[33] The price and the payment specified in the regulatory policy can thus depend only on the report of the firm. The case of observable performance is considered in Section 5.

[33] If the actions of managers were perfectly observable, the manager can be forced to serve the interest of owners, since otherwise he can be replaced with a manager who will do so. In that case, the manager will maximize the profit of the firm as in the models considered above.

4.6.1. *Effort in a managerial model*

In the managerial model the firm is assumed to be operated by a risk neutral manager, who contributes effort a to reduce cost and in doing so incurs a disutility $\psi(a)$ of effort which the regulator does not take into account in its welfare function. The disutility is assumed to be strictly increasing and strictly convex with $\psi(0) = 0$. In the context of the model considered in the previous subsections, suppose that the marginal cost is $c(\theta, a)$, where $c_a < 0$ and $c_\theta > 0$. Assuming that the manager is risk neutral, his utility $V(\hat{\theta}, a; \theta)$ is[34]

$$V(\hat{\theta}, a; \theta) \equiv \pi(\hat{\theta}, a; \theta) - \psi(a) \equiv p(\hat{\theta})Q(p(\hat{\theta})) + T(\hat{\theta})$$
$$-c(\theta, a)Q(p(\hat{\theta})) - K - \psi(a), \tag{4.23}$$

so given a regulatory policy $(p(\theta), T(\theta))$, the manager will choose his effort response function $a(\hat{\theta}; \theta)$ to satisfy the first-order condition:

$$-c_a(\theta, a(\hat{\theta}; \theta))Q(p(\hat{\theta})) - \psi'(a(\hat{\theta}; \theta)) = 0. \tag{4.24}$$

Letting $a(\theta) \equiv a(\theta; \theta)$, the fixed charges function $T(\theta)$ that locally implements a price function $p(\theta)$ is

$$T(\theta) = -p(\theta)Q(p(\theta)) + c(\theta, a(\theta))Q(p(\theta)) + K$$
$$+ \int_\theta^{\theta^+} c_\theta(\theta^0, a(\theta^0))Q(p(\theta^0))\,\mathrm{d}\theta^0 + \psi(a(\theta)). \tag{4.25}$$

Substituting $T(\hat{\theta})$ from (4.25) into (4.23) and maximizing $V(\hat{\theta}, a; \theta)$ with respect to $\hat{\theta}$ and a, assuming that $a(\theta)$ and $p(\theta)$ are differentiable, indicates that the maximum is attained (locally) at $\hat{\theta} = \theta$ and $a(\hat{\theta}, \theta) = a(\theta)$.[35] Then, (4.24) implies that the effort $a(\theta)$ is efficient given the quantity $Q(p(\theta))$. Using the methodology developed in the previous section, the optimal price is

$$p(\theta) = c(\theta, a(\theta)) + (1 - \alpha)\frac{F(\theta)}{f(\theta)}c_\theta(\theta, a(\theta)),$$

[34] To simplify the notation, the compensation of the manager is assumed to equal the profit of the firm. The manager thus may be viewed as an entrepreneur.

[35] If $p(\theta)$ is nondecreasing in θ, the local second-order condition for the report $\hat{\theta}$ is satisfied.

For example, if $c(\theta, a) = \theta\bar{c}(a)$, the price is

$$p(\theta) = \left(\theta + (1-\alpha)\frac{F(\theta)}{f(\theta)}\right)\bar{c}(a(\theta)) = y_\alpha(\theta)\bar{c}(a(\theta)).$$

The choice of effort in a managerial model in which there is no ex post observable is thus efficient given the quantity produced, and the price is distorted from marginal cost only as a result of the marginal information rents associated with the private information of the firm. That is, there is no moral hazard problem when there is no ex post observable and the manager is risk neutral.

4.6.2. *The choice of technology and factor inputs for a value-maximizing firm*

Consider the choice of factor inputs given a production function $G(\kappa, L, \theta)$, where κ and L are capital and labor inputs, respectively. A value-maximizing firm will choose inputs to maximize its profits, and since the firm must satisfy all demand at the price $p(\hat{\theta})$, those inputs will be a function of θ and $\hat{\theta}$ and satisfy:

$$Q(p(\hat{\theta})) = G(\kappa, L, \theta).$$

Letting $L(q, \kappa, \theta)$ denote the labor requirements function, profit is

$$\pi(\hat{\theta}, \kappa; \theta) = p(\hat{\theta})Q(p(\hat{\theta})) + T(\hat{\theta}) - r\kappa - wL(Q(p(\hat{\theta}), \kappa, \theta).$$

The firm will choose its capital input $\kappa(\hat{\theta}; \theta)$ to satisfy:

$$L_\kappa(Q(p(\hat{\theta})), \kappa(\hat{\theta}; \theta), \theta) = -\frac{r}{w},$$

which is the efficient input given the quantity produced. Proceeding as above, the optimal price satisfies:

$$p(\theta) = wL_Q + w(1-\alpha)L_{Q\theta}\frac{F(\theta)}{f(\theta)},$$

and the fixed charges function $T(\theta)$ satisfies (4.11). If θ represents an inefficiency parameter such that the labor requirements function is

$$L = \theta\bar{L}(q, \kappa), \tag{4.26}$$

then the price is

$$p(\theta) = w\left[\theta + (1-\alpha)\frac{F(\theta)}{f(\theta)}\right]\bar{L}_Q(Q(p(\theta)), \kappa(\theta))$$

$$= wy_\alpha(\theta)\bar{L}_Q(Q(p(\theta)), \kappa(\theta)),$$

where $\kappa(\theta) \equiv \kappa(\theta; \theta)$. The price is thus based on the efficient input choices. That is, if the regulator could choose the capital and labor inputs as a function of θ, its choices would be the same as those chosen by the firm. The choice of technology or factor inputs thus does not bias the pricing rule or the efficiency of the regulatory mechanism when there is no ex post observable.

4.7. *A regulated factor input and the Averch–Johnson model*

If the regulator were able to observe a factor input, it could not only base the pricing policy on the report of the firm but it could also specify the input as a function of the report. Besanko (1984) notes that regulators of public utilities have the authority to approve major capital investments of the firms they regulate. He thus considers the case in which the regulator can regulate the price and the observable capital stock of the firm and demonstrates that the resulting regulatory policy has a form analogous to the exogenously-specified regulatory policy in the Averch–Johnson model. In his formulation the regulator is not restricted to choose a policy from the class of rate-of-return policies but instead may choose any relationship between price, and hence profit, and the capital stock of the firm.[36] Since the capital stock chosen by the firm is a function of θ, the regulatory policy can be determined using the method of Subsection 4.2 by choosing functions $p(\theta)$ and $\kappa(\theta)$, and then expressing p as a function of κ. His model specifies a technology of the form in (4.26) and specifies the regulator's objective as the maximization of expected consumer surplus. Besanko demonstrates that for the quantity produced the optimal regulatory policy induces the firm to overcapitalize relative to the efficient capital–labor ratio.[37] The regulator chooses to induce the firm to produce inefficiently in this manner in order to reduce the information rents of the firm.

[36] In Besanko's model, the regulator is assumed to use only a unit price rather than a two-part pricing policy.

[37] As demonstrated in Subsection 4.6.2, the regulator can induce an efficient choice of technology by regulating only the price, but the sacrifice in technical efficiency is warranted by the resulting reduction in information rents.

The optimal regulatory policy may be interpreted in terms of rate-of-return regulation by forming the ratio of profit $\pi(\theta)$ to the capital $\kappa(\theta)$.[38] The resulting rate of return is a decreasing function of the capital employed, which is a property proposed by Klevorick (1966) who labeled it a "graduated allowed rate-of-return" policy. Although the mechanism characterized by Besanko has the features of rate-of-return regulation, it is an endogenous response by the regulator to the private information of the firm when the regulator has the authority to regulate the capital stock. This then provides a prediction of the form of the Averch–Johnson model, but in this case the regulatory mechanism is derived endogenously rather than assumed as a description of practice.

5. Observable performance

The above models involve adverse selection resulting from an asymmetry of information between the regulator and the firm. A feature of these models is that the regulatory mechanism is based only on a report by the firm or equivalently on the quantity that the firm selects to produce given the mechanism offered by the regulator. More realistically, the regulator may be able to observe the actual performance of the firm, or some ex post monitor of performance, and use that information to improve the efficiency of the regulatory mechanism. If there is an observable and verifiable ex post monitor of performance, the mechanism can be based both on an ex ante report and on the ex post monitor. This section extends the above mechanisms to incorporate monitors of performance to improve the efficiency of the self-selection. Basing the regulatory policy on an ex post monitor induces a moral hazard problem if the firm takes an action unobservable by the regulator. As indicated in Subsection 4.6, the regulator can avoid the moral hazard problem by ignoring the observable and basing the regulatory policy only on the report of the firm. The regulator may prefer to induce a moral hazard problem, however, if the efficiency of the mechanism is improved by reducing information rents.

5.1. The ex post observation of private information

As a first step in the development of mechanisms based on observable performance, consider the special case in which the regulator can perfectly observe at the end of the period the actual marginal cost the firm incurs. Since the price must be set before the cost is incurred, the price can only be a function of the

[38]The profit is a decreasing function of θ, but the capital stock may not be monotone in θ.

report, but the regulator can base the fixed charges T on both the report and the actual marginal cost. When cost involves no randomness, any report $\hat{\theta}$ above the marginal cost θ will be detected by the regulator unless the firm creates waste or goldplating ω to "verify" its report. If the regulator is able to observe the sum $\theta + \omega$ and can impose a penalty if $(\theta + \omega) \neq \hat{\theta}$, a sufficiently large penalty would prevent the firm from choosing a report $\hat{\theta}$ that differs from the actual marginal cost $(\theta + \omega)$ it will incur.[39] Thus, the price $p(\hat{\theta})$ is a function only of $\hat{\theta}$, and the fixed charges are a function $T(\hat{\theta}, \theta_\omega)$ of both $\hat{\theta}$ and the observable $\theta_\omega = \theta + \omega$. The profit $\pi(\hat{\theta}, \omega; \theta)$ is thus

$$\pi(\hat{\theta}, \omega; \theta) = p(\hat{\theta})Q(p(\hat{\theta})) - (\theta + \omega)Q(p(\hat{\theta})) - K + T(\hat{\theta}, \theta_\omega). \quad (5.1)$$

An optimal mechanism in this case is $p(\hat{\theta}) = \hat{\theta}$ and

$$T(\hat{\theta}, \theta_\omega) = \int_{\hat{\theta}}^{\theta^+} Q(p(\theta^0))\,\mathrm{d}\theta^0 - \int_{\theta_\omega}^{\theta^+} Q(p(\theta^0))\,\mathrm{d}\theta^0$$

$$-p(\hat{\theta})Q(p(\hat{\theta})) + \hat{\theta}Q(p(\hat{\theta})) + K. \quad (5.2)$$

Given this mechanism, $\omega = 0$ is optimal, and

$$\pi(\hat{\theta}, \omega; \theta) = 0, \quad \forall \theta \in [\theta^-, \theta^+].$$

The mechanism is incentive compatible, so the firm has no incentive to misreport its marginal cost or to waste. Consequently, if the regulator can perfectly observe the expenditures of the firm, first-best efficiency is attainable.

This result is not robust, however. For example, suppose that the actual marginal cost depends on a random variable. In this case the above mechanism cannot be implemented, since the firm cannot guarantee that its actual cost equals its report. In addition to uncertainty affecting costs, the regulator may only be able to observe a noisy monitor of costs, which will also preclude implementing the first-best policy. The following subsections address the mechanism design problem when these limitations are present. The first case considered in Subsection 5.2 is Baron and Besanko's (1984a) extension of the Baron and Myerson mechanism to the case in which the regulator can conduct a costly audit of the actual cost of the firm. The second case considered in Subsection 5.3 is due to Laffont and Tirole (1986) and involves a costless monitor and both an adverse selection problem and a moral hazard problem. The third case considered in Subsection 5.4 is an extension of the Laffont and Tirole mechanism to the case of a managerial model with risk aversion.

[39] The penalty will not be formally incorporated into the model but is assumed to be sufficiently high that it forces the firm to choose ω such that $\theta + \omega$ equals $\hat{\theta}$.

5.2. Auditing of performance

Regulators of public utilities generally have the authority to audit the costs incurred by the firm and may have the authority to impose penalties if the realized costs differ from anticipated costs. Auditing is costly, however, since it involves investigation of costs in a manner sufficiently detailed that they would be verifiable to an independent party such as a court. Baron and Besanko (1984a) extend the adverse selection model of Section 4 to the case in which the regulator has the authority to audit and to impose a penalty $N(\hat{\theta}, C)$ based both on the information $\hat{\theta}$ the firm originally reported to the regulator and on the total cost C incurred by the firm once production has been completed. The price must be set prior to the commencement of production, so price can only be a function of $\hat{\theta}$. The observation of C, however, is useful to the regulator because it permits an inference about the true parameter θ, and that inference can be used to reduce the information rents of the firm. The optimal regulatory mechanism can be determined in a manner analogous to that used in Section 4 with the complication that the imposition of the penalty may cause the individual rationality constraint to be binding for some $\theta < \theta^+$.

The observable cost C incurred by the firm is assumed to be the realization of a random variable $\tilde{C}$ given by

$$\tilde{C} = \tilde{c}q + K,$$

where $\tilde{c}$ is a random marginal cost that depends on the private information θ of the firm. The random variable $\tilde{c}$ induces a density function $h(C|\theta)$ on total cost. The observation of total cost C is thus only imperfectly informative about θ. The penalty $N(\hat{\theta}, C)$ is assumed to be non-negative and bounded above by a constant $\bar{N}$. The bound $\bar{N}$ is to be interpreted as a statutory limitation on the authority of the regulator to impose a sanction. In the context of public utility regulation, a penalty could correspond to the regulator disallowing a cost from inclusion in the revenue requirement.

Auditing is assumed to be costly with the cost A borne by the regulator. Because of this cost, the regulator may prefer not to audit all possible types of the firm and thus will choose whether to audit based on the information the firm reports at the time the price is set. The regulator is thus modeled as choosing the probability $\rho(\hat{\theta})$ that it will audit when the firm reports $\hat{\theta}$. The regulatory mechanism M^A is thus[40]

$$M^A = \{(p(\theta), T(\theta), \rho(\theta), N(\theta, C)), \theta \in [\theta^-, \theta^+]\}.$$

[40] Baron (1985c) applies this approach to the regulation of pollution emitted by a firm that has private information about its abatement costs.

The expected penalty $\overline{N}(\hat{\theta}, \theta)$ faced by the firm when it reports $\hat{\theta}$ is then

$$\overline{N}(\hat{\theta}, \theta) = \rho(\hat{\theta}) \int_{\Gamma} N(\hat{\theta}, C) h(C|\theta) \, dC,$$

where Γ is the support of C which is assumed to be independent of θ. The expected penalty $\overline{N}(\hat{\theta}, \theta)$ thus depends on both the report and the true parameter θ, so the information rents of the firm are affected by the auditing policy $\rho(\theta)$ and the penalty $N(\theta, C)$.

The optimal auditing strategy involves auditing if the firm reports a sufficiently high $\hat{\theta}$ and imposing the maximum allowable penalty $\overline{N}$ if the realized cost is lower than anticipated. More formally, if the density function $h(C|\theta)$ is continuously differentiable and satisfies the monotone–likelihood ratio property,[41] the optimal penalty function is

$$N(\hat{\theta}, C) = \begin{cases} \overline{N}, & \text{if } C < Z(\hat{\theta}), \\ 0, & \text{if } C \geq Z(\hat{\theta}), \end{cases} \tag{5.3}$$

where $Z(\cdot)$ is the inverse of the maximum likelihood estimator $\theta^*(C)$ of θ. For example, if $h(C|\theta)$ is normal and θ is the mean of the random marginal cost $\tilde{c}$, then the penalty is imposed if the observed cost is less than $Z(\hat{\theta}) = \hat{\theta}Q(p(\hat{\theta})) + K$. The maximum penalty is imposed because the regulator's objective function is linear in $N(\hat{\theta}, C)$. Although the firm bears the expected penalty, the regulator must increase $T(\theta)$ to cover the expected penalty, since the firm will participate only if its expected or ex ante profit is nonnegative.

An important feature of this policy is that the penalty in (5.3) is imposed for low, rather than high, realized costs. To understand the rationale for this, recall that the firm has a natural incentive to overstate its cost parameter θ. A low realized cost is evidence that the firm may have overstated its parameter, so the regulator imposes a penalty in that event. Thus, by overstating its parameter, the firm increases the probability that the realized cost will be below the cost $(\hat{\theta}Q(p(\hat{\theta})) + K)$ anticipated for the report it makes. The regulator thus can discourage the firm from overstating its cost parameter by announcing that a penalty will be imposed if the realized cost is lower than expected. Of course, the regulatory policy is incentive compatible, so the firm will actually report truthfully, and the regulator knows this. Once the firm has reported $\hat{\theta}$, the regulator thus prefers to rescind its decision to audit to avoid the auditing cost. The regulator, however, must credibly commit to audit and to impose the penalty if

[41] The density $h(C|\theta)$ satisfies the monotone-likelihood-ratio property if for $\theta^1 > \theta^2$, the ratio $h(C|\theta^1)/h(C|\theta^2)$ is monotone increasing in C. This property is satisfied for a number of commonly-used distributions including the normal.

realized cost is below $Z(\hat{\theta})$ even though it knows that the firm will report truthfully, since if the firm recognized that the regulator might not audit, it would lose its deterrence value. Consequently, this model requires that the regulator be able to commit credibly to the auditing policy.

Baron and Besanko further characterize the optimal auditing and pricing policy for the case in which $\tilde{c}$ is normally distributed with variance σ^2 and mean $\bar{c}(\theta)$. The mean is assumed to be a differentiable, nondecreasing, convex function of θ. The optimal auditing strategy is then to audit if $\hat{\theta}$ is at least as great as θ_A defined by

$$(1-\alpha)\frac{F(\theta_A)}{f(\theta_A)}\frac{\bar{N}}{\sqrt{2\pi}\,\sigma}\bar{c}'(\theta_A) \equiv A. \tag{5.4}$$

The optimal auditing policy is thus a three-stage process. First, the regulator authorizes an audit if the reported $\hat{\theta}$ is greater than θ_A. Second, if an audit is authorized, the realized cost C is compared to the critical point $Z(\hat{\theta})$. Third, if the realized cost is less than the critical point, the maximum penalty is imposed. Otherwise no penalty is imposed.

To interpret the set of reports $\hat{\theta}$ on which the regulator will audit, consider the case in which the individual rationality constraint is binding only at $\theta = \theta^+$. In that case, θ_A has the following properties:

(1) $\partial\theta_A/\partial A > 0$,

(2) $\partial\theta_A/\partial\sigma > 0$,

(3) $\partial\theta_A/\partial\bar{N} < 0$,

(4) $\partial\theta_A/\partial\alpha > 0$.

(1) The greater is the cost of auditing, the smaller is the set on which the regulator will audit, as would be expected.

(2) That set is also decreasing in the standard deviation σ of cost, since the noisier is the cost signal the less valuable is the observation for the inference about θ.

(3) The greater is the maximum penalty $\bar{N}$ that can be imposed, the more effective is the deterrent, so auditing becomes more desirable and the regulator audits over a larger set. In the limit, the first-best outcome can be approximated arbitrarily closely as $\bar{N}$ increases.

(4) The greater is the weight α on the firm's profit in the regulator's welfare function, the smaller is the set over which the regulator will audit. This results because the welfare loss associated with the firm's information rents is reduced as α increases.

An important property of the pricing policy when the regulator can audit is that the price function is independent of the auditing policy if the individual rationality constraints in (4.2) are binding only at the upper bound $\theta = \theta^+$. In this case, the price is $p(\theta) = y_\alpha(\theta)$ as in the model in which there is no auditing. If the expected penalty causes the individual rationality constraint to be binding for some θ less than θ^+, the regulator does not have to distort price from marginal production cost as much as called for by (4.19), because the individual rationality constraint works to reduce the marginal information rents. The price is then equal to $y_\alpha(\theta)$ less an amount equal to the sum of the multipliers on the individual rationality constraints in (4.2) for lower θ. The resulting price can even be below the marginal production cost. Because auditing reduces the information rents, the profit $\pi(\theta)$ of the firm is lower when the regulator can audit than when it does not have that authority.

5.3. *Costlessly observable ex post cost and moral hazard*

Laffont and Tirole (1986) consider a managerial model in which ex post the regulator is able to observe the cost of a firm that has private information θ and takes an unobservable effort decision a. In their model, the cost C incurred by the firm is observable and is specified as

$$C = (\theta - a)q + K + \sqrt{\nu}\,\varepsilon, \tag{5.5}$$

where ε is the realization of a random variable $\tilde{\varepsilon}$ and ν is a parameter that scales the randomness of cost. The manager incurs a disutility $\psi(a)$ of effort, where $\psi(a)$ is a strictly increasing, convex function with $\psi(0) = 0$. Since the regulator does not know θ and is unable to observe effort, even perfect observation of cost does not eliminate the moral hazard problem. The regulator thus faces both adverse selection and moral hazard problems. An important feature of the specification of the cost function in (5.5) is that the marginal rate of substitution of effort for type is independent of the quantity.[42]

Since C is observable, the fixed charges can be based on both $\hat{\theta}$ and C. The price, however, must be set, and the quantity must be produced, before the cost C can be observed, so price can only be a function of the report $\hat{\theta}$.[43] Laffont and Tirole specify their mechanism in terms of the quantity q the firm chooses to produce, given a fixed-charge schedule $T^*(q, c)$ offered by the regulator. They show that if the manager of the firm is risk neutral and $F(\theta)/f(\theta)$ is nondecreasing, the optimal regulatory policy can be implemented using a mechanism composed of a fixed charge schedule that is linear in the observed cost and

[42] This feature allows Laffont and Tirole to establish global incentive compatibility for their mechanism.

[43] A derivation of the Laffont and Tirole mechanism is presented in Appendix B.

nonlinear in the quantity. The fixed charges function $T^*(q, C)$ has the form:

$$T^*(q, C) = b(q) + C + m(q)(\bar{C}(q) - C), \tag{5.6}$$

where $m(q) > 0$ and $\bar{C}(q)$ is a cost target for a firm that produces a quantity q. The firm thus receives the sum of a fixed payment $b(q)$, reimbursement of its cost C, and a bonus for any cost "underrun" ($C < \bar{C}(q)$) or a penalty for any cost "overrun" ($C > \bar{C}(q)$). Since the firm is risk neutral, the moral hazard problem could be eliminated by a fixed-price contract ($m(q) = 0$) in which the firm is paid a lump sum for the quantity delivered; that is, with fixed charges independent of the monitored cost. With a fixed-price contract, however, the regulator bears information costs given in (4.8).[44] Those costs can be reduced by basing the fixed charges on observed costs, and the regulator does so by reimbursing the firm for some but not all of its cost in (5.6).

Laffont and Tirole show that the fraction $(1 - m(q))$ of the cost reimbursed is less than one, so the manager has an incentive to reduce costs by increasing his effort. The fraction of cost reimbursed decreases with output, because with higher output the marginal product of effort increases allowing the function $m(q)$ to be scaled down. That is, for lower θ the greater output naturally mitigates the moral hazard problem by inducing greater effort, so the regulator can use the incentive features of $T(q, C)$ to reduce the information rents. The regulator does so by reimbursing more of the cost. Laffont and Tirole show that, as the regulator's information about θ becomes more precise, the contract in (5.6) approaches a fixed-price contract; that is, the fraction $m(q)$ approaches one. This is the standard result in moral hazard models that with risk-neutral principal the optimal contract involves a lump-sum payment $b(q)$ which induces the agent to expend the first-best level of effort.

In the Baron–Myerson model, the regulator distorts price above marginal cost to reduce the information rents the firm earns. In the Laffont and Tirole model in which cost is observable, the regulator has the same incentive, but the regulator also faces a moral hazard problem. The asymmetric information problem provides an incentive for the regulator to distort price above marginal cost to reduce the information costs. The incentive to exert effort, however, is greater the greater is the quantity the firm produces, since from (5.5) the marginal product of effort is an increasing function of the quantity. The regulator thus has an incentive to respond to the moral hazard problem by distorting price below marginal cost to increase the marginal product. Because the marginal rate of substitution of effort for type is constant, the regulator's incentive to respond to the moral hazard problem is exactly offset by the incentive to respond to the asymmetric informa-

[44] The contract in the Baron–Myerson model is a fixed-price contract.

tion problem.[45] That is, for the case in which the firm is risk neutral, the optimal price satisfies:

$$p(\theta) = \theta - a(\theta), \tag{5.7}$$

where $a(\theta)$ is the firm's effort response function. The marginal information costs to the regulator are thus exactly offset by the marginal gain from inducing more effort, so price is set equal to marginal cost.

Although the mechanism specifies a price equal to marginal cost, the marginal cost is not first-best because the effort $a(\theta)$ of the firm is less than the first-best effort. The effort is also less than the effort that the regulator prefers given the informational asymmetry and the unobservability of effort. That is, if it were possible for a third party to subsidize the effort of the firm, the regulator's welfare function W would be increased. Since effort is too low, the marginal cost is greater than the first-best marginal cost and greater than the marginal cost the regulator prefers given the asymmetric information and moral hazard problems. The higher marginal cost implies that the quantity produced is below the first-best quantity.

Picard (1987) extends the Laffont–Tirole model, specialized for the case of an indivisible project ($q = 1$), by weakening the requirement that the ratio $F(\theta)/f(\theta)$ be nondecreasing.[46] Laffont and Tirole demonstrate that if $F(\theta)/f(\theta)$ is nondecreasing, a linear function $T^*(q, C)$ is optimal,[47] and Picard shows that if $\theta + F(\theta)/f(\theta)$ is increasing, a quadratic payment function can be used to implement the optimal regulatory policy. Even with no assumption on $F(\theta)/f(\theta)$, an efficient mechanism exists if $a(\theta) - \theta$ is nonincreasing, since a quadratic payment function can be used to approximate arbitrarily closely any efficient mechanism. The welfare in these cases is the same independent of the distribution of θ.

5.4. *Cost observability and monitoring for a risk-averse firm*

Baron and Besanko (1987b) consider a managerial model similar to that of Laffont and Tirole but focus on the case in which the firm is risk averse and the cost of the firm is only imperfectly observable because of noise in the monitor of cost.

[45] That is, the multiplier on the moral hazard constraint equals the negative of the multiplier on the derivative of the state variable $\pi(\theta)$. This is demonstrated in Appendix B.

[46] Surplus is taken to be $a - \theta$.

[47] If the regulator has a quantity decision, Laffont and Tirole's assumption that $F(\theta)/f(\theta)$ is nondecreasing appears to be necessary for a mechanism to be implementable with a linear payment function.

The preferences of the manager are expressed as

$$U(\pi) - \psi(a), \tag{5.8}$$

where U is a strictly increasing, concave utility function. In addition to the consideration in the Laffont and Tirole model, risk aversion creates an incentive for risk-sharing to reduce the risk premium the firm requires to participate in the regulatory relationship. The regulatory policy thus involves tradeoffs among responses to risk-sharing, asymmetric information, and moral hazard problems.

Baron and Besanko distinguish between randomness in the costs of the firm and noisiness of the monitor of costs. The random variable $\tilde{\varepsilon}$ in (5.5) is interpreted as randomness of costs due to uncertain factor prices, technology shocks, etc. In addition, even though the true cost C is observed by the firm, the regulator may only be able to observe the realization z of a monitor $\tilde{z}$ of cost. The realization z is assumed to be verifiable, so the regulatory policy can be based on the monitor. As in the model in the previous two subsections, the price can only be a function of the report $\hat{\theta}$, but the fixed charges $T(\hat{\theta}, z)$ can also be based on the monitor.

The monitor $\tilde{z}$ may be a noisy signal of cost due to imperfections in accounting systems or in measurement, so $\tilde{z}$ is modeled as

$$\tilde{z} = \tilde{C} + \sqrt{\xi}\,\tilde{\eta},$$

where $\tilde{\eta}$ denotes the noise in the monitor and ξ is a parameter that scales the noisiness. It is convenient to work with the conditional distribution of C and the unconditional distribution of z, which, for $\tilde{\varepsilon}$ and $\tilde{\eta}$ independent normal random variables with means of zero and variances of one, are given by

$$g(C|z) = N\left((c(\theta, a)q + K)\frac{\xi}{\xi + \nu} + z\frac{\nu}{\xi + \nu}, \frac{\xi\nu}{\xi + \nu}\right)$$

and

$$h(z) = N(c(\theta, a)q + K, \xi + \nu).$$

Here, $N(\mu, \sigma^2)$ denotes the normal density function with mean μ and variance σ^2, and $c(\theta, a)$ denotes the mean of marginal cost, which in the Laffont and Tirole model is specified as $c(\theta, a) = \theta - a$.[48] If $\xi = 0$, the cost of the firm is

[48] The equilibrium in this model can be determined using an extension of the analysis presented in Appendix B.

deterministic, but the noise in the monitor impairs the inference the regulator can draw about the private information θ and the effort a of the manager. If $\nu = 0$, the regulator observes cost perfectly, but it is the randomness of cost that impairs the inference about θ and a.

To indicate the distinction between the randomness of cost and the noisiness of the monitor, consider the two extreme cases: (1) a deterministic cost and a noisy monitor ($\xi > 0$, $\nu > 0$), and (2) a random cost and perfect monitor ($\xi = 0$, $\nu > 0$). In the first case, the firm bears no risk directly, but since the monitor is noisy, the regulator will impose risk on the firm if it bases the fixed charges on the monitor. In the second case, the firm bears risk directly, and the regulator can use the fixed charges to relieve the firm of a portion of that risk. In both cases, the fixed charges will be used to affect the allocation of risk, to provide incentives for the manager to exert effort, and to reduce the information rents that the manager earns.

At one extreme, in the case of a deterministic cost and a noisy monitor, the regulator could make the fixed charges independent of the monitor of cost (a fixed-price contract), which would provide the most efficient risk bearing and the strongest incentive to exert effort. As in the Baron and Besanko (1984a) model of auditing considered in Subsection 5.2, however, the regulator has an incentive to base the fixed charges on the monitor as a means of reducing the rents the firm earns on its private information.[49] The regulator thus may prefer to worsen risk-sharing and moral hazard if the marginal costs of those problems are less than the welfare consequences of the marginal reduction in the information rents.[50] At the other extreme, if the cost of the firm is random and the monitor is deterministic, basing the fixed charges on the monitor can relieve the firm of risk, but improved risk-sharing is achieved only at the expense of diminished incentives for effort. The optimal regulatory policy in both cases involves basing the fixed charges on the monitor, so there are tradeoffs among the three problems that affect the form of $T(\hat{\theta}, z)$. In all cases, however, the equilibrium provides the same incentives from the manager's perspective. For example, the incentive for effort always depends on the share of the actual or monitored cost borne by the firm.

The extent to which the fixed charges vary with the monitor depends on the relative costs of responding to the moral hazard and adverse selection problems. Those marginal costs are measured by the multipliers on the moral hazard

[49] The gain from reducing the information rents is both from the "welfare loss" $(1 - \alpha)$ on any transfer between the firm and consumers and from the reduction in the marginal information costs which allows a lower price and a greater quantity to be produced.

[50] If effort and type are complements, an increase in effort increases the rate at which the marginal cost increases in θ, and this increases the information rents. In this case, the regulator may prefer that the effort of the firm be taxed rather than subsidized.

constraint analogous to (B.4) and on the incentive compatibility constraints analogous to (B.3) as developed in Appendix B. As indicated in the context of the Laffont and Tirole model, if the firm is risk neutral the multipliers have offsetting values. If the firm is risk averse, however, the mulipliers are not equal in general.

To illustrate the effect of risk aversion, consider the case in which the utility function $U(\pi)$ in (5.8) exhibits constant absolute risk aversion. In this case, the first-best regulatory policy, that which the regulator would implement if it knew θ and could observe a, specifies a fixed charges function that reimburses the firm for a proportion $\nu/(\nu + \xi)$ of the monitored cost. Intuitively, when θ is private information and a is not observable, reimbursing a higher proportion of the monitored cost reduces the cost of the adverse selection problem and increases the cost of the moral hazard problem. If, when evaluated at the first-best reimbursement proportion, the marginal cost of responding to the adverse selection problem exceeds the marginal cost of responding to the moral hazard problem, a higher proportion of monitored costs is reimbursed in the equilibrium regulatory mechanism. The price $p(\theta)$ is then greater than the marginal production cost $c(\theta, a(\theta))$ as in the adverse selection model of Section 4.[51] If the marginal benefit from responding to the adverse selection problem is less than the marginal cost of the moral hazard problem, the equilibrium regulatory policy reimburses a smaller proportion of the monitored cost in order to induce more effort. The price in this case is set below the marginal production cost in order to stimulate effort, since the marginal product of effort is proportional to the quantity produced.

6. Dynamic models

6.1. Introduction

The above mechanisms are static in the sense that they involve only one production opportunity. When there is a sequence of production decisions, information may become available over time as uncertainty is resolved and technology and demand evolve. The regulator then may wish to design the mechanism to be responsive to the evolution of information and performance. Responsiveness, however, allows opportunistic behavior by the regulator and the firm, and as Williamson (1975, 1983) has argued, opportunism can result in

[51] If the equilibrium quantity is less than the first-best quantity, the equilibrium effort is less than the first-best effort. In the special case in which the preferences of the firm have a mean–variance representation, the quantity produced and the effort are unambiguously less than the first-best quantity and effort, respectively. See Baron and Besanko (1988).

ex ante inefficiences. For example, if the choice of a pricing policy from the mechanism offered by the regulator in the first period reveals information about the firm's type, the regulator will have an ex post incentive to act opportunistically by fully exploiting that information in future periods. The firm will anticipate this opportunistic behavior and thus will revise its strategy for the first period. As will be demonstrated below in Subsections 6.3 and 6.4, the resulting equilibrium will be ex ante inefficient. Efficiency can be improved only by developing means to limit the opportunism. This requires some means of committing not to act opportunistically when doing so would result in ex ante inefficiency.

The efficiency of the mechanisms used to deal with the dynamics of regulatory relationships thus depends importantly on the ability of the parties to commit to strategies. The significance of commitment has been demonstrated in a number of works,[52] and this section deals with three principal cases. In the first case considered in Subsection 6.2, the regulator is assumed to have the ability to commit credibly to a multiperiod mechanism that will govern the regulatory relationship for the duration of the (finite) horizon. In particular, the regulator can commit to use in any way it chooses the information that will be generated in the implementation of the mechanism. For example, at one extreme it can commit not to use the information it observes, and at the other extreme it can commit to a policy that is fully responsive to that information. In the second case considered in Subsection 6.3, the regulator cannot commit to future policies, so the only recourse of the regulator is to choose a mechanism at the beginning of each period. The third case considered in Subsection 6.4 is intermediate and allows the regulator and the firm to agree to an institutional arrangement in which the regulator, although unable to commit credibly to a multiperiod mechanism, is required to treat the firm "fairly". In exchange, the firm agrees not to quit the regulatory relationship as long as it is treated fairly. That is, in the first two cases, the firm is allowed to decide in each period whether it wishes to participate in the regulatory relationship, whereas in the third case the firm relinquishes its right to quit the relationship in exchange for assurance that it will be treated fairly.

6.2. Commitment to a multiperiod mechanism

6.2.1. Extension of the basic model

The model considered in this subsection is an extension, developed in Baron and Besanko (1984b), of the model in Section 4 in which the firm has private

[52]In the macroeconomics literature, the issue of the optimality of policies in the absence of commitment is referred to as "dynamic consistency" in the terminology introduced by Kydland and Prescott (1977). Roberts (1982, 1984) and Crawford (1988) have also examined the differences between long-term contracts in cases in which commitment is and is not possible.

information about its marginal cost and the regulatory mechanism is a set of pricing policies. The regulator is assumed to have the ability to commit to a mechanism for the duration of the regulatory relationship, so it can specify how the price in each period responds to information that becomes available during execution of the selected regulatory policy. In addition, commitment on the part of the regulator means that it can commit to preclude the firm from operating in future periods if the firm chooses not to participate in a previous period.

The complication in a dynamic model is that the private information of the firm may evolve over time in a manner that is observable only to the firm. Suppose that prior to the choice of the regulatory mechanism the firm knows the marginal cost θ_1 it will have in period 1, and the regulator's prior information is represented by a density function $f_1(\theta_1)$. At the beginning of each subsequent period i, the firm privately observes its marginal cost θ_i, which is given by a function $\theta_i = \theta_i(\theta_{i-1}, \varepsilon) \in [\theta_i^-, \theta_i^+]$, where ε is the realization of a random variable $\tilde{\varepsilon}$.[53,54] The function $\theta_i(\theta_{i-1}, \varepsilon)$ is common knowledge, but only the firm observes the realized θ_i. The distribution function of θ_i will be denoted by $F_i(\theta_i|\theta_{i-1})$ and the density function by $f_i(\theta_i|\theta_{i-1})$. The marginal cost θ_i is assumed to be a nondecreasing function of θ_{i-1}, so an increase in θ_{i-1} shifts the distribution function $F_i(\theta_i|\theta_{i-1})$ downward or $\partial F_i(\theta_i|\theta_{i-1})/\partial\theta_{i-1} \le 0$ for all θ_i for all θ_{i-1}.

Since the firm has private information at the beginning of each period, the regulator faces an adverse selection problem in each period with the complication that the report made in one period provides information about the marginal cost in the next period. The self-selection mechanism designed for each period thus must take into account how the revelation of information in that period influences the rents that the firm earns on the information it will privately observe in the future. This then affects the strategy the firm will employ in selecting a policy from the mechanism offered by the regulator.

A mechanism with commitment specifies at the beginning of the regulatory relationship the price $p_i(\theta_1, \dots, \theta_i)$ and the fixed charges $T_i(\theta_1, \dots, \theta_i)$ in each period i.[55] A mechanism M for a horizon of I periods is thus

$$M = \{(p_i(\theta_1, \dots, \theta_i), T_i(\theta_1, \dots, \theta_i)),\ i = 1, \dots, I,$$
$$\forall \theta_i \in [\theta^-, \theta^+],\ i = 1, \dots, I\}.$$

The strategy of the firm in each period is to report a type $\hat{\theta}_i$ and either to participate or to quit the regulatory relationship. The latter decision can be

[53] To avoid complicating the notation, the support $[\theta_i^-, \theta_i^+]$ is assumed not to depend on θ_{i-1}.
[54] The process that generates the marginal costs is thus Markovian.
[55] When it can do so credibly, the regulator always prefers to commit to a mechanism that will govern performance over the entire horizon of the regulatory relationship.

denoted by ϕ_i with $\phi_i = 0$ indicating that the firm quits and $\phi_i = 1$ indicating that the firm accepts the policy and produces in period i. In the model with commitment developed in this subsection, the regulator prefers to offer policies that the firm will accept, so $\phi_i = 1$, $i = 1, \ldots, I$.[56] The participation decision will thus be suppressed in the subsequent analysis.

Characterization of an equilibrium mechanism is facilitated by the revelation principle which in this case applies in a nested manner as developed in Baron and Besanko (1984b). The method of analysis and the properties of the mechanism can be fully indicated in the context of a two-period model. In the second period the regulator has observed the report $\hat{\theta}_1$, and the firm will report $\hat{\theta}_2$, so the pricing policy is a function of $(\hat{\theta}_1, \hat{\theta}_2)$. The second-period profit $\pi_2(\hat{\theta}_1, \hat{\theta}_2; \theta_2)$ is given by[57]

$$\pi_2(\hat{\theta}_1, \hat{\theta}_2; \theta_2) = (p_2(\hat{\theta}_1, \hat{\theta}_2) - \theta_2) Q(p_2(\hat{\theta}_1, \hat{\theta}_2)) + T_2(\hat{\theta}_1, \hat{\theta}_2) - K_2. \tag{6.1}$$

Incentive compatibility in period two requires that

$$\pi_2(\hat{\theta}_1; \theta_2) \equiv \pi_2(\hat{\theta}_1, \theta_2; \theta_2) \geq \pi_2(\hat{\theta}_1, \hat{\theta}_2; \theta_2),$$
$$\forall \hat{\theta}_2, \forall \theta_2 \in [\theta_2^-, \theta_2^+], \quad \forall \hat{\theta}_1 \in [\theta_1^-, \theta_1^+]. \tag{6.2}$$

Proceeding as in Section 4, a regulatory policy $(p_2(\hat{\theta}_1, \theta_2), T_2(\hat{\theta}_1, \theta_2), \theta_2 \in [\theta_2^-, \theta_2^+])$ for period two is implementable if $p_2(\hat{\theta}_1, \theta_2)$ is a nondecreasing function of θ_2 for all $\hat{\theta}_1$. The profit can then be expressed as

$$\pi_2(\hat{\theta}_1; \theta_2) = \int_{\theta_2}^{\theta_2^+} Q(p_2(\hat{\theta}_1, \theta_2^0))\, \mathrm{d}\theta_2^0 + \pi_2(\hat{\theta}_1; \theta_2^+). \tag{6.3}$$

A policy that satisfies this condition will (locally) induce the firm to report its second-period marginal cost truthfully whatever is the report $\hat{\theta}_1$. The firm will participate in period two if $\pi_2(\hat{\theta}_1; \theta_2) \geq 0$, and since $\pi_2(\hat{\theta}_1; \theta_2)$ is decreasing in θ_2, this can be satisfied by setting $\pi_2(\hat{\theta}_1; \theta_2^+) = 0$.

The mechanism must also specify a period-one policy that takes into account the firm's incentive to misreport its first-period marginal cost not only to obtain a higher first-period profit but also to obtain a higher second-period profit. The

[56] This decision becomes important in Subsection 6.3 when the regulator cannot credibly commit to a mechanism to govern the duration of the regulatory relationship.

[57] A fixed cost K_i is assumed to be incurred in each period.

two-period profit $\Pi(\hat{\theta}_1;\theta_1)$ is defined by

$$\begin{aligned}\Pi(\hat{\theta}_1;\theta_1) &\equiv \pi_1(\hat{\theta}_1;\theta_1) + \beta\int_{\theta_2^-}^{\theta_2^+}\pi_2(\hat{\theta}_1;\theta_2)f_2(\theta_2|\theta_1)\,\mathrm{d}\theta_2 \\ &= (p_1(\hat{\theta}_1)-\theta_1)Q(p_1(\hat{\theta}_1)) - K_1 \\ &\quad + T_1(\hat{\theta}_1) + \beta\int_{\theta_2^-}^{\theta_2^+}Q(p_2(\hat{\theta}_1,\theta_2))F_2(\theta_2|\theta_1)\,\mathrm{d}\theta_2,\end{aligned} \tag{6.4}$$

where $\beta\in[0,1]$ is the discount factor.[58] Incentive compatibility requires that

$$\Pi(\theta_1)\equiv\Pi(\theta_1;\theta_1)\geq\Pi(\hat{\theta}_1;\theta_1),\quad \forall\hat{\theta}_1,\forall\theta_1\in[\theta_1^-,\theta_1^+]. \tag{6.5}$$

An incentive compatible period-one policy, given that the second-period policy is incentive compatible, must satisfy a local condition on profit $\Pi(\theta_1)$ analogous to (4.7) or

$$\frac{\mathrm{d}\Pi(\theta_1)}{\mathrm{d}\theta_1} = -Q(p_1(\theta_1)) + \beta\int_{\theta_2^-}^{\theta_2^+}Q(p_2(\theta_1,\theta_2))\frac{\partial F_2(\theta_2|\theta_1)}{\partial\theta_1}\mathrm{d}\theta_2. \tag{6.6}$$

Since $\partial F_2(\theta_2|\theta_1)/\partial\theta_1\leq 0$, the second term on the right-hand side of (6.6) is nonpositive. The derivative in (6.6) takes into account the effect of a variation in θ_1 both on the first-period information rents and on the second-period information rents given that second-period incentive compatibility is satisfied. The necessary condition for an incentive compatible policy in (6.6) can be integrated to obtain a condition analogous to (4.8):

$$\begin{aligned}\Pi(\theta_1) &= \Pi(\theta_1^+) + \int_{\theta_1}^{\theta_1^+}Q(p_1(\theta_1^0))\,\mathrm{d}\theta_1^0 \\ &\quad -\beta\int_{\theta_1}^{\theta_1^+}\int_{\theta_2^-}^{\theta_2^+}Q(p_2(\theta_1^0;\theta_2))\frac{\partial F_2(\theta_2|\theta_1^0)}{\partial\theta_1}\mathrm{d}\theta_2\,\mathrm{d}\theta_1^0.\end{aligned} \tag{6.7}$$

As in the single-period model, the price in each period-is set equal to the sum of the marginal production and information costs in that period. In the first period, the price is the same as in a static model because the firm has the same information advantage relative to the first period as in a static model. The regulator thus prefers to distort the price above marginal cost θ in the same

[58]The beliefs of the regulator are specified as $f_2(\theta_2|\hat{\theta}_1)$, and in equilibrium $\hat{\theta}_1=\theta_1$, so the beliefs are correct.

for the multiperiod case, so the mechanisms characterized below must be checked to determine if the firm has an incentive to make a nonlocal misrepresentation of its type.

The regulator's objective function analogous to (4.18) can be derived as in Section 4 and is

$$W = \int_{\theta_1^-}^{\theta_1^+} \Bigg\{ \Bigg[\int_{p_1(\theta_1)}^{\infty} Q(p_1^0)\,\mathrm{d}p_1^0 + p_1(\theta_1) Q(p_1(\theta_1)) - y_\alpha(\theta_1) Q(p_1(\theta_1)) - K_1 \Bigg]$$

$$+ \beta \int_{\theta_2^-}^{\theta_2^+} \Bigg[\int_{p_2(\theta_1,\theta_2)}^{\infty} Q(p_2^0)\,\mathrm{d}p_2^0 + p_2(\theta_1,\theta_2) Q(p_2(\theta_1,\theta_2))$$

$$- z_\alpha(\theta_1,\theta_2) Q(p_2(\theta_1,\theta_2)) - K_2 \Bigg]$$

$$\times f_2(\theta_2|\theta_1)\,\mathrm{d}\theta_2 \Bigg\} f_1(\theta_1)\,\mathrm{d}\theta_1 - (1-\alpha)\Pi(\theta_1^+), \tag{6.8}$$

where

$$y_\alpha(\theta_1) = \theta_1 + (1-\alpha)\frac{F_1(\theta_1)}{f_1(\theta_1)} \tag{6.9}$$

and

$$z_\alpha(\theta_1,\theta_2) \equiv \theta_2 - (1-\alpha)\frac{F_1(\theta_1)}{f_1(\theta_1)} \frac{\partial F_2(\theta_2|\theta_1)/\partial\theta_1}{f_2(\theta_2|\theta_1)}. \tag{6.10}$$

Proceeding as in Section 4, the optimal prices satisfy:

$$p_1(\theta_1) = y_\alpha(\theta_1) \tag{6.11}$$

and

$$p_2(\theta_1,\theta_2) = z_\alpha(\theta_1,\theta_2). \tag{6.12}$$

As in the single-period model, the price in each period is set equal to the sum of the marginal production and information costs in that period. In the first period, the price is the same as in a static model because the firm has the same information advantage relative to the first period as in a static model. The regulator thus prefers to distort the price above marginal cost θ in the same manner to deal with the information advantage of the firm. The presence of future periods thus has no effect on the price in the first period.

The regulatory policy in the second period also sets the price equal to the marginal production and information costs, but in this case the marginal information cost depends on what the firm knows ex ante at the beginning of period one about its costs in the second period. For example, if the marginal cost in period two were independent of the marginal cost in period one, the firm's knowledge of θ_1 at the beginning of period one would provide no information about marginal cost in period two. The firm then can extract no information rents for period two, and hence the regulator bears no marginal information cost for period two. More formally, independence of the marginal costs implies that

$$\frac{\partial F_2(\theta_2 | \theta_1)}{\partial \theta_1} = 0, \quad \forall \theta_2, \forall \theta_1,$$

so $z_\alpha(\theta_1, \theta_2) = \theta_2$, and the price in period two equals marginal production cost. Efficiency thus results in every period after the first when the θ_i are independent.

If θ_1 is informative about θ_2, then $\partial F_2(\theta_2 | \theta_1)/\partial \theta_1$ is not equal to zero for all θ_2. The marginal information cost is then nonzero, and the price is distorted away from marginal production cost. If, for example, θ_1 is "fully informative" about θ_2, i.e. $\theta_2 = \theta_1$ so the marginal costs are perfectly correlated, then it can be shown that[59]

$$z_\alpha(\theta_1, \theta_2 = \theta_1) = \theta_1 + (1 - \alpha)\frac{F_1(\theta_1)}{f_1(\theta_1)} = y_\alpha(\theta_1). \tag{6.10a}$$

Consequently, when the marginal cost in the first period is fully informative about the marginal cost in the second period, the optimal regulatory mechanism involves repeating the static policy in each period. The regulator thus does not exploit in period two the information it receives in period one. It is the ability of the regulator to commit to repeat the same policy in each period that is necessary for the regulator to be able to ignore the information revealed in the first period. As will be indicated in Subsection 6.3, if the regulator is unable to commit not to exploit this information, it will act opportunistically and ex ante inefficiency will result.

If knowledge of the marginal cost in the first period is only partially informative about the second-period marginal cost, the distortion of price from marginal cost θ_2 is "between" that of the independent and the perfect correlation cases.

[59] An analogous result obtains if θ_2 is a deterministic function $\theta_2(\theta_1)$ of θ_1.

The pricing policy thus has memory. To illustrate the "informativeness" of θ_1 about θ_2, consider the following specification of second-period marginal cost:

$$\tilde{\theta}_2 = \gamma\tilde{\theta}_1 + (1-\gamma)\tilde{\varepsilon}, \quad \gamma \in [0,1], \tag{6.13}$$

where $\tilde{\theta}_1$, $\tilde{\theta}_2$, and $\tilde{\varepsilon}$ have the same support.[60] For θ_2 such that $F_2(\theta_2|\theta_1) \in (0,1)$, the "informativeness" measure is

$$\frac{\partial F_2(\theta_2|\theta_1)/\partial\theta_1}{f_2(\theta_2|\theta_1)} = -\gamma.$$

The price in the second period is then

$$p_2(\theta_1,\theta_2) = z_\alpha(\theta_1,\theta_2) = \theta_2 + (1-\alpha)\gamma\frac{F_1(\theta_1)}{f_1(\theta_1)}, \tag{6.12a}$$

which is increasing in both θ_2 and γ. The price is thus lower the less informative (lower γ) is first-period marginal cost about second-period marginal cost; that is, the less accurate is the firm's private ex ante information about second-period marginal cost. If $\gamma = 0$, the marginal cost in the second period is independent of the marginal cost in the first period, so the firm has no information advantage relative to the regulator, and the information rents for the second period are identically zero. The regulator thus does not need to distort the price in period two. If $\gamma = 1$, the second-period marginal cost equals the first-period marginal cost, so the regulator has the same information advantage regarding marginal cost in both periods, and the best the regulator can do is to employ the static policy in each period.

The case of perfect correlation of the marginal costs indicates the power of commitment. When the static policy is used in each period, the regulator learns the marginal cost in the first period when the firm selects the regulatory policy corresponding to its marginal cost. The regulator prefers not to utilize that information in subsequent periods, however, because responding to it would increase the information rents by more than the gain in consumer surplus. It is the power to commit not to exploit that information that allows the regulator to repeat the static contract. In Subsection 6.3, the commitment assumption will be relaxed, and the equilibrium contract will be shown to be radically different.

To examine why the regulator prefers to commit to ignore the information revealed in the first period when the marginal costs are perfectly correlated, consider the regulatory policy in which the static policy is employed in the first

[60] For example, the random variables may all be normally distributed. The assumption of normality requires bounding the marginal costs at zero and may require an upper bound on the cost at which the regulator no longer prefers to purchase from the firm. The normality assumption is useful for illustration because the support of θ_2 is independent of θ_1.

period and the regulator fully exploits the information revealed in the first period by setting the second-period price equal to marginal cost. The second-period regulatory policy is thus, writing $\theta_2 = \theta_1$:

$$p_2(\theta_1, \theta_1) = \theta_1 \quad \text{and} \quad T(\theta_1, \theta_1) = K_2. \tag{6.14}$$

The period-two profit of the firm thus equals zero, and the firm will take this into account in making its first-period report $\hat{\theta}_1$. For example, if the firm with marginal cost θ_1 reported in period one that its marginal cost was $\theta_1 + \Delta\theta_1$, where $\Delta\theta_1 > 0$, it would earn profits $\Delta\theta_1 Q(p_2(\theta_1 + \Delta\theta_1, \theta_1 + \Delta\theta_1))$ in the second period. The regulator must respond to this incentive, so the variation in the two-period profit in (6.6) is

$$\frac{\mathrm{d}\Pi(\theta_1)}{\mathrm{d}\theta_1} = -Q(y_\alpha(\theta_1)) - \beta Q(\theta_1). \tag{6.15}$$

The firm thus takes into account the effect of its first-period report on both its first-period and second-period profit. The two-period profit of the firm is then

$$\Pi(\theta_1) = \int_{\theta_1}^{\theta_1^+} \left[Q(y_\alpha(\theta_1^0)) + \beta Q(\theta_1^0)\right] \mathrm{d}\theta_1^0. \tag{6.16}$$

The difference $\Delta\Pi(\theta_1)$ in the information rents between this mechanism in which the information revealed in the first period is fully exploited in the second period and the mechanism in which the static policy is repeated in each period is

$$\Delta\Pi(\theta_1) = \int_{\theta_1}^{\theta_1^+} \beta\left[Q(\theta_1) - Q(y_\alpha(\theta_1))\right] \mathrm{d}\theta_1, \tag{6.17}$$

which is positive when $\alpha < 1$ for all $\theta_1 > \theta_1^-$, since $y_\alpha(\theta_1) > \theta_2$. The greater rents then reduce ex ante welfare. The corresponding difference $\Delta W(\theta_1)$ in welfare conditional on θ_1 is

$$\Delta W(\theta_1) = \beta\left[\int_{\theta_1}^{y_\alpha(\theta_1)} \left(Q(\theta_1^0) - Q(y_\alpha(\theta_1^0))\right) \mathrm{d}\theta_1^0 - (\theta_1 - y_\alpha(\theta_1))Q(\theta_1)\right]. \tag{6.18}$$

The difference in welfare in (6.18) is negative for all $\alpha < 1$ and for all $\theta_1 > \theta_1^-$ as is illustrated in Figure 24.2 where $D(\theta_1)$ denotes the integrand in (6.18). The additional rents in (6.17) that the firm earns thus exceed the gain in consumer surplus resulting from the lower price in period two. The regulator thus prefers to implement the static policy in each period.

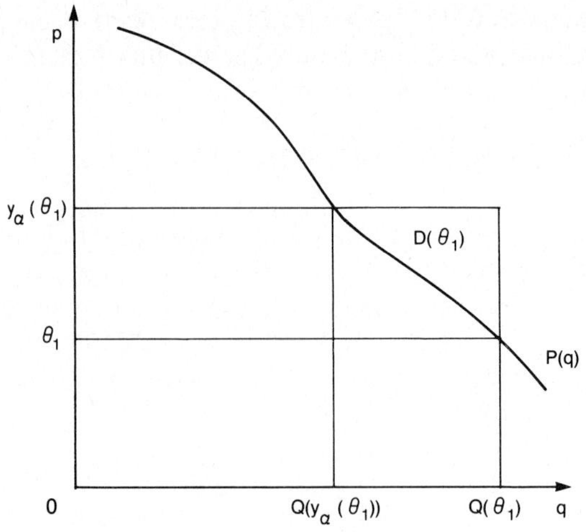

Figure 24.2. Welfare loss with no commitment.

The case in which marginal costs are perfectly correlated across periods stands in opposition to the case in which marginal costs are independent across periods. In the former, the regulator prefers to repeat the static mechanism in each period as a means of reducing the information rents. In the latter, the regulator is able to use marginal cost pricing in each period after the first. Intuitively, the regulator employs marginal cost pricing in the second period because at the beginning of the first period, when the firm chooses a pricing policy from the mechanism offered, the firm has no information advantage relative to the regulator regarding θ_2. The firm thus can earn no rents from the second period, so the regulator need not distort the second-period price from the marginal cost θ_2.

The mechanism, however, must induce the firm to report θ_2 at the beginning of the second period, and to do so, the fixed charges must be specified as

$$T_2(\theta_1, \theta_2) = \int_{\theta_2}^{\theta_2^+} Q(p_2(\theta_1, \theta_2^0))\, d\theta_2^0 + \theta_2 Q(p_2(\theta_1, \theta_2)) + K_2 - p_2(\theta_1, \theta_2) Q(p_2(\theta_1, \theta_2)). \tag{6.19}$$

For the case of independent marginal costs, this is

$$T_2(\theta_1, \theta_2) = \int_{\theta_2}^{\theta_2^+} Q(\theta_2^0)\, d\theta_2^0 + K_2, \tag{6.19a}$$

and the second-period profit $\pi_2(\theta_1; \theta_2)$ in (6.3) equals $T_2(\theta_1, \theta_2) - K_2$. The fixed charges $T_1(\theta_1)$, however, take away the conditional (on θ_1) expectation $E[\pi_2(\theta_1;\theta_2)]$ of the second-period profit. The general expression for $T_1(\theta_1)$ is

$$T_1(\theta_1) = \int_{\theta_1}^{\theta_1^+}\left[Q(p_1(\theta_1^0)) - \beta\int_{\theta_2^-}^{\theta_2^+} Q(p_2(\theta_1^0,\theta_2))\frac{\partial F_2(\theta_2|\theta_1^0)}{\partial\theta_1}\mathrm{d}\theta_2\right]\mathrm{d}\theta_1^0$$
$$+\theta_1 Q(p_1(\theta_1)) + K_1 - p_1(\theta_1)Q(p_1(\theta_1)) - \beta E[\pi_2(\theta_1;\theta_2)], \tag{6.20}$$

and when θ_1 and θ_2 are independent, this is

$$T_1(\theta_1) = \int_{\theta_1}^{\theta_1^+} Q(p_1(\theta_1^0))\,\mathrm{d}\theta_1^0 + \theta_1 Q(p_1(\theta_1)) + K_1 - \beta E[\pi_2(\theta_i,\theta_2)].$$

In the first period, the expectation of the second-period profit is thus deducted from the fixed charges.[61] The profit in the first-period, however, equals the first term in (6.20), so it reflects the rents that the firm earns as a result of its private information about θ_1. In general that information pertains not only to first-period marginal cost but also, through the informativeness of first-period marginal cost, to the second-period marginal cost. When the marginal costs are independent, however, the latter is zero, so

$$\Pi(\theta_1) = \int_{\theta_1}^{\theta_1^+} Q(p_1(\theta_1^0))\,\mathrm{d}\theta_1^0.$$

Since the two-period profit $\Pi(\theta_1)$ of the firm is equal to the first term in (6.20), it is evident that the firm has higher profit the lower is the second-period price $p_2(\theta_1,\theta_2) = z_\alpha(\theta_1,\theta_2)$. Thus, (roughly) the more informative the first-period marginal cost is about the second-period marginal cost, the greater is the profit $\Pi(\theta_1)$.

This analysis can be extended to models in which the regulator has the ability to commit to future regulatory policies and the firm has private information at the time of contracting that is informative about what future marginal cost will be. For example, in Section 9 a model of the selection of a franchise monopolist will be considered in which at the time the regulatory mechanism is chosen the firm has imperfect information about what its marginal costs will be, but the actual marginal cost will not be observed until fixed costs have been sunk. The optimal regulatory mechanism for the selected franchise monopolist is a special case of the mechanism presented in this subsection.

[61] In the regulatory relationship characterized by commitment, transfers are possible across periods.

6.2.2. *Application: Private information after contracting*

The theory of mechanism design in multiperiod models with commitment can be used to determine the optimal regulatory mechanism for a number of important special cases. For example, consider a single-period setting in which the regulator and the firm have symmetric information at the time at which the regulatory mechanism is chosen but in which the firm will observe its marginal cost before production begins. The price can thus be based on a report of marginal cost after the regulatory mechanism has been agreed to but before production commences.[62]

This case may be thought of as involving two periods, the first of which involves no production, and all production takes place in the second period. At the beginning of the first period at the time the regulatory policy is determined, the firm has uninformative private information about what its marginal costs θ_2 will be in the second period. The informativeness measure in (6.10) is thus equal to zero, so the regulatory contract specifies a period-two price $p_2(\hat{\theta}_2)$ equal to the reported marginal cost $\hat{\theta}_2$ and fixed charges given in (6.19) that implement that pricing policy.

Since the firm has no private information at the time it must decide whether to participate, it will participate if its expected profit is nonnegative. The individual rationality constraint thus holds as an expectation rather than conditionally on each possible value of an information parameter.[63] That is,

$$T_1 + \int_{\theta_2^-}^{\theta_2^+} \pi_2(\theta_2) f_2(\theta_2)\, \mathrm{d}\theta_2 \geq 0, \tag{6.21}$$

where the distribution of θ_2 is unconditional and the θ_1 notation is suppressed. The fixed charges T_1 in (6.20) are thus

$$T_1 = -\int_{\theta_2^-}^{\theta_2^+} \pi_2(\theta_2) f_2(\theta_2)\, \mathrm{d}\theta_2. \tag{6.20a}$$

This may be interpreted as a franchise fee paid by the firm to consumers at the time at which the firm agrees to participate in the regulatory relationship. In (6.21) the expected profit net of the franchise fee is thus zero, so the firm is

[62] Baron and DeBondt (1981) consider a related case of the design of a fuel-adjustment mechanism when the regulator and the firm are symmetrically informed at the time the regulatory policy is agreed to but a factor price will subsequently be realized. The regulator is unable to observe the factor price but can observe the unit cost which depends on factor inputs that are unobservable to the regulator. The optimal regulatory policy involves a price adjustment mechanism in response to the observed unit cost.

[63] The firm is not assumed to face any bankruptcy or limited liability constraints. Such constraints are considered in the following subsection.

willing to participate. This mechanism is optimal for all α, so the first-best outcome is attained for any regulatory welfare function.[64,65] That is, the private information that the firm will observe in the future causes no inefficiency.

The firm earns no rents on its information because at the time the mechanism is agreed to the firm and the regulator are symmetrically informed. The mechanism induces the firm to report its true marginal cost once it is observed, and it earns non-negative profit $\pi_2(\theta_2)$ after the franchise fee has been sunk, so it is willing to supply the specified quantity once it observes θ_2. The firm thus has no incentive to quit the regulatory relationship. Although the firm earns rents on its information in the second period, the regulator extracts the expected rent as a franchise fee at the time the mechanism is agreed to, so ex ante profit is zero.

This model can be directly extended to the case in which the manager of the firm takes an unobservable action as in Subsection 4.6.1. Suppose that marginal cost $c(\theta_2, a)$ is a function of θ_2 and effort a, which is unobservable to the regulator. The first-best mechanism above will clearly induce the manager to take the first-best effort level $a^*(\theta_2)$, which satisfies:[66]

$$-c_a(\theta_2, a^*(\theta_2))Q(\theta_2) - \psi'(a^*(\theta_2)) = 0.$$

Consequently, when the regulator and the firm have symmetric information at the time the mechanism is proposed and agreed to, the first-best allocation can be achieved for any regulatory objective even though the firm will subsequently have private information and take an unobservable action.

6.2.3. Limited liability

In models in which the regulator and the firm are symmetrically informed at the time the mechanism is agreed to but in which the firm will obtain information prior to taking an action, the first-best allocation can be implemented using the fixed charges functions given in (6.19) and (6.20a). Once the franchise fee has been sunk, the profits $\pi_2(\theta_2)$ are non-negative, so the firm always has an incentive to produce the specified quantity. A complication may arise, however, if either the firm has an incentive to quit the regulatory arrangement once it observes θ_2 or the firm is unable to fulfill the terms of the policy.

[64] Weitzman (1978) obtained the same result with multiple firms for the case of $\alpha = 1$ and a linear marginal benefits function.

[65] Riordan (1984) obtains a similar result for the case in which the regulator and the firm are symmetrically informed at the time the mechanism is agreed to, but subsequent to the agreement the firm privately observes the realization θ of a random variable $\tilde{\theta}$ that affects demand. He demonstrates that a mechanism exists that results in both the ex ante efficient capacity and the ex post efficient price. This is attainable because information is symmetric at the time at which the agreement is made.

[66] Note that the equilibrium level of effort in (4.24) is second best because the price is distorted above marginal cost.

Sappington (1983b) considers the case in which the firm will be unable to fulfill the terms of the regulatory policy if profit net of the franchise fee falls below a limit L, where L is nonpositive. That is, the firm is able to fulfill the policy only if the realized θ_2 is such that[67]

$$-T_1 + \pi_2(\theta_2) \geq L, \quad L \leq 0. \tag{6.22}$$

He refers to this condition as limited liability.[68,69]

The nature of the optimal mechanism in this case can be determined by noting that the constraint in (6.22) is of the same form as the participation constraint in (4.2) for the case in which the firm has private information prior to contracting. The regulator thus will choose a mechanism that distorts output from the first-best level. The equilibrium mechanism specifies efficient production only for the most efficient type θ^-, and for all other types that produce, output is below the first-best level. These properties of the optimal mechanism are analogous to those of the mechanisms employed in the case in which the firm has private information at the time the regulatory mechanism is chosen. Even though the firm here has no private information at the time the mechanism is agreed to, the first-best allocation cannot be attained because the limited liability constraints force a distortion of price from marginal cost.

Since limited liability as represented in (6.22) can affect the regulatory mechanism, the relevant issue is when such a condition might be present. If the firm could commit to abide by the prearranged terms of the agreement not to quit the relationship, then the constraint would not be present. Similarly, if the firm could pay T_1 ex ante at the time at which the regulatory policy was chosen so that it was sunk by the time θ_2 was observed, the constraint would not be present as indicated in the previous subsection. If the firm did not have the equity to pay T_1 ex ante, it could borrow T_1 in a capital market and repay it with interest, provided that if there were default on the loan payment the lender could take over the firm, observe θ_2, and make the effort a.[70] The explanation for the limited liability condition thus is either an imperfection in the capital markets or an inability of an outsider to observe θ_2 or to make the effort a. That is, either the information or the effort must be specific to the present ownership of the

[67]This constraint can be incorporated directly into the control theoretic formulation in Appendix A.

[68]Similar constraints arise in the study of the breach of contracts. See, for example, Melumad (1988).

[69]In the mechanism characterized in the previous section, the limit L was $L \leq -T_1$, so the firm produces for whatever θ_2 is realized.

[70]The equilibrium loan contract carries an interest rate such that the firm will default with probability one. That is, the firm is sold to a party that can pay the franchise fee ex ante.

firm. This may be characteristic of a managerial model in which the manager has specific ability or observability powers independent of the position occupied.[71]

6.2.4. Observable costs

Sappington and Sibley (1986) consider a dynamic model in which the regulator can at the end of each period perfectly observe the costs incurred by the firm. As in the model in Subsection 5.1, the firm can increase its costs by choosing additional expenditures ω to confirm its reported marginal cost. The regulator is assumed to be able to commit to a mechanism, and the firm is unable to quit the regulatory relationship. The mechanism begins with an exogenous price in the first period. The actual costs in each period are perfectly observable by the regulator, which may impose an infinite penalty on the firm if actual costs differ from its reported cost. The actual costs observed in one period are used as a basis for pricing in the next period, but the observed cost in the final period cannot be so used.

Sappington and Sibley show that the optimal regulatory mechanism for the case in which the marginal cost is the same in each period involves a price equal to reported marginal cost in every period after the initial period with the exception of the final period.[72] In the final period the regulatory policy is the optimal static policy characterized in Subsection 4.2. The fixed charge for the multiperiod mechanism in this case is the fixed charge for the single-period mechanism. This mechanism results in considerable efficiency gains relative to the case in which the regulator cannot observe any aspect of performance. The efficiency gains result both because marginal cost pricing can be achieved in all periods other than the first and the last and because the transfer includes an information rent that is paid in the last period and thus has a present value that is diminished by discounting.

6.3. Multiperiod mechanisms with no commitment

6.3.1. Introduction

The mechanisms in the previous subsection are based on the assumption that the regulator is able to commit to a policy for the duration of the regulatory relationship. The inability of one government to bind a future government to a

[71] In the context of a managerial model, limited liability may also be interpreted as infinite risk aversion for losses below L, and risk neutrality for gains.

[72] Cost must be deterministic and observable without error for this mechanism to be implementable.

particular policy, however, makes commitment to public policies difficult to assure. Any party to a multiperiod relationship has an incentive to act opportunistically, but as Baron and Besanko (1987a) state:

> opportunism may be more characteristic of the policies of public agencies than of private parties because although courts will prohibit inefficient breach by private parties they generally will not proscribe revisions of policies by regulatory or administrative agencies. Instead courts tend to restrict their review to procedure, process, and consistency. Perhaps the greatest impediment to establishing commitment in governmental and regulatory settings arises from electoral competition. Presidential candidates and parties can pledge to preserve or to rescind laws or to force regulatory agencies to alter policies either through the appointment process, executive orders, or the authorization and appropriations process. Similarly, Congress can alter policies as well as initiate new ones. The political incentive to respond to an *ex post* opportunity, even though that opportunity results from an event anticipated under an *ex ante* efficient policy, seems unavoidable in many settings.

If the regulator is unable to commit to a mulitperiod policy, the firm must form expectations about which policies will be adopted in the future. In the context of the self-selection model considered in Section 6, the firm must anticipate the policy the regulator will adopt given what it learns about the firm during previous periods. For example, if the marginal cost of the firm were known to be the same in every period and if the regulatory policy implemented in the first period were fully separating, the regulator would know the marginal cost in every subsequent period. The regulator then has an incentive to exploit fully that information by adopting the policy that is optimal given that information. The firm, of course, recognizes this incentive, and in making its first-period decision it will take into account the policy the regulator will adopt in future periods as a consequence of the information its first-period choice reveals about its marginal costs. The equilibrium concept appropriate for this case in which the regulator cannot credibly commit is a perfect Bayesian equilibrium or sequential equilibrium in which actions must be optimal for the regulator conditional on the information it has at the beginning of each period.[73,74]

[73]The perfectness property was introduced by Selten (1975) and is addressed in Chapter 5 of this Handbook.

[74]Sappington (1986) considers a model in which the regulator wants to motivate the firm to seek information about cost-reducing investment opportunities but is unable to commit to how it will use information it obtains through monitoring the firm's performance. Through monitoring, the regulator can observe the marginal cost the firm will have after it makes its investment, and if the regulator is unable to commit, it will set prices so that the profit of the firm is zero. Recognizing this, the firm has no incentive to seek information about the investment opportunities. If commitment were possible, the regulator could assure the firm that it could earn positive profits if it took the appropriate

If the regulatory policy were separating in the first period, the information of the regulator at the beginning of the second period would be represented by the conditional distribution function $F_2(\theta_2|\theta_1)$. The regulator would then have an incentive to fully exploit that information by choosing the regulatory mechanism that is optimal given that information. That optimal mechanism satisfies the perfectness condition and is simply the single-period mechanism that would be established given that information. The price in the second period is thus of the form of (4.19) with $F_2(\theta_2|\theta_1)/f_2(\theta_2|\theta_1)$ replacing $F(\theta)/f(\theta)$. The firm would recognize that this price would be established in the second period if it were to report its marginal cost truthfully in the first period, and thus it takes into account the period-two consequences of the information it reveals in the first period. The opportunism of the regulator and the response by the firm result in ex ante inefficiency.

This subsection is concerned with the nature of the equilibria when the regulator cannot commit to multiperiod policies and hence is unable to commit not to act in an opportunistic manner.[75] The inability to commit to multiperiod policies can result in equilibria quite different from those with commitment. The objective of this section is to develop the intuition underlying this difference and to indicate the nature of the equilibrium mechanisms. The first case considered is that studied by Laffont and Tirole (1988) in which the marginal cost of the firm is the same in each period. In Subsection 6.3.3 an institutional arrangement is proposed that limits the opportunism and results in improvements in ex ante welfare. The case in which the marginal cost may change over time in an imperfectly predictable manner is then considered in the subsequent subsection.

6.3.2. Perfectly correlated marginal costs $\theta_1 = \theta_2$

With perfectly correlated marginal costs and commitment in a multiperiod model, the firm as in a static model has an incentive to overstate its costs in an attempt to obtain a more profitable regulatory contract. The incentive compati-

---

information acquistion and investment actions. Sappington assumes that although the regulator cannot commit to how information would be used in pricing, it can commit to how costly the monitoring will be. By choosing a costly monitoring technology, the regulator assures the firm that it will not monitor the firm as accurately ex post as it would if that cost were lower. This provides an opportunity for the firm to realize profits, and thus the firm has some incentive to acquire information and to invest efficiently given that information. Employing a costly monitoring technology thus provides some degree of commitment.

[75] Baron and Besanko (1987a) and Roberts (1982) also analyze the case in which the regulator is unable to commit to a multiperiod policy. Using a repeated game approach, Lewis (1986) considers a model of project execution in which neither party can commit to a policy. Tirole (1986a) and Grout (1984) also consider models without commitment in which the second-period outcome is determined by bargaining.

bility constraints in (6.5) thus are binding "upwards", and the fixed charges must be structured to offset the incentive the firm with marginal cost θ_1 has to report its costs as $\theta_1 + \Delta\theta_1$, where $\Delta\theta_1 > 0$. Also, with commitment the regulatory mechanism is always such that the firm's profits were non-negative for all θ_1, so it has an incentive to participate. The participation decision becomes important in the absence of commitment because as indicated next the firm has an incentive to understate its cost in the first period and to quit in the second period. This implies that the incentive compatibility constraints are binding "downwards" as well as upwards.

To illustrate this, suppose that the regulator were to attempt to implement a separating mechanism in the first period. The firm recognizes that if it were to report its true marginal cost in the first period, the regulator would know its marginal cost for all subsequent periods. Then in the second period the regulator could only be expected to implement a policy of marginal cost pricing with the fixed charges equal to the fixed cost, which would yield zero profit for the firm in period two. The two-period profit $\Pi(\hat{\theta}_1; \theta_1)$ under this policy, writing the second-period quantity as a function only of $\hat{\theta}_1$, is

$$\Pi(\hat{\theta}_1; \theta_1) = (p_1(\hat{\theta}_1) - \theta_1)Q(p_1(\hat{\theta}_1)) - K_2 + T_1(\hat{\theta}_1) + \beta(\hat{\theta}_1 - \theta_1)Q(\hat{\theta}_1), \tag{6.23}$$

where $p_2(\hat{\theta}_1) = \hat{\theta}_1$, $T_2(\hat{\theta}_1) = K_2$, $p_1(\hat{\theta}_1) = y_\alpha(\hat{\theta}_1)$, and $T_1(\hat{\theta}_1)$ is

$$T_1(\hat{\theta}_1) = \int_{\hat{\theta}_1}^{\theta_1^+} [Q(p_1(\theta_1^0)) + \beta Q(\theta_1^0)]\, \mathrm{d}\theta_1^0 - (p_1(\hat{\theta}_1) - \hat{\theta}_1)Q(p_1(\hat{\theta}_1)) + K_1. \tag{6.24}$$

The firm has no incentive to overstate its cost, since the payment,

$$\beta \int_{\hat{\theta}_1}^{\theta_1^+} Q(\theta_1^0)\, \mathrm{d}\theta_1^0, \tag{6.25}$$

negates the incentive, created by the exploitation of the information revealed in period one, to overstate marginal cost. It is important to note that when the regulator is unable to commit to a regulatory policy, the period-one fixed charges $T_1(\theta_1)$ must include the incentive payment in (6.25), since the regulator is unable to commit to pay it in period two. That is, the only credible beliefs in period two are that the fixed payments would only cover the fixed cost K_2 in that period.

Although the fixed charges in (6.24) induce the firm not to overstate costs, the firm may have an incentive to understate its costs in the first period and quit in the second period if producing in that period would yield negative profits. To see this, note that the profit function of the firm with the fixed charges given in (6.24) is actually

$$\Pi(\hat{\theta}_1;\theta_1) = (\hat{\theta}_1 - \theta_1)Q(p_1(\hat{\theta}_1)) + \int_{\hat{\theta}_1}^{\theta_1^+} [Q(p_1(\theta_1^0)) + \beta Q(\theta_1^0)]\,\mathrm{d}\theta_1^0$$
$$+\beta \max\{0, (\hat{\theta}_1 - \theta_1)Q(\hat{\theta}_1)\}, \tag{6.26}$$

where, in the last term, the zero results from the possibility of quitting in period two rather than producing $Q(\hat{\theta}_1)$. The right-hand derivative of (6.26) with respect to $\hat{\theta}_1$ equals zero at $\hat{\theta}_1 = \theta_1$, so the firm has no incentive to overstate its costs. The left-hand derivate of (6.26) evaluated at $\hat{\theta}_1 = \theta_1$ is, however,

$$\left.\frac{\partial \Pi(\hat{\theta}_1;\theta_1)}{\partial \hat{\theta}_1}\right|_{\hat{\theta}_1 = \theta_1} = -\beta Q(\theta_1), \tag{6.27}$$

since for $\hat{\theta}_1 < \theta_1$, the last term in (6.26) is zero. The profit function in (6.26) is thus not differentiable, and as (6.27) indicates, the firm has an incentive to understate its costs. This incentive is present because the firm has the incentive to obtain a larger transfer in the first period by reporting $\hat{\theta}_1 < \theta_1$ and then to quit in the second period rather than produce at a price $p_2(\hat{\theta}_1) = \hat{\theta}_1$ that is below its true marginal cost θ_1.[76]

If the regulator were able to commit to a multiperiod policy, it would commit to second-period fixed charges that include the term in (6.25). That would induce the firm to produce in the second period eliminating the incentive to understate costs in the first period. When the regulator is unable to make credible commitments, however, the only credible beliefs about what the regulator will do in the second period is that it will offer fixed charges that cover only the fixed cost and will set price equal to marginal cost. The regulator in this case still must induce the firm not to overstate its cost, so the first-period transfer in (6.24) must include the second-period incentive terms in (6.25). But as indicated in (6.27), this induces the firm to understate its marginal costs. Consequently, a mechanism that employs a separating mechanism in the first period and a mechanism satisfying the perfectness condition in the second period is not feasible because the incentive compatibility constraints cannot be satisfied. This conclusion holds in general for any mechanism that in period one would separate types over any closed interval. The demonstration of this important result is due to Laffont and Tirole (1988) who show that there exists no mechanism that separates the types

[76] Production in the second period would yield a negative profit $(\hat{\theta}_1 - \theta_1)Q(\hat{\theta}_1)$.

on any interval with positive measure.[77] They provide conditions for the existence of an equilibrium and some characterization of the types of equilibria that may exist.

If the regulator is unable to commit to multiperiod policies, it is natural to inquire if the regulator could take actions that would endogenously generate the commitment that would allow it to implement the multiperiod contract optimal with commitment. To do so, the regulator must assure the firm that at the end of the first period it will not revise its policy and revert to marginal cost pricing once it has learned the marginal cost of the firm. The regulator might, for example, post a bond claimable by the firm in the event that the regulator deviated from the multiperiod policy announced at the beginning of the relationship. A bond sufficient to ensure that the regulator would not shirk on this commitment would have to be greater than the difference in second-period welfare under the (perfect) marginal cost pricing policy and the second-period welfare under the equilibrium policy with commitment. With such a bond the regulator would have no incentive to shirk and hence the bond need never be paid. The regulator thus is willing to post it thus guaranteeing its commitment. Such a bond would be sufficient to generate commitment, but any posted bond would be subject to the same political forces addressed above that make commitment difficult to assure. Means of endogenously generating commitment thus seem to be subject to the same type of limitations.[78]

6.3.3. *Perfectly correlated marginal costs and fair regulatory mechanisms*

The inefficiency that results from the opportunism identified above would be expected to generate incentives for the establishment of institutional arrangements that would limit that opportunism and improve efficiency. The characteristics of the resulting institution would be expected to deal with the two causes of the inefficiency: (1) the regulator is unable to give assurance to the firm about how it will be treated under future policies, and (2) the firm can chose whether to participate in each period.

Even though a person cannot commit not to breach a labor contract because the courts will not enforce contracts that are difficult to distinguish from involuntary servitude, a contract between two private parties may be enforceable, particularly if the parties have made reliance expenditures as a consequence of the contract. Similarly, a regulatory authority may have some ability to commit to a pricing policy to the extent that procedural requirements and legal prece-

[77] Note that this result is stronger than the result that the equilibrium mechanism is not separating. It indicates that no separating mechanism is feasible.

[78] Williamson (1983) provides an insightful analysis of endogenous means of generating commitment in private contracting.

dents restrict its ability to alter its policies ex post. For example, Supreme Court decisions such as *Smyth v. Ames 169 U.S.* 466 (1898) and *Federal Power Commission et al. v. Hope Natural Gas Co.* 320 U.S. 591 (1944) provide a lower bound on the earnings of public utilities on used and useful assets employed in a regulated activity. In addition, the procedural requirements of administrative law protect a firm from arbitrary and capricious actions by the regulator. With respect to the firm's ability to withdraw from a regulatory relationship, state statutes generally prohibit a regulated utility from withdrawing assets from regulated services without regulatory approval.[79] As with private contracts, the restrictions placed on regulators by the courts may be intended to yield efficiency gains to a continuing regulatory relationship by limiting opportunism and thereby improving reliance.

Such restrictions could be imposed by legislation, but it is also possible that the regulator and the firm would have incentives to reach a voluntary arrangement in which the firm is offered some protection from the actions of the regulator and, in exchange, limits its ability to withdraw from the arrangement. One such arrangement would involve the firm exchanging its right to withdraw from the regulatory relationship for restrictions on the opportunism of the regulator. A regulatory relationship with this property will be said to be *fair*.[80] Under such an arrangement, however, the regulator still is allowed to choose a policy that is optimal given the information it has as the beginning of each period. Opportunism is restricted by requiring the regulator to choose policies that are compensatory given the information revealed by the firm in earlier periods. Such an arrangement may correspond to the state statutes and Supreme Court decisions referred to above.

In regulatory contexts with informational asymmetries, the adequacy of the profit of a firm must be relative to information that both is observable by all parties and is verifiable by a third party with enforcement powers. The only such information in this context is the report of the firm or equivalently the information revealed by the firm in its selection of a policy from the mechanism offered by the regulator. Thus, the natural fairness condition is that the firm be guaranteed a non-negative profit in each period conditional on the information it reports or reveals in earlier periods. The case considered here is that in which it is common knowledge that marginal cost is the same in each period ($\theta_1 = \theta_2 = \theta$), so if in period one the firm reported $\hat{\theta}_1$, then the period-two profit $\pi_2(\hat{\theta}_1; \hat{\theta}_1)$ for that type is required to be non-negative. In exchange, the firm is not allowed to quit the relationship. That is, if the firm reported that its period-one marginal

[79]See Drobak (1986) for an analysis of the right to withdraw assets.
[80]Greenwald (1984) considers a different fairness arrangement based on the relationship between the market value of the firm and the cost of its assets.

cost is $\hat{\theta}_1$ even though its marginal cost is θ, the firm is required to produce in the second period as long as the second-period regulatory policy would provide a non-negative profit to a firm with marginal cost $\hat{\theta}_1$.

The remaining issue is why a firm would agree to surrender its right to quit a regulatory relationship in exchange for protection against the opportunism of the regulator. At an informal level the firm might so agree because the alternative is unclear. As Laffont and Tirole have shown, an equilibrium in the absence of commitment may have quite complex properties.[81] A firm may well prefer the assurance of a fairness arrangement to an unpredictable outcome. Baron and Besanko (1987a) provide an example in which both the regulator and the firm prefer the fairness arrangement to a policy feasible with no commitment in which all types of the firm are pooled together in the first period.[82] While this is not a general result, both parties may well prefer a regulatory relationship characterized by fairness to one characterized by no commitment.

If the regulator and the firm prefer an arrangement characterized by fairness to one in which there is no commitment, it is natural to ask if they both prefer an arrangement characterized by commitment to one characterized by fairness. As will be indicated below, not only do they have opposing preferences regarding commitment but there exists no transfer between the regulator and the firm that would cause both to agree to implement the commitment policy. Consequently, if fairness arises endogenously in a regulatory relationship in which otherwise no commitment is possible, it would be expected to persist.

The fairness condition prohibits the regulator from offering a policy in the second period that would yield a non-negative profit to a firm with the type revealed in the first period. A formal statement of the fairness requirement distinguishes between first-period mechanisms that are separating and those that induce pooling over sets $\Theta^i \subseteq [\theta^-, \theta^+]$. If a first-period mechanism $M_1 = \{(p_1(\hat{\theta}_1), T_1(\hat{\theta}_1)), \hat{\theta}_1 \in [\theta^-, \theta^+]\}$ is separating so that the firm's response function $\hat{\theta}_1(\theta)$ is invertible, the fairness requirement is that

$$\pi_2(\hat{\theta}_1) \equiv \pi_2(\hat{\theta}_1; \hat{\theta}_1) = p_2(\hat{\theta}_1)Q(p_2(\hat{\theta}_1)) + T_1(\hat{\theta}_1) - \hat{\theta}_1 Q(p_2(\hat{\theta}_1)) - K_2 \geq 0. \qquad (6.28)$$

If the first-period mechanism is pooling on a set Θ^i so that $p_1(\hat{\theta}_1) = p^i$ and

[81] For example, they show that an equilibrium may involve "infinite reswitching" in which a sequence of types that are arbitrarily close together will alternate between two reports $\hat{\theta}^a$ and $\hat{\theta}^b$.

[82] Since no information is revealed in the first period under such a policy, in period two the optimal single-period policy is implemented.

$T_1(\hat{\theta}_1) = T_1^i$ for all $\hat{\theta}_i \in \Theta^i$, then the fairness requirement is

$$\pi_2(\hat{\theta}_2) = p_2(\hat{\theta}_2)Q(p_2(\hat{\theta}_2)) + T_2(\hat{\theta}_2) - \hat{\theta}_2 Q(p_2(\hat{\theta}_2)) - K_2 \geq 0, \quad \forall \hat{\theta}_2 \in \Theta^i. \tag{6.29}$$

Note that fairness allows the regulator to exploit any information revealed in the first period. That is, if the mechanism is fully separating in the first period so that $\hat{\theta}_1 = \theta$, the regulator can offer in period two the single policy $p_2(\hat{\theta}_2) = \theta$ and $T_2(\hat{\theta}_2) = K_2$, which yields the firm zero profit.

One implication of the fairness condition is that it renders feasible the separating policies that cannot be implemented when no commitment is possible. That is, fully-separating policies are feasible with fairness. This does not imply, however, that a fully-separating policy is optimal. The regulator faces a tradeoff between the benefits that accrue from flexible pricing in the first period and the benefits that can be achieved by pooling in the first period as a means of limiting opportunism in the second period. Pooling limits opportunism because the regulator learns only that $\theta \in \Theta^i$ and thus cannot fully exploit the firm in the second period.

The cost associated with pooling in the first period is the reduction in consumer surplus that results because price is not responsive to the marginal cost of the firm. The benefit from pooling is a reduction in the rents earned by the firm by allowing lower quantities to be produced in the second period. That is, with a fully-separating mechanism the regulator would fully exploit the information revealed in the first period by implementing marginal cost pricing in the second period. The fixed charges required to induce the firm to select the policy intended for it is given in (6.24) which results in two-period rents given by

$$\Pi(\theta) = \int_{\theta}^{\theta^+} \left(Q(p_1(\theta^0)) + \beta Q(\theta^0)\right) \mathrm{d}\theta^0. \tag{6.30}$$

If the regulator were to pool in the first period on a set $\Theta = [\theta_a, \theta_b]$, the price $p_2(\hat{\theta}_2)$ in period two would be given by

$$p_2(\hat{\theta}_2) = z(\hat{\theta}_2) \equiv \hat{\theta}_2 + (1-\alpha)\frac{F(\hat{\theta}_2 | \hat{\theta}_2 \in \Theta^i)}{f(\hat{\theta}_2 | \hat{\theta}_2 \in \Theta^i)} = y_\alpha(\hat{\theta}^2) - (1-\alpha)\frac{F(\theta_a)}{f(\hat{\theta}_2)}.$$

Since this price is above marginal cost except at θ_a, the rents in the second period are reduced by pooling in the first period.

To indicate the tradeoff between the benefit and cost of pooling, note that the optimal separating mechanism for the first period is $p_1(\theta) = y_\alpha(\theta)$ with $T_1(\theta)$

given in (6.24). With pooling at a price $\bar{p}$ on an interval $[\theta_a, \theta_b]$, the welfare W^f of the regulator can be written as

$$W^f = \int_{\theta^-}^{\theta^+} \left\{ \int_{p_1(\theta)}^{\infty} Q(p^0)\,\mathrm{d}p^0 - (p_1(\theta) - y_\alpha(\theta))Q(p(\theta)) - K_1 \right.$$

$$\left. + \beta\left[\int_{\theta}^{\infty} Q(\theta^0)\,\mathrm{d}\theta^0 - (\theta - y_\alpha(\theta))Q(\theta) - K_2\right]\right\} f(\theta)\,\mathrm{d}\theta$$

$$+ \int_{\theta_a}^{\theta_b} \left\{ \left[\int_{\bar{p}}^{p_1(\theta)} Q(p^0)\,\mathrm{d}p^0 - (\bar{p} - y_\alpha(\theta))Q(\bar{p})\right] \right.$$

$$+ \beta\left[-\int_{\theta}^{z(\theta)} Q(p^0)\,\mathrm{d}p^0 - (z(\theta) - y_\alpha(\theta))Q(z(\theta))\right.$$

$$\left.\left. + (\theta - y_\alpha(\theta))Q(\theta)\right]\right\} f(\theta)\,\mathrm{d}\theta - (1-\alpha)\Pi(\theta^+), \tag{6.31}$$

where the optimal separating mechanism in the first period is the static mechanism characterized in Section 4. The tradeoff between pooling and separation can be seen in the second integral in (6.31). The term $[\int_{\bar{p}}^{p_1(\theta)} Q(p^0)\,\mathrm{d}p^0 - (\bar{p} - y_\alpha(\theta))Q(\bar{p})]$ in the integrand represents the welfare loss from pooling in the first period that results because price is not responsive to marginal cost.[83] Pooling, however, results in a welfare gain in the second period because pooling allows the price $z(\theta)$ to be implemented in period two rather than the price equal to θ. As demonstrated above, a price equal to marginal cost results in greater information rents (when $\alpha < 1$). The gain from pooling is represented by the second term in the integrand of the second integral in (6.31) and results because the regulator implements the price $z(\hat{\theta}_2)$ rather than θ in the second period. The following analysis provides a characterization of the types of equilibria that can occur when the benefits and costs associated with pooling are considered.

Within the class of fully-separating mechanisms Baron and Besanko (1987a) demonstrate that the optimal mechanism is to implement the price $p_1(\theta) = y_\alpha(\theta)$ in the first period, using the fixed charges in (6.24), and the first-best policy in the

[83] This term is negative, since $p_1(\theta) = y_\alpha(\theta)$ maximizes first-period welfare.

second period.[84] They show that the optimal fully-separating mechanism is an equilibrium under fairness if $\alpha = 1$ in which case the mechanism implements the first-best outcome in each period. The first-best policy is an equilibrium in this case because the rents of the firm do not represent a welfare loss. Fairness thus allows the first-best mechanism to be implemented, whereas with no commitment the first-best policy is infeasible.

Baron and Besanko show that when $\alpha < 1$ the regulator may prefer to pool in period one. They provide an example in which multiple pooling intervals are optimal.[85] Such pooling is more likely to be optimal the lower is α, since then the reduction in rents of the firm resulting with pooling is counted more in the welfare function used by the regulator. Pooling is also more likely to be optimal when the discount factor β is higher, since then the gains from restricting opportunism are greater. Baron and Besanko also show in the context of the example that the pooling intervals are shorter the lower are the costs. This results because the gain in consumer surplus from prices that are responsive to costs is greater for low marginal costs than for high marginal costs. Thus, the gains from pooling are greater at higher marginal costs than at lower marginal costs.

This issue of whether a fairness arrangement would arise endogenously can be analyzed both from an ex ante and an ex post perspective. As indicated above, the comparison will be between the equilibrium mechanism with fairness, as characterized by Baron and Besanko, and with no commitment a first-period mechanism that completely pools the types ($\Theta = [\theta^-, \theta^+]$) in the first-period and then employs the optimal static mechanism in the second period. Since the regulator does not know the marginal cost of the firm, its preferences are determined by the ex ante welfare W. The mechanism with full pooling in the first period and the static mechanism in the second period is a feasible mechanism under fairness, so the regulator prefers fairness to no commitment.

The firm's preferences can be analyzed both from an ex ante and ex post perspective. From an ex post perspective once the firm knows its marginal cost, the firm would voluntarily agree to a fairness arrangement if its profit $\Pi(\theta)$ with fairness is greater than its profit with no commitment. Baron and Besanko demonstrate that compared to this mechanism feasible with no commitment all types of the firm prefer fairness when the profits of the firm are not counted ($\alpha = 0$) in the welfare employed by the regulator. For higher α the types of the firm with high costs prefer no commitment to fairness.

[84] The fairness condition in (6.28) can thus also be thought of as a condition sufficient to make separation feasible when commitment is not possible.

[85] The equilibrium in the fairness case must be supported by off-the-equilibrium path beliefs. The equilibrium in this example is sensitive to the specification of those beliefs. The assumption employed by Baron and Besanko is that each of the types in a pooling interval randomizes its report among the types in that interval.

The decision to enter into a fairness arrangement, however, may be made prior to the firm learning its marginal cost. In that case the firm would compare its ex ante or expected profits under a fairness arrangement to the ex ante profits with no commitment and complete pooling in the first period.[86] Baron and Besanko show in the context of their example that fairness is more likely to be preferred the lower is α and the higher is the discount factor β.

If from an ex ante perspective the firm and the regulator prefer fairness to no commitment, would they both also prefer commitment to fairness if commitment could somehow be assured? The regulator clearly prefers commitment because any mechanism feasible with fairness is also feasible with commitment. Since the equilibrium mechanism with commitment is to repeat the static mechanism in each period, fairness with the optimal separating mechanism results in higher profit in (6.30) because the quantity under fairness is greater in the second period than with commitment. Furthermore, there is no transfer that consumers would be willing to make and the firm would be willing to accept in exchange for agreeing to participate in a relationship characterized by commitment. The ex ante profit is greater with the optimal fully-separating mechanism, but with pooling the comparison is ambiguous. In the example presented by Baron and Besanko the expected profit with pooling is greater than with commitment. In these cases, fairness would be sustainable.

6.3.4. Imperfectly correlated marginal costs

To identify the source of Laffont and Tirole's result that there is no feasible mechanism that is separating for the case in which marginal costs are perfectly correlated, consider the case in which it is common knowledge that marginal costs are independent across periods. Knowledge of the marginal cost in one period thus provides no information about the marginal cost in any other period. Recall that in this case the optimal mechanism when the regulator can commit to a multiperiod policy is to employ the single-period price in the first period and the first-best policy thereafter as indicated in (6.11) and (6.12). When the regulator cannot commit to a multiperiod mechanism, the optimal regulatory mechanism for the independent cost case is to repeat in each period the single-period mechanism characterized in (4.19) and (4.11). At the beginning of each period the firm observes its marginal cost, and given the single-period mechanism, the firm selects the regulatory policy appropriate for its costs. The regulator can do no better than this because it cannot commit to transfers across

[86] The mechanism is still chosen by the regulator after the firm has learned its marginal cost.

periods nor can it commit to offer a particular second-period policy to the firm if it will accept the first-period policy.[87]

The case in which marginal costs are independent indicates that the nonseparation result obtained by Laffont and Tirole is not pervasive. To investigate the robustness of their result, consider the case in which marginal cost θ_2 in the second period is a function of the marginal cost θ_1 in the first period and a random variable $\tilde{\varepsilon}$ or $\theta_2 = \theta_2(\theta_1, \varepsilon)$, where ε is a realization of $\tilde{\varepsilon}$. The induced distribution $F_2(\theta_2|\theta_1)$ of θ_2 conditional on θ_1 is assumed to be common knowledge and to have a support $[\theta_2^-, \theta_2^+]$ that is invariant to θ_1. When this distribution is not degenerate, it is possible that the firm has no incentive to quit the regulatory relationship even when commitment is not possible and the period-one mechanism is separating.

To show this, note that perfectness requires that the price in the second period have the same form as the price in (4.19) for a single-period model with the conditional distribution $F_2(\theta_2|\theta_1)$ replacing the unconditional distribution. Consider the mechanism in which the second-period price is[88]

$$p_2(\theta_1, \theta_2) = \theta_2 + (1-\alpha)\frac{F_2(\theta_2|\theta_1)}{f_2(\theta_2|\theta_1)} \tag{6.32}$$

and the fixed charges are

$$T_2(\theta_1, \theta_2) = \theta_2 Q(p_2(\theta_1, \theta_2)) + K_2 - p_2(\theta_1, \theta_2)Q(p_2(\theta_1, \theta_2)) + \int_{\theta_2}^{\theta_2^+} Q_2(p(\theta_1, \theta_2^0))\,\mathrm{d}\theta_2^0. \tag{6.33}$$

Once the firm observes its second-period marginal cost θ_2, it can earn a profit $\pi_2(\hat{\theta}_1; \theta_2)$, given by

$$\pi_2(\hat{\theta}_1; \theta_2) = \int_{\theta_2}^{\theta_2^+} Q(p_2(\hat{\theta}_1, \theta_2^0))\,\mathrm{d}\theta_2^0, \tag{6.34}$$

by producing in the second period and reporting truthfully. For any period-one report $\hat{\theta}_1$, this period-two profit is strictly positive for any $\theta_2 < \theta_2^+$. Thus, for any report $\hat{\theta}_1$ in period one, the period-two profit in (6.34) provides an incentive to continue rather than quit. Intuitively, if the incentive to continue is stronger than

[87]Ex ante welfare is the same as in the case in which the regulator is able to commit and the firm is known to have the same marginal cost in each period. The ex ante profit of the firm viewed from prior to the point at which the firm learns its marginal cost is also the same.

[88]The ratio $F_2(\theta_2|\theta_1)/f_2(\theta_2|\theta_1)$ is assumed to be nondecreasing in θ_2 for all θ_1.

the incentive to quit as identified in Subsection 6.3.2, a separating mechanism may be feasible even with an inability to make credible commitments. More formally, a separating mechanism can be implemented if the condition in (4.15) for global incentive compatibility is satisfied. That condition is never satisfied if marginal costs are perfectly correlated, is always satisfied if the marginal costs are independent, and may or may not be satisfied with imperfect correlation. Laffont and Tirole (1986a) demonstrate that for small uncertainty about θ_2, that is, near perfect correlation, the regulator never prefers to separate over any closed interval. In that case, separation is too costly. In other cases, a separating mechanism may be both feasible and optimal.

Among the class of separating mechanisms, the optimal mechanism is given by (6.32) and (6.33) and the first-period policies:

$$p_1(\theta_1) = y_\alpha(\theta_1), \tag{6.35}$$

$$T_1(\theta_1) = \int_{\theta_1}^{\theta_1^+}\left[Q(p_1(\theta_1^0)) - \beta\int_{\theta_2^-}^{\theta_2^+} Q(p_2(\theta_1^0, \theta_2))\frac{\partial F_2(\theta_2|\theta_1^0)}{\partial\theta_1}\,\mathrm{d}\theta_2\right]\mathrm{d}\theta_1^0$$
$$+\theta_1 Q(p_1(\theta_1)) + K_1 - p_1(\theta_1)Q(p_1(\theta_1)) - \beta E[\pi_2(\theta_1;\theta_2)], \tag{6.36}$$

where the expected period-two profit is

$$E[\pi_2(\theta_1;\theta_2)] = \int_{\theta_2^-}^{\theta_2^+}\int_{\theta_2}^{\theta_2^+} Q(p_2(\theta_1, \theta_2^0))\,\mathrm{d}\theta_2^0 f(\theta_2|\theta_1)\,\mathrm{d}\theta_2$$
$$= \int_{\theta_2^-}^{\theta_2^+} Q_2(p(\theta_1, \theta_2))F(\theta_2|\theta_1)\,\mathrm{d}\theta_2.$$

This is the optimal separating mechanism under the fairness condition. As in the fairness case, however, it may be possible to improve on this mechanism by pooling in the first period as a means of limiting opportunism.

7. Ex ante competition: The selection of the monopolist

The mechanisms developed above establish regulatory policies for a firm that has already been selected to be the franchise monopolist. More generally, however, the regulator may be viewed as selecting a franchise monopolist from among a set of possible suppliers and then implementing a regulatory policy that responds to information that may be obtained once performance has commenced. The context in which the selection and regulation policies will be considered here involves a first period in which the selection is made and a second period in which production takes place. Although the selection and regulation problems must be dealt with simultaneously, a separation exists between the selection and the regulation phases of the regulatory relationship as will be indicated below. Furthermore, the optimal regulatory or pricing policy is that characterized in the previous section.

For the case in which $\alpha = 1$, Loeb and Magat (1979) propose to resolve the selection problem through an auction in which potential suppliers bid a lump-sum for the right to the monopoly franchise. The franchise carries with it the fixed charges in (3.1) and the obligation to satisfy all demand at the price, equal to marginal cost, the firm chooses.[89] The auction may be progressive where lump-sum bids are made sequentially and in public until no more bids are forthcoming or may be a sealed-bid, Vickery (second-price) auction in which the highest bidder is awarded the franchise but pays an amount equal to the second highest bid.[90] In a symmetric model in which the marginal cost of each potential supplier is drawn from the same distribution, the bid function (a mapping from marginal cost to the bid) of each firm will be the same and will be a strictly decreasing function of marginal cost. The highest bid will thus be made by the firm that has the lowest marginal cost, and that firm will pay an amount equal to the profit that the bidder with the second lowest marginal cost would earn if it were selected. The winning bidder thus earns a rent determined by the difference between its marginal cost and the second lowest marginal cost. For the case in which the regulatory objective is the maximization of total surplus ($\alpha = 1$), this mechanism is efficient and deals effectively with the distributive problem, since the franchise payment can be used to offset a portion of the fixed charges in (3.1) paid under the regulatory policy to the selected firm.[91]

If, however, the regulatory objective is to maximize a weighted function of consumer and producer surplus with $\alpha < 1$, the regulator prefers to distort price from marginal cost in order to improve the distribution of surplus. The optimal mechanism in this case still involves the straightforward combination of an auction with the optimal regulatory policy characterized in the previous sections. To demonstrate this in a more general setting, the model developed by Riordan and Sappington (1987a) will be considered. In their model the regulator is

[89]The Loeb and Magat mechanism was proposed as a non-Bayesian mechanism, since the beliefs of the regulator about the firm's costs have no role in the form of either the regulatory policy or the auction. That is, price is equated to marginal cost for any beliefs the regulator might have about the marginal cost of the selected firm. As indicated above, this is a consequence of the specification of the welfare function that weights consumer and producer surplus equally so that distributional considerations are irrelevant to the design of the mechanism.

[90]See Vickrey (1961) and Milgrom and Weber (1982).

[91]The franchise payment must be redistributed in a manner that does not affect demand.

assumed to be able to commit to both the selection and the regulation policies to be implemented.

Their model includes a set of possible bidders each of which has private, but imperfect, information about the marginal costs that it will incur once it has been selected and has sunk its fixed costs.[92] The firm thus has ex ante private information about its possible marginal costs. Ex post, once selection has occurred and fixed costs are sunk, but before production has begun, the firm will privately observe its actual marginal cost. Since production takes place after the firm observes its marginal cost, the mechanism can base the price, and hence output, on a report on marginal cost.

Let θ_2 denote the marginal cost the firm will incur once it has sunk a cost K in the construction of its facilities. This marginal cost is known neither to the regulator nor the firm at the time of selection but will be privately observed by the firm before production commences. Prior to selection, the firm has private information, denoted by θ_1, that conditions the distribution function $F_2(\theta_2|\theta_1)$ of θ_2, where a higher θ_1 corresponds to higher marginal costs in the sense of first-degree stochastic dominance; i.e. if $\theta_1^1 > \theta_1^2$, then $F_2(\theta_2|\theta_1^1) \le F_2(\theta_2|\theta_1^2)$, $\forall\theta_2$, with the strict inequality holding for some θ_2. Potential supplier i thus has a parameter θ_1^i that is drawn independently from a distribution $F_1(\theta_1)$ that is common knowledge. Each bidder thus knows its own θ_1^i, the distribution of the θ_1^j of the other firms, and $F_2(\theta_2|\theta_1)$. The regulator knows only the distribution $F_1(\theta_1)$, the number n of firms, and the distribution function $F_2(\theta_2|\theta_1)$.

The bidding mechanism specifies a function $\Upsilon(\hat{\theta}_1)$ that determines the payment by the selected firm for the franchise as a function of its report $\hat{\theta}_1$. The winning bidder is the firm that reports the lowest $\hat{\theta}_1$, and if the mechanism induces truthful reports, the lowest cost suplier will be chosen. Since the marginal cost θ_2 will be known to the selected firm prior to production, the regulator at the time of selection commits to a regulatory policy that requires the selected firm to make a report $\hat{\theta}_2$ once its marginal cost has been realized. That report thus conditions the price $p(\hat{\theta}_1, \hat{\theta}_2)$ and the fixed charges $T(\hat{\theta}_1, \hat{\theta}_2)$. The sequence of actions and events is thus that firms learn their θ_1^i's, the regulator commits to the selection–regulation mechanism $M = \{(\Upsilon(\hat{\theta}_1), p(\hat{\theta}_1, \hat{\theta}_2), T(\hat{\theta}_1, \hat{\theta}_2)), \hat{\theta}_2 \in [\theta_2^-, \theta_2^+], \hat{\theta}_1 \in [\theta_1^-, \theta_1^+]\}$, each firm "bids" a $\hat{\theta}_1^i$, and the firm with the lowest $\hat{\theta}_1^i$ is selected. That firm then sinks K, realizes θ_2, and reports $\hat{\theta}_2$ which completes the determination of the price $p(\hat{\theta}_1, \hat{\theta}_2)$ and the fixed charges $T(\hat{\theta}_1, \hat{\theta}_2)$. The equilibrium sought is a Bayesian Nash equilibrium in which each firm i chooses its strategy $\hat{\theta}_1^i(\theta_1^i)$ given the strategies $\hat{\theta}_1^j(\theta_1^j) = \theta_1^j$, $j = 1, \ldots, i-1, i+1, \ldots, n$, of the other firms and given that reporting $\hat{\theta}_2^i = \theta_2^i$ is a dominant strategy once the winner has been determined.

[92] This model thus corresponds to the case in which the firm must build a new plant rather than to the case in which the firm already has a plant in place and knows its costs.

The equilibrium in the Riordan and Sappington model may be characterized by viewing the choice of a regulatory policy and the selection of a firm as two phases of the regulatory process. Suppose initially that the regulator faced only one potential supplier with private information θ_1 that conditions the distribution function $F_2(\theta_2|\theta_1)$ of the marginal cost θ_2. In the context of the theory of commitment presented in Subsection 6.2, the model may be thought of as having two periods. The first period extends from the time the contract is offered to just prior to the sinking of the fixed cost and thus involves the revelation of θ_1 but no production. The second period commences with the sinking of the fixed cost and involves the revelation of θ_2 and the production of a quantity $Q(p(\theta_1, \theta_2))$. The optimal price is thus that given in (6.12), or

$$p(\theta_1, \theta_2) = \theta_2 - (1-\alpha)\frac{\partial F_2(\theta_2|\theta_1)/\partial\theta_1}{f_2(\theta_2|\theta_1)}\frac{F_1(\theta_1)}{f_1(\theta_1)}, \tag{7.1}$$

which depends on the marginal cost and on the informativeness of θ_1 about θ_2.[93] As will be indicated below, this price will also be optimal when the selection phase is incorporated. Consequently, the regulatory policy does not depend on the number n of firms.

The remaining problem for the regulator is to select a firm and to determine the bid function $\Upsilon(\theta_1)$. Viewed from the point in time at which the bidding takes place, the expected profit earned in the second period by the selected firm is given in (6.3), so the value $V(\hat{\theta}_1; \theta_1)$ of the opportunity to bid is

$$V(\hat{\theta}_1; \theta_1) = \left[\int_{\theta_2^-}^{\theta_2^+} Q(p(\hat{\theta}_1, \theta_2))F_2(\theta_2|\hat{\theta}_1)\,\mathrm{d}\theta_2 - \Upsilon(\hat{\theta}_1)\right](1 - F_1(\hat{\theta}_1))^{n-1}, \tag{7.2}$$

where $(1 - F(\hat{\theta}_1))^{n-1}$ is the probability that the other $n-1$ firms have values of θ_1 above $\hat{\theta}_1$ and $\Upsilon(\hat{\theta}_1)$ is the amount the firm pays for the franchise if it is selected. To ensure that the firms bid $\hat{\theta}_1 = \theta_1$, the function $\Upsilon(\theta_1)$ is specified as

$$\Upsilon(\theta_1) = \int_{\theta_2^-}^{\theta_2^+} Q(p(\theta_1, \theta_2))F_2(\theta_2|\theta_1)\,\mathrm{d}\theta_2 + \int_{\theta_1}^{\theta_1^+}\left(\frac{(1 - F_1(\theta_1^0))^{n-1}}{(1 - F_1(\theta_1))^{n-1}}\right)\int_{\theta_2^-}^{\theta_2^+} Q(p(\theta_1^0, \theta_2))\frac{\partial F_2(\theta_2|\theta_1^0)}{\partial\theta_1}\,\mathrm{d}\theta_2\,\mathrm{d}\theta_1^0. \tag{7.3}$$

[93] The fixed charges function that implements this pricing policy is given in (6.20).

The value $V(\theta_1) \equiv V(\theta_1; \theta_1)$ of the opportunity to bid is then

$$V(\theta_1) = \int_{\theta_1}^{\theta_1^+} \int_{\theta_2^-}^{\theta_2^+} Q(p(\theta_1^0, \theta_2)) \frac{\partial F_2(\theta_2 | \theta_1^0)}{\partial \theta_1} \mathrm{d}\theta_2 (1 - F_1(\theta_1^0))^{n-1} \mathrm{d}\theta_1^0. \quad (7.4)$$

This value is a strictly decreasing function of the number n of firms, so more competitors reduces the rents of the selected firm. If θ_1 were uninformative about θ_2, the value $V(\theta_1)$ would be zero, since all firms would make the same "bid". The regulator then may select one at random. The franchise fee in this case equals the expected profit under the regulatory policy, so $V(\theta_1) = 0$.

The regulator will select the firm that reports the lowest θ_1, and viewed ex ante the probability distribution of the winning bid is that of the lowest order statistic θ_1^* which has a density function $f_1^*(\theta_1^*)$ given by

$$f_1^*(\theta_1^*) \equiv n(1 - F_1(\theta_1^*))^{n-1} f_1(\theta_1^*).$$

The expected welfare thus is

$$W = n \int_{\theta_1^-}^{\theta_1^+} \int_{\theta_2^-}^{\theta_2^+} \Bigg\{ \Bigg[\int_{p(\theta_1, \theta_2)}^{\infty} Q(p^0)\, \mathrm{d}p^0 + (p(\theta_1, \theta_2) - \theta_2) Q(p(\theta_1, \theta_2)) - K \Bigg]$$
$$\times f_2(\theta_2 | \theta_1) f_1(\theta_1)$$
$$+ \Bigg[(1 - \alpha) F_1(\theta_1) Q(p(\theta_1, \theta_2)) \frac{\partial F_2(\theta_2 | \theta_1)}{\partial \theta_1} \Bigg] (1 - F_1(\theta_1))^{n-1} \Bigg\} \, \mathrm{d}\theta_2 \, \mathrm{d}\theta_1. \quad (7.5)$$

Maximizing with respect to $p(\theta_1, \theta_2)$ yields (7.1).[94]

An important feature of this mechanism is the separation of selection and regulation. This separation results because the firm does not learn its marginal cost until after the selection has been made and because the regulator is able to commit to the pricing policy that will be implemented once selection has been completed.

Riordan and Sappington (1987b) also consider the case in which the regulator is unable to commit to the pricing policy that will be offered to the firm chosen in the selection phase of the mechanism. After selection, the information of the regulator is represented by $F_2(\theta_2 | \theta_1)$, and the firm can only expect that the

[94] The Loeb and Magat mechanism obtains as a special case when $\alpha = 1$ in which case the price is set equal to marginal cost.

regulator will fully exploit the information available to it. The price $p_2^*(\theta_1, \theta_2)$ is thus given by

$$p_2^*(\theta_1, \theta_2) = \theta_2 + (1 - \alpha)\frac{F_2(\theta_2|\theta_1)}{f_2(\theta_2|\theta_1)}. \tag{7.6}$$

Even though commitment is not possible in this case, the equilibrium is separating, since the firm only has one opportunity to produce and thus cannot employ the strategy identified in Subsection 6.3.

To compare the policy without commitment to the regulatory policy with commitment, consider the example in (6.13) in which $\tilde{\theta}_2$ is a convex combination of $\tilde{\theta}_1$ and $\tilde{\varepsilon}$, which are uniform on [0, 1]. The price $p_2(\theta_1, \theta_2)$ with commitment is then

$$p_2(\theta_1, \theta_2) = \theta_2 + (1 - \alpha)\gamma\theta_1, \quad \text{for } \theta_2 \in [\gamma\theta_1, 1 - \gamma + \gamma\theta_1],$$

and the price $p_2^*(\theta_1, \theta_2)$ without commitment is

$$p_2^*(\theta_1, \theta_2) = \theta_2 + (1 - \alpha)(\theta_2 - \gamma\theta_1), \quad \text{for } \theta_2 \in [\gamma\theta_1, 1 - \gamma + \gamma\theta_1].$$

It is straightforward to demonstrate that the price with commitment is lower than the price without commitment if and only if $\theta_2 > 2\gamma\theta_1$. Consequently, if θ_1 is not very informative (low γ), commitment leads to a lower price, and if θ_1 is highly informative (high γ), commitment leads to a higher price. Since any policy feasible in the absence of commitment is also feasible with commitment (but not vice versa), the regulator is, of course, better off with commitment even though the price may be higher.

In a related model McAfee and McMillan (1986) consider a selection model in which the selected firm makes an unobservable effort which affects an observable cost. They restrict attention to policies that are linear in the observable cost, but they allow the firms to be risk averse with a utility function exhibiting constant absolute risk aversion. Because of these two assumptions the effort taken by the selected firm depends only on the share of the cost reimbursed by the regulator. They provide a characterization of the optimal regulatory policy for the case in which a first-price, sealed-bid auction is employed for selection. The regulator prefers to employ a fixed-price pricing policy to induce effort by the firm, but prefers to use a cost-plus pricing policy to reduce the information rents due to the firm's private information. McAfee and McMillan demonstrate that the closer the policy is to cost-plus, the lower are the initial bids, since the rents appropriable by the firms are lower under such a policy.

In an extension of their observable cost model, Laffont and Tirole (1987) consider the optimal selection and regulatory mechanism for the case in which potential supplier i of an indivisible good has a cost function of the form:

$$C^i = \theta^i - a^i, \quad i = 1, \ldots, n,$$

where a^i is effort. The optimal mechanism selects the most efficient firm, the one with the lowest θ^i, and provides a regulatory policy of the same form as that when there is only one firm. That is, the regulatory policy depends only on the report of the selected firm. The franchise fee, however, may depend on all the bids. As the number of firms increases, the price specified in the regulatory policy approaches the first-best price, since the information rents captured by the firm, and hence the distortion made to reduce the marginal information rents, approach zero. Laffont and Tirole demonstrate that this mechanism can be implemented in dominant strategies through an auction in which the franchise fee depends on the lowest and the next lowest bids (a Vickery auction) using payment functions that are linear in the observed cost as in (5.6). The selected firm captures rents based on the difference between its θ^i and the θ^j of the next most efficient firm.

8. Ex post competition

In the models considered in the previous section, the regulator utilizes an auction as a means of creating an ex ante competion that identifies the most efficient firm. If a firm is already the subject of regulation, the regulator no longer has the opportunity to utilize ex ante competition. It may, however, be able to utilize ex post competition to reduce the information rents and to improve efficiency. For example, the regulator may be able to use the threat of entry or the opportunity to switch to an alternative supplier as a means of improving performance.

Caillaud (1986) considers the case of the regulation of a single firm when there is an unregulated competitive fringe of firms that can also supply the good. This might correspond to the case of a regulated railroad and a competitive trucking industry or to a regulated AT & T and a competitive fringe of long-distance carriers not subject to price or profit regulation. His mechanism utilizes the competitive fringe as a means of controlling the information rents of the regulated firm. The regulated firm has private information about its marginal costs θ as in the model considered in Section 4, and the marginal cost v of the competitive fringe is private information. The regulator can use its prior information about v in its regulatory policy, but the regulator does not have the authority to regulate the fringe and hence cannot induce the fringe to reveal its information ex ante. Ex post, however, consumers can buy from either the regulated firm or the fringe and will do so based on their respective prices.

Consequently, the price that will prevail for the good is the minimum of v and the price established for the regulated firm.

Caillaud demonstrates that the nature of the optimal regulatory policy depends importantly on the relationship between v and θ. In the case in which they are independent, the competitive fringe can be viewed as an option that consumers may exercise if the price established for the regulated firm is higher than the price in the competitive industry. This option is more valuable to consumers the higher is the reported marginal cost of the regulated firm. Viewed from the perspective of the regulator, this option allows the regulator to control better the information rents of the firm through greater distortions of the regulated price from marginal cost. The regulator can set a higher price because the higher is that price the more likely it is that consumers will be able to avoid that price by exercising their option by purchasing from the competitive fringe.

The regulated price in this case is determined as in Section 4 with the modification that the quantity $q(\theta)$ the firm produces satisfies:

$$\begin{aligned} &q(\theta) \text{ s.t. } p(\theta) = E\left[\min\{v, P(q(\theta))\}\right], && \text{if } p(\theta) < E[v], \\ &q(\theta) = 0, && \text{if } p(\theta) \geq E[v], \end{aligned} \tag{8.1}$$

where $P(q)$ denotes the inverse demand function and E denotes expectation. The quantity is thus based on the expected price that will prevail for the good. The quantity is nonincreasing in θ, and if the price $p(\theta)$ exceeds the expected price of the competitive fringe, the regulated firm is not allowed to produce.

Caillaud also analyzes the case in which the marginal cost in the competitive fringe is perfectly correlated with the marginal cost of the regulated firm. A truthful report by the firm of its marginal cost thus identifies for the regulator the marginal cost of the competitive industry. Since the marginal costs are perfectly correlated, the price that will prevail in the market equals $\min\{v, P(q(\theta))\}$. The revenue function of the firm thus has a "kink", and the programming problem of the regulator is nonconvex. Caillaud is able to characterize the optimal regulatory mechanism and show that the regulator may prefer that the competitive industry produce for some θ because the threat that they will produce diminishes the incentive of the firm to overstate its costs and thus reduces the information costs to the regulator. The quantity produced by the regulated firm is a nonincreasing function of θ but may be discontinuous. When the competitive fringe does not produce, the price is that for the optimal static mechanism given in (4.19). On other intervals, the price may be lower or higher than that in (4.19).

Demski, Sappington and Spiller (1986) consider the case in which a regulated firm has private information about its costs which are correlated with the costs of another firm that the regulator could allow to enter the market. The regulator does not know the cost of either firm and thus designs a regulatory mechanism that specifies how much each firm will be allowed to produce. The regulator uses the possibility of entry both as a means of obtaining information from the cost report of the potential entrant, which may be correlated with the private information of the regulated firm, and as an alternative source of output. The information serves to reduce the rents of the regulated firm in the same manner as an audit as considered in Subsection 5.2. The possibility that the potential entrant may be allowed to produce also improves the efficiency of the regulatory mechanism. They show that the reduction in information rents resulting from entry may be sufficient that the mechanism specifies that the entrant produce even though it has higher costs than the regulated firm.

Anton and Yao (1987) consider the case in which a regulator, the Department of Defense in their setting, contracts with a primary source that has private information about its marginal cost. The regulator is able to commit to an initial procurement policy but is unable to commit to a policy for the period after the initial procurement phase has been completed. The regulator then may at that time switch to a second-source supplier, so the regulator makes the reprocurement decision after it has learned the marginal cost of the primary source. Although the regulator cannot commit to a reprocurement policy, it can commit to the mechanism, an auction, to be used to determine if production in the second period will be assigned to the primary source or to the second source. In their model, costs are characterized by a learning curve with no spillover, so the primary source has a cost advantage over a second source. This gives the primary source some assurance that it will be selected as the supplier in the second period. The possibility that a second source may be selected, however, serves to control the strategic advantage of the primary source.

9. Two-sided private information

9.1. *Ex ante private information*

In the models considered above, the private information in the regulatory relationship is "one-sided" in the sense that the firm's type is unknown to the regulator but the regulator's type is known to the firm. The regulator, however, may also have private information that may be of interest to the firm.[95] For example, the regulator may have information about demand that would affect the firm's preferences regarding its selection of a regulatory policy from those comprising the mechanism offered by the regulator. Similarly, the regulator may

[95] Myerson (1983) initiated the study of this class of models which he labeled "informed principal" models.

have private information about its preferences, which may be thought of as corresponding to private information about the weight α it assigns to profit in its welfare function. When private information is two-sided in this sense, the mechanism design may become more complicated because the regulator may be concerned that its announcement of a mechanism will reveal to the firm information that the firm will use to the regulator's disadvantage.

Maskin and Tirole (1986) consider a model in which the regulator has private information which is not an argument of the firm's preference function.[96] For example, if the regulator's private information is about the weight α on profits in the regulator's welfare function this condition is satisfied since the firm's preferences do not depend on α. If, however, the regulator knows the demand function but the firm does not, the regulator's information directly affects the profit of the firm. Their theory pertains to the former and not the latter case.

If the preferences of the regulator and the firm are linear in the revenue $p(\theta)Q(p(\theta)) + T(\theta)$, Maskin and Tirole show that the regulator will employ the same mechanism when it has private information about its type as it would if its type were known to the firm.[97] Consequently, if the regulator knew α but the firm did not, the equilibrium mechanism is that characterized in Subsection 4.2. The regulator thus loses nothing by revealing its information to the firm. Furthermore, the equilbrium mechanism is the same for whatever information the firm may have about α.

More generally, when the preferences of the regulator and the firm are not linear in the payment, the regulator may prefer to conceal its type rather than to have it revealed by the mechanism it offers.[98] The regulator's preferences are represented in general as $W(p, T, \tau^i)$, where τ^i, $i = 1, \ldots, n$, is one of a finite number of types, and the firm's preferences are represented as $V(p, T, \theta^j)$, $j = 1, \ldots, m$, where θ^j is one of a finite number of values. The game considered by Maskin and Tirole involves three stages. In the first stage the regulator offers a mechanism to the firm, and in the second stage the firm either accepts or rejects it.[99] In the third stage both parties announce their types.[100] At the beginning of the first period the firm has prior beliefs, represented by probabilities (ρ_i, $i = 1, \ldots, n$), about the possible types τ^i, $i = 1, \ldots, n$) of the regulator. Upon announcement of the mechanism the firm may revise its beliefs, but if all types of

[96] They label this case as "independent values" and the case in which the firm does care about the regulator's type as "dependent values". The independent values case pertains to adverse selection settings, since if moral hazard is present due to imperfect observability the regulator's information affects the firm's beliefs which then enters into preferences.

[97] The firm is assumed to have one of a finite number of types, and the prior information of the regulator is assumed to be such that the probability of each possible types is positive.

[98] Myerson (1983) refers to this as the principle of inscrutability.

[99] The regulator is assumed to be able to commit to a mechanism, but the firm does not commit to participate.

[100] Attention is restricted here to direct revelation mechanisms.

the regulator prefer in equilibrium to offer the same mechanism, the firm's posterior beliefs will be the same as its prior beliefs. The equilibrium sought is a perfect Bayesian Nash equilibrium in which each player acts optimally at each stage of the game and beliefs are updated according to Bayes' rule and are consistent with the equilbrium strategies and the observed actions.[101] Maskin and Tirole show that a perfect Bayesian Nash equilibrium exists and furthermore that an equilibrium exists in which all types of the regulator offer the same mechanism.[102] If the firm's preferences satisfy the usual sorting condition,[103] there are only a finite number of equilibria in the regulatory game.

Maskin and Tirole's results for two-sided private information are important because if the firm can reasonably be taken to be risk neutral and the regulator employs a surplus measure of welfare the regulator will prefer to reveal its information about α truthfully even when both parties have private information. The firm thus need not consider more sophisticated strategies than to report its type truthfully in response to the announced mechanism. The mechanisms characterized in the previous section then are optimal for whatever information the firm may have about α.

9.2. Ex ante and ex post two-sided private information

In the Maskin and Tirole model both the regulator and the firm have private information at the beginning of the regulatory relationship. In some settings, however, the firm may have private information ex ante, and the regulator may privately observe ex post a parameter that affects either performance or the desirability of alternative strategies. For example, suppose that ex ante the firm knows its marginal cost θ but at the time the regulatory mechanism is announced neither the firm nor the regulator knows the weight α that will be employed by the regulator. That weight will be determined prior to the time at which the pricing policy is to be established and will be privately observed by the regulator. This might correspond to the case in which the firm must construct a plant prior to knowing the basis on which the regulator will establish the regulatory mechanism. The process by which α is determined will not be modeled but instead will be represented by a density function $g(\alpha)$ which is assumed to be positive on $[0,1]$. The regulatory policy is based on both the ex ante and the ex post

[101] To support the equilibrium, beliefs off, as well as on, the equilibrium path are required. The reader is referred to Maskin and Tirole for the specification of the off-the-equilibrium-path beliefs that support the equilibrium.

[102] Their method of analysis involves the ingenious device of constructing a fictitious economy in which the possible types of the regulator trade "slack" in the individual rationality and incentive compatibility constraints. The equilibrium in the game is shown to correspond to the equilibrium in the fictitious economy.

[103] For the specification of costs in (4.13), this sorting condition is satisfied.

information, so a policy $(p(\hat{\theta}, \hat{\alpha}), T(\hat{\theta}, \hat{\alpha}))$ is specified as a function of reports by both the firm and the regulator. The regulator is assumed to be able to commit to the mechanism M defined as

$$M = \{(p(\hat{\theta}, \hat{\alpha}), T(\hat{\theta}, \hat{\alpha})), \hat{\theta} \in [\theta^-, \theta^+], \hat{\alpha} \in [0,1]\}.$$

Because the firm does not observe the ex post private information α, the regulator must assure the firm that it will not be exploited by the regulator misreporting its information in order to obtain a more favorable policy. The regulator thus must structure the regulatory policy so that the firm can be confident that the regulator will implement the policy anticipated in equilibrium by the firm. Since the revelation principle continues to apply to this situation, the regulator will structure its policy so that it has an incentive to report truthfully the information it will receive. At the beginning of the relationship, the firm, in choosing its report, thus can rely on this incentive for assurance about the policy that will be implemented. Riordan and Sappington (1987b) present a theory applicable to this situation. Methodologically, the nested revelation principle approach addressed in Subsection 6.2 forms the basis for the characterization of the equilibrium.

For any report $\hat{\theta}$ by the firm, the regulator will report truthfully $\hat{\alpha} = \alpha$ if the policy is such that

$$W(\alpha|\hat{\theta}) \equiv \int_{p(\hat{\theta}, \alpha)}^{\infty} Q(p^0)\,\mathrm{d}p^0 - T(\hat{\theta}, \alpha) + \alpha\pi(\hat{\theta}, \alpha; \theta)$$

$$\geq W(\hat{\alpha}; \alpha|\hat{\theta}) \equiv \int_{p(\hat{\theta}, \hat{\alpha})}^{\infty} Q(p^0)\,\mathrm{d}p^0 - T(\hat{\theta}, \hat{\alpha}) + \alpha\pi(\hat{\theta}, \hat{\alpha}; \theta),$$

$$\forall \hat{\alpha}, \forall \alpha \in [0,1], \forall \hat{\theta}, \theta \in [\theta^-, \theta^+], \quad (9.1)$$

where $\pi(\hat{\theta}, \alpha; \theta)$ denotes the profit of the firm when the regulator implements the policy corresponding to α. A price $p(\hat{\theta}, \hat{\alpha})$ is implementable if

$$\frac{\mathrm{d}W(\alpha|\hat{\theta})}{\mathrm{d}\alpha} = \pi(\hat{\theta}, \hat{\alpha}; \theta),$$

and the welfare given a truthful report by the firm is thus

$$W(\alpha|\theta) = W(1|\theta) - \int_{\alpha}^{1} \pi(\theta|\alpha^0)\,\mathrm{d}\alpha^0, \quad (9.2)$$

where $\pi(\theta, \alpha) \equiv \pi(\theta, \alpha; \theta)$. The fixed charges function $T(\theta, \alpha)$ that implements

$p(\theta, \alpha)$ can then be obtained from (9.1) and (9.2). Any policy satisfying (9.2) will thus (locally) assure the firm that once the regulator has learned α it will implement the policy corresponding to that α.

The policy will be incentive compatible from the firm's perspective if

$$\pi(\theta; \theta) \geq \pi(\hat{\theta}; \theta), \quad \forall \hat{\theta}, \forall \theta \in [0,1], \tag{9.3}$$

where

$$\pi(\hat{\theta}; \theta) \equiv \int_0^1 \big[p(\hat{\theta}, \alpha) Q(p(\hat{\theta}, \alpha)) + T(\hat{\theta}, \alpha) - \theta Q(p(\hat{\theta}, \alpha)) - K \big] g(\alpha)\, \mathrm{d}\alpha. \tag{9.4}$$

Incentive compatibility requires (locally) that the analog of (4.8) (or (4.7)) be satisfied, so a price function $p(\theta, \alpha)$ is implementable by fixed charges $T(\theta, \alpha)$ such that

$$\int_0^1 T(\theta, \alpha) g(\alpha)\, \mathrm{d}\alpha$$

satisfies the analog of (4.11) and (9.4). The function $T(\theta, \alpha)$ thus must make the policy incentive compatible for both the firm an the regulator.[104] Substitution of $\pi(\theta, \alpha) \equiv \pi(\theta, \alpha; \theta)$, which is the integrand in (9.4), into $W(\alpha | \theta)$ and substitution of the expression analogous to (4.8) indicates that the optimal price is $p(\theta, \alpha) = y_\alpha(\theta)$. The same price will be implemented as in the case in which the welfare weight α is common knowledge. This result is analogous to that obtained by Maskin and Tirole, although the timing of the arrival of information is different. Ex post private information of the regulator about α thus has no effect on the pricing policy. The resulting welfare will be affected, however, since the regulator must satisfy the constraints in (9.1).

10. Non-Bayesian mechanisms

The above mechanisms are based on an underlying information or probability structure that forms the basis for a Bayesian game. The equilibrium mechanism is thus sensitive to the prior information available to the regulator. From a Bayesian perspective this sensitivity is desirable because the regulator is fully utilizing all available information about the firm. From a non-Bayesian perspec-

[104] This analysis is based on local representations of the incentive compatibility conditions, so the resulting policies must be checked to determine if global incentive compatibility is satisfied.

tive, however, the designer of a regulatory institution might prefer a regulatory mechanism that is invariant to the subjective assessments of whoever occupies the position of the regulator. A non-Bayesian mechanism might also be employed if the information structure has sufficiently many dimensions that the optimal mechanism defies analytical characterization. In such situations, a regulator may seek a mechanism that, although not optimal from a Bayesian perspective, has certain desirable properties. Finsinger and Vogelsang (1982) have considered a variety of iterative, non-Bayesian mechanisms with the properties that they converge to marginal cost pricing when the regulator is able to observe ex post either the expenditures or the profit of the firm in each period.[105]

In their model the firm is allowed to choose price and is required to satisfy all demand at that price. The firm is assumed to be fully strategic and to maximize the discounted sum of its net income under the mechanism offered by the regulator. The regulator is assumed to be able to commit to the mechanism and is able to observe the profit of the firm as well as the price and quantity. The regulator does not know the demand and/or cost functions of the firm, however, which are private information of the firm but are known to remain the same in each period. The net compensation or income I_i of the owners or managers of the firm in period i is specified as

$$I_i = \pi_i - \pi_{i-1} + q_{i-1}(p_{i-1} - p_i) + \delta, \tag{10.1}$$

where $\pi_i = P(q_i)q_i - C(q_i)$, $p_i = P(q_i)$, δ is a constant base income, and π_0, p_0, and q_0 are initial parameters specified by the regulator. This compensation function is a linear approximation of the change in total surplus resulting from a change in price from p_{i-1} to p_i, so the firm finds its interests to be aligned with those of aggregate welfare.

The objective of the firm is to maximize the discounted present value I of its income or

$$I = \sum_{i=1}^{\infty} \frac{1}{(1+\rho^i)} I_i,$$

where ρ is the discount rate.[106] The firm will choose q_i to satisfy the necessary

[105] In addition to the mechanism presented here, Vogelsang and Finsinger (1979) have considered mechanisms that either are not immune to strategic behavior by the firm, as demonstrated by Sappington (1980), or require that the firm act myopically. Tam (1981) also provides a mechanism that converges to efficient pricing, but it is myopic in that it requires the firm to maximize current period income rather than the discounted present value of income. See Finsinger and Vogelsang (1985) for an analysis of the Tam mechanism.

[106] Note that the regulator need not know the discount rate used by the firm.

condition:

$$\frac{\rho}{1+\rho}[P'(q_i)q_i + P(q_i) - C'(q_i)] - q_{i-1}P'(q_i)$$

$$+\frac{1}{1+\rho}[P(q_i) - P(q_{i+1}) + P'(q_i)q_i] = 0. \tag{10.2}$$

Because the interests of the regulator and the firm are aligned, in each successive period the firm's choice results in an increase in aggregate welfare. This mechanism leads to efficiency in the limit, as can be seen by noting that at the steady state in which $q_{i-1} = q_i = q_{i+1}$ only a price equal to marginal cost satisfies (10.2).

The strength of this mechanism is that it produces a welfare improvement in each successive period and converges to marginal cost pricing. The mechanism, however, has a number of limitations. First, it is not clear how this mechanism would perform for a nonstationary model in which either the cost function or demand changes over time or in which profit is affected by randomness. Second, measurement or monitoring noise may reduce the efficiency of the mechanism. Third, the mechanism does not utilize either prior information or the information from the observation of profit in each period to improve the form of the mechanism. For example, in each period the regulator observes the profit of the firm and if the firm had private information about its constant marginal cost, the regulator would be able to determine the marginal cost from the observed profit. The regulator could then exploit that information in future periods. The firm would, of course, recognize this and act strategically. The Vogelsang and Finsinger mechanism, however, is based on the assumption that the regulator is able to commit not to exploit this information, but that may not be optimal.[107] Another potential weakness of the mechanism is the determination of the initial parameters π_0, p_0, q_0, and δ. For example, if the firm has increasing returns to scale, the regulator would not know how to set the constant payment δ. Similarly, the firm could participate even if it were inefficient to do so, if δ were set too high. Finally, as with the multiperiod Bayesian mechanisms considered in Section 6, the regulator must be able to commit credibly to the mechanism.

Sappington and Sibley (1988) propose a non-Bayesian mechanism that improves on the Vogelsang and Finsinger mechanism by providing a payment that equals the exact change in consumer surplus from one period to the next. In contrast to the Finsinger and Vogelsang mechanism, this mechanism requires that the regulator and the firm have symmetric information about the demand

[107]Although the Bayesian approach of Baron and Besanko addressed in Subsection 6.2.1 demonstrates that in the case of perfect correlation the regulator never exploits the information, this may not be the case in a non-Bayesian mechanism.

function. Their mechanism is intended to maximize consumer surplus and to deal with any incentive the firm might have to waste resources. The firm is allowed in each period to retain its current profits π_i and receives a payment S_i given by

$$S_i = \int_{p_i}^{p_{i-1}} Q(p)\,\mathrm{d}p - q_{i-1}(p_{i-1} - p_i) + C(q_{i-1}) - q_{i-1}p_i. \tag{10.3}$$

Substituting the expression for operating profit,

$$\pi_{i-1} = p_{i-1}q_{i-1} - C(q_{i-1}),$$

and simplifying yields the income I_i in period i as[108]

$$I_i = \pi_i - \pi_{i-1} + \int_{p_i}^{p_{i-1}} Q(p)\,\mathrm{d}p. \tag{10.4}$$

This expression is analogous to that in Finsinger and Vogelsang's mechanism with the exception that the change in welfare is represented exactly.

Instead of viewing this mechanism as analogous to that of Finsinger and Vogelsang, the Sappington and Sibley mechanism can be more appropriately viewed as an extension of the Loeb and Magat mechanism to a dynamic context. In a static model the only means available to deal with the distribution of surplus is an auction. In a dynamic setting, however, distribution may be dealt with by intertemporal transfers between consumers and the firm. Thus, the firm can be given an incentive for efficiency and the distributive issue can be resolved by taking away in the current period the profit earned by the firm in the previous period. This is apparent in the statement of the firm's net income in (10.4).

To interpret the Sappington and Sibley mechanism, rewrite the last term in (10.4) as the difference between consumer surplus at the prices p_i and p_{i-1}. The income is then

$$\begin{aligned} I_i &= \pi_i + \int_{p_i}^{\infty} Q(p)\,\mathrm{d}p - \pi_{i-1} - \int_{p_{i-1}}^{\infty} Q(p)\,\mathrm{d}p \\ &= TS_i(p_i) - TS_{i-1}(p_{i-1}), \end{aligned} \tag{10.5}$$

where $TS(p_i)$ denotes total surplus. The income of the firm in each period thus is the difference between the total surplus in the current period and the total surplus in the prior period. Maximizing the present value of net income induces the firm immediately to choose price equal to marginal cost and to choose the

[108]Note that when $I_i = 0$ this is also the difference between the profit $\pi(\theta_i)$ and $\pi(\theta_{i-1})$ in (4.8a). The incentive properties of the mechanism thus are the same as that characterized in Section 4.

minimum cost (no waste). The firm will agree to participate in the mechanism if it will earn a nonnegative profit in the first period, and in subsequent periods it will earn zero profits and thus will be willing to participate.[109] This mechanism is thus the dynamic extension of the Loeb and Magat mechanism. Even though Sappington and Sibley state the regulator's objective as the maximization of consumer surplus, the ability to redistribute costlessly provides an equivalence between consumer surplus and total surplus maximization. Except for the problem of establishing the policy in the initial period, the prior information of the regulator is irrevelant to the mechanism design as it is the Loeb and Magat mechanism.

In the case in which the regulator does not know the discount rate employed by the firm, the mechanism results in rents to the firm in the first period and zero rents thereafter when it is common knowledge that the firm has the same cost function in every period. If the regulator knew the discount rate, those rents could be eliminated. The Sappington and Sibley mechanism also gives the firm the incentive to be efficient in every period and to choose efficiently among investments that can lower costs in future periods. Randomness in the firm's costs also does not result in inefficiency if the discount rate is known. This indicates the power resulting from the ability to observe expenditures in each period and to be able to commit to policies. The difficulties associated with ensuring commitment have been addressed in Section 6.

11. Extensions and applications

This section identifies an additional set of issues that have been studied in the context of theory addressed here.

11.1. Multiple regulators

The above models pertain to regulatory settings with a single regulator, but regulatory jurisdictions may be overlapping or different regulators may have control over different aspects of a firm's performance.[110] Baron (1985b) considers the case of a firm such as an electric utility that is subject to regulation by a public utility commission (PUC) responsible for the pricing policy and an environmental regulator (EPA) responsible for controlling a pollution externality. The firm is assumed to have private information about the effectiveness of

[109] The first-period profit results from the choice of the initial parameters.

[110] Bernheim and Whinston (1986) have considered a model with multiple principals in which information is symmetric but the actions of the agent are unobservable.

abatement technologies applied to its production process. The regulators are modeled as having conflicting objectives with the PUC maximizing a weighted sum of consumer surplus and profit and the EPA minimizing a weighted sum of the environmental damage and the abatement burden on the firm. Since the EPA has authority to act unilaterally to deal with the pollution problem and since the PUC has the responsibility to provide the firm with a fair return, the EPA is in a position to act as a Stackelberg leader. Furthermore, since the pricing procedures employed by the PUC are in the public domain, the EPA can anticipate the response of the PUC to any pollution control policy it chooses.

Because of the conflicting objectives of the regulators, both cooperative and noncooperative equilibria are of interest. In the noncooperative equilibrium the EPA sets the maximum allowable emissions fee and mandates an abatement standard that is more stringent than that which the regulators would choose in a cooperative equilibrium. The PUC is forced to respond with prices that are higher than would be set under cooperation. The firm prefers that the regulators not cooperate because it then earns greater rents on its private information. Under plausible conditions the EPA prefers noncooperative regulation because it is better able to serve its own mandate than if it had to take into account the PUC's interests. The PUC prefers cooperative to noncooperative regulation as would be expected.

11.2. Multiple firms

With the exception of those in Sections 7 and 8, the models considered in previous sections pertain to the regulation of a single firm. If the regulator has authority over a set of firms each of which has private information, the regulator may be able to use the information obtained from one firm to improve the regulation of other firms. In the context of the revelation of preferences for public goods, d'Aspremont and Gerard-Varet (1979) provide a modification of a mechanism developed by Groves (1973) that results in an equilibrium in which each agent reports its demand truthfully.[111] If the private information of the firms is correlated and the firms are risk neutral, Cremer and McClean (1985) demonstrate in a bidding model that the regulator may be able to extract all the rents from the firms and to implement the first-best outcome. Demski and Sappington (1984) obtain a similar result in a one-principal, two-agent model with ex ante private information where the agents take unobservable actions. When the agents are risk neutral and their private information is correlated, they show that the first-best outcome is attainable. When the agents are risk averse, the first-best outcome is attained and the principal prefers an equilibrium in which one of the

[111]The individual rationality constraints are not necessarily satisfied in their mechanism.

agents has truthful reporting as a dominant strategy and the other has truthful reporting as a best response to the other agent's strategy. In the context of an agency model with symmetric ex ante information and incomplete observability, Mookherjee (1984) examines the use of relative performance measures when the performance of the agents is correlated.

11.3. Hierarchical relationships

The models analyzed above involve a regulator and a firm and thus represent a hierarchical relationship with one level. Many regulatory relationships involve more levels, however. For example, a cabinet officer or a legislature may supervise the regulatory agency that regulates the firms. Similarly, an agency may regulate a firm whose owners must formulate a contract to motivate managers to serve their interests. These hierarchical relationships involve broader opportunities for strategic behavior than present in the single-level models considered above.[112]

Tirole (1986b) has analyzed a model in which two parties in the hierarchy may collude to the detriment of the third party. For example, the regulator and the firm might collude to serve their own interests rather than follow the agency's mandate or the preferences of the cabinet officer. This, for example, might correspond to capture of the regulator by the firm (or vice versa). The top of the hierarchy would, of course, recognize this possibility and would structure the regulatory relationship to deal as efficiently as possible with this collusion. Tirole's analysis suggests that more complex models may reveal more sophisticated and more realistic behavior on the part of the both the regulator and the firm. For example, the possibility of collusion between the regulator and the firm suggests that the legislature or the executive may wish to change regularly the administrator or the membership on the regulatory commission to diminish the likelihood of collusion. The gains from lessening the likelihood of collusion would have to be balanced against the loss of information associated with regulatory turnover.

11.4. Regulation and bargaining power

The models considered in previous sections assume that the regulator has all the bargaining power in the sense that it is able to offer a mechanism to the firm on a take-it-or-leave-it basis, and the firm has no opportunity to bargain with the regulator over the form of the mechanism. If bargaining power is distributed

[112] Stiglitz (1975), Sah and Stiglitz (1986), and Demski and Sappington (1986) also present models of hierarchical relationships.

differently, the equilibrium mechanism will be affected. Spulber (1988) has characterized mechanisms for differing degrees of bargaining power for the case in which the firm has private information about its costs and consumers have private information about their demand.[113] The regulator then designs a mechanism in response to the distribution of bargaining power. In the case in which the regulator has all the bargaining power, the equilibrium mechanism is a special case of that characterized in Section 4. In the case in which the firm has all the bargaining power, the equilibrium mechanism is that which obtains for an unregulated monopolist as considered by Maskin and Riley (1984).

12. Research directions

The perspective taken in this chapter is basically normative with the regulator modeled as maximizing a welfare function based on consumer and producer surplus and the firm acting strategically given the mechanism adopted by the regulator. The characteristics of regulatory mechanisms and institutions is thus viewed as endogenous to the relationship between the regulatory commission and the firm.[114] The design of regulatory mechanisms in this setting is complicated by incentive problems arising from informational asymmetries, incomplete observability of actions and performance, imperfect monitors of observable variables, and differing risk preferences. The substantial body of theoretical research on these issues has clarified the interrelationships among the incentive problems inherent in regulation and has identified the tradeoffs among the possible responses to them. Important theoretical issues remain particularly pertaining to the dynamics of regulation, to the regulation of several firms, to richer informational structures, and to more descriptive models. At least in the near future, however, this work is likely to be based on the methods employed herein and on the recent advances in game theory and microeconomic theory.

This section is intended to address other directions of research associated with the design of regulatory institutions in the presence of incentive problems. Two directions will be considered: applications to actual regulatory settings and the empirical study of regulatory performance in the presence of incentive problems.

At a conceptual level the theory of regulatory mechanism design is a useful guide to reasoning about applications and about the tradeoffs among the possible responses to incentive problems. The application of these principles, however, is only beginning and can be expected to involve a range of practical complications

[113]The private information in this formulation is an additive component of cost and demand, respectively.

[114]A broader issue would be to explain the locus of regulation in an economy. The explanation undoubtedly rests on theories of market failure but perhaps more importantly on theories of political choice.

that may make precise calculations difficult. In the near term at least this line of theory development may be more directly applicable to the design of institutional features and procedures, such as the fairness condition considered in Subsection 6.3.3. That is, in addition to formulating complex incentive mechanisms, applications may center on the design of institutional properties intended to deal with issues of commitment, ratcheting, monitoring, and performance evaluations.

The application of incentive mechanisms of this nature has a long history in regulation.[115] Many of these mechanisms were introduced during periods of rapid inflation, significant technological change, or a changing regulatory environment such as that created by the antitrust accord that restructured AT&T and the telecommunications industry. For example, even though fuel-adjustment clauses had been used as early as World War I, the rapid increases in fuel prices in the 1970s stimulated a variety of design experiments intended to adjust electricity prices in response to changes in fuel costs.[116] In 1986 and 1987 a number of regulatory commissions began to adopt incentive mechanisms to govern the profits of the regional telephone companies operating in their jurisdistictions. Similarly, regulatory commissions are beginning to take more seriously the deregulation of the electric power industry, and if that transpires, a number of incentive experiments would be designed to deal with the resulting mixture of regulated and unregulated units of power companies.

Experiments such as these provide an opportunity for empirical work of two types. First, researchers may have the opportunity to study the efficiency consequences of various incentive mechanisms using cross-sectional data.[117] Such studies, however, will be complicated by the difficulties in dealing with incomplete information. When information is incomplete, regulation involves mechanisms or schedules of policies, so empirical work must focus both on policies, such as rate-setting formulas and other procedures that specify how reported information is to be used to revise prices, and on how procedures are revised as a function of performance data. Second, researchers may be able to study the institutions established to implement these policies. In particular, institutional properties, such as the ability of regulators to commit to multiperiod policies, may be investigated with the objective of identifying their efficiency consequences.

Empirical studies will be complicated by the difference between the data the econometrician observes and the information available to the parties at the time they took their actions. Even in static contexts the econometrician must be able

[115]See Morgan (1923) for an analysis of early experiments with incentive regulation and Joskow and Schmalensee (1986) for a recent analysis.

[116]These clauses may have been adopted more to respond to cash flow problems of electric utilities due to inflation and regulatory lag than to a desire to promote economic efficiency by basing prices on costs on a continuous basis.

[117]Joskow (1987, 1988) has conducted studies of this nature involving a cross-section of long-term coal supply contracts for electric utilities.

to formulate, or at least make inferences about, the informational asymmetries that were present. Furthermore, care must be taken in the analysis, since in the presence of informational asymmetries the conclusions one might draw from the data may be the opposite of those that would be drawn if information were symmetric. For example, suppose that, after the fact, the econometrician had data on actual costs and the price that had been set in a period. If the price were equal to the actual marginal cost yet information had been incomplete at the time the price had been set, the conclusion that should be drawn is that regulation was inefficient, since price should have been above marginal cost (except in the case of the lowest conceivable cost). Similarly, if the price had been above actual marginal cost, the econometrician could not conclude that regulation had been inefficient. Distinguishing between these two cases may be possible using other data. For example, the econometrician could use data on the profits (rents) of the firm to judge whether regulation had been efficient. That is, profits should be higher under inefficient regulation than under efficient regulation given the same actual costs and information structure. Profits are useful here because, unlike prices, they do not depend directly on the information available to the regulator at the time that prices were established.[118]

Empirical analysis is more complicated in a dynamic setting because it is necessary to determine when information became available. With time series data, however, it may be possible to use the paths of prices and costs to assess the efficiency of regulation. To illustrate this, consider the dynamic model with commitment analyzed in Section 6. If, at the time a regulatory mechanism was adopted, the type of the firm had been known to be persistent (perfect correlation), then a price path that was constant over time would indicate efficient regulation with commitment even if prices remained above costs. If prices ratcheted downward over time, either inefficiency or a limited degree of commitment, such as that characterized by fairness in Subsection 6.3.3, would be consistent with the observation. To complement such an analysis, the extent to which commitment was possible may be assessed by examining whether regulatory procedures had been revised. Other cases could be analyzed in a similar manner as a function of information about the state of the regulator's knowledge at the time the procedures were implemented.

It may also be possible to make inferences from the data about the nature of the regulatory relationship. With the maintained hypothesis that regulators are acting optimally given the information available to them, suppose that the econometrician observed that in each period the regulator employed a pricing mechanism such as that characterized in Section 4 and that prices fluctuated across periods. Then, if marginal costs varied over time yet the firm did not earn rents after the initial period, the data would be consistent with the regulator having the ability to make credible commitments and the type of the firm being

[118]The profit depends, however, on the upper bound θ^+ of possible marginal costs.

random. If, however, the firm earned rents in each period, the data would be consistent with the type being random and the regulator being unable to make credible commitments to multiperiod policies.

As suggested here, even though considerable progress has been made on the theory of the design of regulatory mechanisms and institutions, a wide range of theoretical, applied, and empirical research remains to be conducted.

Appendix A

This appendix presents the control theoretic approach to the solution of the regulator's problem. In this approach the profit function $\pi(\theta)$ is treated as a state variable and the controls are $p(\theta)$, $T(\theta)$, and $\mathrm{d}\pi(\theta)/\mathrm{d}\theta$. The objective function is that in (4.16) which is to be maximized subject to two constraints: (1) that the derivative of the state variable satisfies (4.7) and (2) that the state variable is non-negative for all θ. The Lagrangian $\mathscr{L}$ formed from the Hamiltonian is

$$\mathscr{L} = \left(\int_{p(\theta)}^{\infty} Q(p^0)\,\mathrm{d}p^0 - T(\theta) + \alpha\pi(\theta)\right) f(\theta) + \mu(\theta)(-Q(p(\theta))) \\ +\lambda(\theta)(p(\theta)Q(p(\theta)) - \theta Q(p(\theta)) - K - \pi(\theta)) + \tau(\theta)\pi(\theta), \tag{A.1}$$

where $\mu(\theta)$ is the costate variable associated with $\mathrm{d}\pi(\theta)/\mathrm{d}\theta = -Q(p(\theta))$ in (4.7), $\lambda(\theta)$ is a multiplier, and $\tau(\theta)$ is a non-negative multiplier. The necessary optimality conditions are

$$\frac{\partial \mathscr{L}}{\partial p(\theta)} = -Q(p(\theta))f(\theta) - \mu(\theta)Q'(p(\theta)) \\ +\lambda(\theta)(Q(p(\theta)) + p(\theta)Q'(p(\theta)) - Q'(p(\theta))) = 0, \tag{A.2}$$

$$\frac{\partial \mathscr{L}}{\partial T(\theta)} = -f(\theta) + \lambda(\theta) = 0, \tag{A.3}$$

$$\frac{\partial \mathscr{L}}{\partial \pi(\theta)} = -\mu'(\theta) = \alpha f(\theta) - \lambda(\theta) + \tau(\theta), \tag{A.4}$$

$$\tau(\theta) \geq 0, \tag{A.5}$$

$$\pi(\theta) = p(\theta)Q(p(\theta)) + T(\theta) - \theta Q(p(\theta)) - K. \tag{A.6}$$

From (A.3) the multiplier $\lambda(\theta)$ on the definition of the state variable equals the density function $f(\theta)$, so substituting into (A.4) and integrating yields:

$$\mu(\theta) = \mu(\theta^-) + (1-\alpha)F(\theta) + \int_{\theta^-}^{\theta} \tau(\theta^0)\,\mathrm{d}\theta^0. \tag{A.7}$$

Since the state variable is constrained only to be non-negative, the end points $\pi(\theta^+)$ and $\pi(\theta^-)$ are also to be chosen. From (4.7) the value $\mu(\theta^-) = 0$, since the state variable is a strictly decreasing function of θ. The end point $\pi(\theta^+)$ of the state variable satisfies the transversality condition:

$$\tau(\theta^+)\pi(\theta^+) = 0.$$

To show that the state variable equals zero at θ^+ when $\alpha < 1$, assume that it is positive. This then implies that $\mu(\theta^+) = 0$ which from (A.7) implies that

$$0 = (1 - \alpha)F(\theta^+) + \int_{\theta^-}^{\theta^+} \tau(\theta^0)\,\mathrm{d}\theta^0.$$

Since $F(\theta^+) = 1$ and $\tau(\theta) \geq 0$, a contradiction is obtained when $\alpha < 1$. If $\alpha = 1$, then no contradiction is obtained and $\pi(\theta^+)$ can be chosen arbitrarily. Thus, $\pi(\theta) = 0$ for all α satisfies the necessary conditions. Consequently, $\tau(\theta) = 0$ for all $\theta < \theta^+$. From (A.7) this implies that the costate variable satisfies:

$$\mu(\theta) = (1 - \alpha)F(\theta). \tag{A.7a}$$

Substituting this and $\lambda(\theta)$ into (A.2) yields (4.19). The transfer $T(\theta)$ is then determined by integrating the state equation and using (4.10).

This approach yields a "first-order" solution, since the state equation guarantees only that the incentive compatibility constraints hold locally. The incentive compatibility constraints thus must either be verified directly or compared to the conditions established in (4.12) and (4.15).

Appendix B

This appendix presents a derivation of the optimal regulatory policy for the Laffont and Tirole model. Their approach to determining the optimal mechanism is based on a "concealment set", but instead of presenting that approach, the control theoretic approach of Appendix A will be used in conjunction with the formulation in Baron and Besanko (1987b). The objective of this appendix is to demonstrate that when the firm is risk neutral the marginal cost of responding to the adverse selection problem is exactly offset by the marginal cost of responding to the moral hazard problem in equilibrium.

The uncertain cost $\tilde{C}$ of the firm is assumed to be given by a generalization of (5.5) where

$$\tilde{C} = C(\theta, a, q) + \sqrt{\nu}\,\tilde{\varepsilon}. \tag{B.1}$$

The distribution of $\tilde{\varepsilon}$ induces a distribution on $\tilde{C}$, and the resulting density function will be denoted by $h(C|C(\theta, a, q))$. Only the fixed charges $T(\theta, C)$ and the cost depend on C, so the expected profit of the firm may be written as

$$\pi(\hat{\theta};\theta)=p(\hat{\theta})Q(p(\hat{\theta}))-K-\psi(a)+\int_{\Gamma}[T(\hat{\theta},C)-C]h(C|C(\theta,a,Q(p(\hat{\theta}))))\,\mathrm{d}C. \tag{B.2}$$

Given an incentive compatible policy, the derivative of the state variable $\pi(\theta)$ is

$$\pi'(\theta)=C_{\theta}(\theta,a,Q(p(\theta)))\int_{\Gamma}[T(\hat{\theta},C)-C]h_2(C|C(\theta,a,Q(p(\hat{\theta}))))\,\mathrm{d}C, \tag{B.3}$$

where h_2 denotes the partial derivative of h with respect to its conditioner. The firm will choose its effort $a(\theta)$ to satisfy:

$$\frac{\partial\pi(\theta)}{\partial a(\theta)}=C_a(\theta,a(\theta),Q(p(\theta)))\int_{\Gamma}[T(\hat{\theta},C)-C]\times h_2(C|C(\theta,a(\theta),Q(p(\hat{\theta}))))\,\mathrm{d}C-\psi'(a(\theta))=0. \tag{B.4}$$

The regulator maximizes the objective in (4.16) subject to the constraints in (B.3) and (B.4). The Lagrangian corresponding to (A.1) is

$$\begin{aligned}\mathscr{L}=&\left(\int_{p(\theta)}^{\infty}Q(p^0)\,\mathrm{d}p^0-\int_{\Gamma}T(\theta,C)h(C|C(\theta,a(\theta),Q(p(\theta))))\,\mathrm{d}C+\alpha\pi(\theta)\right)f(\theta)\\&+\mu(\theta)\Big[C_{\theta}(\theta,a(\theta),Q(p(\theta)))\int_{\Gamma}[T(\hat{\theta},C)-C]\\&\qquad\times h_2(C|C(\theta,a(\theta),Q(p(\theta))))\,\mathrm{d}C\Big]\\&+\xi(\theta)\Big[C_a(\theta,a(\theta),Q(p(\theta)))\int_{\Gamma}[T(\theta,C)-C]\\&\qquad\times h_2(C|C(\theta,a(\theta),Q(p(\theta))))\,\mathrm{d}C-\psi'(a(\theta))\Big]\\&+\lambda(\theta)\Big[p(\theta)Q(p(\theta))-K-\psi(a(\theta))\\&\qquad+\int_{\Gamma}[T(\theta,C)-C]h(C|C(\theta,a(\theta),Q(p(\theta))))\,\mathrm{d}C-\pi(\theta)\Big]\\&+\tau(\theta)\pi(\theta),\end{aligned} \tag{B.5}$$

where the multipliers are the same as in (A.1) with the addition of the multiplier $\xi(\theta)$ corresponding to the moral hazard constraint in (B.4).

A necessary optimality condition is obtained by differentiating $\mathscr{L}$ with respect to $T(\theta,C)$ pointwise on (θ, C) or

$$\begin{aligned}\frac{\partial \mathscr{L}}{\partial T(\theta, C)} = & -f(\theta)h(C|C(\theta, a(\theta), Q(p(\theta)))) \\ & +\lambda(\theta)h(C|C(\theta, a(\theta), Q(p(\theta)))) \\ & +[\mu(\theta)C_\theta(\theta, a(\theta), Q(p(\theta))) \\ & \quad +\xi(\theta)C_a(\theta, a(\theta), Q(p(\theta)))] \\ & \times h_2(C|C(\theta, a(\theta), Q(p(\theta)))) = 0, \quad \forall C, \forall \theta. \end{aligned} \tag{B.6}$$

Dividing by h indicates that the first two terms on the right-hand side are independent of C, so the last two terms must also be independent of C. Since h_2/h varies with C, (B.6) can be satisfied only if

$$\mu(\theta)C_\theta(\theta, a(\theta), Q(p(\theta))) + \xi(\theta)C_a(\theta, a(\theta), Q(p(\theta))) = 0, \quad \forall \theta. \tag{B.7}$$

Consequently, the marginal cost $\mu(\theta)C_\theta$ of responding to the moral hazard problem exactly offsets the marginal cost $\xi(\theta)C_a$ of responding to the adverse selection problem. This also implies that

$$\lambda(\theta) = f(\theta), \quad \forall \theta. \tag{B.8}$$

The derivative of the Lagrangian with respect to $p(\theta)$ is

$$\begin{aligned}\frac{\partial \mathscr{L}}{\partial p(\theta)} = & -Q(p(\theta))f(\theta) + C_q\int_\Gamma [-T(\theta, C)]h_2\,\mathrm{d}Cf(\theta) \\ & +[\mu(\theta)C_a + \xi(\theta)C_\theta]C_q\int_\Gamma [T(\theta, C) - C]h_2\,\mathrm{d}C \\ & +\lambda(\theta)\Big[p(\theta)Q'(p(\theta)) + Q(p(\theta)) \\ & \quad +C_q\int_\Gamma [T(\theta, C) - C]h_2\,\mathrm{d}C\Big] = 0. \end{aligned} \tag{B.9}$$

Substituting (B.7) and (B.8) into (B.9) implies:

$$p(\theta) - C_q \int_{\Gamma} Ch_2 \, \mathrm{d}C = p(\theta) - C_q = 0, \tag{B.10}$$

so price equals expected marginal cost.

References

Anton, J.J. and Yao, D.A. (1987) 'Second-sourcing and the experience curve: Price competition in defense procurement', *Rand Journal of Economics*, 18:57–76.

Averch, H. and Johnson, L.L. (1962) 'Behavior of the firm under regulatory constraint', *American Economic Review*, 52:1053–1069.

Bailey, E.E. (1973) *Economic theory of regulatory constraint*. Lexington: Lexington Books.

Bailey, E.E. (1976) 'Innovation and regulation: A reply', *Journal of Public Economics*, 5:393–394.

Bailey, E.E. and Coleman, R.D. (1971) 'The effect of lagged regulation in the Averch–Johnson model', *Bell Journal of Economics and Management Science*, 2:278–292.

Baron, D.P. (1985a) 'Regulatory strategies under asymmetric information', in: M. Boyer and R. Kihlstrom, eds., *Bayesian models in economic theory*. Amsterdam: North-Holland, 155–180.

Baron, D.P. (1985b) 'Noncooperative regulation of a nonlocalized externality', *Rand Journal of Economics*, 16:553–568.

Baron, D.P. (1985c) 'Regulation of prices and pollution under incomplete information', *Journal of Public Economics*, 28:211–231.

Baron, D.P. (1988) 'Regulation and legislative choice', *Rand Journal of Economics* (forthcoming).

Baron, D.P. and Besanko, D. (1984a) 'Regulation, asymmetric information, and auditing', *Rand Journal of Economics*, 15:447–470.

Baron, D.P. and Besanko, D. (1984b) 'Regulation and information in a continuing relationship', *Information Economics and Policy*, 1:267–302.

Baron, D.P. and Besanko, D. (1987a) 'Commitment and fairness in a dynamic regulatory relationship', *Review of Economic Studies*, 54:413–436.

Baron, D.P. and Besanko, D. (1987b) 'Monitoring, moral hazard, asymmetric information, and risk sharing in procurement contracting,' *Rand Journal of Economics*, 18:509–532.

Baron, D.P. and Besanko, D. (1988) 'Monitoring of performance in organizational contracting: The case of defense procurement', *Scandinavian Journal of Economics* (forthcoming).

Baron, D.P. and DeBondt, R.R. (1981) 'On the design of regulatory price adjustment mechanisms', *Journal of Economic Theory*, 24:70–94.

Baron, D.P. and Myerson, R.B. (1982) 'Regulating a monopolist with unknown costs', *Econometrica*, 50:911–930.

Baron, D.P. and Taggart, Jr., R.A. (1980) 'Regulatory pricing policies and economic incentives', in: M.A. Crew, *Issues in public utility pricing regulation*. Lexington: Lexington Books, 27–49.

Baumol, W.J. and Klevorick, .K. (1970) 'Input choices and rate-of-return regulation: An overview of the discussion', *Bell Journal of Economics and Management Science*, 1:162–190.

Bernheim, B.D. and Whinston, M.D. (1986) 'Common agency', *Econometria*, 54:923–942.

Besanko, D. (1984) 'On the use of revenue requirements regulation under imperfect information', in: M.A. Crew, *Analyzing the impact of regulatory change in public utilities*. Lexington: Lexington Books, 39–55.

Besanko, D. and Sappington, D.E.M. (1986) 'Designing regulatory policy with limited information', in: *Fundamentals of Pure and Applied Economics*, Vol. 20. New York: Harwood.

Black, D. (1958) *The theory of committees and elections*. Cambridge: Cambridge University Press.

Bower, R.S. (1981) 'Discussion', *Journal of Finance*, 36:397–399.

Breyer, S. (1982) *Regulation and its reform*. Cambridge: Harvard University Press.

Caillaud, B. (1986) 'Regulation, competition and asymmetric information', working paper, MIT.
Caillaud, B., Guesnerie, R., Rey, P. and Tirole, J. (1988) 'Government intervention in production and incentives theory: A review of recent contributions', *Rand Journal of Economics*, 19:1–26.
Crawford, V.P. (1988) 'Long-term relationships governed by short-term contracts', *American Economic Review*, 78:485–499.
Cremer, J. and McLean, R.P. (1985) 'Optimal selling strategies under uncertainty for a discriminating monopolist when demands are interdependent', *Econometrica*, 53:345–361.
D'Aspremont, C. and Gerard-Varet, L. (1979) 'Incentives and incomplete information', *Journal of Public Economics*, 11:25–45.
Dasgupta, P.S., Hammond, P.J. and Maskin, E.S. (1979) 'The implementation of social choice rules: Some results on incentive compatibility', *Review of Economic Studies*, 46:185–216.
Demski, J. S. and Sappington, D.E.M. (1984) 'Optimal incentive contracts with multiple agents', *Journal of Economic Theory*, 33:152–171.
Demski, J.S. and Sappington, D.E.M. (1987) 'Hierarchial regulatory control', *Rand Journal of Economics*, 18:369–383.
Demski, J.S., Sappington, D.E.M. and Spiller, P.T. (1986), 'Entry in regulated industries: An information-based perspective', working paper, Bell Communications Research.
Drobak, J.N. (1986) 'Constitutional limits on price and rent control: The lessons of utility regulation', *Washington University Law Quarterly*, 64:107–150.
Dupuit, J. (1952) 'On the measurement of the utility of public works', in: *International Economics Papers*, vol. 2. (Translated by R.H. Barbak from 'de al Mésure de l'Utilité des Travaux Publics', *Annales des Ponts et Chaussees*, 2nd series, vol. 8, 1844.)
Finsinger, J. and Vogelsang, I. (1982) 'Performance indices for public enterprises', in: L.P. Jones, *Public enterprise in less developed countries*. Cambridge: Cambridge University Press.
Finsinger, J. and Vogelsang, I. (1985) 'Strategic management behavior under reward structures in a planned economy', *Quarterly Journal of Economics*, 100:263–269.
Greenwald, B.C. (1984) 'Rate base selection and the structure of regulation', *Rand Journal of Economics*, 15:85–95.
Grout, P. (1984) 'Investment and wages in the absence of binding contracts: A Nash bargaining approach', *Econometrica*, 52:449–460.
Groves, T. (1973) 'Incentives in teams', *Econometrica*, 41:617–631.
Guesnerie, R. and Laffont, J.J. (1984) 'A complete solution to a class of principal–agent problems with an application to the control of a self-managed firm', *Journal of Public Economics*, 25:329–369.
Harris, M. and Townsend, R.M. (1981) 'Resource allocation under asymmetric information', *Econometrica*, 49:33–64.
Harsanyi, J. (1967–1968) 'Games with incomplete information played by Bayesian players', *Management Science*, 14:159–182, 320–334, 486–502.
Hart, O. and Holmstrom, B. (1987) 'The theory of contracts', in: T. Bewley, ed., *Advances in economic theory*, 1985. Cambridge: Cambridge University Press.
Joskow, P.L. (1987) 'Contract duration and relationship-specific investment: Empirical evidence from coal markets', *American Economic Review*, 77:168–185.
Joskow, P.L. (1988) 'Price adjustment in long term contracts: The case of coal', *Journal of Law and Economics*, 31:47–83.
Joskow, P.L. and Schmalensee, R. (1986) 'Incentive regulation for electric utilities', *Yale Journal on Regulation*, 4:1–49.
Klevorick, A.K. (1966) 'The graduated fair return: A regulatory proposal', *American Economic Review*, 56:577–584.
Kydland, F.E. and Prescott, E.C. (1977) 'Rules rather than discretion: The inconsistency of optimal plans', *Journal of Political Economy*, 85:473–491.
Laffont, J.-J. and Tirole, J. (1986) 'Using cost observation to regulate firms', *Journal of Political Economy*, 94:614–641.
Laffont, J.-J. and Tirole, J. (1987) 'Auctioning incentive contracts', *Journal of Political Economy*, 95:921–937.
Laffont, J.-J. and Tirole, J. (1988) 'The dynamics of incentive contracts', *Econometrica*, 56:1153–1175.
Lewis, T.R. (1986), 'Reputation and contractual performance in long-term projects', *Rand Journal of Economics*, 17:141–157.

Loeb, M. and Magat, W.A. (1979) 'A decentralized method for utility regulation', *Journal of Law and Economics*, 22:399–404.
Maskin, E. and Riley, J. (1984) 'Monopoly with incomplete information', *Rand Journal of Economics*, 15:171–196.
Maskin, E. and Tirole, J. (1986) 'Principals with private information, I: Independent values', working paper 1234, MIT.
McAfee, R.P. and McMillan, J. (1986) 'Bidding for contracts: A principal–agent analysis', *Rand Journal of Economics*, 17:326–338.
McCubbins, M. and Schwartz, T. (1984) 'Congressional oversight overlooked: Police patrols versus fire alarms', *American Journal of Political Science*, 28:165–179.
Melumad, N. (1988) 'Asymmetric information and the termination of contracts in agencies', *Contemporary Accounting Research* (forthcoming).
Milgrom, P. and Weber, R.J. (1982) 'A theory of auctions and competitive bidding', *Econometrica*, 47:1089–1122.
Mirrlees, J.A. (1971) 'An exploration in the theory of optimum income taxation', *Review of Economic Studies*, 33:175–208.
Mookherjee, D. (1984) 'Optimal incentive schemes with many agents', *Review of Economic Studies*, 51:433–446.
Morgan, C.S. (1923) *Regulation and the management of public utilities*. Boston: Houghton Mifflin.
Myerson, R. (1983) 'Mechanism design by an informed principal', *Econometrica*, 47:61–73.
Myerson, R.B. (1979) 'Incentive compatibility and the bargaining problem', *Econometrica*, 47:61–74.
Niskanen, W. (1971) *Bureaucracy and representative government*. Chicago: Aldine.
Picard, P. (1987) 'On the design of incentive schemes under moral hazard and adverse selection', *Journal of Public Economics*, 33:305–332.
Riordan, M.H. (1984) 'On delegating price authority to a regulated firm', *Rand Journal of Economics*, 15:108–115.
Riordan, M.H. and Sappington, D.E.M. (1987a) 'Awarding monopoly franchises', *American Economic Review*, 77:305–332.
Riordan, M.H. and Sappington, D.E.M. (1987b) 'Commitment and procurement contracting', *Scandinavian Journal of Economics* (forthcoming).
Roberts, K. (1982) 'Long-term contracts', working paper, University of Warwick, UK.
Roberts, K. (1984) 'The theoretical limits to redistribution', *Review of Economic Studies*, 51:177–195.
Robichek, A. (1978) 'Regulation and modern finance theory', *Journal of Finance*, 33:693–705.
Rochet, J-C. (1984) 'Monopoly regulation with two dimensional uncertainty', working paper, Laboratoire d'Economie Politique de l'Ecole Normal Superieure, Paris.
Romer, T. and Rosenthal, H. (1987) 'Modern political economy and the study of regulation', in: E.E. Bailey, ed., *Public regulation: New perspectives on institutions and policies*. Cambridge: MIT Press.
Ruff, L.E. (1981) 'Federal environmental regulation', in: L.W. Weiss and M.W. Klass, *Case studies in regulation: Revolution and reform*. Boston: Little, Brown.
Sah, R.K. and Stiglitz, J.E. (1986) 'The architecture of economic systems: Hierarchies and polyarchies', *American Economic Review*, 76:716–727.
Sappington, D.E.M. (1980) 'Strategic firm behavior under a dynamic regulatory adjustment process', *Bell Journal of Economics*, 11:360–372.
Sappington, D.E.M. (1983a) 'Optimal regulation of a multiproduct monopoly with unknown technological capabilities', *Bell Journal of Economics*, 14:453–463.
Sappington, D.E.M. (1983b) 'Limited liability contracts between principal and agent', *Journal of Economic Theory*, 29:1–21.
Sappington, D.E.M. (1986) 'Commitment to regulatory bureaucracy', working paper, Bellcore.
Sappington, D.E.M. and Sibley, D. (1986) 'Regulatory incentive schemes using historic cost data', working paper, Bell Communications Research.
Sappington, D.E.M. and Sibley, D.S. (1988) 'Regulating without cost information: The incremental surplus subsidy scheme', *International Economic Review*, 29:297–306.
Sappington, D.E.M. and Stiglitz, J.E. (1987) 'Information and regulation', in: E.E. Bailey, ed., *Public regulation: New perspectives on institutions and policies*. Cambridge: MIT Press.
Selten, R. (1975) 'Re-examination of the perfectness concept for equilibrium points in extensive games', *International Journal of Game Theory*, 4:25–55.

Spulber, D.F. (1988) 'Bargaining and regulation with asymmetric information about demand and supply', *Journal of Economic Theory*, 44:251–268.

Stiglitz, J.E. (1975) 'Incentives, risk, and information: Notes toward a theory of hierarchy', *Bell Journal of Economics*, 6:552–579.

Tam, M.-Y.S. (1981) 'Reward structures in a planned economy: The problem of incentives and efficient allocation of resources', *Quarterly Journal of Economics*, 96:111–128.

Tirole, J. (1986a) 'Procurement and renegotiation', *Journal of Political Economy*, 94:235–259.

Tirole, J. (1986b) 'Hierarchies and bureaucracies: On the role of collusion in organizations', *Journal of Law, Economics and Organization*, 2:181–214.

Vickrey, W. (1961) 'Counterspeculation, auctions and competitive sealed tenders', *Journal of Finance*, 16:8–37.

Vogelsang, I. and Finsinger, J. (1979) 'A regulatory adjustment process for optimal pricing by multiproduct monopoly firms', *Bell Journal of Economics*, 10:157–171.

Weitzman, M.L. (1978) 'Optimal rewards for economic regulation', *American Economic Review*, 68:683–691.

Williamson, O.E. (1975) *Markets and hierarchies: Analysis and antitrust Implications*. New York: Free Press.

Williamson, O. (1983) 'Credible commitments: Using hostages to support exchange', *American Economic Review*, 83:519–540.

THE EFFECTS OF ECONOMIC REGULATION

PAUL L. JOSKOW AND NANCY L. ROSE

Massachusetts Institute of Technology

Contents

Handbook of Industrial Organization, Volume II, Edited by R. Schmalensee and R.D. Willig

1. Introduction

This chapter discusses alternative approaches to measuring the effects of "economic regulation" and reviews the empirical literature employing these approaches. By "economic regulation" we refer to both direct legislation and administrative regulation of prices and entry into specific industries or markets. We follow conventional treatment in distinguishing economic regulation from a host of other forms of government intervention in markets, including "social regulation" of environmental, health and safety practices, antitrust policy, and tax and tariff policies.

This distinction is at best a practical necessity. Regulatory activities falling in all these categories share common foundations in welfare economics and political economy, and may affect the same economic variables. Firms typically are subject to all these types of intervention, making it difficult to analyze the effects of one type of regulation in isolation from others. However, given the burgeoning literature on regulatory economics during the last fifteen years, an attempt to provide a complete survey of current knowledge on all regulatory effects could easily fill an entire volume. We therefore focus our discussion on effects of economic regulation. This enables us to restrict our attention to an extensive but reasonably well-defined subset of the literature.

Our survey is intended to provide a framework for evaluating and interpreting empirical studies of regulation, a set of guidelines for those embarking on their own empirical investigations, and a review of significant contributions to this literature. The measurement issues that we discuss arise in empirical analysis of all types of government regulation; we therefore have structured the methodological discussion so that it has broad applicability. While the present study is by no means an exhaustive survey of the literature, it includes numerous examples of the use of different types of data and measurement techniques. These are selected to cover a range of industries and time periods sufficient to give the reader a good feeling for what is known, not known, or in dispute.[1] Where particularly useful, we include references to methodological applications from the social regulation literature. Interested readers should consult Joskow and Noll

[1] Our review reflects the predominantly U.S. focus of the empirical regulation literature; we include references to international or comparative research where relevant. The theoretical and empirical techniques we discuss are broadly applicable to the study of regulation in other countries, though there has been relatively little work of this sort. A partial explanation for this is the tendency for industries that are regulated in the United States to be organized as public enterprises in other countries; see Mitchell and Kleindorfer (1979) and Finsinger (1983). We nevertheless expect major contributions from more extensive analyses of non-U.S. regulatory institutions in the future.

(1981) for a more complete survey of the literature on economic and social regulation through 1980, and refer to the other chapters in this Handbook for analyses of areas beyond the direct focus of this chapter.

The chapter is structured as follows: Section 2 outlines the theoretical bases for identifying and measuring the effects of government regulations. Section 3 develops these frameworks in more detail, discussing theoretical approaches that are of particular relevance for students of price and entry regulation. Section 4 describes four empirical methodologies for measuring the effects of economic regulation. Sections 5 through 9 examine how alternative theoretical frameworks and empirical methodologies have been applied to study the effects of price and entry regulation on each of: prices, costs, technological change, product quality, and the distribution of income and rents. The final section contains a summary and conclusions.

2. The effects of government regulation in general: What are we measuring?

The effects of regulation, whether it is "economic regulation" or "social regulation", are likely to depend on a variety of factors: the motivation for regulation, the nature of regulatory instruments and structure of the regulatory process, the industry's economic characteristics, and the legal and political environment in which regulation takes place. Given the substantial variation in these economic and institutional characteristics, the expected effects of regulation are likely to differ considerably across industries and time. Defining a theoretical framework for analyzing regulation is therefore an important prerequisite to an empirical discussion of regulatory effects. Theory and measurement go hand in hand.

Theoretical research on the economics of government regulation has proceeded from several different perspectives. At one extreme is normative or prescriptive theoretical research, which focuses on when regulation "should" be introduced and what the "optimal" form of regulation is. At the other extreme is a growing body of regulatory research that takes a positive or descriptive perspective, focusing on the economic, political, legal, and bureaucratic forces that lead to government regulation and affect the behavior and performance of regulatory institutions.

Normative research on government regulation can be (roughly) grouped into two branches. The first focuses on identification of "market failures"; that is, imperfections that lead unregulated markets to perform suboptimally relative to some social welfare function (usually the sum of consumer and producer surplus). Natural monopoly, externalities, public goods, information failures, and variations on these themes are standard normative rationales for government intervention into a market economy. The second branch of this literature seeks to develop "optimal" policies for correcting market imperfections (as discussed by Ronald

Braeutigam in Chapter 23 of this Handbook with regard to natural monopolies). Recent research on the incentive properties of different regulatory mechanisms, which explicitly models the information structure of the regulatory environment and the strategic interaction between regulators and those they regulate, has enhanced this literature (discussed by David Baron in Chapter 24 of this Handbook). These extensions recognize that even "good" regulation is imperfect, relative to an ideal in which regulators are costlessly and completely informed about all variables of interest. This helps to set the stage for sound comparative institutional analysis, in which imperfect markets can be compared with imperfect regulation: What is the best that we can do in an imperfect world [Kahn (1979)]?

Positive theories of regulation have matured considerably during the last fifteen years. Historically, positive "public interest" theories of why regulation emerges and how it works were based on normative rationales for optimal intervention [Posner (1974)]: regulators were assumed to maximize social welfare subject to various constraints. In this paradigm, empirical analysis of regulatory effects implicitly becomes both a test of whether or not regulatory institutions are successful in achieving their welfare-maximizing objectives and a basis for quantifying the costs and benefits of regulation. During the past fifteen years, economists have rejected this simplistic model of regulation in favor of richer positive theories of regulatory objectives, processes and outcomes [Stigler (1971), Posner (1974), Peltzman (1976), Wilson (1980), Kalt and Zupan (1984), Noll (1985b)]. These recognize that regulation and regulatory processes respond to complex interactions among interests groups that stand to benefit or lose from various types of government intervention. Specific positive theories of the political economy of regulation then become a possible framework within which the nature and consequences of regulation can be predicted, measured and evaluated. This literature is discussed in more detail in Chapter 22 by Roger Noll in this Handbook.

Empirical analysis of the effects of government regulation can be useful from both normative and positive perspectives. It is, however, important to articulate which framework motivates the analysis. The particular theoretical framework used to develop hypotheses about regulatory effects can have important implications for the nature of the effects one seeks to measure, the formal specification of hypothesis tests, and the collection and use of data. Most importantly, the "effects of regulation" do not mean anything in the abstract. We must ask "the effects of regulation compared to what?". The theoretical framework that leads to measurement questions generally defines (at least implicitly) what the comparative basis for measurement is. It is essential to specify these underlying assumptions about regulatory and firm behavior as well as the base for comparison. Only from this foundation can one formulate and test precise hypotheses and meaningfully interpret the results.

There are several possible benchmarks against which regulated outcomes can be compared. First, regulatory outcomes may be compared to those that would emerge if the industry performed "optimally", as defined by some welfare criterion. Since these "optimal" outcomes may not in practice be attainable, great caution must be exercised in drawing public policy implications from such comparisons.

Second, regulatory outcomes may be compared to the outcomes that would emerge in the absence of price and entry regulation (deregulation or "no regulation"). Two cautions apply to this choice of benchmark. One should not assume that the unregulated regime would be a perfectly competitive regime; many regulated industries have characteristics that make this assumption quite implausible. Moreover, it is important to define what legal institutions (common law, franchising, etc.) actually exist in the "unregulated" regime. "Unregulated" markets may in practice be markets subject to a different form of regulatory restrictions (e.g. municipal franchise regulation rather than state commission regulation), not markets subject to no regulation at all.[2]

Third, one set of regulatory institutions may be compared to some alternative set of regulatory institutions. The alternative could involve minor changes within the context of a particular regulatory process – such as introducing more incentives into cost-of-service regulation [Joskow and Schmalensee (1986)] – or more fundamental changes – such as municipal franchise bidding in place of state commission regulation [Demsetz (1968), Williamson (1976)].

If empirical evidence on the effects of regulation is to be useful for normative evaluations of regulation, it is essential that the benchmark used to measure and articulate regulatory effects be clearly defined. Similarly, tests of competing positive theories of regulation rely on measuring the actual effects of regulation, which also requires precise specification of the benchmark against which regulatory effects are being measured. Each of these benchmarks can provide useful empirical evidence for answering normative and positive questions, but only if the benchmarks are articulated clearly.

3. Alternative frameworks for evaluating the effects of economic regulation

3.1. *Efficient regulation of natural monopolies*

The traditional economic rationale for price and entry regulation is that the production of a particular good or service (or set of goods and services) is

[2] There is, in reality, no such thing as "no regulation". At the very least firms are subject to common and statutory law institutions affecting property rights, liability, and contracts.

characterized by "natural monopoly" [Schmalensee (1979)]. In this case, a single producer minimizes costs, but an unregulated market would lead to prices or costs that are on average too high and to price structures that may be inefficient. Price and entry regulation may be optimal from a normative perspective if: (a) single firm production of one or more goods minimizes costs, i.e. the production function is subadditive over the relevant output range; (b) a firm with a legal monopoly will choose average prices and profits that are too high (excess profits), and individual prices that may be too high or too low (inefficient rate structure); (c) the threat of entry will not effectively discipline a single supplier; and (perhaps) (d) inefficient entry may occur in the absence of a legal monopoly even if, or because, prices are regulated. This rationale has been used to justify price and entry regulation of electricity supply, natural gas transmission and distribution, telephone service, water and sewer service, and cable television service.[3]

In these industries, "good regulation" is supposed to: constrain entry so that the economies of single firm production can be achieved; constrain prices so that the firm earns neither excess nor insufficient profits; and regulate the structure of rates so that individual prices are efficient (at least in a second best sense). When we examine the effects of "costless", well-informed price and entry regulation in industries that are assumed to have natural monopoly characteristics, it seems natural to ask how well regulation achieves these objectives. For example, is the average level of prices constrained below what could be charged by an unregulated monopolist but above the level at which the firm would choose to exit in the long run? Do regulated firms earn normal profits? Is the regulated rate structure efficient in a second-best sense? Empirical analysis of the prices charged and costs incurred by franchised monopolies can, in principle, answer these questions.

3.2. *"Imperfect" regulation of natural monopolies in the "public interest"*

Regulators are unlikely to be perfectly informed, and regulation is unlikely to be costlessly implemented and enforced. When we expand our normative framework to recognize inherent imperfections, the set of potential regulatory effects becomes quite rich. Analysis of practical, as opposed to ideal, regulation must include explicit consideration of the incentive properties of specific regulatory rules and procedures used to set prices, the dynamics of regulation, the control instruments and information available to regulators, and the responses of regulated firms to all of these. Price regulation that sets rates based on the "cost of service" may distort firms' input choices [Averch and Johnson (1962), Baumol

[3]This line of argument could in principle be generalized to encompass markets characterized by "natural oligopoly" or imperfect competition, although there has been little academic interest in doing so.

and Klevorick (1970), Isaac (1982)], or more generally encourage X-inefficiency [Joskow and Schmalensee (1986)]. Regulation may alter the rate and direction of technological change [Capron (1971)]; distort quality choices [Spence (1975)]; change the financial risk faced by the owners of the firm [Brennan and Schwartz (1982)]; and affect the prices regulated firms pay for inputs [Hendricks (1975, 1977), Ehrenberg (1979)]. Finally, regulation is likely to redistribute income among various interested parties. These distributional effects are of particular interest to those who study the political economy of regulation.

3.3. Regulation of multi-firm industries

Natural monopoly rationales have less inherent plausibility for industries in which several firms, rather than a single franchised monopolist, are allowed to provide service. If the production of some good or service has natural monopoly characteristics, regulatory systems that permit or encourage many firms to provide service, subject to economic regulation, must have some other explanation. Regulation in many such industries has been rationalized by "excessive" or "destructive" competition in an unregulated environment (trucking, banking, airlines) or by "natural oligopoly" (railroads), but these arguments are frequently unpersuasive. Skepticism about the need for regulation based on plausible market imperfection rationales leads naturally to an investigation of the causes of regulation and its effects on prices, profits, and market structure. When competing firms operate in a regulated market, the nature of price regulation itself typically changes, and the variety of possible regulatory effects expands. Regulated prices in industries with multiple competing firms generally are based on some measure of industry average costs rather than the costs of each regulated firm [Daughety (1984)]; non-price competition must be carefully incorporated into the analysis [Joskow and Noll (1981)]. While many of the variables that can be affected by regulation are the same as those described for monopoly markets, the nature of regulatory effects may differ considerably from those that emerge when a single legal monopoly firm serves a particular market.

3.4. The political economy of regulation and its implications

While it may be of interest to compare the effects of economic regulation to the ideal "public interest" regulation, this simplistic "normative theory as positive theory" approach does not provide a sound foundation for positive theories of regulation and its effects. The introduction of price and entry regulation, as well as its structure, operation over time, and effects, reflect a complex interplay among interest groups that stand to gain or to lose from different types of regulatory intervention – not efforts to maximize the sum of consumer and producer surplus. Regulatory processes and outcomes depend on the magnitude and distribution of the costs and benefits of various regulatory interventions, the structure of the interests groups affected, prevailing economic conditions, and the nature of political, regulatory and legal institutions within which various groups pursue their self-interest. Regulatory outcomes *may* reflect "public interest" considerations, through the effects of market imperfections on interest group politics, but we cannot *assume* that this will necessarily be the case.

Viewed from this perspective, the nature and magnitudes of regulatory outcomes can be quite complex. Price and entry regulation may lead to prices that are higher or lower than what would emerge in the absence of such regulations. Rather than seeking to provide consumers with the benefits of economies of scale or scope, regulation may protect firms that are not natural monopolies from the threat of competition and lower prices. Rate structures are likely to reflect interest group politics rather than narrow efficiency criteria. New technologies may be discouraged, rather than encouraged, to protect incumbents. The distributional consequences of regulation and changes in regulation become quite important for understanding the nature of the regulatory process itself and how it changes over time. Empirical analyses of the effects of regulation on prices, costs, income distribution, and the like, become central for distinguishing between competing positive theories.

3.5. Summary

These frameworks suggest a diversity of regulatory effects as well as different motivations for and uses of empirical evidence on the impact of regulation. The specific effects of interest will depend on the theoretical model of regulation and firm behavior that characterizes the industry and regulatory process under study. Different theories of regulation will lead to different predictions about the nature and magnitude of its effects, and the nature of regulatory effects will, in turn, have important implications both for making normative judgments as to whether regulation is "good" or "bad", and for distinguishing among alternative positive theories of regulation. We will in the remaining sections focus on measuring the effects of economic regulation on the following indicia of firm and/or market behavior and performance:

(1) The average price level and the structure of prices (e.g. non-uniform and non-linear tariffs, pricing for multi-product natural monopolies).

(2) The static costs of production, including:
- (i) input distortions,
- (ii) X-inefficiency,
- (iii) direct regulatory costs, and
- (iv) input prices paid.

(3) Dynamic efficiency, including the rate and direction of innovation and productivity.

(4) Product quality and variety.

(5) Distribution of income and rents, including:

(i) profitability of regulated firms,
(ii) rent-sharing with factors of production,
(iii) income transfers among customer groups, and
(iv) income transfers among producer groups.

4. Methodologies for measuring the effects of regulation

There are four basic empirical methodologies for measuring the effects of regulation. Although these approaches are not mutually exclusive, each has particular features that may limit or enhance its value in a specific application. These features are highlighted in our discussion below. We make only limited reference to examples from the literature in this section; a broader discussion of studies employing these methods to measure various regulatory effects is deferred to Sections 5 through 9.

The four approaches we consider are:

(1) Comparing regulated and unregulated firms or markets.
(2) Using variation in the intensity of regulatory constraints.
(3) Controlled environment experiments.
(4) Structural estimation/simulation models of regulated firms or markets.

4.1. Comparing regulated and unregulated firms and markets

A simple approach to measuring the effects of regulation is to compare matched samples of "regulated" and "unregulated" firms (or markets). If the only difference between the samples is the nature of the regulatory constraints the firms are subject to, differences in behavior and performance can be attributed to regulation. This approach may rely either on cross-sectional variation, comparing similar firms operating under different regulatory structures, or on time-series variation, comparing the same firms operating under a changing regulatory environment.

The cross-sectional approach most frequently exploits variation in regulatory environments across states, although other sources of regulatory variation also have been analyzed. Differing regulatory regimes across countries [Moore (1976), Finsinger and Pauly (1986)], exclusion of intrastate firms from federal regulation [Jordan (1970)], and statutory exemptions of some firms or markets within a regulated industry may provide alternative sources of cross-sectional variation. Once variations in regulatory jurisdictions are identified, prices, costs, or other performance measures are developed; the difference in their levels between firms operating in "regulated" jurisdictions and those operating in "unregulated" jurisdictions is estimated and attributed to regulation. This type of analysis requires both reasonable variation in regulatory regimes and an ability to control for relevant non-regulatory variations across firms. Stigler and Friedland's (1962) seminal paper on regulated electricity prices in "regulated" and "unregulated" states is a classic example of this method of analysis.

The time-series, or "before-and-after", approach exploits variation in regulatory environments over time. This analysis requires identification of a time period (or periods) during which the regulatory regime changes. The behavior and performance of firms or markets before the regulatory innovation is compared to that after the innovation; the difference is interpreted as the effect of regulation. Effects typically are identified from actual responses of performance measures (prices, costs, innovations) to the introduction or elimination of regulation. This requires data prior to and after the change, and ideally would use a fairly lengthy time series to avoid basing conclusions on possible transitional responses. An alternative approach, available for identifying some, but not all, regulatory effects, is to estimate the *expected* effect of regulatory reforms on performance. This can be accomplished through the use of financial market data and "event study" techniques [see Schwert (1981), Rose (1985a), Binder (1985)].

Either a realization-based or an expectations-based time-series approach is available only when it is possible to identify distinct changes in regulatory regimes and when time-series differences in other relevant variables can be readily controlled for. Peltzman's (1973) study of the effect of FDA regulation of drug efficacy and Rose's (1985a) event study of regulatory rents in the trucking industry are examples of this type of analysis.

Both cross-sectional and time-series analyses involve a common method. First, the dependent variable of interest – such as price, cost, or the rate of technical change – must be defined, and modelled as a function of exogenous economic characteristics that influence performance independent of regulation and a control for the influence of regulation. Regulation generally is measured by a dummy variable indicating whether an observation is drawn from the "regulated" or "unregulated" regime. The effect of regulation is inferred from the sign and magnitude of the coefficient on the regulatory dummy variable.

This dummy variable approach has been used quite widely. Though in theory simple, its implementation and interpretation in practice warrant several cautions. First, it is essential that the differences between the regulatory regimes be carefully articulated. If the "regulated" regime is measured by the existence of state regulatory commissions, for example, it is important that all commissions exercise similar authority over firms' behavior (particularly with respect to price and entry). Treating commissions that have the power to set only minimum (or only maximum) rates as identical to those with authority to set actual rates introduces noise that may bias downward estimates of the difference between "regulated" and "unregulated" firms. Similarly, if firms operating in states without commission regulation are assigned to the "unregulated" sample, the interpretation of any differences in performance depends critically upon whether firms in these states are completely unregulated or controlled by some other set of restrictions. A clear specification of the alternative regulatory regimes, as well as careful inspection of the institutional structures governing firms' behavior in each, is critical to this type of empirical analysis.

Second, care should be taken in controlling for non-regulatory differences between firms or markets. The political economy literature, which develops and tests positive theories of regulation, characterizes the introduction, design, and repeal of regulation as an endogenous choice. This suggests a systematic relationship between economic conditions that affect the behavior and performance of firms and the incidence of regulation. Similarly, regulatory changes may follow upheavals in the distribution of costs and benefits, inducing systematic relationships between economic variables and the nature of the regulatory regime in time-series analyses. This argues strongly for developing a detailed model of the interaction of regulatory structures, economic characteristics of firms or markets, and the behavioral or performance measures of interest. This model should then be used to structure empirical tests of regulatory effects. To the extent that there are systematic differences in important economic characteristics of firms and markets between "regulated" and "unregulated" regimes (across jurisdictions or over time), failure to properly control for these differences may bias the measured effects of regulation.

Time-series analyses involve a third complication: determining the date at which regulatory regimes change. Regulatory statutes may directly restrict firm activity or, more typically, may establish a regulatory agency with a broad mandate to develop specific rules, regulations, and procedures. In either case, "grandfather clauses" and implementation or enforcement lags may cause the actual imposition of significant restrictions on activity to lag behind the nominal date of regulation. These difficulties are compounded for deregulation. In this case, substantial revision of regulatory structures may take place through changes in the administering agency's policies. Moreover, these changes may not occur through formal rulemakings, but may instead be signalled only by decisions in administrative cases. Recent deregulatory experience in airlines, trucking, and banking suggests that such administrative revisions may considerably pre-date congressional legislation.

Expectations-based analyses that use event study techniques must identify the date on which *expectations* about the regulatory regime change, rather than the date the regime actually changes. The effective date of legislation will be much too late for this type of analysis. In addition, it will be difficult to identify regulatory effects from most congressional activity, as congressional votes tend to be well anticipated [see the results in Binder (1985)]. Administrative reforms therefore appear more conducive to expectations-based approaches.

These difficulties with dating regime changes suggest the importance of carefully analyzing the sequence of events leading to major reforms in regulation. Reading the statute creating (or abolishing) the regulation under study, reviewing the contemporaneous trade press discussions of the regulation, and examining the administrative rules, policies, and decisions established by the regulatory agency may help to determine a meaningful date for the regulatory change.

Finally, it may be useful to combine the time-series approach with one of the others described below. In particular, the use of panel data on firms or markets can dramatically improve the power of empirical tests of regulatory effects. Rarely do we expect regulation to have the same effects on all firms at all times. By specifying the determinants of differential effects and employing both time-series and cross-sectional variation, we may obtain stronger results. For example, an industry-wide change in regulation may help some firms and hurt others, depending on their particular economic characteristics. Adding cross-sectional data on firms to the time-series analysis and modelling the regulated–unregulated dummy variable as a function of these characteristics could increase the power of statistical tests of regulatory effects [Rose (1985a), Smith, Bradley and Jarrell (1986)]. Similarly, variations in economic conditions or regulatory intensity over time could be used to add a time-series dimension to the cross-sectional dummy variable tests.

4.2. *Using variations in the intensity of regulation*

In many cases it may not be possible to obtain data on firms or markets that are subject to fundamentally different regulatory regimes. Essentially all states may regulate certain industries, so that distinct cross-sectional variation between "regulated" and "unregulated" environments simply may not exist. There may be no regulatory shock during the time period of interest that makes before-and-after comparisons feasible. In short, we may have observations only on firms and markets subject to qualitatively similar regulatory constraints. This situation clearly is not conducive to the "dummy variable" approach discussed above. Yet there may be *quantitative* differences in the regulatory constraints applied over time and space that, under particular theories of regulation and its effects, would be expected to yield differences in outcomes in one or more dimensions. These variations may arise from differences in regulatory structures or processes, or from the effects of changing economic conditions on regulation. For example, variations in the "tightness" of the rate-of-return constraint have been used, in the context of the Averch–Johnson model, to predict variations in factor input utilization [e.g. Spann (1974)] and productivity growth [Nelson and Wohar

(1983)]. Variations in regulatory resources [Norton (1985)], the structure of specific regulatory instruments and procedures (such as fuel adjustment clauses [Gollop and Karlson (1978)], and the treatment of construction work in progress), and independent ratings of the "quality" of regulatory agencies [Navarro (1982)] have been used to examine the effects of regulation on costs and market values. Variations in the nature of environmental restrictions have been used to measure the costs of environmental regulation [Gollop and Roberts (1983)].

Proper application of this approach requires a detailed understanding of variations in regulatory rules and procedures and the specification of a precise model of how these variations affect the behavioral and performance variables of interest. The cautions discussed with regard to the comparative cross-sectional and time-series approaches also apply. The informational requirements for this approach are much stronger than are the requirements for the comparative "dummy variable" approach. Care must be taken to control for differences in economic conditions that may affect measures of regulatory intensity (such as allowed rates-of-return) independently of the regulatory structure.

Interactions of regulation with changing economic conditions may, when properly modelled, provide an additional way of identifying regulatory effects [Joskow (1974), Carron and MacAvoy (1981), Hendricks (1975), Burness, Montgomery and Quirk (1980), Greene and Smiley (1984)]. In particular, certain regulatory constraints may be binding under one set of economic conditions, but not under another. Implementing this approach requires particular attention to the nature of the regulatory process under study and how it works when economic conditions change. Joskow's (1974) model of state public utility commission behavior provides an example of this approach.

4.3. Using controlled environment experiments

Data generated by actual regulatory and economic conditions may not provide sufficient experimental evidence to estimate the effects of regulation.[4] As an alternative to relying on the "natural experiments" provided by actual experience, evidence from controlled experiments is increasingly used to measure regulatory effects [Smith (1982), Plott (1982), Hausman and Wise (1985), Cox and Isaac (1986)]. These experiments are designed to generate data suitable for testing specific hypotheses about the effects of variations in institutional arrangements and public policies. Two types of experimental evidence are potentially available. Field experiments may be designed to study the behavior of real economic agents. In these, economic conditions or institutional structures are varied in

[4] This is, of course, a potential problem with all econometric work, and not specifically (or more significantly) related to efforts to estimate the effects of regulation.

systematic ways, and behavioral responses are used to quantify the effects of alternative regulatory, public policy, or market arrangements. Field experiments have been conducted to study the effects of a negative income tax, housing subsidy programs, health insurance programs, peak-load pricing [Hausman and Wise (1985)], and the deregulation of the bulk power market [Acton and Besen (1985)]. Field experiments are time-consuming and expensive. Laboratory experiments are an increasingly popular alternative. In these, human (or animal) experimental subjects participate in a set of laboratory "games", designed to provide the subjects with economic conditions that they would face under various market and institutional arrangements. Institutional details can be varied in a way that carefully controls for other causal variables. This approach is used by Hong and Plott (1982), to examine the effects of regulatory pricing rules on inland barge transportation; Rassenti and Smith (1986), to investigate the performance of unregulated wholesale electricity markets; and Cox and Isaac (1986), to evaluate the effects of incentive mechanisms applied to legal monopolies. While experimental techniques have not yet had a major impact on the study of regulation, this approach is certainly promising.

4.4. Structural/simulation models of regulated firms and markets

In all too many cases, none of the previous approaches can readily be used: there are no significant variations in regulatory regimes, in the intensity of regulatory constraints, or in economic conditions that would enable one to measure directly the effects of regulation on behavior or performance. Controlled experiments may be too expensive or complex to perform. We observe regulatory outcomes, but may not have the sample variation to compare these outcomes to a less regulated benchmark. Even when there is substantial sample variation in regulatory incidence, we may lack confidence in our ability to control for important differences that affect both performance and regulation. In these cases, structural models of behavior or performance, combined with simulation techniques, may provide a means of estimating regulatory effects.

As an example, suppose we are interested in determining whether regulatory agencies constrain the prices that franchised monopolies charge below monopoly levels, what the difference is between regulated and monopoly prices, and whether or not the rate structure is "optimal". By estimating the demand and cost functions for these firms, we can compare the average regulated price level to the costs of production to determine the relation between prices and costs. We can solve for the monopoly prices under varying assumptions about the degree of price discrimination and entry restrictions, and compare these simulated prices to the actual prices [Smiley and Greene (1983), Greene and Smiley (1984)]. Finally, we can use the system to solve for second-best non-uniform and non-linear prices, and estimate the welfare gains from more efficient pricing [Brown and Sibley (1986)]. In a similar vein, estimates of firms' production functions, combined with information on input prices, can be used to test whether regulated firms make cost-minimizing input choices.

The success of this approach depends critically upon the ability to identify and accurately estimate demand and cost functions. This task is in some ways easier for firms operating in regulated industries than for those operating in unregulated industries. Regulatory agencies frequently collect detailed firm-level information on revenue, outputs, input prices and quantities, operating costs, capital stocks, investment, and the like. These data often are available over long time periods, and tend to be comparable across firms and over time due to the agency's use of a uniform system of accounts. There are, however, a number of potential impediments.

Estimating demand functions for regulated firms or markets should present no unique difficulties. The issues involved in obtaining consistent demand estimates should be independent of regulatory status; the availability of high-quality data should make this task easier to execute in regulated markets. We are not as sanguine about cost or production function estimation. Estimates of production or cost functions from observed combinations of outputs, inputs, input prices, and costs tend to rely on a number of implicit assumptions, including equilibrium conditions and exogenous factor prices. These may be implausible for many regulated markets.

For example, the bulk of utility investments are long-lived sunk investments with putty–clay technology. Once in place, input proportions are close to fixed, implying that input proportions are likely to be unresponsive to changing input prices. Moreover, expected input prices are unlikely to be constant over time. Assuming static input price expectations, or assuming that the firm is in long-run equilibrium with respect to current input prices, as is often done, will yield unreliable results. Similarly, there is considerable evidence that regulation affects input prices [particularly wages – Hendricks (1975, 1977)] and can directly increase costs by restrictions on factor use (such as inefficient route structures imposed on regulated transportation firms). To the extent that one treats factor prices as exogenous, or fails to model explicitly direct regulatory constraints on production decisions, the resulting cost estimates may be quite misleading. This is not to discourage the use of structural estimation/simulation approaches; we find their careful application quite informative. We urge, however, careful consideration of the assumptions implicit in its implementation, and modifications to account for the peculiarities of the particular regulatory process under study where appropriate.

Although this approach generally is quite information-intensive, in some cases very simple calculations can be instructive. For example, under depreciated original cost ratemaking, the relationship between a utility's stock price and (regulatory accounting) book equity per share varies directly with the relationship between its expected return on investment and cost of capital [see Schmalensee (1986) and the references he cites]. A utility's price-to-book ratio will exceed (fall below) 1.0 if the firm is expected to earn more (less) than its cost of capital, and will equal 1.0 when the utility is expected to earn exactly its cost of capital. Given certain assumptions about earnings and dividend growth paths, the price-to-book ratio and other financial data can be used to estimate the difference between the expected return on investment and the cost of capital, and inferences can be drawn about whether prices are too high or too low and by how much [see Smiley and Greene (1983) and Greene and Smiley (1984)].[5] While this approach applies only to regulated firms subject to depreciated original cost ratemaking, analyses based on Tobin's "q" could provide similar inferences independent of the form of regulatory ratemaking [Lindenberg and Ross (1981), Salinger (1984), Smirlock, Gilligan and Marshall (1984), and Rose (1985b)].

Another simple application of structural models uses asset pricing theory. Regulation may create assets that have value only in a regulated environment, such as operating certificates for regulated trucking companies (i.e. licenses to operate in the specified market), taxicab medallions, radio and television broadcast licenses, crude oil entitlements, and state liquor licenses [Schwert (1981)]. If these assets are traded, their prices will reflect the capitalized value of expected regulatory rents accruing to the holder. Measuring asset values becomes complicated if their sale is bundled with other assets (as is the case with broadcast licenses and taxicab medallions in many jurisdictions); interpreting their value is difficult if they reflect an allocation of scarce resources (such as the broadcast spectrum) as well as regulation-imposed scarcity. These and other issues are discussed at length by Schwert (1981). Despite potential complications, regulatory assets permit a fairly clean test of profitability effects.

5. The effects of regulation on prices

There has been extensive empirical research on the effects of economic regulation on the average level and structure of prices; no simple generalization emerges from this work. Depending on the industry, type of regulation, time period, and norm for comparison, regulation has been shown to increase prices, decrease prices, distort the structure of prices in a variety of different ways, and sometimes to have no significant effect on prices at all. The implications of regulation for

[5]A price-to-book ratio greater than one does not necessarily imply that regulation is too lax. The combination of a modest wedge between prices and costs with regulatory lag may promote static and dynamic cost minimization.

prices therefore depend on the regulatory and economic characteristics of the particular industry being studied.

5.1. Franchised monopoly regulation

We first address research that focuses on "natural monopoly" industries; those for which price regulation combined with de facto franchise exclusivity has been justified on natural monopoly grounds. These include electricity, natural gas distribution and (perhaps) transmission, telephone service, and water and sewer service.[6] Despite the central role of "natural monopoly" in normative theories of regulation, surprisingly few studies have estimated the effects of regulation on the level and structure of prices charged by franchised monopolies. Existing work on price level effects has focused on electricity prices, while analyses of rate structures have covered both electricity and telephone pricing.

Stigler and Friedland (1962) provide the first systematic econometric study of the effects of state commission regulation on electricity prices. They use a comparative cross-sectional methodology to measure average electricity prices in states with state commission regulation of electricity rates relative to prices in states without such regulation, controlling for differences in production costs. The results indicate small and generally insignificant negative effects of regulation on prices, and may suggest a slight increase in the constraining effect of regulation over time. The interpretation of these results highlights two methodological issues. First, insignificant results do not imply that state-regulated prices were identical to unconstrained monopoly prices. During the time period studied by Stigler and Friedland, state commission regulation typically replaced municipal franchise regulation and established clear compensation rules in the case of municipal takeover. The "regulated" dummy variable therefore measures the difference between state regulation and municipal regulation or ownership, not "no regulation". There is little reason to expect this difference to be significantly positive.[7]

[6] These services are not always provided by private for-profit firms, particularly outside the United States. In Europe, government-owned enterprises dominate these industries. In the United States, water and sewer service is typically, but not always, provided by government agencies; municipal and cooperative distribution companies account for about 20 percent of electricity sales [Joskow and Schmalensee (1983)]; gas distribution service is sometimes provided by municipal utilities; and local telephone service is sometimes provided by cooperatives.

[7] The fact that Samuel Insull, the leading electric utility entrepreneur of the day, was a leading proponent of state commission regulation [McDonald (1962)] suggests that state regulation may have led to *higher* electricity profits. Whether this resulted from higher prices to consumers or lower payments to regulators (in the form of non-price concessions or bribes) is unclear.

Second, caution should be exercised in generalizing these findings beyond the time period they cover. In particular, the demand faced by a franchised electric utility in the 1920s and 1930s was probably much more elastic than it was in later years, and the unconstrained monopoly price much lower relative to the cost of production.[8] Alignment of "regulated" and "unregulated" prices may reflect low monopoly power as much as ineffective regulation.

Application of this approach to study contemporary effects of public utility regulation is essentially precluded by the pervasiveness of state commission regulation.[9] One natural alternative to the comparative cross-sectional approach is the structural/simulation methodology, which uses estimates of the cost and demand functions for public utility service to calculate prices under assumptions about industry structure, behavior and performance in the absence (or with a different form) of price and entry regulation. Numerous studies have estimated demand functions for electricity at different levels of aggregation [Taylor (1975), Baughman, Joskow and Kamat (1979)]; others have estimated electric utility cost functions [Christensen and Greene (1976) and the references they cite]. Contemporary estimates of the long-run demand elasticity for electricity average about unity; the short-run demand elasticity is much smaller. This suggests that prices could be profitably raised (to equate MR and MC), implying that regulation constrains electricity prices below monopoly levels.

Demand and cost information can be used to compute unconstrained monopoly prices, as well as first-best and second-best efficient prices, which can then be compared to actual regulated prices. Using this type of approach, Smiley and Greene (1983) and Greene and Smiley (1984) find that unconstrained monopoly prices for electricity are 20–50 percent higher than actual regulated prices. Baron and Taggart (1977) introduce an explicit regulatory constraint into a model of electricity production cost characteristics and electricity demand. Using firm-level data for 1970, they also find that regulation constrains electricity prices below the pure monopoly level. In contrast, Breyer and MacAvoy's (1974) application of this approach to natural gas pipelines suggests little, if any, effect of pipeline regulation on prices.

Utilities' market-to-book ratios for common equity may also provide information on regulated prices, as described in Subsection 4.4. Market-to-book ratios have varied tremendously over time and space [Greene and Smiley (1984)].

[8]Electricity use prior to the 1930s was much more discretionary than it is today. Real electricity rates were quite high; many customers, especially outside of urban areas, had no electricity service; and residential electricity use was largely restricted to lighting. Although industrial use was rapidly expanding, as late as 1925 more than half of industrial electricity consumption was accounted for by self-generation [Edison Electric Institute (1974)].

[9]Some studies have tried to exploit the remaining variation in the interstate incidence of commission regulation to estimate the effects of regulation on the costs of production [Petersen (1975)] and on systematic risk [Norton (1985)]. The idiosyncracies associated with the few states not adopting commission regulation by the 1960s make these results difficult to interpret.

Electric utility market-to-book ratios were generally far above unity in the 1950s and 1960s, fell below unity by the late 1970s, and presently are slightly above unity. There is substantial systematic variation in market-to-book ratios across utilities, at any point in time, which may be a function of firm-specific economic characteristics such as construction program size, magnitude of nominal rate increases, nuclear plant under construction, and excess capacity. These suggest substantial variances in regulatory price effects, although there have been few efforts to relate these variations to regulatory and economic conditions [see Greene and Smiley (1984)]. The endogeneity of allowed rates of return has been empirically modelled by Joskow (1972) and Hagerman and Ratchford (1978). Joskow (1972) finds that allowed rate of return decisions reflect firm financial performance and economic conditions. Hagerman and Ratchford (1978) examine the effects of both financial and political variables on agency decisions, and conclude that economic variables are of most importance in determining allowed returns. These studies highlight the time-specific character of studies of regulatory price effects: results are likely to depend critically upon the economic conditions over the sample period.

Joskow's (1974) study develops an explicit model of the link between economic conditions and regulatory price effects. His model of the behavior of state public utility commissions predicts that the nature of regulatory constraints will vary directly with prevailing economic conditions. With constant or declining nominal costs, the model predicts that regulation will be essentially non-binding. As nominal costs rise during inflationary periods, regulators attempt to minimize or delay price increases, and regulation becomes increasingly constraining. Joskow uses the predictions generated by this model to test the effects of state public utility regulation on electricity prices and electric utility financial performance during different economic regimes. Regulation seems to bind most when nominal costs are rising quickly. These results are confirmed by Greene and Smiley (1984) using more recent data.

Experimental techniques have been used in a limited way to learn more about the price effects and desirability of regulation compared to an unregulated regime. The Federal Energy Regulatory Commission recently sponsored a deregulation experiment for certain short-term wholesale electricity transactions in the southwestern United States [Acton and Besen (1985)]. The experiment did not include a control group, but relied instead on a before-and-after comparative approach. Removing regulatory restrictions appeared to have little effect on prices and quantities, although this may be a consequence of the minimal regulation currently imposed on wholesale transactions of the type covered by the experiment [Joskow and Schmalensee (1983)].

Theoretical research on efficient pricing for natural monopoly services (peak-load pricing, Ramsey pricing, non-uniform pricing, etc.) has led to considerable empirical interest in the rate *structures* established by regulators. This work focuses on both the practical implementation of efficient pricing schemes [Joskow (1976), Turvey (1968), Nelson (1964)] and evaluations of how closely regulated prices conform to these ideals.

The Department of Energy sponsored numerous field experiments during the 1970s, with varying degrees of success [Aigner (1985)]. In one of the better analyses of the experimental data, Acton and Mitchell (1980) use evidence from a Los Angeles experiment to estimate the welfare gains associated with peak-load pricing of electricity for residential customers. They find that, after accounting for the additional costs of metering, the welfare gains from time-of-day pricing are relatively small and are limited to consumers using relatively large amounts of electricity.

Experimental techniques have been used extensively to analyze electric utility rate structures. Brown and Sibley (1986) employ structural estimates of demand and cost to infer the price changes and welfare consequences associated with efficient pricing of telephone service. Mitchell, Manning and Acton (1978) use international variations in the use of peak-load pricing for electricity to identify industry responses to time-of-day pricing. They rely on differences between regulatory outcomes in the United States, where peak-load pricing was rarely used prior to the late 1970s [Joskow (1979)], and public enterprise outcomes in Europe, where extensive use was made of peak-load pricing after World War II.

5.2. *Multi-firm regulation*

Considerably more research has been devoted to estimating the price effects of economic regulation in multi-firm industries such as airlines, trucking, railroads, property/liability insurance, hospitals, natural gas and petroleum wellhead production, certain agricultural commodities, and professions subject to state licensing restrictions. Many of these industries have undergone substantial regulatory reform or deregulation since the mid-1970s. This provides a series of natural experiments for studying the effects of regulation using a time-series approach; the deregulation "shock" makes it possible to observe changes that take place when regulatory constraints on prices and entry are removed or changed in fundamental ways.

In contrast to public utility regulation, regulated prices in many of these industries – particularly airlines, trucking, railroads, natural gas, and property/liability insurance – were in principle based on average cost characteristics for groups of firms, rather than the costs of individual firms. In others, such as licensed professions, entry or supply is regulated and prices are determined by market-clearing conditions. In still others, regulators fix price, but leave supply essentially unrestricted, to be determined by market conditions. Under all these structures, regulation may not entirely eliminate competition, but may instead channel it in directions other than prices. As a result, the effects of regulation on prices may be intertwined with its effects on costs and product quality. We will, however, attempt to focus on price effects in this section, and defer most discussion of cost and quality effects to subsequent sections.

5.2.1. Airlines

In the airline industry, the Civil Aeronautics Board (CAB) set prices and restricted entry into new markets, but firms could still compete in non-price dimensions, particularly on service quality. Douglas and Miller's (1975) analysis of the effects of CAB regulation is particularly noteworthy. This study develops a useful theoretical model of regulation and applies several of the empirical approaches described in Section 4 to measure its predicted effects. Douglas and Miller's work, along with related studies by Levine (1965), Jordan (1970), Eads (1975), and Keeler (1972), shows that, on average, both regulated rates and airlines' service quality choices were too high [see also Bailey, Graham and Kaplan (1985, ch. 1)]. Douglas and Miller compare two aspects of service quality – the proximity of flights to passengers' desired departure times and the probability of being able to obtain a seat on short notice to estimates of the marginal valuation of service quality.[10] Their results indicate that airlines provided higher quality (more costly) service than consumers desired at the margin, implying that average prices were too high. Douglas and Miller also use a "regulated–unregulated" comparative approach [relying on Jordan (1970)], to compare regulated interstate fares with unregulated intrastate fares in California. They report that for comparable routes, CAB regulated fares were higher and average load factors were lower than were unregulated California fares and load factors.

Studies of airline regulation also find that fare structures deviate from efficient pricing rules. Because the CAB's fare formula was not sufficiently sensitive to the effects of market density and distance on costs, fares on longer and denser routes were too high relative to costs, and those on shorter and less densely traveled routes were too low. Regulators also discouraged or prohibited the use of peak-load prices and non-uniform rates, even where these could be justified by cost and demand conditions [Bailey, Graham and Kaplan (1985)]. The deregulation of the domestic airline industry in the late 1970s provides an excellent natural experiment for testing hypotheses about the effects of regulation. While evidence on the effects of deregulation is still being accumulated and analyzed, several recent studies shed some light on the effects of airline regulation on prices

[10] These quality measures are used directly in their simulation analysis, although their other work uses average load factors as a proxy. Average load factors are used to measure quality in most other pre-deregulation studies of airline regulation.

by comparing industry behavior and performance before and after deregulation [Graham, Kaplan and Sibley (1983), Meyer and Oster (1984), Bailey, Graham and Kaplan (1985), Call and Keeler (1985), Morrison and Winston (1986)].

Bailey, Graham and Kaplan compare observed fares to what fares would have been had the CAB fare formula continued to be used. They also compare price changes and cost changes. They find that, on average, fares increased less than did average operating costs and less than they would have under regulation [Bailey, Graham and Kaplan (1985, p. 61)]. Similar results are found by Call and Keeler (1985). Morrison and Winston (1986, pp. 22–24) compare actual 1977 fares to predictions of what 1977 fares would have been under deregulation, and conclude that deregulated coach fares would be on average 10 percent higher, while average discount fares would be 15 percent lower under deregulation.

The permanence of these price declines remains questionable, however. Prices tend to be lower relative to costs in markets that are less concentrated and in markets that are served by one or more of the low cost "no-frills" entrants [Graham, Kaplan and Sibley (1983), Call and Keeler (1985)]. Call and Keeler suggest that the post-deregulation competitive environment is characterized by strategic oligopoly behavior, not contestability. Today, many of the new entrants are no longer independent players in the market. These concentration and entry results are inconsistent with the view that the airline industry is "contestable" and suggest that the recent wave of airline merger activity might reverse the early price declines observed under deregulation.

Deregulation also increased the variance of prices across markets. Fares on long-haul routes and denser routes fell considerably relative to the fares simulated by the CAB's ratemaking formula, while fares on short-haul and less dense routes increased above the levels that would have prevailed under regulation [Bailey, Graham and Kaplan (1985, pp. 54–56)]. Routes that rely heavily on tourists, who arguably have much higher demand elasticities than do business travellers and are more flexible in their choice of departure times, exhibited especially low fares. Whether this reflects efficient peak-load pricing or price discrimination has yet to be determined.

5.2.2. Surface freight transportation

Studies of regulatory effects on prices in the surface freight transportation sector have applied a number of methodologies. Differences in regulatory structures between railroads and trucking appear to have motivated choices of different theoretical frameworks. Trucking regulation was characterized by restrictive entry policy and collectively set rates with rigid price floors; empirical research has focused on price and profit effects, and testing whether regulation cartelized the industry. Rail regulation has been associated with restrictive exit, merger, and maximum rate policies. Empirical rail research has focused on possible modal choice distortions and welfare effects of the regulated rate structure relative to optimal regulation.

The comparative approach has been used extensively in trucking studies. Snitzler and Byrne (1958, 1959) provide one of the earliest regulatory applications of the comparative time-series approach in their studies of the effect of regulation on trucking rates for certain agricultural products. They find that rates for a variety of food products fell by an average of 19–36 percent when a series of court decisions exempted their shipment from price and entry regulation. Sloss (1970) used inter-provincial differences in Canadian trucking regulation with a comparative cross-sectional approach to measure rate effects. He found that average revenue was roughly 7 percent lower in "unregulated" provinces, although the limited cross-provincial variation in regulation and the potential correlation of economic environments with regulation create some difficulties in interpreting this result. Moore (1976) found larger rate differences in his comparative study of trucking regulation in the United States and Europe, but the absence of controls for differences in economic environments may confound the results.

A second set of studies uses asset market data to measure regulatory price effects. The operating certificates required by the ICC to serve a particular market are a classic example of a regulatory asset: they have no intrinsic value apart from the value of regulatory price and entry restrictions. Therefore, significant positive values reflect regulatory rents, implying supracompetitive pricing. Breen (1977), Moore (1978), and Frew (1981) all find evidence of substantial certificate values in the trucking industry. While a number of complications limit confidence in any particular point estimate of the aggregate value of operating certificates, the results of these analyses provide strong evidence of regulatory increases in trucking rates.[11]

Trucking regulatory reforms during the late 1970s and early 1980s provide time-series variation that could be used to identify price effects. Unfortunately, there have been few systematic econometric studies of price behavior over time. Blair, Kaserman and McClave's (1986) comparative time-series study of Florida trucking rates suggests that intrastate deregulation reduced rates by roughly 14 percent. Moore (1986) reports some evidence of price declines coincident with deregulation, but does not attempt to control for changing economic conditions (particularly the 1981–82 recession). Rose (1985a) provides indirect evidence on regulatory price effects, using the variation in regulatory regimes with an event study methodology to test models of regulation. Her evidence is consistent with

[11]Only a small percentage of certificates ever trade; purchases of certificates may be tied to purchases of other firm assets; prices may reflect the value to the purchaser of improving his network configuration or system profitability, not only the excess profits on the certificated route; and certificate sales typically are bundled, with resulting prices reflecting a mixture of routes and commodities with different characteristics.

the "cartelization" view of trucking regulation, and is suggestive of deregulation-induced price declines. Consistent with earlier studies, the effects appear to be largest in the less-than-truckload sector.

Evidence on price effects of ICC rail regulation typically has been ancillary to measurement of the efficiency losses associated with modal choice and output distortions of ICC regulation. The dominant methodology combines structural estimation of cost and demand conditions with simulation techniques. These analyses highlight the importance of clearly specifying the framework within which regulatory effects are to be measured; in particular what is the alternative to current regulation. Numerous studies, because of their focus on efficient allocation of traffic, compare regulated prices to marginal cost prices [Boyer (1977), Levin (1978, 1981), Friedlaender and Spady (1981), Winston (1981), Braeutigam and Noll (1984)]. This benchmark is appropriate if one is interested in understanding deviations from first-best outcomes; however, it may not be feasible, nor is it indicative of unregulated rates. If pricing at long-run marginal cost results in losses [Friedlaender and Spady (1981), Keeler (1983)], first-best outcomes are unlikely to be attainable. This suggests second-best (Ramsey) prices as an alternative benchmark [Winston (1981)]. Since railroads are likely to possess market power in at least some markets, unregulated prices may deviate considerably from marginal cost; we therefore may consider unregulated prices as a third benchmark [Levin (1981)]. The choice depends critically upon what questions we wish to answer.

Most of these studies estimate modal choice demand functions for commodity groups, then either estimate rail and trucking cost functions (Friedlaender and Spady, Winston) or use ICC cost data [Boyer (1977), Levin (1978, 1981)]. These estimates are used to simulate rates and traffic divisions under various behavioral assumptions. Studies that compare regulated rail rates to marginal cost prices typically find that average regulated rail rates are above marginal costs [Boyer (1977), Friedlaender and Spady (1981), Levin (1978, 1981), Winston (1981), Braeutigam and Noll (1984), Keeler (1983)], although there is substantial variation across commodities. These studies find large welfare losses from existing prices relative to first-best prices: estimates center in the range of $900 million to $1.8 billion annually in 1986 dollars. [Braeutigam and Noll's (1984) critique of the methods employed in some of these studies suggests that true welfare losses may be even higher.]

Both regulated and marginal cost rates result in substantial losses for railroads. Levin (1981), for example, estimates railroad rates of return on book value or replacement cost of assets at 0.75–1.6 percent under marginal cost pricing and at roughly 2 percent under ICC regulated rates. This suggests that regulation has held average rates substantially below unregulated levels. Levin's (1981) simulation of unregulated rail rates under a variety of assumptions about rail competitiveness and regulatory cost effects confirms this. For most plausible scenarios, average rail rates would increase under deregulation, with the extent of increase most dependent on the degree of interrailroad competition. The results vary substantially across commodities, suggesting considerable regulatory distortions of the rate structure. Boyer (1981) also analyzes rate structures, by relating regulated rail and trucking rates to characteristics of shippers and shipments. He finds that many cost-based characteristics do not influence rail rates, and argues that the pattern of rates suggests a model of "equalizing discrimination", an ICC policy of equalizing conditions between "advantaged" and "disadvantaged" shippers. His analysis of trucking rates reveals patterns consistent with a cartel model of regulation.

The rail industry, like trucking, underwent substantial regulatory reform during the late 1970s and early 1980s. MacDonald (1986) uses this time-series variation to identify regulatory effects on grain transportation. He notes the difficulty of controlling for other changes taking place during this period (such as declining export demand), but argues that grain shipment rates appear to decline during the 1980s even after allowing for these effects. This is broadly consistent with the results of the earlier simulation-based studies. Friedlaender (1988) also provides an analysis of rail rates under deregulation. Further research along these lines seems desirable.

A final transportation mode – inland barge transportation – has attracted relatively little recent interest, although it has been the subject of one of the few experimental studies directly related to regulatory issues. Hong and Plott (1982) use experimental techniques to compare the properties of negotiated prices to those of a posted price system. This experiment was intended to advise the ICC in their consideration of a regulation that would require carriers on inland waterways to file proposed rate changes with the ICC at least fifteen days before they take effect. Hong and Plott's results suggest that a pre-notification policy leads to higher rates, lower volumes, and less efficiency than a policy that allows carriers to file and use new rates immediately.

5.2.3. Insurance

The effects of rate regulation on property and liability insurance premiums for personal lines (auto, residential fire, homeowners' insurance) have been studied extensively since Joskow's (1973) paper on regulation and competition in the property and liability insurance industry; see Ippolito (1979), Samprone (1979), Smallwood (1975), Walter (1979), Williams and Whitman (1973), Kunreuther, Kleindorfer and Pauly (1983), U.S. Department of Justice (1977), and see Harrington (1984) for a recent survey.[12] Much of this literature uses a comparative approach, exploiting either cross-sectional differences in regulation across

[12] There has been almost no analysis of the effects of regulation on commercial lines of insurance.

states (many states have introduced open competition laws) or time-series variation (much of the deregulation of rates took place after the mid-1970s). The studies show that the effects of rate regulation have varied widely over time and space.

Joskow's (1973) study concluded that the provision of most lines of insurance was structurally competitive, with many suppliers, easy entry and low concentration. Prior approval price regulation appeared to be a "producer protection" initiative by the insurance industry, undertaken after a 1944 Supreme Court decision ruled that the antitrust laws applied to the joint ratemaking activities of the insurance industry. (Earlier court decisions had concluded that insurance was not covered by the antitrust laws.) Joskow examined the effects of New York's introduction of an open rating system in the early 1970s, and found that it led many firms to set rates different from the "standard rates" normally filed by insurance rating bureaus and approved by regulators. He also suggested that price competition from lower cost direct writers [Cummins and Vanderhei (1979)] was partially restricted by regulation, leading to higher rates (and costs) on average. Finally, he hypothesized that non-price competition and excess demand for insurance could be a consequence of regulatory ratemaking procedures that fixed prices but not competition in other dimensions.

Harrington (1984) surveys the voluminous literature since Joskow's 1973 study. The findings of these later studies are mixed. Some discover that rates are lower in unregulated states than in regulated states; others find no effect of regulation; still others find higher rates in unregulated states. Rates charged by direct writers are almost always lower than rates charged by insurers who distribute insurance through agents, and direct writers appear to increase their market shares when pricing constraints are removed. Stringent rate regulation also has adverse supply side effects, forcing some consumers into residual markets (e.g. assigned risk pools) for insurance.

This variation is not terribly surprising, given dramatic changes in the economic conditions faced by property/liability insurance firms. It may be that during the early 1970s, before the acceleration of inflation, regulated rates were higher than competitive market levels and deregulation led to rate reductions. By the late 1970s and early 1980s, rapid inflation could easily have led to a situation in which "regulatory lag" prevented regulated rates from keeping pace with increasing costs, depressing regulated prices relative to competitive levels.[13] This variation would be consistent with the interaction between economic conditions, regulation, and regulatory lag described by Joskow (1974) in the context of electric utility regulation.

[13]Regulatory lag arises when regulators do not continuously adjust prices as cost and profits change. Some regulatory lag is a natural outcome of the administrative process; it can also reflect strategic and political motivations. Rapidly changing nominal costs increase its effects on price/cost relationships. Regulatory lag may have important effects on the incentives firms have to minimize costs and on the quality of service [Joskow and Schmalensee (1986)].

The variation in results may also arise from the inadequacy of a simple dummy variable for capturing differences in regulation across states and the difficulty of measuring prices accurately. In the insurance market, the intensity of regulation varies even among "regulated" or "unregulated" states. Some insurance commissioners have been very consumer-oriented; others have focused on protecting producers. A dummy variable cannot capture these variations. Furthermore, most of these studies approximate prices by loss ratios instead of using actual prices. With free entry and exit, however, long-run loss ratios will tend to equalize, independent of regulatory intensity. Regulatory effects will be manifested by variations in the range of available insurance products, excess demand, and differences in the quality of service. The difficulty of measuring and controlling for these non-price dimensions of insurance output contributes substantially to the wide range of results that have been obtained.

5.2.4. *Energy*

The effects of administrative regulation of field prices of natural gas have been studied extensively. Studies have examined the effects of area rate price ceiling regulation beginning in the early 1960s [MacAvoy (1962, 1971), Breyer and MacAvoy (1974), MacAvoy and Pindyck (1973), Pindyck (1974), Brown (1970), Erickson and Spann (1971)] and the effects of regulations introduced in 1978 by the Natural Gas Policy Act (NGPA) of 1978 [Broadman and Montgomery (1983), Braeutigam (1981), Braeutigam and Hubbard (1986), Kalt and Leone (1986)]. Most of this analysis uses a structural approach, drawing on econometric models of demand and econometric or engineering models of supply to compare regulated outcomes with simulated market outcomes.

There is reasonably broad agreement that the Federal Power Commission's area ratemaking approach, introduced in the early 1960s, kept field prices too low to clear the market, resulting in shortages and inefficient utilization of natural gas. The NGPA tried to correct some of the resulting distortions by instituting an incredibly complex system of field price regulations. These included: extending regulation to intrastate gas; maintaining a uniform national ceiling price at a level far below market-clearing levels; raising ceiling prices for certain supplies of "new gas"; deregulating certain categories of high cost gas; indexing ceiling prices; and phasing out price regulation in 1985 and 1987 for selected categories of gas [Braeutigam and Hubbard (1986, table 4)]. The immediate effect of the NGPA, exacerbated by the dramatic oil price increase in 1979 and 1980, was a sharp increase in prices for unregulated categories of gas. There also is evidence that price constraints led to increased non-price competition in the form of longer contracts and larger take-or-pay provisions for price controlled gas [Hubbard and Weiner (1984), Masten and Crocker (1985), Crocker and Masten (1988)]. During the early 1980s, there was substantial concern that the scheduled 1985 deregulation of certain categories of gas provided for by the NGPA would lead to a sudden increase in prices for these categories of gas, since ceiling prices were far below the Btu equivalent price for oil [Braeutigam (1981, p. 180)]. Instead, the unexpected collapse of oil prices in 1985 and 1986 left many pipelines and distributors with high-cost contracts for gas that they could not market in competition with oil.

5.2.5. Other industries

In a number of industries, supply or entry is directly regulated, but prices are determined by the interplay of demand and (constrained) supply. A prominent example of this type of regulation is agricultural marketing orders. Supply side regulations in agriculture, especially in milk marketing, have been the subject of considerable research [see MacAvoy (1977), Masson and Debrock (1980, 1982), Ippolito and Masson (1978), Shepard (1986)]. These studies tend to rely on structural estimation and simulation approaches. They find that marketing orders, which permit producers to market all output through a common agency, restrict the supply of milk or other agricultural commodities available in certain "prime" markets (e.g. class A fluid milk). This tends to raise prices in primary markets and shift substantial supplies into secondary markets (e.g. powdered milk), thereby forcing secondary market prices below competitive levels. The efficiency losses from these regulations can be quite large (Ippolito and Masson, MacAvoy).

Licensed occupations are a second sector in which regulation imposes entry and related supply-side restrictions without directly regulating price. Interest in professionals subject to state licensing requirements was stimulated by Benham's (1972) study of eyeglass prices, which found that prices were lower in states that allowed professionals to advertise than in states that restricted advertising. Kwoka (1984) finds similar effects in an analysis of advertising's impact on optometrists' prices and qualities. Cady (1976) found a similar result for prescription drugs.

State licensing laws by their very nature provide at least some restriction on entry. However, the strength of these restrictions varies across states, making it possible to measure regulatory effects from interstate variations in regulatory intensity. Shepard (1978) uses an interstate comparative approach to measure dentists' fees in states with licensing reciprocity (i.e. states that waive licensing requirements for dentists licensed in other states) relative to fees in states without reciprocity. He found that states that did not provide for reciprocal licensing (implying more restrictive entry constraints) had dental fees 12–15 percent higher than those in states with reciprocity. Conrad and Sheldon (1982) expanded this analysis to consider commercial practice restrictions on advertising, the number of offices a dentist could operate, and the number of hygienists a dentist could employ, as well as reciprocity regulations. They found that reciprocity restrictions increased fees, but did not find any systematic effects from the other types of restrictions. In contrast, Haas-Wilson (1986) finds that state commercial practice restrictions on optometrists raised quality-adjusted prices by 5–13 percent.

6. The effects of regulation on static costs of production

When regulation is less than ideal, as it necessarily is in practice, its implementation may give rise to a host of production distortions. In this section, we analyze regulatory effects on production costs, focusing on static production efficiency issues: cost-minimizing input proportions, *X*-inefficiency, and direct regulatory cost increases. The effects of regulation on dynamic efficiency (productivity growth and technical change) are covered in Section 7. We begin with a discussion of the evidence on franchised monopoly industries and then consider studies of multi-firm industries.

6.1. Franchised monopoly regulation

Most empirical research on production cost effects of franchised monopoly regulation focuses on the electric power industry. The Averch–Johnson (A–J) model [Averch and Johnson (1962), Baumol and Klevorick (1970), Bailey (1973)], in particular, has motivated a substantial amount of empirical analysis. This simple model of rate-of-return regulation yields clear empirical predictions regarding input utilization: overcapitalization when the allowed rate-of-return exceeds the utility's cost of capital. Papers by Spann (1974), Courville (1974), Petersen (1975), Atkinson and Halvorsen (1980), and Nelson and Wohar (1983), among others, have all sought to determine whether electric utilities employ inputs efficiently and whether regulation induces systematic biases in input mix. Baron and Taggart (1977) test similar regulatory effects in a model that differs from the A–J model and more carefully accounts for financial and tax considerations. Rothwell (1985) provides indirect evidence on A–J effects when he finds that utilities' technology choices are most consistent with a model of net present value (profit) maximizing behavior. These papers typically employ cross-sectional firm- or plant-level data (sometimes both and sometimes as a panel data set) and use variations in regulatory intensity to identify potential effects on production decisions. Nelson and Wohar use aggregate time-series data for the electric power industry, and Petersen also uses a comparative cross-sectional approach, estimating costs in "regulated" versus "unregulated" states.

Spann (1974), Courville (1974), and Petersen (1975) find evidence of significant overcapitalization, consistent with the predictions of the A–J model. Nelson and Wohar's (1983) results are unstable and raise questions about the model and/or the data they utilize. For most time periods their estimates imply a value for the regulatory constraint that is negative, despite the fact that the model they use requires that the value lie between zero and one. For the 1974–78 period they find a significant A–J effect, but given the implausible results for the other periods, the reliability of their specifications and data is uncertain. Baron and Taggart (1977) find undercapitalization, which is inconsistent with the A–J model. Atkinson and Halvorsen (1980) find overcapitalization with regard to the capital/labor ratio, inefficient input utilization with regard to the fuel/labor mix, but efficient input utilization with regard to the capital/fuel ratio. Since capital and fuel account for the bulk of electricity production costs, this suggests that input inefficiency due to A–J type regulatory biases is unlikely to be large. Atkinson and Halvorsen attribute this "negative" result for capital/fuel and fuel/labor to the use of automatic fuel adjustment clauses, and suggest that countervailing distortions are at work. This rationalization seems somewhat implausible, particularly in light of empirical studies of fuel adjustment mechanisms such as Gollop and Karlson (1978), discussed below.

These studies are subject to a number of potential weaknesses. First, the A–J model and other theories of regulation and its effects are theories of the *firm*, not theories of the *plant*. One must be careful using plant-level data to test firm-level theories. Plants are not built and utilized in isolation, particularly in an electric power system. Investment and utilization decisions at the plant level should be evaluated in the context of the overall optimization problem for the firm. Second, we have serious reservations about basing production efficiency conclusions on what are essentially ex post cost functions, particularly when long-lived sunk investments are important, input prices are uncertain and change over time, technological change in generating technology is taking place [Joskow and Rose (1985a, 1985b)], and plant efficiency varies over time [Joskow and Schmalensee (1985)]. Investment decisions should be evaluated by the expected present discounted value of available alternatives at the time the investments are made, not after the fact. The proper way to evaluate fuel and labor utilization decisions ex post is to take the capital stock as given. Except for Baron and Taggart, the literature exhibits little sensitivity to these considerations.

Finally, contemporary analyses of electric utility regulation that rely on comparisons between regulated and unregulated states may have serious identification problems. Few states had not introduced commission regulation by 1970, and these may have atypical characteristics that make it difficult to identify specific regulatory effects. Petersen's comparison of costs between regulated and unregulated states, for example, is quite sensitive to the fact that seven of his nine "unregulated" plants are gas-burning plants located in Texas [McKay (1976)]. These had very low costs during the 1970s, reflecting both locational advantages and the availability of intrastate gas. Attributing to the presence or absence of regulation the cost differences between these plants and coal or oil plants located elsewhere is implausible. We are inclined to agree with McKay's (1976) conclusion that the results of these studies are unreliable.

Despite increasing theoretical interest in incentive effects of regulation [see, for example, Baron and Besanko (1984), Shleifer (1985), Laffont and Tirole (1986) and the studies cited in Chapter 24 by Baron in this Handbook], empirical work in this area is sparse. Much of this literature is based on the recognition that pure cost-plus regulation eliminates firms' incentives to minimize costs or improve efficiency. While few regulatory processes are in fact purely cost-plus, there has been little analysis either of how close existing regulatory procedures are to such a system, or of the extent to which incentive-dampening effects of regulation induce higher costs. Gollop and Karlson (1978) examine the effects of automatic fuel adjustment mechanisms (FAM), and find little evidence of FAM-induced input biases. They do find some FAM-induced X-inefficiency, consistent with predictions of the theoretical models. Joskow and Schmalensee (1986) argue that two features of standard public utility ratemaking – investment prudency reviews and regulatory lag – distinguish regulation from a pure cost-plus contract. The design and adoption of explicit incentive policies, while increasing during recent years, has been somewhat arbitrary, and the effects of these policies are uncertain. As Joskow and Schmalensee point out, many of these schemes may introduce new distortions of firm behavior.

Regulation may also raise firms' costs by increasing financial risk and the cost of capital. The nature of the regulatory process will affect the systematic risk faced by regulated firms and therefore their cost of capital [Brennan and Schwartz (1982)]. These effects may vary with economic conditions if regulatory constraints interact asymmetrically with variations in economic activity. Unfortunately, the likely dependence of the cost-of-capital on specific features of the regulatory process has not been generally recognized by regulatory agencies. This may be a serious problem as regulators consider changes in regulatory rules and procedures that reallocate risk between firms and consumers [Joskow and Schmalensee (1986)]. For example, Clarke (1980) analyzes the effects of fuel adjustment mechanisms on systematic risk, using firm level financial data and a comparative time-series approach. He finds that FAMs reduce regulated utilities' systematic risk, but have little if any independent effect on risk-adjusted stock market values.

Norton (1985) analyzes risk effects of regulation for a sample of electric utilities operating in "strongly regulated", "weakly regulated", and "unregulated" states. He compares "betas" (from a Capital Asset Pricing Model of returns), and concludes that regulation reduces systematic risk. Norton's distinction between "strongly regulated" and "weakly regulated" states is based on differences in the resources devoted to regulation; unregulated firms are in states without commission regulation. This methodology raises two concerns. First, using regulatory "inputs" to distinguish the intensity of regulation across states is arbitrary; characterizing the regulatory environment by its effects seems preferable [Hendricks (1975), Joskow (1974)]. Second, failing to control for differences in economic characteristics across utilities, particularly with respect to cyclical sensitivity of demand, may bias the results. In particular, utilities that depend on cyclical industries (such as steel, coal, and iron mining) for a large fraction of their revenues are likely to have different risk characteristics than will utilities serving largely residential, commercial, and less cyclical industrial loads. Norton's six "unregulated" utilities, located in Minnesota and Texas, may be unusually risky, given their dependence on the highly cyclical iron ore and petrochemical industries.[14]

Despite theoretical interest in franchise bidding as an alternative to traditional commission regulation [Demsetz (1968), Williamson (1976)], there has been relatively little empirical analysis of the consequences of using municipal franchising in place of commission regulation. Williamson's (1976) case study of a cable TV (CATV) franchise illuminates some problems that arise in municipal franchising.[15] Shew (1984) compares the costs of CATV franchising requirements with subscriber benefits and concludes that the franchising process has led to a significant amount of wasteful expenditures. These arise as municipal authorities force potential franchisees to compete over the services they provide to the municipality, rather than on the basis of product price and quality. Rather than yielding optimal prices, municipal franchise bidding results in excessive expenditures on cable facilities that are valued highly by local politicians, but are of lower value to consumers.

6.2. Multi-firm regulation

Many studies examine the cost effects of economic regulation in multi-firm industries. Joskow (1981), Sloan and Steinwald (1980), Sloan (1981) and Melnick, Wheeler and Feldstein (1981) use an interstate comparative approach to evaluate the effects of rate regulation and/or certificate of need (entry) regulation on hospital costs. They generally conclude that rate regulation tends to reduce costs, but that certificate-of-need (entry) regulation does not.

Pre-deregulation studies of airline costs focused primarily on the consequences of quality competition (low load factors), and secondarily on the costs of

[14]In 1983, revenues from large industrial customers accounted for 50 percent of investor-owned utility (IOU) revenues in Minnesota, 36 percent in Texas, but only 28 percent for the United States as a whole [Edison Electric Institute (1983, p. 67)].

[15]Research by Prager (1986) and Zupan (1987) suggests that the contractual problems Williamson identifies have not been very serious in practice, except perhaps in large urban areas franchised since 1980.

inefficient service to small communities and the effects of regulation on labor costs. Comparative time-series analyses including post-deregulation cost data suggest that other regulatory inefficiencies may have been much larger. There have been dramatic changes in airline route structures (hubbing), aircraft utilization, and labor productivity since deregulation [Bailey, Graham and Kaplan (1985, chs. 4, 5 and 8), Morrison and Winston (1986)]. These changes are convincingly attributed to airlines' ability to optimize their routes free from CAB certification restrictions, as well as to competition. More work remains to be done in this area.

Cost effects of ICC regulation of surface freight transportation received considerable attention in the regulation era. Regulatory route restrictions led to considerable inefficiency in the trucking industry. Private carriers and exempt agricultural carriers inherently tend to have unbalanced loads, and regulations that prohibited them from hauling regulated commodities on their return trips made empty backhauls a severe problem [MacAvoy and Snow (1977, pp. 25–26)]. Route and commodity restrictions on regulated carriers (including many one-way authorities) increased their level of empty backhauls and partial loads relative to the unconstrained level; circuitous route authorities and gateway restrictions (which prohibited carriers from travelling via the most direct route) increased route mileage.

Despite widespread agreement on these qualitative effects of regulation, few studies attempt to quantify them. Moore (1975) estimates that unregulated carriers' costs would decrease by $3.2 billion (in 1986 dollars) if their empty backhaul level were reduced to that of regulated carriers. Moore infers cost effects for regulated carriers indirectly, based on assumptions about regulatory price effects and calculations of rents to capital and labor. Combining Moore's (1978) assumptions with a more plausible 10 percent discount rate to translate firms' rents into annual terms implies cost inflation of 8–11 percent of revenues, or roughly $4.5 billion annually in 1986 dollars.[16] These calculations could now be refined using data on deregulated system operations; we await such a study.

Investigations of regulatory cost increases in rail transportation have focused on two areas. The first area is ICC restrictions on route abandonments, which require railroads to maintain service on lightly travelled, unprofitable routes, and result in excessively large systems (from a cost-minimizing standpoint). Friedlaender and Spady (1981) analyze this issue in a structural model of railroad and trucking cost functions and transportation demand functions. Using partial equilibrium analysis, they find that a 10 percent reduction in low-density track would reduce costs by $1.1 billion in 1986 dollars (p. 134; see, however, the caveats on p. 142). Keeler (1983) summarizes various authors' estimates of the

[16] Moore's (1978) own calculations assume an after-tax discount rate of 35 percent (70 percent pre-tax).

total cost of excessive route mileage at $900 million to $1.8 billion in 1986 dollars.

A second major regulatory cost arises from inefficient freight car utilization. Studies typically conclude that the ICC set car rental rates (the rates that railroads pay for using other railroads' boxcars on their system and that shippers pay for keeping cars on their sidings) below their opportunity cost, resulting in too little investment in freight cars and suboptimal utilization rates. To counteract some of these effects, the American Association of Railroads established rules requiring cars to be returned via the most direct routing – which also contribute to inefficient utilization. Estimated annual costs of these inefficiencies range from $2.7 to $3.1 billion in 1986 dollars [Keeler (1983)].

Essentially all the empirical approaches discussed above also have been used to measure the effects of environmental, health, and safety regulations on production costs. Perl and Dunbar (1982), for example, use a simulation approach to estimate the effects of the New Source Performance Standards on the cost of producing electricity. Gollop and Roberts (1983) exploit variations across states in the intensity of environmental constraints on electric generating plants to estimate the costs of sulfur emissions constraints. Joskow and Rose (1985a, 1985b) make use of variations over time and space in power plant emissions scrubbing requirements, as well as variations in intensity of scrubbing, to estimate the costs of scrubbers. The general approaches to estimating the effects of regulation on costs can be applied quite widely to analyze the effects of "social" regulation as well as "economic" regulation.

7. The effects of regulation on innovation and productivity growth

Technological change and innovation has played a central role in increasing real incomes in the United States over time. Several heavily regulated industries have exhibited unusually high rates of productivity growth over long historical periods. These include the electric power industry until 1970 [Joskow and Rose (1985a, 1985b) and Joskow (1987)], the telecommunications industry, the airline industry, and the trucking industry. Others, for example railroads, have poorer productivity records [when correctly measured; see Caves, Christensen and Swanson (1981b)]. There are a number of channels through which price and entry regulation might affect incentives to innovate. Price regulation could change the pattern of expected returns to innovation. Shifting competition from price to non-price dimensions could increase incentives for rapid adoption of product innovations. Restrictions on entry and approval of rates for new services could delay the introduction and slow the diffusion of product, service and process innovations – both directly and indirectly, by raising the costs of introduction and diffusion and reducing the present value of net revenues associated with the innovation [Braeutigam (1979)]. In spite of this, surprisingly little empirical research has been devoted to quantifying the effects of price and entry regulation on innovation and productivity growth.

The existing evidence on the effects of economic regulation on innovation includes anecdotes, case studies, and a few systematic econometric studies. Gellman (1971) documents several examples of how the Interstate Commerce Commission's rate policies delayed the introduction of piggyback rail cars and the "Big John" rail car in the late 1950s and early 1960s. MacAvoy and Sloss (1967) argue persuasively that the adoption of the unit train was delayed considerably by ICC commodity rate restrictions. These conclusions are reinforced by the rapid increase in piggyback rail carriage, multiple car and unit trains after ICC deregulation in the mid- to late-1970s [MacDonald (1986)].

Phillips (1971) argues that CAB regulation of the airlines did not retard innovation, and there is casual evidence to suggest that CAB ratemaking policies encouraged rapid diffusion of larger, faster aircraft. Bailey, Graham and Kaplan (1985) document significant gains in airline productivity after deregulation, but these gains cannot be attributed specifically to an increased rate of technological innovation. Shepherd (1971) hypothesizes that regulation retarded innovation in telecommunications in a variety of different ways, but provides little empirical support for these hypotheses.

A few industry-specific econometric studies have tried to measure regulatory effects on productivity growth and innovation. Nelson and Wohar analyze productivity growth in the electric power industry using an A–J type of model and exploiting variations in the intensity of regulation. They find that regulation had both positive and negative effects on productivity growth, depending on the time period examined. Given the problems they have identifying a meaningful regulatory effect, however, these results should be interpreted cautiously. Joskow (1981) finds that rate and certificate-of-need regulation of hospitals slowed the diffusion of CT scans, and pushed them out of hospitals into physicians' offices [see also Russell (1979)]. Caves et al. (1981a) find that productivity growth in the regulated U.S. railroad industry lagged substantially behind that in the unregulated Canadian railroad industry. During the 1956–1963 period, Canadian railroads averaged 1.7 percent productivity growth, versus 0.6 percent for U.S. railroads. Over 1963–1974, the differences were even more striking, at 4.0 percent versus 0.1 percent. They attribute these differences to the U.S. regulatory environment.

There has been considerably more interest in measuring the effects of environmental, health, and safety regulation on productivity growth and innovation. Peltzman (1973) uses a comparative time-series approach and a simulation approach to measure the effects on new drug introductions of the 1962 amendments tightening the FDA's regulation of the safety and efficacy of prescription drugs. He finds that the costs of reduced innovation, as measured by the reduction in the number of new drugs introduced, greatly exceeds savings from avoiding ineffective drugs; total costs, including the cost of reduced competition, are estimated at 5–10 percent of the annual $5 billion expended on drugs. Wiggins (1981, 1983) presents a related and updated analysis that disaggregates drugs into therapeutic categories [see also Grabowski and Vernon (1983) and Temin (1980)]. He finds that FDA regulations significantly reduced new drug introductions during the 1970s [Wiggins (1981)], and reduced company expenditures on research [Wiggins (1983)].

Christainsen and Haveman (1981) use crude measures of variations in the intensity of federal regulation over time to measure the aggregate effects of "public regulation" on productivity growth. They find that increased regulatory constraints are responsible for about 15 percent of the slowdown in productivity growth in manufacturing between 1973 and 1977 [see also Crandall (1981), Denison (1979), and Siegel (1979)]. The crude measures of regulation used and the almost perfect correlation between increases in regulatory intensity and other economic shocks over time (e.g. energy price increases, inflation, stagnant economic growth, import competition) limit the confidence one can place in these point estimates and suggest the desirability of further, more sophisticated analyses.

It is distressing that so little effort has been devoted to measuring the effects of regulation on innovation and productivity growth. Much of what we do know is now quite dated. The static gains and losses from regulation are probably small compared to the historical gains in welfare resulting from innovation and productivity growth. Further research on what, if any, effect regulation has on the dynamics of productivity growth and the development of new goods and services therefore seems essential.

8. The effects of regulation on product quality

Empirical analyses of regulatory effects on product quality have been fairly limited. The most intensively studied regulation–quality interaction has been in the airline industry, perhaps because we have a good theoretical model of the relationship between quality, price regulation, and the number of competing firms. Following Douglas and Miller (1975) [see also Schmalensee (1977)], the "quality" of airline service is measured by both the frequency of departures (the more departures, the more likely will there be a flight close to a passenger's preferred departure time) and the probability of finding an available seat on the flight closest to the passenger's preferred departure time. Empirical applications usually summarize both dimensions of quality by the average load factor, that is, total passengers divided by seats available on a route (load factors also may capture a third dimension of quality: expected crowding on a flight). Douglas and Miller (1975, chs. 2 and 6) also perform a more sophisticated stochastic simulation involving departures, flight size, and passenger valuations of time.

Most studies [see Douglas and Miller (1975), Keeler (1972), Eads (1975), Graham, Kaplan and Sibley (1983), Bailey, Graham and Kaplan (1985)] find that price regulation induces non-price service competition, yielding equilibria that on average give passengers too much quality; that is, given consumer valuations of service quality, flights are too frequent, load factors are on average too low, and costs are too high. Furthermore, the price/quality relationship depends on the number of competing firms on each route. Routes with large numbers of firms have very low load factors, as service quality competition drives average cost per passenger up to (or above) average revenue per passenger. In monopoly markets, nonprice competition does not occur, so passengers pay relatively high fares and get relatively low quality. In their empirical work, Douglas and Miller show that average load factors vary inversely with the number of airlines certificated to serve a particular route, as predicted by their theory of price-constrained competition. Despite the fact that entry was restricted, the industry did not appear to earn sustained excess profits, or even reasonably stable profits during the regulated era [Douglas and Miller (1975, p. 18), Bailey, Graham, and Kaplan (1985, pp. 23–26)]. Non-price competition, and perhaps supracompetitive labor costs resulting in part from regulation (discussed in Section 9), appear to have ensured that high airline prices did not lead to excess returns for the owners of airline firms.

Deregulation of the airline industry in 1978 provides data for a comparative time-series analysis of service quality. Graham, Kaplan and Sibley compare load factors after deregulation with those observed before deregulation. They find that load factors increased (as expected); based on the traditional models of airline regulation, this should reduce average service quality. However, increased use of peak-load pricing and withholding of high fare seats in anticipation of late reservations mitigated this apparent decline in service quality for time-sensitive passengers. Using a simulation approach, Bailey, Graham and Kaplan also show that convenience did not decrease appreciably after deregulation, despite the increase in average load factors. Morrison and Winston (1986) find that travel time fell in smaller markets and increased in larger markets (for an average increase of 5 percent), while flight frequencies increased in almost all sizes of markets (by 9 percent on average). They conclude that net service quality has improved with deregulation, as has aggregate consumer welfare. Increasing load factors, and hub-and-spoke networks, along with many other supply side changes after deregulation, also have helped to reduce the cost per passenger-mile by increasing productivity.

There is anecdotal evidence to suggest that trucking regulation had adverse effects on product variety, by foreclosing quality-varying rates. Shippers complained that they were disadvantaged by their inability to obtain low rate/low quality or high rate/high quality service [see MacAvoy and Snow (1977, pp. 10–14)]. We are aware of no studies that attempt to quantify these effects.

Joskow (1980) uses a cross-sectional interstate comparative approach to measure the effects of rate and certificate-of-need regulation on the service quality of hospitals. Hospital quality is inversely indexed by the probability that a patient will be turned away because the hospital is full. Joskow argues that the characteristics of hospital insurance and provider reimbursement systems in the 1970s gave hospitals incentives to engage in quality competition. He finds that hospitals located in states that regulated rates and entry had lower service quality than those in states that did not impose such regulations.

Munch and Smallwood (1980) examine the effects of a variety of regulations on the solvency of property/liability insurance firms, using an interstate comparative approach. Solvency is a quality attribute because policyholders prefer to be insured by a company that will be able to pay off if a loss is incurred. Munch and Smallwood find that the probability of insolvency is reduced by state regulations that impose minimal capital requirements on insurers. This reduction is accomplished by making entry at small scale more costly, thereby reducing the number of small entrants. They also find that firms operating in states with rate regulation have a lower probability of insolvency, but that the difference between states with prior approval regulation and those without it is not statistically significant. Frech and Samprone (1980) attempt to estimate the welfare consequences of non-price competition in regulated property insurance markets, but their method for quantifying the regulatory-induced increase in non-price competition leaves much to be desired.

Finally, we note that regulatory agencies have sometimes claimed that regulated electric, gas and telephone utilities systematically build systems with excessively high reliability (quality); in some recent cases, agencies have disallowed cost recovery on plant and equipment deemed to be in excess of "prudent" reserve requirements. Using the model developed by Joskow (1974), Carron and MacAvoy (1981) argue that regulatory quality effects are exactly the opposite. They expect high service quality during periods of increasing productivity and stable prices, when regulatory constraints do not bind. As inflation increases nominal costs and regulators resist price increases, firms reduce their capital investment and therefore their service quality. Carron and MacAvoy (1981, pp. 48–53) cite declining reserve capacities, increasing delays, and increasing equipment problems during the 1970s in support of their argument. While Carron and MacAvoy's argument is intuitively appealing, the evidence they present is incomplete and not entirely convincing. The quality effects of natural monopoly regulation remain uncertain.

9. The distributional effects of regulation and deregulation

Distributional consequences of regulation play a fundamental role in explaining the incidence of regulation and regulatory change, according to modern political economy theories. Alternative regulatory arrangements (including what is popularly called "deregulation") generally imply different distributions of benefits and costs. These distributional effects drive the competition of various interest groups, which in turn determines the nature of regulation through the political process.

Until recently, information on the distributional consequences of regulation was primarily a byproduct of the studies of regulatory price, cost, and quality effects that we have already discussed. In some sense, this is not terribly surprising. Most regulatory research draws on neoclassical economic theories, which focus on economic efficiency. Furthermore, tracing through the ultimate incidence of changes in prices and costs is often quite difficult. Identifying "first-order" winners and losers from regulation and measuring the magnitudes of these effects is, however, practicable; this is the focus of a growing segment of the regulation literature.

A number of authors have analyzed distributional effects of regulation in the context of implicit or explicit tests of political economy models of regulation. Kalt (1981) measures the winners and losers from 1970s petroleum price regulations by comparing the outcomes of regulation with the simulated outcomes in the absence of price regulation. These results are then used to analyze Congressional voting behavior. Kalt finds that both constituents' economic interests and measures of congressmen's ideology are important explanators of votes. A similar approach is used to study the 1977 Surface Mining Control and Reclamation Act (SMCRA) by Kalt (1983a) and Kalt and Zupan (1984). Kalt and Leone (1986) use a simulation approach to examine the effects on regional incomes of deregulation of natural gas prices. Olson and Trapani (1981) attempt to measure the effects of CAB regulation of airlines using a simulation approach that compares regulatory outcomes with various norms. They argue that consumers lost from regulation, aircraft manufacturers benefited, and airlines benefited during some time periods. These issues also have been analyzed for various "social regulations"; see Pashigian (1985) and Oster (1982), for example.

Rather than restrict attention to these tests of political economy models of regulation, we discuss a broad range of evidence on the distributional effects of regulation. We consider four types of regulatory redistributions: transfers to the owners of regulated firms (profits), transfers to factors of production such as labor ("rent-sharing"), transfers among consumer groups, and transfers among producers. Empirical studies of these effects tend to focus on regulated multi-firm industries; evidence from franchised monopoly regulation is discussed where available.

9.1. Profits

Positive theories of regulation predict that regulated firms should, at least in some cases, gain from regulation. This is particularly true where members of the industry were strong advocates of regulatory intervention. As might be expected from the diversity of regulatory price effects, profit effects vary considerably across regulated industries.

A variety of approaches have been used to measure profitability effects. As discussed in Section 3, market values of regulatory assets can provide one of the cleanest tests of regulatory effects on profits. Kitch, Isaacson and Kasper (1971) provide one of the earliest applications of this approach in their study of Chicago taxicab regulation. They use taxicab medallion prices to estimate regulatory rents of $115 million (1986 dollars). Although this approach could be applied to estimate differences in taxicab regulation across municipalities, there has been little additional work in the area. This method has, however, been applied extensively to analyze trucking regulation. Moore's (1978) sample of 23 certificate sales suggests that certificate values are roughly 15 percent of gross revenues. Applying this to aggregate industry revenues in 1972 yields a present discounted value of rents of $5.5 to $7.9 billion in 1986 dollars. Breen's (1977) study of household goods carries operating certificates and Frew's (1981) study of common carrier certificate values also find evidence of substantial certificate values. The sharp decline in certificate values around the period of trucking deregulation confirms the interpretation of certificate values as regulatory rents [Moore (1986), Mabley and Strack (1982)].

A second type of asset market approach, the event study technique, relies on changes in the regulatory environment to analyze regulatory effects. Rose (1985a) uses this approach to analyze the effects of ICC administrative reforms and congressional deregulation on the trucking industry. She finds substantial share price responses to deregulation, with market values of publicly traded general freight carriers declining by 15–19 percent and those of specialized commodity carriers declining by 9 percent. These correspond to a decline of $925 million (1986 dollars) in capitalized rents for the 32 firms in her study, or about 8.8 percent of 1978 gross revenues. Applying the sample rent/revenue ratio to aggregate revenues suggests that the present discounted value of rents earned by the 345 Class I general freight carriers in 1978 was $2.6 billion in 1986 dollars [Rose (1987)].

Levin (1981) uses a structural estimation/simulation approach to estimate regulatory effects on railroad profitability. Although the precise magnitude of effects depends on which competitive scenario is selected, he finds substantial increases in profitability under all but the marginal cost pricing cases. Net income under regulation was $570 million in 1986 dollars, or a 2 percent rate of return on replacement cost of assets. Under moderate competition and deregulation, estimated net income was $3.4 to $11.3 billion (1986 dollars). This suggests substantial transfers *away* from capital under railroad regulation.

Results for the airline industry are mixed. Few studies during the regulatory era specifically address the question of regulatory profits. A number of authors argue that higher prices raised service quality, raising costs and preventing high prices from translating into high profits. While this may indicate that regulatory price policies failed to increase rates of return, regulatory entry policies may have nevertheless raised profits above normal levels [see Schmalensee (1977)]. Indirect support for this view is found in the strong opposition of most trunk carriers to airline deregulation [Kahn (1983)]. Opposite results are found by Morrison and Winston (1986), who find that simulated deregulated profits would have been higher than were 1977 regulated profits. They argue that observed declines in airline profitability in the early 1980s were largely the result of fuel price shocks and macroeconomic conditions, not deregulation.

Natural gas and petroleum price regulations, while not themselves creating rents, have generated enormous rent transfers to and from various interest groups. For example, Kalt (1981) estimates that crude oil price controls reduced the incomes of producers by \$19 to \$65 billion annually (in 1986 dollars) over 1975–1980, and increased the income of refiners by roughly 60 percent of this amount over the period. Smith, Bradley and Jarrell (1986) use an event study technique to estimate refiner gains from the early Crude Oil Allocation Program adopted in response to OPEC's 1973 price increases; their results indicate substantial refiner gains.

9.2. Factor rent-sharing

Many formal models of the effects of regulation and most studies of regulatory effects on prices assume that factor prices are independent of the regulatory environment. This assumption may be invalid for many regulated industries. Regulation may transfer rents to other factors of production, even when capital earns normal returns. Empirical analyses of the effects of economic regulation on factor returns (other than capital) have focused almost exclusively on labor. There are several channels through which the regulatory process may alter the relative bargaining positions of regulated firms and workers. First, to the extent that the regulatory process allows wage increases to be quickly and completely passed through by higher prices, a firm's incentives to be a tough bargainer are diminished, and higher wage settlements may result [Hendricks (1975), Ehrenberg (1979)]. Some forms of price regulation – such as the operating ratio constraint used by the Interstate Commerce Commission to evaluate trucking rates – may reduce the shadow cost of labor, perhaps exacerbating this tendency [see Daughety (1984), Moore (1978)]. We also note that gains by unionized employees may be realized, at least in part, by non-union workers as well. The labor economics literature suggests that union "threat effects", among other factors, tend to raise non-union wages in industries with large union gains [see Lewis (1963, 1986)].

Second, entry restrictions can create a situation in which suppliers that are shut down by a strike cannot be replaced by rival suppliers, because the alternative suppliers are not authorized to provide services in the "struck" markets. This has conflicting effects on the distribution of bargaining power. On the one hand, it may increase union bargaining power by increasing the disruption caused by strikes and the consequent public pressures to settle them [Bailey, Graham and Kaplan (1985, pp. 96–97)]. On the other hand, eliminating the ability of potential competitors to take over a firm's customers during a strike is likely to reduce strike costs to the firm, other things equal, by eliminating post-strike customer defections. This tends to increase the firm's bargaining power vis-à-vis the union.

Third, to the extent that regulation restricts entry, it may be easier to organize a regulated industry and easier to sustain high wages without the threat of entry by lower cost non-union suppliers. Some authors have suggested that entry regulation may enable a union to cartelize an industry and realize monopoly profits for its members [Arnold (1970), Annable (1973)].

Finally, regulation may introduce political considerations into input choice decisions. This will apply to non-labor inputs as well as labor inputs. For example, utilities may be subject to political pressures to buy local products (e.g. coal), rather than cheaper substitutes from suppliers in other states, to bolster the local economy. Depending on the state, they might also come under pressure to use unionized employees when they otherwise might not, or to sign lavish wage agreements [Ehrenberg (1979)].

A number of studies have investigated the effects of regulation on wages. Hendricks (1975) examines wage settlements by electric utilities in the context of three different models of the regulatory process, using an interstate comparative approach. He finds that regulated firms' bargaining incentives and wage settlements depend on the nature of the regulatory constraint they face. Firms operating under a non-binding rate-of-return restraint (due to regulatory lag or benign neglect) are more aggressive bargainers than are firms that expect the regulatory agency immediately to adjust rates to pass through higher wages. As a consequence, wages are lower for utilities that expect to bear increased costs themselves, and higher for utilities that expect regulators to flow through cost increases.

While Hendricks (1975) focuses on differential wage *patterns* within a regulated industry, most subsequent empirical work attempts to measure regulatory effects on average wage *levels*. The evidence on this question is mixed. Hendricks (1977) investigates the distribution of wages for workers across fourteen regulated industries and the unregulated manufacturing sector, using micro-data on individual workers to estimate a conventional human capital earnings equation with controls for occupation, industry concentration, and regulation. For most occupations and most regulated industries, regulation appears to have zero or negative effects on average wage levels. The dominant exceptions are truck drivers in the trucking industry, electricians in radio and television, and possibly certain airline occupational categories; these groups are associated with higher wage levels than in manufacturing as a whole. Carrol and Ciscel's (1982) inter-industry study of executive compensation concludes that executive compensation is significantly lower in regulated industries (utilities and transportation) than in unregulated industries. This work suggests that regulatory wage gains may be limited to certain industries, and may be stronger for workers in certain key occupations (such as drivers in the trucking industry).

A number of other studies explore wages within a particular regulated industry. Ehrenberg's (1979) detailed empirical analysis of New York Telephone Company worker salaries suggests that New York Telephone paid higher wages to many categories of workers. Hendricks (1975, 1977), on the other hand, finds that average levels in the electric utility industry are below those for comparable workers in unregulated sectors. Substantial empirical effort has been focused on wage levels in regulated transportation industries. The relationship between pilots and regulated airlines has been studied extensively [Baitsell (1966), Kahn (1971), Pulsifer et al. (1975)]. The pilots' union has been successful in negotiating extremely attractive wage and work rule arrangements, which appear to have been at least partially a consequence of regulation [Bailey, Graham and Kaplan (1985, pp. 139–147)]. Hendricks, Feuille and Szerszen (1980) use micro data on individual workers and data on characteristics of collective bargaining agreements to investigate the extent of regulated airline workers' gains relative to a manufacturing benchmark. They find that airline workers across a wide variety of occupations have higher mean wages than their manufacturing counterparts, even after controlling for worker quality (see also Bailey, Graham and Kaplan, p. 18). This differential appears to be associated primarily (but not exclusively) with the high levels of unionization and concentration in the airline industry, which may themselves be functions of regulation. Industry responses to deregulation confirm positive regulatory wage effects. Cappelli (1985) reports that virtually all airlines obtained some form of union concessions after deregulation, with concessions concentrated among pilots. Mechanics, whose skills are easily transferable in and out of the airline industry, were least affected by concessions [see also Card (1986)].

Similar analyses have been performed for the trucking industry. Moore (1978) uses a variety of aggregate earnings data and micro data wage equations to estimate union rent-sharing in the regulated trucking industry. Using a 50 percent union wage premium, he calculates Teamster rents from regulation at \$2.6 to \$3.4 billion (in 1986 dollars). There are a variety of problems with inferences based on these simple calculations. In particular, unionized workers in most industries earn higher wages than comparable non-union workers; to attribute the entire union wage premium to regulatory rents requires an explanation for this more pervasive phenomenon. There also are a variety of reasons why cross-sectional estimates probably overstate the level of union premia [Lewis (1986), Rose (1987)].

The deregulation of the trucking industry in the late 1970s and early 1980s provides variation that can be used to estimate the extent of labor rent-sharing more precisely. As in the airlines industry, extensive low-wage, non-union entry (combined with the 1981–82 recession) squeezed existing union carriers. This led to substantial unemployment for union drivers and ultimately resulted in considerable contract concessions by the Teamsters Union [Perry (1986), Rose (1987)]. Econometric analysis of industry wage behavior by Rose (1987) confirms the contract evidence [see also Hirsch (1986)]. Using micro data estimates of industry wage equations for the 1973–85 period, she finds that union wage premia decline from an average of 50 percent over non-union wages during the regulated period to less than 30 percent during the deregulation period. This decline reduces the trucking union premium to the level of the average blue-collar union premium for the economy as a whole. Implied aggregate union losses are $700 million to $1.3 billion per year, or roughly twice the estimated annual losses for owners of trucking firms. Contrary to models of non-union rent-sharing, Rose finds little evidence of non-union wage declines or rent spillovers to truck drivers outside the regulated trucking sector.

Although regulation did not create rents for owners of railroads, labor appears to have gained from regulation, particularly through enhanced union bargaining power. The ICC, for example, required very costly labor protection agreements as a prerequisite to merger approvals [Lieb (1984)]. Rail work rules are among the most restrictive in industry, and tend to enforce higher pay and higher labor requirements. While these cannot be attributed solely to regulation (strong rail unions might have evolved independently of regulation), regulation may contribute to their effect. In the wake of rail consolidations and route rationalizations following deregulation, labor appears to have made limited concessions in some firms, although these do not approach the concessions made by trucking and airline employees [Lieb 1984)].

9.3. Transfers among customer groups

Economic regulation may have important distributional effects across customer groups. The multi-product nature of many regulated industries and political influences on pricing that act through regulatory procedures and appointment processes create a situation ripe with potential cross-subsidies; these frequently are exploited to benefit particular interest groups [Posner (1971)]. Studies of these effects tend to be qualitative. Quantification of inter-customer distributional effects, when available, tends to be an outgrowth of analyses focusing on efficient price structures in regulated industries. These studies are discussed at length in Section 5; we summarize their implications for income transfers below.

Cross-subsidies – i.e. subsidization of some categories of customers by others – is a common theme throughout public utility regulation. For example, it is sometimes argued by industrial customers that the rate structure for electric utilities is skewed toward lower rates for residential and commercial users and higher rates for industrial users, relative to efficient rates. Similarly, implicit coordination of rate-setting between the Federal Communications Commission and state regulatory commissions resulted in telephone pricing procedures that elevated long-distance rates substantially above costs and competitive levels in order to subsidize below-cost prices for local service, and raised urban rates to subsidize rural customers [Johnson (1982), Noll (1985a), MacAvoy and Robinson (1983), Bailey (1986)].

The ability of regulators to maintain such redistributive policies depends critically upon their control over substitute products or suppliers. In the case of telephone pricing, technological advances in microwave communications, combined with court rulings that eliminated AT&T's legal monopoly on long-distance service, created the possibility that high-price long-distance customers would leave the system, forcing price increases on the remaining customers. The subsequent reductions in long-distance prices have decreased, though not eliminated, subsidies of local service; regulators continue to resist rate increases in local service sufficient to cover its appropriable costs [Noll (1985a)].

As noted earlier, the airline fare structure under CAB regulation built in a variety of cross-subsidies. Fares on dense, long-distance routes were elevated substantially above costs, in part to generate profits that could be used to balance below-cost fares in sparse, short-haul markets. Congress and the CAB both were explicit about the protection of air service to small cities. Not only was service deemed essential, but service at "low" fares (relative to costs) was imposed. This was accomplished through both direct subsidies to carriers serving these markets and cross-subsidies of carriers with extensive route networks (enforced by CAB disapproval of carrier abandonment of unprofitable small city routes). Deregulation of prices, entry, and exit has increased fares in low-density, short-haul markets, eliminated air service to a number of small communities, and generally increased service frequency for small cities that have retained air service [Morrison and Winston (1986)]. Rail regulation created similar protection for shippers on low-density routes. Despite costs that appear to have been in excess of service value on many of these routes, the ICC refused to allow railroads to abandon the service, preferring instead to subsidize such service through transfers from capital owners.

Energy regulation created transfers among numerous special interest groups. Kalt (1981) analyzes these effects for petroleum regulation during the 1970s. He finds that regulation established many groups whose energy purchases were heavily subsidized. Regulation-induced shortages gave rise to "priority" consumers, who were given "rights" to more certain production flows, and in some cases, lower prices. Agricultural users, for example, were given high priority, assured supplies; automobile users, low priority, uncertain, and often inadequate supplies [Kalt (1983b)]. Natural gas regulation created similar disparities among customer groups. Rather than increase natural gas prices to avoid chronic shortages during the mid-1970s, regulators relied on rationing. This led to a series of curtailment rules, under which industrial customers typically were shut off the system during shortages, existing residential customers were entitled to unlimited supplies, and new residential customers were excluded from hooking up to the system [Breyer (1982)].

9.4. Transfers among producer groups

Industries are not monolithic, and regulation may benefit some segments of an industry more than (or at the expense of) other segments. The intra-industry distributional effects of regulation have been studied most extensively for social regulation. Pashigian (1984) finds that environmental regulations tend to benefit large firms relative to small firms within an industry. Oster (1982) finds that state generic drug substitution regulations can be explained at least in part by the regulations' differential effects on two groups of firms: large pharmaceutical companies specializing in R&D and patented drugs, and smaller manufacturers specializing in generic drug production. Bartel and Thomas (1986) find that OSHA and EPA regulations have important intra-industry competitive effects that firms may exploit via "predatory" advocacy of particular regulations. There has, however, been little work that has attempted to quantify intra-industry transfers resulting from economic regulation.

In the case of the trucking industry, ICC regulation protected regulated carriers at the expense of exempt or partially exempt carriers. Rules restricting contract carriers to no more than eight shippers limited the size and expansion possibilities of contract carriers. Prohibiting private carriers from using owner-operators or sub-leasing their equipment and drivers on return trips to avoid empty backhauls increased their costs vis-à-vis regulated carriers. Owner-operators were limited to exempt commodities, or required to sign long-term contracts with regulated carriers. Contract and private carriers' dissatisfaction with ICC regulation in the late 1970s led to a conflict within the American Trucking Associations (ATA) over the ATA's lobbying position on deregulation initiatives, and ultimately may have contributed to the success of deregulation initiatives.

Similar intra-industry disagreements may have been operative in airline regulation. Kahn (1983) argues that a number of air carriers believed that regulatory route restrictions constrained their business opportunities by more than it constrained their competitors. These included Pan Am, which was confined to overseas operations by the CAB, and a number of intra-state and commuter carriers, which were precluded from expanding service by the CAB's restrictive entry policy and long-standing refusal to certificate new trunk service. In contrast to the major trunks, these airlines basically supported deregulation.

Energy price and allocation regulations appear to have had substantial distributional effects across producers. Inter-state regulation of natural gas prices resulted in large transfers away from inter-state producers relative to exempt intra-state producers. This situation changed with enactment of the Natural Gas Policy Act of 1978 (NGPA), which extended the Federal Energy Regulatory Commission's jurisdiction to intra-state wellhead prices. The NGPA's complicated set of prices based on different categories of natural gas resulted in benefits to some wellhead producers and losses to others [Braeutigam and Hubbard (1986)].

As discussed earlier, Kalt (1981) finds that crude oil price regulations created an enormous pool of rents, which regulators divided among various producer and consumer interest groups. Initial regulations in 1973 resulted in large rents for refiners with historical ties to "old", price-controlled oil. This system was replaced by the Entitlements Program, which redistributed income among refiners. This tended to raise the income of refiners who depended largely on imported crude oil, and lower the income of refiners who had access to domestic crude. In addition, a number of arbitrary redistributions, such as the "Small Refiner Bias", were built into the system [Kalt (1981, 1983b)]. Smith, Bradley and Jarrell (1986) combine an event study with an economic model of oil regulation to analyze the joint effects of the OPEC price hike and U.S. oil regulations on producers. Their results, like Kalt's, suggest that prior to the entitlements program, crude oil price regulation created large transfers from U.S. crude producers to those U.S. refiners with substantial access to price-controlled crude oil.

10. Conclusions

Systematic empirical analysis of the effects of economic regulation originated with Stigler and Friedland's 1962 paper, which sought to measure the effects of state commission regulation of franchised electric utilities. Stigler and Friedland found that commission regulation had little or no effect on electricity prices. Since 1962 there have been several hundred scholarly studies of the effects of economic regulation. These have analyzed a broad range of industries, measuring regulatory effects against a number of different benchmarks, and using different types of data and a variety of empirical methodologies. This empirical analysis has coincided with the development of both positive and normative theories of regulation and its effects.

The empirical regulation literature of the last twenty-five years clearly demonstrates that regulation frequently has substantial impacts on the behavior and performance of regulated firms. It is, however, impossible to generalize simple propositions about the effects of economic regulation; we cannot, for example, conclude that economic regulation always leads to lower prices than would emerge in the absence of regulation. The nature and magnitude of regulatory effects vary substantially, depending on the structure of the regulatory process, the industry being examined, and the economic environment. The diversity of observed regulatory effects should not be surprising. The term "economic regulation" covers many different types of economic control applied to quite diverse industries with a variety of objectives. Several common themes emerge from the empirical analyses, however.

(1) The effects of economic regulation often differ considerably from the predictions of "public interest" models, which presume that regulation is intended to ameliorate market imperfections and enhance efficiency. This conclusion follows not simply from the observation that regulation is the outcome of a political process, but from analyses of the impacts of regulatory intervention.

(2) In classical "public utility" industries, price regulation generally constrains prices below the level an unconstrained monopolist *with a legal exclusive franchise* would choose. The structure of prices and distribution of revenues across classes of customers often reflect distributional and political objectives, however, rather than efficiency objectives. Furthermore, regulated prices may not be lower than prices would be under a fundamentally different industry structure with multiple firms and free entry.

(3) In regulated markets with multiple competing firms, the effects of entry regulation on prices are more complex. In some industries (airlines, surface freight transportation, insurance), price and entry regulation seem to have been introduced to protect incumbents for competition. Despite this intent, the ability of price regulation to transfer income to the owners of the regulated firms has been sharply constrained by non-price competition and factor rent-sharing. Institutional inertia further limits the benefits of regulation through time, as regulated firms are constrained from adapting to the introduction of competing products and suppliers. The immutability of regulation can transform protectionism into strangulation, as in the railroad industry. Regulation often persists despite the apparent absence of economic rents because regulation has so distorted industry structures that changes would lead to large losses for incumbents [McCormick, Shugart and Tollison (1984)].

In other multi-firm industries, price regulation has been introduced primarily to protect consumers from precipitous price increases. This is true of natural gas, petroleum, hospitals, and to some extent electric utilities with expensive nuclear plants. These regulatory initiatives appear to be self-limiting. At some point, efforts to keep prices below market-clearing levels cannot be sustained. With prices below the marginal cost of additional supplies, shortages develop and the quality of service deteriorates. These effects generate intense pressures for regulatory reform.

(4) Economic regulation has important direct and indirect effects on the costs of production and the quality of service. Regulatory influences on input choices, X-inefficiency, and technological change tend to increase costs. Regulation also alters the quality and variety of services, although these effects often are difficult to quantify. It tends to increase service quality through non-price competition when regulated prices in structurally competitive industries are above competitive levels. Regulation may lower service quality when its intention is to keep prices below their market-clearing levels.

(5) Simplistic "producer capture" models, which view regulation as a cartelization device by which firms transfer income from consumers to producers, are just that – too simplistic. The distributional impacts of regulation are complex and vary with economic conditions and across industries. Moreover, labor appears to be an important beneficiary in a number of industries; perhaps more so than owners of regulated firms. Price and entry regulation seem to be especially conducive to the development of strong unions that can use their bargaining power to exact higher wages.

(6) Although the performance of regulated firms is sensitive to prevailing economic conditions, regulatory structures are quite impervious to exogenous economic forces. Regulatory systems tend to respond only to profound changes in the economic and political environment. The massive economic disruptions of the 1930s gave rise to a vast array of federal regulations, most of which persisted through the next forty years. The recent wave of federal regulatory reforms arose from the substantial supply shocks and macroeconomic disturbances of the 1970s, which have been characterized as the most severe disruptions since the 1930s. These reforms have dismantled or refigured much of the 1930s federal regulatory apparatus.

Our understanding of the effects of economic regulation has advanced considerably over the last twenty-five years, but many questions remain unresolved. The profound changes in both regulatory institutions and economic conditions during the past decade provide a valuable opportunity to answer some of these questions, through careful analysis of the effects of these changes. A number of recent studies have measured early responses to regulatory reforms. In some cases, however, these may be observing transition behavior, rather than a steady-state response to a new regulatory environment. Further analysis of the behavior and performance of industries that have experienced major changes in regulation will be invaluable in discerning permanent impacts.

With the decline of U.S. federal regulatory efforts, the research payoffs to more intensive study of state regulation and to comparative studies of industrial performance in a variety of regulatory and ownership settings may be substantial.

State regulation of some industries has expanded to fill the void created by federal deregulation. These regulations are seldom uniform across states; growing experimentation and diversity at the state level provides valuable variation through which we can measure the effects of regulation. This research will proceed most productively if we improve our measurement of differences in the intensity and types of regulation across states, as well as developing better controls for differences in the economic characteristics of regulated firms. Inter-county comparative studies are more difficult, but as other developed economies consider "privatization", deregulation, and regulatory reforms, there is probably much to be learned by comparing the outcomes of different approaches to industrial ownership and control.

Finally, the large collection of empirical measurements of regulatory effects developed over the last twenty-five years provides a data base to better distinguish among competing theories of the political economy of regulation. Much of the research that tests alternative positive theories of regulation has focused on legislative voting behavior (almost exclusively at the federal level), and particularly on the relationship between legislative voting behavior and constituent interests. This work is interesting and important. We do not find it surprising, however, that Congressional voting behavior reflects constituent interests. Nor do we find it surprising that the discretion of regulatory agencies is sharply constrained by political considerations. This tells us simply that regulation has effects on various economic variables, that these effects have distributional impacts that create constituent interests, and that groups representing diverse interests respond in the political arena. Interest group politics is not, however, per se inconsistent with a "public interest" view of regulation (whatever that means) or with competing general "private interest" theories. The work on the political economy of regulation must inevitably be carefully related to the effects of economic regulation and the way economic regulation is accomplished. The politics and economic consequences of regulation are intertwined in complex ways. Further effort to fold more traditional analysis of the effects of economic regulation into analyses of the political economy of regulation seems essential.

References

Acton, J.P. and Besen, S.M. (1985) 'Regulation, efficiency, and competition in the exchange of electricity', report R-3301-DOE, Rand Corporation, Santa Monica.

Acton, J.P. and Mitchell, B.M. (1980) 'Evaluating time-of-day electricity rates for residential customers', in: B.M. Mitchell and P.R. Kleindorfer, eds., *International symposium on public policy for regulated monopolies and public enterprises: European and United States perspectives*. Lexington: Lexington Books.

Aigner, D.J. (1985). 'The residential electricity time-of-use pricing experiments: What have we learned?', in: J.A. Hausman and D.A. Wise, eds., *Social experimentation*. Chicago: University of Chicago Press.

Annable, J.E. (1973) 'The ICC, the IBT, and the cartelization of the American trucking industry', *Quarterly Review of Economics and Business*, 13:33–47.

Arnold, T.R. (1970) 'The Teamsters Union as a determinant of the structure of the trucking industry', unpublished Ph.D. dissertation, Department of Economics, Syracuse University.

Atkinson, S.E. and Halvorsen, R. (1980). 'A test of relative and absolute price efficiency in regulated industries', *Review of Economics and Statistics*, 62:81–88.

Averch, H. and Johnson, L. (1962) 'Behavior of the firm under regulatory constraint', *American Economic Review*, 52:1052–1069.

Bailey, E.E. (1973) *Economic theory of regulatory constraint*. Lexington: Lexington Books.

Bailey, E.E. (1986) 'Deregulation: Causes and consequences', *Science*, 234:1211–1216.

Bailey, E.E., Graham, D.R. and Kaplan, D.P. (1985) *Deregulating the airlines*. Cambridge: MIT Press.

Baitsell, J.M. (1966) *Airline industry industrial relations: Pilots and flight engineers*. Cambridge: Harvard University Press.

Baron, D.P. and Besanko, D. (1984). 'Regulation, asymmetric information, and auditing', *Rand Journal of Economics*, 15:447–470.

Baron, D.P. and Taggart, R.A. (1977) 'A model of regulation under uncertainty and a test of regulatory bias', *Bell Journal of Economics*, 8:151–167.

Bartel, A.P. and Thomas, L.G. (1987) 'Predation through regulation: The wage and profit impacts of OSHA and EPA', *Journal of Law and Economics*, 30:239–264.

Baughman, M.L., Joskow, P.L. and Kamat, D.P. (1979) *Electric power in the United States: Models and policy analysis*. Cambridge: MIT Press.

Baumol, W.J. and Klevorick, A.K. (1970) 'Input choices and rate-of-return regulation: An overview of the discussion', *Bell Journal of Economics and Management Science*, 1:162–190.

Benham, L. (1972) 'The effect of advertising on the price of eyeglasses', *Journal of Law and Economics*, 15:337–352.

Binder, J.J. (1985) 'Measuring the effects of regulation with stock price data', *Rand Journal of Economics*, 16:167–183.

Blair, R.D., Kaserman, D.L. and McClave, J.T. (1986) 'Motor carrier deregulation: The Florida experiment', *Review of Economics and Statistics*, 68:159–164.

Boyer, K.D. (1977) 'Minimum rate regulation, modal split sensitivities, and the railroad problem', *Journal of Political Economy*, 85:493–512.

Boyer, K.D. (1981) 'Equalizing discrimination and cartel pricing in transport rate regulation', *Journal of Political Economy*, 89:270–286.

Braeutigam, R.R. (1979) 'The effect of uncertainty in regulatory delay on the rate of innovation', *Law and Contemporary Problems*, 43(1):98–111.

Braeutigam, R.R. (1981) 'The deregulation of natural gas', in: L.W. Weiss and M.W. Klass, eds., *Case studies in regulation*. Boston: Little, Brown.

Braeutigam, R.R. and Hubbard, R.G. (1986) 'Natural gas: The regulatory transition', in: L. Weiss and M. Klass, eds., *Regulatory reform: What actually happened*. Boston: Little, Brown.

Braeutigam, R.R. and Noll, R.G. (1984) 'The regulation of surface freight transportation: The welfare effects revisited', *Review of Economics and Statistics*, 66:80–87.

Breen, D. (1977) 'The monopoly value of household-goods carrier operating certificates', *Journal of Law and Economics*, 20:153–185.

Brennan, M.J. and Schwartz, E.S. (1982) 'Consistent regulatory policy under uncertainty', *Bell Journal of Economics*, 13:506–524.

Breyer, S.G. (1982) *Regulation and its reform*. Cambridge: Harvard University Press.

Breyer, S.G. and MacAvoy, P.W. (1974) *Energy regulation by the Federal Power Commission*. Washington, D.C.: Brookings Institution.

Broadman, H.G. and Montgomery, W.D. (1983) *Natural gas markets after deregulation*. Washington, D.C.: Resources for the future.

Brown, K. (1970) *Regulation of the natural gas production industry*. Baltimore: Johns Hopkins University Press.

Brown, S.J. and Sibley, D.S. (1986) *The theory of public utility pricing*. Cambridge: Cambridge University Press.

Burness, H.S., Montgomery, W.D. and Quirk, J.P. (1980) 'Capital contracting and the regulated firms', *American Economic Review*, 70:342–354.

Cady, J.F. (1976) 'An estimate of the price effects of restrictions on drug price advertising', *Economic Inquiry*, 14:493–510.

Call, G.D. and Keeler, T.E. (1985) 'Airline deregulation, fares, and market behavior: Some empirical evidence', in: A.F. Daughety, ed., *Analytical studies in transport economics*. Cambridge: Cambridge University Press.

Cappelli, P. (1985) 'Competitive pressures and labor relations in the airline industry', *Industrial Relations*, 24:316–338.

Capron, W.M., ed. (1971) *Technological change in regulated industries*. Washington, D.C. Brookings Institution.

Card, D. (1986) 'The impact of deregulation on the employment and wages of airline mechanics', *Industrial and Labor Relations Review*, 39:527–538.

Carroll, T.M. and Ciscel, D.H. (1982) 'The effects of regulation on executive compensation', *Review of Economics and Statistics*, 64:505–509.

Carron, A.S. and MacAvoy, P.W. (1981) *The decline of service in the regulated industries*. Washington, D.C.: American Enterprise Institute.

Caves, D.W., Christensen, L.R. and Swanson, J.A. (1981a) 'Economic performance in regulated environments: A comparison of U.S. and Canadian railroads', *Quarterly Journal of Economics*, 96:559–581.

Caves, D.W., Christensen, L.R. and Swanson, J.A. (1981b) 'Productivity growth, scale economies, and capacity utilization in U.S. railroads', *American Economic Review*, 71:994–1002.

Christainsen, G.B. and Haveman, R.H. (1981) 'Public regulations and the slowdown in productivity growth', *American Economic Review*, 71:320–325.

Christensen, L.R. and Greene, W.H. (1976) 'Economies of scale in U.S. electric power generation', *Journal of Political Economy*, 84:655–676.

Clarke, R.G. (1980) 'The effects of fuel adjustment clauses on systematic risk and market values of electric utilities', *Journal of Finance*, 35:347–358.

Conrad, D.A. and Sheldon, G.G. (1982) 'The effects of legal constraints on dental care prices', *Inquiry*, 19:51–67.

Courville, L. (1974) 'Regulation and efficiency in the electric utility industry', *Bell Journal of Economics and Management Science*, 5:38–52.

Cox, C. and Isaac, R.M. (1986) 'A new mechanism for incentive regulation: Theory and experiment', working paper 86-15, Department of Economics, University of Arizona.

Crandall, R.W. (1981) 'Pollution controls and productivity growth in basic industry', in: T. Cowing and R. Stevenson, eds., *Productivity measurement in regulated industries*. New York: Academic.

Crocker, K.J. and Masten, S.E. (1988) 'Mitigating contractual hazards: Unilateral options and contract length', *Rand Journal of Economics*, 19 (forthcoming).

Cummins, J.D. and Vanderhei, J. (1979) 'A note on the relative efficiency of property-liability insurance distribution systems', *Bell Journal of Economics*, 10:709–719.

Daughety, A. (1984) 'Regulation and industrial organization', *Journal of Political Economy*, 92:932–953.

Demsetz, H. (1968) 'Why regulate utilities?' *Journal of Law and Economics*, 11:55–65.

Denison, E.F. (1979) 'Pollution abatement programs: Estimates of their effects upon output per unit input', *Survey of Current Business*, 59:58–59.

Douglas, G.W. and Miller, J.C. (1975) *Economic regulation of domestic air transport: Theory and policy*. Washington, D.C.: Brookings Institution.

Eads, G.C. (1975) 'Competition in the domestic trunk airline industry: Too much or too little', in: A. Phillips, ed., *Promoting competition in regulated markets*. Washington, D.C.: Brookings Institution.

Edison Electric Institute (1974, 1983) *Statistical yearbook of the electric utility industry*. Washington, D.C.: Edison Electric Institute.

Ehrenberg, R.G. (1979) *The regulatory process and labor earnings*. New York: Academic.

Erickson, E.W. and Spann, R.M. (1971) 'Supply response in a regulated industry: The case of natural gas', *Bell Journal of Economics and Management Science*, 2:94–121.

Finsinger, J., ed. (1983) *Economic analysis of regulated markets*. New York: St. Martin's Press.

Finsinger, J. and Pauly, M., eds. (1986) *Economics of insurance regulation: A cross-national study*. New York: St. Martin's Press.

Frech, III, H.E. and Samprone, Jr., J.C. (1980) 'The welfare loss of excess nonprice competition: The case of property-liability insurance regulation', *Journal of Law and Economics*, 23:429–440.
Frew, J.R. (1981) 'The existence of monopoly profits in the motor carrier industry', *Journal of Law and Economics*, 24:289–315.
Friedlaender, A.F. (1988) 'Efficient rail rates and deregulation', mimeo.
Friedlaender, A.F. and Spady, R. (1981) *Freight transport regulation*. Cambridge: MIT Press.
Gellman, A.J. (1971) 'Surface freight transportation', in: W.M. Capron, ed., *Technological change in regulated industries*. Washington, D.C.: Brookings Institution.
Gollop, F.M. and Karlson, S.H. (1978) 'The impact of the fuel adjustment mechanism on economic efficiency', *Review of Economics and Statistics*, 60:574–584.
Gollop, F.M. and Roberts, M.J. (1983) 'Environmental regulations and productivity growth: The case of fossil-fueled electric power production', *Journal of Political Economy*, 91:654–674.
Grabowski, H.G. and Vernon, J.V. (1983) *The regulation of pharmaceuticals: Balancing the benefits and risks*. Washington, D.C.: American Enterprise Institute.
Graham, D., Kaplan, D.P. and Sibley, D. (1983) 'Efficiency and competition in the airline industry', *Bell Journal of Economics*, 14:118–138.
Greene, W.H. and Smiley, R.H. (1984) 'The effectiveness of utility regulation in a period of changing economic conditions', in: M. Marchand, P. Pestieau and H. Tulkens, eds., *The performance of public enterprises: Concepts and measurement*. Amsterdam: Elsevier Science Publishers B.V.
Haas-Wilson, D. (1986) 'The effect of commercial practice restrictions: The case of optometry', *Journal of Law and Economics*, 29:165–186.
Hagerman, R.L. and Ratchford, B.T. (1978) 'Some determinants of allowed rates of return on equity to electric utilities', *Bell Journal of Economics*, 9:46–55.
Harrington, S. (1984) 'The impact of rate regulation on prices and underwriting results in the property-liability insurance industry: A survey', *Journal of Risk and Insurance*, 51:577–623.
Hausman, J.A. and Wise, D.A., eds. (1985) *Social experimentation*. Chicago: University of Chicago Press.
Hendricks, W. (1975) 'The effect of regulation on collective bargaining in electric utilities', *Bell Journal of Economics*, 6:451–465.
Hendricks, W. (1977) 'Regulation and labor earnings', *Bell Journal of Economics*, 8:483–496.
Hendricks, W., Feuille, P. and Szerszen, C. (1980) 'Regulation, deregulation, and collective bargaining in airlines', *Industrial and Labor relations Review*, 34:67–81.
Hirsch, B.T. (1988) 'Trucking regulation, unionization, and labor earnings: 1973–1985', *Journal of Human Resources*, 23:296–319.
Hong, J.T. and Plot, C.R. (1982) 'Rate filing policies for inland water transportation: An experimental approach', *Bell Journal of Economics*, 13:1–19.
Hubbard, R.G. and Weiner, R.J. (1984) 'Regulation and bilateral monopoly: Long term contracting in natural gas', mimeo.
Ippolito, R. (1979) 'The effects of price regulation in the automobile insurance industry', *Journal of Law and Economics*, 22:55–89.
Ippolito, R.A. and Masson, R.T. (1978) 'The social cost of government regulation of milk', *Journal of Law and Economics*, 21:33–66.
Isaac, R.M. (1982) 'Fuel adjustment mechanisms and the regulated utility facing uncertain fuel prices', *Bell Journal of Economics*, 13:158–169.
Johnson, L.L. (1982) 'Competition and cross-subsidization in the telephone industry', Rand Report R-2976-RC/NSF, Rand Corporation, Santa Monica.
Jordan, W.A. (1970) *Airline regulation in America: Effects and imperfections*. Baltimore: Johns Hopkins University Press.
Joskow, P.L. (1972) 'The determination of the allowed rate of return in a formal regulatory hearing', *Bell Journal of Economics and Management Science*, 3:632–644.
Joskow, P.L. (1973) 'Cartels, competition and regulation in the property-liability insurance industry', *Bell Journal of Economics*, 4:375–427.
Joskow, P.L. (1974) 'Inflation and environmental concern: Structural change in the process of public utility price regulation', *Journal of Law and Economics*, 17:291–327.
Joskow, P.L. (1976) 'Contributions to the theory of marginal cost pricing', *Bell Journal of Economics*, 7:197–206.

Joskow, P.L. (1979) 'Public utility Regulatory Policy Act of 1978: Electric utility rate reform', *Natural Resources Journal*, 19:787–809.

Joskow, P.L. (1980) 'The effects of competition and regulation on hospital bed supply and the reservation quality of the hospital', *Bell Journal of Economics*, 11:421–447.

Joskow, P.L. (1981) *Controlling hospital costs: The role of government regulation*. Cambridge: MIT Press.

Joskow, P.L. (1987) 'Productivity growth and technological change in the generation of electricity', *Energy Journal*, 8(1):17–38.

Joskow, P.L. and Noll, R. (1981) 'Regulation in theory and practice: An overview', in: G. Fromm, ed., *Studies of public regulation*. Cambridge: MIT Press.

Joskow, P.L. and Rose, N.L. (1985a) 'The effects of technological change, experience, and environmental regulation on the construction cost of coal-burning generating units', *Rand Journal of Economics*, 16:1–27.

Joskow, P.L. and Rose, N.L. (1985b) 'The effects of technological change, experience, and environmental regulation on the construction cost of coal-burning generating units: 1981–82 update', MIT Energy Lab Report MIT-EL-017WP.

Joskow, P.L. and Schmalensee, R.L. (1983) *Markets for power: An analysis of electrical utility deregulation*. Cambridge: MIT Press.

Joskow, P.L. and Schmalensee, R.L. (1985) 'The performance of coal-burning electric generating units in the United States: 1960–1980', *Journal of Applied Econometrics*, 2:85–109.

Joskow, P.L. and Schmalensee, R.L. (1986) 'Incentive regulation for electric utilities', *Yale Journal on Regulation*, 4:1–49.

Kahn, A.E. (1970, 1971) *The economics of regulation*. New York: Wiley.

Kahn, A.E. (1979) 'Applications of economics in an imperfect world', *American Economic Review*, 69:1–13.

Kahn, A.E. (1983) 'Deregulation and vested interests: The case of airlines', in: R. Noll and B. Owen, eds., *The political economy of deregulation*. Washington, D.C.: American Enterprise Institute.

Kalt, J.P. (1981) *The economics and politics of oil price regulation: Federal policy in the post-embargo era*. Cambridge: MIT Press.

Kalt, J.P. (1983a) 'The costs and benefits of federal regulation of coal strip mining', *Natural Resources Journal*, 23:893–915.

Kalt, J.P. (1983b) 'The creation, growth, and entrenchment of special interests in oil price policy', in: R. Noll and B. Owen, eds., *The political economy of deregulation: Interest groups in the regulatory process*. Washington, D.C.: American Enterprise Institute.

Kalt, J.P. and Leone, R.A. (1986) 'Regional effects of energy price decontrol: The roles of interregional trade, stockholding, and microeconomic incidence', *Rand Journal of Economics*, 17:201–213.

Kalt, J.P. and Zupan, M.A. (1984) 'Capture and ideology in the economic theory of politics', *American Economic Review*, 74:279–300.

Keeler, T. (1972) 'Airline regulation and market performance', *Bell Journal of Economics*, 3:399–424.

Keeler, T. (1983) *Railroads, freight, and public policy*. Washington, D.C.: Brookings Institution.

Kitch, E.W., Isaacson, M. and Kaspar, D. (1971) 'The regulation of taxicabs in Chicago', *Journal of Law and Economics*, 14:285–350.

Kunreuther, H., Kleindorfer, P. and Pauly, M. (1983) 'Insurance regulation and consumer behavior in the United States – the property and liability industry', *Journal of Institutional and Theoretical Economics*, 139:452–472.

Kwoka, Jr., J.E. (1984) 'Advertising and the price and quality of optometric services', *American Economic Review*, 74:211–216.

Laffont, J.-J. and Tirole, J. (1986) 'Using cost observations to regulate firms', *Journal of Political Economy*, 94:614–641.

Leffler, K.B. (1978) Physician licensure: Competition and monopoly in American medicine', *Journal of Law and Economics*, 21:165–186.

Levin, R.C. (1978) 'Allocation in surface freight transportation: Does rate regulation matter?', *Bell Journal of Economics*, 9:18–45.

Levin, R.C. (1981) 'Railroad rates, profitability, and welfare under deregulation', *Bell Journal of Economics*, 12:1–26.

Levine, M. (1965) 'Is regulation necessary? California air transportation and national regulatory policy', *Yale Law Journal*, 74:1416–1447.

Lewis, H.G. (1963) *Unionism and relative wages in the United States*. Chicago: University of Chicago Press.

Lewis, H.G. (1986) *Union relative wage effects*. Chicago: University of Chicago Press.

Lieb, R.C. (1984) 'The changing nature of labor/management relations in transportation', *Transportation Journal*, (Spring):4–14.

Lindenberg, B. and Ross, A. (1981) 'Tobin's *q* ratio and industrial organization', *Journal of Business*, 54:1–32.

Mabley, R. and Strack, W. (1982) 'Deregulation – a green light for trucking efficiency', *Regulation*, July/August:36–42, 56.

MacAvoy, P.W. (1962) *Price formation in natural gas fields*. New Haven: Yale University press.

MacAvoy, P.W. (1971) 'The formal work-product of the Federal Power Commissioners', *Bell Journal of Economics and Management Science*, 2:379–395.

MacAvoy, P.W. (1973) 'The regulation-induced shortage of natural gas', *Bell Journal of Economics*, 4:454–498.

MacAvoy, P.W., ed. (1977) *Federal milk marketing orders and price supports*. Washington, D.C.: American Enterprise Institute.

MacAvoy, P.W. and Pindyck, R. (1973) 'Alternative regulatory policies for dealing with natural gas storage', *Bell Journal of Economics*, 4:454–498.

MacAvoy, P.W. and Robinson, K. (1983) 'Winning by losing: The AT&T settlement and its impact on telecommunications', *Yale Journal on Regulation*, 1:1–42.

MacAvoy, P.W. and Sloss, J. (1967) *Regulation of transport innovation*. New York: Random House.

MacAvoy, P.W. and Snow, J.W., eds. (1977) *Regulation of entry and pricing in truck transportation*. Washington, D.C.: American Enterprise Institute.

MacDonald, J.M. (1987) 'Competition and rail rates for the shipment of corn, soybeans, and wheat', *Rand Journal of Economics*, 18:151–163.

Masson, R.T. and Debrock, L.M. (1980) 'The structural effects of state regulation of fluid milk', *Review of Economics and Statistics*, 63:479–487.

Masson, R.T. and Debrock, L.M. (1982) 'The structural effects of state regulation of retail fluid milk prices – a reply', *Review of Economics and Statistics*, 64:534–536.

Masten, S.E. and Crocker, K.J. (1985) 'Efficient adaptation in long-term contracts: Take-or-pay provisions for natural gas', *American Economic Review*, 75:1083–93.

McCormick, R.E., Shugart, III, W.F. and Tollison, R.F. (1984) 'The disinterest in deregulation', *American Economic Review*, 74:1075–1079.

McDonald, F. (1962) *Insull*. Chicago: University of Chicago Press.

McKay, D. (1976) 'Has the A-J effect been empirically verified?' Social science working paper 132, California Institute of Technology.

Melnick, G.A., Wheeler, J.R.C. and Feldstein, P.J. (1981) 'Effects of rate regulation on selected components of hospital expenses', *Inquiry*, 18:240–246.

Meyer, J.R. and Oster, C.V. (1984) *Deregulation and the new airline entrepreneurs*. Cambridge: MIT Press.

Mitchell, B.M. and Kleindorfer, P.R., eds. (1979) *International Symposium on Public Policy for Regulated Monopolies and Public Enterprises: European and United States perspectives*. Lexington: Lexington Books.

Mitchell, B.M., Manning, W. and Acton, J.P. (1978) *Peak load pricing: European lessons for U.S. energy policy*. Cambridge: Ballinger.

Moore, T.G. (1975) 'Deregulating surface freight transportation', in: A. Phillips, ed., *Promoting competition in regulated markets*. Washington, D.C.: Brookings Institution.

Moore, T.G. (1976) *Trucking regulation: Lessons from Europe*. Washington, D.C.: American Enterprise Institute.

Moore, T.G. (1978) 'The beneficiaries of trucking regulation', *Journal of Law and Economics*, 21:327–343.

Moore, T.G. (1986) 'Rail and trucking deregulation', in: L.W. Weiss and M.W. Klass, eds., *Regulatory reform: What actually happened*. Boston: Little, Brown.

Morrison, S. and Winston, C. (1986) *The economic effects of airline deregulation*. Washington, D.C.: Brookings Institution.

Munch, P. and Smallwood, D. (1980) 'Theory of solvency regulation in the property and casualty insurance industry', in: G. Fromm, ed., *Studies in public regulation*. Cambridge: MIT Press.

Navarro, P. (1982) 'Public utility regulation: Performance, determinants and energy policy impacts', *Energy Journal*, 3:119–149.

Nelson, J.R., ed. (1964) *Marginal cost pricing in practice*. Englewood Cliffs: Prentice-Hall.

Nelson, R.A. and Wohar, .E. (1983) 'Regulation, scale economies, and productivity in steam-electric generation', *International Economic Review*, 24:57–78.

Noll, R.G. (1985a) 'Let them make toll calls: A state regulator's lament', *American Economic Review*, 75:52–56.

Noll, R.G. (1985b) *Regulatory policy and the social sciences*. Berkeley: University of California Press.

Norton, S.W. (1985) 'Regulation and systematic risk: The case of electric utilities', *Journal of Law and Economics*, 28:671–686.

Olson, C.V. and Trapani, J.M. (1981) 'Who has benefited from regulation of the airline industry?', *Journal of Law and Economics*, 24:75–94.

Oster, S. (1982) 'The strategic use of regulatory investment by industry subgroups', *Economic Inquiry*, 20:604–618.

Pashigian, B.P. (1984) 'The effect of environmental regulation on optimal plant size and factor shares', *Journal of Law and Economics*, 27:1–28.

Pashigian, B.P. (1985) 'Environmental regulation: Whose self-interests are being protected?', *Economic Inquiry*, 23:551–584.

Peltzman, S. (1973) 'An evaluation of consumer protection legislation: The 1962 drug amendments', *Journal of Political Economy*, 81:1049–1091.

Peltzman, S. (1976) 'Toward a more general theory of regulation', *Journal of Law and Economics*, 19:211–240.

Perl, L. and Dunbar, F. (1982) 'Cost-effectiveness and cost-benefit analysis of air quality regulation', *American Economic Review*, 72:208–213.

Perry, C.R. (1986) *Deregulation and the decline of the unionized trucking industry*. Industrial Research Unit, The Wharton School, University of Pennsylvania, Philadelphia.

Petersen, H.C. (1975) 'An empirical test of regulatory effects', *Bell Journal of Economics*, 6:111–126.

Phillips, A. (1971) 'Air transportation in the United States', in: W.M. Capron, ed., *Technological change in regulated industries*. Washington, D.C.: Brookings Institution.

Pindyck, R.S. (1974) 'The regulatory implications of three alternative econometric supply models of natural gas', *Bell Journal of Economics*, 5:633–645.

Plott, C.R. (1982) 'Industrial organization theory and experimental economics', *Journal of Economic Literature*, 20:1485–1527.

Posner, R.A. (1971) 'Taxation by regulation', *Bell Journal of Economics and Management Science*, 2:22–50.

Posner, R.A. (1974) 'Theories of economic regulation', *Bell Journal of Economics and Management Science*, 5:335–358.

Prager, R.A. (1986) 'Firm behavior in franchise monopoly markets: The case of cable television', unpublished Ph.D. dissertation, Department of Economics, MIT.

Pulsifer, R. et al. (1975) *Regulatory reform, report of the CAB special staff*. Washington, D.C.: Civil Aeronautics Board.

Rassenti, S.J. and Smith, V.L. (1986) 'Electric utility deregulation', working paper 86-3, Department of Economics, University of Arizona.

Rose, N.L. (1985a) 'The incidence of regulatory rents in the motor carrier industry', *Rand Journal of Economics*, 16:299–318.

Rose, N.L. (1985b) 'Unionization and regulation: The division of rents in the trucking industry', working paper no. 1684-85, Sloan School of Management, MIT.

Rose, N.L. (1987) 'Labor rent-sharing and regulation: Evidence from the trucking industry', *Journal of Political Economy*, 95:1146–1178.

Rothwell, G. (1985) 'Comparing models of electric utility behavior', social science working paper 588, California Institute of Technology.

Russell, L.B. (1979) 'Regulating the diffusion of hospital technologies', *Law and Contemporary Problems*, 43:26–42.

Salinger, M.A. (1984) 'Tobin's q, unionization, and the concentration–profits relationship', *Rand Journal of Economics*, 15:159–170.
Samprone, Jr., J. (1979) 'Rate regulation and nonprice competition in the property and liability insurance industry', *Journal of Risk and Insurance*, 46:683–696.
Schmalensee, R.L. (1977) 'Comparative static properties of regulated airline oligopolies', *Bell Journal of Economics*, 8:565–576.
Schmalensee, R.L. (1979) *The control of natural monopolies*. Lexington: D.C. Heath.
Schmalensee, R.L. (1986) 'A note on depreciation and profitability under rate-of-return regulation', mimeo.
Schwert, G.W. (1981) 'Using financial data to measure the effects of regulation', *Journal of Law and Economics*, 24:121–159.
Shepard, L. (1978) 'Licensing restrictions and the cost of dental care', *Journal of Law and Economics*, 21:187–202.
Shepard, L. (1986) 'Cartelization of the California–Arizona orange industry, 1934–1981', *Journal of Law and Economics*, 29:83–124.
Shepherd, W.G. (1971) 'The competitive margins in communications', in: W.M. Capron, ed., *Technological change in regulated industries*. Washington, D.C.: Brookings Institution.
Shew, W,.B. (1984) 'Costs of cable television franchise requirements', National Economic Research Associates, mimeo.
Shleifer, A. (1985) 'A theory of yardstick competition', *Rand Journal of Economics*, 16:319–327.
Siegel, R. (1979) 'Why has productivity slowed down', *Data Resources Review*, 1:1.59–1.65.
Sloan, F.A. (1981) 'Regulation and the rising cost of hospital care', *Review of Economics and Statistics*, 63:479–487.
Sloan, F.A. and Steinwald, B. (1980) 'Effects of regulation on hospital costs and input use', *Journal of Law and Economics*, 23:81–110.
Sloss, J. (1970) 'Regulation of motor freight transportation: A quantitative evaluation of policy', *Bell Journal of Economics*, 1:327–366.
Smallwood, D.E. (1975) 'Competition, regulation, and product quality in the automobile insurance industry', in: A. Phillips, ed., *Promoting competition in regulated markets*. Washington, D.C.: Brookings Institution.
Smiley, R.H. and Greene, W.H. (1983) 'Determinants of the effectiveness of electric utility regulation', *Resources and Energy*, 5:65–81.
Smirlock, M., Gilligan, T. and Marshall, W. (1984) 'Tobin's q and the structure–performance relationship', *American Economic Review*, 74:1051–1060.
Smith, R.T., Bradley, M. and Jarrell, G. (1986) 'Studying firm-specific effects of regulation with stock market data: An application to oil price regulation', *Rand Journal of Economics*, 17:467–489.
Smith, V.L. (1982) 'Microeconomic systems as an experimental science', *American Economic Review*, 72:923–955.
Snitzler, J.R. and Byrne, R.J. (1958) 'Interstate trucking of fresh and frozen poultry under agricultural exemption', marketing research report 316, U.S. Department of Agriculture.
Snitzler, J.R. and Byrne, R.J. (1959) 'Interstate trucking of frozen fruits and vegetables under agricultural exemption', marketing research report 316, U.S. Department of Agriculture.
Spann, R.M. (1974) 'Rate of return regulation and efficiency in production: An empirical test of the Averch–Johnson thesis', *Bell Journal of Economics and Management Science*, 5:38–52.
Spence, M.A. (1975) 'Monopoly, quality, and regulation', *Bell Journal of Economics*, 6:417–429.
Stigler, G.J. (1971) 'The theory of economic regulation', *Bell Journal of Economic and Management Science*, 2:3–21.
Stigler, G.J. and Friedland, C. (1962) 'What can the regulators regulate: The case of electricity', *Journal of Law and Economics*, 5:1–16.
Taylor, L.D. (1975) 'The demand for electricity: A survey', *Bell Journal of Economics*, 6:74–110.
Temin, P. (1980) *Taking your medicine: Drug regulation in the United States*. Cambridge: Harvard University Press.
Turvey, R. (1968) *Optimal pricing and investment in electricity supply*. Cambridge: MIT Press.
U.S. Department of Justice (1977) *Federal–State regulation of the pricing and marketing of insurance*. Washington, D.C.: American Enterprise Institute.
Viscusi, W.K. (1985) 'Consumer behavior and the safety effects of product safety regulation', *Journal of Law and Economics*, 28:527–554.

Walter, J. (1979) 'Regulated firms under uncertain price change: The case of property and liability insurance companies', *Journal of Risk and Insurance*, 46(2):5–21.

Wiggins, S.N. (1981) 'Product quality regulation and new drug introductions: Some new evidence from the 1970s', *Review of Economics and Statistics*, 63:615–619.

Wiggins, S.N. (1983) 'The impact of regulation on pharmaceutical research expenditures: A dynamic approach', *Economic Inquiry*, 22:115–128.

Williams, C.A. and Whitman, A. (1973) 'Open competition rating laws and price competition', *Journal of Risk and Insurance*, 40:483–496.

Williamson, O.E. (1976) 'Franchise bidding for natural monopoly – in general and with respect to CATV', *Bell Journal of Economics*, 7:73–104.

Wilson, J.Q. (1980) *The politics of regulation*. New York: Basic Books.

Winston, C. (1981) 'The welfare effects of ICC rate regulation revisited', *Bell Journal of Economics* 12:232–244.

Zupan, M.A. (1987) 'Reneging by cable operators on their franchise promises: Opportunism or economic necessity', mimeo.

Chapter 26

THE ECONOMICS OF HEALTH, SAFETY, AND ENVIRONMENTAL REGULATION

HOWARD K. GRUENSPECHT AND LESTER B. LAVE

Carnegie-Mellon University

Contents

Handbook of Industrial Organization, Volume II, Edited by R. Schmalensee and R.D. Willig

1. Introduction

1.1. Economists' disinterest in externalities

Economists have long recognized the theoretical possibility of externalities and their role in disrupting the efficiency of competitive equilibrium. More recently, the incentive and appropriability features of information markets have raised questions regarding the efficiency of the private market as a mechanism for generating and disseminating information.

Environmental pollution clearly constitutes an externality. Moreover, in a setting where information is imperfect and held asymmetrically, the regulation of environmental externalities will inevitably become intertwined with problems of information. Health and safety decisions typically involve few direct externalities, although there can be important public good aspects. When public goods are important, basing private decisions regarding health and safety matters on an information set that reflects the shortcomings of private information markets may produce inefficient outcomes. Thus, externalities, public goods, and the shortcomings of private information markets which stem in large measure from the nonappropriability of information, provide a theoretical justification for health, safety, and environmental regulation (HSE).

In practice, however, economists have tended to emphasize the positive role of unfettered markets in attaining objectives such as efficient allocation and growth. By giving little attention to externalities and information, most economists implicitly assumed them to be unimportant, or at least of no more than second-order importance. After Pigou (1920), externalities were seen to pose no new theoretical issues; for example, Arrow (1983) characterizes externalities as simply a problem with incomplete markets. Few economists saw phenomena such as the devastating air pollution in Pittsburgh in 1948 and in London in 1952 as compelling attention. We assumed that the doctrine of caveat emptor would handle dangerous or defective products and polluted neighborhoods. Workers would select jobs and consumers would select housing with the preferred amount of risk, based on market generated wage and rent differentials that reflected safety and health risks (along with the other attributes of jobs and housing) [Oi (1974), Viscusi (1983b), Harrison and Rubinfeld (1978)].

The economic paradigm stresses making tradeoffs rather than meeting a lexicographic hierarchy of needs. An economic consumer would not strive for a totally pristine environment or products with no safety and health risks. As long as there are positive marginal costs in improving along these dimensions, utility from other desirable goods and services would lead to choosing a somewhat polluted environment. Externalities and inefficiencies in private information markets may provide a theoretical basis for regulation, but there is no guarantee that a practical regulatory program will move society towards the Pareto frontier. We are acutely aware of the direct costs of government regulation as well as the potential evils of discretionary government actions that tend to reflect politics, individual wealth-seeking behavior, or merely arbitrary forces. This leads economists to demand large efficiency losses from externalities or information market failures before recommending government action.

In practice, the bias against intervention is reflected in such mundane matters as how GNP is measured [Nordhaus and Tobin (1972)]. A despoiled environment is not reflected in GNP and even occupational injury and disease is reflected only indirectly, if at all. The GNP measure is biased and glosses over issues such as the conditions under which economic growth is good. Since it fails to address the negative aspects of urban concentration and industrial growth, the economic paradigm directs the attention of policy-makers away from these issues, encouraging them to regard these concerns as largely illegitimate or irrelevant.

A series of public scandals led to the creation of the Food and Drug Administration in 1906 and the periodic amendments that have strengthened the law. Adulterated food and drugs were the initial target, although the FDA later was charged with ensuring that food and drugs were safe, and, in the modern era, that drugs were effective. The National Highway Transportation Safety Administration was created in 1966 to make highways safer; the Occupational Safety and Health Administration was created in 1969 to protect workers; the Environmental Protection Agency was initiated in 1970 to clean the environment; the Consumer Product Safety Commission was created to ensure the safety of all products [Lave (1980)].

1.2. An increased public demand for regulation

By the end of the Second World War, business leaders in Pittsburgh saw that pollution was choking economic activity and set out to curtail it. Organizations such as the Ford Foundation and Resources for the Future supported economic inquiry into these externalities that made notable contributions [Kneese and Bower (1972)]. Public values began to shift in the mid-1960s with an increase in concern for air and water quality, the environmental effects of pesticides, and highway safety. HSE problems were not getting markedly worse in the 1960s; indeed, there are some indicators of improvements in indices such as air pollution. Why, then, was there such an abrupt shift in public concerns? One explanation revolves around the superiority (income elasticity greater than one) of HSE attributes [Lave (1980)].

By the 1960s sustained economic growth had produced high incomes and most people had attained a reasonable standard of material welfare. A more receptive public was presented with new data on DDT concentrations in human tissues and milk, data on the effect of DDT on the ability of hawks to lay eggs, and fragmentary data on the road handling of Corvairs. Carson (1962) and Nader (1965) raised public awareness and catalyzed dissatisfaction. "Environmentalists" and "consumerists" used the fragmentary data to broaden the inquiry from DDT to all pesticides, to air and water quality, and to health problems more generally.

Earth Day 1969 demonstrated the extent of public concern. The public demanded that the federal government take charge of what they perceived to be important neglected problems. Over the course of a decade, Congress created several new regulatory agencies and enacted legislation that gave these agencies a central role for the first time in highway safety, safety of consumer products, controlling air and water pollution, and occupational safety and health.

The conditions of the 1960s led to more general concern for health and safety. For example, in 1962 Congress significantly strengthened the powers and broadened the authority of the Food and Drug Administration. The FDA not only was to determine if drugs were safe, it was to decide if drugs were effective in combating disease.

1.3. Regulatory reform

By 1980, economists and business leaders had affirmed that HSE regulation was costly, both in terms of the direct budget and the indirect costs imposed on the economy [Ruff (1978), Weidenbaum and deFina (1978), Environmental Protection Agency (1979), Denison (1979), Lave (1980)]. Since regulations were not designed with cost effectiveness and efficiency in mind, it is hardly surprising that they failed to meet these criteria. Studies also showed that the goals of the legislation had not been achieved. There were not "zero discharges into the waterways", air quality was not good enough to "protect the most sensitive group in the population with an ample margin of safety", and working men and women had not been "assure[d] insofar as practicable that no employee will suffer diminished health, functional capacity, or life expectancy as a result of his work". The problems were much more difficult than either the public or Congress had appreciated. The rhetoric of zero risk and a pristine environment had little mirror in reality. Neither the economic models nor practical wisdom had much to say about how to bring regulation under control while satisfying public desires.

Economic deregulation of the airlines, trucks, railroads, banks, and financial markets generally met with public approval [Bailey et al. (1985), Derthick and Quirk (1985), Joskow and Noll (1981), Robyn (1987)]. Surveys revealed that people continued to desire improvements in health, safety, and the environment and were prepared to pay for them. Discontent with the federal agencies stemmed from frustration with their heavy-handed and inefficient manner of operation rather than from opposition to their goals. What was needed was not euthanasia for the HSE agencies, but rather regulatory reform that addressed the major problems.

1.4. A zoology of concerns

The material in this chapter is organized by issues, with difficulties and examples given in each section. We now list the issues and refer the reader to the section where each is discussed.

We begin by considering the *efficiency of implementation mechanisms*, the most inherently "economic" of the issues. Section 2 reviews the extensive pure and applied theory work on efficient and cost-effective regulation. The primary motivation for environmental regulation is the recognition that environmental quality is itself a public good. Mechanisms for handling environmental externalities in a perfect information context have received some attention. However, most of the recent pure and applied theory on efficient or cost-effective regulation focuses on information issues that are pervasive in the real world, such as uncertainty surrounding cost and benefit functions and incentives to reveal private knowledge. While information issues are prominent in environmental regulation models, they complicate a problem that would exist even in a perfect information setting. In contrast, health and safety regulation is driven primarily by the perception of information problems in private markets. In Section 2 we consider environmental regulation first, and then move to the literature on health and safety regulations.

Beginning in Section 3 we consider a host of economic issues surrounding actual regulation that arise outside of the context of the stylized regulatory models examined in Section 2. *Goal-setting*, the determination of how safe is safe enough, and how clean is clean enough, is a primary issue. Congress and the agencies have not given clear answers to these questions because there is no public consensus about answers. Having failed to answer the questions directly, Congress has retreated to seeking answers through defining the *process of deciding issues* (Subsection 3.3). For example, Congress requires agencies to publish information about what areas they are thinking of regulating, to publish preliminary regulations and then to hold hearings on them, and to publish final rules. Congress has given standing to virtually anyone to challenge the rules during the hearings process or in federal courts after they are finalized. The courts have reacted by examining not only whether agency actions followed due process and statutory authority, but also whether the actions seem reasonable

[Stewart (1975)]. The President (through executive order) requires agencies to do benefit–cost analyses of important rules and to explain why the most cost-effective solution was not proposed. The resulting process is extremely cumbersome, requiring large amounts of professional work and a great deal of time to issue a final rule. In virtually every case the rule is challenged in federal court, so that judges often become the final arbiters of what is in the public interest.

Goal-setting often involves the striking of a balance between *paternalism* (Subsection 3.2) and reliance on responsible individual judgment. Much of health and safety regulation is concerned with overriding private decisions in order to protect individuals from themselves. Paternalism poses difficulties both for goal-setting and for implementation. For goal-setting, it implies that we know better than an individual what is in his best interest [Lave (1987a)]. For implementation, as Prohibition demonstrated, it is hard in a generally free society to force large numbers of people to comply with a rule to which they object.

Another issue is *equity*: the allocation of risk and the cost of regulation (Subsection 3.1). Economists give short shrift to equity since it is subjective, controversial, and economic theory provides no unique insights. However, equity is the focus of politicians and of political decisions [Wilson (1980)]. The neglect of equity has left economists able to say little in normative or descriptive terms about regulations in practice. Political economists have begun to remedy this oversight by investigating voting behavior and the role of narrowly defined self-interest in political decisions [Downs (1957), Buchanan and Tullock (1975), Romer and Rosenthal (1984), Crandall (1983), Peltzman (1983), Pashigian (1985)].

The remainder of the chapter focuses on issues that arise in implementing regulatory programs. Section 4 deals with the quantification and valuation of benefits. Section 5 examines the discipline of the market and its feedbacks. In shaping proposals for efficient regulation, academic economists usually neglect *administrative simplicity* and *transparency*. Economists design policies to appeal to a philosopher-king (or rather an economist-king) rather than to a diverse constituency of voters, interest groups, and politicians. Yet, almost all people, except economists and some "Chicago" lawyers who believe in the free market more than most economists themselves, fail to see how economic incentives will call forth desired behavior as quickly and comprehensively as command-style regulation. Given the difficulty of overcoming public mistrust of economic approaches to regulation, a push for regulatory reform is attractive only if significant improvement over the status quo is possible (Subsection 5.1).

Regulation, in either present or improved form, also raises several issues beyond the scope of the inherently static models considered in Section 2. Among these are the impact of regulation on the investment and technology choices of firms in the regulated sector (Subsection 5.2) and its effect on the behavior of those whom it is designed to protect (Subsection 5.3). Since one industry or activity may be regulated under multiple programs, the problem of contradictory regulation may also arise (Subsection 5.3). The distributional impact of regulation and its effect on the overall economy, considered in Subsections 5.5 and 5.6, are also central implementation issues.

Finally, there are also a host of *noneconomic issues*, or issues that are less explicitly economic (Section 6). For example, environmental impact statements, the development of the field of risk analysis, the gains and losses associated with regulatory due process, and judicial and administrative review have had profound effects on the economics of HSE regulation.

2. A gallery of externalities and information management approaches

2.1. Externalities

From an economist's perspective, consideration of the sufficient conditions for the optimality of competitive equilibria is a natural starting point for an examination of HSE issues. One of the great accomplishments of modern economics is specificatio⁻ of sufficient conditions under which a competitive equilibrium is Pareto optimal [see Arrow (1983), Stiglitz (1983)]. These sufficient conditions are not a good description of the U.S. economy. Monopoly power, information asymmetries, and externalities can each negate the optimality of competitive equilibrium. Both economic regulation (considered by Joskow and Noll in Chapter 27 in this Handbook) and HSE regulation may be viewed as attempts to correct market failures.

The importance of these deviations was recognized long before the sufficient conditions were demonstrated. Although monopoly has been an important part of economic theory from the beginning, fruitful models of externalities are of recent origin. In particular, Pigou (1920) described externalities and argued that they could be treated via taxes and subsidies. In contrast to Pigou, Coase (1960) gave prominent attention to the role of private negotiation as a means of achieving efficiency in situations involving externalities. In his view the essential role of government in externality problems is limited to providing a clear allocation of property rights to provide a basis for subsequent private negotiations. Negotiation has its place when there are few parties involved and complete information. The need for mechanisms with lower transactions costs for situations combining large numbers with imperfect and asymmetric information is readily apparent (e.g. a situation where the externality is a public good for a sizable group).

Consider a regime in which firms hold the right to generate sulfur dioxide pollution, a major cause of acid rain. An individual damaged by the impact of acid rain on his favorite mountain fishing lake might be unable to identify a negotiating partner from the numerous and distantly located sources of the problem. Even where a negotiating partner could be identified, the free rider problem (among those who would benefit from a reduction in the externality level) sharply reduces the likelihood that potential Pareto improving deals between externality sources and victims will actually be consummated. Note that similar problems arise when victims hold the right not to be damaged, so that externality sources are liable.

Either direct negotiation or enforcement of victims' rights through the courts engender high transactions costs. When the courts hold firms liable for damages, firms can be expected to cut their externality output. However, because a liability scheme tries to compensate victims for actual damage sustained, it makes victims less anxious to forestall damages by undertaking efficient avoidance behavior.

Given the limited applicability of direct negotiation in all but a few externality problems and the informational economy of competitive market systems, it is natural to consider how other approaches, such as government intervention through the market mechanism, might be used to reach efficient outcomes.

2.2. *Optimal regulation of environmental pollution*

2.2.1. *Full information regulation*

Baumol and Oates (1975) present a Pigouvian taxes–subsidies approach to indicate how government might handle environmental externalities. They characterize the market equilibrium of a system that includes potential compensation payments to those impacted by externalities and a charge on the externality itself. They show that the first-order conditions characterizing the market solution can be made to coincide with those for Pareto optimality by pricing the externality at a rate equal to the sum of marginal damages across all victims while providing no damage-related compensation to those victims. The charges deter firms from generating externalities that can be eliminated at a marginal cost below the marginal damage imposed, while the absence of compensation ensures efficient damage avoidance by the victims.

Knowledge of both the victims' damage functions and the externality producers' cost functions is required to set the optimal Pigouvian tax. With this information in hand, the regulatory authority could directly limit each firm to the externality level it would choose under an optimal tax rather than impose the tax itself. Indeed, from the polluter's perspective, such command and control regulation would result in a more favorable income distribution than that achieved under optimal externality taxes.

2.2.2. Regulation with incomplete information

In a full information world, there is no efficiency basis for choosing among price-oriented, quantity-oriented or mixed regulation. However, regulators rarely have perfect knowledge. There are significant uncertainties in estimates of the dose–response functions that form the basis of the damage function. Firms generally have imperfect information about their abatement cost functions and may also have an incentive to misrepresent the information they do have in dealings with the regulator. A major strand in the literature has examined how imperfect or asymmetric information affects the choice of regulatory instruments.

The number of communication rounds and the complexity of the regulatory messages play an important role in the design of regulation when there is imperfect or asymmetric information. With an unlimited number of rounds, regulators might rely on a tatonnement process using either simple price or quantity regulation. Reactions to the policy settings at each stage might reveal information that could be used to adjust the settings. This would allow for eventual convergence to optimal regulation, assuming full adjustment of firms to the announced price. Alternatively, the regulator could issue contingency messages whose instructions would depend on the state of the world (say, the control costs for various pollution sources) actually realized.

Neither multiple iterations nor contingent messages are observed features of extant regulatory programs. The absence of continual fine tuning may be due to the fact that firms often incur large and irreversible fixed costs in responding to a particular level of regulation. An electric utility may build either a dry or wet sulfur dioxide scrubber depending on the tax or standard adopted, but cannot convert one type into the other as regulation changes. Also, because fixed investment is involved, a considerable interval of time must often pass before the impact of the initial regulatory settings is revealed.

Fixed costs that must be incurred before the state of the world is fully realized are also a problem for state-contingent regulatory schemes. Also, the states on which regulation must be conditioned represent the control cost functions for the externality producing firms, which may never be revealed to the regulatory authority. Finally, in a multifirm setting, state-contingent regulation would directly tie the regulation of each firm to the entire set of cost realizations.

Following regulatory practice, most attention has focused on the practice of having regulators request information from regulatees before they set standards (or fees). Some models envision more than one round of such information requests, and all need to ask whether regulatees are motivated to gather and provide complete, accurate information. The focus has been on models where communication is restricted to one or two rounds and the regulator can issue a rule with only a simple message specifying a price (externality tax), a quantity (a standard), or some mixture. Weitzman (1974, 1978) and Roberts and Spence (1976) treat the one-round case in which the center transmits a single message or set of messages to the regulated population. Kwerel (1977) considers the two-round case in which the firms send information to the center which uses it as an input in formulating its own regulatory message. Dasgupta, Hammond and Maskin (1980) consider both one- and two-round communication. The results obtained in this literature are outlined below.

2.2.3. *Prices versus quantities*

With one-round communication and noncontingent messages the regulator is generally incapable of attaining a Pareto efficient outcome. Instead, he seeks to minimize the expected deviation from efficiency. In Weitzman (1974) the marginal control cost function of the single firm producing an externality is not known to the regulator, who is limited to the choice between a pure tax or a pure standards approach. Figure 26.1 illustrates the case where the regulators' uncertainty relates to the location of a linear marginal cost function. Assuming that the marginal cost uncertainty is symmetric around MC_{E}, p_{E} is the best tax, and q_{E} is the best standard. However, neither p_{E} nor q_{E} is efficient when realized marginal costs differs from MC_{E}. If marginal costs are high (MC_{H}), a tax of p_{E} provides less than the efficient level of externality abatement (q_{H} vs. q_{H}^*) while a standard of q_{E} provides too much. However, if costs are low (MC_{L}) a tax of p_{E} results in excessive externality removal (q_{L} vs. q_{L}^*), while a standard of q_{E} provides too little removal. From Figure 26.1, it is apparent that standards will yield smaller expected deviations from efficiency than taxes when marginal benefits have a steeper slope than marginal costs and that taxes minimize expected deviations from efficiency when the reverse is true. Intuitively, when the marginal benefits function is steep, the socially optimal level of externalities is relatively insensitive to cost conditions and the welfare losses associated with departures from the optimal level are large, favoring a standards approach over a tax approach which, with a relatively flat marginal cost function, could result in large deviations from the optimal externality level if either high or low marginal costs are realized.

Laffont (1977) emphasizes the distinction between information gaps between the regulated firm and the regulator and genuine uncertainty, with only the former having relevance to the choice of regulatory instruments. In addition to the cost-side information gap considered by Weitzman, Laffont allows for those affected by externalities as well as those who generate them to have information unavailable to the regulator. In this context, a third regulatory option of setting a price for consumers and subsequently transmitting their quantity choice to the producers is considered along with Weitzman's taxes and direct quantity standards. In a structure with information gaps on both sides, he finds that direct

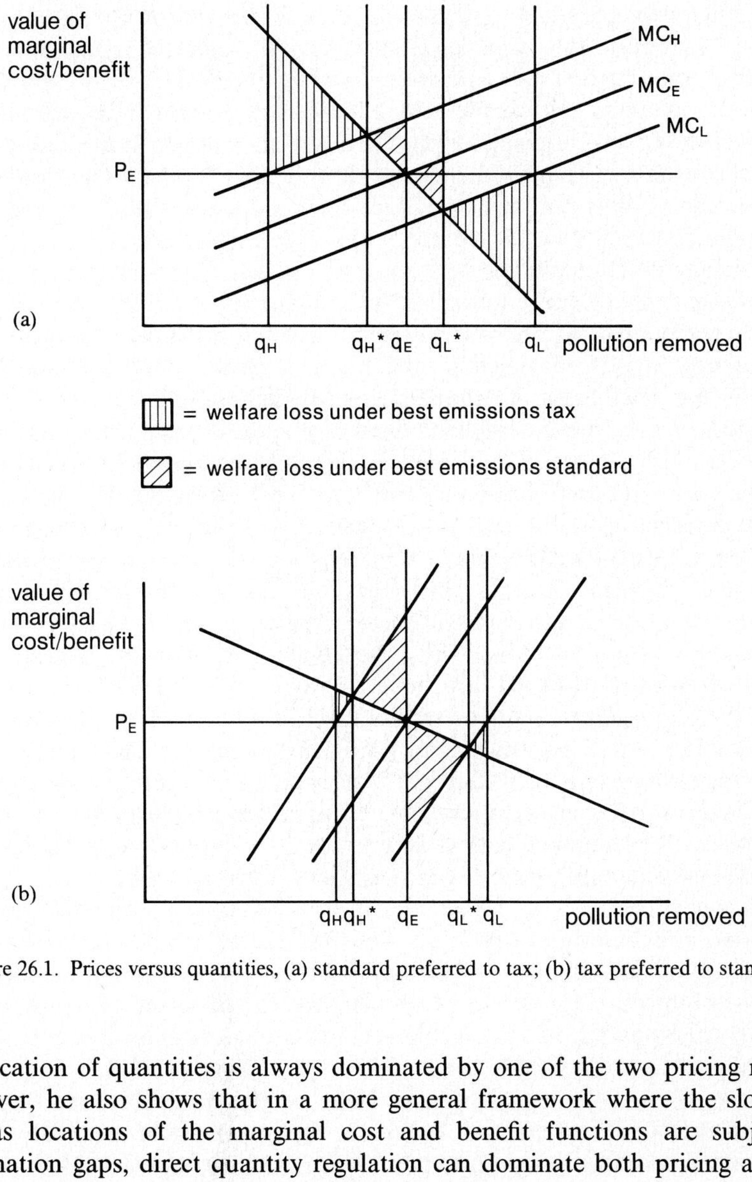

Figure 26.1. Prices versus quantities, (a) standard preferred to tax; (b) tax preferred to standard.

specification of quantities is always dominated by one of the two pricing modes. However, he also shows that in a more general framework where the slopes as well as locations of the marginal cost and benefit functions are subject to information gaps, direct quantity regulation can dominate both pricing alternatives.

In a pollution externality context, there are likely to be a large number of firms simultaneously subject to regulation. With many firms, a tax system, even if it results in a socially inefficient aggregate externality level, has the desirable property that marginal costs of abatement are equalized across firms. A quantity scheme that sets individual standards for each firm does not have this desirable property. However, the issuance of transferable property rights provides an alternative specification for a quantity scheme that does retain this feature, relying on a competitive market to allocate the permits in a manner that minimizes the cost of reaching the specified aggregate target. The choice between a tax scheme and marketable permits would still depend on the factors identified in Weitzman's single-firm analysis. Since marketable permits are at the implementation frontier we will consider them in some detail below.

Weitzman (1978) derives the best one-round policy in a multi-firm setting with quadratic cost and benefit functions. This policy incorporates both price and quantity components whose relative weight depend on the relative slopes of the marginal cost and benefit functions, the interdependence of the cost uncertainties across the regulated firms, and the degree of substitutability between the externality outputs of the different regulated firms in the social benefit function.

The relationship between the weight on the quantity term and the slopes of the marginal cost and benefit functions follows his 1974 article. Ceteris paribus, high positive correlation among the cost realization across firms favors an increased weight on the quantity component, since all firms are likely to err in the same direction in response to price signals. In a pollution externality context, one might expect control costs to have a strong positive correlation across sources. A high degree of substitutability in the benefit function between the (externality) outputs of different regulated firms tends to favor price regulation by increasing the focus on aggregate output rather than its components. The degree of substitutability across sources will vary with the specific application. For global or regional pollutants, such as fluorocarbons or acid rain precursors, externalities from a large set of firms may be nearly perfect substitutes. With local pollutants, an increase in externality output at one location coupled with an offsetting reduction elsewhere may lead to large swings in realized benefits.

Weitzman's policy is one example of a general result due to Dasgupta, Hammond and Maskin (1980). They find that the best policy with one-round communication presents each regulated firm with a nonlinear tax function that renders its objective (profit) function identical to the expected social welfare function. Such tax schemes are implementations of the public choice revelation mechanisms of Groves (1973), Clarke (1971), and Vickrey (1960).

Mendelsohn (1984) adds endogenous technical change to the basic Weitzman (1974) model. Technical change compounds the variability of externality abatement outcomes under price regulation. When marginal costs are low, so that abatement overshoots the socially optimal level under price regulation, firms overinvest in cost-reducing technical change, because the returns to technical investment depend on the volume of abatement to which it can be applied. By lowering the cost of abatement, technical progress increases the margin of overshooting. Conversely, when price regulation leads to undershooting the social optimum there is a tendency to reduce investment in technical change, compounding the undershooting. In sum, the extra degree of freedom in a model with endogenous technical change is used in a socially undesirable manner under price regulation. In contrast, quantity regulation which holds the level of abatement constant results in a stable technical investment decision regardless of the realization of the underlying cost uncertainty.

2.2.4. *Revealing regulation*

Even though the best one-round policy leads each of the regulated firms to pursue the social objective, the full information social optimum will not be attained because the cost expectations for the entire set of firms on which the tax function for each of them is based differ from the actual cost realizations.

With two-round communication, the regulator can close the information gap by seeking cost information from the firms prior to imposing regulation. If firms can be induced to report truthfully, the regulator can reach the ex post optimum by using the true cost reports rather than expected costs as the basis for regulation. Since the regulator never observes true costs, each firm will provide a cost report that minimizes its total cost of regulation under the regulatory scheme it anticipates will be applied. Pure price or quantity regulation will not induce truthful reporting. If firms anticipate that the center will set an externality tax on the basis of the cost reports, they have an incentive to underestimate costs, so that a low tax is set. If firms anticipate the center will regulate through a quantity target, they will overstate costs to secure a high target. However, if regulators commit themselves to the policy outlined in Weitzman (1978) or Dasgupta, Hammond and Maskin (1980), so that each firm faces the social objective plus or minus a lump-sum payment, truthful revelation will be a dominant strategy. The only difference from the one-round case is that the first best can actually be attained. Such mechanisms have not, to our knowledge, been employed in any public choice or externality context, and it is unclear whether such systems are implementable given the sheer complexity of their administration and the budget balance and equity issues inherent in tailoring a revealing tax for each polluter.

An alternative mechanism in which truth-telling is a Nash equilibrium, but not dominant, strategy, has been proposed by Kwerel (1977). Based on the cost reports of the firms, C, and its own estimate of the damage function, D, the regulator determines the pollution level at which the marginal reported cost of pollution abatement and its own estimate of the marginal benefit of pollution abatement are equal and sets the number of pollution licenses at this level. The licenses are traded competitively among firms with each being required to hold licenses sufficient to cover their actual pollution levels. For licenses held in excess of actual pollution, the regulator pays a subsidy equal to its estimate of the marginal benefit of abatement given full utilization of the license stock it has issued. Thus, if L licenses are issued the market price of licenses will be $\max[D'(L), C'(L)]$, with the first term reflecting the subsidy rate to holders of excess licenses and the second term reflecting the value of abatement cost avoidance to the regulated firms. If $D''(L) > 0$ and $C''(L) < 0$, so that the marginal benefit of abatement rises and the marginal cost of abatement falls as the aggregate allowable pollution level is increased, the price of licenses is minimized by issuing a quantity of licenses, L^*, equal to the Pareto optimal pollution level based on the cost reports made to the regulator. If the initial distribution of licenses does not depend on reported costs, so that cost reports do not have income effects, the sum of abatement and license costs is minimized when the license price is minimized. Therefore, truth-telling is a Nash equilibrium strategy for firms seeking to minimize their total cost of regulation.

2.3. *Cost effectiveness*

The foregoing discussion is framed in terms of attaining Pareto optimality or of minimizing expected deviations from optimality at a fairly high level of abstraction. Regulatory practice raises separate issues that are not considered in these frameworks. Rather than pursue optimality, the issue is whether we can improve current practice taking into account the political, informational, and institutional constraints present in applied problems. Perhaps the most glaring feature in regulatory practice is the wide divergence of opinion as to the benefits of externality control. When health effects are at issue, the chemical, spatial, and temporal relationships between primary emissions and pollutants may be poorly understood. The dose–response relationship between pollution and health effects, especially where chronic diseases with long latency periods are involved, is also subject to considerable uncertainty [Morgan et al. (1984)]. Finally, even if consensus estimates of the magnitude of mortality and morbidity effects could be attained, their valuation is fraught with controversy. The valuation of aesthetic, vegetation, and materials benefits are also highly controversial, calling into question the notion of a generally accepted benefit function, perhaps surrounded by some uncertainty, that is implicit in discussions focused on the goal of Pareto optimality. Efficiency may be a natural objective in a world where distributional concerns can always be handled through lump-sum taxation. In reality, redistribution is difficult and expensive and so the distributional effects of a program matter a great deal.

Thus, regulatory targets are usually set through the political process, not through the use of some grand optimization calculus. While the political debate can be improved by attempts at calculating social optima, perhaps a greater contribution can be made by taking the politically set objectives as given and devising a cost-minimizing approach to reaching them, thereby pursuing the goal of cost effectiveness rather than optimality.

Montgomery (1972), following earlier work by Dales (1968), evaluates the role of tradable permits as a means of attaining cost-effective externality abatement. An objective defined in terms of the pollution level measured at a set of monitoring points can be attained at least cost through the competitive trading of pollution licenses among firms whose emissions cause pollution. This least-cost property is independent of the initial allocation of pollution licenses. However, since an individual firm would need to hold licenses for each receptor where its emissions contributed to measured pollution, an important prerequisite for such a system would be a set of commonly accepted dispersion and conversion models that could be used to make the translation from emissions at the plant site to environmental impacts at the receptor sites. Our knowledge of conversion processes varies widely across pollutants. Dispersion is inherently uncertain. The density of the monitoring site network, the importance of long-range transport for the pollutant in question and the cutoff point used for determining de minimis effects would together determine the number of markets in which each emitter would be required to hold licenses.

In contrast to pollution licenses, emission licenses confer a right to emit pollutants. Under an emission license scheme, there is one market for the emissions of each pollutant or pollution precursor. However, one-for-one trading of emissions licenses raises the problem of "hotspots" if emissions become concentrated at certain locations within the relevant airshed or watershed. To avoid hotspots, the regulator must set trading terms for each possible transaction such that no trade results in an increase in measured pollution at any receptor point. Provided that the hotspot problem is avoided, emission licenses appear to provide a simpler mechanism than pollution licenses, since there is no need to hold licenses for each individual receptor site. The cost of this simplicity may be a loss in cost effectiveness: in contrast to the pollution license scheme, competitive markets do not yield cost-effective attainment of the pollution targets. The problem is lumpiness, since avoiding hotspots at one location may require trading terms in the emissions license market that cause the target to be exceeded at other locations. In a pollution license scheme this "excess" attainment could be sold to some other polluter; in the emissions license context it is wasted.

While theoretical models of tradable permits have generally assumed perfectly competitive behavior in permit markets, a small number of large sources are responsible for a large share of some pollution externalities that have attracted regulatory attention. For this reason, individual firms may hold market power in tradable permit markets, especially where the pollutant being regulated has relatively localized effects. Hahn (1984) presents an analysis in which permit trading results in cost-effective abatement under perfect competition but fails to do so when there is a strategic player in the permit market unless the regulator endows the strategic player with precisely the efficient number of permits before trading opens. Of course, if the regulator knew the efficient allocation of emissions ex ante, there is no need to allow for trades at all. Deviations in either direction from this correct initial allocation will increase the total cost of attaining the target. To minimize the adverse impact of market power on efficiency, Hahn and Noll (1982) propose a zero revenue auction scheme that puts all firms on the same side of the market in the initial market period, but avoids imposing costs on them as a group by reallocating revenues from the initial permit auction according to a fixed rule to avoid income effects.

2.4. *Modeling health and safety regulation*

This subsection aims to examine the underlying economic basis for safety and health regulation. Several features of occupational choice and consumer product decisions dictate an analysis distinct from that applicable to environmental regulation. Unlike environmental quality, health and safety are not in themselves inherently public goods, so there is no prima facie case that the pre-regulation outcomes place too low a weight on these attributes (exceptions are dams, nuclear power plants, etc. where risk is inherently spread over many people). With heterogeneous preferences and income levels, the set of activities and outputs arising from the decisions of utility-maximizing consumers and profit-maximizing firms could be expected to embody significant variation in achieved health and safety levels.

Another difference from environmental regulation arises in the role of private legal action as a substitute or complement to regulation. Stewart and Krier (1978) note that private lawsuits against polluters have not had widespread impact on polluters' behavior. In health and safety matters, where the relevant parties and the extent of damages can be more readily identified, private litigation plays a significant role, and the potential for litigation may lead parties to alter their behavior. The role of the litigation system and the allocation of rights between the consumer/worker and the producer/employer are considered in Subsection 2.4.1.

A final difference from environmental regulation arises from the greater involvement of individual consumers or workers in the realization of safe or healthful outcomes. It is not enough for firms to offer appropriate products and working environments – consumers and workers should also take an appropriate level of "care" in their activities. Because of the need for care, health and safety regulation raises the question of moral hazard if regulation induces consumers and workers to react to regulation by behaving in a riskier fashion [Evans and Schwing (1985)].

What rationale (aside from paternalism as described below) is available for substituting the judgment of the regulator for that of the individual agents? Two broad types of market failures form the basis of the argument for intervention. First, since even in a world with efficient information markets, individual agents do not bear the full costs of adverse health and safety impacts, they will undertake an excess amount of unsafe and unhealthful activities in the absence of regulation. Second, the nature of information as a commodity suggests information markets are likely to fail in the absence of government intervention. The demonstration of information market failure alone may justify interventions that provide information directly or force private agents to do so. However, the case for direct regulation of product characteristics as a useful response does not follow from the mere demonstration of informational failure. Consumer heterogeneity and the risks of paternalism weigh heavily against this approach. Despite this, OSHA and CPSC focus almost exclusively on product characteristic regulation. The literature on information is reviewed in Subsection 2.4.2.

2.4.1. Accidents, litigation, and regulation

The goal of consumer product and occupational health and safety regulation is to reduce the occurrence and severity of accidents, a term defined broadly to include unintended harmful effects resulting from exposure to or use of a product as well as product failure. The division of the costs of accidents between the parties involved, and between those parties and society at large, can influence the decisions and behavior surrounding activities that have the potential for resulting in an accident. (Such activities may be called risky.) Two types of decisions are relevant: the decision to engage in a particular activity and the level of care exercised in an activity. Regulation provides an ex ante method of affecting these decisions, while litigation is an ex post tool. From an economic perspective, the primary issue is whether the litigation system provides workers and employers with the proper incentive to engage only in risky activities whose value is sufficiently great to offset the harm they may cause. To the parties involved, the matter of income distribution, not efficiency, appears to be of pre-eminent importance.

Oi (1973) considers the market for products with a positive failure probability to determine the impact of liability allocation across producers and consumers on decisions in an environment where the size of the loss associated with product failure varies across consumers. When they are liable, each consumer's choice among products offering different combinations of price and reliability reflects his information regarding the size of the loss incurred in the event of failure. When they are liable, producers are required to indemnify actual losses in the event of failure, so that the size of losses in the event of failure do not affect consumer decisions. Unless they are allowed to discriminate among consumers, the shift to producer liability forces producers to offer a package of product plus full insurance and affects the market allocation. Although the Coase theorem would hold with symmetric discrimination possibilities across alternative liability regimes, it does not hold given ordinary barriers to producer discrimination. Oi's demonstration that the adoption of producer liability can actually force reliable products out of the market belies the notion that producer liability necessarily promotes healthier or safer market outcomes.

In Oi's model, as in Shavell (1982) (who considers how insurance affects producer incentives to make socially appropriate expenditures on risk reduction), the consumer/worker and the producer/employer are both perfectly informed regarding the risks inherent in the product or activity. Furthermore, should an accident or product failure occur, it is unerringly associated with one product or activity. Yet, in many risky situations the causation of harm (accidents) is beset with uncertainty. Cancers occur naturally, but may also be induced by personal behavior (smoking and diet) and occupational exposure to carcinogens. The claim of a smoker with a family history of cancer against an asbestos manufacturer for lung cancer presents a classic case of uncertain causation.

Court suits for liability tend to have an all-or-nothing character. The plaintiff must prove by a preponderance of the evidence that his disease was caused by the defendant. When this is done, he is entitled to receive full compensation (some states use contributory negligence to make awards proportional to contribution). Unfortunately, this is too simple a model. Smoking and asbestos exposure are multiplicative factors in causing lung cancer. For an asbestos insulator who smokes, what is the cause of the lung cancer? Precisely this issue has been addressed in asbestos suits with the courts having a difficult time deciding what was responsible for the lung cancer. The same situation has arisen for men who received direct exposure to ionizing radiation during military testing in the 1940s and 1950s. Radiation is known to cause cancer. However, are the cancers that have appeared in some of these men thirty years after exposure due to the radiation or to other factors?

Congress ordered the National Cancer Institute to figure out the proportional risks for various kinds of cancers: How much of a contribution was made by exposure to radiation during the atomic bomb tests and how much by subsequent exposures, such as smoking, occupational exposures, and heredity? Rall et al. (1985) used the substantial knowledge about the effects of ionizing radiation to come up with just such a model. Lagakos and Mosteller (1986) describe the model and respond to several critics. A similar approach has now been taken for asbestos [Chase et al. (1985)]. There are substantial questions about whether this approach can be used in the current legal system and whether either experts or juries would find it appealing.

The impact of the legal system on behavior depends on its features. Shavell (1985) considers a situation in which activities generate benefits and possibly losses that can both be measured in monetary terms. Under a strict liability standard, parties are held liable for accident losses they cause whether or not they exercised care. If there is no uncertainty as to the causation of accidents, agents will undertake only those activities whose benefits exceed expected accident losses. Such behavior will maximize the expected value of the activities in question, which is the desired outcome if society is risk neutral. Under a negligence rule, agents cannot be held liable unless they fail to exercise care in a situation where care "should" have been exercised. (The desirability of care-taking can be determined through a criterion that compares the cost of care to the resulting reduction in expected loss.) In this system, agents can protect themselves from liability simply by taking care, even if the costs of care-taking plus expected losses exceed the benefits of the activity in question. Thus, the negligence system fails to promote decisions that favor only those activities with positive expected net benefits.

If there is uncertainty over causation, a situation that arises in many cases of interest, behavior depends on the legal regime (strict liability or negligence), the rule used to resolve the uncertainty, and on the portion of the loss that is paid by the parties that may have caused the accident. Under strict liability, a more likely than not rule (a common criterion for liability) attempts to determine if the probability that an observed accident results from a particular risky activity exceeds a threshold level (often 1/2). If the threshold is exceeded, the party undertaking the activity is held liable for the entire loss. Application of this rule can result in a risky activity being pursued at a level that is either too low or too high depending on whether its probability of causation falls below or above that necessary to trigger liability. Under negligence, where taking care makes a party judgment proof, there may be either too much or too little care taken, with the outcome again depending on the relationship between the triggers and the levels.

A proportional liability standard is shown to induce the correct level of risk-taking and care. Proportional liability is usually developed in the terms of liability-splitting among parties known to be the potential source of damages suffered by the plaintiff, so that, if occupational exposure is thought to cause 20 percent of cancers in a particular category of employees, the employer would be held liable for 20 percent of the resultant damages. *Sindell vs. Abbott*, a recent case involving DES, divided damages to a cancer victim whose mother had taken an unidentified brand of the synthetic cancer-causing hormone among the multiple suppliers in proportion to their market shares, even though none of the suppliers could be held liable under a more-likely-than-not test and only one of them was the actual source of the drug.

Shavell (1984) considers the choice between litigation, regulation, and a mix of the two. In a model where litigation always leads to a "correct" verdict in which the injurer will be held liable for the actual amount of harm caused (no punitive damages), he considers whether parties will undertake optimal expenditures on care. The answer is no for two reasons. First, the injured party may not undertake litigation, especially under American practice where each side is responsible for its own costs in civil litigation regardless of the ultimate verdict.

Second, the potential injurer recognizes that he is "judgment proof" beyond the level of his wealth and insurance coverage, so does not take potential liability in excess of wealth into account in choosing his behavior.

The regulatory alternative involves setting a standard that is the same for all parties engaged in the activity, even though the risk of harm varies across parties. The optimal standard equals the level of care that is first best for a party that poses an average risk of harm. The choice between standards and liability hinges on the same factors that arise in Weitzman's prices and quantities framework. In particular, the more dispersed the potential for harm across parties the less attractive is a uniform standard. Conversely, the more important the wealth constraint as a barrier to recovery, the less attractive is a pure liability system. Shavell finds that a mixed system of liability and standards is at least weakly superior in inducing desirable care patterns to either the pure liability or pure standards approach. In fact, regulatory programs do not foreclose the possibility of private lawsuits, so that parties with a high potential for causing harm have an incentive to exceed the applicable standards.

The real-world litigation system does not always produce correct verdicts, and sometimes provides punitive damages. For this reason it is possible that the pursuit of health and safety issues in the courts alone may result in outcomes that are excessively safe from a welfare perspective. A *New England Journal of Medicine* editorial defined a litogen as a chemical which does not harm health but does lead to lawsuits regarding harm. Several recent actions, such as the withdrawal of contraceptive foams and the anti-nausea drug Bendectin from the market despite the lack of scientific evidence of health or safety problems, and the threatened withdrawal of whooping cough vaccine suggest that in some cases regulation may be needed to temper, rather than supplement, the tort system.

In Shavell's models, the only concern is the cost of the accident itself. Calabresi (1970) posits a more general framework that considers secondary and tertiary costs as well as the primary cost examined by Shavell. The secondary cost concept recognizes that the welfare impact of a given accident will depend on the extent to which accident costs are spread and in some cases on the timing of the mechanism for making accident-related transfers. Thus, one advantage of no-fault schemes is that they allow for the immediate financing of therapeutic measures that may lessen the permanent disability resulting from a given accident injury. Spreading also tends to reduce the secondary costs of accidents, which is one explanation for insurance. However, spreading may attenuate incentives to take care by externalizing the cost of accidents, so that secondary and primary cost avoidance may be in conflict. Tertiary costs arise from the administration of the system for allocating accident costs. The high level of tertiary costs associated with litigation to determine fault in accidents was another prime motivation for the adoption of no-fault systems. Generally, any comparison between regulation and liability as alternative paths to desirable levels of health and safety practice must consider the role of administrative cost.

2.4.2. The market for information

In environmental regulation information considerations add complexity to a market failure that would exist without them. In health and safety regulation information *is* the problem. Information is a "commodity" useful in making product or occupational choice decisions. Many authors have noted that this commodity has features that thwart the operation of efficient markets. First, information is a public good in the sense that the seller cannot appropriate the value of his product. Indeed, each buyer of information instantly becomes a competitor who can provide the product to other potential buyers. For this reason, the seller often cannot anticipate a volume of sales sufficient to justify the cost of gathering information in the first place. Second, even if dissemination among potential buyers can be controlled (say they are geographically dispersed), information is a natural monopoly. Information will likely be sold at a price far in excess of the near-zero marginal cost of dissemination. Third, in many contexts, information about specific products is produced jointly with the products themselves, so that the product supplier is the least-cost source of product information. Yet, product suppliers may not be credible sources of information given the incentive to provide only favorable data to buyers in the product market. Imperfect information also underlies the phenomenon of moral hazard, since due care can be enforced only if worker/consumer behavior can be perfectly monitored.

It is important to distinguish inherent uncertainty that is correctly perceived by all market participants from a situation involving misperceptions. Akerlof (1970) provides examples in which correctly perceived uncertainty disrupts the operation of economically useful markets. The problem of adverse selection is illustrated in the market for automobiles, where the consumers' inability to distinguish "lemons" from good cars drives good cars out of the used-car market. Counteracting institutions, such as warranties and reputations, can provide signals of quality that can help overcome the problem of uncertain quality.

Spence (1977) develops a model where homogeneous consumers, who may be risk neutral or risk averse, misperceive product quality. After characterizing the socially optimal quality level and risk allocation, he finds that ordinary producer liability cannot be employed to reach the optimum. The addition of a second instrument, in the form of a fine payable to the state in addition to the liability payment to consumers, can be used to reach the optimum. However, the optimal fine depends on the sensitivity of consumer perceptions of quality to changes in actual quality, which may be difficult to assess. With heterogeneous consumers, it is even more difficult to reach the optimum, which can involve the production of multiple qualities that should be consumed by specific groups of consumers. There is also the problem of moral hazard if consumers who are insured by producers can affect the probability of product failure. Alternative approaches that do not require the regulator to perceive consumer perceptions, such as direct regulation and the provision of official product quality information to consumers, also have shortcomings in realistic settings. Spence's results highlight the near impossibility of reaching an optimum through regulation in a setting where misperceptions play an important role.

Shapiro (1982) looks at the quality choice of a profit-maximizing firm in a dynamic setting involving consumer misperceptions. If a product is purchased frequently and consumers can experience product quality, firms weigh the current cost savings associated with low quality against the adverse effect of a poor reputation on future sales and profitability. The faster consumers update their perceptions, the more closely the quality level offered by profit-maximizing producers approaches the perfect information limit. Informational regulation may be interpreted as an effort to facilitate the learning process. However, the welfare implications of imperfect information, and efforts to redress it, are unclear because imperfect information may occur in tandem with other market failures. For example, if producers with market power set product prices above marginal cost, a social surplus objective may be served when consumers over-estimate product quality, which leads them to buy more at the going price than they would if perfectly informed (an example of the theory of the second best). Shapiro also considers the case where firms can adjust quality over time, and shows that firms may choose to either improve quality monotonically towards the perfect information limit or to oscillate quality in cycles of building and milking a reputation.

3. Goal-setting

3.1. Social goals

A significant advantage of the market as a mechanism for allocating goods is that each consumer can take account of his preferences and income level when choosing how much of each good to consume. Individually, we may be unable to "understand" why anyone would choose to buy some of the goods and services offered, but we are not directly affected by the choices. At the opposite end of the spectrum, a family situation where the tastes of one or two adults are imposed on children poses a sharp contrast to the market model. The unfortunate consequences of continuing to attempt to impose parental tastes on older children and adolescents are all too familiar. Any system that increases individual choice for responsible adults has important advantages. When the Food and Drug Administration first banned cyclamates and then saccharin, the public outcry forced Congress to rescind the ban in favor of labeling and individual choice.

Unfortunately, when public or quasi-public goods are considered, decisions made by individuals on the basis of their private incentives do not add up to a beneficial social decision; individuals must agree on the provision of these goods, even when they are not provided uniformly. For example, air quality is uniform over a neighborhood, but some neighborhoods are much more polluted than others. Air quality cannot be tailored to the preferences of each individual, but instead must reflect the tastes of all who either experience the air pollution or who cause it. In this situation, goal-setting must be collective and there is the problem of defining some sort of social utility function (or its equivalent). Having a small number of actors may not expedite solution because of the issues associated with bargaining.

3.1.1. Setting risk goals

One area of particular controversy involves setting risk goals. Douglas and Wildavsky (1982) show that what is perceived to be risky and what is an acceptable risk are largely determined by culture. While this observation helps to put the current difficulties into perspective, it does not help to manage risks within our culture [Fischhoff et al. (1981)]. Extreme and conflicting views such as Perrow's (1984) position that our technology has increased the potential for disaster, the U.S. Council on Environmental Quality (1980) finding that the Earth's resources were being used up quickly, or Simon and Kahn's (1984) conclusion that the world is getting richer, less risky, and generally better, promote the suspicion that investigators' biases play an important role in many analyses.

Congress's position (in 1958 and the early 1970s) seemed to be that no risk was tolerable [Lave (1981b)]. In this mood it instructed the Food and Drug Administration that "no substance shown to cause cancer in animals or humans could be added to food" (the Delaney Clause). Congress directed the Environmental Protection Agency to set primary air quality standards that "protected the most sensitive group in the population with an ample margin of safety". The Occupational Safety and Health Administration was instructed to "assure insofar as practicable that no employee will suffer diminished health, functional capacity, or life expectancy as a result of his work".

These zero-risk goals have proven dysfunctional to the agencies, since they cannot reduce most risks to zero and are left without a sensible basis for setting priorities. Left to their own devices, several agencies have gone through goal-setting processes. The Food and Drug Administration (1982) decided that a food contaminant estimated to lead to less than one additional cancer per million lifetimes constitutes a de minimis risk and would not be considered a carcinogen under the Delaney Clause. The Federal Aviation Administration (1980) has implicitly set safety goals by adopting a value (approximately \$500 000) for the social benefit of preventing a premature fatality. It uses this value in benefit–cost analysis. The Nuclear Regulatory Commission (1983) has gone through an explicit goal-setting process for commercial nuclear power plants and has set goals. It decided that nuclear power plants should not increase the risk of either immediate death or cancer by more than 0.1 percent (one part in 1000) over the levels prevailing without the plant; it also bounded the likelihood of a core melt, even if such a mishap would cause no injury to the surrounding population.

Most agencies have avoided dealing explicitly with goal-setting, but have not attempted to regulate risks to zero. Almost inevitably, this means that agencies are sued because the regulations they set are not sufficiently protective. In deciding a challenge to OSHA tightening the exposure standard for benzene, the Supreme Court (1980) used a common law doctrine that the "law does not concern itself with trivia" to assert that agencies cannot regulate a de minimis risk. Apparently, the hope was that there would be some general agreement on what constitutes a trivial risk so that agencies could avoid cases where the risk is already trivial and use this as an upper bound for a risk goal.

Unfortunately, defining what is a trivial risk has proved to be no easier than defining a risk goal. Perhaps the most helpful research has been an examination of past federal agencies' decisions, with an attempt to draw a common pattern out of decisions [Milvy (1986), Byrd and Lave (1987), Travis et al. (1987)]. This "common law" approach to inferring risk goals may eventually arrive at helpful generalizations, but there is still a good deal of noise in current decisions.

3.1.2. The political economy of regulation

Most of the early HSE legislation was formulated with a "polluter must pay" principle; it seemed naive, however, to assume that the public would not bear the cost. Measuring even the first round incidence of HSE policies is difficult. Some calculations are shown below in Section 5.

The formulation of HSE goals is supposed to be the task of our elected representatives in Congress and state legislatures. Setting such goals is controversial and, since representatives like to be re-elected, they rarely face the issues and give helpful guidance. In some cases Congress has provided only the most general rhetoric; in other cases, Congress has set specific standards and time tables. Only in rare cases does Congress actually specify goals that would serve to guide a regulatory agency which is supposed to be implementing policy set by Congress. The language of social and economic regulatory statutes, and representatives of the agencies charged with carrying them out, frequently invoke the public interest as the basis for regulation. However, the number of passionate advocates of regulation is not consistent with the diffuse distribution of its public benefits. An explanation is needed of how the political support necessary to implement and maintain programs of regulation is generated.

Stigler (1971) and Peltzman (1975) argue that regulation is actually promoted by interest groups seeking private benefits, and that administering agencies are captured by private interests, whom they serve in return for support in the political arena. This capture theory is most directly applicable to economic regulation. The political economy literature is relevant to goal formulation in terms of who the agency actually serves, who controls the agenda, and the roles played by the courts and other actors. Peltzman (1983), Crandall (1983), and Pashigian (1985) have argued that concern for preserving jobs and other aspects of direct economic self-interest were major factors influencing Congressional votes on the Clean Air Act and other major pieces of environmental legislation. Ackerman and Hassler (1981) describe a coalition of eastern coal producers and environmentalists who put together the 1977 Clean Air Act Amendments so as to force continued use of eastern coal while taking steps to lower emissions in the west and eventually to lower emissions in the east.

Although social regulation is popularly perceived as placing an uncompensated burden on the entire regulated sector, it can yield significant rents to at least a portion of the industry being regulated. Maloney and McCormick (1982) present an event analysis of stock market returns for the cotton textiles and metal refining and smelting industries for periods in which they were subject to new regulations by OSHA and EPA. They attribute their finding of abnormal excess returns associated with regulation to the nonuniformity of its impact across firms. Worker health standards in the cotton textile industry were particularly costly for existing small firms and potential small entrants, providing a competitive edge to the large firms. In the metals refining and smelting industry, regulation blockaded entry, thereby reducing potential competition and raising the returns of existing facilities. Neumann and Nelson (1982), Pashigan (1984), and Bartel and Thomas (1985) also find that regulation imposes disproportionate costs on small or nonunionized firms to the benefit of their large or unionized competitors.

From the earliest stage, it was clear to Congress that HSE regulation would impose major costs and disruptions on the economy. This led to thinking about where to impose the (initial) burden. One general principle was to impose the greatest burden on yet-to-be-built plant and equipment, with mild or no burdens on existing plant and equipment. This "new source" bias has been shown to be inefficient, leading in some cases both to higher costs and to delays in the time required to achieve a given objective that depends on average rather than marginal performance [Gruenspecht (1982)]. It is also a natural source of rents for existing facilities in many contexts.

3.2. Paternalism revisited

Paternalism, not market failure, is the primary motivation behind much HSE regulation. While individuals demand safety, they generally demand less than others desire them to have, particularly for teenagers and young men [Winston and Mannering (1984)]. The installation and use of seat belts provides a clear example. Recent analyses show that state mandatory belt-use laws have been effective both in increasing safety belt use and in reducing deaths and injuries [Latimer and Lave (1987)]. A benefit–cost analysis of safety belts assuming 100 percent usage shows they are extremely beneficial, while one at 10–15 percent use shows they are not worthwhile [Lave (1981a)]. The federal government has required that all new cars sold since the 1967 model be equipped with safety belts. There has never been a federal requirement that these safety belts be buckled, although about half the states have enacted such laws since 1984. By 1984, only about 10–15 percent of occupants were buckling their belts and so the effectiveness in practice of an extremely helpful device was negligible.

If there are economies of scale in installing safety belts or concern that people other than the first purchaser have their choices constrained by that person's decisions at the time of purchase (e.g. passengers or subsequent owners might not have the opportunity to wear safety belts), there might be justification for requiring that all cars be manufactured with belts. Beyond equipping the cars with belts, there are few externalities associated with individual use of these belts. To be sure, society pays for the medical costs of those who are injured and pays to support the dependents of someone who is killed, but these externalities could be handled via insurance [Lave (1987a)].

Paternalism is also clear in decisions that something beyond providing information to workers about risk is required to optimize occupational safety. The Occupational Safety and Health Administration has favored lowering the concentration of toxic chemicals around a worker, rather than permitting the worker to be protected by a personal protective device (since they fear workers usually will not wear such devices); the agency favors requiring worker training, even though workers know they are in hazardous situations and need information. Indeed, few people other than economists and libertarians seem to regard it as even questionable that governments would not act to regulate large risks rather than provide workers with information.

3.3. *Defining social goals through process*

The more than 200 million Americans, millions of businesses, and the multiple roles of people as consumers, workers (employed in jobs from heavy manufacturing to personal services), and citizens combine with the cultural diversity of the United States to ensure that no consensus can be reached on nonvacuous HSE goals. Congress has tended to fill the preambles of HSE legislation with rhetoric that reflects wishes rather than goals. In practice, Congress has legislated administrative procedures and decision frameworks, rather than clearly stated goals. By requiring that agencies inform the public that they intend to consider an area, hold public hearing on proposals, and specify the basis for their decisions, Congress has ensured that decisions reflect the many views in society. However, such complicated procedures eliminate the possibility of quick, simple regulations. By requiring that agencies listen to a broad spectrum of concern and be responsive to it, Congress implicitly asks agencies to make compromises. The Administrative Procedures Act makes it clear that agencies are serving a political function, not just making narrow technical decisions.

In many cases, Congress has directed regulatory agencies to give little or no attention to the costs of abatement. For example, the Clean Air Act precludes examination of the cost implications of achieving the primary air quality standards. Some acts permit indirect consideration of abatement costs by mandating that regulations must be "practicable." In other situations, Congress specifies that agencies find the best available control technology. Occasionally, Congress or the President have required that decision alternatives be scrutinized via benefit–cost analysis.

Implicit in these decision frameworks is Congressional goal-setting, since it constrains the nature of the resulting decisions. Lave (1981b) has set out a series of decision frameworks and identified the nature of the HSE goals implicit in each. Apparently, Congress finds it less controversial to specify a decision process than to specify a sharp goal.

A useful framework for examining HSE decisions recognizes the multiple goals and seeks to determine if all can be satisfied, or what proposals satisfy almost all goals. Four criteria for good policy discussed above are economic efficiency, equity, administrative simplicity, and transparency. These criteria refer to getting the marginal conditions for cost minimization correct, making sure that the proper people pay or receive the benefits, minimizing the level of resources required for administration, and ensuring that the route by which the program achieves its purposes is clear to the public.

In the absence of sharp social goals, we are left with weak, contradictory goals or goals defined by process. A system without sharp goals will appear to lack direction and be out of control, leading to demands that new procedures be instituted to bring it under control and tighten its focus. Since HSE regulation affects many economic and social decisions that had previously been outside government control, such as where to locate a factory and what production technology to use, these demands cannot easily be satisfied.

There have also been calls for broad spectrum regulatory reform, including proposals to implement benefit–cost tests, regulatory budgets, and regulatory calendars [Noll (1971)]. Several books have been written about the attempt to control HSE regulation [White (1981), Miller and Yandle (1979), Viscusi (1983b), Litan and Nordhaus (1983), Wilson (1980)]. These often have a narrow disciplinary focus, with the economists focusing on efficiency and concluding that

HSE regulation is not efficient, or the political scientists noting that HSE regulation is not very different from previous social movements.

4. Quantification and valuation of benefits

4.1. Quantifying the benefits

Any systematic approach to reforming HSE regulation requires that both benefits and costs be quantified. Laying out the costs is relatively straightforward, although far from trivial. Quantifying the benefits is much more difficult [Freeman (1979), Kneese (1984), National Science Foundation (1985a)]. While people could be expected to know a dirty environment or unsafe workplace when confronted with it, a major regulatory program requires more precise and objective measurement of the externalities and identification of the causes of harm. But even measuring air or water quality requires a judgment as to which pollutants are of interest [National Academy of Sciences (1984), Lave and Upton (1987), Peskin and Seskin (1975)]. Even where this appears easy, further judgment is required regarding measurement targets and techniques. For example, the sulfur dioxide and particles that are emitted when burning coal were recognized as important pollutants at an early date [Ruff (1978)]. Yet, the focus of concern has shifted from sulfur dioxide itself to acid sulfates, the products of sulfur dioxide reacting with other gases in the atmosphere. Similarly, the initial way in which particles were measured, total mass per unit volume, put the focus on the largest particles, since a particle of diameter 100 micrometers has one million times the mass of a 1 micrometer particle. However, it is the smaller particles that have the greatest effects on health and visibility, requiring a different set of measurements and different control standards.

Although the textbooks assume that economists get their quantification of effects from scientists and engineers, in fact economists play a leading role in estimating the effects of air pollution [Chappie and Lave (1982), Lave and Seskin (1977), Mandelbaum (1985), Mendelsohn and Orcutt (1979), Watson and Jaksch (1982)], water pollution [Page et al. (1976)], auto safety [Arnould and Grabowski (1981), Crandall and Graham (1984), Crandall et al. (1986), Lave and Weber (1970)], and in other areas [O'Byrne et al. (1985)].

To date, the predominant benefits of HSE regulation come from mitigating human health problems. Health effects are quantified via risk assessment using a diverse set of tools to analyze the effects of air pollution on health, the number of lives that might be lost from a nuclear mishap, the effects of environmental carcinogens on health, and the risks of highway transport (see Section 6 on risk assessment below).

4.2. Valuation of nonmarket goods and services

Once the risks have been quantified, the next step is to translate them into a single metric, presumably dollars. If valuing injury and disease in dollars is offensive, one metric might be used for benefits while another (dollars) could be used for costs. Even this approach requires a way of comparing slight with serious injury and disease with death. How many broken legs are comparable to paraplegia? How many days of being confined to bed are equivalent to death? Some people answer that these degrees of injury are not comparable, that any number of broken legs is better than paraplegia and that being confined to bed permanently is better than death. Is there some level of pain over some period of time that would be worse than death [Zeckhauser and Shepard (1976)]?

A further problem involves comparing injury across people. For example, would having a million people with broken legs for 70 years each be worse than one of them being a paraplegic? Is one death not better than a million people being confined to bed all of their lives? Indeed, a principal difficulty is constructing a weighting function that relates all injury and disease states to each other. Given such a function, it is less difficult to translate the outcomes into dollar terms.

Economists manage to present their ideas in the worst possible light by speaking of this as the "dollar value of life", managing to confuse premature death with slavery and other ethical issues. Schelling (1968) shows that valuation should be conceptualized as a lottery whose payoffs include no untoward outcome with high probability and injury or death with low probability. The correct question is then: How much would each person be willing to pay to lower the probability of death or injury?

Most economists are aware of the distinction and accept Schelling's concept, but still refer to the "dollar value of life". This sort of insensitivity, as well as the bizarre discussions about the equivalence of broken legs and cancer deaths and dollar value of making a species such as the snail darter extinct, leads environmentalists, politicians, and the public more generally to be extremely suspicious of benefit–cost analysis [Kelman (1981), Campen (1986)].

The history of attempts to model these issues is filled with muddled concepts [Rice and Cooper (1967), Hartunian et al. (1981)]. For example, one of the earliest questions was: What dollar amount should be paid to an injured worker or his heirs after an unfortunate event? Before this question can be answered, a more important question is: Who was at fault? If the employer was negligent, there is outrage that he did not take greater care to prevent the injury. Indeed, there is the real possibility of criminal prosecution for negligence. If the fault was the employer's, the worker should receive a generous settlement. If the fault is the worker's, the employer would not have to pay any amount. If fault has been put aside in favor of a no-fault system, the amount that should be given would be intermediate between the previous two cases.

To be able to decide how much of a settlement the worker and his heirs should receive, one needs to specify the issues with some care and precision. Unfortunately, economists have been searching for general purpose answers that would fit all circumstances in which someone was hurt.

An improvement on the original approach, but one that is not generally useful, is to infer the implicit valuation put on premature death in the work setting. A number of studies have estimated the increment in wages associated with an increase in risk, after accounting for other relevant factors affecting the wage rate [Thaler and Rosen (1976), Jones-Lee (1976), Linnerooth (1979), Bailey (1980), Graham and Vaupel (1981), Arthur (1981), Viscusi (1983b, 1986a), Olson (1981), Smith (1982), Dickens (1984)]. These studies find that workers have put actuarial values on their lives that range from about \$250 000 to \$10 million. The valuation is sensitive to the risk level of the job being considered, since the worker population already reflects self-selection of workers into jobs with risk characteristics that match individual preferences. In any case, these estimates are sensitive to the precise circumstance and question asked, and so are not readily generalized to other circumstances.

People can be asked for their willingness to pay to avoid premature death [Schelling (1968)]. Again, the question presumably must be quite precise to get a meaningful estimate. There is also the difficulty of posing a hypothetical question in a form that the respondent has never encountered [Cummings et al. (1986), Kahneman et al. (1982)].

Still more controversial than valuing injury and premature death in dollar terms is valuing extinction of a species or deteriorations in environmental quality in dollar terms [Cummings et al. (1986)]. How much is it worth to prevent extinction of the snail darter? How much is it worth to have an additional sunny day in which one can see 20 miles instead of 10? How much is it worth to have a remote lake, rarely visited by people, not become so acidic that fish are killed? At the very least, it is difficult to pose these questions so that people find them meaningful and can give answers in which they would have confidence. The difficulty is probably deeper, making a willingness-to-pay survey inappropriate for such abstract issues.

The willingness-to-pay literature has developed many estimates of relevant parameters. However, it is unclear what to do with the resulting estimates. Are college sophomores in Cheyenne, Wyoming, representative of the entire population? How sensitive are the valuations to the precise event that is the focus? How sensitive are they to the background level, e.g. one additional clear day among 50 as against among 250? Several methods are used to derive estimates, from analysis of actual choices to surveys or interviews. Inevitably, one has reservations about the responses people give when asked how many hypothetical dollars they would be willing to pay to stop a hypothetical event.

5. Implementation issues

5.1. How much room for improvement?

Economists tend to emphasize efficiency, giving less attention to such other attributes as equity, administrative simplicity, and transparency. Some proposals promise efficiency, but are so complicated to administer that the promise could never be fulfilled. Thus, the key question for regulatory reform is the extent to which current regulation is inefficient. Unless there is a great deal of room for improvement, more efficient alternatives will not be politically attractive.

While we know of no direct estimate of the efficiency losses from design standards and occupational licensure, we believe they are large. Design standards are enacted to control quality but serve to impede innovation; the temptation is great to write standards that eliminate competition. While occupational licensure is motivated as a quality assurance mechanism, it quickly gets directed toward limiting entry and creating monopoly rents. Regulation and licensure also pose barriers to innovation, since innovators must persuade regulators as well as customers that their product is safe and desirable. Regulation might be thought of as imposing a vast amount of inertia on the system.

Economists have sought mechanisms to handle the externalities and information problems that do little to restrict competition. For example, performance standards can achieve the desired level of quality and protection with fewer restrictions than design standards. Requiring people to disclose their training and qualifications can substitute for licensure. Information disclosure is one of the more important alternatives to regulation [Baram (1982)]. As we saw in Subsection 2.4, tort law will not generally result in optimal efficiency when a product or occupation has health and safety risks. It is an open question whether tort law will give rise to a more efficient solution than direct regulation.

In evaluating water pollution control regulation, Kneese and Schultze (1975) found that an effluent fee system would save 40 percent over the system of point-by-point effluent limits used to protect water quality. The Federal Aviation Agency, in moving from a system of direct and nontransferable allocation of landing slots at congested airports to a scheme allowing for trades and sales among airlines, was able to accommodate expanding air travel despite the disruptions caused by airline deregulation and the mass dismissals of air traffic control workers in the aftermath of an illegal strike.

Both simulation evidence and analyses such as those cited above emphasize the static benefits of adopting economic approaches to regulation. Yet, the limited use of approaches based on fees or trading of rights has been exclusively motivated by dynamic concerns – such as how to accommodate new pollution sources in areas where existing sources are already pushing against inflexibly set environmental quality targets. In the complete absence of transferability, existing sources can be induced to "make room" for new polluters only by tightening the standards they face. In addition to drawing the opposition of existing sources, such an effort will inevitably spark disputes over the distribution of the extra reductions.

Starting from a position in which existing sources have already made irreversible investments in particular technologies and operate activities of widely varying economic value, a planner would face great difficulty in devising an efficient plan even if there were no distributional effects to account for. Faced with the Scylla and Charybdis choice between revising standards or spurning growth opportunities, regulators have opted for a limited market mechanism – the offset system. In areas where environmental constraints are binding, new sources can enter provided that offsetting emissions reductions from other polluters are obtained. Relying on a voluntary transaction between the "buyers" and "sellers" of offsets circumvents the difficulty of imposing new standards, and provides an incentive for those existing sources able to accommodate growth at relatively low cost to reveal themselves. The offset system serves to promote incremental, but not global, rationality. The bubble policy, another quasi-market approach used in environmental programs, allows for intraplant trading of emission rights across point sources so long as the aggregate externality output is kept below the sum of the individual point source standards. A single bubble at a New Jersey chemical plant was estimated to have saved $12 million in capital costs and $3 million in annual operating costs. Total bubble savings to date are estimated to be in the $1 billion range.

5.2. Dynamic issues in regulation

Virtually all of the models discussed in Section 2 are intended to provide insights of the "comparative statics" variety. The usefulness of comparative statics as a guide to policy may be limited by the importance of the adjustment process in the actual implementation of programs. For example, tightening new source standards beyond some point may actually increase the aggregate level of externalities. Such an outcome is possible because a differentiated regulatory structure may extend the economic lifetime of existing sources subject to less stringent regulation. In a regime of differentiated regulation, short- and long-term regulatory objectives may be in conflict.

5.2.1. *Technology-forcing*

The modern view of innovation focuses on the importance of demand pressure in determining the direction of innovation, of having a ready market for the innovation. In the absence of regulation, there is little or no demand for abatement technology and so no R&D effort. Even when the law specified that EPA will require the "best available control technology", there is a long step between innovation, regulatory change, and orders for the new control technology. One common method of spurring technology development is to impose regulations that cannot be met using existing technologies (as with automobile emissions), or to mandate a particular technology rather than a specific performance level (as with scrubbers for coal-fired boilers). While "technology-forcing" might be justified by attainment of a highly valued target, it poses credibility problems that are not generally considered in the prices versus standards literature. In the event that unforeseen difficulties or foot-dragging result in the failure of new abatement technologies to become available when needed, the regulator must either shut down those firms that cannot comply or back off from the standard. Knowledge that the latter approach will inevitably be favored over the former retards technology development efforts. The best known example of such a "credibility crisis" in regulation, the failure of the domestic automobile industry to comply with the scheduled 1977 standards, was solved through statutory action to revise the standard under pressure of a threatened shutdown of the industry. Price-type systems are inherently less subject to such dynamic inconsistency considerations but are not immune. Ford and General Motors have lobbied hard to secure the rollback of corporate fuel economy standards rather than pay substantial fines for failing to attain the mandated level of fuel economy. The fines would have been costly, but would not have shut down the industry.

The requirement for specific technologies poses other difficulties. Obviously, it focuses R & D on specific approaches even though a more diffuse effort might uncover better alternatives. Second, it places little emphasis on operating and maintenance behavior, even though these are key determinants of the effectiveness of abatement. Crandall (1983) finds that a significant fraction of mandated pollution control equipment is not even hooked up. The notion substituting technology standards for monitoring effort is a poor tradeoff in most cases.

5.3. *Risk compensation*

Will people react to regulation by changing their behavior? Peltzman (1975) examines the impact of automobile safety regulation on realized safety. He finds evidence of risk compensation behavior in the form of driving less carefully. Although drivers themselves are safer despite their offsetting behavior, pedestrians and bicyclists who do not directly benefit from the safety equipment on cars experience a rise in fatalities and injuries. Overall, Peltzman finds that safety measures do not have a net safety payoff. While providing a striking example of the need to consider human feedback to regulation and more generally the importance of the level of care, there is significant controversy surrounding Peltzman's empirical findings [Graham and Garber (1984), Evans and Schwing (1985)]. Other studies have not found evidence of significant risk compensation, or have even found evidence of positive feedback whereby safety equipment, by reminding drivers of safety concerns, actually induce them to drive more safely. A recent study by Viscusi (1985) examing the impact of child-resistant safety caps on poisoning rates found strong evidence of risk compensation on the part of parents in the form of less safe placement and leaving drug bottles open. Indeed, the proportion of aspirin poisonings involving safety capped bottles actually exceeded the proportion of aspirin sold in such bottles by the end of Viscusi's observation period, suggesting that safety topped bottles increase rather than decrease the poisoning rate.

5.4. *Contradictory regulation*

Since Congress and the regulatory agencies deal with one case at a time, there is no reason to expect even rough consistency among actions. For example, in 1966 Congress expressed its concern for highway safety by creating a federal agency that would regulate safety-related design of automobiles and have the power to mandate safety equipment. In 1970 Congress expressed its concern for air quality by setting emissions constraints for automobiles. In 1975 Congress expressed its concern for fuel economy by mandating fuel efficiency standards for cars. Each piece of legislation was a logical reaction to the conditions prevailing at the time and what the public desired. At first sight, they appear to have nothing in common save that they all deal with automobiles.

However, enhancing safety generally requires increasing the weight and size of automobiles; other things equal, larger cars are safer [Lave (1981a, 1984)]. Unfortunately, fuel economy is inversely related to vehicle weight. Thus, increasing fuel economy leads to smaller vehicles which, other factors held constant, are less safe. Finally, curtailing vehicle emissions lowers the efficiency of the engine and hurts fuel economy.

The contradictions or secondary implications are important. For example, the fuel economy penalty from the increase in weight due to the package of safety features essentially doubles the implicit cost of preventing a premature death. The situation can be thought of as attempting to maximize social welfare as a function of safety, emissions, fuel economy, performance–comfort, and price, where the factors are not independent. Congress's actions were each equivalent to taking a simple derivative, as if social welfare were a function of only one of the attributes. The resulting solution is demonstrably inefficient. A better solution could be achieved by recognizing the structure of the problem and optimizing by taking partial derivatives, i.e. recognizing the spillover effects. Inevitably, this requires assuming values for the various interactions, but even choosing somewhat arbitrary values is better than assuming the interactions are zero. The systems' optimization comes from recognizing the interdependence explicitly and solving the set of equations of partial derivatives simultaneously.

5.5. Effects on the economy

Denison (1979, 1985) has estimated the effect of HSE regulation on productivity. Pollution abatement was estimated to lower productivity growth by 10 percent over half a decade. Smith and Sims (1985) estimate the effects of environmental regulation in Canadian breweries to be large; unregulated firms had productivity growth of 1.6 percent per year while regulated firms had growth of −0.008 percent. Crandall (1981) also finds a large effect of regulation on productivity. Hartman, Bozdogan and Nadkarni (1979) examine the effects of environmental regulations on the copper industry in the face of increasing demand; the regulations imposed a large burden on the industry which was largely shifted to consumers through an inelastic demand [see also, Gallop and Roberts (1983), Highton and Webb (1984), Maloney and Yandle (1984), Peskin et al. (1981), Viscusi (1983a)].

The effects on inflation can be estimated by examining the direct increase in cost due to this regulation. There is much casual speculation about the effect on international competitiveness, unemployment, and growth, but little formal investigation. Clearly, if some nations have less stringent HSE regulations, their direct manufacturing costs would be lower, until they created an environment so polluted that workers were sickened. These nations would have a comparative advantage in exporting dangerous, environmentally polluting goods. The quantitative advantage is likely to be small given that the estimated increase in the cost of HSE regulation for various products is small [Denison (1979), Environmental Protection Agency (1979), Ruff (1978)].

5.6. *Distribution of HSE benefits and costs*

Since the cost of environmental programs run in the tens of billions of dollars per year, and since it is unlikely that the costs would be spread uniformly or in proportion to income across families, economists have been interested in estimating the distribution of costs and benefits by attributes such as geographic location and income. Knowing the costs borne by each industry, budget studies can be used to estimate how the immediate costs will be borne. Longer run adjustments are almost impossible to predict. These techniques have been applied by Freeman (1977), Gianessi and Peskin (1980), Gianessi, Peskin and Wolff (1979), Harrison (1975), and Peskin (1978). As might be expected, they find that those living in some areas pay more than four times the national average, while those living in other areas pay almost nothing. Although amounts rise with family income, as a proportion of income, they fall sharply. This result leads to asking whether some of the pollution control efforts should not be paid for out of general tax revenues so as to get a more equitable distribution of costs. Benefits are also quite unevenly distributed, both geographically and by income.

Great care must be taken with these estimates of distributional implications. Carried to extremes, they could indicate the net cost to each Congressional district, each income group, and so on. Such calculations will goad people to focus on these particular costs and benefits, rather than on the national interest.

6. Noneconomic issues

Noneconomists view HSE regulation as almost entirely unrelated to economics. For the most part, economics enters only as a constraint on how stringent the regulation can be. Perhaps the most important of the environmental requirements has been requiring environmental impact statements. Although these are regarded as having no economic content, they are so central that they must be discussed.

Estimating the benefits of health and safety regulation requires quantifying the risks. While risk estimation is normally outside the province of economists, there is such large uncertainty associated with the estimates that economists must understand the nature of these estimates in order to use them sensibly.

6.1. *Environmental impact statements*

The environmental impact statement (EIS) was introduced by the National Environmental Policy Act of 1969. An EIS is required of all federal government projects that might affect environmental quality. The EIS has been attacked as time-consuming, wasteful, and as serving no useful purpose, other than delay. Taylor (1984) makes the case that the EIS was designed to sensitize federal decision-makers to the impact of their projects on environmental quality and that it has done an admirable job. Thus, Taylor uses a satisficing framework to examine what will get bureaucrats to give attention to environmental concerns. He sees government officials as either exceedingly busy or otherwise occupied. It takes a Congressional or Presidential act to change their behavior and get them to extend their consideration to a wider class of issues.

6.2. *Risk analysis and management*

Much of the early HSE legislation was intended to lower risks to zero. It quickly became apparent that zero risk was unattainable so that good decision-making requires knowing the risks associated with various concentrations of toxic chemicals or situations in which injury could occur. A large literature has grown up on assessing the risks of accidents, chronic disease, and acute disease [National Science Foundation (1985b), Covello et al. (1986)]. The methods used include fault and event trees, probabilistic risk assessment, and statistical analysis.

A good deal of work has been done on estimating the risks to people [Office of Technology Assessment (1977), Lave (1982, 1987), Marcus (1983), Office of Science and Technology Policy (1985)]. Unfortunately, the uncertainty associated with the point estimates is generally large.

One of the particular problems has been estimating the risks associated with hazardous facilities, such as nuclear plants or toxic waste dumps. Although the risks are generally low compared to risks commonly faced, people do not want these risky facilities nearby. Economists have taken an active role in trying to find ways to transfer some of the social benefit to the individuals who must bear the risk [Kunreuther and Kleindorfer (1986), Mitchell and Carson (1986), Smith and Desvousges (1986a)].

7. Conclusion

Public concern and scientific research on health, safety, and environmental externalities finally lured a number of economists to apply their tools and models to these issues. The materials balance model of Kneese, Ayres and d'Arge (1970) and the environmental models of Baumol and Oates (1982) are examples of incorporating HSE externalities into standard economic models. These enriched models have attracted a good deal of attention from both theorists and applied economists.

Nonetheless, our review of the economics of health, safety, and environmental regulation cites work of a large number of people trained in disciplines other than economics. The lesson appears to be that we economists are narrowly bound by our models and view of what are interesting problems and approaches. When a movement as sweeping and important as the environmentalist–consumerist movement occurs, economists should not be complaining two decades later that government programs are not efficient; we should have done more to show how to improve the efficiency and effectiveness of these social programs.

Tackling HSE issues is inherently difficult, since they involve some of the thorniest issues in economics: paternalism, public goods, information, incentives for innovation, uncertainty, valuing nonmarket goods and services, and modeling unanticipated consequences of actions. Indeed, the set of issues is so large and fascinating, it would provide employment for a great many theorists. At the danger of missing the most important issues, we suggest that investigations of setting social goals, pursuing the valuation of nonmarket goods and services, and some of the interaction mechanisms between firms and regulators are worth greater attention.

In less than two decades, the economics of HSE regulation has come from somewhat sterile arguments about Coase versus Pigou to a rich array of models, parameter estimates, and policy advice. Experience has shown that sometimes taxes and subsidies were the best route, sometimes direct bargaining among concerned parties was best, and more often a wide range of new approaches was needed. We hope and expect that current problems will continue to intrude in economic models to enrich our thinking and remind us how much we are needed.

References

Ackerman, B. and Hassler, G. (1981) *Clean coal/dirty air*. New Haven: Yale University Press.

Akerloff, G. (1970) 'The market for lemons: Qualitative uncertainty and the market mechanism', *Quarterly Journal of Economics*, 84:488–500.

Arnould, R. and Grabowski, H. (1981) 'Auto safety regulation: An analysis of market failure', *Bell Journal of Economics*, 12:27–48.

Arthur, W.B. (1981) 'The economics of risks to life', *American Economic Review*, 71:54–64.

Arrow, K.J. (1983) 'The organization of economic activity: Issues pertinent to the choice of market versus nonmarket allocation', in: R.H. Haveman and J. Margolis, eds., *Public expenditure and policy analysis*. New York: Houghton Mifflin.

Bailey, E.E., Graham, D.R. and Kaplan, D.P. (1985) *Deregulating the airlines*. Cambridge: MIT Press.

Bailey, M.J. (1980) *Reducing risks to life: Measurement of the benefits*. Washington, D.C.: American Enterprise Institute.
Baram, M.S. (1982) *Alternatives to regulation*. Lexington: Lexington Books.
Baron, D.P. (1985) 'Noncooperative regulation of a nonlocalized externality', *Rand Journal of Economics*, 16:553–568.
Baron, D.P. and Myerson, R. (1982) 'Regulating a monopolist with unknown costs', *Econometrica*, 50:911–930.
Bartel, A.P. and Thomas, L.G. (1985) 'Direct and indirect effects of regulation: A new look at OSHA's impact', *Journal of Law and Economics*, 33:1–26.
Baumol, W. and Oates, W. (1975) *The theory of environmental policy*. Englewood Cliffs: Prentice-Hall.
Baumol, W.J. and Oates, W.E. (1982) *The theory of environmental policy*. Englewood Cliffs: Prentice-Hall.
Brown, J. (1973) 'Towards an economic theory of liability', *Journal of Legal Studies*, 2:323–350.
Buchanan, J.M. and Tullock, G. (1975) 'Polluters' profits and political response: Direct controls versus taxes', *American Economic Review*, 139–147.
Byrd, D. and Lave, L. (1985) 'Significant risk is not the antonym of de Minimum Risk', in: C. Whipple, ed., *De Minimum Risk*. New York: Plenum.
Byrd, D. and Lave, L. (1987) 'Managing health risks: The role of 'significant' and 'de minimis' concepts', in: *Issues in Science and Technology*.
Calabresi, G. (1970) *The cost of accidents: A legal and economic analysis*. New Haven: Yale University Press.
Campen, J.T. (1986) *Benefit, cost, and beyond: The political economy of benefit–cost analysis*. Cambridge: Ballinger.
Carson, R. (1962) *Silent spring*. New York: Houghton Mifflin.
Chappie, M. and Lave, L.B. (1982) 'The health effects of air pollution: A reanalysis', *Journal of Urban Economics*, 12:346–376.
Chase, G.R., Kotin, P., Crump, K., and Mitchell, R.S. (1985) 'Evaluation for compensation of asbestos-exposed individuals', *Journal of Occupational Medicine*, 27:189–198.
Clark, E.H. (1971) 'Multipart pricing of public goods', *Public Choice*, 8:19–33.
Coase, R.H. (1960) 'The problem of social cost', *Journal of Law and Economics*, 3:1–44.
Council on Environmental Quality (1980) *The global* 2000 *report to the President: Entering the* 21*st century*. Washington, D.C.: U.S. Government Printing Office.
Covello, V.T., Menkes, J. and Mumpower, J. (1986) *Risk evaluation and management*. New York: Plenum.
Crandall, R.W. (1981) 'Pollution controls and productivity growth in basic industries', in: T.G. Cowing and R.E. Stevenson, eds., *Productivity measurement in regulated industries*. New York: Academic.
Crandall, R.W. (1983) *Controlling industrial pollution*. Washington, D.C.: Brookings Institution.
Crandall, R.W. and Graham, J.D. (1984) 'Automobile safety regulation and offsetting behavior: Some new empirical estimates', *American Economic Review*, 74:328–331.
Crandall, R.W., Gruenspecht, H.K., Keeler, T.E. and Lave, L.B. (1986) *Regulating the automobile*. Washington, D.C.: Brookings Institution.
Cummings, R.G., Brookshire, D.S. and Schulze, W. (1986) *Valuing public goods: The contingent valuation method*. Totowa: Rowman and Allanheld.
Dales, J.H. (1968) *Pollution, property, and prices*. Toronto: University of Toronto Press.
Dasgupta, P., Hammond, P. and Maskin, E. (1980) 'On imperfect information and optimal pollution control', *Review of Economics Studies*, 47:857–860.
Denison, E.F. (1979) *Accounting for slower economic growth: The United States in the* 1970*s*. Washington, D.C.: Brookings Institution.
Denison, E.F. (1985) *Recent USA productivity*. Washington, D.C.: Brookings Institution.
Derthick, M. and Quirk, P.J. (1985) *The politics of deregulation*. Washington, D.C.: Brookings Institution.
Dickens, W.T. (1984) 'Differences between risk premiums in union and nonunion wages and the case for occupational safety regulation', *American Economic Review*, 74:320–323.
Douglas, M. and Wildavsky, A. (1982) *Risk and culture: An essay on the selection of technical and environmental dangers*. Berkeley: University of California Press.

Downing, P.B. and White, L.J. (1986) 'Innovation in pollution control', *Journal of Environmental Economics and Management*, 13:18–29.

Downs, A. (1957) *An economic theory of democracy*. New York: Harper.

Environmental Protection Agency (1979) 'The cost of clean air and water', report to Congress, EPA, Washington.

Evans, L. and Schwing, R.C. (1985) *Human behavior and traffic safety*. New York: Plenum.

Federal Aviation Administration (1980) 'Airport crash/fire/rescue (CFR service cost and benefit analysis)', DOT/FAA/AS 80-2, Department of Transportation, Washington.

Fischhoff, B., Lichtenstein, S., Slovic, P., Derby, S.L. and Keeney, R.L. (1981) *Acceptable Risk*. London: Cambridge University Press.

Fischhoff, B., Slovic, P. and Lichtenstein, S. (1983) 'The 'public' vs. the 'experts': Perceived versus actual disagreements about the risks of nuclear power', in: V. Covello, G. Flamm, J. Roderick and R. Tardiff, eds., *Analysis of actual versus perceived risks*. New York: Plenum.

Food and Drug Administration (1982) 'Policy for regulating carcinogenic chemicals in food and color additives', *Federal Register*, 49:130.

Freeman, A.M. (1977) 'The incidence of the cost of controlling automotive air pollution', in: F. Juster, ed., *The distribution of economic well-being*. Cambridge: Ballinger.

Freeman, A.M. (1979) *The benefits of environmental improvement: Theory and practice*. Baltimore: Johns Hopkins University Press.

Gianessi, L.P. and Peskin, H.M. (1980) 'The distribution of the costs of federal water pollution control policy', *Land Economics*, 56:86–102.

Gianessi, L.P., Peskin, H.M. and Wolff, E. (1979) 'The distributional effects of uniform air quality policy in the United States', *Quarterly Journal of Economics*, 93:281–301.

Gollop, F.M. and Roberts, M.J. (1983) 'Environmental regulations and productivity growth: The case of fossil-fueled electric power generation', *Journal of Political Economy*, 91:654–674.

Graham, J.D. and Garber, S. (1984) 'Evaluating the effects of automobile safety regulation', *Journal of Policy Analysis and Management*, 3:206–222.

Graham, J.D. and Vaupel, J.W. (1981) 'The value of life: What difference does it make?', *Risk Analysis*, 1:89–95.

Groves, T. (1973) 'Incentives in teams', *Econometrica*, 41:617–663.

Gruenspecht, H.K. (1982) Differentiated regulation: The case of auto emissions standards', *American Economic Review*, 72:328–331.

Hadden, S.G. (1986) *Read the label: Reducing risk by providing information*. Boulder: Westview Press.

Hahn, R. (1984) 'Market power and transferable property rights', *Quarterly Journal of Economics*, 99:753–765.

Hahn, R. (1986) 'Trade-offs in designing markets with multiple objectives', *Journal of Environmental Economics and Management*, 13:1–12.

Hahn, R. and Noll, R.G. (1982) 'Designing a market for tradable emission permits', in: Magat, ed., *Reform of environmental regulation*. Cambridge: Ballinger.

Harrison, D. and Rubinfeld, D. (1978) 'Hedonic housing prices and the demand for amenities', *Journal of Environmental Economics*, 5:81–102.

Harrison, Jr., D. (1975) *Who pays for clean air*. Cambridge: Ballinger.

Hartman, S.R., Bozdogan, K. and Nadkarni, R.M. (1979) 'The economic impacts of environmental regulations on the U.S. copper industry', *Bell Journal of Economics*, 10:589–618.

Hartunian, N.S., Smart, C.N. and Thompson, M.S. (1981) *The incidence and economic costs of major health impairments*. Lexington: Lexington Books.

Highton, N.H. and Webb, M.G. (1984) 'The effects on electricity prices in England and Wales of national sulphur dioxide emission standards for power stations', *Journal of Environmental Economics and Management*, 11:70–83.

Hirshleifer, J. and Riley, J.G. (1979) 'The analytics of uncertainty and information – an expository survey', *Journal of Economic Literature*, 17:1375–1421.

Huber, P. (1983) 'The old–new division in risk regulation', *Virginia Law Review*, 69:1025–1107.

Ireland, N.M. (1977) 'Ideal prices versus quantities', *Review of Economic Studies*, 44:183–186.

Jarrell, G. and Peltzman, S. (1985) 'The impact of product recalls on the wealth of sellers', *Journal of Political Economy*, 93:512–536.

Jones-Lee, M.W. (1976) *The value of life: An economics analysis*. Chicago: University of Chicago Press.
Joskow, P.L. and Noll, R.G. (1972) 'Regulation in theory and practice and efficient pollution control programs', *Journal of Economic Theory*, 5:395–418.
Joskow, P.L. and Noll, R.G. (1981) 'Regulation in theory and practice: An overview', in: G. Fromm, ed., *Studies in public regulation*. Cambridge: MIT Press.
Kahn, H. and Simon, J.L. (1984) *The resourceful earth: A response to global* 2000. New York: Blackwell.
Kahneman, D., Slovic, P. and Tversky, A., eds. (1982) *Judgment under uncertainty: Heuristics and biases*. New York: Cambridge University Press.
Keeton, R., Connell, O'J. and McCord, J. (1968) *Crisis in car insurance*. Urbana: University of Illinois Press.
Kelman, S. (1981) 'Cost–benefit analysis: An ethical critique', *Regulation*, 5:33–40.
Kelman, S. (1983) 'Economic incentives for environmental policy', in: T.C. Schelling, ed., *Incentives for environmental protection*. Cambridge: MIT Press.
Kneese, A.V. (1984) *Measuring the benefits of clean air and water*. Washington, D.C.: Resources for the Future.
Kneese, A.V., Ayres, R.U. and d'Arge, R.C. (1970) *Economics and the environment: A materials balance approach*. Washington, D.C.: Resources for the Future.
Kunreuther, H. and Kleindorfer, P.R. (1986) 'A sealed-bid auction mechanism for siting noxious facilities', *American Economic Review*, 76:295–299.
Kneese, A.V., Ayres, R.U. and d'Arge, R.C. (1970) *Economics and the environment: A materials balance approach*. Washington, D.C.: Resources for the Future.
Kunreuther, H. and Kleindorfer, P.R. (1968) 'A sealed-bid auction mechanism for siting noxious facilities', *American Economic Review*, 76:295–299.
Kwerel, E. (1977) 'To tell the truth: Imperfect information and optimal pollution control', *Review of Economic Studies*, 44:595–601.
Laffont, J.-J. (1977) 'More on prices versus quantitites', *Review of Economic Studies*, 44:177–182.
Lagakos, S.W. and Mosteller, F. (1986) 'Assigned shares in compensation for radiation-related cancers', *Risk Analysis*, 6:345–358.
Latimer, E. and Lave, L.B. (1987) 'Initial effects of the New York state auto safety belt law', *American Journal of Public Health*, 77:183–186.
Lave, L.B. (1980) 'Health, safety, and environmental regulations', in: J. Pechman, ed., *Setting national priorities: Agenda for the* 1980*s*. Washington, D.C.: Brookings Institution.
Lave, L.B. (1981a) 'Conflicting objectives in regulating automobiles', *Science*, 212:893–899.
Lave, L.B. (1981b) *The strategy of social regulation: Decision frameworks for policy*. Washington, D.C.: Brookings Institution.
Lave, L.B. (1982) *Quantitative risk assessment in regulation*. Washington, D.C.: Brookings Institution.
Lave, L.B. (1983) 'An economic approach to protecting worker health and safety', *American Industrial Hygiene Association Journal*, 44:A22–A25.
Lave, L.B. (1984) 'Controlling contradictions among regulations', *American Economic Review*, 74:471–475.
Lave, L.B. (1987a) 'Injury as externality: An economic perspective of trauma', *Accident Analysis and Prevention*, 19:29–37.
Lave, L.B. (1987b) 'Health and safety risk analysis: Information for managing risks', *Science*.
Lave, L.B. and Seskin, E.P. (1977) *Air pollution and human health*. Baltimore: Johns Hopkins University Press.
Lave, L.B. and Upton, A.C. (1987) *Toxic chemicals, health, and the environment*. Baltimore: Johns Hopkins University Press, forthcoming.
Lave, L.B. and Weber, W.E. (1970) 'A benefit–cost analysis of auto safety features', *Applied Economics*, 2:265–275.
Levin, M. (1985) 'Statutes and stopping points: Building a better bubble at EPA', *Regulation*, 9:33–42.
Linnerooth, J. (1979) 'The value of human life: A review of the models', *Inquiry*, 17:52–74.
Liroff, R.A. (1986) *Reforming air pollution regulation: The toil and trouble of EPA's bubble*. Washington, D.C.: The Conservation Foundation.

Litan, R.E. and Nordhaus, W.D. (1983) *Reforming federal regulation*. New Haven: Yale University Press.

Loeb, M. and Magat, W. (1979) 'A decentralized method for utility regulation', *Journal of Law and Economics*, 22:399–404.

Maloney, M. and McCormick, R. (1982) 'A positive theory of environmental quality regulation', *Journal of Law and Economics*, 35:99–123.

Maloney, M.T. and Yandle, B. (1984) 'Estimation of the cost of air pollution control regulation', *Journal of Environmental Economics and Management*, 11:244–263.

Mandelbaum, P. (1985) *Acid rain: Economic asessment*. New York: Plenum.

Marcus, G. (1983) 'A review of risk assessment methodologies', Committee on Science and Technology, U.S. House of Representatives, ninety-eighth Congress, first session, serial B.U.S. Government Printing Office, Washington, D.C.

Mendelsohn, R. (1984) 'Endogenous technical change and environmental regulation', *Journal of Environmental Economics and Management*, 11:202–207.

Mendelsohn, R. and Orcutt, G. (1979) 'An empirical analysis of air pollution dose–response curves', *Journal of Environmental Economics and Management*, 6:85–106.

Miller, J.C. and Yandle, B. eds. (1979) *Benefit–cost analyses of social regulation: Case studies from the Council on Wage and Price Stability*. Washington: American Enterprise Institute.

Milvy, P. (1986) 'A general guideline for management of risk from carcinogens', *Risk Analysis*, 6:69–80.

Mitchell, R.C. and Carson, R.T. (1986) 'Property rights, protest, and the siting of hazardous waste facilities', *American Economic Review*, 76:285–290.

Montgomery, D.W. (1972) 'Markets in licenses and efficient pollution control programs', *Journal of Economic Theory*, 5:395–418.

Morgan, M.G., Morris, S.C., Henrion, M., Amaral, D.A.L. and Rish, W.R. (1984) 'Technical uncertainty in quantitative policy analysis – a sulfur air pollution example', *Risk Analysis*, 4:201–216.

Nader, R. (1965) *Unsafe at any speed*. New York: Grossman.

National Academy of Sciences (1984) *Toxicity testing: strategies to determine needs and priorities*. Washington, D.C.: National Academy Press.

National Science Foundation (1985a) *Benefits estimation: The state-of-the-art*. Washington, D.C.

National Science Foundation (1985b) *Risk analysis: The state-of-the-art*. Washington, D.C.

Neumann, G. and Nelson, J.P. (1982) 'Safety regulation and firm size: The effects of the Coal Mine Health and Safety Act of 1969', *Journal of Law and Economics*, 35:183–189.

Nichols, A.L. (1984) *Targeting economic incentives for environmental protection*. Cambridge: MIT Press.

Noll, R.G. (1971) *Reforming regulation: An evaluation of the Ash council proposals*. Washington, D.C.: Brookings Institution.

Nordhaus, W. and Tobin, J. (1972) 'Is growth obsolete', in: *Economic growth, fiftieth anniversary colloquium*, vol. 5, New York: National Bureau of Economic Research, 4–17.

Nuclear Regulatory Commission (1983) 'Safety goals for nuclear power plants: A Discussion Paper', NUREG-0880, Washington, D.C.

O'Byrne, P.H., Nelson, J.P. and Seneca, J.J. (1985) 'Housing values, census estimates, disequilibrium, and the environmental cost of airport noise: A case study of Atlanta', *Journal of Environmental Economics and Management*, 12:169–178.

Office of Science and Technology Policy (1985) 'Chemical carcinogenesis: A review of the science and its associated principles', *Federal Register*, 50(50):10372–10442.

Office of Technology Assessment (1977) *Cancer testing technology and saccharin*. Washington, D.C.: U.S. Government Printing Office.

Oi, W. (1973) 'The economics of product safety', *Bell Journal of Economics and Management*, 4:3–29.

Oi, W. (1974) 'On the economics of industrial safety', *Law and Contemporary Problems*, 38:538–555.

Olson, C.A. (1981) 'An analysis of wage differentials received by workers on dangerous jobs', *Review of Economics and Statistics*, 63:561–572.

Owen, B.M. and Braeutigam, R. (1978) *The regulation game: Strategic use of the administrative process*. Cambridge: Ballinger.

Page, T., Harris, R.A. and Epstein, S.S. (1976) 'Drinking water and cancer mortality in Louisiana', *Science*, 193:55–57.

Pashigan, P. (1984) 'The effect of environmental regulation on optimal plant size and factor shares', *Journal of Law and Economics*, 37:1–28.
Pashigian, B.P. (1985) 'Environmental regulation: Whose self-interests are being protected?', *Economic Inquiry*, 23:551–584.
Peltzman, S. (1975) 'The effects of automobile safety regulation', *Journal of Political Economy*, 83:677–725.
Peltzman, S. (1983) 'An economic interpretation of the history of congressional voting in the twentieth century', Center for the Study of the Economy and the State, University of Chicago.
Perrow, C. (1984) *Normal accidents*. New York: Basic Books.
Peskin, H.M. (1978) 'Environmental policy and the distribution of benefits and costs,' in: P. Portney, ed., *Current issues in U.S. Environmental Policy*. Baltimore: Johns Hopkins University Press.
Peskin, H.M. and Seskin, E.P., eds., (1975) *Cost benefit analysis and water pollution policy*. Washington, D.C.: Urban Institute.
Peskin, H.M., Portney, P.R. and Kneese, A.V. (1981) *Environmental regulation and the U.S. economy*. Baltimore: Johns Hopkins University Press.
Pigou, A.C. (1920) *The economics of welfare*. London: Macmillan.
Rall, J.E., Beebe, G.W., Hoel, D.G., Jablon, S., Land, C.E., Nygaard, O.F., Upton, A.C. and Yalow, R.S. (1985) *Report of the National Institutes of Health Ad Hoc Working Group to develop radioepidemiological tables*. Washington, D.C.: National Institutes of Health Publication no. 85-2748.
Reilly, R.J. and Hoffer, G.E. (1984) 'Will retarding the information flow on automobile recalls affect consumer demand?', *Economic Inquiry*, 21:444–447, 1–16.
Rice, D. and Cooper, B. (1967) 'The economic value of life', *American Journal of Public Health*, 57:1954–1966.
Roberts, M. and Spence, M. (1976) 'Effluent charges and licenses under uncertainty', *Journal of Public Economics*, 5:193–208.
Robyn, D. (1987) *Braking the special interests: Trucking deregulation and the politics of policy reform*. Chicago: University of Chicago.
Romer, T. and Rosenthal, H. (1984) 'Voting models and empirical evidence', *American Scientist*, 71:465–473.
Ruff, L.E. (1978) 'Federal environmental regulation', in: *Study on federal regulation*, vol. 6, *Framework for regulation*, Appendix, Senate Committee on Governmental Affairs. Washington, D.C.: U.S. Government Printing Office.
Schelling, T. (1968) 'The life you save may be your own', in: S. Chase, ed., *Problems in public expenditure analysis*, Washington, D.C.: Brookings Institution.
Schelling, T.C., ed. (1983) *Incentives for environmental protection*. Cambridge: MIT Press.
Shapiro, C. (1982) 'Consumer information, product quality, and seller reputation', *Bell Journal of Economics*, 13:20–35.
Shavell, S. (1982) 'On liability and insurance', *Bell Journal of Economics*, 13:120–132.
Shavell, S. (1984) 'A model of the optimal use of liability and safety regulation', *Rand Journal of Economics*, 15:271–280.
Shavell, S. (1985) 'Uncertainty over causation and the determination of civil liability', *Journal of Law and Economics*, 38:587–609.
Simon, J.L. and Kahn, H. (1984) *The resourceful Earth: A response to global* 2000. New York: Basil Blackwell.
Slawson, W.D. (1986) 'The right to protection from air pollution', *Southern California Law Review*, 59:667–808.
Smith, J.B. and Sims, W.A. (1985) 'The impact of pollution charges on productivity growth in Canadian brewing', *Rand Journal of Economics*, 16:410–423.
Smith, R.S. (1982) 'Protecting workers' safety and health', in: R.W. Poole, Jr., ed., *Instead of regulation*. Lexington: Lexington Books.
Smith, V.K. and Desvousges, W.H. (1986a) 'Asymmetries in the valuation of risk and the siting of hazardous waste disposal facilities', *American Economic Review*, 76:291–294.
Smith, V.K. and Desvouges, W.H. (1986b) *Measuring water quality benefits*. Boston: Kluwer–Nijhoff.
Spence, M. (1977) 'Consumer misperceptions, product failure, and producer liability', *Review of Economic Studies*, 44:561–572.

Spulber, D.F. (1985) 'Effluent regulation and long run optimality', *Journal of Environmental Economics and Management*, 12:103–116.
Stewart, R.B. (1975) 'The reformation of American administrative law', *Harvard Law Review*, 88:1667–1813.
Stewart, R.B. and Krier, J.E. (1978) *Environmental law and policy*. Indianapolis: Bobbs–Merrill.
Stigler, G.J. (1971) 'The theory of economic regulation', *Bell Journal of Economics*, 2:3–21.
Stiglitz, J.E. (1983) 'Risk, incentives and insurance: The pure theory of moral hazard', *The Geneva Papers on Risk and Insurance*, 8:4–33.
Supreme Court of the United States (1980) *Industrial union department, AFL-CIO v. American Petroleum Institute*. 448 U.S. 607.
Taylor, S. (1984) *Making bureaucracies think: The environmental impact statement strategy of administrative reform*. Palo Alto: Stanford University Press.
Thaler, R. and Rosen, S. (1976) 'The value of saving a life: Evidence from the labor market', in: N. Terleckyz, ed., *Household production and consumption*. New York: Columbia University Press.
Tietenberg, T.H. (1985) *Emissions trading: An exercise in reforming pollution policy*. Washington, D.C.: Resources for the Future.
Travis, C.C., Richter, S.A., Crouch, E.A.C., Wilson, R. and Klema, E.D. (1987) 'Cancer risk management: A review of 132 federal agency decisions', *Environmental Science and Technology*, 21:415–420.
U.S. Council on Environmental Quality (1980) *The global 2000 report to the President: Entering the 21st century*. Washington, D.C.: U.S. Government Printing Office.
Vickrey, W. (1961) 'Counterspeculation, auctions, and competitive sealed tenders', *Journal of Finance*, 16:8–37.
Viscusi, W.K. (1978) 'Wealth effects and earnings premiums for job hazards', *Review of Economics and Statistics*, 60:408–418.
Viscusi, W.K. (1979) 'Job hazards and worker out rates', *International Economic Review*, 20:29–58.
Viscusi, W.K. (1983a) 'Frameworks for analyzing the effects of risk and environmental regulations on productivity', *American Economics Review*, 83:793–801.
Viscusi, W.K. (1983b) *Risk by choice: Regulating health and safety in the workplace*. Cambridge: Harvard University Press.
Viscusi, W.K. (1984a) 'The lulling effect: The impact of child-resistant packaging on aspirin and analgesic ingestions', *American Economic Review*, 74:324–327.
Viscusi, W.K. (1984b) *Regulating consumer product safety*. Washington D.C.: American Enterprise Institute.
Viscusi, W.K. (1984c) 'Structuring an effective occupational disease policy: Victim compensation and risk regulation', *Yale Journal on Regulation*, 2:53–81.
Viscusi, W.K. (1985) 'Consumer behavior and the safety effects of product safety regulation', *Journal of Law and Economics*, 38:527–554.
Viscusi, W.K. (1986a) 'The determinants of the disposition of product liability claims and compensation for bodily injury', *Journal of Legal Studies*, 15:321–346.
Viscusi, W.K. (1986b) 'The impact of occupational safety and health regulation, 1973–1983', *Rand Journal of Economics*, 17.
Viscusi, W.K., Magat, W.A. and Huber, J. (1986) 'Informational regulation of consumer health risks: An empirical evaluation of hazard warnings', *The Rand Journal of Economics*, 17:351–365.
Watson, W.D. and Jaksch, J.A. (1982) 'Air pollution: Household soiling and consumer welfare losses', *Journal of Environmental Economics and Management*, 9:248–262.
Weidenbaum, M.L. and DeFina, R. (1978) 'The cost of federal regulation of economic activity', American Enterprise Institute for Public Policy, RM-88, Washington, D.C.
Weitzman, M. (1974) 'Prices versus quantities', *Review of Economic Studies*, 41:477–491.
Weitzman, M. (1978) 'Optimal rewards for economic regulation', *American Economic Review*, 68:683–691.
White, L.J. (1981) *Reforming regulation: Processes and problems*. Englewood Cliffs: Prentice-Hall.
Wilson, J.Q., ed. (1980) *The politics of regulation*. New York: Basic Books.
Winston, C. and Mannering, F. (1984) 'Consumer demand for automobile safety', *American Economic Review*, 74:316–319.
Zeckhauser, R. and Shepard, D. (1976) 'Where now for saving lives?', *Law and Contemporary Problems*, 40:5–45.

INDEX